PHILOSOPHY
AN INTRODUCTION
TO THE ART
OF WONDERING

THIRD EDITION

PHILOSOPHY
AN INTRODUCTION TO THE ART OF WONDERING

JAMES L. CHRISTIAN
Department of Philosophy, Santa Ana College, Santa Ana, California

HOLT, RINEHART AND WINSTON

New York   Chicago   San Francisco   Philadelphia
Montreal   Toronto   London   Sydney
Tokyo   Mexico City   Rio de Janeiro   Madrid

The cover illustration is a map of the solar corona obtained by the Orbiting Solar Observatory-7 (OSO-7) and presented on a computerized color display. The brighter the color, the greater the quantity of ionized gas in the corona. The hottest colors are white, the cooler colors are turquoise and black. The "polar caps" may be as much as 1,800,000 degrees F, while hot spots in the sun's equatorial region may rise to temperatures of 72 million degrees F during solar flares. Photo courtesy of NASA.

Publisher	*Ray Ashton*
Aquisitions Editor	*David P. Boynton*
Senior Project Editor	*Peggy Middendorf*
Production Manager	*Patrick Sarcuni*
Art and Design	*Robert Kopelman*

Library of Congress Cataloging in Publication Data

Christian, James Lee, 1927-
    Philosophy.

    Includes bibliographies and index.
    1. Philosophy—Introductions.   I. Title.
BD21.C56 1981   100   80-26147
ISBN 0-03-047416-7

Philosophy: An Introduction to the Art of Wondering, third edition by James L. Christian
Acknowledgments for the use of quoted materials are given on pages 571–584.
Copyright © 1981 by CBS College Publishing
© 1977 by Holt, Rinehart and Winston
© 1973 by Rinehart Press, 5643 Paradise Drive, Corte Madera, Calif. 94925
A division of Holt, Rinehart and Winston, Inc.
Address correspondence to:
383 Madison Avenue, New York, N.Y. 10017
All rights reserved
Printed in the United States of America
Published simultaneously in Canada
1 2 3 4 146 9 8 7 6 5 4 3 2 1
CBS COLLEGE PUBLISHING
Holt, Rinehart and Winston
The Dryden Press
Saunders College Publishing

PRELUDE

The following pages
may cause you to wonder.
That's what philosophy is.
Wondering.

To philosophize
is to wonder about life—
about right and wrong,
love and loneliness,
war and death,
about freedom, truth, beauty, time . . .
and a thousand other things.

To philosophize
is to explore life.
It means breaking free
to ask questions.
It means resisting
easy answers.
To philosophize
is to seek in oneself
the courage to ask
painful questions.

But if, by chance,
you have already asked
all your questions
and found all the answers—
if you're sure you know
right from wrong,
and whether God exists,
and what justice means,
and why men fear and hate and pray—
if indeed you have done your wondering
about freedom and love and loneliness
and those thousand other things,
then the following pages
will waste your time.

Philosophy is for those
who are willing to be disturbed
with a creative disturbance.

Philosophy is for those
who still have the capacity
for wonder.

DEDICATIONS

EDWIN PRINCE BOOTH

Though it comes too late, thank you for showing me why we must tirelessly seek out the profoundly human element in all events since only therein can their meaning be found. . . .

ARNOLD TOYNBEE   In memorium: October 22, 1975

Thank you for the passion to see all existence as a single phenomenon without losing sight of the most minute details—*this* cave painting, *this* footnote, *this* flower in *this* crannied wall. . . .

HERMAN and ANNE

Thank you each for a parent's love, and more; for faith, hope, strength, phone calls, and countless instances of critically timed support. There are no words to express my appreciation of you both. . . .

BARBARA, my wife

Thank you for your faith in, and unwavering dedication to, the completion of our book; for an incisive intellect which can clarify even the muddiest of philosophical problems; for a rare creative brilliance in the understanding of psychodynamic processes; for the relentless reminders to relate helium-filled abstractions to real people; . . . for loving me.

CREDIT/BLAME/ACKNOWLEDGMENTS

from the Preface to the First Edition / February 1973

I have written this book for my philosophy students . . . and for all who are caught up in the wonderment of life—its mystery, its enormity, its diversity.

All of us wonder, sometime or often, about our place within the existential ecosystem. What we are asking is how we can relate most happily to ourselves, to others close about us, to fellow creatures with whom we share our delicate planet, and to our mind-boggling, pulsating, multibubble universe. We burn with an urgency to know all that can be known, but we search for a *method* to help us assimilate that knowledge with insight.

A philosophy text should offer cautious counsel to all who would seek intelligent, nonpartisan guidance on the life-and-death questions of human existence; but many textbooks are found wanting in the face of life's final questions.

Eliot Aronson notes that so many of our students ask us what time it is, and we respond by presenting to them the history of time-keeping from waterclocks to wristwatches. By the time we finish, they have turned elsewhere to ask their questions.

And J. B. Priestley hurts when he reminds us that the man who shouts "My house is on fire!" may not be able to define precisely what he means by *my* and *house* and *is* and *on* and *fire*, but he may still be saying something very, very important.

That's why this book has been written.

* * * * * * *

For an author to attempt to pay his debts is sheer folly . . . but I must try. I owe so much to so many who have understood and lent me strength. As I scribbled out my ideas, it was a continual surprise to discover that so many of the notions I assumed to be my own turned out to have developed from seeds planted by others, and really belong to them. Such insights spread through my being like colored dye, their sources too easily forgotten.

To several generations of philosophy students: Thank you for a myriad of ideas, wrestlings, ponderings; for gathering volumes of materials; for critical suggestions for the book in its developmental phase (you were not always gentle, but you *were* always helpful).

To colleagues: Thank you for your encouragement; for taking time to read portions of the typescript; for your assistance in developing illustrations. A special thank you to Dave Hartman and Ron Smith.

To the men at Rinehart Press—Dick Raihall, Greg Hubit, and Emmett Dingley: Your professionalism never wavered and your warmth as men was never compromised by the pragmatics of production. As Managing Editor, Greg Hubit has handled the book's complexities in a way which insured that the final product would be faithful to the original dream. A special word of appreciation to Alden

Paine: Your perceptive guidance at the inception of this project meant more than we can say.

To some special people who, in a variety of ways, are part of this book, thank you . . . many times over: Terry Allen, Bob Baker, Carol Weber, Marge Hennen, Court Holdgrafer, Nancy Jones, Don Meyer, Bob Moore (photographer par excellence), Jill Olson, Bob Putman, Doris Sauter, Dorothy Symms, John Velasquez, Larry West.

To all who granted permission to use materials, our sincere appreciation. Due credit has been noted at the back of this book, and we earnestly hope there have been no oversights. Many individuals have given us more than perfunctory responses, and, in extra ways, gave us their time, help, and, in some cases, friendship. We would like to acknowledge those extra courtesies: Ray Bradbury, John Buechler, Abner Dean, Houston Harte, Jay W. Klug, Kelly Lange, Stanley Miller, Cyril Ponnamperuma, Maarten Schmidt, Ralph Solecki, Joseph Stacey, Harry Torczyner, Helmut Wimmer.

To some other people—perplexing innocents all, but wise—who are very special: Cathy, Dane, Carla, Marcia, Sherrie, Reinar, Laurie, Shawna, Shannon, Linda. Somehow, there were those of you who understood. *Thank you.*

MOREOVER . . .
from the Preface to the Second Edition / January 1977

This book is a teaching instrument, a collection of teaching materials which, at one point or another, raises most of the classical problems of philosophy as well as many contemporary and relatively new philosophical questions. All materials in this book can be employed, analytically and synoptically, to perform the numerous tasks required by classroom philosophic activity.

Some chapters include empirical data that we would normally subsume under Psychology, Biology, Chemistry, and the like. It helps enormously, I have found, if philosophy students have a common fund of information, however brief, on a few specific problems before they plunge into a philosophic discussion of them.

* * * * * *

In a variety of ways, many more individuals have now become a part of this book, and I am deep in debt to them: Peter Angeles, Fred Bender, Richard Doss, Devon Edrington (my longest-standing critic/supporter), Donald Heidt, Harold Hoyt, Robert McCall, George Sessions, Roger Sullivan. A very special thank you to Dr. Alice Bergel for the most comprehensive critical scrutiny any book ever received.

At Holt, Deborah Doty and Terry O'Reilly have given skillful and gentle editorial guidance throughout this revision; and Jeanette Ninas Johnson, who brings it all together, has been a joy to work with.

THIRD EDITION / MOREOVER . . .

Besides a general updating and the omission of less useful materials, two noteworthy changes have been made in this edition: it contains 32 chapters rather than 40, and 12 brief biographies have been added.

As for the chapters, those omitted from the second edition are: 1-3, 2-3, 3-3, 4-4, 5-4, 6-2, 7-2, 8-2. (Some of this material has been absorbed into adjacent chapters; and part of 4-4 was transposed to 5-3.) On a semester schedule especially, 32 chapters should prove more manageable.

As for the biographies, most are fairly conventional: Marcus, Plato, Aristotle, Camus, Hume, James, the Buddha, Merton, and Sagan. (The scenarios in the Sagan biography are from the televised segments of the PBS series *Cosmos,* not the book.) The "vignettes" of Socrates, Confucius, and Empedocles are constructed in the genre of the historical novel: settings imagined and some dialogue composed, but with all ideas and dramatis personae based on fact. In connection with a few of the biographies, a comment or reference is in order.

Merton: In addition to *The Seven Storey Mountain* and *The Asian Journal,* the new biography by Monica Furlong is highly recommended: *Merton: A Biography* (Harper, 1980).

The Buddha: While fact and myth are inseparable in all accounts of the Buddha's life, this picture of Siddhartha is drawn from various Nikayas in the Sutta Pitaka and therefore has the best chance of containing a modicum of historical fact. The reconstruction of his spiritual odyssey and teaching follows the analysis of Rune E. A. Johansson, *The Psychology of Nirvana* (Doubleday Anchor, 1969).

Confucius: This "moment of truth" by the riverbank is fiction, but it reflects a specific time and condition in Kung's life (c. 484 B.C. when he was 67 years old); and the events alluded to are historic. All utterances of Kung and Tze-lu are quotations (or paraphrases) from the *Analects.* At about this time Kung was summoned home to Lu by Duke Gae, and the records indicate that he achieved a position of honor and subsequently edited the Five Classics.

Empedocles: The Aetna scene is fantasy, but the characters are historical and the orations of Empedocles are quoted from later records. Sources: W. K. C. Guthrie, *A History of Greek Philosophy* (Cambridge, 1962–1965) and Philip Wheelwright, *The Presocratics* (Odyssey Press, 1966).

* * * * * * * *

My gratitude continues to the many individuals acknowledged in the first and second editions. Now, I'm indebted to many more.

To each of my colleagues who has performed first aid and/or major surgery on portions of the book: Richard Sneed, Lee Layport, Steve Eastmond, Doug Toohey, John Goerger, William Phipps. Thank you.

To Dr. Robert W. Smith for being a travel-guide in many worlds and co-conspirator in this one; and for strength and friendship.

To Dr. Ronald M. Huntington III for being general counsel in all things religious and philosophical; and for scholarship and unerring guidance.

To Stewart Munson III / Illustrator for drawing the original portraits for this edition and for allowing me to be in at the inception of an exciting career in the arts.

At HRW, to David Boynton for persistent encouragement and for keeping the machinery moving; to Peggy Middendorf for handling the endless details of production with grace and style.

Lastly, and firstly, to my wife Barbara, an enormous debt that remains unpaid and unpayable. There comes a time when the involvement of one's mate/companion in the very fabric of a book reaches such proportions that the notion of a "single author textbook" is a literal half-truth. For a full decade now substantial portions of this book have been enriched by the depth and breadth of her intellect, so that, in its final form, this book stands as a joint labor of love.

Santa Ana, California   J. L. C.
January 1981

CONTENTS

WHAT DO YOU MEAN PHILOSOPHY??

For man, the unexamined life is not worth living.

SOCRATES

°Synoptic. *From the Greek* sunoptikos, *"seeing the whole together" or "taking a comprehensive view." The attempt to achieve an all-inclusive overview of one's subject matter. See Chapter 1–4 and glossary.*

Understanding man and his place in the universe is perhaps the central problem of all science.

DUNN AND DOBZHANSKY

The meaning of life is arrived at . . . by dark gropings, by feelings not wholly understood, by catching at hints and fumbling for explanations.

ALFRED ADLER

1   Sometime, at your leisure—if you want to know what philosophy is—go into a large bookstore and browse. Check a variety of books in psychology, anthropology, physics, chemistry, archeology, astronomy, and other nonfiction fields. Look at the last chapter in each book. In a surprising number of cases, you will find that the author has chosen to round out his work with a final summation of what the book is all about. That is, having written a whole book on a specialized subject in which he is probably an authority, he finds that he *also* has ideas about the larger meaning of the facts that he has written about. The final chapter may be called "Conclusions," "Epilogue," "Postscript," "My Personal View," "Implications," "Comments," "Speculations," or (as in one case) "So What?" But in every instance, the author is trying to elucidate the larger implications of his subject matter and to clarify how he thinks it relates to other fields or to life. He has an urge to tell us *the meaning* of all his facts *taken together*. He wants to share with us the *philosophic implications* of what he has written.

When he does this, the author has moved beyond the role of a field specialist. He is a philosopher.

2   This is a textbook in synoptic° philosophy. It is an invitation to ponder, in the largest possible perspective, the weightier, more stubborn problems of human existence. It is an invitation to think—to wonder, to question, to speculate, to reason, even to fantasize—in the eternal search for wisdom. In a word, synoptic philosophy is an attempt to weave interconnecting lines of illumination between all the disparate realms of human thought in the hope that, like a thousand dawnings, new insights will burst through.

By its very nature, philosophy is a do-it-yourself enterprise. There is a common misunderstanding that philosophy—like chemistry or history—has a content to offer, a content which a teacher is to teach and a student is to learn. This is not the case. There are no facts, no theories, certainly no final truths which go by the name of "philosophy" and which one is supposed to accept and believe. Rather, philosophy is a skill—more akin to mathematics and music; it is something that one *learns to do*.

Philosophy, that is, is a *method*. It is *learning how* to ask and re-ask questions until meaningful answers begin to appear. It is *learning how* to relate materials. It is *learning where* to go for the most dependable, up-to-date information that might shed light on some problem. It is *learning how* to double check fact-claims in order to verify or falsify them. It is *learning how* to reject fallacious fact-claims—to reject them no matter how prestigious the authority who holds them or how deeply one would personally like to believe them.

3   The student should be aware that philosophy has never been just one kind of activity with a single approach to a single task. Rather, there have been many kinds of philosophy: the quiet philosophy of the

sage who sees much but speaks little because language cannot hold life; the articulate, noisy dialectics of Socrates; the calm, logical apologetics of Aquinas; the mystical philosophy of Plotinus and Chuang-tzu; the mathematical philosophy of Russell and Wittgenstein.

Each school of philosophy has concentrated upon some aspect

Morally, a philosopher who uses his professional competence for anything except a disinterested search for truth is guilty of a kind of treachery.

BERTRAND RUSSELL

PEANUTS®   By Charles M. Schulz

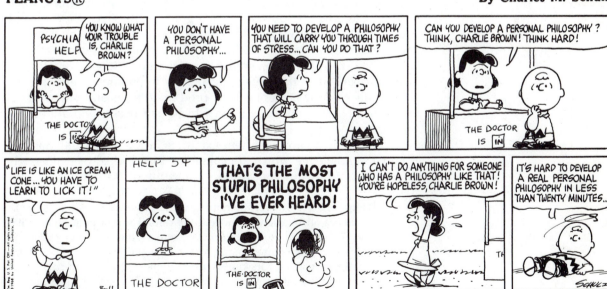

of man's knowledge. Logical/analytical philosophy has worked long and hard on the confusion which vitiates so much of our thinking and communicating. Pragmatism has concentrated on finding solutions to problems of man's social existence. Existential philosophy has been concerned with making life meaningful to each, unique individual. Activist schools argue that philosophers spend too much time trying to make sense of the world and too little time trying to change it. Several schools of philosophy, Eastern and Western, challenge the individual to turn away from an alienating society and to seek harmony with Nature or Ultimate Reality.

Each kind of philosophy has made an immense contribution to its area of concern. Each was doubtless a part of the *Zeitgeist*—"the spirit of the age"—which gave it birth and to which it spoke.

The present unhappy condition of human knowledge calls for the application of a synoptic methodology. We now possess vast accumulations of specialized knowledge in countless fields, but these fields remain isolated from one another. Yet it is increasingly clear that many of our urgent problems can be understood only when the specialized information from a variety of these separate fields is integrated and "seen together"—synoptically. It is only then that we can develop realistic solutions to these complex problems.

4 It is often said that philosophers engage in two basic tasks: "taking apart"—*analyzing* ideas to discover if we truly know what we think we know (and we don't)—and "putting together"—*synthesizing* all our knowledge to find if we can attain a larger and better view of life (we can).

But in practice philosophers do a lot more than this. They talk a lot. They carry on dialogues with anyone who comes within range. And they argue a great deal. Not the usual kinds of argument in which egos fight to win, but philosophical arguments in which they attempt to clarify the reasoning that lies behind their statements; and no one cares about winning since, in philosophical arguments, everyone wins.

They also ask one another for definitions to be sure they're thinking clearly; and they push one another to pursue the implications of their ideas and statements. They prod themselves and others to examine the basic assumptions upon which their beliefs and arguments rest.

Philosophers are persistent explorers in the nooks and crannies of human knowledge which are commonly overlooked or deliberately ignored. It is an exciting but restless adventure of the mind.

5 Philosophers, however, do not engage in this critical task just to make nuisances of themselves. Indeed, the central aim of philosophers has always been . . . to construct a picture of the whole of reality, in which every element of man's knowledge and every aspect of man's experience will find its proper place. Philosophy, in short, is man's quest for the unity of knowledge: it consists in a perpetual struggle to create the concepts in which the universe can be conceived as a *uni-*

verse and not a *multi*verse. The history of philosophy is the history of this attempt. The problems of philosophy are the problems that arise when the attempt is made to grasp this total unity. . . .

It cannot be denied that this attempt stands without rival as the most audacious enterprise in which the mind of man has ever engaged. Just reflect for a moment: Here is man, surrounded by the vastness of a universe in which he is only a tiny and perhaps insignificant part—and he wants to *understand* it. . . .

WILLIAM HALVERSON

6   In one respect, philosophic material can be deceptive. Since it deals with life by examining the sort of questions we ask every day, some of the subject matter will have an easy, familiar ring.

The fact is that synoptic philosophy must be as diligently studied as any other subject, not to remember data, but to set the mind in motion toward developing larger concepts, connecting ideas, and seeing through and beyond mere words and facts.

In a sense, intellectual growth *happens to us;* it is not really something that we do. But it happens to us only when our minds are given a chance to operate on their terms. They take their own time to process information and to begin developing a web of interconnecting lines of illumination among their materials. This undertaking is partly conscious, of course; but largely it is an unconscious process. This is why much philosophic insight just happens, as though the light moves from the depths upward and not from the rational conscious downward.

Only disciplined study with an open mind will produce philosophic awareness. Insight and consciousness still come only with relentless labor. In this age of instant everything, there is still no instant wisdom, unfortunately.

7   No two of us possess precisely the same information, or see things from the same viewpoint, or share the same values. Therefore, each of us must do synoptic philosophy in his own unique and personal way. A student entering upon the activity of philosophizing may need to be on guard against developing a world-view which resembles, a bit too closely, the prepackaged philosophy of life belonging to someone else or to some institution. Most of us are philosophically lazy, and it is easy to appropriate another's thoughts and rationalize our theft. The British logician Wittgenstein warned us that "a thought which is not independent is a thought only half understood." Similarly, a philosophy of life that is not the authentic product of one's own experience is a philosophy only half understood.

Nor will any of us succeed in developing a finished philosophy; for as one changes with life, so does one's thinking. A philosophy *of life* must change *with life.* Doing philosophy is an endless activity.

For this reason, this textbook is merely an example of synoptic philosophy. This is the way I have had to do it because of *my* perspectives, *my* interests, *my* areas of knowledge, *my* personal concerns, and

Here we are in this wholly fantastic Universe with scarcely a clue as to whether our existence has any real significance. No wonder then that many people feel the need for some belief that gives them a sense of security, and no wonder that they become very angry with people like me who say that this security is illusory. But I do not like the situation any better than they do. The difference is that I cannot see how the smallest advantage is to be gained from deceiving myself.

FRED HOYLE

"There is an old saying that philosophy bakes no bread. It is perhaps equally true that no bread would ever have been baked without philosophy. For the act of baking implies a decision on the philosophical issue of whether life is worthwhile at all. Bakers may not have often asked themselves the question in so many words. But philosophy traditionally has been nothing less than the attempt to ask and answer, in a formal and disciplined way, the great questions of life that ordinary men put to themselves in reflective moments."

TIME, JANUARY 7, 1966

my limitations. But *your* world-view will be different because it will be *yours,* and *yours alone.*

This is why my attempt to do synoptic philosophy is, at most, a guideline showing how it might be done; at least, the expression of a hope that, someday, in your own way, you will resolve the contradictions of your own existence—both of knowing and of being—and proceed to see life in a larger, more fulfilling way.

As soon as man does not take his existence for granted, but beholds it as something unfathomably mysterious, thought begins.

ALBERT SCHWEITZER

One can tell for oneself whether the water is warm or cold.

I CHING

Uno itinere non potest perveniri ad tam grande secretum.

"The heart of so great a mystery can never be reached by following one road only."

Q. AURELIUS SYMMACHUS
Relatio Tertia

THEAETETUS: Yes Socrates, I stand in amazement when I reflect on the questions that men ask. By the gods, I do! I want to know more and more about such questions, and there are times when I almost become dizzy just thinking about them.

SOCRATES: Ah yes, my dear Theaetetus, when Theodorus called you a philosopher he described you well. That feeling of wonder is the touchstone of the philosopher, and all philosophy has its origins in wonder. Whoever reminded us that Iris (the heavenly messenger) is the offspring of Thaumas (wonder) wasn't a bad genealogist.

Plato/*Theaetetus*

A sense of wonder started men philosophizing, in ancient times as well as today. Their wondering is aroused, first, by trivial matters; but they continue on from there to wonder about less mundane matters such as the changes of the moon, sun, and stars, and the beginnings of the universe. What is the result of this wonderment, this puzzlement? An awesome feeling of ignorance. Men began to philosophize, therefore, to escape ignorance. . . .

Aristotle/*Metaphysics*

PART I

THE FINE ART OF WONDERING

To grow into youngness is a blow. To age into sickness is an insult. To die is, if we are not careful, to turn from God's breast, feeling slighted and unloved. The sparrow *asks* to be seen as it falls.

Philosophy must try, as best it can, to turn the sparrows to flights of angels, which, Shakespeare wrote, sing us to our rest.

RAY BRADBURY

The World-Riddle

Have You Ever Wondered . . .

- Why, when a commercial jet crashes, some people blame the airlines while others blame God?

- Why so-called natural events take place?

- Whether life is meaning-full or meaning-less?

- Whether human life is essentially a comedy or a tragedy?

- Whether a human being— e.g. *you*—can be truly happy?

- Whether death is—or can be made—meaningful?

- Whom you can turn to for the answers to your deepest questions about living?

JUST IN CASE . . .

1   Shortly before a solar eclipse was to occur in central India, an Indian physicist—who was also a member of the Brahmin caste—was lecturing to his students at the university. He told them precisely when the event would begin and described in detail how the moon's orbit would take it between the sun and the earth. In their city there would be only a partial eclipse, but on a wall map he pointed out the path of totality as it moved across the terrestrial globe to the north of them. They discussed such things as the corona, solar flares, the beauty of annular rings, and the appearance of Bailey's beads during

that rare total eclipse. Some of the students from the rural villages had heard stories about a Giant Dragon that swallowed the sun, but their teacher's lucid presentation of celestial mechanics had dispelled any fears they might have felt.

Having dismissed his class, the professor returned to his village and, since he was a Brahmin, assumed his duties as a priest. Around his shoulders he draped the vestments of his office and began counting through his string of beads, calling aloud the names of the gods. A goat was beheaded in sacrifice to Kali, the Black Goddess, the cause and controller of earthquakes, storms, and other evil things, and the archenemy of demons. Prayers were offered to her that she might frighten away the Dragon. "Glory to Mother Kali," the priest and people chanted.

While in the classroom there was nothing illogical about describing the solar eclipse in terms of celestial mechanics; neither was there anything wrong in offering a gift to the Black Goddess—*just in case* . . .

THE HUMAN CONDITION

2   To sensitive spirits of all ages, life is filled with cruel contradictions and bitter ironies. Human experience is capricious and our finite minds are not able to see enough of life *at one time* for us to know for sure what is going on. We see only fragments of life, and never the whole. We are not unlike children struggling with a jigsaw puzzle handed to us as a cosmic joke.

Just under the surface of the entire human enterprise, implicit in all we think and do, there lies the eternal question: *What is the meaning of existence?* It is the ultimate question of all Mankind, yet it must be reopened by each of us in our turn. If we refuse to take the contradictions of life for granted; if we can't accept prepackaged solutions; if we can't persuade ourselves to accept a mere fragment of life as the whole of life—then for all of us, the question persists. While we may have great difficulty finding satisfactory answers to it, we also know that there is no escape from it.

3   On the real-life scene where the human tragicomedy plays itself out, our question splits into two further practical questions. Stated positively: How can we make life worth living? Stated negatively: How can we prevent life from turning into tragedy?

Through the ages, man has sought clues to life's meaning through his religions and philosophies. To date they have given us immense help, but a contemporary overview of Mankind's quest supplies us with a superabundance of answers, so many answers in fact that we can't decide among them. Some would attempt to evade the problem by a "leap of faith" into a garden of plastic flowers, while others play a sort of religious roulette. But such arbitrary shortcuts fail to face the essential complexity of human existence.

Philosophy, when superficially studied, excites doubt; when thoroughly explored, it dispels it.

FRANCIS BACON

The most important thing . . . we can know about a man is what he takes for granted, and the most elemental and important facts about a society are those that are seldom debated and generally regarded as settled.

LOUIS WIRTH

°Information on illustrations, along with sources and credits, will be found on pages 579–584.

Philosophy is the eternal search for truth, a search which inevitably fails and yet is never defeated; which continually eludes us, but which always guides us. This free, intellectual life of the mind is the noblest inheritance of the Western world; it is also the hope of our future.

W. T. JONES

Every man, whether he is religiously inclined or not, has his own ultimate presuppositions. He finds he cannot live his life without them, and for him they are true. Such presuppositions, whether they be called ideologies, philosophies, notions, or merely hunches about life, exert creative pressure upon all conduct . . .

GORDON ALLPORT

Furthermore, after a more critical reexamination, we discover that most of man's religions and many of his philosophies have concluded that, in the final analysis, life-in-this-world is *not* worth living. At best it's but a time of troubles to be endured until we can reach something better.

Today, that's a conclusion we find difficult to live with.

4   In Panshin's *Rite of Passage* the heroine, a young girl, states candidly: "If you want to accept life, you have to accept the whole bloody universe." She may be right. But how can we really "accept" a universe of wild and destructive contradictions? After all, we seem to be as ambivalent about ultimate realities as the Indian physicist/priest.

The natural world is not the contradiction today that it was some four centuries ago before the birth of the New Science. We are fairly secure in our general mathematical descriptions of the physical universe. Our "scientific laws" will undergo continued refinement, of course, and there is little doubt that we will discover new realms, or new dimensions, of realities. But there is such a high degree of consistency to our experience of nature's operations that we have arrived at the point of accepting a naturalistic world-view *for nature.* With this physical universe—from galaxies and gravity fields to television and laser beams—we have made our peace. Though our comprehension of nature is far from complete, we can live with the foundations of understanding so far secured. The unintegrated cosmos which challenged the existence of ancient men and eluded their understanding is no longer a bewildering problem to us.

Our serious problems, therefore, lie buried somewhere within the protoplasmic venture which we call "life." To borrow a phrase from Buckminster Fuller, the puzzlement seems to be that this protoplasmic experiment came without an instruction manual.

5   Long before the birth of modern psychology, there were perceptive individuals who felt stirrings from the depths of the human organism, but it was left to Sigmund Freud to launch the fantastic journey into the inner world. As the Viennese doctor shook loose the secrets of the human psyche, it was no longer deniable that the subconscious mind, quite without our conscious permission, pushes us headlong into all forms of irrational behavior. The subconscious mind is a vast depository for emotionally charged experience which, for one reason or another, we cannot face; and these repressed elements determine to a large extent how we feel, think, and behave.

But, to realize that we do countless things without understanding why—this can be a soul-jarring discovery. We are manipulated, like puppets on a string, by inner forces over which we have little control. We scurry about in frenzied activity, accomplishing little else than satisfying the whims of the shadowy slavedriver. Not knowing our motivations, we don't understand what we do; and much of the time our striving brings little fulfillment.

Mankind's common instinct for reality . . . has always held the world to be essentially a theatre for heroism.

WILLIAM JAMES

There is a coherent plan in the universe, though I don't know what it's a plan for.

SIR FRED HOYLE

I have one longing only: to grasp what is hidden behind appearances, to ferret out that mystery which brings me to birth and then kills me, to discover if behind the visible and unceasing stream of the world an invisible and immutable presence is hiding.

NIKOS KAZANTZAKIS

"This is all there is."

Perhaps here is one source of the meaninglessness of our lives. We have no clear notion of what we are after, but we plunge blindly ahead in search of something.

6   "Good morning," said the little prince.

"Good morning," said the railway switchman.

"What do you do here?" the little prince asked.

"I sort out travelers, in bundles of a thousand, said the switchman. "I send off the trains that carry them: now to the right, now to the left."

And a brilliantly lighted express train shook the switchman's cabin as it rushed by with a roar like thunder.

"They are in a great hurry," said the little prince. "What are they looking for?"

"Not even the locomotive engineer knows that," said the switchman.

And a second brilliantly lighted express thundered by, in the opposite direction.

"Are they coming back already?" demanded the little prince.

"These are not the same ones," said the switchman. "It is an exchange."

"Were they not satisfied where they were?" asked the little prince.

"No one is ever satisfied where he is," said the switchman.

You philosophize when you reflect critically upon what you are actually doing in your world. What you are doing is, of course, in the first place, living. And life involves passions, faiths, doubts, and courage. The critical inquiry into what all these things mean and imply is philosophy.

JOSIAH ROYCE
The Spirit of Modern Philosophy

René Magritte, *Castle of the Pyrenees*, 1959.

And they heard the roaring thunder of a third brilliantly lighted express.

"Are they pursuing the first travelers?" demanded the little prince.

"They are pursuing nothing at all," said the switchman. "They are asleep in there, or if they are not asleep they are yawning. Only the children are flattening their noses against the windowpanes."

"Only the children know what they are looking for," said the little prince. "They waste their time over a rag doll and it becomes very important to them; and if anybody takes it away from them they cry . . ."

"They are lucky," the switchman said.

SAINT-EXUPÉRY
The Little Prince

7   In Freud's world, life is at once a blessing and a curse, for *eros* (the life-force) is pitted in mortal combat against *thanatos* (the death-wish).

On the one hand, we possess drives toward self-preservation which countermand almost all other impulses. We fear the cessation of breath and sense. "Let me not see the death which I ever dread!" cried the hero of the Gilgamesh Epic three thousand years ago. While alive, we dream our dreams, work toward our goals, and feel the joyous pain of activity and growth. All this indicates the depth of our hunger for life; we will fight to the death in order to live. *Eros.*

On the other hand, "To exist is to suffer," taught the Buddha, and we have devised ingenious ways of escaping existence. We sense a futility in our dreams; an inner voice chides us for yearning for goals we can't achieve. We often have an empty feeling when we hold in our hands something we have fought for, wondering why we wanted it. All around we see loneliness, surd hatreds, and pointless sadisms. Mephistopheles speaks for many: Hell is no fable, for *this life IS* hell. Away from all this, we are pulled toward death, as though it would be a blessing to have done with it. *Thanatos.*

Out of frustration, perhaps we ought to ask whether the essential implication of so many of man's religions and philosophies might be correct after all—the implication that the human condition is uninhabitable. Perhaps it really is possible that there is something inherently wrong. Perhaps Norman Brown is close when he calls man a "disease." It's not inconceivable that self-destruction, in some sense, is already an accomplished fact.

Albert Schweitzer once wrote that he remained optimistic because hope is an indispensable ingredient of daily life, but that when he took a long look at human history he could not escape the gloom of pessimism.

When asked if he were "optimistic these days about the state of the world," Alan Watts replied: "I have to be. There is no alternative. For if I were to bet, I would bet that the human race will destroy itself by 2000. But there's nowhere to place the bet."

"Realistic people" who pursue "practical aims" are rarely as realistic or practical, in the long run of life, as the dreamers who pursue their dreams.

HANS SELYE

To lose one's life is a little thing and I shall have the courage to do so if it is necessary; but to see the meaning of this life dissipated, to see our reason for existing disappear, that is what is unbearable. One cannot live without meaning.

ALBERT CAMUS

The idea that so much suffering can be in vain is intolerable to me, it kept me awake all night: I'm awake now. . . .

ANDRÉ GIDE

THE SEARCH FOR MEANING

8   Modern men are caught in an "existential vacuum," writes Viktor Frankl, a feeling of

> the total and ultimate meaninglessness of their lives. They lack the awareness of a meaning worth living for. They are haunted by the experience of their inner emptiness, a void within themselves. . . .
>
> The existential vacuum is a widespread phenomenon of the twentieth century. This is understandable; it may be due to a twofold loss that man had to undergo since he became a truly human being. At the beginning of human history, man lost some of the basic animal instincts in which an animal's behavior is embedded and by which it is secured. Such security, like Paradise, is closed to man forever; man has to make choices. In addition to this, however, man has suffered another loss in his more recent development: the traditions that had buttressed his behavior are now rapidly diminishing. No instinct tells him what he has to do, and no tradition tells him what he ought to do; soon he will not know what he wants to do.

9   The search for life, if it is to succeed, must be an individual odyssey. Each of us is caught in the philosophical enterprise. There is not one of us who is not trying to make sense of his existence, and at some level of our being each is seeking fulfillment. Our experiences come pouring into us in endless variety and they do not come neatly packaged and labeled. Each one of us must select and assimilate, organize and arrange, value and apply. So we are all philosophers by default, not by choice.

To be sure, we must seek the guidance of others who have searched; we can listen to those who have found answers that work *for them.* But in the last analysis, no one else can donate an insight to us. It has to be indigenous, grown from native soil.

Nor is our quest for meaning a quixotic tilting after windmills. There are many who find, to some degree, what they are seeking; they find the clues that set them in the right direction. When we listen to their recounting of what has happened in their lives, we cannot doubt the depth of meaning to which their insights have led them.

Each of the following men, at some point in his search, found an answer or a perspective which affected the quality of his entire existence.

10   After working through the long hot days with his patients at the Lambaréné hospital, Albert Schweitzer would retire to his cluttered study in the evening and take up again the problem from which he could not escape. He was attempting to discover a positive ethical principle upon which civilization could be securely grounded.

> For months on end I lived in a continual state of mental excitement. Without the least success I let my thought be concentrated, even all

"There is no hope."
"We're both alive. And for all I know, that's hope."

HENRY II
The Lion in Winter

The story of Eden is a greater allegory than man has ever guessed. For it was truly man who, walking memoryless through paths of sunlight and shade in the morning of the world, sat down and passed a wondering hand across his heavy forehead. Time and darkness, knowledge of good and evil, have walked with him ever since. . . .

LOREN EISELEY

Albert Schweitzer

through my daily work at the hospital, on the real nature of world- and life-affirmation and of ethics, and on the question of what they have in common. I was wandering about in a thicket in which no path was to be found. I was leaning with all my might against an iron door which would not yield.

While in this mental condition I had to undertake a longish journey on the river. . . . Slowly we crept upstream, laboriously feeling—it was the dry season—for the channels between the sandbanks. Lost in thought I sat on the deck of the barge, struggling to find the elementary and universal conception of the ethical which I had not discovered in any philosophy. Sheet after sheet I covered with disconnected sentences, merely to keep myself concentrated on the problem. Late on the third day, at the very moment when, at sunset, we were making our way through a herd of hippopotamuses, there flashed upon my mind, unforeseen and unsought, the phrase, "Reverence for Life." The iron door had yielded: the path in the thicket had become visible. Now I had found my way to the idea in which world- and life-affirmation and ethics are contained side by side! . . .

The world-view of Reverence for Life follows from taking the world as it is. And the world means the horrible in the glorious, the meaningless in the meaningful, the sorrowful in the joyful. However it is looked at it remains to many a riddle.

But that does not mean that we need stand before the problem of life at our wits' end because we have to renounce all hope of comprehending the course of world-events as having a meaning. Reverence for Life brings us into a spiritual relation with the world which is independent of all knowledge of the universe. . . . It renews itself in us every time we look thoughtfully at ourselves and the life around us.

Reverence for Life. "In that principle my life has found a firm footing and a clear path to follow."

11   The editors of *Psychology Today* wrote a brief note after the death of Dr. Abraham Maslow. In it they remarked that he had "a joyful affirmation of life that surged through the long tapes he often dictated for us, encouraging *Psychology Today* to explore questions that have no easy answers. Much as we loved this beautiful man, we did not understand the source of his courage—until the last cassette came in."

On that tape, they say, Dr. Maslow

talked with intense introspection about an earlier heart attack that had come right after he completed an important piece of work. "I had really spent myself. This was the best I could do, and here was not only a good time to die but I was even willing to die. . . . It was what David M. Levy called the 'completion of the act.' It was like a good ending, a good close. I think actors and dramatists have that sense of the right moment for a good ending, with a phenomenological sense of good completion—that there was nothing more you could add. . . .

Life is the life of life.

Bhagavata Purana

Abraham Maslow

"My attitude toward life changed. The word I used for it now is the post-mortem life. I could just as easily have died so that my living constitutes a kind of an extra, a bonus. It's all gravy. Therefore I might just as well live as if I had already died.

"One very important aspect of the post-mortem life is that everything gets doubly precious, gets piercingly important. You get stabbed by things, by flowers and by babies and by beautiful things—just the very act of living, of walking and breathing and eating and having friends and chatting. Everything seems to look more beautiful rather than less, and one gets the much-intensified sense of miracles.

"I guess you could say that post-mortem life permits a kind of spontaneity that's greater than anything else could make possible.

"If you're reconciled with death or even if you are pretty well assured that you will have a good death, a dignified one, then every single moment of every single day is transformed because the pervasive undercurrent—the fear of death—is removed. . . . I am living an end-life where everything ought to be an end in itself, where I shouldn't waste any time preparing for the future, or occupying myself with means to later ends

Abe's message ended there.—The Editors.

12   Dr. Gordon Allport has written, in the preface to Viktor Frankl's book *Man's Search for Meaning:*

As a longtime prisoner in bestial concentration camps [Viktor Frankl] found himself stripped to naked existence. His father, mother, brother, and his wife died in camps or were sent to the gas ovens, so that, excepting for his sister, his entire family perished in these camps. How could he—every possession lost, every value destroyed, suffering from hunger, cold and brutality, hourly expecting extermination—how could he find life worth preserving? . . .

From [Frankl's] autobiographical fragment the reader learns much. He learns what a human being does when he suddenly realizes he has "nothing to lose except his so ridiculously naked life." Frankl's description of the mixed flow of emotion and apathy is arresting. First to the rescue comes a cold detached curiosity concerning one's fate. Swiftly, too, come strategies to preserve the remnants of one's life, though the chances of surviving are slight. Hunger, humiliation, fear and deep anger at injustice are rendered tolerable by closely guarded images of beloved persons, by religion, by a grim sense of humor, and even by glimpses of the healing beauties of nature—a tree or a sunset.

But these moments of comfort do not establish the will to live unless they help the prisoner make larger sense out of his apparently senseless suffering. It is here that we encounter the central theme of existentialism: to live is to suffer, to survive is to find meaning in the suffering. If there is a purpose in life at all, there must be a purpose in suffering and in dying. But no man can tell another what this purpose is. Each must find out for himself, and must accept the responsibility that his answer prescribes. If he succeeds he will continue to grow in spite of all indignities. Frankl is fond of quoting Nietzsche, "He who has a *why* to live can bear with almost any how."

A philosophy is the expression of a man's inner character.

WILLIAM JAMES

Viktor Frankl

To see and accept the boundaries of the human mind without vain rebellion, and in these severe limitations to work ceaselessly without protest—this is where man's first duty lies.

NIKOS KAZANTZAKIS

WHY-QUESTIONS

13   Our urge to ask ''Why?'' seems irresistible. If, for example, an avalanche plunges down the mountainside burying sixty schoolchildren in a few seconds, is it humanly possible for the families of the children not to ask *why* it happened?

Nor is a naturalistic answer satisfying, even though a scientifically adequate one may be quite possible: ''The avalanche was produced by a week of especially warm days alternating with cold nights. Much snow melted during those days, and when the water refroze at night the expanding ice gradually loosened the snowbank. The slide occurred during the daytime because melting snow finally produced enough water to weaken the last friction spots holding the snowbank to the mountainside. The snow gave way and cascaded down the slope.''

Such an explanation is scientifically sound. However, at the mass funeral service for the children, imagine in your mind the presiding clergyman presenting the scientific/naturalistic explanation for the tragedy—and stopping there.

Does this not prove Frankl's thesis that, above all else, man must find meaning in his living and, finally, in his dying?

ZORBA. Why do the young die? Why does anybody die, tell me?

SCHOLAR. I don't know.

ZORBA. What's the use of all your damn books? If they don't tell you that, what the hell do they tell you?

SCHOLAR. They tell me about the agony of men who can't answer questions like yours.

NIKOS KAZANTZAKIS
Zorba the Greek

---

14   It would be comforting to know that life has meaning; it would feel good to know that ''nothing happens without a purpose.'' But our need for meaning leads us to find easy and absurd answers to our why-questions.

In the year A.D. 410 when the city of Rome fell to Alaric the Goth, the ''pagans'' blamed the Christians for having abandoned the true gods of Rome; but Saint Augustine spent a dozen years writing *The City of God* to show that the fall of Rome was a part of God's plan to vanquish paganism and establish the Reign of God.

In November of 1755 one of the world's worst earthquakes struck Lisbon. In a few minutes, more than thirty thousand people were killed. The event occurred on All Saints' Day when churches throughout the land were filled with worshippers. French clergymen interpreted the disaster as punishment for the sins of the Portuguese.

Andrew Wyeth, *Christina's World*, 1948. Collection, The Museum of Modern Art, New York.

Protestants blamed the event upon the tyranny of the Catholics, while the Roman clergy laid the event to the fact that there were so many Protestant heretics in Catholic Portugal. In England John Wesley, the founder of Methodism, in a sermon entitled "The Cause and Cure of Earthquakes," blamed original sin as "the moral cause of earthquakes, whatever the natural cause may be . . . ."

In April 1970, after the near-tragic *Apollo XIII* lunar mission was aborted, an American political leader stated on national television that mission failure was a warning from God that man is not to attempt further ventures into space. "A warning," he said; man's next attempt would result in tragic consequences.

THE WORLD-RIDDLE

15   In a hotel in East Africa, weary hunters relax from their safaris into the veld. In the hotel lounge one finds a comfortable set of sofas covered with zebra skins, and on one wall hang several lion skins sep-

Life is a comedy to those who think, a tragedy to those who feel.

RACINE

arated by a dozen or so Masai spears spread out as a fan. Higher up, on all four walls of the lounging area, are mounted heads of game animals. One looks up at the heads of the great African antelopes: elands with long, straight horns; kudus with screw-twisted spires; dainty gazelles; stately sables with long, back-curving horns; and wildebeests with short upturned hooks. Other sentinels which look down upon visitors include the legendary African buffalo whose horns cover its forehead and spread widely on either side; a rhinoceros with double-horns rising from its snout; and a warthog with ivory tusks coming out of either side of its lower jaw and curling over its nose. Various smaller game animals are mounted between the larger heads.

Down through evolutionary time, each animal has developed a means of defense and/or killing. The overwhelming and singular thrust of evolution seems to have been to produce some mechanism of survival against attackers: horns to hold predators at bay; spiked tusks to rip apart and kill; fangs, claws, sharp hooves; thick skins, powerful jaws; sleek, strong legs for running and jumping.

Each animal must exist in unending competition with other creatures that would kill it. Species prey upon species. Nature is, after all, "red in tooth and claw."

No single animal had anything to say about it. It possessed no "freedom" to choose a "life-style." Its place in the scheme of nature is entirely determined for it. What a strange, impertinent thought—that any single, individual animal *could* have had freedom to *choose* its own life-style or to determine its "role" in life.

What forces would design creatures to prey upon one another and, at the same time, instill into each creature the capacity for intense pain and suffering?

And what an unbelievable, ironic condition: in this "deadly feast of life," each of us, in order to exist, must *eat* living things which harbor the same life-drive we possess. *Life feeds upon itself!*

16   Desmond Morris is quite sure that our problems are genetic in origin. In *The Naked Ape* he refers to the "deep-seated biological characteristics of our species" and contends that certain patterns of social behavior "will always be with us, at least until there has been some new and major change in our makeup."

"Species that have evolved special killing techniques for dealing with their prey seldom employ these when dealing with their own kind." But man's trouble, writes Konrad Lorenz, "arises from his being a basically harmless omnivorous creature, lacking in natural weapons with which to kill big prey, and, therefore, also devoid of the built-in safety devices which prevent 'professional' carnivores from abusing their killing power to destroy fellow members of their own species. . . ."

The "Law of the Jungle," writes Morris, is that you don't kill your own kind. "Those species that failed to obey this law have long since become extinct."

Marcus Aurelius
Philosopher-King

Plato wrote that philosophers must become kings or kings philosophers before nations shall have peace. He was describing, five centuries early, the fourteenth emperor of Rome, Marcus Aurelius. Becoming emperor of the Roman Empire was a fair bid for immortality; but Marcus is most remembered for the sort of personal qualities that transform otherwise mundane souls into saints.

What was great about Marcus was that he succeeded in living-in-the-world while refusing to compromise his ideals with the petty obsessions of lesser men; and what made this possible was his philosophy of life: a set of convictions, rationally derived, about how *his life* should be run *by him*. His only writing—random reflections commonly called *Meditations* but which he referred to as *Things Written to Himself*—is an exercise in self-discovery. It is one man's instruction manual for living.

He was born in Rome of an old Spanish family and named Marcus Annius Verus. Both parents died while he was still a child, and he was fondly adopted, at seventeen, by his uncle Antoninus, a patrician and warrior soon to be the next emperor of the Empire. As Antoninus' heir, Marcus, too, was destined to become emperor. At eighteen he was given the title of Caesar and made consul. Thus Marcus felt presentiments of responsibilities to come—heavy burdens for a youth in his late teens.

Marcus was slender and graceful and wore a bland expression. He was a good athlete and hunter, a gifted painter, and a disciplined student of rhetoric and literature. Bright and sensitive, he loved nature and delighted in trips to the countryside. His was the gentle spirit that might have chosen to be a recluse, meditating in quietude. He loathed the pomp and ceremonials of state and cared nothing for personal power.

His presentiments of weighty responsi-

Marcus Aurelius   *Faustina*

bilities came true. Most of his ruling years were spent fighting back invasions on the northern frontier and quelling revolts. After defeating the Parthians in the east, his soldiers, returning through Syria, brought back a plague which swept the Empire and decimated the Roman population. At home Marcus was beset with family turmoil. His wife Faustina ranked low on intellect but high on infidelity. She birthed thirteen children, most of whom Marcus dutifully accepted as his. Eight of them died in infancy. Not one member of his family shared his intellectual interests. He was lonely and alone at the center of the civilized world.

Since the age of eleven he had been attracted to the Stoic philosophy, and finally, at twenty-five, he vowed his full devotion to philosophic study—for as long as the world would let him. Throughout his life he alternated between carrying his worldly obligations—which he met energetically, resourcefully, and with common sense—and nourishing his spiritual life. When his duties became oppressive, Marcus would return to his thoughts in stolen hours, late at night, in a tent pitched beside a battlefield, and there, by candlelight, continue his reflections.

It was during times such as these, while fighting the Germanic tribes along the Rhine-Danube frontier, that Marcus wrote his *Things to Himself,* in Greek. Will Durant writes: "This glimpse of a frail and fallible saint, pondering the problems of morality and destiny while leading a great army in a conflict on which the fate of the Empire turned, is one of the most intimate pictures that time has preserved of its great men."

While encamped in Vienna, in the nineteenth year of his reign, Marcus was stricken ill. He beckoned his son to his bedside and outlined strategies for holding off the invaders. Death, an old invader long stayed, was near. He abandoned further food and drink. On the sixth day he rose from his couch, led his son Commodus outside his tent and presented him to his armies as their new emperor. Then he returned to his tent, lay down, and died. He was fifty-nine. The date was March 17 of the year A.D. 180.

Earlier he had written: "Do not act as if you were going to live ten thousand years. Death hangs over you. While you live, while it is in your power, be good."

He had borne the burdens of empire, the alienation of family, the stress of life and the specter of death—yet through it all had maintained his sensitivity, his decency, his humanity.

His body was returned to Rome in a final triumphal march.

As Marcus saw it, *the problem* was finding a way to live in the world and not be destroyed by it. To be sure, his soul longed to escape from the tragedies of life (in good Buddhist fashion), but escape, for him, was not a moral option. "Men seek retreats for themselves—houses in the country, by the seashores, in the mountains; and you too are apt to desire such things very much. But this is altogether a mark of the most common sort of men." By contrast, wise men are called to live "the life of the social animal" and be responsible to their fellow human beings, to whom they belong.

The answer, Marcus reasons, lies in a two-fold commitment. First, people must live-in-the-world by playing whatever roles Fate assigns to them. "All the world's a stage," Shakespeare would later write, "And all the men and women merely players. . . ." Whatever the roles we are cast into, it is a sacred duty that we play our parts well.

We must understand, clearly, that we have little choice of the roles we play. Fate decrees them. Marcus, for instance, did not *choose* to be emperor or to marry Faustina; he did not *choose* to fight the Parthians or Quadi. These events are merely passing scenes in the playing-out of the drama. Therefore, he concludes, we should proceed with fearless *apatheia* to play whatever roles we are given . . . and ignore the rest.

Marcus writes: "Do you see me unhappy because thus-and-so has happened to me? Not at all. Rather, I am happy *despite* its happening to me. Why? Because I continue on, free from pain, neither crushed by the present nor fearing the future. For events such as this happen to every human being."

Along with this acceptance of roles, we must make another commitment: Each of us must look to the well-being of his inner world, for it's here that we may find peace. This is our true retreat, and we had best see to it that the place is habitable. Each one of us is the sole and final caretaker of "this little plot that is thyself."

The wise man "will not go against the Divinity which is planted in his breast; but rather he will preserve his deepest inner self in tranquility. He will, above all, preserve his own autonomy and integrity, and not let anything alienate him from himself."

"This then remains," Marcus reminds himself: "Remember to retire into this little territory of the inner self—your own world (which is all there is)—and there be free, and observe the passing world as a human being. . . ."

---

17   It was in early spring when Captain Jacques Cousteau's oceanographic vessel *Calypso* anchored off the shore of a southern California island. One night his crewmen noticed a churning of the waters and the ship's lights were turned on. In the water were millions of squid, six to ten inches long. Cousteau and his men had accidentally discovered the breeding ground of the sea arrows. The small squid returned here in cycles of two or three years to mate, lay their eggs, and die. Arriving on the scene by the millions, they milled around, waiting.

Then a frenzy of mating began. The females had developed their eggs in tubular egg-cases. Now as the sea arrows darted about, males would grab females and hold them fast in their arms. A special tentacle was used to insert a capsule of sperm under the mantle of the female. The mating continued for days.

Then the females extracted the elongated egg-cases from their bodies and attached them in clusters to the rocks below, where the cases slowly swayed, like fingers covering the bottom of the ocean. Each female would carefully place six to eight egg-cases in position. With the last case attached, her time was finished; she went limp and died. The males, fertilization completed, had already died.

A few days later Cousteau's divers scoured the bottom for signs of life. Of the millions of squid that had made the waters alive, nothing survived. As though covered with snow, the ocean bottom was white with the bodies of the squid. They had fulfilled their purpose, and it was all over. All that the divers found were acres of egg-cases, now covered with a leathery skin to protect them. Inside each egg-case another generation of sea arrows waited to be born. They would come singly out of their eggs, begin to grow, move out to sea and continue the cycle of life. Then at their appointed time, they would return to

The world's a failure, you know. Someone, somewhere, made a terrible mistake.

Mission Impossible
CBS-TV

The world has always been ruled by Lucifer. The world is evil. Call his name, my love. Call the name of Lucifer.

Ritual of Evil
NBC-TV

From what is presently known, Homo sapiens—the modern form of man—has existed on earth for approximately a hundred thousand years in numbers large enough to constitute a population. Barring catastrophic accidents, it can be expected that man will continue living on earth for many millions of years. Using a somewhat fanciful kind of arithmetic, it can be calculated from these figures that the present age of humanity corresponds to very early childhood in the life of a human being. Pursuing still further the same farfetched comparison, reading and writing were invented a year ago; Plato, the Parthenon, Christ, date from but a few months; experimental science is just a few weeks old, and electricity a few days; mankind will not reach puberty for another hundred thousand years. In this perspective, it is natural that so far mankind should have been chiefly concerned with becoming aware of the world of matter, listening to fairy tales, and fighting for pleasure or out of anger. The meaning of life, the problems of man and of society, become dominant preoccupations only later during development. As mankind outgrows childhood, the proper use of science may come to be not only to store food, build mechanical toys, and record allegories, myths, and fairy tales, but to understand, as well as possible, the nature of life and of man in order to give more meaning and value to human existence.

RENÉ DUBOS
The Torch of Life

I have one longing only: to grasp what is hidden behind appearances, to ferret out that mystery which brings me to birth and then kills me, to discover if behind the visible and unceasing stream of the world an invisible and immutable presence is hiding.

NIKOS KAZANTZAKIS
The Saviours of God

I would write of that prehistoric life when man was knit close to nature. I would describe the people who were brothers of the red earth and the red rock and the red streams of the hills. . . . I would show you the unknown, the hideous shrieking mystery at the back of this simple nature. Men would see the profundity of the old crude faiths which they affect to despise. I would make a picture of our shaggy, sombre-eyed forefather who heard strange things in the hill silences. I would show him brutal and terror-stricken, but wise, wise, God alone knows how wise!

JOHN BUCHAN

the breeding ground as their parents had done to meet their destiny and die.

In the last days of the squid's life, two of the *Calypso's* crewmen, swimming the bottom, came upon a female trying to push the last egg-case from her body. Gently they helped her by pulling out the case and attaching it to a rock. Then, joining the rest of her sea arrow family, she too died.

18   The instinct to fulfill the breeding cycle is so deep that no single sea arrow could thwart or change it. The "meaning of existence" for the squid is species-wide; it is provided by its instinctual makeup.

Is it conceivable that man has been totally separated from that evolutionary past when the instincts determined all significant behavior? If our problems are species-wide (as Morris and others believe), is it not possible that there also exist impulses-to-meaning—goal-directed instincts—which are species-wide? Might there not be such leftover urges moving in us, pulsing in the dimmest reaches of our being so that we are unaware of them, yet determining still our most basic behavioral patterns?

As a psychologist, Abraham Maslow believed he had discerned such drives. He was convinced that the human being has within him a pressure (among other pressures) toward unity of personality, toward spontaneous expressiveness, toward full individuality and identity, toward seeing the truth rather than being blind, toward being creative, toward being good, and a lot else. That is, the human being is so constructed that he presses toward fuller and fuller being.

[There is] a single ultimate value for mankind, a far goal toward which all men strive. This is called variously by different authors self-actualization, self-realization, integration, psychological health, individuation, autonomy, creativity, productivity, but they all agree that this amounts to realizing the potentialities of the person, that is to say, becoming fully human, everything that the person *can* become. . . .

19   It is still not out of the question that man, unique among living things, lies free and lost. Perhaps Sartre is right in saying we are ''condemned to be free.'' Perhaps there is no God, no Goddess, no Spirit, no Fate, no Moral Law, no phylogenetic urge-to-life, no instinct—and no meaning.

Perhaps Kierkegaard was right: ''There is no truth, except truth *for me.*'' The nihilistic existentialists have consistently held that the cosmos is depressingly meaningless and human society absurd. Our lives can achieve meaning only if we boldly grasp the choices before us and make whatever meaningful responses we can.

To be sure, many of us wake up each morning—and wonder why.

20   Richard Strauss composed the great tone poem *Also Sprach Zarathustra* in the spring and summer of 1896 and based it on passages from Nietzsche's book of the same title, written a dozen years earlier. Strauss himself wrote:

I meant to convey by means of music an idea of the development of the human race from its origin, through various phases of its development, religious and scientific, up to Nietzsche's idea of the Superman. The whole symphonic poem is intended as an homage to Nietzsche's genius. . . .

Will the mind of man ever solve the riddle of the world? A few calm introductory bars, and already the trumpet sounds, *pp*, their solemn motto C–G–C, the so-called World-Riddle theme which, in various rhythmic guises, will pervade the whole symphonic poem through its very end. The simple but expressive introduction grows quickly in intensity and ends majestically on the climactic C major chord of the organ and full orchestra. . . .

And then comes the mystical conclusion which, ending in two different keys, aroused much controversy when the work was first performed. While the trombones stubbornly hold the unresolved chord C–E–F-sharp, the violins and upper woodwinds carry upward the Theme of the Ideal to higher register in B major . . . the pizzicati of the basses all the while sounding repeatedly the C–G–C of the World-Riddle. *Evidently the great problem remains unsolved.*

Life's but a walking shadow, a
  poor player
That struts and frets his hour upon
  the stage.
And then is heard no more. It is a
  tale
Told by an idiot, full of sound
  and fury.
Signifying nothing.

SHAKESPEARE
Macbeth

Nil desperandum
There's no cause for despair

HORACE

Wise men come ever promising
The riddle of life to know.
Wise men come. . . .
Ah, but over the sands,
The silent sands of time
They go. . . .

KISMET

From ''The Sands of Time'' by Robert Wright and George Forrest. © 1953 by Frank Music Corp. Used by permission.

REFLECTIONS—

1 The Indian physicist/priest seems to be involved in a contradiction. (It's difficult to sympathize with him, of course, because you and I never let ourselves get caught in such dilemmas.) How would you characterize his contradiction? What philosophic assumptions might we infer from his behavior? Would you call him a hypocrite? Can he believe, logically and simultaneously, in *both* world-views implied by his actions?

2 "To sensitive spirits of all ages, life is filled with cruel contradictions and bitter ironies" (Sec. 2). List some of these contradictions and ironies which you have come across in your own experience.

3 When we ask whether life has meaning, what precisely are we asking? What is "meaning"? Is our question essentially logical or psychological? (Or both?) What might be the source(s) of meaning? How would we *know* if life has meaning?

4 What do you understand to be meant by the term "why-question"? In your opinion, why do we have such a deep impulse to ask why-questions? What assumptions must we make in order to render such questions meaningful? Do you think why-questions are asked universally by all men, or are they asked more in our Western tradition because of specific religious assumptions about "the meaning" of events?

5 Ponder the implications of Schweitzer's "Reverence for Life," Maslow's "post-mortem life," and Frankl's conviction that the search for meaning is the key to life. Is there a common *ethic* implied in these three convictions? Would they all lead to a common goal or to a similar kind of experience?

6 Imagine that among the millions of squid (Sec. 17), one of the sea arrows became a philosopher. If you could ask it (in Squidanese) about "the meaning of life," what do you think it might reply? Ask the same question—as vividly as your imagination will allow—of the Saturn V moon rocket (see Prelude), the man-ape (p. 16), and Christina (see Wyeth's painting, p. 11).

7 The fact that "life feeds upon itself" strikes some as being a puzzling *theological* contradiction. Why might it be considered a theological problem and not merely a philosophical problem?

8 What if you decide that life is without meaning—what would this mean to you personally? Do you think your life would be worth living? (Why, incidentally, are you attempting to answer this question?)

Furthermore. . .

BONHOEFFER, DIETRICH, *Letters and Papers from Prison.* Macmillan, 1962.

CARROLL, LEWIS, *Alice in Wonderland* and *Through the Looking Glass.* (Any editions.)

FRANKL, VIKTOR E., *Man's Search for Meaning.* Washington Square, 1963.

JASPERS, KARL, *Socrates, Buddha, Confucius, Jesus.* Harcourt, 1962.

MAUGHAM, W. SOMERSET, *The Razor's Edge.* Pocket Books, 1946.

PIRSIG, ROBERT M., *Zen and the Art of Motorcycle Maintenance.* Bantam, 1975.

SALTEN, FELIX, *Bambi.* (Several paperback editions available.)

SCHNEIDER, FRANZ, and CHARLES GULLANS (trans.), *Last Letters from Stalingrad.* Signet, 1961.

SCHWEITZER, ALBERT, *Out of My Life and Thought.* Holt, Rinehart and Winston, 1961.

The Spirit of Philosophy

Have You Ever Wondered . . .

- Whether questioning the existence of the gods is a wise thing to do?

- What "wisdom" is and how you can acquire it?

- Why there seem to be so many different opinions about every issue?

- Why there have been virtually no women philosophers?

- If it's good to be a "doubter" or a "skeptic" or a "cynic"?

- What the difference is between "faith" and "belief"?

- What the "existentialist" philosophy is all about?

THE LOVE OF WISDOM

1   The word *philosophy* comes from two Greek words: *philein* ("to love") and *sophia* ("wisdom"), implying that a philosopher is (or should be) a "lover of wisdom." Among countless definitions of "philosophy" this is still one of the simplest and best.

2   And so, the would-be philosopher unabashedly admits that he wants to become wise. The wisdom he seeks, however, is not merely the acquisition of facts to dispel ignorance. Rather "wisdom" is the

"Then you believe in an afterlife?"
"Slow up! I don't *'believe'* anything. I *know* certain things— little things, not the Nine Billion Names of God—from experience. But I have *no* beliefs. Belief gets in the way of learning."

ROBERT HEINLEIN
Time Enough for Love

19

antonym of (and antidote for) "foolishness." It is indeed the "fool" who may acquire volumes of information yet not know how to use it. To be "wise" is to possess the understanding and skill to make mature judgments about the use of human knowledge in the context of daily life.

But this sort of wisdom is elusive. It dissolves when desired too desperately, and in times of need it can become paralyzed. Wisdom is not unlike the Tao: if defined too precisely, it will lose its essence; if sought too diligently, it will be missed.

Nevertheless, the philosopher at least knows what he is looking for: *wisdom*.

3   "Wisdom! What wisdom? . . . I certainly have no knowledge of such wisdom, and anyone who says that I have is a liar and wilful slanderer." Thus Socrates begins his defense when brought to trial in Athens in 399 B. C.

Socrates (469–399 B. C.)

> You know Chaerephon, of course. . . . Well, one day he actually went to Delphi and asked this question of the god [Apollo]. . . . He asked whether there was anyone wiser than myself. The priestess replied that there was no one. . . .
>
> When I heard about the oracle's answer, I said to myself "What does the god mean? Why does he not use plain language? I am only too conscious that I have no claim to wisdom, great or small; so what can he mean by asserting that I am the wisest man in the world?". . .
>
> After puzzling about it for some time, I set myself at last with considerable reluctance to check the truth of it in the following way. I went to interview a man with a high reputation for wisdom. . . . Well, I gave a thorough examination to this person—I need not mention his name, but it was one of our politicians that I was studying when I had this experience—and in conversation with him I formed the impression that although in many people's opinion, and especially in his own, he appeared to be wise, in fact he was not. . . . I reflected as I walked away: "Well, I am certainly wiser than this man. It is only too likely that neither of us has any knowledge to boast of; but he thinks that he knows something which he does not know, whereas I am quite conscious of my ignorance. At any rate it seems that I am wiser than he is to this small extent, that I do not think that I know what I do not know."
>
> From that time on I interviewed one person after another. I realized with distress and alarm that I was making myself unpopular. . . . After I had finished with the politicians I turned to the poets, dramatic, lyric, and all the rest. . . . It seemed clear to me that the poets were in much the same case; and I also observed that the very fact that they were poets made them think that they had a perfect understanding of all other subjects, of which they were totally ignorant. So I left that line of inquiry too with the same sense of advantage that I had felt in the case of the politicians.
>
> Last of all I turned to the skilled craftsmen. I knew quite well that I had practically no technical qualifications myself, and I was sure that I should find them full of impressive knowledge. . . . But, gentlemen, these professional experts seemed to share the same failing which I had noticed in the poets; I mean that on the strength of their

technical proficiency they claimed a perfect understanding of every other subject, however important. . . .

The effect of these investigations of mine, gentlemen, has been to arouse against me a great deal of hostility. . . . This is due to the fact that whenever I succeed in disproving another person's claim to wisdom in a given subject, the bystanders assume that I know everything about that subject myself. But the truth of the matter, gentlemen, is pretty certainly this: that real wisdom is the property of [Apollo], and this oracle is his way of telling us that human wisdom has little or no value. It seems to me that he is not referring literally to Socrates, but has merely taken my name as an example, as if he would say to us "The wisest of you men is he who has realized, like Socrates, that in respect of wisdom he is really worthless."

PLATO
The Apology

THE GREEK MIRACLE

4   The birth date of philosophy and science is usually taken to be 585 B.C., for about that time a philosopher named Thales made an assumption which broke with the world-view of his day. He assumed that all things were made of a single substance (Thales thought it might be water) and that the processes of change come from within the substance itself. Thales seems to have thought that the principle of motion and change was inherent in the basic material of which the universe is made.

Now why is this assumption significant? Before Thales, physical events were explained by supernatural causes. Since the cosmos was inhabited by all sorts of gods and goddesses, godlets, demigods, demons, ancestral ghosts, and a host of other spirits good and bad, it was reasonable to conclude that all events of human experience occured *because they had been willed.*

If lightning struck, Zeus had hurled another thunderbolt. When the sun moved through the heavens, all knew that Apollo was driving it in his fiery chariot. If the Greeks lost the battle of Troy, or if Jason's ship slipped safely between the rocks of Scylla and the whirlpool of Charybdis, then the Olympians were playing games again.

And so, before the time of these first philosophers, all *natural* events were attributed to *supernatural* causes. G. K. Chesterton once remarked that for those holding the ancient world-view, the sun moved across the sky each day only because God got up before the sun and said to the sun, "Sun, get up and do it again."

The first philosophers were not quite satisfied with all this. Perhaps they realized that if, to every question you can ask, you get but a single answer ("The gods willed it"), then in fact you know nothing meaningful or useful. So the Milesian philosophers (Thales and his pupils Anaximander and Anaximenes) sought a different *kind* of explanation: when they asked about the cause of events, *they made the assumption* that the answer might be found in "nature" or within matter itself. In other words, they deliberately ignored the unpredictable wills of the anthropomorphic Greek deities.

This assumption marks the beginning of knowledge in the

Thales (fl. 585 B.C.)

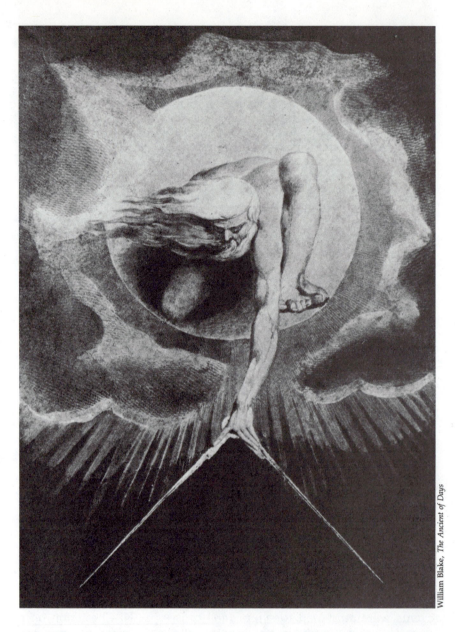

William Blake, *The Ancient of Days*

West. This is the breakthrough that has been called "the Greek miracle."

5   Men of Athens, I know and love you, but I shall obey God rather than you, and while I have life and strength I shall never cease from the practice and teaching of Philosophy. . . . I am that gadfly which God has attached to the state, and all day long and in all places am always fastening upon you, arousing and persuading and reproaching you. . . . I tell you that to do as you say would be a disobedience to God, and therefore I cannot hold my tongue. Daily to discourse about virtue, and about those other things about which you hear me examining myself and others is the greatest good of man. The unexamined life is not worth living. . . . In another world I shall be able to con-

PEANUTS®

By Charles M. Schulz

© 1969 by United Feature Syndicate, Inc.

tinue my search into true and false knowledge. . . . In another world they do not put a man to death for asking questions: assuredly not.

PLATO
The Apology

Flight from insecurity is catastrophic to any kind of human growth. To flee from insecurity is to miss the whole point of being human. It is to miss, at any rate, the whole point of religion.

PETER BERTOCCI

FREEDOM TO WONDER AND TO ASK QUESTIONS

6   Philosophy and freedom of inquiry were born together. Neither has ever existed without the other. If we possess freedom, we inquire. But if our freedom to inquire is too limited, freedom, which is rightly a condition, becomes itself the goal for which we are willing to fight and die.

Throughout Western history, of course, religious sentiment has resisted critical inquiry into certain questions the final answers to which were allegedly known. The question of God's existence, for example, was not considered debatable. In more recent times there has been opposition to investigation into the nature of man, especially his evolutionary origin and the operations of his inner world. The possibility of synthesizing life in the laboratory has also been feared and fought. In such areas scientists have long since probed where others feared to search and have reduced the *mysterium* to quantitative analysis.

For the philosopher, as for the scientist, there is no holy ground—unless indeed *all* is Holy Ground.

7   Despite our background of Greek rationalism, reason in the Western world has had a difficult time. In the Judeo-Christian tradition it is made clear that we are saved by faith and not by our rational intellects or academic credentials.

The epitome of the righteous man was Abraham, who was willing to go so far as to kill his son Issac *in order to obey* the word of his God, Yahweh. He assumed no right (according to the story in Genesis 22) to question the command; there was no chance of his debating with Yahweh the morality of the order. (However, read Genesis 18:20–33 where Abraham—yes, Abraham—carried on a running argument with God about a similar moral issue—and won!) In sacrificing

Love is a strong word, but not, I think, too strong for a passion which scorns the harlotry of fantasy and demands that those dedicated to an austere beauty should be faithful even unto death. The love of truth—which must not be confused with love of certainty—has seldom made much appeal to religious minds.

HECTOR HAWTON

Isaac, absolute obedience was required, and because of his submission Abraham has been held up as the ideal "Man of Uprightness" for more than three thousand years. Salvation is a reward for faith and obedience.

8   In the gospel tradition, Thomas is the example of what we are not to be, if we can help it. Thomas doubted. He wanted better evidence than he had before believing something reported to him by others, that is, before he *could* believe emotional second-hand reports of an event which, at first glance, seemed extremely improbable. Eventually "doubting Thomas" was told to place his hands in the wound in Jesus' side so that then he too might believe. But this skepticism is not commendable, for Jesus is reported to have said, "Blessed be those who have not seen me and yet believe!" (John 20:29).

Similarly, Saint Paul had grave misgivings about human wisdom and those who seek it. It appears that he had a rather sour experience with some Stoic and Epicurean philosophers in Athens. "Where now is your philosopher? Your scribe? Your reasoner of today?" he wrote to the Corinthian Christians. "Has not God made a fool of the world's wisdom?" A similar word of caution was sent to his friends in the Lycus Valley: "Take care that nobody exploits you through pretensions of philosophy. . . ."

Time and again, Paul found that philosophers were the hardest minds to sway, and, despairing of their lack of understanding, he moved on to the towns where he could find people who had the capacity for faith.

9   Reason and knowledge are of little value in achieving salvation, according to orthodox Western theology. On the contrary, they can be a positive hindrance. We are saved by *faith*. Redemption is for the illiterate as much as for the educated. For in Christ, Paul reminds us, there is neither Jew nor Gentile, male nor female, slave nor free. "In union with Christ, all men are one." In matters of salvation, that is, all men of faith are equal.

The Church Fathers and Scholastic philosophers, of course, followed Paul's lead. Saint Augustine (A.D. 354–430) alway asserted the primacy of faith: *Fides proecedit intellectum*, "Faith must exist before one can understand." Augustine "never abandoned or depreciated reason," writes a church historian; "he only subordinated it to faith and made it subservient to the defence of revealed truth. Faith is the pioneer of reason, and discovers the territory which reason explores."

Saint Anselm of Canterbury (1033–1109) took the same position. *Credo ut intelligam*, "I believe in order to understand." Revealed truth must first be accepted, and in the light of that certainty one can then know how to interpret all else. The revealed truth cannot itself be subject to doubt.

Peter Abelard (1079–1142) disagreed and stoutly declared it was the other way around. Understanding comes first, and only then can one decide what to believe. Abelard was not afraid of questions and doubts: "For by doubting we come to inquiry, by inquiry we discover the truth."

Our Reason is capable of nothing but the creation of a universal confusion and universal doubt: it has no sooner built up a system than it shows you the means of knocking it down. It is a veritable Penelope, who unpicks during the night the tapestry that she has woven during the day.
Accordingly, the best use that one can make of philosophical studies is to recognise that it is a way that leads astray, and that we ought to look for another guide, which we shall find in the light of Revelation.

PIERRE BAYLE (1647–1706)

The real tragedy that may occur in any of our lives is not the losing of our faith. . . . The real tragedy is *not* to lose our faith . . . to be satisfied, to be smug and content, to have arrived . . . .

BERT C. WILLIAMS

St. Paul in Athens

I do not seek to understand in order that I may believe, but I believe in order that I may understand, for of this I feel sure, that, if I did not believe, I would not understand.

ST. ANSELM

Needless to say, Augustine and Anselm won, and Abelard lost. We speak of *Saint* Augustine and *Saint* Anselm, but we do not say "Saint" Abelard.

10   In a postscript to *A Study of History*, Arnold Toynbee conjures an imaginary Hindu who scolds Christianity for its rational self-immolation.

> "I feel little respect for the Christian application of thought to Christianity because your Christian thinkers do not dare to have the courage of their conviction. The characteristic virtue of thought is to follow the argument whithersoever it may lead; if thought flinches from fulfilling this first commandment of intellectual honesty, it commits a stultifying sin against its own nature; and this is the moral infirmity by which your Christian thinking is invalidated. Your imposing *Summa Theologiae* is confined within the prison-walls of a mythology which your hearts have dictated to your heads; and in matters of religion Christianity allows the Intellect to operate only under a perpetual edict serving notice 'Thus far and no farther.' What is the World to think of a Christian intelligence that consents to work under conditions that make nonsense of the Intellect's essential function? . . . I am proud—however high your Christian judgement may rate the moral price—that my Hinduism does not sacrifice honest thinking to prejudiced sentiment."

11   "My trade is to say what I think," said Voltaire. We might add that the philosopher's vocation is to think what he pleases, and then to speak and write what he thinks. He cannot in good faith accept any restraint upon his professional calling. For economy and efficiency, of course, he will choose how he limits himself and how he articulates his questions, but he will resist any external threat to his freedom of inquiry.

In this spirit, he will grant to all others the same freedom he insists upon for himself. To turn again to Voltaire, a well-known, but little-heeded, line is attributed to the French philosopher: "I do not agree with a word that you say, but I will defend to the death your right to say it."

EITHER/OR . . .

12   Time and again, when we want to understand ourselves, we find that we must return to the two great traditions which together make up our Western heritage. Like intellectual archeologists, we have to chip at the clay and brush away the dust from the remains of our buried past.

Countless ideas inherited from our two ancestral worlds—Greco-Roman and the Judaic—have been harmonized into a coherent world-view, and Western life has been richer for it. But like a dissonant undercurrent, a few Greek and Judeo-Christian beliefs have remained stubbornly incompatible, and thinkers have tried in vain to work out some sort of coexistence.

The most ordinary misinterpretation of faith is to consider it an act of knowledge that has a low degree of evidence. . . . If this is meant, one is speaking of belief rather than of faith. . . . Almost all the struggles between faith and knowledge are rooted in the wrong understanding of faith as a type of knowledge which has a low degree of evidence but is supported by religious authority. One of the worst errors of theology and popular religion is to make statements which intentionally or unintentionally contradict the structure of reality. Such an attitude is an expression not of faith but of the confusion of faith with belief.

PAUL TILLICH

Voltaire (1694–1778)

It is only charlatans who are certain. . . . Doubt is not a very agreeable state, but certainty is a ridiculous one.

VOLTAIRE

Socrates

The Wisest Man Alive

"You know Chaerephon, of course?"

I had heard of him, but it really wasn't a question. I nodded.

"Well, Chaerephon once had the audacity—and really, that's what it was: audacity!—to go into the Temple of Apollo out at Delphi and ask the oracle that question: 'Of all men alive, who is the wisest?' And the priestess—or perhaps Apollo himself—had the gall to answer: 'The wisest man alive is Socrates of Athens.' "

Socrates was smiling, faintly, with an expression of impish irony, I thought, and perhaps sadness, but not humor. Four bailiff-guards watched from the portico above, waiting for the king-archon to summon him back into the court to proceed with the penalty part of the trial.

Socrates had been pacing, but now he sat down in the corner of the stone bench opposite me. Some of his friends stood nearby, in small groups, talking anxiously or glancing, in benumbed silence, at this impressive figure. He had already been convicted—though barely, by a vote of 280 to 220; and shortly he would be hailed back into the chambers before the same tribunal, this time to suggest some

appropriate punishment and, perhaps, to plea for leniency.

Almost six hours have passed since we first heard the reading of the staggering indictment, brought against Socrates by Anytus—so long considered to be a moderate and respectable citizen—proclaimed loudly by Anytus'

Silenus

spokesman, young Meletus, to the five hundred freemen who constitute the jury: "Socrates is guilty," he declared in forensic tones, "first, of not honoring the gods of the City of Athens and of introducing new and strange religious practices; and, secondly, of corrupting the youth of our City." Then in ringing rhetoric: "The prosecution demands the death penalty."

It was spring in the year of Laches, and the warming sun was casting afternoon shadows. Socrates wore sandals and the same white, threadbare robe he wore year round. He had a broad face, flattish nose, and thick lips—a countenance, Alcibiades often said, that strikingly resembled the masks of Silenus one sees in stone carvers' shops, masks with pipes and flutes in their mouths. He was balding, with locks of gray hair around the fringe and a thick, silver-gray beard. He was stocky and his tanned skin was firm for a man of seventy years.

At the moment he was pensive, and the fiery eyes that normally glared from the Silenus-mask were closed in thought.

This is the man, I recalled, who has wandered the streets of Athens for almost half a century, forcing men to think, reasonably and honestly, about what they claim to know.

This is the man who has associated with, and been honored by, the great men and women of Hellas. He was a friend to Pericles, our greatest statesman, and to his beautiful Aspasia. He was admired by the tragic poet Euripides and mocked—but then befriended—by the comedic poet Aristophanes. His companionship has been sought by such intellectual lights as Protagoras, Archelaus, Aristippus, Antisthenes, and Euclides. And he was the teacher of Alcibiades the Traitor.

This is the man who distinguished himself for courage time and again during the long wars with Sparta. At the siege of Potidaea he had saved the wounded Alcibiades from certain death. At the retreat from Delium Socrates stood his ground against the Boeotian troops; and, so the story goes, the ferocious appearance of this oxlike hoplite, in full infantry gear, waving his spear and glaring at them, caused the enemy to rout and run from the field. His courage and strength have become as legend-

ary as his embarrassing honesty and towering intellect.

I recall hearing Xenophon tell of the time Socrates lost his way in the winding streets of Athens and asked, "Where does one go to buy groceries?" After giving him directions, Xenophon received the further inquiry, "And where does one go to learn to become an honest man?" When no answer was forthcoming, Socrates beckoned: "Come with me, and I'll show you."

Socrates shook his head. "In the name of God, how many are the lies they tell about me! But the oracle did not lie. This has been clear to me for more than thirty years now. What makes a man truly wise? Only his realization of how much he doesn't know. And again today I've discovered the truth of the oracle's words. My learned accusers—they *know* everything. The know *everything*, that is, except how little they know."

I too have visited Delphi. With scores of other pilgrims I walked along the Sacred Way that winds through the olive groves in the wide valley below Mount Parnassus; and I trembled with awe as I watched the Pythian priestess, balanced on a three-legged bronze throne, inhaling the pungent vapors of a simmering brew of laurel leaves and delivering oracles. Whenever she spoke, the attending priests would pass on Apollo's answer to some pilgrim's eager question.

On that auspicious occasion, years ago, the divine oracle had replied to Chaerephon's inquiry: "Socrates is the wisest man alive."

The coolness of evening was drifting in from the sea. Socrates gathered the woolen folds of his tunic close around him and settled back into the corner of the bench to await their call.

I wondered what he would say when he stood before the jury for the last time. Whatever it might be, I knew he would say it with grace and style.

Still, I feared for him.

Beloved Pan, and all ye other gods who haunt this place, give me beauty in the inward soul; and may the outward and inward man be at one. May I reckon the wise to be the wealthy, and may I have such a quantity of gold as none but the temperate can carry.

SOCRATES
Plato, *Phaedrus*

In time, the true meaning of the oracle dawned on Socrates. The meaning was that mankind are universally ignorant of the one thing it is most imperative to know, how to conduct their lives aright, how to "tend" their own souls, and "make them as good as possible," and they are universally blind to this ignorance. Socrates is the one exception; if he, too, does not possess this supremely important knowledge, he knows its importance, and he knows his own ignorance of it; he is, at least, the "one-eyed" in a kingdom of the "blind," and the wisest of men, as men go. This is why he feels it a duty laid on him by God to persist in seeking the supreme knowledge, and to try to induce any man, fellow-citizen or stranger, who will listen to him to seek it with him.

A. E. TAYLOR
Socrates

Wherefore, O judges, be of good cheer about death, and know of a certainty that no evil can happen to a good man, either in life or after death, and that he and his are not neglected by the gods. . . . The hour of departure has arrived, and we go our ways—I to die, and you to live. Which is better God only knows.

SOCRATES
The Apology by Plato

This was the end of our comrade, . . . a man, as we would say, of all then living we had ever met, the noblest and the wisest and the most just.

PLATO
Phaedo

The trial of Socrates represents something more than a mere historical event that could not possibly happen again. The trial of Socrates is a charge leveled at the type of intellectual questioning that seeks out the true problems lying outside everyday mediocrity. When Socrates tormented the Athenians like a gadfly, he prevented them from sleeping peacefully, from relaxing with their ready-made solutions to moral and social problems. By astonishing us, Socrates prevents us from thinking along the old lines that have been handed down to us and have become habits. Thus Socrates stands at the very opposite end of the scale from intellectual well-being, easy conscience, and beatific serenity. For all who think that the evidence of authority ought to prevail over the authority of evidence, that order and stability cannot permit the crimes of nonconformity and "lèse-société," Socrates could only have been an enemy. . . .

JEAN BRUN
Socrates

All in all he was fortunate: he lived without working, read without writing, taught without routine, drank without dizziness, and died before senility, almost without pain.

WILL DURANT
The Story of Civilization

We have now, in this chapter, encountered basic assumptions about life, involving ultimate commitments, which are logically and psychologically incompatible. For almost two millennia we have been torn by the conflict. Despite all healing attempts by some of the West's greatest minds, we are still intellectually dichotomized.

The Greek commitment is to reasoned inquiry into the nature of existence. This commitment has enabled us to understand the natural world we live in and to lay the foundations for an understanding of man.

On the other hand, the Judeo-Christian commitment has been to religious beliefs which lie beyond human understanding. What has been revealed by the Infinite Mind cannot be comprehended by finite minds; the "mysteries of faith" will remain beyond our grasp, for "we see through a glass, darkly." Our purpose in life should not be to analyze the Infinite or synthesize life's fragments. Rather, our goal should be "to get into a right relationship with God," to do his will through faith, and to look forward to an eternity which will transcend this mortal existence.

And so, for many, it is either/or. Here the road forks and one may be forced to choose the road he will travel. Many have tried to blaze a way between them, but no clear path has yet been found.

13   In this dichotomy, the philosopher generally chooses the company of Socrates. The philosopher has no doubt about the transforming power and the pragmatic virtue of religious belief, but he believes that courageous inquiry, and growth from the knowledge thereby gained, hold out greater hope for both personal fulfillment and the future of Mankind.

"I have said some things," Socrates once remarked, "of which I am not altogether confident. But that we shall be better and braver and less helpless if we think that we ought to inquire, than we should have been if we indulged in the idle fancy that there was no knowing and no use in seeking to know what we do not know—that is a theme upon which I am ready to fight, in word and deed, to the utmost of my power."

14   The philosopher engages in doubt as a *modus operandi*. He insists upon doubting a fact-claim to force it to defend itself. For exam-

A point of view can be a dangerous luxury when substituted for insight and understanding.

MARSHALL MCLUHAN

Why is the Universe as it is and not something else? Why is the Universe here at all? It is true that at present we have no clue to the answers to questions such as these. . . . But throughout the history of science, people have been asserting that such and such an issue is inherently beyond the scope of reasoned inquiry, and time after time they have been proved wrong. . . . All experience teaches us that no one has yet asked too much.

FRED HOYLE

Descartes (1596–1650)

ple, René Descartes used "methodical doubt" as the foundation of his philosophical system. He doubted everything he could in the hope of arriving at some "fact" that he could not further doubt. When he discovered such a "fact" (*Cogito, ergo sum,* "I think, therefore I exist"), he began to build deductively upon that certified first principle. This brand of doubt has played a significant role in all the knowledge-gathering sciences. A historian once said that the beginning of *all* knowlege is a "good healthy doubt."

A COMMUNITY OF SEEKERS—

To my way of thinking, a college is a community of seekers—a community of those devoted not solely to the appreciation and preservation of the past, but dedicated to the discovery of greater truth. It is a community of those who do not believe that *all* truth has been found in *any* area—who refuse to invest any particular statement, book, creed, institution, or person with finality or infallibility. It should be a community of those who are completely dedicated to the best that they know but believe that there is a better-to-be-known in all areas. Persons in such a community should be doubters and sceptics in the sense that they suspend judgement and question all assumptions and conclusions, so that each one will be forced to justify itself before the bar of critical analysis. Such attitudes are never apt to win friends or to influence people among that segment of society that believes that it has the truth.

BERT C. WILLIAMS

There have been four general ideas of what philosophers are supposed to be doing. They can be classified as (1) synoptics, (2) activists, (3) antinomians, and (4) analytics.

THE SYNOPTIC PHILOSOPHERS

The synoptic philosophers have in common the desire "to see life steadily and to see it whole" (Whitehead) or, at least, to understand every event in the largest possible way (James). Commonly we find the synoptic philosophers having a very wide range of interests and concerns. They are usually fascinated by almost all areas of human knowledge. They will have special interests, of course, but they will delve into all sorts of knowledge to better obtain an overview of life and the problems they wish to work on.

15   In the spring of the year 334 B.C., as Alexander the Great was setting off across Asia to conquer the world and bring the gift of Greek civilization to all Mankind, Aristotle left his home town in Thrace and returned to Athens to establish his own school of learning. In a green

Aristotle (384–322 B.C.)

grove just ouside the city, near a temple dedicated to Apollo Lyceus, he founded the Lyceum. It had a campus, classrooms, a chapel, covered walkways, and shaded gardens. In time it also contained the Western world's first great library, a museum of natural history, and a zoological garden.

During morning hours Aristotle lectured to his students in technical subjects as they strolled along the pathways. (For this they came to be nicknamed Peripatetics or "the Strollers.") In the afternoons he lectured on popular subjects to crowds from outside the school. At dinner teacher and students dined together and often held symposia. Aristotle reserved his evening hours for his own research and writing.

Out of this atmosphere emerged our first empirically° grounded synoptic philosophy.

16 Aristotle was the first great *synoptic* philosopher. His mind ranged over every known realm of human knowledge, and he produced brilliant, creative writing in every field. Drawing upon the immense amount of empirical data collected by his students and sent to him by Alexander from foreign countries (one report has it that Alexander set a thousand men collecting specimens of flora and fauna for Aristotle's laboratories and museums), Aristotle was also the West's first true scientiest.

While hundreds of Aristotle's writings have been lost, some forty works survive. He wrote extensively in what we would call the *natural sciences* (physics, astronomy and cosmology, geology, meteorology), the *life sciences* (biology, anatomy, physiology, genetics), and *social sciences* (psychology, politics, ethics), the *practical arts* (oratory and rhetoric), and *"philosophy"* (logic and epistemology, esthetics, theology, metaphysics).

His synoptic mind was continually at work weaving these vast areas of knowledge into a coherent philosophical system that served as the framework for man's thinking until the beginning of the scientific revolution. "He is probably the only human intellect that has ever compassed at first hand and assimilated the whole body of existing knowledge on all subjects, and brought it within a single focus—and a focus, at that, which after more than two thousand years still stands as one of the supreme achievements of the mind of man."

17 One goal of synoptic philosophy is the development of an empirically sound and rationally coherent world-view to serve as an operational model for the interpretation and valuation of all our experience. Such a world-view provides unity and consistency to the whole of life.

A common result of synoptic activity is what Dr. Robert Fischer has called "an ecology of understanding": the discovery that all knowledge is related and that any rigid compartmentalization of data ("chemistry," "biology," "psychology," etc.) is artificial and eventually self-defeating. Knowledge is seen to be a unity, an "ecological system" in which all parts must be understood in relation to one another.

°Empirical, empiricism. *In philosophy the word "empiricism" is defined in two distinct ways. (1) It refers to knowlege acquired by our senses only. (2) "Empirical" is often used to refer to any knowledge gained by human experience (not merely sense experience). This wider definition would include dreams, emotions, religious experiences, and so on.*

In these pages, unless otherwise noted, these terms will be used only in the narrow sense, as in (1) above: "empirical" knowlege is gained alone through the senses. See glossary.

As knowledge grew, fear decreased; men thought less of worshiping the unknown, and more of overcoming it.

WILL DURANT
The Story of Philosophy

Certainly, the characteristic activity of the mind, from the formation of a general idea to the great system of Philosophy, from the humblest perception to the laws of Science and the Uniformity of Nature itself, from the vaguest conception of spirit to the monistic unity of the Supreme Personality of Religion, is the endeavor to create 'wholes' in thought, to organise experience into some form or other of coherent totality.

ARNOLD TOYNBEE

THE ACTIVIST PHILOSOPHERS

18   The *activist* philosophers believe that the philosophic enterprise must be a part of life itself and that the philosopher cannot be a mere spectator of life's tragicomic drama. He may not have auditioned for a role in the drama, but he has been cast nevertheless. He can no more resign from the cast than he can resign from the human race.

There are at least three distinct varieties of activist philosophers: (1) the prophetic activists, (2) the pragmatists, and (3) the existentialists. Each, however, insists on participation in the human drama for quite different reasons.

19   The *prophetic°* activists contend that the task of philosophy is to bring about drastic reforms in social conditions; human suffering in all its forms must be dealt with *now*. Karl Marx, for example, became disillusioned with the ivory-tower philosophy in vogue in nineteenth-century Germany, a grandiose metaphysics of human history which was blind to the concrete realities of day-to-day human experience. Indeed, much German philosophy (and especially Hegelian idealism) hardly acknowledged the existence of the individual per se.

Against such dehumanizing theories, there arose numerous reactions, Marx's among them. Marx wrote that "philosophers have only *interpreted* the world differently: the point is, however, to *change* it." He therefore developed a philosophy of history in which change (and the doctrine of "inevitable progress") was the central idea. "Marx's aim," writes Erich Fromm,

> was that of the spiritual emancipation of man, of his liberation from the chains of economic determination, of restituting him in his human wholeness, of enabling him to find unity and harmony with his fellow man and with nature. Marx's philosophy was, in secular, nontheistic language, a new and radical step forward in the tradition of prophetic Messianism; it was aimed at the full realization of individualism, the very aim which has guided Western thinking from the Renaissance and the Reformation far into the nineteenth century.

Since our main concern here is to describe what philosophers are supposed to be doing, it is of interest to note that Marx the man was more philosopher than revolutionary. "A man whose whole creed was one of action," notes Untermeyer, "he spent practically all his time in libraries." To be sure, he had himself engaged in social action in Paris and Brussels, but the last thirty years of his life were spent writing in the British Museum and in a dingy two-room London apartment. Instead of taking action he philosophized about it.

This is not to be taken as an indictment. On the contrary, it suggests that philosophy and social activism may be competing preoccupations. One can do one or the other, or one can alternate from one to the other, but it appears doubtful that both activities can be carried on effectively at the same time.

Heretofore philosophers have only *interpreted* the world differently: the point is, however, to *change* it.
                                        KARL MARX

°The word "prophetic" is used here in its original sense as referring to those who, with a passion for justice, advocate a crash program of social reform. This is precisely the position of the prototypical prophets of the Old Testament such as Amos, Isaiah and Jeremiah. By definition a "prophet" was a "spokesman of God," but his social function was to initiate social change by courageously exposing the corruption and the corruptors. While the scriptural prophets were not philosophers in any precise sense, their social concerns and actions were the same as those of the activist philosophers dealt with here.

Karl Marx (1818–1883)

20   The American *pragmatists*° represent a second reaction against the prevailing German idealism. "Damn the Absolute!" was William James's response to Hegel's idea that history is the manifestation of the "Absolute Mind" of God. James believed that philosophers should get down to the task of solving the problems of life. Too long have they been playing around with metaphysical speculations. An idea is to be judged by its "cash value," wrote James; and philosophical concepts should be evaluated in terms of their practical consequences.

It has often been noted that pragmatism could only have been born on American soil, since it reflects the spirit of the nineteenth century, the frontier spirit of individualism, self-reliance, and practicality. Americans had traditionally been castigated by European thinkers as "long on action but short on thought." William James successfully argued that it was time for a carefully thought-out philosophy of action which would deal candidly with real issues.

James's down-to-earth attitude sometimes shocked staid academicians. "This universe will never be completely good as long as one being is unhappy," he said, and added, "or as long as one poor cockroach suffers the pangs of unrequited love."

°Pragmatism. *From the Greek* pragma, *"deed" or "action." An American philosophical movement associated with Peirce, James, and John Dewey. The basic theme of pragmatism is that ideas have meaning only in relation to the practical results which they effect.*

William James (1842–1910)

21   The *existentialists*° have all shared the basic belief that life has meaning only when it is fully experienced. Life is not a thing to be thought, but an existence to be lived. To think and to exist are quite different things, and most philosophers have sold their existence for a handful of thoughts. To watch someone else enjoy a sunset or experience love may not be without value; but it's a world away from enjoying the sunset and feeling love within and for oneself.

The existentialist becomes involved in life, therefore, not primarily to change the world or even to solve its problems but in order to discover, for himself, the meaning of existence.

Søren Kierkegaard, the "father of existentialism," and all subsequent existentialists have criticized traditional philosophy as a collection of astute observations by "spectators." It therefore has a hollow ring, for it has missed life.

The existentialists believe that the only "reality" that is worthwhile is experience—what takes place personally and uniquely in the inner world of each of us. Moreover, since neither past nor future exist, the concrete present is where the full intensity of life is to be found. The advice of the existentialist, therefore, is to live life and not let it pass by while meditating on it.

°Existentialism. *A school of philosophy arising during World War II, but drawing heavily from the long-neglected writings of Kierkegaard (1813–1855). One central theme of existentialism is that the only realistic understanding of life comes from focusing upon the moment-by-moment, concrete existence of individual persons, especially their inner worlds. All intellectual speculation is secondary to the experiencing organism involved in living.*

THE ANTINOMIAN PHILOSOPHERS

22   Not all philosophers would agree that social action is the noblest of human activities. The *antinomian*° philosophers have held that a realistic assessment of the human condition necessarily leads anyone concerned with the quality of his existence to withdraw from the world. Western monastics, of course, have disengaged themselves

°Antinomian. *From the Greek* anti, *"against," and* nomos, *"law"; hence, "against the law." In the widest sense (as used here), it refers to those who deliberately choose to exist outside the accepted norms of society.*

A page from Kierkegaard's *Journals*.

from the world since at least the second century before Christ. Hindus revere the *sannyasin* who enter the forests to meditate, their ultimate goal being total withdrawal into the trance-state of *nirvana*. Zen and Theravada Buddhists share similar attitudes toward life-in-this-world.

The best known Western critics of society are perhaps Jean-Jacques Rousseau and Henry David Thoreau. Both contended that a return to nature and the simple life is necessary to preserve one's self and sanity. Both, however, were sensitive to social ills and neither managed to withdraw from the world for very long.

The true antinomian philosophers are such men as Diogenes the Cynic and Chuang-tzu the Taoist.

23   *Antinomianism—Western Style.* After Athens' Golden Age was over, many diverse philosophical schools were born. One such school, the Cynics, was founded by Antisthenes. He held his classes in a gymnasium outside Athens and catered to the poor, the illegitimate, and the foreign-born. He taught without fees, lived simply, and dressed shabbily. Socrates once said to him, "Antisthenes, I can see your vanity through the holes of your cloak."

"I can't decide whether to go to the orgy or listen to Socrates."

His most famous pupil was Diogenes, who had tried banking in Asia Minor, failed, and came to Athens. He was forced to beg, and Antisthenes helped him rationalize his condition into a philosophy. He gathered the accouterments of a beggar—old clothes, a bowl, and a staff—and lived in a large tub in the courtyard of an Athenian temple. His only companions were dogs.

The Cynics disdained culture and ridiculed sophistic learning. They rebelled against the customs and codes of society. They wandered from place to place, evangelically denouncing the absurdities and corruptions of society and preaching a simple, back-to-nature existence in which all Mankind could be one family.

Diogenes tried to practice what he preached. He slept on the ground or in his tub, eating whatever he could beg. He tried never to hurt anyone. Above all he wanted to be free—free of material possessions, relationships, traditions, laws. In fact, he recognized no laws, so he could neither obey nor disobey them. Freedom of speech was most important to him and he made much use of it, coarsely and wittily. He never thought of himself as a Greek (he wasn't) and considered himself as belonging to Mankind alone.

There is a legend to the effect that Diogenes often walked the streets of Athens with a lantern in his hand, looking—in vain—for an honest man.

24 *Antinomianism—Eastern Style.* The Taoist philosopher Chuang-tzu is considered by many to be the greatest sage that China has produced. We know little about his life, but as we listen to his thoughts we can feel the working of a wise and subtle mind.

Chuang-tzu lived in the state of Meng about 300 B.C. He became famous and could have held high office, but he disdained society, power, and wealth. He was irreverent toward pompous authorities and ridiculed all schools of philosophy (he never dreamed that his philosophy would become a "school"). He was especially critical of Confucian teachings because they produced obedient, cultured, "virtuous" men who were empty inside. Such men could play to perfection the artificial games of social custom, but they had lost the freedom for authentic, spontaneous behavior. They were imprisoned by arbitrary rules and social niceties.

Chuang-tzu wanted none of this. He preferred to watch the merry go-around from a distance. "The life of things passes by like a rushing, galloping horse, changing at every turn, at every hour. What should one do, or what should one not do? Let the changes go on by themselves!"

25 Chuang-tzu with his bamboo pole was fishing in the river. The prince of Chu sent two officials to offer him formally the post of Prime Minister.

Chuang-tzu held his bamboo pole. Still looking into the river, he said, "I am told there is a sacred tortoise which has been dead now some three thousand years. Wrapped in silk, in a shrine on an altar in the temple. What do you think: Is it better to give up one's life and

leave a sacred shell as an object of veneration in a cloud of incense three thousand years, or is it better to live as a plain turtle wagging its tail in the mud?''

"For the turtle," replied one of the officials, "it is better to live and wag its tail in the mud!"

"Then, begone!" ordered Chuang-tzu. "I too will stay here and wag my tail in the mud!"

26   Thomas Merton, an interpreter of the writings of Chuang-tzu, was a Trappist monk. Reflecting upon the philosophy of Chuang-tzu he sensed a familiar way of life. Father Merton wrote:

> I have been a Christian monk for nearly twenty-five years, and inevitably one comes in time to see life from a viewpoint that has been common to solitaries and recluses in all ages and in all cultures. . . . There is a monastic outlook which is common to all those who have elected to question the value of life submitted entirely to arbitrary secular presuppositions, dictated by social conventions, and dedicated to the pursuit of temporal satisfactions which are perhaps only a mirage. Whatever may be the value of "life in the world" there have been, in all cultures, men who have claimed to find something they vastly prefer in solitude.

If you wish to converse with me, define your terms.

VOLTAIRE

Faith is believin' things that nobody in his right mind would believe.

ARCHIE BUNKER
All in the Family

THE ANALYTIC PHILOSOPHERS

27   From its beginning, one of the central concerns of Western philosophy has been the *analysis* of ideas. The origins of logic° are pre-Socratic, but the special preoccupation with problems of clear thinking dates from Socrates himself. Much of his time was spent in asking questions about words, ideas, and beliefs and discovering the fallacies which mar a large part of our thinking.

Aristotle, however, is considered the founder of formal logic. He invented the syllogism and wrote the first textbook in logic. Since his time new systems of logic have been devised, including systems of symbolic logic which have had practical application in business fields and computer science.

Twentieth-century philosophical logic has had an ambiguous career. One name, however—Wittgenstein—has dominated the field for nearly a half-century.

°*Logic. From the Greek* logike, *"the art of reasoning." In philosophy the word "logic" is a technical term referring to the study of valid inference. It is the disciplined study of the techniques of clear thinking. (Furthermore, the word* valid *is a technical term, used in logic, to refer to any idea which has been correctly inferred from other given statements.)*

28   There were two creative periods in the life of Ludwig Wittgenstein, each of which culminated in a complex system of philosophy. His first period began in 1912 when he became a student of Bertrand Russell at Cambridge University; it ended in 1921 with the publication of an epoch-making (but remarkably brief) treatise entitled *Tractatus Logico-Philosophicus.* Subsequently he published almost nothing, as though his philosophic search had reached its end.

Then a second period of creative philosophizing began in 1929 when he returned to Cambridge, first as a student, then as a teacher. Out of his teaching a new philosophy was born, which resulted in his *Philosophical Investigations,* published posthumously in 1953.

Ludwig Wittgenstein (1889–1951)

WHERE ARE THE WOMEN?

A mere glance through the history of philosophy shows a glaring absence. *Where are the women?* Didn't women become philosophers? Weren't they just as concerned as men with problems of human existence?

Most civilizations have been men's worlds, and those professions likely to bring fame have been closed to the female of the species. Few women became military heroines, for instance; and on the rare occasions when they did (Joan of Arc comes to mind) they did so along paths quite outside society's *modus operandi*.

And so it was with philosophy. There was but one profession which encouraged women to make the most of their intellectual capacities and cultural interests. Since the classical Greeks fostered intellectual attainments in its male citizenry to a degree previously unknown in the Western world, it is not surprising that there arose a class of women trained to be the intellectual companions of such men of culture and ability. They comprised history's highest class of courtesans and were appropriately called *hetairai*, "companions." They alone, it seems, enjoyed the requisites for philosophizing: adequate leisure time, professional incentive, and freedom from the traditional child-bearing role expected of women. A few of these courtesans transcended whatever social stigmata they encountered and became renowned intellectuals in the highest philosophical and literary circles of their times.

Aspasia (c. 470–410 B.C.) was one of the most effective women's liberationists of all time. She opened a school of philosophy and rhetoric for women in Athens and did much to advance their education and encourage their emergence into public life. The great men of her era, including Pericles and Socrates, attended her lectures. She became the mistress of Pericles and their home became a center of Athenian culture.

Of *Diotima* we know very little, but in Plato's *Symposium* Socrates states that he was her pupil and says: "There is a speech about Love which I heard once from Diotima of Mantineia, who was wise in this matter and many others."

Leontium became the concubine of Epicurus and through her voluminous writing established herself as an articulate philosopher and, when necessary, a defender of womanhood. *Arete*, daughter of the fa-

Aspasia

mous hedonist philosopher Aristippus, was apparently not a courtesan. She succeeded her father as head of the Cyrenaic school of philosophy, wrote some 40 books, and achieved such distinction that she became known as "The Light of Hellas."

The supremely brilliant and beautiful *Hypatia* (A.D. 370–415) became head of the famed school of Neoplatonism in Alexandria. Her fame spread through her lectures, teaching and erudite writing. She was murdered by an outraged mob of Christians—ostensibly because of her liaison with Orestes, the prefect of Alexandria—and thus became the first woman philosopher to die for her beliefs.

Through the centuries other women became the intellectual lights of their times, though most of them moved merely on the periphery of philosophy per se. Among them: the Empress Theodora, wife of Justinian; Eleanor of Aquitaine; Marguerite d'Angoulême, Queen of Navarre; and Queen Christina of Sweden (who dispatched a warship to persuade René Descartes to come to Stockholm to establish an academy for her). In our century, for whatever reasons, the names are only slightly on the increase: Susanne Langer, L. Susan Stebbing, Simone de Beauvoir, Ayn Rand.

Now that life-styles are changing and women are breaking free of the cultural traditions which have heretofore predetermined their roles, it will be interesting to see if history begins to record a greater equality among those who professionally confess to being, not merely lovers, but "lovers of wisdom."

His first period was devoted primarily to logic and logical systems, while his second period dealt entirely with the analysis of everyday language. The testimony to his genius is that each of his systems—esoteric, technical, and demanding—has strongly influenced the course of twentieth-century philosophical thought.

For this reason Wittgenstein occupies a singular place in the history of philosophy, having first at an early age written a work which exercised a decisive influence on the philosophical thought of his time, and then, in his mature years, rejecting his early theory and producing a second theory which, for sheer originality, stature and influence, is even more important than the first.

Wittgenstein and subsequent language analysts have been convinced that most philosophical puzzlements are the result of sloppy use of language. Their task, therefore, is to analyze the function of language so that questions can be precisely constructed to which exact answers can be given. Only then can we know clearly what we are thinking and saying.

As Wittgenstein saw it, philosophy should not engage in synoptic or speculative tasks. Rather, its goal should be to help us think more clearly and precisely about anything and everything. Philosophy is therapy for our linguistic neuroses.

Because his whole being was so consumed with passionate thought, Wittgenstein could not give lectures as other university teachers do. To lecture in the ordinary way is to expound, or repeat what has already been thought; and to repeat a thought is not to think it, at any rate, not to think it with Wittgenstein's kind of intensity. So instead of giving conventional lectures, Wittgenstein *thought* what he said as he spoke. He did not reproduce what he had prepared before. And it was precisely because he went through this process of thinking in such a fresh, powerful and concentrated way, in the presence of his students, that he earned their respect, and even something approaching veneration.

Of course his lectures were not elegant in style or form; they were a kind of research, which really serious students—and only such attended Wittgenstein's lectures—found strangely inspiring. For them it was like being in the workshop of a great master where they could witness, and perhaps even participate in, the creation of new and often exhilarating thoughts.

A professor has his students and, if he is the founder of a school, his followers. Wittgenstein had both, but he also had disciples. It was perhaps not difficult to become his disciple because of his magnetic and compelling personality and because of the orginality and depth and fervor of his thought. Wittgenstein was conscious of this, and regretted it. A disciple's spiritual dependence on his master at best hinders independent thought, and, at worst, prevents it. And a thought which is not independent is a thought only half understood. . . .

JUSTUS HARTNACK

A page from the *Principia Mathematica* by Bertrand Russell and Alfred North Whitehead.

A page from Wittgenstein's *Tractatus*.

SOMEONE MUST KEEP WATCH

30   There seems to be a motif, a pattern, which runs through the lives of almost all the great philosophers; it is a thread so fine that it might be overlooked. With few exceptions, their lives exhibit an alternation: a *withdrawal* from life-in-the-world, then a *return* to the world of men to apply in some way the insights they have gained. It is the ebb and flow of both psychic and physical energy, the alternation of the active and the passive—the Yin and the Yang.

On the one hand, the existentialist is very close to the truth. If one is merely a "spectator" of life, then his observations cannot be very meaningful; they are only second-hand. Apart from a full participation in life where "he laughs all his laughter and cries all his tears," one's philosophizing will not have the mark of life on it.

At the same time, the antinomians must be heard. Unless one can withdraw from life sufficiently to keep his experience in perspective, his insights cannot be trusted. To be sure, this is not easy, for when one has become involved in the human drama, reestablishing an overview may require considerable courage.

Yet a Yin-Yang alternation might be a very workable solution if one can manage it. Life is to be lived; but without the solitude which one finds in the desert, the forest, the mountains, by the seashore or in the study, the meaning of life will almost inevitably be missed. Wrestling with the Ultimate often seems to be preeminently a private affair.

31   In this tribal world, someone must still keep watch. He must stand apart, as best he can, to try to keep life in perspective. The party members won't do it, nor will the fearful, the brainwashed, the prejudiced, or the bigoted. But there must be someone.

There must be someone who remains sensitively aware of the essential humanness in every position that human beings take.

There must be someone who tries to stay as close to *all* the realities as possible, someone who tries, keeps on trying, and who will not give up.

And there is some value in knowing just that—that in this world of adversary rhetoric and close-minded partisanship there is someone who will struggle against being manipulated and polarized.

He will only partially succeed. He may reach moments of greater clarity and then fall back into a one-sided point of view, but then he will (like Kant) arouse himself from his "dogmatic slumbers" and start to work again fitting together the pieces of the jigsaw puzzle.

My propositions are elucidatory in this way: he who understands me finally recognizes them as senseless, when he has climbed out through them, on them, over them. (He must so to speak throw away the ladder after he has climbed up on it.) He must surmount these propositions; then he sees the world rightly. Whereof one cannot speak, thereof one must be silent.

WITTGENSTEIN

Truly, philosophers play a strange game. They know very well that one thing alone counts, and that all their medley of subtle discussions relates to one single question: why are we born on this earth? And they also know that they will never be able to answer it. Nevertheless, they continue sedately to amuse themselves. Do they not see that people come to them from all points of the compass, not with a desire to partake of their subtlety, but because they hope to receive from them one word of life? If they have such words, why do they not cry them from the housetops, asking their disciples to give, if necessary, their very blood for them? If they have no such words, why do they allow people to believe they will receive from them something which they cannot give?

JACQUES MARITAIN

Keep me from the wisdom that does not weep, and the philosophy that does not laugh . . . .

KAHLIL GIBRAN

REFLECTIONS—

1 Socrates came to some clear conclusions after he had investigated several men who laid claim to being wise. Do you think his observations were accurate about the claims we make? In the last analysis, according to Socrates, what makes a person wise?

2 Summarize in your own words the philosophic breakthrough that has been called "the Greek miracle." Why is this naturalistic methodology so important in the gathering of information? Or, conversely, what would happen to human knowledge if the naturalistic assumption were not followed?

3 Summarize in your own way the nature of the "Western dilemma" regarding human knowledge (Sec. 12). Is it "either/or" for you personally, or have you discovered a pathway between the two traditions?

4 Without attempting a precise definition of religion at this point, do you think it possible for a philosopher who insists upon the freedom to inquire into *everything* (including religious axioms and "revealed truths") to also be religious?

5 Suppose a philosopher inquires into the existence of God (and all do, sooner or later). If he concludes that God exists, is he still a philosopher? If he concludes that God doesn't exist, does he cease to be religious? Do one's philosophic credentials depend upon the questions he asks or the answers he arrives at?

6 Pure speculation, but . . . *if* there had been as many women philosophers as men, in what ways do you think Western thought (philosophical and theological) might have been different? (Besides p. 37, see sidenote on p. 134).

7 It is easy to see how the different endeavors described in this chapter can all make contributions to our knowledge of life and how to live it; but how can these quite different enterprises *all* be philosophy? In other words, what essential commonalities are shared by all these "schools" of philosophy? What makes each position distinctive?

8 At least six different kinds of philosophic activity and temperament are summarized briefly in the foregoing pages. Which of these "ways of philosophy" do you find—at this point in your own odyssey—to be most congenial and meaningful? Can you tell why?

9 What is Kierkegaard implying when he remarks (p. 35 QM) that "the skipper of a fishing-smack knows his whole cruise before sailing, but a man-of-war gets its orders only on the high seas"?

10 Jacques Maritain indicts philosophers for hypocrisy and even cruelty (p. 39 QM). There is but a single ultimate philosophical question, he says: "Why are we born on this earth?" Yet philosophers, says Maritain, know they cannot answer the question. What responses might be given to Maritain (who was a Catholic philosopher and theologian) by (a) a synoptist, (b) an existentialist, (c) a prophetic activist, and (d) an antinomian?

11 Do you agree with the suggestion of your text (p. 32) that philosophy and social activism may be "competing preoccupations"?

12 There is a brief description of the philosopher's calling in Sec. 31. Do you find this description meaningful, or are you uncomfortable with it? Tell (yourself) why you feel as you do.

Furthermore . . .

ADLER, MORTIMER J., *The Conditions of Philosophy*. Delta, 1967.

BARRETT, WILLIAM, *Irrational Man*. Anchor, 1962. (On existentialism.)

BONTEMPO, CHARLES J., and S. JACK ODELL (eds.), *The Owl of Minerva: Philosophers on Philosophy*. McGraw-Hill, 1975.

CORNFORD, F. M., *From Religion to Philosophy: A Study in the Origins of Western Speculation*. Harper, 1958.

DESCARTES, RENÉ, *Discourse on Method*. (A number of paperback editions available.)

DURANT, WILL, *The Story of Philosophy*. Washington Square, 1952.

FRANKFORT, HENRI, et al., *Before Philosophy*. Penguin, 1949.

FROMM, ERICH, *Marx's Concept of Man*. Ungar, 1961.

HYLAND, DREW, *The Origins of Philosophy*. Putnam, 1973.

KINGSLEY, CHARLES, *Hypatia*. Dutton, 1907. (An enjoyable historical novel, essentially accurate.)

MAIMONIDES (1135–1204), *Guide for the Perplexed*. Dover, 1904.

MALCOLM, NORMAN, *Ludwig Wittgenstein: A Memoir*. Oxford, 1958.

MARTÍ-IBÁÑEZ, FÉLIX, *Tales of Philosophy*, Dell, 1969.

McDERMOTT, JOHN J. (ed.), *The Writings of William James*. Modern Library, 1968.

MERTON, THOMAS (interp.), *The Way of Chuang Tzu*. New Directions, 1965.

PLATO, *The Last Days of Socrates*. Penguin, 1969. (Or any editions of Plato's dialogues containing these accounts of Socrates' trial and final month of life).

RANDALL, JOHN HERMAN, *The Role of Knowledge in Western Religion*. Beacon, 1958.

TAYLOR, A. E., *Socrates*. Anchor, 1953.

TILLICH, PAUL, *The Dynamics of Faith*. Harper, 1957.

TROXELL, EUGENE A., and WILLIAM S. SNYDER, *Making Sense of Things*. St. Martin's, 1976.

DE UNAMUNO, MIGUEL, *The Tragic Sense of Life* (1913). Dover, 1921.

How to Philosophize/ Analysis

Have You Ever Wondered . . .

- What an "idea" is?

- Why Charlie Brown is such a great philosopher?

- Why some people have good luck and others seem to have only bad luck?

- What "luck" is?

- How to go about analyzing an "idea"?

- What an "insight" is?

- Why Lucy is such an ardent feminist?

- Whether there exists a Universal Moral Law?

MEANING-EVENTS

"There's no use trying," said Alice: "one can't believe impossible things."

"I dare say you haven't had much practice," said the Queen. "When I was your age I always did it for half an hour a day. Why sometimes I've believed as many as six impossible things before breakfast."

LEWIS CARROLL

1   Philosophy's role in our lives—in fact its sole reason for being—is to deal with *meaning*, and it works with questions of meaning at all levels of experience. In its ultimate concerns it deals with the meaning of life. (Viktor Frankl is correct: we cannot live our lives without meaning.) This is the final obligation of philosophy: to search out, faithfully and tenaciously, the ultimate meaning by which we live. Philosophy would be derelict if it turned away from this ultimate responsibility.

At more routine levels we talk about mundane kinds of meaning-events: we wonder about the meaning of ideas and facts; of words and sentences; of gestures, events, and accidents; of hypotheses, models, and theories; of policies and programs; and of nasty remarks: "Now what did he *mean* by *that?*"

Philosophy spends most of its waking time searching out *hidden meanings*, that is, meanings that are tucked away in our ideas and statements, but which, for one reason or another, escape our notice. By "hidden meanings" is meant such things as the (unseen) implications of our comments, the unexamined assumptions that (unknown to us) underlie and shape our thinking, and the different (unobserved) meanings that we give to words when we employ them in different contexts.

Never accept a fact until it is verified by a theory!

SIR ARTHUR EDDINGTON

Pythagoras was the first person who invented the term "Philosophy," and who called himself a philosopher.

DIOGENES LAERTIUS

WONDER/CONFUSION/PATIENCE/WISDOM

"Confusion" is an intitial phase of all knowledge, *without which one cannot progress to clarity*. The important thing for the individual who truly desires to think is that he not be overly hurried but be faithful at each step of his mental itinerary to the aspect of reality currently under view, that he *strive to avoid disdain for the preliminary distant and confused aspects* due to some snob sense of urgency impelling him to arrive immediately at the more refined conclusions.

JOSÉ ORTEGA Y GASSET
The Origin of Philosophy

The teacher's obligation is to be patient enough to permit deliberation and decision by each of those he is trying to help. If his students do not choose, each in the light of his own contingent existence and his own limitations, they will not become ethical beings; if they are not ethical beings—in search of their own ethical reality—they are not individuals; if they are not individuals, they will not learn.

SØREN KIERKEGAARD
The Point of View

Philosophy, as Plato and Aristotle said, begins in wonder. This wonder means a dim awareness of the useless talent, some sense that antlikeness is a betrayal. . . .

Philosophy means liberation from the two dimensions of routine, soaring above the well known, seeing it in new perspectives, arousing wonder and the wish to fly. Philosophy subverts man's satisfaction with himself, exposes custom as a questionable dream, and offers not so much solutions as a different life.

A great deal of philosophy, including truly subtle and ingenious works, was not intended as an edifice for men to live in, safe from sun and wind, but as a challenge: don't sleep on! there are so many vantage points; they change in flight: what matters is to leave off crawling in the dust.

WALTER KAUFMANN
Critique of Religion and Philosophy

Is it wise to assume that every solution has a problem or that every answer has a question?

JLC

(Don't confuse this search for "hidden meanings" with a pathological form of paranoia which hears in the statements of others sinister meanings which, in fact, *aren't there*. By contrast, philosophic analysis attempts to make explicit the implicit meanings that *are there*.)

2   There are two general ways in which philosophy has approached the search for meaning. These two methods are *analysis* and *synthesis*—taking apart and putting together, or, as one philosopher phrased it, "digging deeper and flying higher" when thinking about ideas, perceptions, and other meaning-events.

In this chapter we'll be "digging deeper" into ideas—working with various forms of philosophic analysis. In the following chapter we'll deal with the activity of synoptic synthesis—attempting to play jig-saw puzzler, fitting the pieces of life's complex puzzle together in order to try to see general outlines of the whole, complete picture.

PHILOSOPHIC ANALYSIS

3   To analyze is to separate something into its component parts to find out what it's made of. News commentators "analyze apart" a political speech to discover hidden implications not readily apparent to us listeners. We "analyze apart" water and find that it's composed of atoms of hydrogen and oxygen; then we "analyze apart" a hydrogen atom and find that it's composed of a proton and an electron; and so on—such analysis continues until we reach the desired level of comprehension or an impasse.

What is "life's meaning" composed of? Among other things, it's made up of bits and fragments of human knowlege—literally millions of pieces of information. These "bits and fragments" are ideas, facts, fact-claims, stories, myths, concepts, notions, mental images, memories, doctrines, beliefs, theories, and much, much more—all melded together into a personal *universe*. Each individual's world-view is a unique mosaic assembled from the millions of data-bits which constitute his own personal knowledge.

Much as the physicist works with elements, atoms, and particles to understand what the universe is made of, the philosopher analyzes the "bits and fragments" of human knowledge in order to find out what they're composed of and to be able to conclude, in "the last analysis," whether we really know what we think we know.

4   Later in this chapter we'll be using a Charlie Brown cartoon strip to illustrate philosophic analysis. This episode is rich in hidden implications, and Charlie Brown's baseball team offers us an authentic slice-of-life. Our analysis can apply to our real-life situations.

At this point read through the following seven-frame episode— just to enjoy it; then we'll stop-the-world and think about it.

There is not *a* philosophical method, though there are indeed methods, like different therapies.

WITTGENSTEIN

[Speculative philosophy is] the endeavor to frame a coherent, logical, necessary system of general ideas in terms of which every element of our experience can be interpreted.

ALFRED NORTH WHITEHEAD

History is the story of the defiance of the unknown and of what happens when man tries to extend his reach. Such defiance is necessary because conventional wisdom has never been good enough to run a civilization.

NORMAN COUSINS

The paramount distinction between human and animal intelligence, so far as we know, lies not in complexity, or profundity, or creativity, or memory, but in man's capacity for conceptual thought, and his power to see ahead. . . . Both foresight and the capacity to form a mental concept reflect the same intellectual capacity: imagination.

ROBERT ARDREY

It's important to note that Charlie Brown's baseball/seminar is *not* a philosophic discussion. Each person says his thing, and no one connects; no one hears anyone else. The "dialogue" is only a collection of monologues; and consequently the so-called discussion is unproductive. Each speaker is going his own way all by himself (and herself—sorry, Lucy).

Yet the strip as a whole gives one a philosophic feeling. Several of the statements, quite by themselves, are ultimate in their implications: "Man is born to trouble. . . ." "A person who never suffers, never matures." "If a person has bad luck it's because he's done something wrong." These isolated comments are philosophical in the best sense; and such pearls have made CB and Company "everybody's favorite philosophers."

The problem we face is how to turn this collection of soliloquies into a philosophic dialogue that goes somewhere. As for CB's ball team, it's probably hopeless. But in our daily conversations we can do it, if we want to. The answer lies in applying a disciplined awareness to this sort of idea-game. All that is required is a touch of system and method.

All acquisition of knowledge is an enlargement of the Self, but this enlargement is best attained when it is not directly sought.

BERTRAND RUSSELL

PRELIMINARY STEPS

5   Making one's way into philosophic analysis is a bit like altering one's consciousness (Eastern style): take three deep breaths, relax, and let the mind do its work. To move into a philosophic mode of consciousness, it helps to proceed along a sequence of four steps.

(1) First, *stop-the-world.*° All our minds are flooded with meaning-events: ideas, memories, percepts, concepts, beliefs, theories,

°*The phrase "stop-the-world" is from Carlos Castaneda's accounts of the*

Yaqui sorcerer Juan Matus; and the notion here of stopping the world is not dissimilar to the teaching of Don Juan. See Castaneda, Journey to Ixtlan, *pp. 291ff.*

dreams, plans—ad infinitum. There are *too many* events; there is *too much* meaning. Our minds can't catch them all, ponder them, and then assimilate them meaningfully into our philosophy of life. Look again at CB's baseball game: note *how much meaning* is expressed. It's the same in all our conversations. Too much is going on for our minds to handle.

When working with written materials, it is relatively easy to stop-the-world. We are onlookers. We can, from the outside, go back and forth over the meaning-events, as often as we need to, until we see. It's different with living dialogue. Ongoing conversations are difficult to slow down. But whether we are sideline observers or involved participants, any good discussion will cover too many meaning-events to be assimilated and analyzed.

One way to stop-the-world is to let the verbal exchanges roll on while making mental note of essential points or meaningful ideas, and then returning to them. In this way, we can stop-the-world sufficiently to allow us to develop a synoptic overview of the discussion. We can then range back and forth over it in a way not unlike what we can do with the CB cartoon-strip sequence.

Stopping-the-world is an inner process. The real world won't slow down for us. In fact, it tries to wriggle free and race onward, demanding that we keep up and that we *not* pause to really see what is going on. But each of us can say, "I want to see. And *I will* the world to stop *until I see.*" If we don't stop-the-world the parade of meaning-events marches on. Meaning-full ideas will pass us by.

> If the only tool you have is a hammer, you tend to treat everything as if it were a nail.
>
> ABRAHAM MASLOW

6   (2) Next, *decide what and how.* Having stopped-the-world, we can then decide *what* meaning-events we want to deal with, and *how* to deal with them. This is a deliberate decision each of us can make. *We* decide what appears most meaning-full to us, and *we* decide what sort of philosophic analysis *we* want to engage in. We can choose, each of us, "what eyes to see with."

Whether we are analyzing written materials or live conversation, certain ideas will always be more meaningful than others; by contrast the rest will seem trivial, and we won't want to waste our time on them. Perspectives change, of course, and we may find later that seemingly insignificant ideas have become meaningful. This trial-and-error way of learning what is significant is all part of the philosophic process and should be taken in stride.

> The important point for us to see is that it is the unconscious that determines what the conscious impulse and the conscious action shall be.
>
> JOHN HOSPERS

Along with *what* ideas we decide to analyze goes the choice of *how* we decide to analyze them. Philosophic analysis takes several forms, and we are free to choose the kind of analysis that we feel might give us the insight and awareness that we want. (More on the different kinds of philosophic analysis later in this chapter.)

7   (3) *Zero in on an idea.* The proverbial definition of a scientist as the specialist "who knows more and more about less and less" applies equally to the philosopher-analyst. Our subject matter is delimited by gazing long and intently at specific ideas. We zero in on an idea, give it full attention, and by living with it for a while we begin to see the hidden meanings involved in the idea. The idea is "illuminated"; it gives up its secrets. We see implications that were there all the time but which had to be "inferred out" through concentrated effort on our part.

Some understanding of how our minds work is helpful. Ideas don't yield up all their secrets the first time they're asked. After analyzing an idea for a while, it often helps to leave it for a time and return to it later. We can then think ourselves more deeply into the idea. While we allow our conscious mind to rest, the subconscious continues to process information. Given the chance, the deeper intuitive levels of our minds can become allies in the analytic process. Contrary to popular (Western) belief, productive thinking is carried on at many levels. We deprive ourselves of much mental efficiency if we fail to make use of them all.

8   (4) *Think about it*. Having zeroed in on a promising idea, philosophic analysis begins by thinking about it. This is the essence of philosophy—thinking about it. Each of us lives in a world-view that contains countless ideas, beliefs, values, opinions, clichés, thinking habits, and so on, which, if carefully examined, we would toss out in a minute. Like proverbial rotten apples, they spoil the cleanness and coherence of our philosophy of life. If we could rid ourselves of them, then the philosophic ideas by which we guide our lives would be sounder and more meaningful; and, as a result, we would all be more honest with ourselves. There is immeasurable pragmatic value in being able to think clearly, accurately, and with awareness.

Don't let anyone kid you into believing that concentrated thought on an idea is easy, and that something has gone awry in your intellectual habits if you can't instantly plunge into an idea and, with nonchalant brilliance, see all its component parts. It takes motivation; it takes practice; it takes hard labor and time.

In order to get our thinking processes started, there is a variety of starter-games we can play on ourselves, or on others. One way to begin is to ask questions about the idea. Is it stated clearly or ambiguously? Does the idea need a context to be made clear? What words need defining? Does the idea involve fact-claims? Does it make value-judgments? How can I decide if it's true? Whether true or not, is the idea valid? And so on—there is no end to the questions that can be asked about even the simplest meaning-event.

PHILOSOPHIC DIALOGUE

9   Asking such questions initiates *philosophic dialogue*. This may be internal dialogue during which each of us can "talk it over with one's self," or interactive dialogue between self and others. If internal, we can talk ourselves through an idea; we can ask ourselves questions about it; we can, as it were, explain it to ourselves or, in imagination,

---

Give to the intellect, wisdom to comprehend that one thing; to the heart, sincerity to receive this understanding; to the will, purity that wills only one thing.

KIERKEGAARD

The essence of Zen is to learn to do just one thing at a time.

WILLIAM W. BLAKE

It is much easier to bury a problem than to solve it.

WITTGENSTEIN

Eastern and Western epistemology are united in reminding us that when we are thinking we are not experiencing outside ourselves.

WILLIAM W. BLAKE

Plato

The First Educator

He was born in Athens on the 7th of Thargelion in the first year of the 88th Olympiad—May 29, 427 B.C. His father, Ariston, traced his lineage to Codrus, the last king of Athens; and his mother, Perictione, traced hers to Solon, Athens' greatest lawgiver. His was an illustrious heritage, and he moved with statesmen, playwrights, artists, and philosophers all his life.

His name was Aristocles, but with good reason his coach nicknamed him Plato—from the Greek word *platon,* meaning "broad-shouldered"; and he excelled in sports and wrestled in the Isthmian games at Corinth. But he was multi-talented and distinguished himself in every field. He fought in three battles during the Peloponnesian wars and was decorated for bravery.

At 21, Plato was caught up by the charismatic brilliance of Socrates and dedicated himself to philosophy, which he called "a precious delight"; and though he was to be Socrates' pupil for only eight years, their association would set the course of Western thought for the next two thousand years.

When Athens was finally garrisoned by the Spartans in 404 B.C., Plato—already horrified at the inhumanity of war, the tyranny of oligarchs, and the bestiality of mobs—saw the Athenians further degraded by their own ruthlessness and greed. He wrote: "Whereas at first, I had been enthusiastic about a political career, now all that I could do is to watch, helplessly, this chaotic world around me." This experience of the Absurd turned personal when, at 29, he witnessed the trial and execution of his teacher. Socrates was convicted on trumped-up charges of impiety and corrupting youth and was put to death with a cup of poison hemlock. "This is the end of our comrade," Plato later wrote, "a man, as we would say, of all then living we had ever met, the noblest and the wisest and the most just."

Plato seems to have made a serious attempt to put the Athenian nightmare behind him. He traveled for a dozen years, visited Italy and Sicily—where he absorbed Pythagorean metaphysics—possibly sailed to Cyrene and Egypt, and returned home to Athens about 388 B.C. He was 40. Within the year he established the school that would occupy him the rest of his life: the Academy, the first institution of higher learning in the Western world. (The Academy endured for more than 900 years. In the year A.D. 529 it was closed by the Byzantine emperor Justinian because, in his eyes, it was a stronghold of paganism.)

At the age of 60 Plato was invited back to Syracuse to educate the new king, Dionysius II. He also hoped to field-test the theories of social psychology he had described in *The Republic*. But the young king proved uneducable and political intrigues drove the philosopher back to Athens.

After another (failed) mission to Syracuse when he was 67, Plato attended the Olympic games (in July), then came home to Athens to settle for the rest of his life, teaching and writing. His greatest works, in which he used Socrates as his literary hero, had been written before he was 40; they included *The Apology, Crito,* and *The Republic*. During this last period he wrote *Parmenides, Theaetetus,* the *Laws,* and others. He was by this time universally admired and honored.

On his 80th birthday one of his pupils invited the master to a wedding feast. He attended, and the tale is told that he danced at the party, into the night. Eventually he took leave of his students and withdrew to rest. He died in his sleep. According to tradition, it was the first year of the 108th Olympiad—347 B.C.

The Academy: The Search for Universal Ideas

Plato's life is marked by two supreme achievements: the establishment of the Academy and the immortalizing of Socrates in writing. Both have profoundly influenced the Western world. Of the two, Plato would have considered his school the most important.

The Academy was located on several acres of public park on the outskirts of Athens, about a mile northwest of the Dipylon Gate. The site contained olive trees, statues, and temples named for the legendary Greek hero Academus—hence its name. Also on the grounds were lecture halls, classrooms, and a shrine of learning—a sort of chapel, built by Plato himself, dedicated to the worship of the Muses, those nine daughters of Zeus who were the inspiring spirits of all the arts and sciences. Adjacent to the grounds was a large

sports gymnasium. The land was purchased for Plato by his friends.

Here Plato gathered about him a circle of serious students and organized them into a disciplined educational community. Young men and women came from all parts of the Greek world and dedicated themselves to a demanding program of study that included literature, history, music, mathematics and geometry, and philosophy. They were to be educated, not trained. Through intellectual and moral development they were to become qualified leaders of the state. They lived close by, off campus. They paid no fees, but their parents gave generous gifts so that, after a few years, the school was heavily endowed. The students were Hellas' finest youth, and they stayed on for years, or even for a lifetime, engaged in rigorous study and research.

Plato had a fiercely clear vision of what he had to do: educate young men and women to seek the truth, with the hope that they would then be qualified to assume positions of leadership in the world where they could put that truth to work.

By the time Plato started his school, he had already witnessed a lifetime of tragedy. Human beings, he had observed, have an unfortunate tendency to see everything through the narrow slits of their defensive armor. We operate from a reduced point of view, while claiming virtual omniscience. Out of irrationality, or on the basis of false or inadequate information, or because of myths and fallacies, we draw lines of separation, erect fortresses, and go to war.

While lies and limited information can alienate people, a clear understanding of universal truth would bring men together. Plato believed that truth—if it *is* truth—must be universal. There can be but one truth—or one set of truths—for all men. It follows that if men understand things as they really are—that is, if they possess the truth—then they could no longer divide themselves into parochial encampments, and, out of ignorance and arrogance, so bitterly fight with one another, with words and/or swords.

Over the entrance to the Academy Plato had inscribed the words *MEDEIS AGEOME-TRETOS EISITO,* "Let no one without geometry enter here." This inscription implies more than its literal meaning. Geometry (which includes mathematics) is *the* universal science. It is Plato's metaphor for the search for universal truth.

Thus, Plato is the founder of rational philosophy, and philosophy, Plato would say, is the art and science of developing universal ideas.

What are ideas?

An idea is an abstract concept manufactured by the mind to enable it to handle a large number of particular observations. For instance, my experience of one lonely meadowlark singing from a fencepost is a single direct perception; but my notion of bird (that is, bird-in-the-abstract, "birdness"—what all birds have in common) is an idea—a universal idea. The first is my *perception* of a real object (meadowlark); the latter is my *conception* of an idea (bird).

How do we develop universal ideas?

Suppose I have actually seen only six crows and ten turkeys. I will indeed have an idea of "bird" (which will include only whatever characteristics crows and turkeys have in common); but my idea can't be very accurate (or very useful) because I haven't experienced enough birds. It's a beginning, but it's too limited.

Now, say that I add a hundred finches, a thousand gulls, and a pair of pelicans. Having experienced *more* birds, I have a *more accurate* idea of bird. But suppose that I have actually seen millions of birds of all kinds during my lifetime. My idea of bird will be more inclusive, more accurate, more universal—and more useful.

In daily life, our (mis)use of ideas is a calamity. What happens is this. Athenians have seen only seagulls and terns; so they will tell you that they have a clear idea of bird. Alexandrians have seen vultures, kites, and ibises; so they too have a clear notion of bird, so they say. And Latins from Italy have just as clear an idea of bird, too, for they have seen finches, sparrows, and sanderlings. Each has a "clear notion of bird." But what is likely to happen when Athenians, Alexandrians, and Latins get together to discuss "birds"? They will all have different *ideas* of what bird is, and, since they're only human—and if they don't take time out to clarify and define their ideas—they will soon be arguing and fighting because each knows that the others' bird-idea is wrong.

Going to battle over something as trivial as our differing ideas of bird seems silly. But what about our (similarly incomplete) ideas of justice, virtue, morality, decency, right, wrong, sin, evil, pleasure, happiness, loyalty, selfishness, pride, human nature—and countless other ideas, including Faith, Hope, and Love . . . and Goodness, Truth, and Beauty? Plato observed that everyone seems to have different notions of what these things are; and we seem to be possessed by a diabolical drive to fight over them before trying to discover the root of our differences.

Plato is convinced that men will stop fighting only when they understand the truth about things. This is the task of philosophy and the goal of education. To philosophize is to exchange and refine ideas by talking about them, through dialogue. If Athenians and Spartans could have talked over their ideas of honor and justice, perhaps they would never have had to fight over them.

"Until philosophers are kings, or the kings and princes of this world have the spirit and power of philosophy . . . cities will never rest from their evils—no, nor the human race . . . ."

Plato is philosophy, and philosophy Plato.

Ralph Waldo Emerson

Over the centuries, a special, almost mystical aura has surrounded Plato, the pupil and interpreter of Socrates, as perhaps the strongest spiritual presence in the Western world before the coming of Jesus of Nazereth.

William Harlan Hale
The Horizon Book of Ancient Greece (347)

Plato's wide-ranging mind was subtle, searching, and his dialogues laid the foundation of many modern sciences and philosophies: his Socrates insisted on analyzing individual instances before proposing generalizations; political theory, economics, aesthetics, and sociology can be traced back to Plato, as can measures of town planning and public health that were later borrowed by the Macedonians and Romans. His *Republic* alone qualifies Plato for immortality; the book is replete with theology, ethics, psychology, theory of art, communism, feminism, birth control, eugenics.

Félix Martí-Ibáñez
Tales of Philosophy (33)

Looking back over this body of speculation we are surprised to see how fully Plato anticipated the philosophy, the theology, and the organization of medieval Christianity . . . . Plato is . . . a pre-Christian Puritan. He distrusts human nature as evil, and thinks of it as an original sin tainting the soul. He breaks up into an evil body and a divine spirit that unity of body and soul which had been the educated Greek ideal of the sixth and fifth centuries; like a Christian ascetic he calls the body the tomb of the soul. . . . He adopts, in his last works, the other-worldly tone of a converted and repentant Augustine. One would almost say that Plato was not Greek if it were not for his perfect prose.

Will Durant
The Story of Civilization (II.523)

Until philosophers are kings, or the kings and princes of this world have the spirit and power of philosophy, and political greatness and wisdom meet in one, and those commoner natures who pursue either to the expulsion of the other are compelled to stand aside, cities will never have rest from their evils—no, nor the human race . . . .

Plato
The Republic (V.473)

we can explain it to others. This is the secret of many successful thinkers: they have learned how to carry on a productive internal dialogue. (You also understand now why philosophers are often seen talking to themselves.)

Since the time of Socrates' street-corner conversations in Athens, philosophic dialogue has generally been thought of as interactive dialogue, a particular kind of verbal repartee in which two or more persons explore a meaning-event together. They explain it to one another, ask each other questions about it, and exchange all sorts of ideas and insights. Interactive dialogue is not all that different from internal dialogue, except in the obvious way: dialogue between two or more minds requires the use of ambiguous communicative symbols, and one can never know precisely what another is thinking. (But do we *always* know what we ourselves are thinking?)

10   Interactive dialogue can take the form of adversary dialogue or supportive (nonadversary) dialogue. The goal of *adversary dialogue* is to force participants to clarify and defend their ideas. It is an inherent part of the adversary system in philosophy (as it is in scientific method) for one thinker to attempt to disprove another's idea or hypothesis. If a notion can be shown to be false or invalid, then everyone gains, since in philosophy (as in science) the goal is not to win an argument but to attain the truth. Likewise, if the ideas can be satisfactorily defended, then again everyone is the winner.

In *supportive dialogue* the defense posture is replaced by one of mutual aid in exploration. Two or more minds think parallel, as it were, in analyzing a meaning-event. They ask questions of self and others alike, sharing ideas and insights along the way. Fortunately, our minds are not shaped by the same mold. We see different things in the joint exploration process. Shared insights expand the understanding and awareness of each person. The inherent polarization of the adversary approach is lacking in supportive dialogue. Each individual shares his own doubts, thought problems, fallacies, trial-and-error mistakes, and so on, just as readily as he shares his insights. A mistake that is shared can often be as valuable as an insight. Everyone knows henceforth of at least one mistake to avoid.

These, then, are useful preliminary steps leading to philosophic analysis (and sometimes also to synoptic synthesis). Stop time, stop our darting minds, stop words—stop-the-world. Focus on a specific meaning-event, zero in, and think about it. Think about what? Meaning(s). To philosophize is to think about meaning-full events.

GENERAL PHILOSOPHIC ANALYSIS

11   Philosophers engage in many different kinds of analysis. Some analytic procedures are rigorous and formal, even mathematical. Some are logical and linguistic. Some are pragmatic and practical. Others are semantic, introspective, or existential. All methods are valuable. They help us clarify our thinking, weed out errors, recondition bad thinking

---

Understanding the world for a man is reducing it to the human, stamping it with his seal. . . . The truism "All thought is anthropomorphic" has no other meaning. Likewise, the mind that aims to understand reality can consider itself satisfied only by reducing it to terms of thought.

ALBERT CAMUS

Philosophers start out with growing pains, and end up with hunger pangs.

ED MCDERMOTT

Man is a symbolic animal.

ERNST CASSIRER

An idea once born never dies. It may grow feeble under the battering of other ideas. It may gather dust upon some library shelf. But sooner or later someone is going to shake off that dust and look at the forgotten idea once again. And lo and behold! here precisely is what he has been searching for these many years.

T. K. MAHADEVAN

habits, and expand our awareness of the meaningful events of consciousness°.

A general philosophic analysis makes use of many methods, depending on need. Usually the specific method to be used is chosen spontaneously as the analysis proceeds.

Let's return to Charlie Brown and his theological seminary and run a general analysis on some of the meaning-events in the seven-frame episode.

Frame One. Charlie Brown: "We're getting slaughtered again, Schroeder." CB is obviously agitated, frustrated. His statement is emotional, not informative and not rational—which is quite in order: one of the essential functions of language is "to let off steam." "Why do we have to suffer like this?" We might wonder why he's taking the game so seriously. Does he really *have to suffer?* It's only a baseball game (isn't it?). Yet, typically, we all take our roles seriously (too seriously?)—even in games.

Charlie Brown is probably just being existential, venting his momentary frustrations; his "suffering" is not deep. If we could leap into the frame and say, "Hey, Charlie Brown, it's only a ball game. You don't *have* to 'suffer like this.' Hang loose!" he would probably reply that *he knew that.* After which he would dust off his cap and get on with the game.

°*For an example of conceptual/logical analysis, see page 518.*

The philosopher does sometimes get so interested in his technique that he forgets the human interest that may first have led him and his students to philosophy; the student suffers from impatience to get to the main point. Some philosophers are like pianists who play only scales; on the other hand some students are like beginners in music who are so anxious to play Beethoven that they resent having to learn scales.

LEWIS WHITE BECK

Science is the attempt to make the chaotic diversity of our sense-experience correspond to a logically uniform system of thought. . . . The sense-experiences are the given subject-matter. But the theory that shall interpret them is man-made. . . . hypothetical, never completely final, subject to question and doubt.

ALBERT EINSTEIN

Beginning to think is beginning to be undermined.

ALBERT CAMUS

Frame Two. "Man is born to trouble as the sparks fly upward." Schroeder's response has interesting implications. First, he makes an ultimate comment about the human condition in apparent reply to CB's momentary outburst. Did Schroeder respond to what Charlie Brown really said? Not at all.

One of the values of philosophy is to help us learn when to take things seriously, and when not to. To give ultimate responses to existential comments is to miss the mark—that is, if good communication is our goal; and conversely, to give trivial answers to ultimate questions about the human condition is equally, and more painfully, to miss the mark. To learn to philosophize, therefore, involves learning to weigh meanings and to respond at appropriate levels.

Another interesting thing about Schroeder's response is that he quotes from authority. (The quotation marks indicate that he knows what he's doing.) We quote our authorities out of various motives, but in this case Schroeder isn't quoting the Bible in a one-upmanship game or as a dogmatic putdown. He has turned to Job for a well-formulated insight into the problem of human suffering, and he's gone to a good source. In the world's great literature, the Book of Job stands high in its treatment of the problems of human suffering and theodicy (the problem of reconciling the existence of suffering with the goodness and compassion of God).

Furthermore, Schroeder's quotation from Job contains a commonly held religious doctrine. It is to be found in many of man's great historical religions, preeminently in Buddhism. The Buddha's "Four Noble Truths" eloquently contend that to exist at all *is* to suffer; and one ceases to suffer only when one ceases to exist. Suffering is inevitable, as natural as sparks flying upward from a blazing wood fire. The Buddha's mission in life was to help all creatures who exist to find a pathway out of their suffering condition; and that pathway out is to gradually diminish all wants, all cravings *(tanha)*. When all our creaturely needs are eradicated, suffering will cease.

Frame Three. It seems odd that Linus would know, off the top, the exact source of this quotation; but youngsters often surprise us with scraps of knowledge they're not supposed to have. Perhaps this frame serves only to inform Charlie Brown (and us) where the quotation is from. However, knowing Linus, perhaps it's not odd after all.

Frame Four. Linus persists in holding the discussion at an ultimate level with his comment about the human condition, but Lucy has entered the picture, so the dialogue can't last for long. In her unique way Lucy comes on strong with another widely held religious doctrine. She states succinctly the concept of a universal "moral law," the sort of you-reap-what-you-sow doctrine found in numerous religious traditions (Judaic, Christian, Islamic, Hindu) and philosophical systems (notably the Stoic).

Lucy has some confused ideas which language analysis will straighten out. "If a person has bad luck," she says, "it's because he's done something wrong." Lucy is linguistically confused and doesn't know it. Professor Peter Angeles takes Lucy to task this way: "If someone has 'bad luck,' then you cannot linguistically connect this with 'because he's done something wrong.' Luck is non-intentional. If it does have the element of intentionality or deliberateness, then it cannot properly be called luck. No one 'gives' you luck. You *have* luck. The very meaning is one of coincidence, of undesigned change or good fortune. It is a contradiction to say that someone (God or the Universe) gives you, or that you have, bad luck because of something wrong you have done. I can see doing something (wrong?) and then viewing it as leading to 'bad luck,' but not the other way around."

We could dwell at length on Lucy's pronouncement. She is here reiterating the late Judaic doctrine that if one sins then he will suffer, while if he is pious in his faith then he will live a long and prosperous life. The doctrine is found throughout the scriptural writings called "Wisdom Literature" (Proverbs, Ecclesiastes, and Job). For example:

> Blessings are upon the head of the righteous;
> But sorrow will cover the face of the wicked.

The original sin of metaphysics is to read the features of language into the world.

JOHN SEARLE

Sit down before fact as a little child, be prepared to give up every preconceived notion, follow humbly wherever and to whatever abysses nature leads, or you shall learn nothing.

T. H. HUXLEY (1825–1895)

The Agnostic's Prayer: "Oh, God, if there is a God, save my soul, if I have a soul."

ERNST RENAN

You see me as an atheist. God sees me as the loyal opposition.

WOODY ALLEN

The things which exist around us, which we touch, see, hear and taste, are regarded as interrogations for which an answer must be sought. . . .

JOHN DEWEY

It is a terrible thing, Tolstoi said, to watch a man who doesn't know what to do with the incomprehensible, because generally he winds up playing with a toy named God. Pasteur saw nothing particularly terrifying or unsatisfying about this situation, saying that the only thing to do in the face of the incomprehensible is to kneel before it. But that which is most incomprehensible of all is not a distant planet but the human mind itself; kneeling under these circumstances may represent the ultimate vanity.

NORMAN COUSINS

Reverence for Yahweh prolongs life;
But the years of the wicked will be shortened.

No harm can befall the righteous;
But the lives of the wicked are full of misfortune.

This doctrine constitutes the major theme of the Book of Job (as Schoreder and Lucy well know—see next frame). Some version of Lucy's moral law has infused Western Judeo-Christian thinking for more than twenty-five hundred years. Even today, after tragedy has torn at their lives, we commonly hear people ask, "What have I done to deserve this?"

This doctrine is also found in Hinduism and Buddhism—the Law of Karma, the "law of sowing and reaping." One's behavior in this life determines his status in his next incarnation. Note the difference between the Western and Eastern doctrines. The Judaic version holds that divine rewards and punishments will occur in this life, while the Indian accounts contend that the karmic consequences will be incurred in the next life. The Hindu caste system rests upon this cosmic law: if an individual has accumulated bad karma in this life, he will be reborn at a lower level in the next, perhaps as an outcast or in animal form.

By this time an analytic mind has a lengthy list of questions. Does moral causality such as this really exist? Can we validly infer that when an individual suffers he has committed some wrong? Does this apply also to groups? If this is truly the case, then it logically follows that, whenever we suffer, we should try to remember what specific sin brought on the suffering. We should try to isolate the "sinful cause," do penance for it, and avoid such causal behavior in the future. The converse would also be true. Whenever good things come our way, we should try to determine what we did that was so good that brought about happy results. We should conclude that we must be as good and pious as possible so as to causally assure only desirable consequences.

Above all else, since the philosopher *wants to be sure* of the facts upon which his understanding is based, he wants to know: How can I know if such a moral law really exists? The Book of Job says it does. So do the Bhagavad Gita and the Quran. And so may other religious and philosophical writings. But to a philosopher all this is no more than hearsay—notions derived from other people who may or may not know any more about the subject matter than we do. In fact, they all may be trapped in one of those "unexamined assumptions" which need to be brought into the open and tested in the arena of human experience. So, how can I know for sure that such a law governs my existence? What empirical evidence can I find to support the hypothesis that such a law exists? How would I go about gathering evidence for or against the idea? (Isn't there already a body of evidence against it? Aren't we surrounded by "sinners"—and how do we define "sinner"?—who strike it rich and get off scotfree? And aren't we acquainted with many gentle, loving people for whom tragedy and suffering never cease?)

If such moral causality does exist, what might be its source? Would that source necessarily be divine? or supernatural? How could we know for sure? Lucy says "That's what I always say!" But it has the familiar ring of a doctrinaire pronouncement: just accept it—never mind the facts. The philosopher can't live with that.

Another question: The notion of a moral law has been very widely held. Does universal agreement on an idea ever make it right? The answer must be No. "Can eighty million Frenchmen be wrong?" The answer must be Yes. Lucy—or any of us—may be in good company; we may enjoy the support of an overwhelming majority. But none of this makes an idea right or satisfies our honest inquiry as to whether such a moral law does, in fact, exist.

Frame Five. Schroeder seems to have recently reviewed the Book of Job.° But Lucy interrupts with another theme: "What about Job's wife?" She may be playing the feminist. We could open up an enormous range of questions from the chauvinism of Judeo-Christian myths which figure patriarchal father-deities and the consequent secondary status of women to the philosophic rationalizations of female inferiority. But focusing strictly on Lucy's comment, we might ask

5

what it is that Job's wife doesn't get enought credit for. A careful reading of the Job story shows that his wife is really on the wrong side and only contributes to Job's suffering.

6

Wherever it is possible to find out the cause of what is happening one should not have recourse to the gods.

POLYBIUS

°*By this time, you too may want to read up on Job, his friends, and his problems (his friends are his problems). You might begin by reading the folk-story framework—the prose prologue (the first two chapters) and prose epilogue (the last ten verses of the book). Then enjoy the intermediate poetic explorations at your leisure.*

Men talk because men have the capacity for speech, just as monkeys have the capacity for swinging by their tails. For philosophers, as for other human caddis flies, talk passes the time away that would otherwise hang like a millstone about a man's neck. Tellurians in general, and philosophers in particular, swing from day to day by their long prehensile tongues, and are finally hurled headlong into their silent tombs or flaming furnaces.

HERMAN TENNESSEN

°See pp. 127f

Philosophy is at once the most sublime and the most trivial of human pursuits. It works in the minutest crannies and it opens out of the widest vistas. . . . No one of us can get along without the far-flashing beams of light it sends over the world's perspectives.

WILLIAM JAMES

°For an example of communications analysis, see pp. 255ff.

An undefined problem has an infinite number of solutions.

ROBERT A. HUMPHREY

Frame Six. This discussion of the human condition has fragmented into several seminars clustered about the pitcher's mound. One comment has worthwhile implications, and again it's Schroeder's: "I think a person who never suffers, never matures . . ."—another doctrine. This notion was formulated by the Greek tragedian Aeschylus as "the law of Pathei Mathos." Aeschylus wrote that "Zeus has laid it down that man shall learn by suffering and alone by suffering."° There is abundant evidence to support the conclusion that, while there may be no "law" that dictates how we must learn wisdom, it is almost always the case (because of "human nature"?) that we face the truly difficult questions of life only when suffering forces us to. For instance, the philosopher Schopenhauer contended that without our consciousness of death there would be no philosophy. Schroeder's comment that "suffering is actually very important" might be a significant insight into the wellsprings of wisdom.

Lucy has missed the point. "Who wants to suffer? Don't be ridiculous!" No one *wants* to suffer, of course, but our task, since we *have* to suffer, is to turn our suffering into growth and not allow it to make us cynical or sour. Will Durant has written that those who suffer much become either very bitter or very gentle. Existential philosophers argue passionately that we individuals possess the freedom of choice to decide how we will respond to the human tragedies in which we are caught: we can *choose* to turn bitter and hostile, or we can *choose* to mature into more authentic, humane beings.

Here linguistic assistance is called for. Is the word "suffer" used with the same meaning by Charlie Brown (F-1: "Why do we have to suffer like this?"), by Linus (F-4: "The problem of suffering is a very profound one."), and by Lucy (F-6: "Who wants to suffer?")? Clearly not. As they talk to (or at) one another, the same word has been used but the meanings have shifted. As onlookers we can stop the debate, define the terms in their contexts, and determine whether shifts in meaning have taken place from one frame to another.° We can see that as the meanings changed they failed to hear (that is, understand) one another; and their not-hearing has resulted in the arguments they're now having. Typical. This is one of the reasons we get into prolonged time-wasting debates. We don't listen carefully to *the meanings* that others give to their symbols. They use a familiar word, giving it specific meaning in a specific context; but this word, equally familiar to us, reminds us of *other meanings* which, derived from our own unique experience, we have given to the term. Thus by association the symbol shifts its meaning. Hence our failure to communicate and our endless, fruitless debates.

Frame Seven. Charlie Brown's pensive finale: "I have a theological seminary." Could CB have just as well said "I have a philosophy seminar?" or "My baseball game has turned into a philosophers' convention?" What distinguishes theology from philosophy? Apparently they both deal with the ultimate questions of life. Does that make them essentially the same? Is there a definable difference between the two disciplines?

7

To Charlie Brown's dejected comment, the logician Peter Angeles makes a pungent retort: "No ball game . . . just a seminary. That's right—and insofar as you've got only a theological seminary going on in that baseball field, you won't get the game played. Amen."

12 Having taken time *to think about* this cartoon-strip debate, reread the frames from the beginning, slowly, without attempting very much analysis. Read it through several times. Ask yourself whether your overall awareness of what is going on has expanded as a result of your analysis. As you read, do you see more and hear more than you did the first time you read it? You should be able to see hidden assumptions and spot definitional problems. You can see how communication breakdowns become the source of frustration and argument. You may tune in feelings and other meaning-events (Charlie's frustration, Lucy's hostility) more than before. And first steps have been taken into ultimate philosophic questions such as the universal "moral law" and the "law of Pathei Mathos."

While making a general analysis of CB's seminar, what we actually did was to make random use of several analytic methods. Among these were several kinds of logical analysis, language analysis, semantic and existential analysis, and others. But if we wish, and if the materials require it, we can single out any one of these methods and apply it.

Classical or formal logic was invented by Aristotle and attempts to establish the principles of valid inference—the so-called rules of right reasoning. In learning how to think correctly, of course, we also learn to spot the fallacies which result from our bad thinking habits. Modern forms of logic may be rigorously formal—symbolic and mathematical logic, for example; or they may be informal and pragmatic.

Much modern critical analysis focuses on language, its use and abuse. The goal of ordinary language analysis is to show that most philosophical problems can be solved—or dissolved—by better understanding the structure of the language we use in daily discussion.

The critical analyst assumes an "on guard" stance; but critical analysis is not a nihilistic discipline, despite the negative connotation

You will never succeed in getting at the truth if you think you know, ahead of time, what the truth ought to be.

MARCHETTE CHUTE

A French politician once wrote that it was a peculiarity of the French language that in it words occur in the order in which one thinks them.

WITTGENSTEIN

of the words "critic" and "criticize." The verb "to criticize" derives from the Greek root *krinein* which means "to place under judgment" or simply "to question." To be "critical" of an idea means only that it is to be carefully weighed so we can be sure of its validity, its verity, or its value. If it passes muster, then a new data-bit has been admitted to the growing realm of human knowledge. But if the idea can't "stand up under criticism," then a rotten apple has been removed from the barrel.

REFLECTIONS—

1 According to this chapter, the role of philosophy in our lives is to deal with meaning. How many different kinds of meaning can you list? As for "the meaning of life," would you still define the phrase about the same way you did after reflecting on Chapter 1-1?

2 By way of summary, recast in your own thoughts what is intended by *analysis* and *synthesis*. How do we go about analysis? How do we go about synthesis? What are the goals in each case?

3 Most of the time we plunge spontaneously into our mental tasks, so this chapter suggests some preliminary steps to doing philosophy. In your case, would they work? What do you think of the idea that we must "stop-the-world" before we can zero in on ideas because the world—like a speeded-up movie film—is buzzing too rapidly for us to deal with the meaning-events taking place around us? How would you stop *your* world in order to deal with it meaning-fully?

4 There is an essential difference in the psychology of learning between adversary dialogue and supportive dialogue. What is the goal of adversary dialogue? Of supportive dialogue? Do these two modes of operation make good clear sense to you? Could you alternate from one to the other, depending upon the requirements of the situation?

5 General philosophic analysis is a very practical kind of activity; so before the mood and method fades away, practice this kind of analysis in the first appropriate conversations that present themselves. Remembering the preliminary steps, practice until you acquire a feel for it and it begins to work for you.

6 The question is posed in Sec. 12, after having gone through the ball-team debate, "do you see more and hear more than you did the first time you read it?" Your overall awareness should have expanded. Was this the case? If yes, could you achieve these results in your day-to-day conversations?

Furthermore . . .

ALSTON, WILLIAM P., *Philosophy of Language*. Prentice-Hall, 1964.

CORNMAN, JAMES W., and KEITH LEHRER, *Philosophical Problems and Arguments*. Macmillan, 2nd ed. 1974.

EMMET, E. R., *Learning to Philosophize*. Penguin, 1968.

FLESCH, RUDOLF, *The Art of Clear Thinking*. Collier, 1962.

GOROVITZ, SAMUEL, et al., *Philosophical Analysis: An Introduction to Its Language and Techniques*. Random House, 1965.

LITTLE, WINSTON W., et al., *Applied Logic*. Houghton Mifflin, 1955.

REID, CHARLES L., *Basic Philosophical Analysis*. Dickenson, 1971.

RORTY, RICHARD (ed.), *The Linguistic Turn: Recent Essays in Philosophic Method*. Chicago, 1970.

SHIBLES, WARREN, *Philosophical Pictures*. William C. Brown, 1969.

How To Philosophize/ Synoptic Synthesis

Have You Ever Wondered . . .

- Whether you could be (or want to be) a "philosopher"?

- Whether you are in charge of your education or your education is in charge of you?

- (Whether you're in charge of your life or whether life is in charge of you?)

- Whether you really WANT "to know more and more about less and less" OR really WANT "to know less and less about more and more"?

- Whether there are benefits in being a generalist?

- Whether there are dangers in being a specialist?

AND HE WANTS TO UNDERSTAND IT

Learning is not the accumulation *of scraps of knowledge. It is a* growth, *where every act of knowledge develops the learner . . . .*

HUSSERL

1   The goal of synoptic philosophy is what the Greek words imply: *sun-optikos*, "seeing (everything) together," and *philein-sophia*, "to love wisdom." Put these root-words together and the message comes out clear: Synoptic philosophy is the love of the wisdom that comes from achieving a coherent picture of everything seen together—a vision of the whole of life.

2   "A vision of the whole of life"—! Could any human undertaking
be grander, or more grandiose? William Halverson writes that "this
attempt stands without rival as the most audacious enterprise in which
the mind of man has ever engaged. Just reflect for a moment: Here is
man, surrounded by the vastness of a universe in which he is only a
tiny and perhaps insignificant part—and he wants to *understand*
it. . . ."°

3   We want to understand it, of course, because we must. Being
what we are, it isn't a matter of choice. If we have eyes to see, then
we must see; if we have ears, then we must hear. There are at least
three reasons for this necessity, and all are ontological.

First, seeing life holistically is a matter of survival. Imagine some
animal at home in its environmental niche with all the normal, routine
life-and-death events going on around it. The more it can perceive of
these events, and *the more accurately it can perceive them,* then the better
it can adjust. Developing a realistic sense of priorities—to be able to
distinguish between significant and insignificant events, between the
dangerous and the benign—means survival. This is just as true for
abstract man as for the wild fox and the wallaby. Investing our energies in consequential events rather than trivialities requires a wisdom
born of perspective.

°See p. xix

To grow into youngness is a blow.
To age into sickness is an insult.
To die is, if we are not careful, to
turn from God's breast, feeling
slighted and unloved. The sparrow
asks to be seen as it falls.
   Philosophy must try, as best it
can, to turn the sparrows to flights
of angels, which, Shakespeare
wrote, sing us to our rest.

RAY BRADBURY

When a speculative philosopher
believes he has comprehended the
world once and for all in his
system, he is deceiving himself;
he has merely comprehended
himself and then naively projected
that view upon the world.

C. G. JUNG

But man has a need which (we think) goes beyond the deer and the dolphin: the need for meaning. For man a meaning-less existence is a contradiction. Intuitively we have known that the well-lived life—the meaning-full life—results from what we humans call wisdom. By definition wisdom *is* the understanding of life and how to live it; and for as long as men have sought wisdom it has been apparent that wisdom is correlated to our capacity to *perceive more* and *understand more*.

Lastly, this drive to create a personal universe has still deeper origins. Each of us harbors within a pressure to achieve psychological wholeness, and our passion for wholeness in knowledge is a part of this drive. Unity of personality and unity of knowledge are two aspects of the same goal. What do we feel if we see on a table a jig-saw puzzle half finished or a painting left undone? We assume—we *know*—that any enterprise, once begun, ought to be completed. An unfinished story nags at us. An unfinished letter haunts us. An unfinished sentence, left dangling in mid-air, leaves us waiting, and when

LIFE ON A PICTURE-PUZZLE

4   Think of life as a jig-saw puzzle with an enormous number of pieces, and think of synoptic philosophy as our attempt to fit the puzzle together. This puzzle didn't come to us sealed in a cardboard box with an illustration on the cover, so we really don't know what the picture on the puzzle will turn out to be.

To be sure, we have been told what the picture is. But this is the problem. So many people have told us, on the best authority, what picture is *really* on the puzzle, and they describe different pictures. We must draw the logical conclusion that they, too, have not yet attained a glimpse of the whole picture.

Our ultimate goal is clear: to fit *all* the pieces together so we can attain a clear look at the picture. But it's an incredibly complex puzzle, and we may never succeed in getting the whole picture pieced together. Attempts thus far have failed, though many have been able to assemble scattered clusters. You and I may succeed in filling a few random spaces or joining together a small group of pieces here and there. Still, for all of us, at this point in the progress of human understanding, the total picture is diffuse, with light and dark shades that don't yet make sense. The task requires endless patience. If, in the meantime, we can enjoy just working the puzzle, that might be a sufficiently rewarding compromise.

So, the goal of synoptic philosophy is to see the picture on the puzzle—the whole picture, nothing less; and to see it clearly, unmistakably, and realistically.

5   The metaphor of the picture-puzzle helps to clarify several characteristics of synoptic philosophy.

The first, of course, is that the goal of synoptic synthesis is to see the whole picture. It won't settle for a fragmented view of scat-

---

One can be positive of one's own way that it leads to the goal and not that others cannot. That would be a species of dogmatism.

T. R. V. MURTI

One thing, at least, seems clear: the quest for "the total picture," the struggle to discern the unity that we instinctively believe must somehow lie behind the apparent inconsistencies of our little fragments of knowledge . . . will go on, with or without the cooperation of professional philosophers. It may turn out that those philosophers who of late have found their profession somewhat sterile and unchallenging will find a renewed interest in their work if the quest for unity comes once again to be accepted as the *raison d'être* of the philosophical enterprise.

WILLIAM HALVERSON

All philosophy begins—as the ancient Greeks so well knew—with astonishment and wonder.

KURT REINHARDT

tered designs; nor will it allow itself to be seduced into believing that any mere fragment is really the whole picture. The mandate of synoptic philosophy is to keep working with the jig-saw pieces until the picture is seen and the puzzle is resolved.

The philosopher of history Arnold Toynbee has written that, as of the latter part of the twentieth century, we are collectively in transition to a new world-view in which our dominant perception will be that of being meaningful parts of a larger universe. These new ties contrast sharply with the old world we are now leaving, in which the dominant sense of consciousness was for each of us to believe we were complete, self-contained universes within ourselves.

To use the puzzle metaphor, most of us have heretofore taken up residence on a single piece of the jig-saw puzzle. We lived out our life/times on this small picture plot; we put down roots and became intimately familiar with the design of one small bit of reality. Eventually we came to believe that our cardboard square was the most important piece in all the puzzle; the rest of the vast scene was to be judged from the perspective of our own mini-puzzle. The final illusion followed close behind: we convinced ourselves that our single puzzle-piece was in fact the whole of reality—the total picture.

To escape this predicament, synoptic philosophy encourages each of us to wander over the puzzle, visiting neighboring parts and trying to see how the pieces of the puzzle all fit together. It urges us to travel from square to square until it becomes clear that no single part is in fact the whole. Only by wandering over the puzzling terrain restlessly and observantly—like itinerant Flatlanders—can we arrive at an honest conclusion as to what the whole of reality is like.

6   The way in which philosophic analysis and philosophic synthesis work together is also implicit in the picture-puzzle analogy.

Although a synoptist wants to stand back and ponder the whole picture, he finds that he must spend much of his time close-up working with singular pieces of the puzzle—turning them, scrutinizing them, studying them. Philosophic analysis works with each microscopic area of the giant puzzle until it is clearly understood.

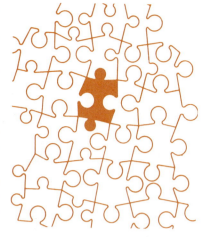

Knowledge of the world demands more than just seeing the world. One must know what to look for in foreign countries.

IMMANUEL KANT

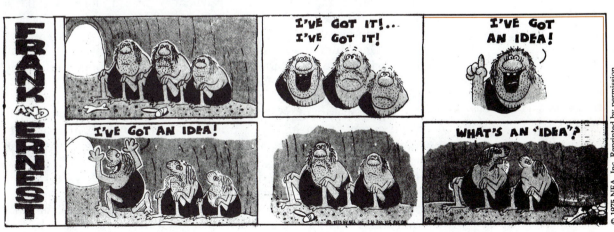

Analysis generally precedes synthesis. We must first make sure each piece really belongs in the puzzle. (Ever work on a jig-saw puzzle where someone had mixed in pieces from another puzzle?) The analyst familiarizes himself with each fragment so that, at some later time, he stands a good chance of recognizing where it fits in.

Leaving aside the puzzle analogy, what we find is that "the bugs" must be worked out of so many of our ideas before we can confidently put them to use. What's the point in wasting time trying to synthesize an idea into our philosophy of life if in fact it is false, or involves a fallacy, or is a trivial value-judgment?

°*By the way, did you personally come to a final decision on the matter?*

For instance, take Lucy's notion of a universal moral law. Remember how complex the problem was and how much clarification was needed before we could decide, in good conscience, whether to adopt the idea?° This was a factual matter, a what-is-really-the-case kind of problem. Other such factual questions usually requiring analytical assistance are: Does God exist? How could we know? Is there personal immortality? What makes religious beliefs "right" or "wrong"? How can subjective selves "know" the objects/events of the real world? In terms of freedom and determinism, should I be held personally responsible for everything I do?

Equally confusing, and in need of analysis, are value-questions: Can we ever justify the deliberate killing of another human being (as in self-defense, or when an individual goes berserk; in euthanasia or capital punishment; in war, in a "wrong" war, in a revolution against oppression)? Can we justify the deliberate killing of animals (a species nearing extinction, our pets, dolphins, whales)? Can we justify abortion, the nonpayment of taxes, disobeying unjust laws or disobeying just laws under special circumstances? Or, more broadly, what makes any action "right" or "wrong"?

My young men shall never work. Men who work cannot dream, and wisdom comes in dreams. . . .

SMOHALLA (INDIAN PROPHET)

Philosophic analysis becomes especially useful in our very personal dilemmas. Was I justified in lying to someone who trusts me? Should I feel guilty about having sex (or enjoying sex) at the "wrong" time and place? (And exactly what makes the time and place "wrong"?) Is cheating on exams ever justified (not rationalizable, but justifiable)? I don't love someone whom I "should" love—a child, a husband or wife, a parent; am I a "bad" person (or ungrateful, or neurotic, or immoral)?

Only after analysis has been performed on such questions—all of which hide a multitude of complexities—can synoptic philosophy go to work fitting the pieces into the whole puzzle.

From the cowardice that shrinks
   from new truth,
From the laziness that is content
   with half-truths,
From the arrogance that thinks it
   knows all truths,
O God of Truth, deliver us.

Ancient prayer

7   The history of philosophy is the record of men and women who were caught up in just such problems. Many of them invested lifetimes in the same questions we face today. After all, they shared "the cruel contradictions and bitter ironies" of the human condition, and their guidance can be of enormous help to us.

But the philosophers of the past can't do our work for us. They moved within the possible world-views of their times. Given the data-limitations and the conceptual schemes within which they had to think, they phrased questions and found answers as best they could; and we honor their accomplishments when we draw upon their work.

By contrast, we have at our service vast quantities of empirical data and pragmatic concepts not available to those of past ages. Our lives overflow with an abundance of knowledge that would have made Aristotle and Bacon and Spinoza ecstatic, and we are self-defeating philistines if we take this wealth of knowledge for granted.

You and I face the all-too-human temptation to become dependent upon thinkers of the past for answers to our philosophic inquiries, and with scarcely half an effort we can rationalize our dependence: These were great intellects, after all; they had special gifts; they had leisure time to reflect upon such problems—and so on. We can easily kid ourselves into believing that the great problems of life have long been solved.

Recall Wittgenstein's warning that when we repeat another's thought it indicates a failure to think it for ourselves, and that dependence on the thinking of others "at best hinders independent thought, and at most, prevents it. And a thought which is not independent is a thought only half understood. . . ."

Synoptic philosophy is a *now* philosophy. We live in the present, not in the past. It is the meaning of *our* lives we must live, not the meaning of the great lives of the past, and not "the Meaning of Life" as others believed they saw it. History serves us; we are not here to serve history. We must make use of the best facts and ideas available to us *now* in assembling our own jig-saw puzzles.

By and large, the pensive minds of the past were wise. They would be content to have us use their ideas when we can and let us lay them to rest, appreciatively, when they are no longer serviceable.

THE ANNIHILATION OF BOUNDARIES

8   Since at least the time of Aristotle, synoptic philosophy has been the ultimate interdisciplinary enterprise. When Aristotle and his peripatetic students were walking and talking along the paths of the Lyceum, subject-matter specialization had not yet begun, and knowledge was not yet "organized apart" into countless categories—biology, psychology, physics, and so on. Aristotle still looked with awe and wonder upon all human knowledge. His adventuresome mind was still free, not yet trained to function along carefully defined boundary-lines, not yet cluttered with classification systems that fragment human understanding into competing disciplines.

It has been said that Aristotle was the last Western thinker that could actually know all that there was to be known. Before his time there wasn't much to know; and after him there was far too much. Specialization became inevitable.

But it's important to realize that *life* is *not* specialized. Life is "interdisciplinary." Vocationally we may be electronics engineers, or neurosurgeons, or accountants; but when not practicing our profession

Something forever exceeds, escapes from statement, withdraws from definition, must be glimpsed and felt, not told. No one knows this like your genuine professor of philosophy. For what glimmers and twinkles like a bird's wing in the sunshine it is his business to snatch and fix. . . .

WILLIAM JAMES

**He who knows does not speak;
He who speaks does not know.**

TAO TEH CHING

we "revert" to the human condition and find ourselves thinking like generalists again.

Synoptic philosophy is a reflection of life. We *are*, each and every one of us, sociology and anthropology and history and geography. We *are* physics (put your finger into a light socket and feel). We *are* astrophysics and cosmology (we feel silvery-moon sentiments by night and get sunburns by day). We *are* biology and biochemistry and genetics (unless the stork story is true, after all). We *are* psychology and physiology and psychophysiology (ever guzzle a martini or suffer a brain concussion?) We *are* all these things, and there is *nothing* in human knowledge that we *are not*. So when we engage in synoptic thinking we are returning to life. Life cannot specialize. It remains just what it was before the human mind fragmented it: totalic, whole.

9   In the academic system, as in life, synoptic philosophy erases the mental barriers that separate branches of knowledge. Academic divisions are pragmatic ways of organizing our vast accumulations of data and of keeping specialists out of one another's domains. Most of the time they are indispensable, and the specialized sciences will continue to make immeasurable gains. But dividing lines must be removed when they cease to be helpful, and in all synthesizing activities they become counterproductive. They fragment our understanding.

"Something there is that doesn't love a wall," wrote Robert Frost; and this is the byline of the synoptist. He resists the permanent posting of all boundary-lines. The rigid compartmentalization of knowledge is arbitrary, after all; and in an age of new problems the disparate fields of data must be reassembled if we are to find viable solutions.

Currently no other specific discipline can be found in the curriculum whose essential function is to draw all the areas of knowledge back together and interrelate them. Academic programs continue to be characterized by pragmatic divisions of labor: the chemist must not encroach on the biologist who must not encroach on the psychologist, and so on. As a result, students commonly receive replies such as, "That question belongs in psychology, not here in biology," meaning: "By classification, that question is outside my field of specialization. Go ask some other specialist."

Furthermore, when we choose a major, the demanding requirements force us to forego and forget all the other fascinating stores of knowledge. While mastering our chosen specialty, whatever interest we have in other fields must be put aside; we remind ourselves that we can return to them at some later time. So, by practical necessity, specializations become mutually exclusive. There is little encouragement to develop holistic habits of thinking during our years of formal education.

Synoptic synthesis focuses specifically on our thinking habits. It helps each person develop the habit of erasing imaginary boundaries; it tears down mental walls that hamper free access to needed fields of

We need people who can see straight ahead and deep into the problems. Those are the experts. But we also need peripheral vision and experts are generally not very good at providing peripheral vision.

ALVIN TOFFLER

There is today—in a time when old beliefs are withering—a kind of philosophical hunger, a need to know who we are and how we got here. There is an ongoing search, often unconscious, for a cosmic perspective for humanity.

CARL SAGAN

information. This means reconditioning ourselves to think through arbitrary barriers, to turn to all disciplines for data, and to ask interdisciplinary questions.

10   Doesn't all this mean that the synoptic philosopher is attempting to know everything, to become omniscient—to play God? Isn't the attempt to attain a vision of the whole of life beyond the capacity of finite human minds?

The answer to the first question is that the synoptist never tries "to know everything." He makes no attempt to memorize the reams of hard data that have accumulated in the specialized fields. Happily, it is not uncommon to become excited about a field and find oneself drawn in deeper than first intended. Still, the synoptist remains a layman when it comes to specialized details, and he doesn't let himself forget this fact.

The task of the synoptist is to keep himself informed on the latest *conclusions, general principles, hypotheses, models, and theories* that emerge from the work of the field specialists. He is not himself a field specialist, and he is not in competition with them since he is not a knowledge-gatherer in the sense they are. He makes use of the data they labor to discover; hence he is always in their debt. He is also at their mercy, of course; and he hopes that he turns to the right specialists for information. If he listens to wrong sources and receives wrong answers, then, in effect, he ends up with jig-saw pieces that don't belong in the puzzle; and he may waste considerable time trying to fit in pieces that won't fit.

The second question—Can the human mind attain "the holistic vision"?—presupposes a degree of faith.° At present the complexity of "all that is" boggles our minds; total comprehension seems like a fuzzy dream. However, the holistic vision is probably not an unrealistic goal *for the human race*. Not that we have a choice. Since this drive is ontological, we will continue to work for it both individually and collectively because we cannot do otherwise. In our own short life/times the most we can hope for is partial success. But even a little progress, at the personal level, proves immensely rewarding.

At present history is on the side of optimism. The story of man's attempt to gather a fund of empirical knowledge and to discover the truth about himself and his world has, in the longer-range perspective of history, just begun; and human understanding is advancing so rapidly on all fronts that any oddsmaker would advise placing our bets on the continued capacity of the human mind to understand, in principle, the fundamental nature of man and his universe. True, this judgment could be wrong. Gray matter may have unsuspected limits; and the real world could turn out to be too intricate to be reduced to human abstractions. Still, *understanding* requires *general principles*, not details. (The details can be handled by our computers so that we can concentrate on understanding.) According to present evidence the human capacity for conceptualization is quite adequate to the task.

°*You may find it helpful to check the glossary for a philosophic definition of the word "faith."*

Although Omar Khayyam may have claimed that the results of his studies were that he "evermore came out by the same door as in I went," he neglected to notice that he was facing a different direction when he came out.

RONALD HUNTINGTON

Aristotle

The First Scientific World-View

Three supreme moments illuminate Aristotle's life. Any one of them would have assured his immortal value to the human race.

First, Aristotle journeyed to Athens when he was 18, enrolled in the Academy, and became a student of Plato. He had come from Stagira, a small colonial town on the Aegean coast of northern Greece. His father had been court physician to the king of Macedonia. Aristotle had accompanied his father, Nichomachus, and mother, Phaestis, to the capital city of Pella sometime during early childhood, but returned to Stagira after their deaths. He was born in 384 B.C.

Aristotle performed brilliantly at the Academy. Plato called him "the Mind" of the school and referred to his living quarters as "the bookworm's house," apparently because Aristotle had accumulated an enviable library of scrolls. These were years for maturing, for mastering his subject matter, and for clarifying his own ideas. Plato had developed a comprehensive and coherent world-view—the first Western thinker to do so; and Aristotle had fully absorbed it; but he had to exorcise it from his psyche—the two men possessed quite different temperaments—before he could move on to develop his own empirical world-view.

Aristotle left the Academy at 38 and sailed to Asia Minor to join an old friend who had become ruler of the city-state of Atarneus. For three years Aristotle lived there and, at 40, married the king's niece, Pythias. Sometime thereafter they moved to the island of Lesbos, where Aristotle continued to study the marine life of the Aegean shores. We would like to know if he sat by the tidepools, dissected sponges, talked with fishers, and kept notebooks and drawings. At any rate, his writings reveal an accurate knowledge of the marine biology of this part of the world.

Aristotle's marriage was apparently happy but short-lived, for Pythias died sometime after the birth of their daughter. Later in life Aristotle married again—her name was Herpyllis—and they had two children, Nichomachus (named for Aristotle's father) and a daughter (who remains anonymous to us).

When he was 42 the second historic event occurred in Aristotle's life: He received a royal summons from King Philip to return to the Macedonian court as teacher to Philip's son Alexander. The Crown Prince was only 13, but within six years he was to assume the throne and marshal the military might of a united Greek world against the Persian Empire. After his lightning conquest of the known civilized world, we remember him as Alexander the Great.

Aristotle taught Alexander for three years. "History leaves us free to believe (though we should suspect these pleasant thoughts) that Alexander's unifying passion derived some of its force and grandeur from his teacher, the most synthetic thinker in the history of thought; and that conquest of order in the political realm by the pupil, and in the philosophic realm by the master, were but diverse sides of one noble and epic project—two magnificent Macedonians unifying two chaotic worlds" (Will Durant, *The Story of Philosophy*, p. 52).

In the spring of 334 B.C. the third momentous event of Aristotle's life began: He sailed to Athens to set up his own school, the Lyceum, an institution for higher learning which would last for almost 800 years. He chose acreage in the northeastern outskirts of the city that included a shady garden, covered walkways, and a public gymnasium on the grounds of a temple dedicated to Apollo Lyceus—Apollo the Lightgiver. Not being a citizen, Aristotle did not possess property rights, so he was forced to rent the land and buildings for his school. The gymnasium was one of the three large recreation halls in the city at that time; and no doubt Aristotle's students sometimes dashed into his classrooms, a minute late, fresh from workouts in the sports arena.

Aristotle was 50 when he opened the Lyceum. He was a gentle, sensitive man and an inspiring teacher. For a dozen years he oversaw the institution, directed research programs, taught, and wrote. He lectured as he wandered through the grounds of the park and under covered walkways called *peripatoi* (his students became known as the Peripatetics, "the Strollers"). During morning hours he lectured on technical subjects; in the afternoon he presented open-air lectures to the public on popular topics such as rhetoric and politics. During the evenings he conversed and wrote.

In contrast to Plato's Academy, which stressed mathematics and geometry, the Lyceum was designed as a center for scientific research and the teaching of scientific method. Heavy emphasis was placed on the natural sciences, especially biology. Aristotle found he had to be a collector and curator in order to be a scientist. He and his students carried on their own field work, and historians tell us that Alexander helped by putting his soldiers to work in newly conquered lands gathering flora and fauna for the museums. In and around his buildings Aristotle built up a zoo and botanical garden, and inside the school he developed laboratories and a voluminous library. As in today's textbooks, Aristotle used anatomical diagrams to illustrate his observations, and these were put up on the walls of the Lyceum, just as they are in modern classrooms. Thus, Aristotle had available an abundance of material to make a scientist jubilant. He turned his attention to virtually every subject.

He wondered about the stars, planets, sun and moon, the mountains and oceans, heat and cold, rain, snow, clouds, thunder and lightning, and rainbows.

He investigated plants and animals, and the relationships of living things, including ecological systems and animal behavior; mollusks, fishes, insects, birds, mammals; organs for sense perception and locomotion, mating, and reproduction; diseases and disorders.

He reflected on mind and emotions, men and women, love and genes. He pondered perception, conception, words and meanings, and fallacies; poetry, sculpture, and music. He studied written constitutions and power politics; he evaluated various forms of government such as the monarchy, aristocracy, and timocracy.

Doubtless Aristotle derived immense enjoyment from delving into the mysteries of our world, but his gathering of facts was incidental and unimportant. What he was seeking was understanding, and his knowledge of particulars enabled him to generalize.

Therefore, from his observations he developed abstract concepts of motion, change, actuality, potentiality, process or becoming, and causality; geological time, biological evolution, and entelechy (biological purposiveness—our genetics); systems of classification, concepts of truth and validity, definitions, categories, *archai* (first principles, axioms), deduction and induction; concepts of virtue, justice, human nature, the soul *(psyche),* and happiness *(eudaimonia);* concepts of form and substance, teleology, causality, and a Prime Mover.

We can judge, from our vantage point, that Aristotle succeeded in laying foundations for the sciences of physics, astronomy, and meteorology; taxonomy, biology, forensic pathology, and animal psychology; psychology, epistemology and logic, and esthetics; political science and ethics; and, finally, metaphysics— the philosopher's unified field theory for understanding his universe.

Add to all this a picture of the man reflecting, writing, and lecturing on more popular subjects such as education, rhetoric and grammar, mathematics and geometry, statecraft, drama and literature, and the art of living the good life.

Aristotle was a true scientist—an honest mind seeking empirical data from which to build explanatory hypotheses; and he was a true philosopher—a wonderer who surrendered lovingly to his curiosity about life.

All hell broke loose in Athens when Alexander died in 323 B.C. Aristotle had remained an alien in the eyes of the Athenians, a colonial Greek from the north too closely associated with the Macedonian conqueror. After Alexander's death the Macedonian party was ousted from power, and the wrath of the citizenry turned against Aristotle. He was charged with atheism (as was Socrates). At this juncture he was offered protection by an old friend, so Aristotle retreated to Chalcis on the island of Euboea, some 50 miles north of Athens. He had tolerated this exile for barely a year when he died in 322 B.C., aged 62.

We possess the text of Aristotle's will. He made the usual bequests, provided for his children and his servants (he freed some slaves), expressed gratitude for the affection of Herpyllis, and asked that the remains of Pythias be placed in the tomb beside his.

HOW TO DO SYNOPTIC PHILOSOPHY

11   How does one go about "doing" synoptic philosophy?

One good way to begin is to place yourself in the center of what we'll call the "synoptic wheel." In your imagination, look outwards in all directions from that center. Around the rim of the wheel are all the knowledge-gathering disciplines known to man, plus various arts and skills and some philosophic specializations. This schematic is merely one way of visualizing our philosophic predicament: when we feel overwhelmed by life's stubborn questions and don't know which way to turn for help, then spin the synoptic wheel and ask the specialists to share their knowledge and insights.

Note the general areas that are represented on the wheel.

In working through a problem, a synoptist would move along a sequence of steps something like the following.

(1) Having come across a philosophic problem (or having been

"Everything I have taught you so far has been an aspect of *not-doing,*" Don Juan went on. "A warrior applies *not-doing* to everything in the world, and yet I can't tell you more about it than what I have said today. You must let your own body discover the power and the feeling of *not-doing.*"

CARLOS CASTANEDA
Journey to Ixtlan

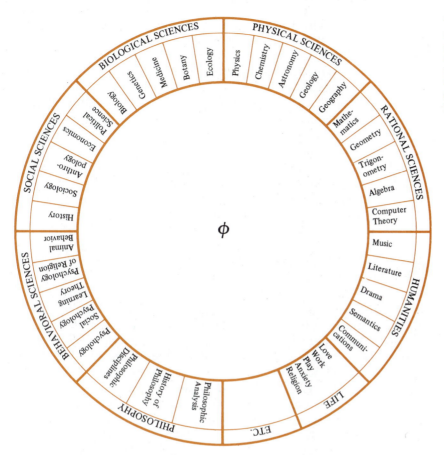

°*The Greek letter phi (φ) is commonly used as a symbol for philosophy. When placed at the center of the synoptic wheel it will be used to stand for synoptic philosophy, for the problem being worked on, and for the philosopher doing the work (namely, you).*

run down by one), first proceed as far as possible with philosophic analysis, clarifying and drawing out all the hidden meanings that you can, dissolving the problem completely if that is possible.

Then, to the extent that time and materials permit, find out what philosophers of the past have thought about the problem. In the history of philosophy, most of the problems you and I must deal with have been pondered, time and again, from many different perspectives; and these earlier treatments can lighten our labors by enlightening our thoughts. Uniquely valuable insights are often provided by individuals who, in some special way, were bothered by, and became caught up in, a particular problem.

Once a problem is posed, it may be necessary to rephrase the question in a variety of ways before we can get it to reveal what kinds of information will help solve it. (There is *no* question that *can't* be asked in many ways. The following exchange: ''Does God exist?'' ''What do you mean by the question?'' ''I mean just what I said: Does God exist?''—this exchange is quickly ushered out of any philosophic discussion.) The synoptist tries to develop an intuition for asking and reasking questions from different angles until they point to the data that would illuminate them.

(2) From your vantage point in the center of the synoptic wheel, ask yourself what fields seem most likely to contain information related to your problem. Begin by just asking questions about the problem and how it might connect, one by one, to the various fields in the rim of the schematic. For instance . . .

Question: Does God exist? (First, ask yourself if your question is honestly intended as a genuine question. Do you really *want* an objective answer? Or do you want an "objective" answer only if it agrees with what you already "know"? Whatever the question may be, if you already know the answer *beyond any possible doubt,* then one must entertain second thoughts about its being a true philosophic question.) If it's an authentic question, then *go to psychology,* and ask questions of this kind: What do "religious experiences" seem to imply regarding the existence of a God? What about mystical experiences such as Saint Theresa's "golden arrow," and pentecostal "ecstasy," and "spirit possession"? Can the multitude of deity-images in man's religions be understood in terms of our psychological needs?

Then *go to linguistics,* and ask: What does the word "god" refer to? Does it refer to reality or only to other words? Whence does it derive its meaning for you? for the Buddhist? for the native American Indian? What other names could you use for your God—matter, force, spirit, wind,° love, power—? *Go to physics:* Are there any real objects/events that can't be explained in terms of known physical forces? Can the origins of matter be accounted for apart from the idea of a Prime Mover or Creator? *Go to history:* Is there documented evidence of past events that necessitate the hypothesis of supernatural intervention? Can we discern any sort of pattern or "dramatic plot" in human history that indicates direction, guidance, planning, or purpose?

Go to biology: Can life processes be explained in terms of natural biochemical events? Is there any event in DNA genetics, speciation, or evolutionary modeling that necessitates the hypothesis of a supernatural or a "vital impulse"? *Go to medicine:* Do there exist well-documented cases of healings which cannot be explained by medicine or by our understanding of the human psychophysical organism? If so, how must we define the word "miracle"? *Go to exobiology:* Is your image of God anthropomorphic—that is, humanoid? In what form might deity appropriately manifest itself to advanced alien beings on other planets? *Go to astronomy:* What concept of deity is possible in the incomprehensibly vast universe that we know today? *Etcetera . . . .*°

This is but the briefest sampling of *the kinds* of questions that would have to be asked before such a question could be answered. Without doubt the task feels formidable, but it can also be one of our most exciting adventures. To perform the synoptic task well, one must keep up with what is going on in various fields and be willing to listen to *anyone* who is in possession of helpful information.

Having made this kind of preliminary question-asking survey, the next step is to go to these promising fields and gather information. Remember that the synoptist is looking for conclusions, hypotheses,

---

Perhaps the major challenge to philosophy in the last decades of the twentieth century is whether it can face the future imaginatively and creatively or whether it will simply be content with a status as a second-order discipline, able only to analyze and evaluate the concepts and ideas of other disciplines.

RICHARD DOSS

°*Note the meanings given to the Greek word* pneuma, *p 495-Box*

Reason is ⁶/₇ of treason.

JAMES THURBER

°*Be only as literal as you need to be when it says "go to biology" or chemistry, physics, or whatever. None of us can promptly go and digest a textbook in every field. What is meant is to turn to that general subject matter and find whatever materials you can, whether they be technical, textbook, or popular. All that is important is that we obtain dependable information.*

and models currently used by field specialists. As you gather materials, keep asking questions, relating the data to your central problem and cross-relating insights from the fields themselves.

(3) Next, criss-cross from field to field, drawing "interconnecting lines of illumination" as you go, stopping often to refocus new ideas on your initial problem to see whether the sort of understanding you are after is beginning to emerge.

Moving from first question to final answer is often a long journey. In fact, doing synoptic philosophy is much like starting a trip where all you know is where you are now and where you want to arrive—namely, at the best answer possible at this time. The route by which you'll get there is not at all clear, and philosophic journeys can rarely be neatly penciled on a map ahead of time. So, just set off down the road. If you come to a side road pointing to new information, turn that way. Travel till you come to new intersections of knowledge or see a sign pointing in still another direction. Don't be afraid to wander without a map. Let the journey unfold gradually, just as it wishes. The facts will lead us where we need to go.

(4) Lastly, back away from the problem you've been working on and try to see it in a larger way. Since it is so easy for us to lose perspective, stand back as often as needed and ask yourself whether the whole picture can be better seen now that you have invested considerable thought in analyzing and synthesizing the problem.

Such a view of the larger picture is not easily achieved in less than twenty minutes. Our minds will weave the silken strands into a beautiful tapestry, but they will do so in their own good time. What is important is that *we attempt* to see larger blocks of life and that *we develop the habit of trying* to think in ever larger frames as we work through the problem.

This attempt to see the full-scale picture on life's puzzle creates certain dangers about which we need to be forewarned. So, word of caution #1: Don't be forced into saying you see more of the puzzle than you really do. The temptation to see what others insist *is* the picture on the puzzle can be great; and it may require no small amount of courage on our part to say, and to continue to say: " I can't *see* that part of the puzzle yet." Or: "I know that factual information in that area is still nonexistent, and no one can be absolutely sure about it at this time. It's too soon to persuade ourselves that we can see what isn't there." We all know how difficult it is to keep on saying "I don't know" when so many people around us are positive that *they* know the answers and keep proclaiming them to us, loudly. The gentle admonition of Confucius has a healing touch: "One can tell for oneself whether the water is warm or cold."

Word of caution #2: Considerable self-knowledge is required for us to resist the pressures of *our own needs* to have answers which, in fact, we don't have. Our cultural conditioning has made us believe we are supposed to "have convictions" about most everything, or at least to "have an opinion." (If we don't we're apathetic.) So the need to

The *Shri Yantra* is employed in meditation by Hindu worshippers known as Shaktas. It is a symbol of wholeness. Ultimate Reality is represented by the dot in the center, and the rest of reality is symbolized by triangles (consciousness and energy) and lotus petals (the material universe). The outer square contains gates through which the mind of man can enter into the deeper levels of wholeness.

The thrust of Western intellectual development since the sixteenth and early seventeenth centuries has been to fragment knowledge. . . . Now we know that isolated specialization is no longer realistic and perhaps even suicidal. We are being forced again to think in holistic terms. All knowledge is once again an ecological system.

EDWARD B. FISKE

Academic philosophers, ever since the time of Parmenides, have believed that the world is a unity. . . . The most fundamental of my intellectual beliefs is that this is rubbish. I think the universe is all spots and jumps, without unity, without continuity, without coherence or orderliness or any of the other properties that governesses love . . . it consists of events, short, small and haphazard. Order, unity, and continuity are human inventions, just as truly as our catalogues and encyclopedias.

BERTRAND RUSSELL

prepare answers to meet our own competitive/survival situations is great. Knowing ourselves, recognizing our motives, and remaining wary lest these personal pressures push us into claiming more than we should—all this is not easy. But it's necessary, not just so we can play a defined role, but in order to be honest with ourselves about what, in fact, we actually know and don't know.

As one logician puts it, all but a small portion of our thinking is need-oriented; it is determined and guided by numerous subjective factors. "To become a sound thinker it is necessary not only to school yourself thoroughly in certain techniques but also to understand fully the nature and operation of subjective factors and to take special measures for reducing their influence."

In the last analysis, we serve both ourselves and others best if we refuse to detour from our goal of knowing "what is." If we are cavalier with facts or play loose with value-judgments, it becomes difficult for us to live with ourselves; and unless we play fair with our experiences, others have no good reason to believe us or respect our judgment.

Unless the synoptist remains loyal to his vision of seeing nothing less than the whole puzzle-picture, then there is really no one left in this (existentially absurd?) world who continues to strive to know the full story. The World-Riddle is largely abandoned to those who intently gaze at some small portion of the jig-saw picture and proclaim to the rest of us that they have discovered the Whole. And we'd better believe it.

The real world is increasingly seen to be, not the tidy garden of our race's childhood, but the extraordinary, extravagant universe described by the eye of science.

HERMAN J. MULLER

THE SYNOPTIC VENTURE: RISKS AND REWARDS

12   The risks of specializing are many, but, since specialization is the order of the day, we don't commonly become aware of them—except in a painful way, and too late. One risk is that the more one specializes in a narrow field the more he tends to neglect a general knowledge of life that is necessary just to remain human. The proverbial definition of the scientist—"the one who knows more and more about less and less until he knows everything about nothing"—is apt for every specialist. A narrow field too often signals a narrow mind. A fulfilling life is far more likely for the individual who develops a balanced awareness of the requirements of living.

Another frequent result of specialization is the loss of the ability to communicate. Encapsulation is the commonest of all human diseases, with a mortality rate second to none. If we have failed to nourish the shared experiences of life, there may be nothing to bridge the chasms between us. The statement is commonly made that specialists tend to be lonely people, and this is probably true.

Brand Blandshard, a contemporary philosopher, once warned would-be specialists to keep their lines of communication in good repair.

> The more deeply you penetrate into the mineshaft of your own science, the more isolated and lonely you are with regard to those interests that mark the growing point of your mind. I admire beyond words the scientific acumen that made it possible for Planck to define the value of *h*, for example. But if I were to sit down for a talk with someone, and he were to focus the discussion on *h*, the tête-à-tête would be brief, for as far as I am concerned, *h* is not discussible.
>
> What are the grounds on which men generally can meet? They are the experiences that all men have in common. All of us, however humble, have had experiences of suffering and exaltation, of inspiration and depression, of laughter and pain that would, if we could only express them, make us, too, poets and essayists. Indeed, literature consists of just such experiences expressed as we should like to express them if we could. . . .
>
> It is well to be a specialist; it is better to be a good human being. . . .

13   The synoptist is vulnerable to equally perilous risks. Perhaps the most uncomfortable is the likelihood of being considered (and called) a dilettante by specialists. Whenever we turn to a specialist for information, we are, from his viewpoint, "only a layman"—never the authority, never the expert. We always appear to be at a strategic disadvantage. Because we try to know something (the basic conclusions) about everything (the basic disciplines), we can easily leave the impression that our concerns are shallow and that our currents never run deep.

A far greater danger, however, is that we might actually become

If there is any science man really needs it is the one I teach, of how to occupy properly that place in creation that is assigned to man, and how to learn from it what one must be in order to be a man.

IMMANUEL KANT

We need and sometimes want to make a persistent attempt to think things through. In this, we should be grateful for any help that we can get. . . . Philosophy begins in a natural curiosity that will not be satisfied with what we already know or think we know; according to Aristotle, it begins in wonder. "Hast any philosophy in thee, shepherd?" The answer is, Yes, but it needs cultivating.

LEWIS WHITE BECK

dilettantes—random dabblers in all things known and unknown. The difference between a dilettante and a synoptist lies in the way the synoptist weaves his data into a coherent world-view. Dabblers and dilettantes are known for dipping and picking at bits of information in order to be in a position—over hors d'oeuvres and a demitasse—to impress others with their range of erudition. By contrast, the stance of the synoptist is to admit, to himself and others, what he doesn't know; and in the context of all that there is to be known, he is aware that his abysmal unknowing is nothing to boast about. The goal of the synoptic empiricist is not to collect bits and pieces, but to weave the strands of knowledge into a glowing tapestry.

A double-edged risk is the fact that specialists become irritated with the way laymen—however honorable their intentions—tend to misunderstand and misuse the discoveries from their fields. They are (rightly) wary of having their work "popularized" and distorted. That fear can be calmed, of course, only by the honest, accurate handling of the data derived from their specialized fields. We are morally justified in asking their help only if we are willing to assimilate their materials with intelligence and integrity.

14   The rewards of the synoptic venture are, for the most part, intensely personal, having to do with what we are, or can become, as human beings.

One reward is learning to "think bigger." From its inception, a prime concern of philosophy has been the fact that the parameters of human thought—for all of us, all the time—are very, very narrow. Larry Niven, a science-fiction writer, put it perfectly: The trouble with people who live on a planet is that the inhabitants tend to think small.

MAN'S TRUE FUNCTION

If the great design of the universe had wished man to be a specialist, man would have been designed with one eye and a microscope attached to it which he could not unfasten. All the living species except human beings are specialists. The bird can fly beautifully but cannot take its wings off after landing and therefore can't walk very well. The fish can't walk at all. But man can put on his gills and swim and he can put on his wings and fly and then take them off and not be encumbered with them when he is not using them. He is in the middle of all living species. He is the most generally adaptable but only by virtue of his one unique faculty—his mind. Many creatures have brains. Human minds discover pure abstract generalized principles and employ those principles in the appropriate special cases. Thus has evolution made humans the most universally adaptable, in contradistinction to specialization, by endowing them with these metaphysical, weightless invisible capabilities to employ and realize special case uses of the generalized principles. . . .

All the biologicals are converting chaos to beautiful order. All biology is antientropic. Of all the disorder to order converters, the human mind is by far the most impressive. The human's most powerful metaphysical drive is to understand, to order, to sort out, and rearrange in ever more orderly and understandably constructive ways. You find then that man's true function is metaphysical.

BUCKMINSTER FULLER

And when we think small, we never quite succeed in arranging life's events into an efficient priority system that promises optimal growth and fulfillment. We don't think big enough to know what's important in our lives and what's not important, what to invest our time and energy into and what to ignore.

Synoptic philosophy is an antidote for small thought. As a result, many of life's problems—what we *thought* were life's problems—simply dissolve and disappear. Seeing the larger picture gives us the perspective and power to screen out trivial, inconsequential events.

Synoptic thinking also produces greater awareness in our perception of daily life. All of us want to be more than we now are: we want to be brighter (by 30 IQ points, maybe 40!); we want a greater comprehension of life's painful events; we want more intensely pleasurable "peak experiences, " more adventures, and so on. In a word, we all harbor a deep desire for *more life,* both in quantity and quality. Synoptic philosophy moves in that direction by laying solid foundations for such experiences; it hears this ontological cry for help. Synoptic thought leads to a greater awareness of oneself, and hence to an understanding of others. This in turn means better communication—and less alienation, isolation, and loneliness. Other things being equal, these are good foundations for greater fulfillment within the context of the human condition; and this may be the most we can reasonably expect in one (short) life/time.

Another reward is the fact that both our conscious and unconscious operations move more efficiently within a coherent world-view that is relatively free of internal contradictions and conflicts. Internal conflict means stress and a loss of psychological energy. If there is internecine strife going on between the ideas and feelings which constitute the cognitive contents of our character structure, then much of the energy potentially available to us for living is bound up in the inner struggle. We have "built-in headwinds"; we can't get off the ground. A world-view that works well for us is one whose component elements have ceased carrying on a running battle inside us and have begun to work together.

A final note: learning can be (*can* be) one of life's most exciting adventures. Catch a glimpse, just once, of the new discoveries taking place along today's frontiers—it is humbling, thrilling, mind-boggling . . . and addictive! It is difficult not to want to share the action.

Each of us is free, if we wish, to become an epistemic amateur—a knowledge-lover—and to touch the incredible adventures which are breaking in astronomy, psychology, molecular biology, planetology, oceanography, physics, history, and so on. These are vistas which the specialists know but can't share with us until we decide to open ourselves to their worlds. Even if some of these fields have heretofore been anesthetized by boring teachers and dull classes, the ability to rediscover them and to rekindle in ourselves a sense of wonderment—this may be a measure of our growth and, perhaps, of our capacity for life.

The fish trap exists because of the fish: once you've gotten the fish, you can forget the trap. . . .
Words exist because of meanings: once you've gotten the meanings, you can forget the words.

CHUANG-TZU

As to the question whether any general empirical propositions may correctly be described as *certain,* the answer will depend upon the meaning assigned to the word "certain.". . . We cannot claim that any inductive statement is beyond the possibility of correction or revision, or that the behavior of future unobserved instances can in any case of induction be unconditionally guaranteed in advance.

JOSEPH BRENNAN

A generalized body provided by a million years of evolution, and now a mind which can see the pattern of the woods as well as individual trees. Can this combination help to answer the question: "Who am I and where am I going?"
The man at the Information Booth looks puzzled but not altogether dubious.

STUART CHASE

Isaac Asimov

"I CAN FLOAT OVER THE ORCHARD AS IN A BALLOON"

15   *Epilog.* Few individuals understand better than Isaac Asimov what the synoptic vision is all about. His 225 books—written as specialist, knowledgeable authority, or just excited layman—range over nearly all conceivable subjects—the sciences, history, literature, religion, and, of course, science-fiction. As the following autobiographical note indicates, he has been unable, try as he may, to retreat from the synoptic vision.

Science, before 1800, was like an orchard: tame, well laid-out and ordered; fragrant and fruit-bearing. One could wander through it from end to end observing its various parts; and from a neighboring hill, one might even see the entire scheme, and appreciate it.

But by 1800, the wanderers note that the busy planters, gardeners, and cultivators had done their work so well that parts of it had grown dark and foreboding. Order was still there; indeed the intricate network of relationships was more refined, more subtle, and more fascinating than ever; but the proliferating branches had begun to shut out the sky.

And then there came the shock of realizing that the orchard was too large. One could no longer pass through it from end to end—not without getting lost and walking in circles back to one's starting point. Nor was the neighboring hill any longer of use, for it, too, was covered by orchard now.

So some of the observers, some of the lovers of the beauty of order, abandoned the orchard altogether; while others compromised by confining themselves to narrow sections of the orchard, then to narrower sections and still narrower sections.

Now, the orchard of science is a vast globe-encircling monster, without a map, and known to no one man; indeed, to no group of men fewer than the whole international mass of creative scientists. Within it, each observer clings to his own well-known and well-loved clump of trees. If he looks beyond, it is usually with a guilty sigh.

And just as an organism in the embryonic stages seems to race through the aeons of evolutionary development, from the single cell to ultimate complexity, in mere weeks or months; so the individual scientist in the course of his life repeats the history of science and loses himself by progressive stages, in the orchard.

When I was young, the neighborhood public libraries were my source material. I lacked the intelligence and purpose to be selective, so I started at one end of the shelves and worked my way toward the other.

Since I have an inconveniently retentive memory, I learned a great many things in this way that I have since labored unsuccessfully to forget. One of the valuable things I learned, however, was that I liked nonfiction better than fiction; history better than most other varieties of nonfiction; and science even better than history.

By the time I entered high school, I had restricted myself largely to history and science. By the time I entered college, I was down to science.

In college, I found I was expected to choose among the major disciplines of science and select a "major." I flirted with zoology and then, in my second year, made chemistry a firm choice. This meant not much more than one chemistry course per semester, but when I entered graduate school, I found that all my courses were chemistry of one sort or another, and I had to choose among them with a view toward doctoral research.

Through a series of developments of absorbing lack of interest (as far as these pages are concerned), I found myself doing research on a biochemical topic. In that area of study I obtained my Ph.D., and in no time at all I was teaching biochemistry at a medical school.

But even that was too wide a subject. From books to nonfiction, to science, to chemistry, to biochemistry—and not yet enough. The orchard had to be narrowed down further. To do research, I had to find myself a niche within biochemistry, so I began work on nucleic acids. . . .

And at about that point, I rebelled! I could not stand the claustrophobia that clamped down upon me. I looked with horror, backward and forward across the years, at a horizon that was narrowing down and narrowing down to so petty a portion of the orchard. What I wanted was all the orchard, or as much of it as I could cover in a lifetime of running.

To be sure, rebellion at this stage is often useless. Specialization has taken hold firmly and one dare not leave its confines. The faculty of participating in life outside one's special field has atrophied. . . .

I have never been sorry for my stubborn advance toward generalization. To be sure, I can't wander in detail through all the orchard, any more than anyone else can, no matter how stupidly determined I may be to do so. Life is far too short and the mind is far too limited. But I can float over the orchard as in a balloon.

I see no signs of an end; I make out very little detail. The precious intricacy one can observe by crawling over half an acre is lost to me.

But I have gains of my own, for occasionally I see (or seem to see) an overall order, or an odd arabesque in one corner—a glimmering fragment of design that perhaps I would not see from the ground.

> **Knowledge is never finished.**
>
> *MERLEAU-PONTY*

> **Of all the disorder-to-order converters, the human mind is by far the most impressive.**
>
> *BUCKMINSTER FULLER*

REFLECTIONS—

1 Rephrase in your own (meaningful) way the essential goals of synoptic philosophy and make your own assessment of the rewards of the synoptic venture. Would your thinking and feeling change if you could achieve the rewards mentioned in this chapter? Are you willing to accept the risks?

2 What is meant by saying that synoptic philosophy is a "now" philosophy? What is the relationship of synoptic philosophy to the history of philosophizing? To assist you in your own philosophic tasks, what benefits would you gain by becoming acquainted with the history of philosophic thought?

3 What is the relationship of philosophic analysis to synoptic synthesis? Does the metaphor of the picture-puzzle help to clarify how they relate? Are these two activities inherently in competition, or do they cooperate with and complement one another?

4 As a synoptic philosopher, how would you respond to the charge of being a dilettante? How would you answer the accusation that you were trying to know everything and, hence, to "play God"?

5 Are you in agreement with the statement that most of the significant questions of life are interdisciplinary by nature and that we are already in the habit, in daily life, of drawing information from many sources to solve our problems? In your judgment, is it accurate to describe synoptic philosophy as "a disciplined form of what we do all the time"?

6 Do you agree with the suggestion that the compartmentalization of knowledge, although pragmatic, is an arbitrary mental habit and that all knowledge is interrelated? "We need a discipline which, by its nature and calling, will help us put our fragmented world of knowledge back together." Do you find this notion congenial?

7 Choose some philosophic problem that is of personal concern to you; sketch a rough synoptic wheel, place the problem in the center, and then jot down the areas in the wheel where you might find relevant data to help solve the problem. Develop the habit of using the synoptic wheel during your philosophic wondering through the rest of this book. Try to be aware of any resistance you may feel to breaking over the imaginary walls separating areas of thought that you've not been in the habit of relating, or of any reluctance to interrelate fields that might reveal discord and conflict— theology and physics, for instance (see back to pp. 2–3 or ahead to pp. 509 ff.), or anthropology and ethics.

Furthermore . . .

ABEL, REUBEN, *Man Is the Measure*. Free Press, 1976.

ASIMOV, ISAAC, *View from a Height*. Lancer, 1963.

FABUN, DON, *The Dynamics of Change*. Prentice-Hall, 1967.

NOTT, KATHLEEN, *Philosophy and Human Nature*. Delta, 1974.

SIU, R. G. H., *The Portable Dragon: The Western Man's Guide to the I Ching*. MIT Press, 1971.

TOULMIN, STEPHEN, *Knowing and Acting: An Invitation to Philosophy*. Collier, 1976.

PART II

THE CONDITION AND THE ODYSSEY

Philosophy is man's quest for the unity of knowledge: it consists in a perpetual struggle to create the concepts in which the universe can be conceived as a *universe* and not a *multiverse*. . . . This attempt stands without rival as the most audacious enterprise in which the mind of man has ever engaged: Here is man, surrounded by the vastness of a universe in which he is only a tiny and perhaps insignificant part— and he wants to *understand* it. . . .

WILLIAM HALVERSON

2-1

Predicament/ Illusion

Have You Ever Wondered . . .

- Which religion is the true religion?

- Which race is the truly superior race?

- Whether or not your own philosophy of life is true?

- Why human beings differ so much in their beliefs and opinions?

- Whether the world is going to come to an end tomorrow? (or by next January, anyway?)

- Whether an individual who claims to be God is (necessarily) sane or (necessarily) insane?

- Whether tribalism and nationalism produce positive results?

THE COHERENT WORLD-VIEW

1   Each of us has a world-view—merely because we're human. A world-view is a more or less coherent, all-inclusive frame of reference through which one sees the world; it is a subjective attempt to provide unity and consistency to the totality of one's experience. Since we cannot tolerate excess fragmentation, we must attempt to find an inclusive structure which will harmonize as much of our experience as possible.

The last creature in the world to discover water would be the fish, precisely because he is always immersed in it!

RALPH LINTON

For most human beings, a world-view is a given. We are born into it and live within it; we rarely break out of it or even realize that it exists. By and large this inherited framework contains all the essential ingredients for a meaningful existence: social structures which act as guidelines for relating to others; clear-cut value systems of right and wrong; codes indicating acceptable and unacceptable behavior; language, legends, and hero stories which provide group identity; myths which answer a multitude of ultimate questions about the world we live in. Any world-view that can provide all these life-giving elements must be considered a successful world-view.

> Every man takes the limits of his own field of vision for the limits of the world.
>
> *SCHOPENHAUER*

2   It is one of the purposes of philosophy to help the individual build a world-view that is functional. We each possess what we might call a naive world-view in which many elements remain unsynthesized. The threads of experience have yet to be woven together into a harmonious picture; loose ends remain. Our "collection" of experiences is a hodge-podge of contradictions in values and beliefs.

The ideal world-view will be internally consistent, pragmatically realistic, and personally fulfilling. Philosophy can suggest guidelines and provide materials toward achieving this goal.

There is no implication here that there can be but a single viable world-view. Such a claim would be patently false, for many exist for our examination. While individuals within the same culture tend to share similar world-views, every world-view is in fact unique, personal, and (hopefully) the product of one's own labors.

> Archetypes come to the fore again and again in history, always presuming at each moment of history that the particular form in which they find themselves is the only one that is "true" and "eternal."
>
> *IRA PROGOFF*

THE EGOCENTRIC PREDICAMENT

3   In the year 1910 an American philosopher, Ralph Barton Perry, published in a philosophical journal an article entitled "The Ego-Centric Predicament." Perry wanted to make a specific point about our knowledge of real° objects/events. Western philosophers have long debated whether such external realities in some way depend upon, or are changed by, our perception of them. As a philosopher might ask: What is the metaphysical° status of real objects/events? What is the real world like apart from our perception of it? Or can we ever know for sure what such objects/events really are as things-in-themselves?

Using very lucid logic, Perry made what seems an obvious point: to know what any real object/event is, we have to perceive it. We can never observe things in their "original" state as they might exist apart from our perception of them. How then can we know whether our perception of them changes them? In our knowledge of the real world, therefore, we are in a logical predicament, and a "predicament" by definition is a problem situation to which there is no solution.

°*Refer to the Glossary for an explanation of* real, reality, *and* realism.

°Metaphysics. *The study of the nature of ultimate reality and the dynamic principles (natural, supernatural or other) by which reality exists.*

°Epistemology, epistemological
(often shortened to epistemic). The
branch of philosophy specializing in the
study of knowledge and the acquisition
of knowledge.

St. Augustine looked at history
from the point of view of the early
Christian; Tillemont, from that of
a seventeenth-century Frenchman;
Gibbon, from that of an
eighteenth-century Englishman;
Mommsen, from that of a
nineteenth-century German. There
is no point in asking which was
the right point of view. Each was
the only one possible for the man
who adopted it.

R. G. COLLINGWOOD

The Prayer of the Little Ducks

Dear God,
give us a flood of water.
Let it rain tomorrow and always.
Give us plenty of little slugs and
other luscious things to eat.
Protect all folk who quack and
everyone who knows how to
swim. Amen.

CARMEN DE GASZTOLD

"Faites qu'il pleuve demain et tou-
jours."

As we shall see when we move into epistemology° and examine carefully the nature of human knowledge, these questions about our understanding of the real world are not as far out as they might seem.

4   Let's reexamine the "egocentric predicament" from another standpoint and proceed quite beyond the point Perry was making.

From birth till death each of us is locked into a physical organism from which there is no escape. We are caught in a body which contains all our perceptual and information-processing equipment. Each of us, for as long as we live, is confined within a particular system and we will be able to experience life only in terms of that singular system. This is an obvious limitation, but it's one we fight: who wants to be imprisoned in a narrow cell only six feet high for the duration of one's existence, with no hope of escape?

Yet apparently we must resign ourselves to this condition. No matter how much we would like to jump out of our skins, enter into another person's perceptual shell, and peer out at the world from his center, we can't. We are always reminded that we shall have but a single vantage-point from which we can assess existence.

It therefore appears to be an immutable fact that we can never know how existence is experienced by any other living creature.

5   The egocentric predicament entails an illusion. For the duration of our mortal existence we must occupy a physical organism; we must "occupy" a *point* in space and time. And herein lies *the egocentric illusion,* for it appears to each of us that our center is the hub of the whole universe; or conversely, it appears to each of us that the entire cosmos revolves around that point in space/time which we occupy.

This egocentric illusion continues to follow us no matter where in space/time we move our center. If I should move my center to Tokyo or the South Pole, it would appear *to me* as though the universe had shifted its center to accommodate me. If I should travel to a planet in the Andromeda galaxy, some 2 million light-years distant from our Milky Way galaxy, it would still appear to me that the cosmos revolved around my ego-center.

Perceptually, of course, *I am* the center of *my* universe, but not of *the* universe. Yet I *perceive* myself as *its* center. This illusion is not limited to human beings. Every living organism with conscious perception would share in the egocentric illusion because it would occupy *its* point in space/time. Every such creature would be enclosed within its physical organism, and so the universe would appear to revolve around it.

If any living creature really thinks of itself as the point-center of the cosmos, there is an illusion in that consciousness. No one of us is the center of the universe any more than a billion other creatures are in fact cosmic centers.

In a word: every living, conscious creature experiences itself to be the true center of the cosmos, but in truth the cosmos has no center.

Rather, the cosmos is filled with creatures which share the illusion that they are cosmic centers.

ARISTOCENTRIC CLAIMS

6   At this point almost all us humans take a further step which our nonhuman fellow creatures probably do not. Taking the egocentric illusion seriously, we proceed to make *aristocentric claims.*° Whenever any creature fails to correct for his egocentric illusion and begins to feel that he really is the center of the universe, and further, if he feels that he *should* be treated by others *as though he were the center*, then he has taken a giant step beyond the illusion itself. He is making an aristocentric claim, an unjustified claim to superiority. In various ways he may conclude that he is special, and insist that the cosmos has favored him. He may claim that in some way his existence has special meaning, that he has a special knowledge or message, or is endowed with special grace or powers. In every case we can suspect that he has failed to make allowance for the illusion that all of us share.

  We rarely make such aristocentric claims in the singular, for if any one of us should say, "I am the center of the cosmos" we would probably be laughed out of our illusion. So we make the aristocentric claim in the first person plural that *"We* are special," that *"We* are the Favored Ones of the cosmos," and we can reinforce one another's claim so that it's believable. It feels good to be special and belong to a special group, and if our numbers are large we might even persuade the world to take us seriously. When the claim is made collectively, we can avoid the absurdity of standing naked and alone with an indefensible "I AM."

°Aristocentric, aristocentrism. *An inordinate claim to superiority for oneself or one's group. From the Greek* aristos (*superlative of* agathos, *"good") meaning "the best of its kind" or "the most to be valued," and* kentrikos, *from* kentron, *"the center of a circle."*

Much of what has been written in English-speaking countries in the last ten years about the Soviet Union, and in the Soviet Union about the English-speaking countries, has been vitiated by this inability to achieve even the most elementary measure of imaginative understanding of what goes on in the mind of the other party, so that the words and actions of the other are always made to appear malign, senseless, or hypocritical.

EDWARD HALLETT CARR

Mircea Eliade tells of the group of Australian aborigine nomads who on their wanderings carried a pole with them which they planted in the middle of each new settlement to constitute "the center of the world." When missionaries invaded their territory and took away the pole, as mere superstition, the Australian tribe withered away and died; its members had lost the center of their world.

WILFRID DESAN

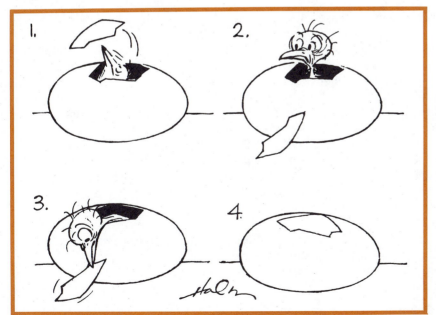

A. CAMUS

Albert Camus
Man and the Absurd

During the darkest days of World War II the discouraged spirits of Frenchmen were heartened by a series of anonymous articles written by an editor of the underground newspaper *Combat*, the voice of the resistance movement during the Nazi occupation of France. At the very moment when the world was turned upside down, they recognized a courageous intelligence at work, speaking to those who, in the midst of madness, could still reason. Someone was still trying to make sense of an insane world.

Also during the war two disturbing novels—*The Stranger* and *The Myth of Sisyphus*—had been written by a 29-year-old philosopher named Camus. They dealt with the crushing absurdities we humans find ourselves facing, simply because we exist.

It wasn't until after the war, in 1946, that the world discovered the resistance editor and the young author to be the same man. France had a new philosopher and a new hero. American newsmagazines reported that a tidal wave of philosophy had engulfed Paris, that sidewalk cafes had again become marketplaces of ideas, and that riots had resulted from heated philosophic debates. Albert Camus, now 32, became, almost overnight, the voice and the conscience of the new movement.

Camus was born in Algeria in 1913. Three images from that world, he wrote, dominated his life: the hot Algerian sun, the cool Mediterranean sea, and the silent, suffering mother. When Albert was a year old his father was killed in the war, and his illiterate mother supported her family in poverty and loneliness, and in silence, for she was deaf and had a speech impediment.

Education was a cherished commodity and, with difficulty, relying on odd jobs and well-deserved scholarships, Camus graduated from the University of Algiers. At 23 he submitted his master's thesis on the interplay of early Christian and Greek thought. Then in 1937, at 24, he published his first book, *The Wrong Side and the Right Side*, a work dominated by themes of death, alienation, loneliness, and the human soul trying to wrest meaning from all this.

At 25 he became a journalist and, later, night editor with an Algerian newspaper. With the outbreak of the war he worked as a reporter in Paris; but when Paris was overrun by the Germans, Camus and the staff members of

Paris-Soir transferred operations to Lyons. There he was married to Francine Faure. They moved to Algeria briefly, but Camus returned to Paris, the Allies invaded North Africa, and the couple was separated for the remainder of the war.

Camus joined *Combat* and wrote vigorously against all these "absurdities." He labored to develop an ethic of resistance. Without denying the patent fact of the world's madness, he attempted to go beyond a mere acceptance of the Absurd, and beyond a fashionable ethical relativism, to arrive at some position that would provide a moral anchor for men at war.

Following the war Camus became disenchanted with the reestablishment of the same old systems and, after some futile attempts to influence French and Algerian politics, he withdrew from public life to write. Among his most compelling works are his early books, *The Stranger* and *The Myth of Sisyphus*; a second philosophic work, *The Rebel*; plus *The Plague*, *The Fall*, numerous essays, short stories, and plays, including *Caligula*.

In 1951 an interviewer described Camus: "There is a discreet smile on his tormented face, a high, wrinkled forehead beneath very dark crisp hair, a manly, North African face that has grown paler in our climate. A discreet but frequent smile, and his rather deep voice is not afraid of humorous inflexions."

In 1957 Camus received the Nobel Prize for literature. With some of the prize money he bought a modest house in southern France, where he could retreat and work in a more congenial atmosphere. While returning to Paris with a friend on January 4, 1960, he was killed in an automobile accident. He was 47.

Camus' philosophy is built around the concept of "the Absurd"—which is his comprehensive description of the human condition and our predicament. Camus begins by analyzing *the feeling* of the Absurd and proceeds to develop the philosophy implied by it.

The problem lies in the individual's relationship to the world. Man is not absurd, and the world is not absurd. It's at the interface between man and the world that the Absurd is encountered. At this interface there is discord—a friction, a grating, a destructive interaction between two surfaces that don't match. This interface is given, and we're trapped. We dream dreams that the world is not designed to fulfill. We long for honesty, but neither the world nor the human system is equipped for honesty. We long for—indeed our natures demand—a just world; but the world couldn't care less about our dreams of justice. This is the absurd condition. (What Camus intends by the term "Absurd" may not be clear to some of us; but Frenchmen who lived with the breakdown of values during the Nazi occupation would recognize immediately what he means.)

But we don't deserve all this. It's not fair. We are born innocent, prepared to love and to live. We long for—and we truly deserve—a good world; but the world is not good. It victimizes and defeats us by the sheer weight of its insanity. Still, in the end, crying out in bewilderment and rage, our fundamental feeling of innocence remains, alive and invincible.

Now, given this inescapable condition, the question we face is how to live. A clear awareness of the Absurd is merely the diagnosis, a starting point. "What Camus is attempting to do," writes David Denton, "is to find a way of living which faces the absurd without trying to hide behind either rationalism or irrationalism, these two competing gods of philosophy. The question becomes, given the absurd reality and an extremely limited knowledge, is it possible to live with an attitude of optimism?" The philosophy of the Absurd, writes Camus, is "a lucid invitation to live and to create, in the very midst of the desert." Optimistically—"in the midst of the desert"? How?

We begin by accepting the absurd nature of the interface between our inner subjectivity and the real world. We must deny neither. We must avoid commiting physical suicide—the negation of the subjective side—and philosophical suicide—the manipulation of our perceptions of the world so that it appears congenial.

Having accepted the Absurd, the response must be revolt. "Accepting the absurdity of everything around us is one step, a necessary experience: it should not become a dead end. It arouses a revolt that can become fruitful." Revolt is a method, Camus emphasizes, a procedure, not a doctrine. It can help us "discover ideas capable of restoring a relative meaning to existence. . . ."

Revolt means abandoning the rigid categories of thought—the parochial world-views, the angular perspectives, the limiting beliefs, the defining doctrines; the conceptual and semantic distortions that make us lie; the arbitrary dos and don'ts of an immoral world in which we heretofore sought a moral existence. Revolt means refusing to cooperate with a society that would impose its dishonesties upon us and with a universe that would crush our dreams.

The results are freedom and innocence. In revolting, one becomes free: he can do whatever he wishes. There are no absolutes or moral laws, no abiding criteria for branding any act right or wrong. All is permitted, for all is *equally* right *and* wrong. And, in this condition, one recovers innocence, because he is now free to do all things without guilt. The guilt condition is a part of the Absurd; and by revolting the individual frees himself from the guilt matrix. He reaffirms his innocence.

Having regained innocence, the individual is then free to rely upon his senses to live a full life for himself and others. The senses, and not abstractions, become the essential criteria for understanding life and for living it.

Camus' final challenge, then, is to live existentially. His ontology is a personal resistance movement against the Absurd requiring clarity and courage. It means never abandoning the present for the future or living off the past. It means trusting one's empirical experience as a guide for what is good and right.

Camus' humanism is a freedom fighter's personal declaration of war against an absurd world. In both epistemology and ethics, it's a call—always to the individual—to revolt and transcend.

For me "The Myth of Sisyphus" marks the beginning of an idea which I was to pursue in The Rebel. It attempts to resolve the problem of suicide, as The Rebel attempts to resolve that of murder, in both cases without the aid of eternal values which, temporarily perhaps, are absent or distorted in contemporary Europe. The fundamental subject of "The Myth of Sisyphus" is this: it is legitimate and necessary to wonder whether life has a meaning; therefore it is legitimate to meet the problem of suicide face to face. The answer, underlying and appearing through the paradoxes which cover it, is this: even if one does not believe in God, suicide is not legitimate. Written fifteen years ago, in 1940, amid the French and European disaster, this book declares that even within the limits of nihilism it is possible to find the means to proceed beyond nihilism. In all the books I have written since, I have attempted to pursue this direction. Although "The Myth of Sisyphus" poses mortal problems, it sums itself up for me as a lucid invitation to live and to create, in the very midst of the desert.

Albert Camus; from the preface to *The Myth of Sisyphus*

The Teacher

Camus was interviewed by Gabriel d'Aubarède in 1951. His "Encounter with Camus" was published in the May 10 issue of *Les Nouvelles littéraires*.

D'Aubarède mentions Camus' passionate sensitivity to the drama of the twentieth century. It is "this sensitivity which has given you the attention and trust of a large section of young people. In turn, the new generation looks on you today as one of its masters. . . ."

(This time, the author of *The Plague* laughs out loud.)

A master, already! But I don't claim to teach anybody! Whoever thinks this is mistaken. The problems confronting young people today are the same ones confronting me, that is all. And I am far from having solved them. I therefore do not think that I have any right to play the role you mention. . . .

What are young people looking for? Certainties. I haven't many to offer them. All I can say definitely is that there is a certain order of degradation I shall always refuse. I think this is something they feel. Those who trust me know that I will never lie to them. As to the young people who ask others to think for them, we must say "No" to them in the clearest possible terms.

That is all I have to say.

I summarized *The Stranger* a long time ago, with a remark that I admit was highly paradoxical: "In our society any man who does not weep at his mother's funeral runs the risk of being sentenced to death." I only meant that the hero of my book is condemned because he does not play the game. In this respect, he is foreign to the society in which he lives; he wanders, on the fringe, in the suburbs of private, solitary, sensual life. And this is why some readers have been tempted to look upon him as a piece of social wreckage. A much more accurate idea of the character, or, at least, one much closer to the au-thor's intentions, will emerge if one asks just *how* Meursault doesn't play the game. The reply is a simple one: he refuses to lie. To lie is not only to say what isn't true. It is also and above all, to say *more* than is true, and, as far as the human heart is concerned, to express more than one feels. This is what we all do, every day, to simplify life. He says what he is, he refuses to hide his feelings, and immediately society feels threatened. He is asked, for example, to say that he regrets his crime, in the approved manner. He replies that what he feels is annoyance rather than real regret. And this shade of meaning condemns him.

For me, therefore, Meursault is not a piece of social wreckage, but a poor and naked man enamored of a sun that leaves no shadows. Far from being bereft of all feeling, he is animated by a passion that is deep because it is stubborn, a passion for the absolute and for truth. This truth is still a negative one, the truth of what we are and what we feel, but without it no conquest of ourselves or of the world will ever be possible.

One would therefore not be much mistaken to read *The Stranger* as the story of a man who, without any heroics, agrees to die for the truth. . . .

Albert Camus, January 8, 1955, from the preface to *The Stranger* (Published as a preface to the American University edition, 1956)

7   Writing as sociologists, Paul Horton and Chester Hunt use the term "ethnocentric" when referring to any form of aristocentricism. They write:

All societies and all groups assume the superiority of their own culture. . . . We are ethnocentric because (1) we are so habituated to our culture's patterns that other patterns fail to please us; (2) we do not understand what an unfamiliar trait means to its user and therefore impute our reactions to him; (3) we are trained to be ethnocentric; (4) we find ethnocentrism a comforting defense against our own inadequacies. Ethnocentrism (1) promotes group unity, loyalty, and morale, and thereby reinforces nationalism and patriotism; (2) protects a culture from changes, including those needed to preserve the culture; (3) reinforces bigotry and blinds a group to the true facts

Just as it is possible to have any number of geometries other than the Euclidian which give an equally perfect account of space configurations, so it is possible to have descriptions of the universe, all equally valid, that do not contain our familiar contrasts of time and space.

BENJAMIN WHORF

WORLD-VIEW I   The Primitive

I live in a capricious world, unpredictable and dangerous. Evil spirits hide in caves, ponds, woods, and sometimes in animals and people. I must be careful not to offend the evil spirits. I try to make them stay away from my fire and the door of my hut. The spirits of my ancestors will help me. All that happens—the storm and the rains, the green maize, a good hunt, my success in battle, the getting of many cattle, wives and children—all these are mine because I perform the rites of our ancestors and keep favor with the good spirits. The witchdoctor also helps.

WORLD-VIEW II   The Hindu

At last I am born a Brahmin and I therefore know that I lived a good life in my last incarnation. Perhaps now I can achieve moksha so that I shall not return again in mortal flesh. I shall therefore practice diligently, spending many hours daily in meditation. The world of maya around me will vanish and my soul will know the joy and peace of nirvana. Vishnu will aid me. Glory to thee, god of the lotus-eye! Have compassion upon me!

WORLD-VIEW III   Early Christian

I live on the brink of Eternity. The long cosmic struggle between the forces of Light— who dwell in the Heavens above—and the forces of Darkness—who dwell below—is nearly finished. God's plan for the ages is about to be fulfilled with the destruction of Satan. In Christ there will be no more death. We have been chosen to be the Children of Light and we will dwell with Him in His Kingdom. His only Son, Yeshua the Messiah, was the herald of God's Reign, and we must finish our earthly tasks quickly for His Reign is about to begin. Ἀμήν, ἔρχον κύριε Ἰησοῦ. Amen, return quickly, Lord Jesus.

WORLD-VIEW IV   The Taoist

I weary of the ways of men and I seek serenity by the waterfall and in the forest. Wherever men gather together, there are too many. The forces of yang and yin thrust them about and society is roiled as a muddy torrent. Let them begone! In the quietness of my solitude I shall seek the Tao, or rather the Tao shall seek me. Wu-wei—quiet now; no striving, no longing, no fear. Let me be filled with the tranquility of silence and inaction; let me be immersed in Tao. Why should existence be like a drawn bow?

WORLD-VIEW V   Western Scientific

I live in a universe of matter in motion. The universe seems to follow consistent patterns which we can formulate into workable "laws" and describe with mathematical and geometrical terms. We now believe that life originated through natural processes and developed according to the principles of evolution. We exist in an "open" universe, containing billions of galaxies and, most likely, millions of planets sustaining intelligent life-forms. Man is unique, but he is also an integral part of nature and of natural processes which operate throughout the universe. With further scientific understanding man will be able to control his own destiny and mold his future.

about themselves and other groups, sometimes preventing their successful adjustment to other groups and cultures.

8 The ultimate in aristocentric claims was recorded by a psychiatrist in the case of three men each of whom claimed to be Christ and God. All three were institutionalized as paranoid schizophrenics whose "delusions of grandeur" had taken the form of messianic fantasies.

Dr. Milton Rokeach wanted to know what adjustments these three men would make if placed together. After all, each was making the final exclusive claim: "I alone am God." The agony of their encounter was recorded by Rokeach in his book *The Three Christs of Ypsilanti*.

At their first meeting each man was asked to introduce himself. Joseph obliged: "Yes, I'm God." Clyde admitted that "God" and "Jesus" were two of his six names. Leon stated that he was Lord of Lords and King of Kings, and added: "It also states on my birth certificate that I am the reincarnation of Jesus Christ of Nazareth. . . . "

Rokeach notes that "the confrontations were obviously upsetting."

> Clearly, all of them felt threatened. The profound contradiction posed by others' claims had somehow penetrated deeply, to become transformed into an inner conflict between two primitive beliefs: each man's delusional belief in his own identity and his realistic belief that only one person can have any given identity. Many times Joseph said: "There is only one God"; and Clyde said: "I'm the only one"; and Leon said: "I won't deny that you gentlemen are instrumental gods—small 'g.' But I'm the only one who was created before time began."

Each of the Christs of Ypsilanti ultimately made similar adjustments. Each decided that his godly qualities of compassion and magnanimity allowed him to accept the fact that the other two men were mentally disturbed. Each came around to a "compassionate acceptance" of the other deluded mortals.

9 Dr. Rokeach writes:

> Clyde and Joseph and Leon are really unhappy caricatures of human beings; in them we can see with terrible clarity some of the factors that can lead any man to give up realistic beliefs and adopt instead a more grandiose identity.
>
> And they are caricatures of all men in another sense too. I believe it was the German philosopher Fichte who pointed out years ago that to some extent all of us strive to be like God or Christ. One or another facet of this theme is to be found in a good deal of Western literature—for example, in the writings of Sherwood Anderson, William Faulkner, and Dostoevsky. Bertrand Russell said it best of all: "Every

Man can either remain within his "accidental" reference frame and unquestioningly accept the meaning it has to offer, or he can boldly emerge from his psycho-epistemological cocoon and broaden his reality image. The need for man to break out of his capsule is crucial, for encapsulation may well be the essence of contemporary man's spiritual emptiness.

JOSEPH R. ROYCE

Dense, unenlightened people are notoriously confident that they have the monopoly on truth.

JOSHUA LOTH LIEBMAN

Each individual is his own center, and the world centers in him.

KIERKEGAARD

A human self cannot be brought into harmony with Absolute Reality unless it can get rid of its innate self-centredness. This is the hardest task that Man can set himself; but, if he accomplishes it, his reward will be far more than proportionate to the toil and pain of the spiritual struggle. In giving up self-centredness he will have felt as if he were losing his life; but in achieving this act of self-sacrifice he will find that he has really saved his life, because he will have given his life a new centre, and this new centre will be the Absolute Reality that is the spiritual presence behind the phenomena.

ARNOLD TOYNBEE

ARISTOCENTRISM: Religion

"Thereupon Abram fell on his face: and God said to him, 'This is my covenant with you: . . . I am establishing my covenant between myself and you and your descendants after you throughout their generations as a perpetual covenant, to be God to you and your descendants." [Gen. 17:3—4, 7]

"If we wish to compare our people with foreigners, we find that although we are only their equals or even their inferiors in other matters, in religion—that is, in the cult of the gods—we are far superior." [Cicero]

"Do Jehovah's Witnesses believe theirs is the only true faith?"

"Certainly. If they thought someone else had the true faith, they would preach that. There is only 'one faith,' said Paul." [Milton G. Henschel, a Witness]

"The Catholic religion claims to be a supernaturally revealed religion. What is more important, it claims to be the one and only true religion in the world, intended for all men, alone acceptable to God." [*Toward the Eternal Commencement, 1958*]

"Japan is the divine country. . . . This is true only of our country, and nothing similar may be found in foreign lands. That is why it is called the divine country." [Kitabatake, a Shinto]

"Crinkled hills freckled with kraals plunge to the Nsuze River. In this region lies the legendary birthplace of a man called Zulu—which means 'heaven.' In the early 1600's he founded a clan that bears his name, and thus became progenitor of the Zulus, the 'People of Heaven.'" [*National Geographic*]

Man is encapsulated. By encapsulated I mean claiming to have the whole of truth when one has only part of it. By encapsulated I mean looking at life partially and proceeding to make statements concerning the whole of life. And by encapsulated I mean living partially because one's daily activities are based on a world-view or philosophy of life which is meager next to the larger meaning of existence.

JOSEPH R. ROYCE

It is pitiful to see so many Turks, heretics, and infidels following in their fathers' track, for the sole reason that each has been conditioned to believe that this track is the best. This accident of birth is also what decides everyone's condition in life, making one man a locksmith, another man a soldier, etcetera.

BLAISE PASCAL

man would like to be God, if it were possible; some find it difficult to admit the impossibility."

EGOCENTRIC ILLUSIONS IN TIME AND SPACE

10   This egocentric illusion which we all share produces within us distorted perspectives. Consider, for instance, the *egocentric illusion in time*. Our life-*times* are short in the perspective of geological time or human history, yet we tend to think of all existence in terms of our alloted span.

Time overpowers our minds. Are we really convinced that the fossil trilobite from Cambrian eras darted about on the ocean sand, alive and well, running from enemies and seeking food? Holding in one's hand the fossil animal, 500 million years old, staggers our time sense. And what of our australopithecine ancestors only 5 million years ago or the Sumerian clay-writers of five thousand years ago? Were they really flesh and blood like us, laboring, getting angry, telling lies, making love, laughing at tall stories, getting stoned, and fearing death? Most of us are almost—but not quite—convinced that their existence was real.

It is very easy to fall into the belief that things happening during our lifetimes have never happened before. *Our* times we take to be the norm, or the culmination of history, or the best times, or the worst times, or whatever. We may forget, or not care to know, that the same beliefs have been shared by all who breathe.

ARISTOCENTRISM: *Race*

"Of old the Hellenic race was marked off from the barbarian as more keen-witted and more free from nonsense." [Herodotus]

A gray-bearded Kirghiz patriarch stated that the heart of a Kirghizian is superior to that of any other race of people, and, he added, "the heart is what really matters in men."

A modern Mexican painter inscribed a beautiful work with the words: "Through *my* race will speak the Spirit."

True history begins from the moment when the German with mighty hand seizes the inheritance of antiquity." [H. S. Chamberlain]

"We the Black Nation of the Earth are the NUMBER ONE owners of it, the best of all human beings. You are the Most Powerful, the Most Beautiful and the Wisest." [Elijah Muhammad, referring to Black Muslims]

"Everything great, noble, or fruitful in the works of man on this planet, in science, art, and civilization . . . belongs to one family alone. . . . History shows that all civilization derives from the white race, that none can exist without its help, and that a society is great and brilliant only so far as it preserves the blood of the noble group that created it." [Le Comte de Gobineau]

---

11   We are equally prone to a distorted perspective because of the *egocentric illusion in space.* Wherever we locate our space-occupying organism, the space around us takes on vividness and clarity and contains all things of significance for us; our life-space becomes the center of all things good, and more distant regions somehow lack the reality of our vicinity.

The most important shrine in the Greek world was at Delphi with its temple where the god Apollo revealed himself. Emissaries and pilgrims came from all around the Middle Sea to discover his will. When prophesying, the young priestess of the temple sat on a bronze tripod over an opening in the rock floor. This opening was the *omphalos*, the "navel" or center of the universe. From this "navel" arose a narcotic incense which induced an ecstatic trance in the priestess. While the young lady was out of her mind, Apollo could speak his.

This spatial predicament gives rise to various claims of sacred ground or holy lands. The Shintos, for instance, believed that the Japanese islands are "The phenomenal center of the universe," created by

BRITANNUS (shocked): Caesar, this is not proper.
THEODOTUS (outraged): How?
CAESAR (recovering his self-possession): Pardon him Theodotus: he is a barbarian, and thinks that the customs of his tribe and island are the laws of nature.

GEORGE BERNARD SHAW
Caesar and Cleopatra

"You have to leave something."

The word for China is composed of two characters meaning "middle" and "country"; that is to say, China is the geographical center of the Earth.

the primeval gods Izanagi and Izanami. "From the central truth that the Mikado is the direct descendant of the gods, the tenet that Japan ranks far above all other countries is a natural consequence. No other nation is entitled to equality with her. . . . " The Chinese made a similar claim: China was "the Middle Kingdom," that is, the center of the flat disc-shaped earth. Everything praiseworthy was found at that center; the farther one traveled from China the less civilized and respectable all things became.

The egocentric illusion in space contributes to various forms of tribalism and nationalism. We tend to devalue the lands and people which remain at a distance geographically and, therefore, psychologically. On the maps of human experience, distant space is still inscribed *terra incognita*.

12   At the prehuman level is seems very unlikely that any animal could have sufficient self-awareness to assess its own existential condition. Without the capacity for abstract reflection on experience, no creature could hope to rise above or out of its egocentric world-view.

Man, however, can develop such self-awareness. He can comprehend and transcend. ''To understand our ethnocentrism will help us to avoid being so gravely misled by it. We cannot avoid *feeling* ethnocentric, but with understanding, we need not *act* upon these irrational feelings.''

Human growth requires the transcendence of our egocentric il-

Indeed, I do not forget that my voice is but one voice, my experience a mere drop in the sea, my knowledge no greater than the visual field in a microscope, my mind's eye a mirror that reflects a small corner of the world, and my ideas—a subjective confession.

CARL G. JUNG

By permission of Bill Mauldin. Copyright 1944.

''Th' hell this ain't th' most important hole in th' world. I'm in it.''

lusions and, by an act of moral courage, the reconditioning of our aristocentric feelings and beliefs.

The spiritual struggle in the more exclusive-minded [Western] half of the world to cure ourselves of our family infirmity seems likely to be the most crucial episode in the next chapter of the history of Mankind.

ARNOLD TOYNBEE

13   To achieve an efficient balance between a useful pride in our own culture and subcultures and a realization of the real qualities of other groups is a difficult task. It requires both an emotional maturity which enables the individual to face his world without the armor of exaggerated self-esteem and an intellectual realization of the complexity of cultural processes. There is no guaranteed way to achieve this maturity. . . . But unless we can understand and control our ethnocentric impulses, we shall simply go on repeating the blunders of our predecessors.

HORTON AND HUNT

REFLECTIONS—

1 Ponder Abner Dean's drawing on page 98: "You have to leave something." *Why???*

2 The egocentric predicament and the egocentric illusion are descriptions of epistemological and ontological conditions. (Check your glossary here if you need to.) Do you recognize these concepts as accurate descriptions of your experience?

3 Define *aristocentrism* as you understand it. Have you ever felt the urge to make aristocentric claims? Have you ever been victimized by the aristocentric claims of others?

4 Can you think of other examples of aristocentric thinking and feeling similar to those illustrated in this chapter (pp. 96 and 97)?

5 Reflect on the various kinds of aristocentric claims that we make and their roots in the egocentric predicament and illusion. Do you honestly think there is any way that we, as individuals, can learn to transcend such limitations and cease to make such inordinate claims?

6 In your opinion, what are some of the greatest dangers involved in aristocentrism? What might be some of the benefits of maturing beyond the *need* to make aristocentric claims?

7 Reflect on the five world-views briefly stated on page 94, remembering that there are countless others also. Which world-views are best? Which world-views are correct? Consider the possibility that some one world-view is *the correct* world-view; by what standards or criteria could we decide which set of aristocentric claims are the true and correct claims?

8 The story of "the three Christs of Ypsilanti" is more than a case study. It is a metaphor. As metaphor what does the account say to you about the claims and rationalizations that universally characterize the human species?

Furthermore . . .

DE GASZTOLD, CARMEN BERNOS, *Prayers from the Ark*. Viking, 1962.

ELIADE, MIRCEA, *The Sacred and the Profane: The Nature of Religion*. Harcourt, 1959.

HOFFER, ERIC, *The True Believer*. Mentor, 1958.

ROKEACH, MILTON, *The Three Christs of Ypsilanti*. Knopf, 1964.

ROYCE, JOSEPH, *The Encapsulated Man*. Van Nostrand, 1964.

TOYNBEE, ARNOLD J., *An Historian's Approach to Religion*. Oxford, 1957.

2-2

Self/Autonomy

Have You Ever Wondered. . .

- How much of you is you?

- What it means to "be yourself"?

- Whether "loving yourself" is a virtuous or (as some religions tell us) selfish thing to do?

- Whether you really are a "self" at all? or a "person"?

- What a "perfectly adjusted" person might be like?

- Whether you can grow out of being "self-conscious"?

- Whether you have a strong sense of identity?

HOW MUCH OF ME IS ME?

All education is self-discovery.

RAY BRADBURY

1   At this moment in space/time, I *think I* know *who* I am and where *I am.* As I (the Greek word for "I" is *ego*) write these lines, I am attached to a large desk in my study. The time is 11:40 p.m., and a fireplace blazes in the background.

But as *you* read these lines, where in space/time are you? *Who* are *you*? And what are *you* experiencing? We think it takes a "who" to experience—we can assume so for now—but it might not be too absurd to inquire later if *you* and *I* are whos at all.

The accurate, realistic assessment of self resulting from acceptance makes possible the use of self as a dependable, trustworthy instrument for achieving one's purpose.

ARTHUR W. COMBS

2   Philosophers who have attempted serious thinking about the nature of the "self" have encountered formidable ambiguities. Normally, one would turn to the field specialists for some hard facts, but in this case psychiatric and psychological literature is of little help. The word "self" seems to be given an endless variety of meanings. Some-

102

"How much of me is me?

According to Zen, awareness of oneself dawns gradually, step by step. A Zen master of the twelfth century, Kakuan, drew the "ten oxherding pictures" to represent this progression toward enlightenment. The bull symbolizes the dynamic prinicples of life and truth; the ten bulls suggest the sequence of steps in "the realization of one's true nature."

[PAUL REPS]

1. The Search for the Bull

In the pasture of this world, I endlessly
push aside the tall grasses in
 search of the bull.
Following unnamed rivers, lost
 upon the
interpenetrating paths of distant
 mountains,
My strength failing and my vitality
 exhausted,
I cannot find the bull.
I only hear the locusts
 chirring through the forest at
 night.

Comment: The bull never has been lost. What need is there to search? Only because of separation from my true nature, I fail to find him. In the confusion of the senses I lose even his tracks. Far from home, I see many crossroads, but which way is the right one I know not. Greed and fear, good and bad, entangle me.

times it is used to mean the whole of one's being, including all mental and physical operations. Sometimes it refers only to mental activity (conscious and unconscious) and excludes the body. Sometimes "self" refers to an organizing psyche which determines how one thinks, feels, and behaves. And sometimes "the self" is only a mental construct used to describe observable behavioral patterns.

So, what is a "self"? Or, perhaps more to the point, when I ask who I am, am I(!) asking a meaningful question at all?

3 *From the Movie "Cleopatra."* At the end of a glorious career, Mark Antony, lying mortally wounded in the arms of Cleopatra, speaks of his impending death as "the ultimate separation of my self from myself." Apparently he means that his "genius"-self is about to separate from his physical-self, since it was current Roman belief that each man possesses a *genius* (and that each woman possesses a *juno*), a sort of individual spiritlike essence, distinct from the physical body, which gives him identity and has the power to protect him. But we can't be sure what he is saying.

News Item. A man is indicted for embezzlement, but he is never caught and lives under an assumed name in another state for twenty-six years. Then, by a freak move, a relative turns him in. "Yes," he confesses, "I did it."

But did he? After twenty-six years, in what sense is he the same "self"? He does not have the same name; having lived for a quarter-century under a different name, he has developed a new identity. Nor does he have the same body; we are told the human body completely renews itself every seven to ten years. The "person" (that is, personality, self-image, behavioral style) has changed; with the passing of so many years he *feels* like a different person.

How much of the original person—"self" or "body"—still exists at all? To be sure, he does possess a memory of a past event. Does that make him guilty? But what if, through repression, he has blocked the painful event from his mind and has no memory of the crime? Is *he* guilty, despite his (?) confession?

From "The Sixth Sense" **(ABC-TV).** The doctor hypnotizes the young lady on the witness stand and regresses her (?) to a time on the afternoon of the previous Thursday and asks her (?) where she (?) is. "I (?) am sitting on a rock by the lake." "What do you (?) see?" "I (?) am not really at the lake. I (?) am in the large mansion looking at the man I (?) am about to kill." "But you (?) were not in the mansion, were you (?)?", he (?) persists. "No, I (?) was sitting at the lake." "Yes," he (?) answers, "I (?) know, because I (?) was sitting beside you (?)."

Would you care to try to figure out who is speaking to whom about whom and who is doing what when and where?

A SENSE OF SELF

4 What each of us can become during our life/time is determined by two fundamental conditions: (1) the degree to which we experience a more or less consistent sense of self or identity, and (2) whether the feelings we have developed about that self are predominantly good.

These conditions are of crucial importance during our earlier years. If the environment in which we are nurtured inhibits the development of an integrated self and/or instills negative feelings about that self—self-hate in its many forms—then the quality of our existence can be permanently damaged. It is quite possible at a later time to face our inner problems and develop belatedly a sense of self and a feeling of self-worth; but the therapeutic path is often prolonged and painful.

5   The identity question—"Who am I?"—must be persistently asked by each of us during our separation years. We all go through an "identity crisis" beginning near the onset of puberty. In the early teen years no adolescent has a consistent feeling of being a self. Besides the fact that he still identifies with authorities, it is also during these years that dramatic physiological and emotional changes are taking place, and there is a correlated upheaval in the psyche. Body and self are both changing and developing.

During these years, separation from the decision-making, behavior-setting authorities normally takes place. Each developing self begins to discover his own feelings and thoughts; he must explore his own "style" of doing things. As he experiences more and more spontaneous and authentic expressions of his own being, he begins to feel a sense of identity. He finds that there is a consistency and a distinctiveness in the way he behaves, thinks, and feels. This is a gradual process, not to be accomplished overnight. Throughout these years of separation, it is essential that the question "Who am I?" be continually asked, not explicitly in words, but implicitly in all that self-in-process-of-becoming does.

2. Discovering the Footprints

Along the riverbank under the trees,
  I discover footprints!
Even under the fragrant grass I see
  his prints.
Deep in remote mountains they are
  found.
These traces no more can be hidden
  than one's nose, looking heaven-
  ward.

Comment: Understanding the teaching, I see the footprints of the bull. Then I learn that, just as many utensils are made from one metal, so too are myriad entities made of the fabric of self. Unless I discriminate, how will I perceive the true from the untrue? Not yet having entered the gate, nevertheless I have discerned the path.

I have had to experience so much stupidity, so many vices, so much error, so much nausea, disillusionment and sorrow, just in order to become a child again and begin anew.

                 HERMAN HESSE
                 Siddhartha

We judge ourselves by what we feel capable of doing, while others judge us by what we have already done.

                 LONGFELLOW

One of the best known Western statements that there is no such entity as a self is from the philosopher David Hume (1711–1776). The more he meditated on the problem, the more he became convinced that the "mind" or "self" is nothing other than a "bundle of perceptions," that is, the totality of perception. He wrote: "There are some philosophers who imagine we are every moment intimately conscious of what we call our *self;* that we feel its existence and its continuance is existence; and we are certain, beyond the evidence of a demonstration, both of its perfect identity and simplicity. . . . For my part, when I enter most intimately into what I call *myself,* I always stumble on some particular perception or other of heat or cold, light or shade, love or hatred, pain or pleasure. I never can catch myself at any time without a perception, and never can observe anything but the perception. When my perceptions are removed for any time, as by sound sleep, so long am I insensible of *myself,* and, may truly be said not to exist."

3. Perceiving the Bull

I hear the song of the nightingale.
The sun is warm, the wind is mild,
   willows are green along the shore,
Here no bull can hide!
What artist can draw that massive
   head, those majestic horns?

Comment: When one hears the voice, one can sense its source. As soon as the six senses merge, the gate is entered. Wherever one enters one sees the head of the bull! This unity is like salt in water, like color in dyestuff. The slightest thing is not apart from self.

I am convinced that each human being is unique and that he has a right to be his own separate self.

AARON UNGERSMA

Scientific knowledge of the self is not real knowledge. . . . Self-knowledge is possible only . . . when scientific studies come to an end, [and the scientists] lay down all their gadgets of experimentation, and confess that they cannot continue their researches any further. . . .

D. T. SUZUKI

"What do you recommend for someone going through the agony of soulsearching and inner criticism?"

6   Selfhood develops, or is allowed to develop, as one perceives his "self" in action, as one thinks his own thoughts and feels his own feelings. The commonest problem most of us face lies in the fact that conflicting elements have been "programmed" into us by various authorities. Few if any of us have been guided by consistent authority. Most of us have grown up under the guidance of two or more "significant others" whose beliefs and values differed. What they demanded of us varied. Since we were dependent upon them, we had to take their standards seriously and accede to them.

So, as separation takes place and freedom is experienced, these diverse elements must be integrated into a "self." Gradually it must become a harmonious, smoothly operating system. After some years of practice in experiencing one's self in action, he should feel a sense of identity. Then he can say meaningfully, "I know who I am."

To borrow an analogy from space technology, the self becomes an "onboard guidance system." The system cuts the umbilical cord and goes on internal power. It functions automatically, runs smoothly, and operates on schedule.

A SENSE OF WORTH

7   The second major condition which determines the quality of existence is the feeling one develops about his self. In general, if things go right for us, then we develop positive feelings: self-worth, self-esteem, self-love. Whatever the terms, we are referring to a cluster of constructive feelings which we develop about the self and the things the self does.

One who has these positive feelings feels privileged at being who he is and what he is; he enjoys living with himself.

How we feel about our selves strongly reflects how others felt about us during our earliest years. If we were loved, then we feel lovable; we can love our selves. If we were accepted, then we feel acceptable; we can accept our selves. If we were trusted, then we feel trustworthy; we can trust our selves. If our very existence was valued, then we feel valuable; we value our selves.

It is impossible to escape the severe fact that we are wholly dependent upon the feeling-reflections of others during these early stages of development.

8   The self concept, we know, is learned. People learn who they are and what they are from the ways in which they have been treated by those who surround them in the process of their growing up. This is what Sullivan called learning about self from the mirror of other people. People discover their self concepts from the kinds of experiences they have had with life—not from telling, but from experience. People develop feelings that they are liked, wanted, acceptable and able from having been liked, wanted, accepted and from having been successful. One learns that he is these things, not from being told so but only through the experience of being treated as though he were so.

ARTHUR W. COMBS

9   One who has been loved during his formative years develops a love of self. There is a common confusion between "self-love" and "selfishness." Self-love is neither a narcissistic obsession with one's physical or intellectual qualities nor egotism, the inordinate desire to look out for one's own interests at the expense of others.

Erich Fromm writes:

> If it is a virtue to love my neighbor as a human being, it must be a virtue—and not a vice—to love myself, since I am a human being too. There is no concept of man in which I myself am not included. A doctrine which proclaims such an exclusion proves itself to be intrinsically contradictory. The idea expressed in the Biblical "Love thy neighbor as thyself!" implies that respect for one's own integrity and uniqueness, love for and understanding of one's self, cannot be separated from respect and love and understanding for another individual. The love for my own self is inseparably connected with the love for any other being. . . . Love of other and love of ourselves are not alternatives. On the contrary, an attitude of love toward themselves will be found in all those who are capable of loving others.

10   In summary, if we are among the fortunate ones for whom things have gone right on both scores—in our sense of identity and self-esteem—then we can be sure that some of the following things have happened to us.

We were loved and not rejected; therefore, we are lovable.

4. Catching the Bull

I seize him with a terrific struggle.
His great will and power are inexhaustible.
He charges to the high plateau
*   far above the cloud-mists,*
Or in an impenetrable raving he stands.

Comment: He dwelt in the forest a long time, but I caught him today! Infatuation for scenery interferes with his direction. Longing for sweeter grass, he wanders away. His mind still is stubborn and unbridled. If I wish him to submit, I must raise my whip.

The member of a primitive clan might express his identity in the formula "I am we"; he cannot yet conceive of himself as an "individual," existing apart from his group. . . . When the feudal system broke down, this sense of identity was shaken and the acute question "who am I?" arose.

ERICH FROMM

5. *Taming the Bull*

The whip and rope are necessary,
Else he might stray off down some
  dusty road.
Being well trained,
  he becomes naturally gentle.
Then, unfettered, he obeys his mas-
  ter.

Comment: **When one thought arises,
another thought follows. When the
first thought springs from enlightenment, all subsequent thoughts are
true. Through delusion, one makes
everything untrue. Delusion is not
caused by objectivity; it is the result of subjectivity. Hold the nose-
ring tight and do not allow even a
doubt.**

**Here Phaethon lies: in Phoebus'
care he fared and though he
greatly failed, more greatly dared.**

OVID

We were given consistent guidelines for learning social behavior.

We learned that we were of value for what we *were*, and not for
what we *did*. Unacceptable behavior was not confused with *being* unacceptable as selves.

As we were ready to cope with new experiences, we were allowed the freedom to explore life, on schedule, a little at a time.

We were provided with the support which enabled us to handle
hurt and failure without loss of self-esteem.

We were allowed to express our feelings honestly, even verbally,
without fear of punishment for having such feelings.

We tested boundaries—within and without—and developed realistic estimates of their limits.

We were encouraged to integrate periods of instability and
change as a natural part of our growth.

We gradually found that we could exist independently and
apart from our parents' protection.

Eventually we came to terms with a separate identity and felt
comfortable with our own value systems and beliefs.

11   Most of us never move beyond *self*-consciousness. During the
Who-am-I? stage we are never quite sure how we are going to respond
to people, symbols, or situations. We have been accustomed to reacting as others have conditioned us, but now the question becomes:
"How would I really respond to it in *my* way?" So, we try out new
forms of behaving and explore new experiences. "Do *I* like liver and
onions?" "How do *I* feel about him?" "Do *I* really *believe* that?"

While working through the identity problem we are forced,
therefore, into self-consciousness. But after one has developed a congenial style of behavior, then he no longer wonders how he will respond, nor does he plan his responses: he merely responds. He asks
himself less and less how he thinks and feels about things: he simply
thinks and feels. So the self-consciousness that was a necessary part of
the developmental phase begins to fade away.

12   Buddhism is explicitly committed to the doctrine of *anatta*, "no
self." The "self" is an illusion. The Buddhist believes that the feeling
of individuality is an acculturated condition. The "ego" is the unfortunate result of a bit of social programming which has persuaded us
that we are separate and distinct identities.

The egoless state is one of pure spontaneous experience. Ide-
ally, the good Buddhist, through years of disciplined practice, attempts to banish any culturally conditioned "self" that says "This is
good" or "This is the proper way to behave" or "This is my way of
doing things." Rather, spontaneous behavior is above and beyond acculturation; it is impersonal because it is not culturally produced or
ego-defined. It is a way of experiencing everything in an unmediated

way. On can look at a candle and experience the pure flame, not as subject-object, but as direct unmediated experience, as though the experiencer were impinging directly upon the flame.

We in the West are habituated to putting a name to everything so we can store it away, call it back, talk about it, or reexperience it dimly at a later time. The Easterner values more the quality of the original experience without any sort of conceptual or verbal intervention.

The Buddhist point of view, therefore, is that the ego interferes with pure experience, and once one begins to know pure experience, he no longer has a need for ego to mediate it.

The Buddhist has a strong self behind the no-self. That is, with careful definition, we can say that the very strong self (Western) that has passed beyond self-consciousness to spontaneous experience has reached a state similar to the Buddhist no-self state. If one has succeeded in developing a self-system that works smoothly and harmoniously, then the identity question has become meaningless. Enjoying the strong feeling of unity pervading all his experience, he has forgotten that he "has" a self.

THE AUTONOMOUS SELF

13 The word "autonomy" refers to one's ability to function independently in terms of an authentic self. The measure of one's autonomy is his capacity to determine his own behavior and make decisions consonant with what he truly is, in contrast to behavior which conforms to norms set by others which may be discordant with his own existential needs.

The ability to make autonomous decisions presupposes several things. First, it requires an awareness of one's needs, and this comes only from experience. It means being able to recognize one's own feelings and to sort out authentic needs from acculturated needs, or acculturated beliefs *about* needs.

Another requisite is the courage of self-affirmation. To accept all that one is, and especially those aspects of one's self which are objectionable (to authorities or peers), imperfect (to perfectionist parents), and unacceptable (to society), takes courage. Self-acceptance always contains an implied "in spite of": "I affirm my existence in spite of my bad habits, short temper, dependence needs," or whatever. This courage grows as we experience self-affirmation in concrete situations.

A third requisite is an understanding of the culture-patterns within which one has lived his existence. Without recognition of the beliefs and values which one has unknowingly followed, it is difficult to separate autonomous behavior from conformity.

14 How does one experience his existence if he has achieved autonomy?

6. Riding the Bull Home

Mounting the bull,
 slowly I return homeward.
The voice of my flute intones
 through the evening.
Measuring with hand-beats the
 pulsating harmony, I direct the
 endless rhythm.
Whoever hears this melody will join
 me.

Comment: **This struggle is over; gain and loss are assimilated. I sing the song of the village woodsman, and play the tunes of the children. Astride the bull, I observe the clouds above. Onward I go, no matter who may wish to call me back.**

Self-acceptance comes only to those who have the courage to investigate the areas where their self-doubts reside. Viewed a little differently, many self-doubts represent uncertainty about one's ability to do something one regards as important. The person who seeks self-acceptance *directly* is motivated to try such things, to explore his potential and develop his capacities.

GAIL AND SNELL PUTNEY

7. The Bull Transcended

Astride the bull, I reach home.
I am serene. The bull too can rest.
The dawn has come. In blissful re-
pose,
Within my thatched dwelling
I have abandoned the whip and
rope.

Comment: All is one law, not two.
We only make the bull a temporary
subject. It is as the relation of rab-
bit and trap, of fish and net. It is a
gold and dross, or the moon
emerging from a cloud. One path
of clear light travels on throughout
endless time.

Rast ich, so rost ich.
(When I rest, I rust.)

German Proverb

The self has to be achieved; it is
not given. All that is given is the
equipment and at least the
minimal (mother and child) social
environment. Since the self is
achieved through social contact, it
has to be understood in terms of
others. "Self and other" is not a
duality because they go so together
that separation is quite impossible.

EARL C. KELLEY

For one thing, in terms of identity, he knows who he is and who he isn't. He feels like a whole self, and there is no felt need to engage in competitive behavior to preserve his identity. It feels genuine. He doesn't feel like an empty shell having to pretend that there is something inside. A self—someone—dwells inside. This is the feeling of being integrated.

One with a clear sense of self knows his likes and dislikes. He has a distinct personal feeling of right and wrong; he does not operate on borrowed guidelines labeled "moral" by others. Nor does he experience a sense of panic that he might be easily persuaded to do what he does not want to do or, more important, to be what he is not. In occasional situations, of course, he will choose or even be forced *to do* things which he does not want or like to do; but he knows that—short of brainwashing—he can never be forced *to be* what he is not.

15   When someone feels like a whole self, he also has a feeling of authenticity. He feels genuine rather than phony. His behavior doesn't feel like playacting, as though all his social interactions were merely speaking lines from an endless drama.

Out of an authentic self, authenticity comes, and therefore he can be honest with others, freely and by choice and not from a compulsion to obey formalistic rules. In normal relationships he finds no need to be manipulative or indirect. Nor will he use his honesty to hurt others.

For the authentic person the game-playing patterns of social relationships take on a different meaning. He may decide that he will play games—social roles, rank roles, political strategies, good-manners games, and so on; but his playing will not be infused with a seriousness or compulsiveness ("uptightness"). They are not panic-plays since there is no inner need to play them; there is no do-or-die emotional investment in them. He plays games deliberately as situations demand, plays them with an awareness of the game-structure and the prevailing rules. He can accept the games and follow the rules, but he doesn't use rules, policies, laws, or legalisms to meet neurotic needs: to avoid taking responsibility, making decisions, or relating honestly with others.

An important result of the authentic feeling is that he is not afraid to "look inside himself" or to allow others to see and know him. He has no need to use formalities to prevent others from knowing him. He can remove his masks if he so wishes, as if to say, "This is what I am." If he should be rejected, his life is not shattered. The integrity of his self remains intact and his self-worth is not seriously affected.

16   A clear sense of identity often results in a relaxed existence. All of life loses some of its anxiety and tension. In knowing who one is, one does not have to fight the inner battles of an identity crisis. There is no compulsion to prove to others what he is or what he can do. (This does not mean that he can't be effectively competitive when the situation calls for it.) He does not need to prove to others his worth; that's already firmly established within himself.

This feeling of security creates an openness to new ideas. He is the opposite of the self that has undergone closure, has an answer to every question, and has finalized all his ideas. Paradoxically, a strong sense of identity enables him to experiment with new ideas, experiences, and lifestyles. He is not threatened by them. He will try on new ways of life and new ideas to see if they fit. If they don't, he is free to discard them; if they do, he has become richer for it. If they are not for him, then he is left with a better understanding of others' ideas and ways.

17   In an article entitled "The Fully Functioning Personality," Dr. S. I. Hayakawa summarized the studies of two well-known humanistic psychologists—Abraham Maslow and Carl Rogers—on the subject of the human potential. The two scientists had attempted independently to find out what qualities those people had in common who were actually using an unusually high degree of their capabilities. Maslow called them "self-actualizing" individuals; Rogers used the terms "fully functioning person" and "creative person"; Hayakawa settled on the term "genuinely sane person." In any case, there were six distinct characteristics shared by all such people:

(1) Actualized individuals are not "well-adjusted" in the sense that they conform to social norms; but neither are they rebellious against society. They can conform or not conform, as the situation calls for it, because neither is important in itself. What is important is that they possess their own well-developed behavioral norms.

(2) They are unusually open to what is going on inside themselves. They experience fully their own thoughts and feelings. Self-awarenes is great; self-deception is minimal. They are realistic about themselves and resort to few myths about themselves or life.

(3) They are not bothered by the unknown. They can be comfortable with disorder, indefiniteness, doubt, and uncertainty. They don't have to know all the answers. They can accept "what is" without trying to organize and label neatly all of life's contents.

(4) They are remarkably existential: they enjoy the present moments of life more fully, not as means to future ends, but as ends in themselves. Their lives are not a perpetual preparation for the future; they enjoy living now.

(5) They are creative individuals, not merely in customary roles such as painters or musicians, but in all that they do. The commonest things—from conversing to washing dishes—are all performed in a slightly different, more creative way. Their own distinctive style touches everything they do.

(6) Actualized persons are "ethical in the deepest sense." They

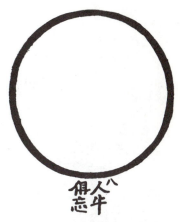

8. Both Bull and Self Transcended

*Whip, rope, person, and bull—
   all merge in No-Thing.
This heaven is so vast no message
   can stain it.
How may a snowflake exist in a
   raging fire?
Here are the footprints of the patriarchs.*

Comment: **Mediocrity is gone. Mind is clear of limitation. I seek no state of enlightenment. Neither do I remain where no enlightenment exists. Since I linger in neither condition, eyes cannot see me. If hundreds of birds strew my path with flowers, such praise would be meaningless.**

Happiness is the emotional state that accompanies need satisfaction.

   GAIL AND SNELL PUTNEY

The General shook his head. "You've been out of school all these years, and what have you learned? Don't you know raw ability will never take you to the top?"
"I'd rather be myself than be at the top," said Beller. "I like to know what I think when I go to bed at night."

   CHRISTOPHER ANVIL

I may climb perhaps to no great heights, but I will climb alone.

   CYRANO DE BERGERAC

9. Reaching the Source

*Too many steps have been taken
  returning to the root and the
  source.
Better to have been blind and deaf
  from the beginning!
Dwelling in one's true abode,
  unconcerned with that without—
The river flows tranquilly on
  and the flowers are red.*

Comment: From the beginning, truth is clear. Poised in silence, I observe the forms of integration and disintegration. On who is not attached to "form" need not be "re-formed." The water *is* emerald, the mountain *is* indigo, and I see that which *is* creating and that which *is* destroying.

rarely follow the superficial, conventional norms of moral behavior. They consider the majority of so-called moral issues to be trivial. Their ethical concern is expressed in a positive, constructive attitude toward all people and all things. Since they easily identify with the conditions of others, they care, and their caring is the wellspring of their ethical nature.

REFLECTIONS—

1 As you reflect on the case of the man indicted for embezzlement (*"News item,"* p. 104), what is your conclusion? Was he the same person (self) twenty-six years later? Might the philosophical, psychological, physiological, ethical, and legal answers be different? Which answer(s) is/are correct? (This problem is not merely hypothetical: remember Leon Uris' *QB VII?*)

2 After a thoughtful perusal of Abner Dean's drawing on p. 103—"How much of me is me?"—what responses, intellectual and emotional, do you have?

3 Summarize in your own words David Hume's concept of the self (p. 105–Box). Drawing upon your knowledge of psychology and other modern disciplines, do you think Hume was essentially right or wrong? In either case, how would you describe "the self"?

4 "What each of us can become during our life/time is determined by two fundamental conditions. . ." (Sec. 4). Is this statement in accord with your observations of others and your experience of your self?

5 Review the suggestions regarding how one might experience his existence if he has achieved a significant degree of autonomy (Secs. 14–17). Is this description meaningful to you? Are there points here that you strongly agree or disagree with?

6 What is meant by "self-love"? Why is it so important? Contrast self-love with egotism, selfishness, and narcissism.

7 The study by Hayakawa of the "fully functioning personality" (Sec. 17) provides an interesting profile of more actualized individuals and gives a clue, perhaps, to our own potential. What is your response to the six qualities described? Can you see how each would contribute to the greater actualization of the person? Would you want to possess these qualities? Do you now possess these qualities? To what degree?

8 Pretend that you are an Eastern sage, and gaze patiently at the Zen oxherding pictures. As a Westerner (if you are), how far can you meaningfully go in accepting this account of the search for one's "true nature"? Can you accept Step 7, for example? Is Step 8 meaningful? Can you state in your own words what is implied in Steps 9 and 10?

Furthermore . . .

BRONOWSKI, JACOB. *The Identity of Man.* Natural History Press, 1971.
CASTELL, ALBUREY, *The Self in Philosophy.* Macmillan, 1965.

FROMM, ERICH, *The Art of Loving.* Bantam, 1963.

HALL, CALVIN S., and GARDNER LINDZEY, *Theories of Personality.* Wiley, 1970.

MYERS, GERALD E., *Self: An Introduction to Philosophical Psychology.* Pegasus, 1969.

POWELL, JOHN, *Why Am I Afraid to Tell You Who I Am?* Argus Communications, 1969.

ROGERS, CARL, *On Becoming a Person.* Houghton-Mifflin, 1961.

SAMPSON, EDWARD E., *Ego at the Threshold: In Search of Man's Freedom.* Delta, 1975.

10. In the World

Barefooted and naked of breast,
I mingle with the people of the world.
My clothes are ragged and dust-laden, and I am ever blissful.
I use no magic to extend my life;
Now, before me, the dead trees become alive.

Comment: Inside my gate, a thousand sages do not know me. The beauty of my garden is invisible. Why should one search for the footprints of the patriarchs? I go to the market place with my wine bottle and return home with my staff. I visit the wine shop and the market, and everyone I look upon becomes enlightened.

Change/Growth

Have You Ever Wondered . . .

- Whether you can honestly know (understand) yourself?

- Whether there might be some things about oneself that one shouldn't know?

- Whether you are a different "person" in different relationships?

- Why men (that is, "real men") are not supposed to cry?

- What happens to us when we are not loved?

- Whether you are one "person" or many "persons"?

- Whether it might be good, for all of us, if we could be like little children again?

- If it's possible to have too much curiosity?

Harlow and friend

WHEN THINGS GO WRONG

1   Dr. and Mrs. Harry F. Harlow have for years studied the growth patterns of rhesus monkeys. In the Primate Laboratory of the University of Wisconsin, the Harlows discovered that their monkeys have a developmental sequence which, under normal conditions, produces mutually beneficial social behavior. The young monkeys' emotional development must proceed in this order: (1) affection and security, (2) fear and adjustment, and (3) social-sexual interaction. If this growth

sequence is disrupted, then tragic results, in varying degrees, take place in the inner worlds of the young monkeys.

2   Affection and security are basic to the monkey's earliest stages of growth. Normally he first knows these feelings in relation to his mother. She is the prime source of comforting reassurance as he begins to experience the world about him.

The Harlows found that if a monkey is separated from its mother at birth, but is given the chance to live and develop with age-mates, then affectional ties can grow between them. Emotional bonds are established as they play together.

> Young monkeys that have not been permitted to establish relationships with other infants are wary of their playmates when finally allowed to be with them, and these deprived monkeys often fail to develop strong bonds of affection. Yet monkeys that have been deprived of mother love but provided with early contacts *can* develop ties with their peers which seem comparable to the bonds formed by mother-reared infants.

3   The worst thing that can happen is for a young monkey to be deprived of both his mother and his playmates. If this happens, no bonds of affection and trust can develop.

> Fear is the overwhelming response in all monkeys raised in isolation. Although the animals are physically healthy, they crouch and appear terror-stricken by their new environment. . . . They cringe when ap-

The unforgivable sin is not to become all that you can as a human being, given the circumstances of life that we have to accept.

R. D. LAING

If you begin by sacrificing yourself to those you love, you will end by hating those to whom you have sacrificed yourself.

GEORGE BERNARD SHAW

The supreme ideal of Greece is to save the ego from anarchy and chaos. The supreme ideal of the Orient is to dissolve the ego into the infinite and to become one with it.

KIMON FRIAR

115

Hell is—other people

NIETZSCHE

proached and fail at first to join in any of the play. During six months of play sessions, they never progress beyond minimal play behavior, such as playing by themselves with toys. What little social activity they do have is exclusively with the other isolate in the group. When the other animals become aggressive, the isolates accept their abuse without making any effort to defend themselves. For these animals, social opportunities have come too late. Fear prevents them from engaging in social interaction and consequently from developing ties of affection.

If young monkeys are reared in isolation for a long period of time—for up to twelve months—then their lifetime behavior is seriously affected, and it appears that little or nothing can undo the damage.

As one goes through it
one sees that the gate one
   went through
was the self that went through
   it. . .

R. D. LAING

4   We continued the testing of the same six- and twelve-month isolates for a period of several years. The results were startling. The monkeys raised in isolation now began to attack the other monkeys viciously, whereas before they had cowered in fright. . . . The monkeys which had been raised in the steel isolation cages for their first six months now were three years old. They were still terrified by all strangers, even the physically helpless juveniles. But in spite of their terror, they engaged in uncontrolled aggression, often launching suicidal attacks upon the large adult males and even attacking the juveniles—an act almost never seen in normal monkeys of their age. The passage of time had only exaggerated their asocial and antisocial behavior.

In those monkeys, positive social action was not initiated, play was nonexistent, grooming did not occur, and sexual behavior was not present at all or was totally inadequate. In human terms, these monkeys which had lived unloved and in isolation were totally unloving, distressed, disturbed and delinquent.

Throughout our studies, we have been increasingly impressed by the alternative routes monkeys may take to reach adequate social behavior, which by our criteria includes affection toward peers, controlled fear and aggression, and normal sexual behavior. In protected laboratory conditions, social interaction between peers and between mother and child appears to be in large part interchangeable in their effect on the infant's development. A rhesus can surmount the absence of its mother if it can associate with its peers, and it can surmount a lack of socialization with peers if its mother provides affection. Being raised with several age mates appears to compensate adequately for a lack of a mother. . . .

After numerous and varied studies at the University of Wisconsin, we have concluded that unless peer affection precedes social aggression, monkeys do not adjust; either they become unreasonably aggressive or they develop into passive scapegoats for their group.

Why are Americans so hungry for
the approval of others?
   The adjusted American lacks
self-approval; that is to say, he has
not developed a self-image that he
can believe is both accurate and
acceptable. To do so he would
require successful techniques for
creating an accurate and acceptable
self-image through honest
introspection, candid association,
and meaningful activity. The
patterns to which he has adjusted
do not include such techniques.
Instead, the culture abounds with
misdirections, which the adjusted
American acquires. . . . Perhaps
above all he learns to seek self-
acceptance indirectly, by seeking
to substitute the good opinions of
others for self-approval. It is thus
that he becomes "other-directed."

GAIL AND SNELL PUTNEY

5   The Harlows are writing of rhesus monkeys, not man; and all careful scientists are wary of extrapolating their findings from experiments with one species to any different species. However, there is evidence that human developmental patterns are quite similar.°

°See Chapter 2-4, sections 4 through 6.

PEANUTS

THOSE DREAMS I HAVE AT NIGHT ARE GOING TO DRIVE ME CRAZY

LAST NIGHT I DREAMED THAT LITTLE RED-HAIRED GIRL AND I WERE EATING LUNCH TOGETHER...

BUT SHE'S GONE..SHE'S MOVED AWAY, AND I DON'T KNOW WHERE SHE LIVES, AND SHE DOESN'T KNOW I EVEN EXIST, AND I'LL NEVER SEE HER AGAIN ...AND...

I WISH MEN CRIED..

For human beings, as with the Harlows' monkeys, normal psychosocial development appears to follow a sequential order: (1) reasurance/security/trust → (2) courage/aggression/exploration → (3) self/autonomy/maturity.

If this growth sequence is interrupted or the requisites not provided at any stage, we too become disturbed creatures cringing in the corner of life with our hands over our faces.

When things go wrong, one wonders whether the young monkey is more fortunate than human young. The monkey's behavior is a spontaneous expression of need-deprivation; it is doubtful that he

Man is something more than a carcass loosely coupled with a ghost.

SIR CYRIL BURT

"You've made me very happy."

wonders why he is "disturbed." He simply is. But our *self*-consciousness becomes acutely painful; *we know* (most of us) that something has gone wrong, and *we* wonder why.

> It makes all the difference whether one sees darkness through the light or brightness through the shadows.
>
> *DAVID LINDSAY*

6   When things have gone very wrong for us and need-deprivation has been acute, the image we develop of ourselves is distorted, confused, inaccurate. Having developed without reassurance and support, we remain vulnerable to the varied, inconsistent responses of others. Nor do we move through the normal stages of growth. There is no period of separation from authority during which we evolve a healthy reliance on our own thoughts and feelings. We are held at a level where the tenuous "mirror-images"—what others think and feel about us—continue to reinforce a fragmented self. We become alienated from the potentially authentic self, the remnants of which still cry out from deep inside.

> All children paint like geniuses. What do we do to them that so quickly dulls this ability?
>
> *PICASSO*

7

If, very early, we do not receive love, we quickly know that we are unlovable.

If we are rejected, by word or deed, we learn to reject ourselves.

If we find that what we *do* is more important than what we *are*, then doing the "right thing" becomes all important; in fact, we strive desperately *to be* what *we do*.

> My mother does not love me. . .
> I am bad because she does not
>   love me
> She does not love me because I am
>   bad
>
> *R. D. LAING*

If our parents are permissive so that we see them as "not caring," we will feel unwanted and worthless.

If our parents "care" too much, especially when they call it "love," then we may never establish self-reliance.

If we are given behavioral ultimatums that demand repression of authentic feelings, we will develop inauthentic selves which comply to required specifications.

If we have been denied the warmth we crave, we will carry with us the ache of an insatiable emptiness.

THE MASKS WE WEAR

> If one has succeeded in aligning his neuroses with his goals so that his neuroses are working *for* him, it is next to impossible for him to empathize with the person whose neuroses are still working *against* him.
>
> *JLC*

8   Few of us are fortunate enough to have had parents who appreciated our early spontaneous expressions of life and self and, at the same time, taught us to "play the games" of adjustment to other norms outside the home. How many mothers prefaced a lecture on cleanliness with a word or two about the social realities we would face—for instance, when preparing us to attend a friend's party—without instilling in us the idea that "dirty" itself is bad and "clean" is inherently good?

Yet it's an idea which children can grasp at a remarkably early age. "If you want to go to Suzy's party, then Suzy's mother will want you to look clean. I want you to look clean too. I'm happy you enjoy playing in the mud, but this is the way of the world, so let's wash up."

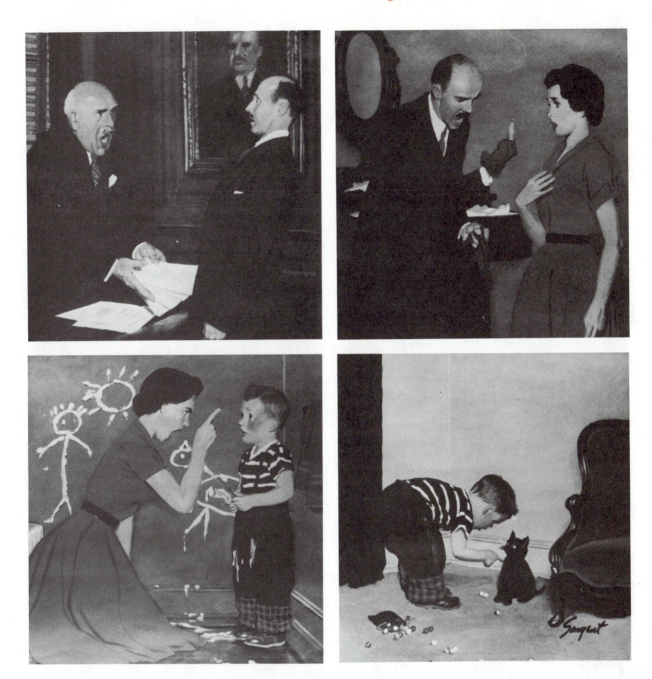

   This is a reality-perspective that permits the child to enjoy playing in the mud and at the same time choose to "play the games" required in order to attain a goal, in this case attending Suzy's party.

9   Far more than other creatures, man has the capacity to be "many
things to many people." As the situations call for it, we can be different "persons" or wear different masks (the work *person* is from the
Latin *persona*, meaning "mask"). Some of us become quite adept

Nothing is more wondrous than a
human being when he begins to
discover himself.

CHINESE PROVERB

at putting on masks or switching masks; thus we can ensure that we always have ready a *persona* that is acceptable. It effects minimal rejection by any other person or group.

But the price we pay is very dear. In the process of switching masks, we may discover that there are *nothing but* masks; indeed they may begin to feel familiar and genuine, all of them. And if someone should demand, "Will the *real* self please stand up?" we find to our horror that there is no one there. It is not uncommon to make the discovery during some personal crisis that an authentic self never developed. If we glimpse this may be the case, in panic we may seize our masks and fit them more tightly, reluctant to remove them ever again.

The feeling that one does not know "who he is" may be intuited by ourselves and inferred by others, but it is perhaps the last thing that we will confess to ourselves or others. The pain which our masks cover is too great for anyone to see. We can't risk being open. We are ever fearful that someone might see beneath our masks and discover . . . *nothing.*

I WILL NOT STOP TILL I KNOW

10   Oedipus is the prototype of the man who gains knowledge about himself and pays the ultimate price. The issue in the drama is: Shall Oedipus know what he has done? Shall Oedipus know who he is and what his origins are? . . .

Oedipus is a hero precisely because he will let no one stand in the way of his knowledge about himself. He is the hero because he faces his own reality. He cries out with pain again and again, but he repeats, "I will not stop till I have known the whole."

ROLLO MAY
Love and Will

11   Deep within the unconscious mind of man, there moves a longing to recover the innocence of childhood, a condition that he nostalgically (mis)interprets as a state of blissful happiness. Intuitively, we sense that with knowledge comes insight, and with insight comes pain. Most of man's religions have in their mythologies some place or state where he may reenter into that paradise of unknowing where suffering will cease. The Garden of Eden was a paradise only as long as the fruit of *knowledge* remained untouched. It would have been better to be innocent, the story seems to say, than to know the pain of understanding. Once innocence has been lost, however, there is no return.

Once we possess knowledge we must leave the Garden of Eden, and we leave it forever.

12   *To be innocent is not to know.* To be innocent is to be childlike, and to be childlike is to be unaware of certain facts or experiences. A

". . .We are what we pretend to be, so we must be careful about what we pretend to be."

KURT VONNEGUT, JR.
Mother Night

I do not understand my own actions.

ST. PAUL

Every time you teach a child something you keep him from reinventing it.

JEAN PIAGET

Pablo Picasso, *Girl before a Mirror*, 1932. Collection, The Museum of Modern Art, New York. Gift of Mrs. Simon Guggenheim

child does not have certain information at his disposal which he can use, information which others do have; and all decisions related to those areas have to be made by others.

Therefore, to be innocent is to be dependent. If one cannot make his own decisions, others must. This is a normal condition for a child, and he accepts it. This vulnerability puts him at the mercy of those he depends upon; if his basic self-needs are met, however, this is a happy dependency.

Dependence requires trust and faith. For the innocent child there is no alternative. He must trust the decisions others make for him, that those decisions are right and good; and he must accept on faith information given to him, that it is right and true.

Dependence requires obedience. Wherever there is dependency, obedience is demanded, but if trust is not a part of that dependency relationship, then obedience is given grudgingly. With trust, however, obedience is given willingly, even joyfully. There is no need to question the authority to whom one submits.

Innocence is an instrument of control. Knowledge and know-how are potentially dangerous assets—dangerous to all who possess them but lack maturity to use them for good, and dangerous to any who wish to maintain a state of control. Parents guard their children against certain kinds of knowledge and experiences until they are "old enough" (that is, until they are aware and responsible) to make constructive use of it. A child may be told to do things he does not understand, or that he does not want to do; but obedience to authority is necessary since authorities (that is, those *with* knowledge) can make more realistic judgments. Obviously, in matters of destiny, it could be tragic if a child were forced to make critical decisions he is not yet equipped to make.

So, while we are children, we think like children—innocently: without information and awareness. We order our experience along simple lines and our behavior is guided by those we depend upon.

GROWTH AND INSECURITY

13   Desmond Morris employs two helpful concepts to describe the innate alternating feelings of fear and curiosity: neophobia and neophilia.

By *neophobia* he means that we are afraid of new objects, unfamiliar behavioral patterns in others, strange feelings in ourselves, or any other new and threatening elements of life that we do not understand. It is completely natural to be afraid of the unknown. To experience fear in the presence of potential danger has obvious survival value. Life may be likened to our moving forever on the edge of darkness, not knowing what exists just beyond the immediate circle of experience.

We can understand, too painfully, the first experiences of the infant monkeys described by the Harlows. When placed in a room

Selfishness is not living as one wishes to live. It is asking others to live as one wishes to live.

OSCAR WILDE

We pay a heavy price for our fear of failure. It is a powerful obstacle to growth. It assures the progressive narrowing of the personality and prevents exploration and experimentation.

JOHN GARDNER

That hatred springs more from self-contempt than from a legitimate grievance is seen in the intimate connection between hatred and a guilty conscience.

ERIC HOFFER

I contradict myself. I am large. I contain multitudes.

WALT WHITMAN

. . . Only that life is worth living which develops the strength and the integrity to withstand the unavoidable sufferings and misfortunes of existence without flying into an imaginary world.

NIETZSCHE

cluttered with unfamiliar objects and without any mother or comforting "home base" to return to, the young monkey was unable to explore the room with its formidable array of unknowns. His fear was too great, and he could only huddle in the corner of the room with his hands over his eyes.

But when given the security of a mother, or even the comfort of a soft blanket or surrogate mother, to which he could periodically return for reassurance and security, then step by step the monkey would explore the room's contents. An object would be touched, handled, played with; then the monkey would return to the mother (or blanket) for a security "rest period," then explore another object, and so on until all objects were familiar. Little by little, he would reduce his fear of all the objects in the room.

Individuals are able to trust their total organismic reaction to a new situation because they discover to an ever-increasing degree that if they are open to their experience, doing what "feels right" proves to be a competent and trustworthy guide to behavior which is truly satisfying.

When a person is open to experience there is a maximum of adaptability, a discovery of structure in experience, a flowing, changing organism of self and personality, It means discovering the structure of experience in the process of living the experience.

And as he lives and accepts these widely varied feelings, in all their degrees of intensity, he discovers that he has experienced *himself*, that he is *all* these feelings.

CARL ROGERS

Open people are free to devote their energies to what is positive and constructive. They can and do set more realistic goals for themselves. Their levels of aspiration are more likely to be in line with their capacities. They are more likely to achieve their goals because those goals are more realistic.

Openness to experience and acceptance refer not only to acceptance of events outside the person's self but equally to the individual's perceptions of self. The adequate person is less defensive and does not bar from perceptual organization what is true about self.

The accurate, realistic assessment of self resulting from acceptance makes possible the use of self as a dependable, trustworthy instrument for achieving one's purposes.

ARTHUR W. COMBS

The strongest principle of growth lies in human choice.

GEORGE ELIOT

When he knew, from his own experience, that nothing in the room held any danger for him, he could then move about the room without fear. He had succeeded in making all the unknowns a part of his world.

14   *Neophilia* is a strong counter-impulse to neophobia. We are fascinated by the new and the unknown; we are drawn to new objects, new experiences, new ways of living—drawn by "curiosity" and by a sense of adventure and excitement. It is the neophilic impulse that provides us the possibility of growth. If our desire to explore the unknown is overwhelmed by fear, then we withdraw. We return to our corner. But if we have enough security when we need it, then we can explore more and more of the unknowns, assimilate them, explore some more, widen our horizons, and grow.

This kind of growth is open; it has no limits. There are always new worlds to be explored, new adventures to become excited about, new ways of living to be experienced, new ideas to be discovered, new problems to be solved.

15   The *static concept of security* may be pictured by thinking of the oyster inside its shell, the frightened person behind his neurotic defenses, or prewar France behind the Maginot Line. The main idea in the static concept of security is to build up enough protective walls and to sit still inside them. The "search for security" for many people still is the task of building and mending walls around themselves.

The *dynamic concept of security* can be pictured by thinking of a skillful and self-confident driver speeding home in the traffic stream along Bayshore Highway. He knows that the highway is dangerous; he knows that he may encounter drunken drivers or cars with faulty brakes, and he knows that a slight error in judgment at sixty miles an hour may result in his not getting home at all. Nevertheless, he is not insecure, he is not frightened; in fact, this daily confrontation of danger doesn't worry him at all, because his security in this dynamic and dangerous situation depends not on walls to protect him from danger, but on internal resources—skill, knowledge, experience, flexibility—with which he knows he can cope with danger.

S. I. HAYAKAWA

16   With a positive view of self, one can risk taking chances; one does not have to be afraid of what is new and different. A sturdy ship can venture farther from port. Just so, an adequate person can launch himself without fear into the new, the untried and the unknown. A positive view of self permits the individual to be creative, original and spontaneous. What is more, he can afford to be generous, to give of himself freely or to become personally involved in events. With so much more at his command, he has so much more to give.

Truly adequate people possess perceptual fields maximally open to experience. That is to say, their perceptual fields are capable of change and adjustment in such fashion as to make fullest possible use of their experience.

ARTHUR W. COMBS

THE ANSWER-GIVERS

17   A variety of institutions and individuals specialize in providing us with the answers before we have asked the questions. The rationale for doing this is always altruistic: they want to protect us from dangerous ideas or bad influences; they must prevent our doing the wrong things; they wish to guide us into the right paths of feeling, thinking, and behaving. They give us answers because, they would say, we have a "need to know."

The actual fact is that answer-givers have a need to persuade. One of their goals is to contain us within a state of innocence and

Be like the promontory against which the waves continually break, but it stands firm and tames the fury of the water around it.

MARCUS AURELIUS
Things Written to Himself

My own belief is that man has the capacity as well as the desire to develop his potentialities and become a decent human being, and that these deteriorate if his relationship to others and hence to himself is, and continues to be, disturbed. I believe that man can change and keep on changing as long as he lives.

KAREN HORNEY

The passion for truth is silenced by answers which have the weight of undisputed authority.

PAUL TILLICH

thereby establish control over us. Their true motivation is disguised by perhaps the commonest of human rationalizations: that they are really helping us. Indeed, the claim that we need the answers can become so widely accepted that, without raising further questions, we too assume the claim to be true.

The price of such answer-giving is very high.

It prevents the individual from having to wrestle personally with life's problems and to ask the questions that lead to emotional and intellectual growth. Once trained to accept given answers, one may never learn how to formulate meaningful questions in terms of who he is or what life means to him.

Moreover, one who has been conditioned to accept answers tends to develop a rigid conceptual framework which undergoes early closure to new ideas and experiences. He knows if he lacks an answer, the authority can supply it. All he must do is ask for the answer instead of asking the question. Nor can he question the answer. It is common to find individuals who can repeat verbatim the "correct" answers, but when questioned about their meaning, they reveal little understanding; and if pressed, their only recourse is to fall back on other "remembered" answers.

One who has been protected in this way has been prevented from knowing both the "agony of insight" and the "ecstasy of growth." He has been preassured that no painful questions will have to be faced.

CRISIS OF AUTHORITY

18   The date: A.D. 2198. The speaker: Mia, a young girl who has just survived "The Trial," a rite-of-passage which prepares youth to face themselves and their world.

> It was only after I came back from Trial that I came to a notion of my own as to what maturity consists of. Maturity is the ability to sort the portions of truth from the accepted lies and self-deceptions that you have grown up with. It is easy now to see the irrelevance of the religious wars of the past, to see that capitalism in itself is not evil, to see that honor is most often a silly thing to kill a man for, to see that national patriotism should have meant nothing in the twenty-first century, to see that a correctly-arranged tie has very little to do with true social worth. It is harder to assess as critically the insanities of your own time, especially if you have accepted them unquestioning for as long as you can remember, for as long as you have been alive. If you never make the attempt, whatever else you are, you are not mature.

ALEXEI PANSHIN
Rite of Passage

The surest way to corrupt a young man is to teach him to esteem more highly those who think alike than those who think differently.

NIETZSCHE

It is only in emotional and spiritual crises of suffering that people will endure the pain and anxiety involved in digging out the deep roots of their problems.

Psychology Today

If it were not for the neurotics, there would be very little work accomplished in this world.

ARTHUR P. NOYES

19   One of the major roadblocks to autonomy is failure to achieve separation from authority. This is the failure to outgrow our dependence upon those who have nourished us; we prolong our need of them and rely upon them to make our decisions and provide directives for our behavior. Long past separation-time we continue to operate in terms of their values. Dependence, of course, means security; in a dependent state there is much of life we need not face and many responsibilities we need not assume. It is comfortable to maintain dependence and conform to BTF-patterns° that are not ours.

The longer dependence lasts, the more difficult separation becomes. Unless, sometime, we experience the feeling of being a separate self, the very idea of autonomy may remain meaningless.

20   The self that longs for autonomy—the self that longs for a life of its own—will not easily be put down. If the authorities are reluctant to relinquish control and/or if the separating self cannot outgrow its dependency, then the separation process is often prolonged and may reach crisis proportions. But paradoxically, as long as there is pain, there is hope; the separation process has not been abandoned.

This "crisis of authority" is felt on both sides. For the self that is fighting for autonomy, the severance of the umbilical cord brings fear and guilt. He is doing the very thing the authorities find unacceptable. He is behaving "badly" or "wrong." One commonly feels like a traitor in abandoning the values and beliefs of the authority-figures; and, unavoidably, the authorities will be hurt. They may experience a sense of failure, perhaps of betrayal. The crisis of separation is often as painful for the authorities as it is for the separating self, for authorities have as difficult a time letting go as the self has in cutting loose. An authority-figure, after all, must *be* an authority or his role—the role he has defined for himself and identified with—vanishes. He often feels (unconsciously) that his purpose in life will be lost if he is not needed by others; and if others do not *need* him then there will be no basis for a relationship with him. He will be alone. Therefore, authorities frequently bind us to them in an effort to give their own lives meaning. If seen from this perspective, it becomes clear that the dependency-ties go in *both* directions.

DEVELOPING SELF-AWARENESS

21   If the recovery of the whole self is to be one's goal, then the development of self-awareness is a prerequisite. If we sense that things have not gone right either in the development of identity or self-worth, and we genuinely want growth to take place, then self-knowledge is essential and some very deliberate choices will have to be made in terms of that knowledge.

°BTF-patterns *is a convenient abbreviation which will be used to refer to all the elements which are interwoven to create selves and societies. Behavior, thought, and feeling—these are the three elements of human experience which are judged to be acceptable or unacceptable, right or wrong. Also, the single symbol "BTF" implies the important fact that behavior, thought, and feeling are ultimately inseparable and operate together.*

Aggression and hostility are so clearly defensive and protective drives. However, in humans hostility can readily turn against the self and become self-destructive, even as it can fuse with sexual impulses to become sadism.

THEODORE LIDZ

The ultimate goal of the educational system is to shift to the individual the burden of pursuing his own education.

JOHN GARDNER

There seems to be a sort of progress in awareness, through the stages of which every man—and especially every psychiatrist and every patient—must move, some persons progressing further through these stages than others. One starts by blaming the identified patient for his idiosyncrasies and symptoms. Then one discovers that these symptoms are a response to—or an effect of —what others have done; and the blame shifts from the identified patient to the etiological figure. Then, one discovers perhaps that these figures feel a guilt for the pain which they have caused, and one realizes that when they claim this guilt they are identifying themselves with god. After all, they did not, in general, know what they were doing, and to claim guilt for their acts would be to claim omniscience. At this point one reaches a more general anger, that what happens to people should not happen to dogs, and that what people do to each other the lower animals could never devise. Beyond this, there is, I think, a stage which I can only dimly envisage, where pessimism and anger are replaced by something else—perhaps humility. And from this stage onward to whatever other stages there may be, there is loneliness.

GREGORY BATESON
"Language and Psychotherapy"

The highest duty of the writer, the composer, the artist is to remain true to himself and let the chips fall where they may.

JOHN F. KENNEDY

What's to say? I have the feeling that everybody knows everything so far as human interaction goes, and that we only choose to ignore or to forget. That's why social science is so hard to teach. The people I love best are the ones who dig daffodils as well as ancient history. . . .

JOHN M. SHLEIN

A great many people are neurotic today, and the neuroses are caused by the fact that their talents, their unique potentialities, have not been used. They are "spinning their wheels" in life because they have not grown as they could have grown, because they have not used the gifts they have . .

AARON UNGERSMA

It is not uncommon to find ourselves experiencing repeatedly the same dominant negative emotions as we live through a variety of activities in time: anxiety, fear, anger, frustration, depression. We may engage in sundry projects and numerous relationships, expecting (or perhaps just hoping) that something will happen to change how we feel. But it doesn't happen. In our honest moments we can confess to a hunger for life, but something inside holds us where we are. At the deepest emotional level, it is always the same.

22   Where does one begin? A deceptively simple answer: We begin here and now. We begin with the sum of all that we are.

When we are open to experiencing our selves precisely as they are—rather than expending energy feeling anxious or guilty over what they are not—a change in feeling can take place. An awareness of all that we contact inside must be brought into our consciousness. Whatever our shortcomings (on whatever criteria they are judged to be "shortcomings"), these too must be accepted as part of one's self. Here deliberate choice comes in. There are unpleasant things stored in the inner worlds of all of us, and we may be tempted to ignore them; but with self-awareness, we can deliberately choose to stay a moment, recognize heretofore repressed events, and begin the process of "decharging" them.

A fact about emotion is that it changes when it is permitted expression and can run its course. When one allows himself to feel a feeling, and no longer permits himself the dangerous luxuries of repression and rationalization, then genuine change can follow.

For example, the monologue might heretofore have gone like this: "I feel sad. I don't want to feel sad, so I will pretend I don't feel sad. Others won't notice and I can fool myself as well." If we play this kind of game with our emotions, the sadness in this case is repressed and has little chance to change. It will remain stored as a charged energy-system within the psyche. This is true, of course, for all the bitter emotions—anger, hatred, frustration, fear, and so on.

On the other hand, the monologue might proceed: "I feel sad. I don't want to feel sad, but I'll not deny what exists. Rather I will feel the full force of the feeling and let it run its course. It will fade away by itself." This way, when we *choose* not to repress an emotion, we find that it will diminish and we can move on to better feelings. Nothing is repressed which can return later and wreak vengeance for not having been dealt with honestly.

In this way, with self-awareness and deliberate choice, one can begin to integrate all that he is. These are first steps in the recovery of a wholeness which most of us, living in a fragmenting world, have to some degree lost and forgotten.

Mary had a little lamb,
One and one made two.
Candles on a birthday cake,
Blow them out and your wish
   comes true.
Does she love me, does she not?
Tell me, daisy, do.
   Oh, to be a child again!
Oaks from acorns grew,
One and one made two.
   I believed it all, didn't you?©

ANTHONY NEWLEY
and LESLIE BRICUSSE

THE LAW OF "PATHEI MATHOS"

23   Men have long been aware that growth never comes without a price: pain. The Greek tragedian Aeschylus thought of man as subject to an "epistemic law" decreed by the god Zeus "who has laid it down that wisdom comes alone through suffering." Charlie Brown put it more succinctly after Linus lost his faith in the Great Pumpkin: "In all this world there is nothing more upsetting than the clobbering of a cherished belief."

The agonies of insight are not strangers to any of us.

The agony of discovering you are not one but many people, created in the images of those who have mattered most to you.

The agony of having your childhood's faith crumble at the very moment when you needed it most to sustain you.

The agony of doubting what you knew was right, and wondering if what you knew was wrong just could be right.

The agony of watching your children enter new worlds you cannot enter, and cannot accept, yet cannot completely condemn.

The agony of listening to your children condemn all that you believe in and tried to teach them.

The agony of feeling like a traitor to your parents when you find you must abandon their cherished beliefs because, for you, they are not true.

The agony of having to unlearn and relearn what you learned because what you were taught is no longer true.

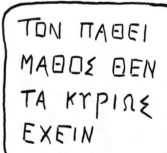

THE LAW OF PATHEI MATHOS

Zeus, who taught men to think, has laid it down that wisdom comes alone through suffering.

AESCHYLUS

PEANUTS ®

The agony of hating others for making you what you are, yet knowing in your honest moments that they could not have done otherwise.

The agony of being concerned, when others are not.

24   It is a painful insight to discover that one holds a belief because one needs the belief, and not because the belief is true. This is the sort of insight one would like to make go away, like a bad dream or clouds on a rainy day.

But this sort of insight, which comes with self-awareness, is the most difficult to dispel. When the process has begun by which one begins to examine the nature of the need which the belief fulfills, it follows that one asks whether the belief is *also* true—and often finds that it is not. The insight into the nature of the need has, for all pragmatic purposes, destroyed the efficacy of the belief.

Our pain can be especially sharp when the insight has destroyed the belief while our need for it is still alive. The head has said, "You can no longer believe it, for now you see through it." But the rest of one's being cries out in emptiness for what is has lost.

This is the cry of the soul that still needs healing but has discovered that the healers have lost their power. This is a Saint Paul, torn with conflict, realizing that the Law of Moses only increased his guilt. This is a Luther, still yearning for peace of soul, but finding that his faith in the sacraments has failed him and they cannot bring him peace.

This is the agony of alienated selves who have found themselves cut off from their roots, still longing for something *worth* believing in, but discovering that the old gods are gone and there is nothing to take their place.

25   You ask me how I became a madman. It happened thus: One day, long before many gods were born, I woke from a deep sleep and found all my masks were stolen—the seven masks I have fashioned and worn in seven lives,—I ran maskless through the crowded streets shouting, "Thieves, thieves, the cursèd thieves."

Men and women laughed at me and some ran to their houses in fear of me.

And when I reached the market place, a youth standing on a

[Speaking of "Longstreet" (ABC-TV), author Stirling Silliphant said that the series is] an existentialist statement based on the conviction that people who cannot suffer can never grow up, never discover who they really are.

TV Times

I will not let you (or me) make me dishonest, insincere, emotionally tied up or constricted, or artifically nice and social, if I can help it.

EUGENE T. GENDLIN

Edvard Munch, *The Scream*, 1893.

house-top cried, "He is a madman." I looked up to behold him; the sun kissed my own naked face for the first time. For the first time the sun kissed my own naked face and my soul was inflamed with love for the sun, and I wanted my masks no more. And as if in a trance I cried, "Blessed, blessed are the thieves who stole my masks.

Thus I became a madman.

KAHLIL GIBRAN

REFLECTIONS—

1 Ponder (and *feel*) the drawing by Abner Dean on p. 202. Comment?

2 The developmental sequence of young monkeys—and by implication of human beings (Secs. 1–5)—makes a sort of sound common sense. Put into your own words why, in terms of psychological development, the sequence seems to be so important.

3 According to the Putneys (p. 116-QM), Americans are "hungry for the approval of others." Does that make sense to you? Why are we this way?

4 Do you agree with the statement (Sec. 9) that "the price we pay is very dear" for wearing masks? As you see it, what is that price?

5 It isn't uncommon to hear someone say, "I don't know who I am." What do you think this person is trying to say? Have you ever said this?

6 Ponder the pictures on page 119. These paintings were entitled "Passing the Buck" by the artist, Dick Sargent. To use the psychological term, this series depicts the displacement of hostility. Psych it out: *Why* do we *displace* our hostilities in this manner?

7 What do you think of Oedipus' vow to himself—"I will not stop until I understand myself"? Is this a noble goal, in your estimation? Does this determination of Oedipus frighten you? What are its dangers? What are its rewards?

8 Criticize the analysis of the meaning of innocence in Sec. 12. Where in this description do you find yourself (if at all)? Is the state of dependence an *enjoyable* state?

9 Interpret and evaluate the following statement by Carl Rogers (p. 122-Box): "When a person is open to experience . . . it means discovering the structure of experience in the process of living the experience."

10 Ponder the painting by Picasso (p. 120) entitled "Girl before a Mirror." How many persons (remember that the Latin word *persona* means "mask"—see p. 119) are in the painting? How many persons do you think the girl perceives?

11 Contrast the two kinds of security described by Hayakawa (Sec. 15). Do these concepts apply in any specific way to your own behavior, especially to the way you tend to face new experiences?

12 Zero in on the problem of dealing with those who would "provide us with the answers before we have asked the questions" (Sec. 17). Do you agree with the problem as stated in this chapter? How would you suggest that we confront such answer-givers?

13 Note the sequence of stages in Gregory Bateson's "progress in awareness" (p. 126-Box). Restate in your own terms the steps he describes. Does Bateson's description sound like an accurate accounting of the way we grow?

14 As you reflect on the so-called Law of Pathei Mathos (pp. 127, 128), are you inclined to agree that there exists such a human pattern that might be thus designated as a "law"? What is meant by "suffering" in this case? Can you describe the human pathways by which suffering could lead to wisdom?

Furthermore . . .

ALLPORT, GORDON, *Becoming.* Yale University Press, 1955.

COMBS, ARTHUR W. (Chmn, 1962 Yearbook Committee), *Perceiving, Behaving, Becoming.* ASCD (Association for Supervision of Curriculum Development, NEA), 1962.

HEINLEIN, ROBERT, *Stranger in a Strange Land.* Berkley, 1968.

HOOPES, NED E., *Who Am I?: Essays on the Alienated.* Dell, 1969.

JOSEPHSON, ERIC and MARY, *Man Alone: Alienation in Modern Society.* Dell, 1962.

JOURARD, SIDNEY M., *The Transparent Self: Self-Disclosure and Well-Being.* Van Nostrand, 1964.

PRATHER, HUGH, *Notes to Myself.* Real People Press, 1970.

PUTNEY, SNELL, and GAIL PUTNEY, *The Adjusted American: Normal Neuroses in the Individual and Society.* Harper, 1966.

ROGERS, CARL and BARRY STEVENS, *Person to Person: The Problem of Being Human.* Real People Press, 1967.

ROGERS, RAYMOND, *Coming into Existence: The Struggle to Become an Individual.* Dell, 1967.

RUBIN, THEODORE I., *Compassion and Self-Hate: An Alternative to Despair.* David McKay, 1975.

RUITENBEEK, HENDRICK M., *The Individual and the Crowd: A Study of Identity in America.* Mentor, 1964.

SHOSTROM, EVERETT, *Man, the Manipulator.* Bantam, 1968.

STEVENS, JOHN Q., *Awareness.* Real People Press, 1971.

UNGERSMA, AARON, *Escape from Phoniness.* Westminster, 1969.

WATTS, ALAN, *Psychotherapy East and West.* Mentor, 1963.

———. *The Book: On the Taboo against Knowing Who You Are.* Collier Books, 1967.

2-4

Life/Time

Have You Ever Wondered. . .

- Whether women might be "mistakes" (as Aristotle and St. Thomas believed)? Or whether, maybe, men just might be the real "mistakes"?

- Why, when you're a five-year-old and your mother says, "Wait here, I'll just be a minute"—it takes foreverever-everevererererrrrrrr?

- Whether your life, as a whole, is unfolding according to some plan?

- Whether the oft-talked-about "stages of life" are facts or fictions?

- "What you want to be when you grow up"?

- What people mean when they talk about the "mid-life crisis"?

- What it feels like when time—your time—is truly "running out"?

ALL THE WORLD'S A STAGE . . .

1 To see life whole is to experience life in a very special way, but this is a difficult vision to attain.

Each single life/time is a living drama played out in space and time against the backdrop of eternity.

> *All the world's a stage*
> *And all the men and women merely players,*

The curiosity of the human race is most evident in children. A child's innocent question will often give the adult to pause, and ponder carefully the answer. But there are other things than answers to be careful of when dealing with a child. . . .

JACK WILLIAMSON

They have their exits and their entrances;
And one man in his time plays many parts.

In each life, the curtain has arisen and the play is in progress. But not having read the script, the plot of the drama remains unknown. We can't foresee the acts that lie ahead—or when the play will end—because, as in living theater, the plot is developed extempore as line follows line and scene follows scene.

2   On rare occasions, however, we are able to see and feel, in a single sweep of comprehension, the whole of a life/time. Such a vision may flash through our minds after reading a biography or after watching a drama. Ofttimes at a funeral we are left in a reflective mood as we stand, for a short moment, at the end of a life just completed.

When the biography is closed—when the third-act curtain has been rung down—only then can the play be seen in its entirety. Every part relates to, and sheds light upon, every other part. For life *is* an unfolding drama. Scene follows scene, each illuminating what has gone before and pointing toward developments that lie ahead. We can trace the major motifs of later life back to their beginnings. We can see the inception of strengths that are to bring fulfillment and flaws that are to bring failure. We can point to the decisions that made all the difference.

To see life whole allows us to ponder the mystery of human existence with a special kind of awareness. The feeling of absolute finality forces upon us a reordering of values. We frequently feel that, in effect, "it has put things in perspective."

What would it be like if each of us could stretch our conceptual limits to reflect upon our life/time as a completed biography?

THE GROUNDPLAN

3   It is quite within the realm of possibility for us to view *the basic groundplan* which our lives follow. The capricious details of daily existence are unpredictable, to be sure; but we have within us a psychophysiological timetable which provides the plot of the human drama. Quite apart from contingencies and variables, we *can* see our own lives as a whole.

Current thinking in the human sciences tends to avoid dividing the life-cycle into neat, clearly defined "stages." Rather, life is phasic in nature; it is a continuum, with each phase emerging out of the previous phase. Distinct events occur more or less at scheduled times. There does in fact exist a clear psychophysiological growth-progression that is universal and constitutes the groundplan for the entire human life-cycle.

Erik Erikson and others have emphasized the fact that life unfolds in a sequence of challenges which must be resolved. Each challenge is a genetically programmed, psychophysiological readiness to incorporate *specific experiences* into our developing selves. As each

challenge is successfully met, growth takes place and we can move ahead, on schedule, to face the next readiness period. Each phase of our lives literally grows out of the successful completion of the previous challenge. The precise schedule of these challenges is unique to each individual and determines the phasic nature of life.

The following sections should be read in a special way with a specific goal in mind. That goal is to feel the whole of a life-cycle, to see the human enterprise, from birth till death, in a single vision, as One. Perhaps reading rapidly through all the sections several times would accomplish this better than studying details which, in this case, are of secondary importance.

INFANCY TO CHILDHOOD

4   *Infancy.* During the first twelve to fifteen months of life, we awaken to the world about us. We are wholly dependent; our needs must be met by others. Therefore, the crucial challenge of this phase is the development of a feeling of trust, and the depth of our trust depends upon how well we are cared for. Whether we develop this capacity at all is out of our hands; we are pawns of our environment.

If these months are pleasant times, then we begin to open ourselves to life. We can feel hunger, pain, loneliness—whatever is authentic—and know that there will be someone to fulfill our needs. There is someone who cares. Thus we learn in a very natural way to be ourselves and to remain open to the actions of others. We trust them. By contrast, if the environment is capricious or hostile, we become fearful; we remain on guard; we cannot afford to open ourselves to others. Quite realistically, we have no grounds for trusting.

This phase is critical. If we don't develop trust and openness during this period, then severe conflicts lie ahead. Some personality theorists go much further and believe that if we don't experience love during this early period, then love is lost from our lives forever. We will never love—or be loved.

5   *Early Childhood.* A new phase begins when we learn to stand, walk about, and get into things. Better motor control brings whole new worlds within range of our curious hands. We venture into new rooms, play with new toys (*everything* is a toy), and find drawers and cupboards to explore.

The essential challenge of early childhood is striking a balance between an unbounded freedom to do anything (which *we* want) and the necessary limits and controls (which *others* want)—parameters within which we must exist. Guidelines must be consistent and firm. Our neophilic impulse to explore must not be dampened, but we must learn to accept limits; we must learn to live with the frustrations of not being able to do everything we want. If we can find a satisfactory balance between freedom and restriction, then we can continue, safely and happily, to explore the world about us. But if there is too much

Our days, our deeds, all we achieve or are, Lay folded in our infancy. . .

JOHN TROWBRIDGE

He whom love touches not, walks in darkness.

PLATO

For young children it is primarily experience that determines character, but for the more mature person it is character that determines experience.

HAIM GINOTT

Immortal God! What a world I see dawning! Why cannot I grow young again?

ERASMUS

freedom, we will learn to resist all authority that would impose any limitations upon us; or if there is too much restraint, then we gradually lose the urge to explore life and give in to a neophobic passivity. Either extreme sets us up for problems which will return to bother us at a later time.

6   *Middle Childhood.* The next challenge is a different kind: it is the discovery that other people come in two varieties—and that we do too. We awaken to the fact that, physiologically, we are different from others in our family and from friends.

The psychological challenge of this phase is the successful acceptance of ourselves as boy or girl within the context of all our relationships. That is, we proceed to clarify and understand our sex-role identity. With positive guidance from authorities, our sex-role is accepted without undue stress or guilt. We begin to feel that being a girl or a boy is natural and good, that it was not a mistake or terrible accident that we were not born of the other sex.°

Those who employ Freudian concepts hold that there is also an Oedipal conflict to be resolved at this stage. The daughter finds herself in profound competition with her mother as she comes to realize they are of the same sex; similarly, the son feels a competitiveness toward his father—each for the love and sex-role approval of the other parent. The resolution of these conflicts leads to a new set of relationships all around, based upon the realities of sex-identity.

7   *Late Childhood.* About the age of six there begins a longer, smoother period of growth that lasts until the beginning of adolescence, a duration of five or six years. It is a time for consolidation of the growth-gains we have made so far. It is a sort of rest period from the ordeals of rapid change. However, if earlier growth-challenges

°*I hesitate (but only briefly) to mention that this was precisely the view of Aristotle and Saint Thomas Aquinas. Both believed that women are mistakes. According to the latter, nature always tries to produce a male, but a female results when something goes wrong* (mas occasionatum); *more than that, she is a defective and accidental creature* (deficiens et occasionatum). *No philosopher, as far as I know, has suggested that men are also mistakes, though I'm sure a very interesting argument could be constructed to support the notion.*

TOKEN SEPARATION

Several recent, extensive studies suggest that the number of adolescents who achieve a decisive articulation of the self is diminishing. Elizabeth Douvan and Joseph Adelson found that a serious testing of values and ideology occurs only in a minority of adolescents. It appears that real independence is accomplished in lower-class and some upper-middle-class youngsters because these two extremes are so different from the core adolescent culture. But in studying the "silent majority" of adolescents, they found only token parent-child conflict and therefore token maturity and autonomy. They found that the peer group for many adolescents is only used to learn and display social skills—a kind of playpen designed to keep the children out of harm's way. Although for many the peer group is an arena for confrontation of self, for many more it acts to hinder differentiation and growth.

Developmental Psychology Today

haven't been effectively resolved, this "rest period" may be a sort of catch-up time for further resolution of these conflicts.

During this calmer time, if all goes well, there is a deepening sense of identity as the distinctive elements of our personalities become more coherent. Personality is still developing, to be sure; it is still shaky and tender. Our selves are not yet firmly grounded. Therefore, if our environment is especially hostile and rejecting at this time, painful feelings of inadequacy can result. Acceptance by our peers at this point is important; we seek it aggressively, though not often directly. We want to feel that we are like others, and that others approve of us.

If all goes well during this stabilizing phase, then the stage is set for the next critical ordeal of our life-cycle: adolescence.

THE ADOLESCENT YEARS

8   *Early Adolescence.* With the sudden physiological growth that initiates adolescence, we enter a time of "storm and stress," an upheaval that affects not only us but the lives of all who are within range.

Adolescence is transition. Heretofore, each of us has been a child. We have been treated as children, and our thoughts and emotions have been those of a child. We have been passing through the conflicts characteristic of childhood.

All this rapidly changes as the transition to adulthood begins. We identify increasingly with adults, and others treat us more and more as young adults. We are being thrust into adulthood. The allurement of freedom and independence beckon, but self-doubt and fear of responsibility draw us back. Adolescence is marked by spurts of growth and regression. All the while, the lingering little-boy or little-girl feelings haunt us; we are pulled and torn, not knowing from day to day which—and who—we are.

The prime challenge of early adolescence is the acceptance of the physiological and obviously sexual changes our body undergoes. For a time we may feel like spirits inhabiting an alien organism. It changes almost daily; it is erratic and unpredictable. Alterations in body chemistry intensify our emotions, and many of them are new to us. Hormonal changes bring on dramatic, uncontrollable mood-swings.

As if all this weren't enough, we are hit by an excruciating realization that society has *norms* for our sexual characteristics and behavior. Society, we discover, expects us to grow in a specific way, and we anxiously wonder whether we will ever measure up to its standards. Underlying all this is a diffuse, undefined, all-pervasive sexual uneasiness.

But eventually, with encouragement, we adjust to these drastic changes and accept this new body. We find—with mixed feelings—that others begin to respond differently to this body. A young woman faces the fact of her sexual attractiveness with embarrassment, self-

To pretend to satisfy one's desires by possessions is like putting out a fire with straw.

Chinese Proverb

Self and personality emerge from experience. If they are open to their experience, doing what "feels right" proves to be a competent and trustworthy guide to behavior which is truly satisfying.

CARL ROGERS

consciousness, and delight; a young man begins to have exhilarating sexual feelings, but they may be compromised by anxiety, guilt, and bewilderment.

In summary, the central challenge of early adolescence is to be able to hold on tight while our bodies and emotions undergo dramatic alterations, carrying us through the transition into adulthood, and getting us ready for mating and parenting.

9   *Mid-adolescence.*   During mid-adolescence physical and psychological turmoil continues, but as we feel more like adults our preoccupation shifts to the problem of independence from authority—that is, independence from other adults. This is the challenge of separation. Feeling increasingly like separate persons, we set out on our own. In the language of space technology, it is time to go on internal power. We venture further in our exploration of life, experimenting with a variety of new experiences. It is a time of trial and error, savoring successes but learning to accept failure when we don't achieve our goals. Independence means learning to set goals for ourselves, and inevitably some will be unrealistic. The challenge is learning to accept failure without feeling like failures—that is, without loss of self-esteem. Gradually we learn how to set more realistic goals.

Separation often involves a painful and prolonged revolt against authority, against parents and other immediate "controllers" (real or imagined) and also *symbols* of control. But while seeking independence we commonly displace our feelings toward all authorities who, we think, might keep us from gaining the desired separation. It is perhaps a hackneyed phrase, but "the crisis of authority" still describes accurately the experience of mid-adolescence. The more we have been restricted and repressed, the louder our protests and the sharper our attacks against the restraints and the restrainers; or if not permitted direct attack, then the greater will be our use of scapegoats.

The separation process produces great ambivalence. We feel loyalty to those who have cared for us, and separation is painful for everyone. And when others are hurt (we usually say that "*we* hurt *them*," though in fact this is not the case at all), then we feel guilt. To ease our guilt-feelings we seek the approval of those we hurt; that is, we want to be forgiven. But we cry out for the very thing that can't be given. Parents and authorities feel rejected, too; they usually don't understand, and can't accept, our "separating behavior." A part of the individuating process, therefore, is learning to accept without excess remorse and guilt the fact that we have to proceed with the separation *without the approval* of the significant-others involved in the process. Depending upon the maturity of our parents, it is easy to see how manipulative games and bitter conflicts can complicate the mid-adolescent years and often thwart altogether the successful establishment of separate identities. Indeed, for years to come, our parents can linger on in us, and we in them, in a perpetual, agonizing entanglement.

It is quite possible, Octavian, that when you die, you will die without ever having been alive.

MARK ANTONY
"Cleopatra"

So many people die before they really begin to live.

AARON UNGERSMA

Adolescence is a kind of emotional seasickness. Both are funny, but only in retrospect.

ARTHUR KOESTLER

When I put on roller skates, I was as tall as Bette and everyone looked shorter. Then I realized that's how we look to Bette all the time.

SHANNON CHRISTIAN

Be patient . . . because it wasn't your parents who made the world.

ARNOLD TOYNBEE

WHAT TIME IS IT?

It is a common experience that time for a child seems to pass much more slowly than time for the adult. A year goes by rapidly for a man compared to his recall of childhood years. Seymour Kety has reviewed available information, obtained by the nitrous-oxide technique, on over-all cerebral blood flow and oxygen consumption in man, and finds a distinct correlation of these functions with age. He reports a rapid fall in both circulation and oxygen consumption of the brain from childhood through adolescence followed by a more gradual but progressive decline through the remaining age span. Slowing of cerebral oxygen consumption with advancing years would, according to our considerations, make time appear to pass faster in old age, as indeed it does.

HUDSON HOAGLAND

Percepts of space and time are related to metabolic rate since changes in the latter bring about concomitant perceptual changes. Physiological clocks run fast when metabolic rate is increased, while clock time is over-estimated, subjects arrive early to appointments, time appears to pass more slowly. When the physiological clocks run slowly (corresponding to a decrease of metabolic rate), clock time is underestimated, subjects arrive late to their appointments, time flies by rapidly, the days seem to fly by "like magic."

Another manifestation of the relation between metabolic rate and time sense is exemplified by Lecomte du Noüy's experiments [involving healing of tissue]. . . .du Noüy calculated the impression of "our passage" in time for a twenty- and fifty-year-old man to be four and six times faster respectively than for a five-year-old child.

ROLAND FISCHER
J. T. FRASER (ed.)
The Voices of Time

During these troublesome times, we seek the support and understanding of our peers; and an important feature of the mid-adolescent years is "peer-conformity." The more we are misunderstood and rejected by our parents, the more we need the support of our peers who are themselves having similar experiences. They can understand.

10   *Late Adolescence.*   If these challenges have been met with continued self-esteem, then late adolescence will be characterized by a strong sense of self. We feel more like distinct, whole persons.

With a smoothly functioning self, we can successfully take on ever-greater responsibilities. Indeed, we enjoy responsibility and the satisfactions it brings. Underlying all of life's sundry experiences is a developing strength which carries us through.

If we are on schedule, and our feelings about both body and self are positive, then we will have developed, smoothly and naturally, the capacity for intimacy, not merely sexual intimacy, but a sense of honesty and openness in all our relationships. The capacity for sexual intimacy is but a single—thought often a central—manifestation of the comprehensive capacity for trusting, empathizing, and sharing. The better we feel about ourselves the more we long for intimacy with others.

Therefore, the challenge of late adolescence is the consolidation of a sense of self in relating to other persons, in developing a capacity for intimacy, and in gradually laying to rest our doubts and fears about

Youth is the age of extremes: "if the young commit a fault it is always on the side of excess and exaggeration." The great difficulty of youth (and of many of youth's elders) is to get out of one extreme without falling into its opposite. For one extreme easily passes into the other. . . .

ARISTOTLE
(Summary by Durant)

I can, therefore I am.

SIMONE WEIL.

No task is more difficult for youth than allowing their elders to live with their myths; nor any task more difficult for adults than allowing youth their quest for their own myths.

JLC

what we can accomplish as unique selves, newly emerged on the scene and ready for life.

THE MATURING YEARS

Chronological age is arbitrary. Everyone is many ages at the same time.

SHARI FOX

11   *Early Adulthood*   (about 20–30). Before the advent of the 1970s, life-span research had concentrated almost exclusively on the phases from infancy through adolescence; little careful study had been made of life's adult stages. When research began in these phases, results were surprising and some earlier assumptions were removed from textbooks.

Daniel Levinson, a professor of psychiatry at Yale, has branded as false the belief that if we know what happened during an individual's childhood, then the rest of his life is generally predictable. "Psychologists speak as if development goes on to age six, or perhaps eighteen. Then there's a long plateau in which random things occur, and then, at around age sixty or sixty-five, a period of decline sets in to be studied by gerontologists." This picture of the human life-span is little more than a widely held myth. An abundance of new information has shown the adult decades to be as exciting as childhood and as turbulent as adolescence, offering fully as many storm-filled opportunities for change and growth. Based on current knowledge, says Levinson, "there *is* something called adult development, an unfolding, just as there is earlier" during our growing-up years.

The early-adult phase is primarily a time of mating and parenting, but the basic challenge of this stage is the development of one's capacity for intimacy. Both physically and psychologically we are prepared for intimacy and sexual activity (they are *not* synonymous) and the rearing of offspring. Intimacy is not only the capacity for fulfilling sexual companionship, but is more basically a quality of openness and trust which is essential to both marriage and the well-being of the offspring.

This phase of life is characterized by one writer, Linda Wolfe, in this way: "This is a time of life when spouses are wooed and wed, and when adolescent friendships are cast off if they no longer seem desirable, or consolidated if they seem worthy of future investment." New dependencies are established which replace old ones.

Dr. Levinson describes this as a time of "getting into the adult world." We experiment with society's defined roles, rules, and responsibilities. This can be a time for creation and productivity, a time to channel one's creative energies into a variety of activities, of which parenting may be only one. Many of us choose our vocations at this time, as well as various long-lasting avocations. All are ways of expressing the essence of our own personalities. Our creative urges can be realized in art forms, in the professions, in roles which serve others, in competitive business ventures, in sports, and so on.

During these years we may achieve for the first time a clear pic-

> One of the reasons why mature people are apt to learn less than young people is that they are willing to risk less. Learning is a risky business, and they do not like failure.
>
> *JOHN GARDNER*

> A man without the love of a good woman is like a squeaking gate on a white picket fence.
>
> *L. L. TAYLOR*

© by Sidney Harris/American Scientist, Volume 67, Number 3, May–June 1979, page 336.

"But you can't go through life applying Heisenberg's Uncertainty Principle to *everything*."

ture of the capacities and limitations that we will have to live with for the rest of our lives. We may find that we must accept some basic limitations. At the same time we can develop a feeling for our growth potential and begin to set realistic goals in terms of what we truly are.

12   *Intermediate Adulthood*   (roughly 30–40). The age of 30, give or take a year or two, is another time of transition which, for some, mounts to a "growth crisis" which jars us out of our ruts and forces us to face new alternatives. The basic factor in this transition is a feeling that some sort of change is imperative. Stagnation is felt to be a real possibility and must be avoided. Dr. Roger Gould describes it as a feeling that some deep and personal side of the self "is striving to be accounted for." It is a time for the reassessment of priorities, relationships, commitments, and goals. Men and women both develop the feeling that the careers and life-styles they have settled into have somehow become too restrictive, too confining. Such roles are perceived to be "a violation or betrayal of a dream they now had to pursue" (Levinson's words). Marriages that were apparently stable often become strained; marriage partners turn elsewhere for companionship and fulfillment. Women frequently discover that they have fallen into the "suburban housewife syndrome" and proceed to change their roles by seeking outside interests—taking a job, returning to classes, thinking of a career. "This brief transitional period may occasion considerable inner turmoil—depression, confusion, struggle with the environment and within oneself—or it may involve a quieter reassessment and intensification of effort" (Levinson).

Following this initial transition, the thirties are best described as a time for settling down and seeking stability. Inner turmoil now vanishes: the adolescent search for identity and the early-adult quest for intimacy are past. Life turns outward; concerns become more objective. Men and women both become concerned about their "niche" in society and about advancing their careers.

The late thirties are frequently characterized by a renewed search for autonomy. During mid- and late-adolescence our strivings were directed toward the discovery of self and autonomy; but during our twenties some of our gains are lost. No sooner do we separate from parents than we reestablish dependencies with mates and mentors, and, like belated obligations, these must eventually be dealt with. One's success in finding a compatible mate is felt and faced earlier. But now, during the late thirties, there emerges a strong need to break dependency-ties with older mentors, especially those in one's job or profession. To accomplish this men and women commonly switch jobs and even relocate themselves vocationally and geographically.

The essential challenge of this phase of life is one of growth and accomplishment in the world. If we can assume responsibilities with assurance and skill, then the attainment of goals can bring deep satisfaction. We can enjoy the fruits of our labors. Autonomy and self-esteem can deepen. Our children grow. Social and material gains are

---

If you don't know where you are going, you will probably end up somewhere else.

LAWRENCE J. PETER

---

*Nel mezzo del cammin di
  nostra vita
Mi ritrovai per una selva
  oscura,
Che la diritta via era smarrita.*

In the middle of the journey of our life I came to myself in a dark wood where the straight way was lost.

DANTE

Time . . . Time. I bound it up in a little equation and it has never forgiven me! You see . . . I disprove my own theory. My energy leaves me in quantum bursts. My mass . . . approaches zero. And time . . . time approaches the speed of light.

From "Dr. Einstein before Lunch"
ERNEST KINOY

"I have an important appointment."

made. With increased knowledge and skill in living, we can experience an ever-widening expansion of awareness. These can be fulfilling years.

They can also be dangerous years. If we make unrealistic demands upon ourselves, set unattainable goals, and slide into a pattern of failure, then life, to some degree, can become hellish, and trouble may lie ahead. Furthermore, if we become so absorbed in attaining social and material goals that we neglect to set goals that would promote the growth of ourselves as persons, then the stage is set for us to approach the upcoming years unprepared and empty.

For looming just ahead is a crucial challenge which will largely determine whether the rest of our life/time will be worth living.

13 *Middle Adulthood* (about 40–50). The challenge of the middle years can be the most precarious time of life since the turmoil of the adolescent transition. This also is a time of transition. This "mid-life crisis"—which begins around 40, give or take a few years—now calls upon all the resources we have been able to develop.

The middle years are a time of taking stock. One arrives at a point where he no longer *assumes* youthfulness; he no longer takes it for granted. He realizes that the youthful phase is passing and that there is nothing he can do about it. The essential challenge might be stated: "I have lived up the first half of my life/time, and I realize there

Middle age has been defined as the period of life when you do new things less and less and cease to do old things more and more.

JOHN CHANCELLOR
NBC Nightly News

"I don't know anything."
"The beginning of wisdom, as they say. When you're seventeen you know everything. When you're *twenty*-seven if you *still* know everything you're still seventeen."

RAY BRADBURY
Dandelion Wine

141

is only so much time left and my life will end. I *experience* that I am mortal. I will die. Now, what do I really want to do with the rest of the time I have left?"

Underlying the mid-life crisis is a deeply felt anxiety that is completely democratic: it comes alike to rich and poor, introverts and extraverts, successful entrepreneurs and social dropouts. It is ontologi-

The familiar lament, "I don't know who I am," once thought to belong only to the crisis of adolescence, to be resolved by the adult stage, is heard not only from teenagers but from adults of all ages. . . . A sad commentary on this is the increasing number of suicide attempts on the part of lonely aged people. Education, status, "success," material security or lack of it, seem to have little bearing upon the high degree of suffering, unhappiness, and loneliness found in the life of those who have found no focus of identity or pattern of meaning in their existence.

AARON UNGERSMA

The biologist looks at the worst aspects of aging, which tends to trouble people.

F. MAROTT SINEX

SUNRISE, SUNSET . . .

Is this the little girl I carried?
Is this the little boy at play?
I don't remember growing older.
When did they?
When did she get to be a beauty?
When did he grow to be this tall?
Wasn't it yesterday when they were small?

Sunrise, sunset,
Sunrise, sunset,
Swiftly flow the days.
Seedlings turn overnight to sunflowers,
Blossoming even as we gaze.
Sunrise, sunset,
Sunrise, sunset,
Swiftly fly the years,
One season following another,
Laden with happiness and tears.

What words of wisdom can I give them?
How can I help to ease their way?
Now they must learn from one another,
Day by day.
They look so natural together,
Just like two newlyweds should be.
Is there a canopy in store for me?

Sunrise, sunset,
Sunrise, sunset,
Swiftly flow the days.
Seedlings turn overnight to sunflowers,
Blossoming even as we gaze.
Sunrise, sunset,
Sunrise, sunset,
Swiftly fly the years,
One season following another,
Laden with happiness and tears.

SHELDON HARNICK
Fiddler on the Roof

cal; it is a part of our being human. Failure to negotiate the rough seas at this time portends discontent, while success brings the promise of further growth and greater fulfillment.

Whatever one's state in life, a time of introspection begins. The worldly symbols of success may have been attained, but such accomplishments feel empty and meaningless. "There's more to life than this. There must be. I don't know what it is, but I'm going to find out." Thus an inner anxiety—"Is this all there is?"—is translated into new forms of action: "What have I got to lose?"

Typically, you find a businessman who has spent his life in management, banking, or the like; or a blue-collar worker who has been a responsible provider and "solid citizen." By all criteria he is to be judged successful and commended by society's standards. Inside, however, he experiences a sense of unfinished business. He's sure that he has so far lived the kind of life he should have lived: he chose a vocation, established himself, attained a degree of security and stability. But in all of this he senses a contradiction. In effect, he is saying: "I'm successful, but there's something missing from my life. I've *accomplished* something, but Im not sure that I've *become* anything. As a person I feel that, somehow, I got left behind."

Typical also is the housewife and mother. It gradually dawns that she has neglected her own life. There are things she wants to do, and the time has come for her to pursue her own interests. She has devoted years to the defined tasks of housewife and/or mother. She has more or less fulfilled society's expectations of her role and responsibilities. But in doing so, she finds that she has denied many of her own profoundly human needs. At the very worst, she may have discovered that Shaw's bitter axiom is true: "If you begin by sacrificing yourself to those you love, you will end by hating those to whom you have sacrificed yourself."

One study revealed that almost ninety percent of the over-35-year-old women attending college are there because they are unhappy with their lives and have become uneasy with the state of their personal growth. Many expressed their discontent in some such words as these:

> When I graduated from high school I was thinking of a career, and I went to college at the time to prepare for it. But in my first year I met my husband and we got married. I dropped out and took a job so my husband could continue his education. By the time he finished his degree and got a job we had two children.
>
> But that was more than ten years ago. Now that the children are older I feel strongly that I should go back to school and pick up where I left off.

All these women indicated they never gave up hope of completing their education. In recent years most of them came to see their marriage/family condition as an interlude in (or interruption of) their own "fulfillment as human beings."

Treasure each other in the recognition that we do not know how long we shall have each other. . . .

JOSHUA LOTH LIEBMAN

"There is no hope."
"We're both alive. And for all I know, that's hope."

HENRY II
The Lion in Winter

Here I am, fifty years old and I don't know what I want to be when I grow up.

PETER DRUCKER

Oh, and by the way, the morning low-clouds will clear by mid-afternoon. . . .

LORNA AMES

We dare not call ourselves philosophers, and yet we all are, aren't we, or we could not get out of bed in the morning. Unless you plan, the night before, to be alive at dawn, you will not stir.

RAY BRADBURY

Thank God mirrors don't have memories . . .

ROBERT W. SMITH

"It's all over, and you're out of danger."
"How can I be out of danger if I'm not dead?"

Rachel, Rachel

Several events may coalesce and contribute to the onset of this stock-taking period. (1) Our children may have achieved separation and we are no longer needed as parents. We have been freed of long-term responsibilities which have been taken for granted. Not to be needed in this familiar role can initiate an "agonized reappraisal" of our purpose in living. (2) With this change of roles, husband and wife often encounter one another for the first time in many years. They find that they are not the same selves. Without knowing it, both have changed, and rather suddenly their relationship undergoes an "agonized reappraisal." Often a new relationship must develop. We may also find that we have moved in different directions, and the reestablishment of the intimacy essential to carry us through later years without profound loneliness may be difficult. It may be doubly difficult if such intimacy was never accomplished in the young-adult years.

To some extent, men and women differ in their experience of this middle-years challenge. Menopause may force upon a woman a self-image crisis which a man is spared. If a woman's primary feelings of worth have long been associated with her role as a mother, then the loss of her childbearing capacity—which frequently coincides with the time when her children reach young adulthood, leave home, and no longer need her as a mother—may create severe readjustment problems.

Physical appearance is also a common cause of self-image problems. If a girl's feelings of self-esteem derive primarily from her physical/sexual attractiveness, then as she sees these qualities fade, her self-esteem may also fade. She may feel that she possesses no other qualities which could be a realistic basis for any continued self-esteem. She may feel an irreparable, tragic loss. She may spend her later years trying to recapture the attractiveness which she (and, she believes, others) so valued during the mating years. She may try to perpetuate the image of physical/sexual attractiveness which others can see has vanished. Coquettishness at 22 may be quite in order; at 55 it indicates a confusion of roles and may appear to others as a painful anachronism.

At 40 or 45 a man may note that some gray hair is showing and that younger people are calling him "sir." He may smile to himself and recognize that others' responses toward him are changing. (He may also misinterpret the "sir" and think it has something to do with respect.) Just as a woman may attempt to perpetuate the myth of youthful beauty, a man may try to recapture the image of a youthfulness which is passing away.

Failure to deepen one's sense of autonomy and authenticity during the middle-years—as opposed to the single-minded pursuit of external accomplishments—renders the future precarious. The foundations of integrity upon which the deeper experiences of our later years must build are shaky in the extreme. This is a vital matter in the inevitable aging process which we all experience.

Autonomous men and women who have practiced authenticity will be more realistic. Having never attempted to be other than what they are, they can accept change just as it comes, without myth. The autonomous individual values himself; others' responses to him may change, but his self-esteem remains intact. The later years can arrive more smoothly without problems reaching crisis proportions.

Having weathered the mid-life transition, the rest of the forties becomes a period of restabilization and renaissance. Roger Gould calls it a time of "relief from the internal tearing apart of the immediately previous years." It is a time of calm. Marriages generally become more stable. Men and women turn more to their mates for understanding, sympathy, and affection. Tragedy and loss can be accepted with patient strength and without the rage and remorse of early years.

Therefore, the central challenge of the middle years is the cluster of decisions regarding how we want to live and what we want to become during the rest of our lives. The resolution of the middle-years challenge depends largely upon our capacity to reset meaningful goals for ourselves *in terms of who we are and the life/time we have left to us.*

14 *Later Adulthood* (from 50 or 55 on). If the middle-years' challenge has been met with some degree of success, then the later-adult years can be fulfilling. We will continue to grow, to actualize our goals, and simply to enjoy life. Our physiological processes will begin to decline; we may be afflicted with a variety of ailments. But today we know that in most instances our intellectual and emotional capacities can remain viable, and even expand. These faculties—the very substance of our existence—need not fade. To be sure, faculties that were never developed may dim completely, but if our essential faculties have been used optimally, then there is no necessary decline of the quality of our existence with the decline of the somatic organism.

Men and women can meaningfully be called "adults" now. The lingering tendency to blame one's parents for our problems finally ceases. We perceive them, or remember them, with appreciation, as having done their best. There is frequently an enjoyment of human relationships not possible for us during earlier, fiercely competitive years. There is an increased awareness of our mortality, and acceptance of it. Our creativity often reaches greater heights, as though obstacles had been removed; personal and professional accomplishments continue, or increase. This has been called a time of "mellowing and warming up," and there is often the feeling that one has succeeded, at last, in sorting out life's trivialities and knowing what is genuinely of worth and meaning.

Indeed, the later years can usher us into a *quality of experience* which can rarely come at an earlier time. This can be a new sense of ultimacy in all that we are and do. We may feel a yearning, aching, profound beauty in our experience of simple things, and see previously unnoticed patterns of meaning in nature, and find new perspectives on, and a belated appreciation of, other people. The very fact of existence itself—not merely human life, but all life, and all existence—can become a glorious mystery that one feels privileged to participate in—"a cosmic drama, and I am actually a part of it!" If life has been a

"I want to live forever—or die in the attempt."

JOSEPH HELLER
Catch-22

"You don't stop playing because you grow old. You grow old because you stop playing."

"DAD" MILLER (105 YEARS OLD)
Glendale Federal Savings
(TV Commercial)

What makes old age hard to bear is not a failing of one's faculties, mental and physical, but the burden of one's memories.

SOMERSET MAUGHAM

truly expansive adventure, then in these later years there can be an unspeakable love of life—measured by awareness, sagacity, and calm—which we would not exchange, if we could, for the physical vitality of the early years.

The seventh and eighth decades of our life/times may also bring a feeling of resolution, a time for wrapping up some of life's enterprises, a sort of tying up of loose ends. But at the same time, we may well feel the urge to savor all that life can offer. If we have been truly existential throughout our life/time, we will enjoy the warmth and intimacy of human relationships as much, or perhaps more, than ever before.

Admittedly, the other side of this coin is not uncommon. When conflicts from the middle years continue unresolved, then these later years may be filled with despair and disillusionment. If intimacy was never reestablished during the middle years, a shallowness and distance may characterize all our later relationships, resulting in an all-pervasive loneliness which is one of life's true tragedies: *the unrelated person.*

15   The adult who lacks integrity in this sense may wish that he could live life again. He feels that if at one time he had made a different decision he could have been a different person and his ventures would have been successful. He fears death and cannot accept his one and only life cycle as the ultimate of life. In the extreme, he experiences disgust and despair. Despair expresses the feeling that time is too short to try out new roads to integrity. Disgust is a means of hiding the despair, a chronic, contemptuous displeasure with the way life is run. As with the dangers and the solutions of previous periods, doubt and despair are not difficulties that are overcome once and for all, nor is integrity so achieved. Most people fluctuate between the two extremes. Most, also, at no point, either attain to the heights of unalloyed integrity or fall to the depths of complete disgust and despair.

Even in adulthood a reasonably healthy personality is sometimes secured in spite of previous misfortunes in the developmental sequence. New sources of trust may be found. Fortunate events and circumstances may aid the individual in his struggle to feel autonomous. Imagination and initiative may be spurred by new responsibilities, and feelings of inferiority be overcome by successful achievement. Even later in life an individual may arrive at a true sense of who he is and what he has to do and may be able to win through to a feeling of intimacy with others and to joy in producing and giving.

ERIK ERIKSON

16   It is not uncommon in our later years for us to return to some form of religion which we may have forgotten or neglected during our earlier years. Cynics will accuse us of trying to "play it safe" or to get comforted because of our fear of death. There is some truth in this, of course, but there is far more. It is an expression of our longing for ultimacy in our later time of life. Many of us enter the later years with-

Here lies Dion, a pious man; he lived 80 years and planted 4000 trees.

LATIN EPITAPH

Speaking of the shadows at Shea Stadium: "It gets late early out there . . . ."

YOGI BERRA

The life so short, the craft so long to learn.

HIPPOCRATES

The medical evidence is mounting that human beings should be allowed to quit the race when there is no more hope of winning.

WALTER CRONKITE
CBS Radio News

Learning is ever in the freshness of its youth, even for the old.

AESCHYLUS

ELEGY

One brought me the news of your
   death, O Herakleitos my friend,
And I wept for you, remembering
How often we had watched the
   sun set as we talked.

And you are ashes now, old friend
   from Halikarnassos,
Ashes now:
         but your nightingale
         songs live on,
And Death, the destroyer of every
   lovely thing,
Shall not touch them with his
   blind all-canceling fingers.

KALLIMACHOS

out profound "spiritual" (that is, ultimate) resources. Life has absorbed our energies in other concerns. We are limited in the ways we know of probing the ultimacy, the depth, the meaning of existence which is intuited as somehow essential to the successful completion of life. For very many of us, the only practical solution may be to return to the religion we knew at an earlier time. A great deal of the late return to religion is precisely that: returning to an earlier stage of life. However, a more resourceful resolution of the challenge of the middle years ("What do I really want out of life?") can lead on to far more effective and meaningful forms of ultimacy. It could make possible the flowering of one's own unique and profoundly personal existence. In any case, this religious emphasis should be seen as an attempt to explore the meaning of life and to achieve, in the short time left, an ultimacy which life has heretofore not attained.

17   *The Final Phase.*   For some of us—though not all—there is a final phase to our life-cycle. It begins when we must face the fact that our own death is imminent. This is not merely the realization that one is mortal. Rather, this is the acceptance of the absolute fact that our own life/time has almost run out. Now the feeling may become very strong that we must take care of unfinished business and come to terms with the fact that our cessation of consciousness is near. Dying is much in our thoughts and death-symbols pervade our dreams—a clock without hands, perhaps, as in Ingmar Bergman's *Wild Strawberries*.

If we have lived a long life, we are prepared for our own momentous death-event by having lived closely with death for some years. Others around us have died, more and more of those we have known; loved ones, friends, colleagues, acquaintances, notable contemporaries. This living with death is an essential time of preparation for our own death-event. It serves to diminish feelings of fear and dread.

There may also be a reliving of past events, a replaying of our memories. We are frequently critical of the person who begins "to live in the past," and, of course, if we develop such a habit long before the final phase, then it is probably a sign of premature withdrawal from life. During the final phase, however, it is natural and normal. Partly it is an attempt to see the life/time drama in perspective, and to write a good completion. But partly it is a final preparation for the death-event. It is a recapitulation, a sort of browsing through the storehouse of a lifetime of activities, a savoring of one's accomplishments, a final inventory of life's experiences—and taking mental note of what we will leave behind.

THE SHRIEK OF IVAN ILYTCH

18   In a scene from Tolstoy's *Death of Ivan Ilytch*, the man is ill and dying. As he reflects upon the meaninglessness of his death, what now hits him so forcefully is the meaninglessness of his life. When the pointless absurdity of his petty life dawns fully in his consciousness, he shrieks. *"For the last three days he screamed incessantly."* Then a blessed rationalization comes to his rescue. After all, he had lived a conventional kind of life; he had achieved the material and social success others expected of him. So on his deathbed ambivalent fragments of his squandered life wander randomly through his mind.

> "What do I want? . . . To live? How? . . . Why, to live as I used to— well and pleasantly." . . . And in imagination he began to recall the best moments of his pleasant life. But strange to say none of those best moments of his pleasant life now seemed at all what they had then seemed. . . . And the further he departed from childhood and the nearer he came to the present the more worthless and doubtful were the joys. . . . "It is as if I had been going downhill while I imagined I was going up. And that is really what it was. I was going up in public opinion, but to the same extent life was ebbing away from me. And now it is all done and there is only death." . . "Maybe I did not live as I ought to have done." "But how could that be, when I did everything properly?" . . . And whenever the thought occurred to him, as it often did, that it all resulted from his not having lived as he ought to have done, he at once recalled the correctness of his whole life and dismissed so strange an idea.°

Do not go gentle into that good
    night,
Old age should burn and rave at
    close of day;
Rage, rage against the dying of the
    light.

DYLAN THOMAS

°You may wish to proceed to Chapter 8-3 (Death/Immortality) from this point.

EMERGING . . .

There is a tide, by no means constant but strong enough to note, which carries a number of great artists away from the youthful vigor and impertinent complexities with which they made their reputations and toward a firm simplicity, even serenity, in their last works. It is always an achieved simplicity; no beginner could obtain it. In Matisse's paper cutouts and Picasso's beaming eroticism, in "Oedipus at Colonus" and the simple folk tune that concludes Beethoven's last quartet, there is the ease and quietness of an artist who, having mastered his craft, can afford now to come out on the other side.

Newsweek, January 3, 1972

When a man is made to retire after a lifetime of good work, he'd better take his gold watch and hurry to the undertaker. There'll just be time for a down payment.

L. L. TAYLOR

REFLECTIONS—

1 **The purpose of this chapter is to help you "to feel the whole of a life-cycle, to see the human enterprise, from birth till death, in a single vision, as One" (p. 133). Having read through the chapter, jot down your immediate responses, emotional as well as intellectual, to whatever holistic perspective you attained. What are your most meaningful insights?**

2 **Remember that Aristotle and St. Thomas Aquinas shared the belief that women are mistakes (p. 134 sidenote). Would you care to counter-argue these male chauvinists by developing the case that it's really the male of the species who is the mistake? It *can* be done. (For openers, note that the anthropologist**

Ashley Montagu wrote a widely acclaimed book entitled *The Natural Superiority of Women*.)

3 Most of us are familiar with the popular proverb, "Today is the first day of the rest of your life." How do you think one might appropriately respond to this maxim if he is 5 years old? 18 years old? 40 years old? 65 years old? 94 years old?

4 Reread the observation from *Developmental Psychology Today* on p. 134. Do you agree with the Douvan-Adelson conclusion? If so, what do you think are the causes of this widespread "token separation"?

5 Focus on two challenges that one encounters during a full lifetime: the challenge that you are currently involved in, and one which you are not presently facing (preferably one that lies ahead). Describe in the most personal way what these challenges mean to you. Is there a contrast between your understanding of these two challenges? In other words, to what degree can any of us comprehend a challenge we have not yet faced ourselves?

6 If you think of life metaphorically as a "path" or "road," can you locate yourself with some accuracy somewhere (somewhen) along that path? Did you personally go through the earlier challenges as described in this chapter?

7 Ponder the drawing by Abner Dean on p. 141: "I have an important appointment." Comment? Does this drawing apply to anyone you know? Do you think you might actually show the drawing to someone and say, "There, that's you!"? What sort of response do you think you would get?

Furthermore . . .

AXLINE, VIRGINIA M., *Dibs: In Search of Self*. Ballantine, 1967.

BRADBURY, RAY, *Dandelion Wine*. Bantam, 1964.

LIDZ, THEODORE, *The Person*. Basic Books, 1968.

MAAS, HENRY, and JOSEPH KUYPERS, *From Thirty to Seventy*. Jossey-Bass, 1974.

MacIVER, R. M., *The Challenge of the Passing Years: My Encounter with Time*. Simon and Schuster, 1962.

SHEEHY, GAIL, *Passages: Predictable Crises of Adult Life*. Dutton, 1976.

STEICHEN, EDWARD, *The Family of Man*. Museum of Modern Art, 1955. (Striking photographic essay. Several editions available.)

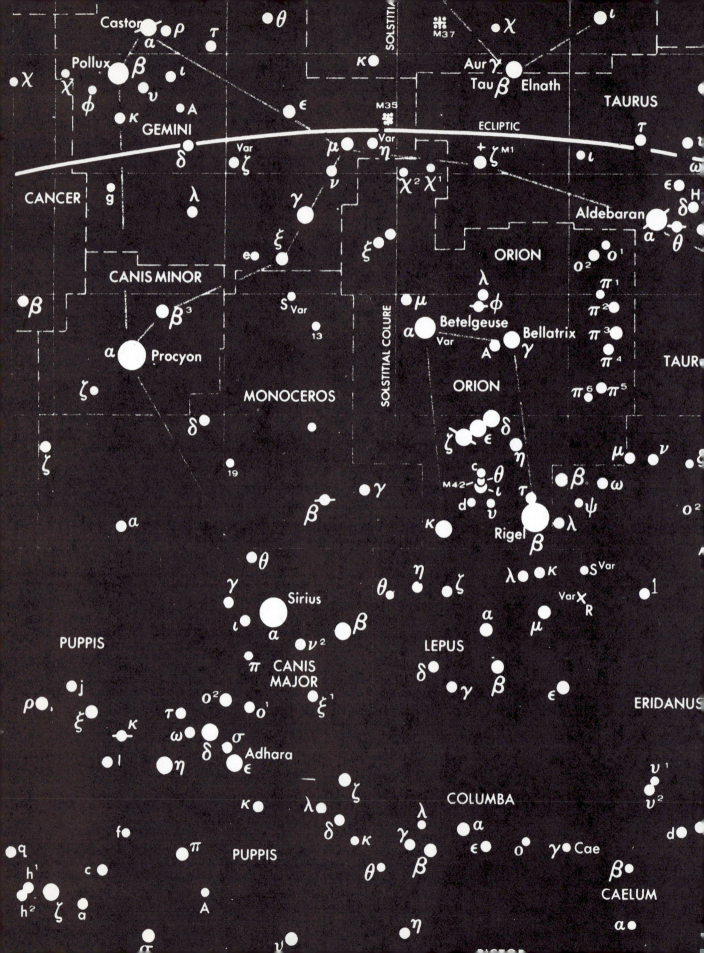

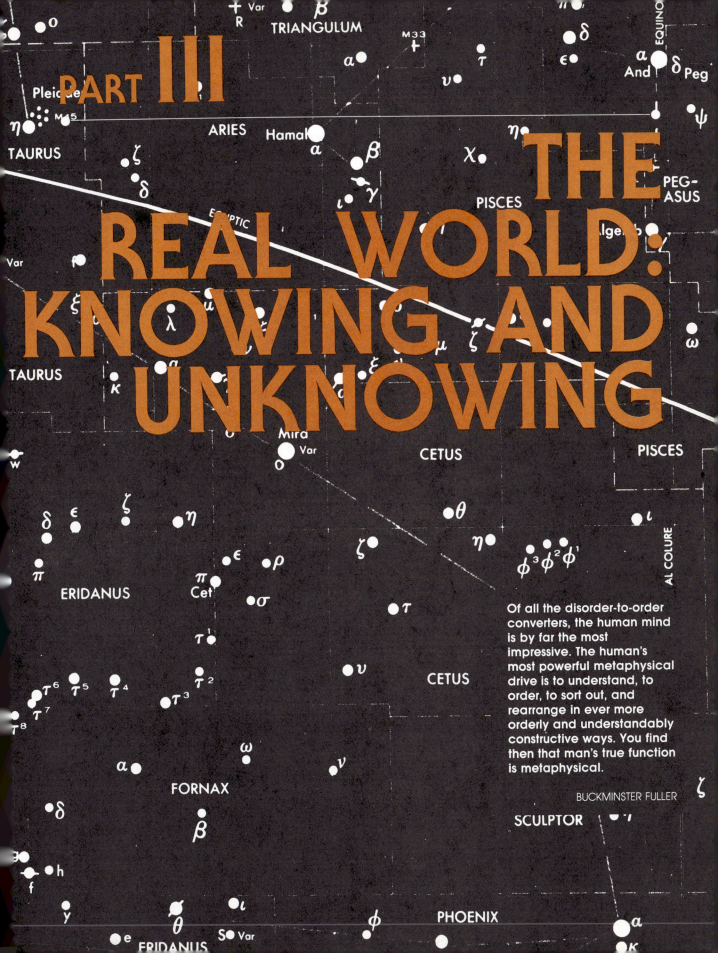

PART III

THE REAL WORLD: KNOWING AND UNKNOWING

Of all the disorder-to-order converters, the human mind is by far the most impressive. The human's most powerful metaphysical drive is to understand, to order, to sort out, and rearrange in ever more orderly and understandably constructive ways. You find then that man's true function is metaphysical.

BUCKMINSTER FULLER

Knowledge

Have You Ever Wondered. . .

- What the "real world" is really like?

- Whether you do in fact know what you think you know?

- Whether "seeing is believing"—truly?

- Whether people see things that aren't there?

- What it means to be "reasonable"?

- Where you store all your memories while you're not thinking about them?

- Whether you do anything because of "instinct"?

- Whether mental telepathy exists?

EPISTEMIC AWARENESS

1   All of us begin our philosophizing from a state of *epistemic naivety*, a condition in which we have not yet begun to question the origins, structure, and dependability of our information. To be sure, some of us may have discovered we were wrong about some things, or we may have "outgrown" certain beliefs; but few of us have peered deeply into the fundamental operations of the information-processing system we call "the mind."

   Epistemology is the branch of philosophy defined as "the study of human knowledge." In exploring this field we are touching one of evolution's fundamental mechanisms of survival, for it is by knowledge that we orient ourselves in the world. Accurate knowledge of our

> We have to live today by what truth we can get today, and be ready tomorrow to call it falsehood.
>
> WILLIAM JAMES

154

two worlds—the real° world and the inner world—correctly informs us of the conditions we must cope with. To know true facts is to survive; not to know, or to assess one's environment wrongly, is to lose the fight for survival.

With the examination of the sources, nature, and accuracy of our knowledge, we begin to develop *epistemic awareness*, a more informed understanding of what we know and don't know.

2   We face two serious epistemological problems. (1) How can we determine which facts are true? (2) How can we determine which facts are important?°

Since we are victimized by fragmented, pressurized information, we must find a way to double check fact-claims. We must learn somehow to screen out the fictions but let in the facts. *On what criteria can we decide what are facts and what are false claims?*

Secondly, among the billions of bits of information at our fingertips, we can't distinguish high-priority data. There *are* facts that are important; there *are* causes that are crucial; there *are* ideas that work. But which? Since not all facts are of equal importance at a given time, we are forced to make value-judgments. *What criteria can we use for deciding what is more important, what less?*

3   Each of us has stored away in his repertoire hundreds of thousands of bits of knowledge, most of which, needless to say, we can't remember when we want to. What is the source of all these facts? How do they get into our heads and into our memory-banks?

Almost everything that we know originates from four basic sources. The first, our *senses*, can be considered our primary source of information. Two other sources, *reason* and *intuition*, are derivative in the sense that they produce new facts from data already supplied to our minds. The fourth source, *authority*, is by nature secondary, and second-hand facts prove to be the most difficult to handle. Beyond these four sources there may well be others; but if so, knowledge derived from them remains, at present, extremely problematic, and many of the sources are seriously to be doubted.

THE SENSES: EMPIRICAL KNOWLEDGE

4   *The Senses.* The fundamental source of all knowledge is our own senses. Throughout our earlier years, this remains our dominant source of information about ourselves and our environment. As beginners in life we "learn by doing," and doing in large part means to see, to hear, to taste, to feel, and so on. Our senses are exploratory organs; we use them all to become acquainted with the world we live in.

We learn that candy is sweet, and so are sugar, jam, and maple syrup. Lemons are not, and onions are not. The sun is bright and blinding. Glowing coals in the fireplace are beautiful if you don't touch them. Sounds soothe, warn, or frighten us. Through millions of single

°Real, realism. *Recall that the word "real" is a technical term in philosophy. See glossary.*

Most of the greatest evils that man has inflicted upon man have come through people feeling quite certain about something which, in fact, was false.

BERTRAND RUSSELL

°*This latter problem will be dealt with in Chapters 4-3, 5-2, 5-3, and 5-4. In the present chapters we will work on the first question only: How can we decide what is true?*

Richard Lippold, *Variation Number 7*, 1949–1950. Collection, The Museum of Modern Art, New York. Mrs. Simon Guggenheim Fund.

If you cannot convince me that there is some kind of knowable ultimate reality, or if you cannot convince me that there are certain absolute values by which I can live my life, I shall commit psychological suicide. That is, either convince me that there is "one truth" or one right way of doing things, or I shall conclude that everything is meaningless and I will not try any more.

JOSEPH ROYCE (describing the reality-image of contemporary man)

°Empirical, empiricism. *See definitions on page 31 and in the glossary.*

Philosophy begins when one learns to doubt—particularly to doubt one's cherished beliefs, one's dogmas and one's axioms.

WILL DURANT

The eyes believe themselves; The ears believe other people.

Chinese Fortune Cookie

°*The word "feeling" does double duty, of course, by referring to sense responses (specifically to touching: "I can feel his pulse") and to emotions ("I feel sad"). The unfortunate fact is that confusion reigns through much technical material (especially in psychological, psychiatric and physiological literature) on the usage of "sensation" and "feeling." In these pages the term "sensation" will always refer to "sense-responses" and never to emotions or to sense-responses with emotional resonances. The word "feeling" will generally refer to emotional feelings; but on rare occasions it will refer to touch-sensing. Context will make clear which meaning is intended.*

sense-events we build a fabric of empirical° information which helps us interpret, survive in, and control the world about us.

Three of our senses—sight, sound, and smell—give us information about events and objects which lie at a distance, while two of the classical "five senses"—taste and touch—inform us about happenings in the immediate vicinity of our sensors. In the perspective of evolutionary survival, this arrangement has obvious benefits.

We have developed specialized sense receptors to perform four of these functions: eyes, ears, taste buds, and olfactory cells. By contrast, the sense of touch does not involve any specialized, strategically positioned organ; touching sensations take place all over our bodies. These "cutaneous sensors" are specialized, however; different types of nerve endings respond to different stimuli. Separate sensors are activated by heat, cold, touch, pressure, and cell damage (which we experience as pain). Nerve endings which react to one of these stimuli generally do not respond to the others. Taken together, all these "touching senses" give us a great deal of data which we put to immediate use in our assessment of real objects/events going on at close range.

These can be called *objective senses* since they tell us about the external world.

5   We also possess numerous *subjective senses* which inform us about our inner world. "Visceral senses" line the inner surfaces of our bodies. They are found in the mouth, along the digestive tract, and on the surfaces of some organs. Without such senses we would not experience a variety of sensations ("feelings"°) which we take for granted, such as headaches, stomachaches, or appendicitis pains. The latter nuisances might be considered minor losses if we didn't have them, but however much they hurt, the warning signals they send us are requisite to adjustment and survival.

Another group of subjective senses have nerve endings in our muscles, tendons, and joints. These are the "proprioceptive sensors" which tell us when our muscles are stretched or contracted; through them we sense if a hand is open or closed, which way our head is turned, and whether our knees are bent. Physical coordination is determined to some extent by these senses.

Another subjective sense is equilibrium. Located in the inner ear, it enables us to maintain our balance within a gravity field and tells us if we are moving or are at rest. We utilize the same principle in a carpenter's level.

This by no means exhausts the list of senses, subjective or objective. We human beings, along with all other living creatures, develop senses whenever conditions make it possible in order to enable us to acquire a bit more information about our two worlds, thus refining our operations and improving our adjustments.

6   Our senses present us with a serious credibility problem. Is there any way we can be sure that they are "telling us the truth" about the two worlds they represent? Can we *believe* what our senses seem to tell us?

At this point in our inquiry, the answer must be a reluctant no. Our senses do not give us a "true picture" of the real world; they give us an "operational picture." In fact, we can begin to construct an accurate picture of objective reality only after meticulous correction of the sense data which our senses transmit to us (to "us"—that is, to our minds). We now know that there are numerous inherent "deceptions" and "translations" in the data-transmission processes of the senses. Unfortunately, most of us never get around to making adequate corrections. We remain *naive realists.*°

To follow knowledge like a
  sinking star,
Beyond the utmost bound of
  human thought.

                    TENNYSON
                    Ulysses

°Naive realism. *The uncritical
acceptance of one's sense data as
representing accurately the real world;
a sort of "blind faith" in what one's
senses seem to tell him.*

KNOWLEDGE FROM OTHERS

7   *Authority.*   Other people are continual sources of information. Such information, however, is always second-hand knowledge—or third-, fourth, or *n*th-hand knowledge. It is all "hearsay." The farther it is removed from our own personal experience, the more caution we must exercise before accepting a fact-claim.

Certain specific classes of knowledge necessarily come to us from the testimony of others. All our historical knowledge we acquire this way. Since the "past" doesn't exist in reality, it isn't subject to empirical observation. We must rely upon those who personally witnessed the living episodes and have recorded, orally or in graphic form, accounts of the events which they believed important. Historical knowledge begins for us when we attempt to re-create in our minds images of, and ideas about, those events. Our reliance upon others for *all* the input about those events is an inescapable dependency.

Most of our knowledge of the sciences also comes to us by authority. We can't personally repeat every experiment, so we must trust the specialists and accept, though sometimes provisionally, the discoveries they record for us. Careful workers in the sciences document their researches in such manner that if we wish to double check the fact-claims ourselves we can obtain the necessary information to do so. Knowing that a fact can be double checked gives one better reason to trust the scientists' work.

By authority also we receive a good deal of knowledge from the society in which we live, but it can't be accepted uncritically. Every culture is a carrier of traditions, folklore, "common knowledge," and "common sense" which must be carefully screened before one can feel assured that he possesses dependable information.

8   How can we be sure that the "facts" others give us are true? In the face of conflicting fact-claims, how can we decide which authorities to follow? In a word, whom can we trust?

There is no simple answer. We *must* accept large amounts of knowledge which have been accumulated over the centuries; we would be personally impoverished without it. The solution lies in

Most of our assumptions have
outlived their uselessness.

                    MARSHALL MCLUHAN

Yes, reason is an imperfect instrument, like medical science, or the human eye; we do the best we can with it within the limits which fate and nature set. We do not doubt that some things are better done by instinct than by thought: perhaps it is wiser, in the presence of Cleopatra, to thirst like Antony rather than to think like Caesar; it is better to have loved and lost than to have reasoned well. *But why is it better?*

WILL DURANT

"How about five do's and five don'ts?"

Anyone who conducts an argument by appealing to authority is not using his intelligence; he is just using his memory.

LEONARDO DA VINCI

knowing how to apply checkout criteria to fact-claims and in maintaining an ever-vigilant, critical spirit. If one possesses the skill to check at will any fact-claim, and if one has learned when to be wary of those who would seduce him into accepting *their* "facts" without supplying evidence or sound reason—if one commands this equipment, he will feel far more confident in handling the knowledge which comes his way.

There is another, and perhaps more insidious, danger involved in relying upon others for knowledge. Most of us are prone to the development of dependencies. We commonly select one or two authorities, invest our trust in them, and indulge our laziness to the absurd point of accepting all they tell us. Despite the fact that developing one's critical skills is hard work, those who wish to feel more secure in their knowledge will avoid dependencies which inhibit personal inquiry and growth.

The universe is not to be narrowed down to the limits of the Understanding,—but the Understanding must be stretched and enlarged to take in the image of the Universe as it is discovered.

FRANCIS BACON

REASON: USING KNOWN FACTS . . .

9   *Reason.*   Our reasoning faculties can be a source of true facts. "Reason" might be defined as the process of using known facts to arrive at new facts. Hence, if we start with data which we are sure of, we can apply deductive or inductive procedures and arrive at new information which we did not have before.

If you are traveling in Mexico City and your travel guide reads, "One peso is equal to about 5¢ in U.S. money," you can readily find out how much your breakfast is going to cost if the menu reads, "Huevos Rancheros—35 pesos." It doesn't take much reasoning to discover that your eggs will cost you $1.75. Note merely that your conclusion—

It would be impudent to tell intelligent, grown-up people how to think.

RUDOLF FLESCH

that you are considering a $1.75 breakfast—is new knowledge, making possible a new understanding. Reasoning itself, therefore, can produce new facts.

The two general forms of reasoning are deduction and induction. *Deduction* is the process of drawing out (making explicit) the implications of one or more premises or statements of fact. If one *infers* correctly what the premises *imply*, then his inference (conclusion) is said to be "valid." *Induction* is the procedure of developing general explanatory hypotheses to account for a set of facts. In scientific induction one projects universal principles—for instance, concluding that *all* planetary orbits are parabolic—after having actually examined only a few cases.

Notice that in deduction, the conclusion *necessarily* follows from the premises. (For example: All cats are blue. Tom is a cat. Therefore, Tom is *necessarily* blue.) By contrast, when using inductive reasoning one's working hypothesis is always tentative; it is always subject to change whenever further facts are obtained. (For example: "I have seen only six cats, and they were all blue. I must conclude, tentatively, that *all cats* must be blue." All it takes in this case is the observation of one yellow cat to strike a fatal blow to a viable hypothesis. Inductive conclusions, therefore, are always subject to change.)

There are common abuses involved in both deductive and inductive reasoning. Deductive procedure applies primarily to mathematics, geometry, and to systems of logic with clearly defined terms. Yet we often try to apply deduction to our familiar, ambiguous everyday words and then arrive at convenient conclusions which in no way follow from the premises.

The weakness of induction results mainly from our failing to realize that it always gives us *probable* knowledge and never *certain* knowledge. Take another example: If one should witness five auto accidents in the period of an afternoon, all involving the same make and model of car, most of us would be tempted to conclude that something is mechanically haywire with this particular make and model. This conclusion would be an inductive hypothesis, with apparent validity. But it is not a *certain* conclusion; it is only a possible and probable explanation. Add five more accidents with the same make and model. Is one more certain of the validity of the hypothesis? Yes, but only *more* certain, not (and never) absolutely. Now what happens to the neatly working hypothesis when you discover that six of the ten drivers were driving on the wrong side of the freeway?

The induction problem forever haunts us. How many instances of a class must be observed before one can be *really sure*? Having experienced two uncoordinated woman-drivers, am I justified in making a generalization about woman-drivers? (For too many men, a sampling of two seems to justify such a generalization. Women, of course, never make this sort of error.)

In scientifically controlled investigations with a large and representative sampling, one can often eliminate competing hypotheses and run up the probability factor for the correct explanation. Nevertheless,

I have had my solutions for a long time, but I do not yet know how I am to arrive at them.

KARL FRIEDRICH GAUSS

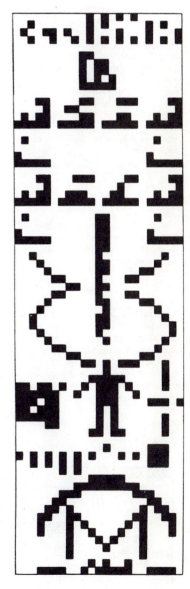

°For further explanation of inductive reasoning, note the problem of the robins'. eggs on pages 419ff. See also the case of the dead TV set on page 199.

the hypothesis shall always remain a *probable explanation,* and nothing more.°

INTUITION: KNOWLEDGE FROM THE SUBCONSCIOUS

10   *Intuition.* Although the word *intuition* calls up varied connotations, when carefully defined it can be considered a source of knowledge. Intuition refers to insights or bits of knowledge which emerge into the light of consciousness from the deeper subconscious. It is not uncommon to have sought-for ideas pop into our minds while consciously thinking about quite different things. We know that the subconscious mind can perform complex operations which the conscious mind, burdened with the task of mediating sense data, cannot handle.

An American theologian, Francis McConnell, recalls an instance of intuition when he was about fifteen and in high school. He had been assigned several algebra problems for homework and was having no trouble with them until the last problem became obstinate. He wrestled with it in prolonged frustration, but it would not give in, and finally, very late, he gave up and went to bed. Upon awaking the next morning the solution popped immediately into his mind. It dawned on him that his subconscious mind had continued to work on the problem while his conscious mind slept.

Having discovered such a helpful faculty, he decided to take full advantage of it. The next evening he glanced briefly over his algebra assignment, promptly forgot it, and went to sleep. Needless to say, when the morning came there were no solutions. McConnell recalls the lesson he learned: the subconscious mind can do creative work, but it must be treated fairly. It must be given adequate data to work with and also, perhaps, more than a little coaxing.

11   Sometimes intuition is experienced as an emotional feeling. We often say something like "I have the feeling he's not telling the truth," and it may be just that: a feeling, but a feeling in the process of informing us of a true fact.

"I have a feeling it's going to rain." Perhaps such a statement rests on subliminally collected sense data subconsciously synthesized, giving us a "feeling" about a real condition we could not consciously recognize.

> **Why is a single instance, in some cases, sufficient for a complete induction, while in others myriads of concurring instances, without a single exception known or presumed, go such a very little way toward establishing a universal proposition? Whoever can answer this question knows more of the philosophy of logic than the wisest of the ancients, and has solved the problem of Induction.**
>
> *JOHN STUART MILL*

> **The more extensive a man's knowledge of what has been done, the greater will be his power of knowing what to do.**
>
> *DISRAELI*

> **To myself I seem to have been only like a boy playing on the seashore, and diverting myself and now and then finding a smoother pebble or a prettier shell than ordinary, while the great ocean of truth lay all undiscovered before me.**
>
> *SIR ISAAC NEWTON*

PEANUTS®   **By Charles M. Schulz**

Occasionally we hear someone say, "I have a feeling something bad is going to happen." It's a presentiment, a foreboding. Jung suggested that the unconscious can correlate data in such a way that it can "foresee" events which the conscious mind, being preoccupied with perception and immediate concerns, cannot "feel." Strictly speaking, such feelings would not be precognitive insights, but rather premonitions derived from current data; but such premonitions, when accurate, would become genuine sources of knowledge.

The principal weakness of intuition and feeling as sources of knowledge is that the insights they produce are as likely to be wrong as right. If left to intuition, most algebra problems would remain unsolved. Intuitive fact-claims must be carefully double checked before credentials are issued.

ARE THERE OTHER SOURCES OF KNOWLEDGE?

12   Fact-claims have been made against other possible sources. For various reasons all of them are problematic, not the least because, in theory, most of them cannot be double checked at all.

(1) *Instinct.* There was a time when "instinct" was used to account for an "inherited pattern of behavior" in both animals and humans. Its existence in man is very doubtful, however, and the term is little used today. Even if it should prove to exist, it would not be a knowledge of facts, but a know-how system of survival behavior.

(2) *Racial Memory.* Evidence in support of racial memory is meager, though the concept has been developed by Dr. Carl Jung in his theory of the "collective unconscious." Granting that such memories might exist, and that they could be inherited, the archetypal images described by Jung are diffuse and seem to be devoid of any specific fact-claims.

(3) *Extrasensory Perception.* ESP in its several forms is commonly claimed to be a source of knowledge. About 20 percent of Americans relate experiences of telepathy, clairvoyance, or precognition. There is accumulating scientific evidence that some forms of ESP may exist, but at present we know very little about them. No viable unifying hypothesis seems to be developing which would account for all the varied ESP phenomena. Although it might eventually turn out to be a source of verifiable fact-claims, our present understanding of ESP is so incomplete that we must consider the source with great caution.

(4) *Anamnesis* ("recollection") refers to remembrance of things from a previous existence. The notion was held by several Greek philosophers, notably Pythagoras and Plato; and the "transmigration of souls" (*samsara*) is a basic Hindu doctrine. There are many recorded cases of individuals "remembering" people and places from previous lifetimes. If indeed anamnesis does exist, however, it is safe to say that for most of us it is inconsequential; our knowledge of any previous existence has long since faded away.

(5) *Supernatural revelation* has been a universal source-claim;

If a thing moves, then it must move either in the place where it is or in a place where it is not. But it cannot move where it is nor can it move where it is not; therefore it cannot move.

ZENO THE ELEATIC
(Formulated by William and Mabel Sahakian)

We only think when we are confronted with a problem.

JOHN DEWEY

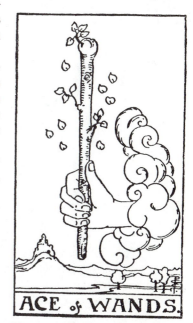

ACE of WANDS.

Man is a credulous animal and tends to believe what he is told. Historically, philosophers . . . have taken great pains to point out that authority is at least as important a source of error as it is of knowledge.

JOSEPH BRENNAN

every variety of human knowledge has been attributed to God or the gods. As a source of verifiable information, the supernatural in any form raises enormous problems. Time and again we are blocked when we try to make our way back to the primary personal experience where the facts would have originated. Historical documentation invariably presents a credibility barrier. All this aside, however, *if* there is a supernatural order of reality, and *if* facts truly derive from such a source, they would be subject to the same checkout criteria which we apply to all other fact-claims. Their source would not exempt them from having to prove their truth-value.

(6) *Spiritualism.* Many books have been written allegedly containing information from discarnate spirits, communicated by mediums, fortune tellers, ouija boards, and the like. When such fact-claims can be checked they frequently turn out to be untrue. There are few "facts" from a discarnate world which cannot be better accounted for on known psychological principles, and most of those few remaining "facts" can be explained in terms of some form of telepathic phenomena. While it cannot be ruled out as a source of knowledge, it is difficult at present to feel much confidence in any known form of spiritualism.

(7) *Occult Sources.* Astrology, Tarot, and other occult sources are commonly believed to give us certain kinds of information. According to present knowledge, it is doubtful that there are any objective phenomena operating to reveal "facts" to us. This does not rule out the possibility of subliminal influences which may indeed exist, but any fact-claims deriving from the whole range of the occult are at present quite precarious.

BELIEVING IS SEEING

A psychologist employed seven assistants and one genuine subject in an experiment where they were asked to judge how long was a straight line that they were shown on a screen. The seven assistants, who were the first to speak and report what they saw, had been instructed to report unanimously an evidently incorrect length. The eighth member of the group, the only naive subject in the lot, did not know that his companions had received such an instruction, and he was under the impression that what they reported was really what they saw. In one third of the experiments, he reported the same incorrect length as they did. The pressure of the environment had influenced his own semantic reaction and had distorted his vision. When one of the assistants, under the secret direction of the experimenter, started reporting the correct length, it relieved that pressure of the environment, and the perception of the uninformed subject improved accordingly.

J. SAMUEL BOIS
The Art of Awareness

REFLECTIONS—

1 What is epistemology? Make a list of some of the questions which this field of inquiry attempts to answer.

2 What do you understand to be meant by the terms "epistemic naivety" and "epistemic awareness"? As you reflect on your own knowledge-condition, do you feel that these terms apply to you?

3 Note the two basic epistemological problems (Sec. 2). Is it clear to you at this point why these are so important? Can you summarize briefly your understanding of each?

4 This chapter lists the four classic sources of knowledge: senses, authority, reason, and intuition. But what about the other suggested sources (Sec. 12)? Do you have evidence that any of these are also dependable sources of knowledge? Can you think of still other sources which should be given serious consideration?

5 Each of the four basic sources of information, when not employed with great care, can deceive us and give us false data. Therefore we must be wary and remain critical. What specific dangers must we guard against when using each source?

6 "The induction problem forever haunts us" (Sec. 9; see also p. 418, Sec. 4). What is "the induction problem" and why might it so haunt us?

7 Page 157, QM: "Most of our assumptions have outlived their uselessness." What do you think Marshall McLuhan (who is a pun-master) is trying to tell us?

8 Will Durant asks an interesting question about the use of reason (p. 158–QM). How would you answer his question?

9 On p. 161–QM, Zeno the Eleatic confronts us with one of his mind-boggling logical paradoxes. How would you resolve this one?

Furthermore . . .

HAMLYN, D. W., *The Theory of Knowledge.* Anchor, 1970.

JONES, W. T., *The Sciences and the Humanities: Conflict and Reconciliation.* University of California Press, 1967.

ROTH, MICHAEL D., and LEON GALIS, *Knowing: Essays in the Analysis of Knowledge.* Random House, 1970.

SANTAYANA, GEORGE, *Scepticism and Animal Faith.* Dover, 1955.

SELLERS, WILFRED, *Science, Perception, and Reality.* Humanities Press, 1963.

SHAFFER, JEROME A., *Reality, Knowledge, and Value.* Random House, 1971.

YOLTON, JOHN W., *Theory of Knowledge.* Macmillan, 1965.

Senses/Reality

Have You Ever Wondered . . .

- Whether that famous tree that fell when no one was around to hear it made any sound?

- Whether our senses tell us accurately what is going on in the real world?

- What is in fact "real" and "not-real"?

- Whether a yellow grapefruit might be perceived as, say, purple?

- Whether the real world looks the same to other creatures—say, to a dolphin, a deer, a butterfly?

- Whether aliens from another planet would "see" things the way we do?

WE NEVER SEE THE REAL WORLD

1   Our senses constitute our interface with reality. The word *interface* is a modern term used to describe the boundary of contact between adjacent realms; it is the common surface where two areas of activity meet. Thinking in these terms, it is our senses which make up the surface-contact between our subjective world of experience and the objective world of reality. The phenomena that take place along these two surfaces are what concern us here, for now we face directly the problem of the nature of our interface with reality.

What is going on where these two worlds meet?

2   Our senses are *transducers*. A transducer is any substance or device which converts one form of energy into another. A lightbulb, for

> Learning? certainly, but living primarily, and learning through and in relation to this living.
>
> *JOHN DEWEY*

164

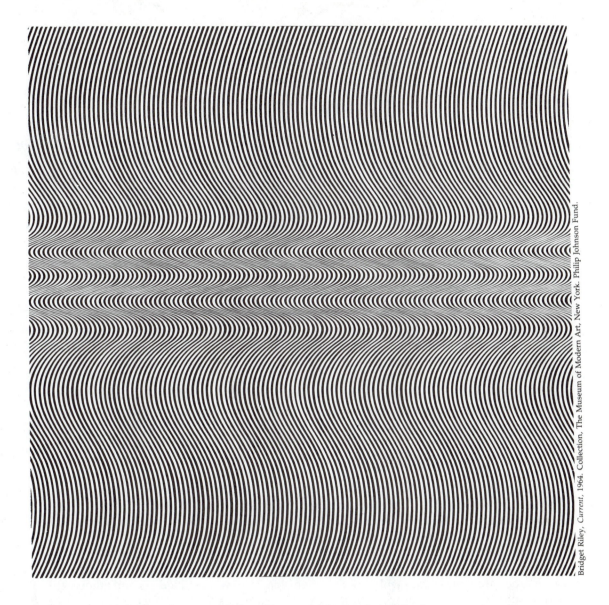

Bridget Riley, *Current*, 1964. Collection, The Museum of Modern Art, New York. Philip Johnson Fund.

instance, converts electricity into light. (You and I know that *light* does not run through the cord which is plugged into the wall outlet, but a primitive tribesman might arrive at the belief—with excellent reason— that if he cut the cord, light would spill out.)

In our technological world we are surrounded by transducers. A hotplate changes electrical energy into heat, but eggbeaters, blenders, and power-mowers convert that same electrical energy into mechanical motion. Conversely, heat is used in nuclear power plants to produce electricity. Geiger counters convert radiation into sound—audible warning clicks. Tape recorders convert air waves into electrical impulses which are converted into magnetic lines of force which are stored in the oxides on the tape. Batteries change chemical energy into electrical energy, and solar cells convert light into electrical energy. An

A philosopher riding through the countryside on a train once leaned over to peer long and hard out the window. When asked what he saw, he replied that he was looking at a half of twenty sheep, and that he was wondering how he could find out about the other half.

An uneducated child and a trained astronomer, both relying on the naked eye and their twenty-twenty vision, will literally *see* a different sky.

HERMAN TENNESSEN

David Hume
The Scottish Skeptic

A typical Scot in all but his philosophy, David Hume was born and raised on the family estate of Ninewells near Edinburgh. His father died when David was but a year old, so his mother, a woman of force and conviction, brought him up in the rigid Calvinism of the Scotch Presbyterian Church. Four hours of church services each Sunday, plus morning prayers and table grace.

Hume entered the University of Edinburgh at twelve, but dropped out three years later without getting a degree. At about sixteen, on his own, he plunged headlong into philosophy and literature and read voraciously. He confides in us: "I found a certain boldness of temper growing in me, which was not inclined to submit to any authority in these subjects." He was in love with learning, but he loved too seriously, became saturated, and suffered a mild breakdown at nineteen.

Wisely, he attempted to change his lifestyle, first by getting a job in business, then by avoiding his books for a while and traveling. But he could not stay away very long. In 1734 we find him hard at work again in the library of the Jesuit College of La Flèche in France. After three years of intense labor he completed his first masterpiece, *A Treatise of Human Nature*

(he is 26). He returns to England with his manuscripts, confident and excited. His publisher, however, insists that numerous "offensive" passages (one on miracles, for instance) be excised before he will print it, so two years pass before it is published. When finally it is published, Hume is nonplussed by the public response—or lack of it. He complains that "never literary attempt was more unfortunate than my Treatise of Human Nature. It fell dead-born from the press, without reaching such distinction as even to excite a murmur among the zealots."

As the years pass brilliant works flowed from his pen, and everywhere he offended the offensible. He was vilified as an atheist (he wasn't) and attacked by clerics for casting doubt on immortality (which he did). His analysis of causality and induction raised the wrath of scientists and rationalists. His multi-volume *History of England* irritated all political parties. For unpopular opinions and "shocking ideas" he was twice denied professorships at Edinburgh.

Hume calmly went his own way through all this, friendly to everyone, tolerant of opinions that differed with his. His open mind saw much. He possessed a keen sensitivity to hypocrisy, paradox and irony; he had a sense of the ridiculous in human affairs. But all his insights were tempered with gentleness, humor, and cheerful optimism.

By 1750 Hume was famous, much admired, even loved by a few who could love; he was fêted in salons, visited by celebrities, wined by kings. He loved Paris. His versatile intellect was more at home in the atmosphere of the Enlightenment than in an England that took itself too seriously or a Scotland where a Calvin *redivivus* still longed to light fires under heretics like Hume. Yet even in his home in Edinburgh, he lived happily within his circle of loyal friends.

When a friend scolded Hume for not being the gentle spirit he once was, Hume corrected him: "I am still a mild and temperate man. A sober, discreet, virtuous, frugal, regular, quiet, good-natured man with a bad character."

In the spring of 1775 Hume's health quickly failed. With calm spirit and clear mind he wrote an eight-page autobiography, *My Own Life*. Death came on August 25, 1776.

"He was an atheist," someone remarked at his funeral.

"No matter," another replied. "He was an honest man."

In the Western philosophic tradition Hume is considered a staunch empiricist. He believed that all dependable human knowledge must be derived from, and be verified by, sense perception. Our best reasoning is worthless if one is working from personal beliefs or fashionable ideas that can't be traced to empirical experience.

It doesn't follow from our dependence upon sense perception that our observations give us an accurate knowledge of reality. Far from it: a knowledge of metaphysical essences — things-as-they-really-are — forever eludes us. Using the raw data of sense perception, our minds go their merry way, constructing impressions and ideas that we are likely to accept as pictures of real objects/events; but we are deceived, for, in the final analysis, we possess nothing more than subjective notions.

Hume's criticism focuses on a concept that we daily take for granted: the idea of causality. We just assume that the "principle of causality" governs the universe. Every cause has an effect and every effect a cause, and we rest content that we "understand" events if we know their cause(s); they have been "explained" to our satisfaction.

Event-B is caused by event-A. He broke his leg *because* he was careless. The trees are budding *because* it's spring. The bacon burned *because* it was overcooked. The plane crashed *because* it struck a power-line. His temperature is 101° *because* he is sick. The phone is ringing *because* someone is calling. In every case we would feel that we *understood why* event-B took place; we accept event-A as "the explanation."

Hume asks us to take a second look at what we actually observe. What we find, he says, is that A and B are closely associated in our minds; wherever we have found B we generally found A, and vice versa. We also associate A and B together within a mentally acceptable time frame in which A always precedes B. Now, this is all that we observe. What we don't see is causality. This idea of causality is a creation of the mind based on nothing more than the habit of associating A and B.

Furthermore, the habit of association can become so strong that we come to believe that event-A and event-B are necessarily connected, that A *must* be followed by B. Heating water to 212° causes it to boil—necessarily? Toss a rock into the air and gravity causes it to fall—necessarily? Hume contends there are no grounds for the idea of necessity. On the contrary, because we made an A-B association in the past gives us no rational grounds for assuming any necessary A-B association in the future. Moreover, for most causal sequences, we commonly observe A *not* followed by B, and B *not* preceded by A; so there is no necessary relationship between the two events. The engine started *because* I turned the key in the ignition. But: I turn the key in the ignition and the engine *must* start? Not at all.

Thus, Hume concludes that no event in the world can be shown to be necessarily connected to any other event—a conclusion quite the opposite of our assumptions about daily experience, and one with implications for everything from research on the causes of cancer to the equations of physics (Natural Law), to our religious doctrines.

Consider the following statements: He recovered because Lord Buddha had compassion upon him. The eclipse took place because Kali made it happen. The flood occurred because Zeus was angry. He died because God willed it.

Such statements are empirically meaningless because the causal event-A can't be observed at all. What we have is a series of B-events without any observable A-events. We may well continue to accept the statements, however, because they take a causal form that appears acceptable. Because of this familiar form alone, they may satisfy.

"In thus locating the necessity of causal connectedness in the mental process itself, rather than in the external objects, Hume . . . has brought to modern philosophy a fundamental shift in perspective. In preference to speculating about the objective laws of the universe, he has analyzed the subjective laws of mental behavior. . . .

". . . Hume himself was the first to admit that his philosophical experiment left the validity of scientific method in doubt, the pervasive unity of our experience unexplained, and the existence and nature of a coherent self or personality unaccounted for. He insisted again and again that he was no happier with these results than were his critics. Nevertheless, he preferred a humble confession of ignorance to the dogmatic pretensions of some of his opponents—a cautious empiricism to a fallacy-ridden rationalism" (Philip Wheelwright, *Five Philosophers*, pages 104ff.).

David Hume

---

electroencephalograph converts brain waves (electrical) into squiggly lines on paper or dancing curves on an oscilloscope. Finally, there is chlorophyll, one of nature's grand transducers, which converts light into chemicals used in living processes.

And then there are fireflies, who spend a large percentage of their waking time (our sleeping time) converting biochemical energy into light.

In trying to distinguish appearance from reality and lay bare the fundamental structure of the universe, science has had to transcend the "rabble of the senses."

LINCOLN BARNETT

3   A transducer, then, converts *one kind of energy* into a *different kind of energy*.

Each of our senses is a living transducer. So our question becomes: What kind of energy goes into the sense/transducer, and what kind of energy comes out? Or, to put it differently: (1) What is the energy input? (2) What is the energy output? and (3) How does the sense-converter do it?

If we can answer these questions, we can discover what actually is taking place along that boundary-surface which constitutes our interface with reality.

Let's answer question (2) immediately and return to the others later. From all our known senses, the output is the same: it is electrochemical energy which propagates along the neural pathways. So far as we know at present, the impulses which leave our senses and move toward the central nervous system and into the brain are in every case the same. What then makes the difference in our experience if the impulses are all the same? Only the location in the brain to which the message-impulses are carried. Visual sensors, for example, send impulses to the back tip of the occipital lobe; sound sensors send their messages to another area of the brain located on the top inner fold of the temporal lobe; and so on, for every sense we have. Each sensory area of the cortex "knows how" to convert the electrochemical impulses into the "right" experiences.

Now, what if we should "get our wires crossed"? That is, what if we should have nerve fibers ending in the wrong area of the brain? If that should happen, the brain would *misinterpret* the impulses. If touch receptors sent their messages to the "cold center" in the cortex, the lightest touch would be felt as a cold sensation. In one laboratory experiment, scientists crossed the nerve fibers of the right and left rear feet of a white rat; when the pain sensors in the right foot were stimulated, the rat would jerk away the left foot, and vice versa.

If the nerve fibers from our eyes could be crossed with the nerve fibers from our ears, then undoubtedly we would "hear" colors and "see" sounds.

4   It is apparent that the gathering of information by our senses is a complex process, with many a possible slip twixt the energy input and the final experience. To clarify the problem, let's use one sense as an analogue.

A round, contented, bright yellow grapefruit lies in the fruit bowl on the table. Now, no matter how hard you try, it is a fact that you can never see the grapefruit—or touch, smell, or taste it.

What you *see*, of course, are light quanta which strike the grapefruit and are reflected back to your eyes. "White" light (that is, light of all wavelengths together) from some source such as the sun or a lightbulb strikes the surface of the grapefruit which, because of the molecular structure of its surface material, absorbs all the wavelengths of the spectrum *except* the "yellow" wavelengths (in the vicinity of 5600 to 5800 angstrom units), which are reflected back and reach your eyes. So, what do we *see*? Only the reflected light from the object, never the object itself.

5   Now, what are "light waves"? The best we can say is that they are electromagnetic waves of different lengths which travel at a speed of about 186,000 miles per second. *The waves themselves are colorless*, but the cones embedded in the retinas of our eyes are stimulated by the various wavelengths of radiation and send impulses to the visual centers of the cortex, *where they are interpreted as colors*. Human retinas possess three kinds of cones, which are sensitive, respectively, to three

It's funny how the colors of the real world only seem really real when you viddy them on the screen.

ALEX
A Clockwork Orange

These sensory limitations, and the resulting failure to comprehend fully much of Nature, may be only a local deficiency. On the basis of the new estimates of the great abundance of stars and the high probability of millions of planets with highly developed life, we are made aware—embarrassingly aware—that we may be intellectual minims in the life of the universe. I could develop further this uncomfortable idea by pointing out that sense receptors, in quality quite unknown to us and in fact hardly imaginable, which record phenomena of which we are totally ignorant, may easily exist among the higher sentient organisms of other planets.

HARLOW SHAPLEY

basic wavelengths, the wavelengths we interpret as red, blue, and green—the three primary colors for light (notice the three colors of phosphor dots on a color TV screen).°

THE MIND MANUFACTURES EXPERIENCE

6   From these facts, two conclusions must be drawn which are of great significance for understanding the nature of our knowledge.

(1) *Color is an experience in our minds*. It is the experiential finale to a long and complicated process of transduction. The energy input to our visual transducers is uncolored electromagnetic radiation which enters our eyes with wavelengths (in the visual spectrum) of about 3800 to 7200 angstroms. Our transducer/cones identify the various wavelengths and send electrical messages along the neural pathways to the visual center of the brain. There and then *only* we see color.

(2) A corollary: *There is no color whatever in the external world of things*. Look around you. That grapefruit only *appears* to be yellow. All the colors you "see"—however beautiful, enchanting, stimulating they seem to you—are only experiences in your mind. The ocean is not deep blue, the pine forest is not green, and the aurora borealis does not scintillate with cosmic colors.

And there is no color in the rainbow.

7   This transduction pattern holds true for all our senses, and for all possible senses which we can imagine.

Sound.   Once there was a famous tree in a forest, a tree that decided to fall when no one was around. It did its very best to make a noise; it wanted to be heard. But it went down to defeat. It did indeed set up quite a vigorous series of waves in the summer air, waves that alternately rarefied and compressed the air as they moved outward. But there was no sound in the land.°

Taste.   Chemical substances penetrate the surface cells of our tastebuds, which apparently respond to only four basic "tastes": sweet, sour, salty, and bitter. All the flavors of our gastronomic spectrum are merely combinations of these four. But note: there is no taste to the chemical substances; they are only molecular structures. There is no "sweetness" in the peppermint candy, no "saltiness" in the sodium chloride, and no "sourness" in a lemon.

Smell.   Gaseous molecules permeate the linings of the olfactory membranes in the upper nasal passageway. Precisely how the molecules manage to stimulate such a variety of "odor messages" is not understood, but our conclusion is again clear: there is no scent in the rose nor salty odors from the spray of the breakers on the beach. All the sweet fragrances of Samarkand are merely experiences in the mind.

°*Textbooks in the physical sciences occasionally define certain wavelengths with a certain color. This is an expediency for the sake of simplicity, but it is a conceptual fallacy. Modern physical theory consistently shows that physical entities—atoms, molecules, electromagnetic waves, etc.—cannot possess the qualities which we experience.*

Things which we see are not by themselves what we see. . . . It remains completely unknown to us what the objects may be by themselves and apart from the receptivity of our senses. We know nothing but our manner of perceiving them. . . .

IMMANUEL KANT

°*It is reported that a chipmunk, sunning on a rock at the top of the hill, had his transducers going, and that he heard the sound of a crash in the valley below. One transducer can make all the difference between sound and eternal silence.*

It is impossible to explain . . . qualities of matter except by tracing these back to the behavior of entities which themselves no longer possess these qualities. If atoms are really to explain the origin of color and smell of visible material bodies, then they cannot possess properties like color and smell. . . . Atomic theory consistently denies the atom any such perceptible qualities.

WERNER HEISENBERG

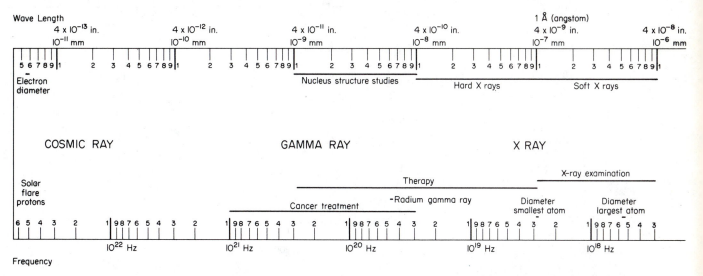

Wave Length

| 4 x 10⁻¹³ in. | 4 x 10⁻¹² in. | 4 x 10⁻¹¹ in. | 4 x 10⁻¹⁰ in. | 1 Å (angstom) | 4 x 10⁻⁸ in. |

COSMIC RAY   GAMMA RAY   X RAY

Nucleus structure studies · Hard X rays · Soft X rays

Electron diameter

X-ray examination

Therapy

Solar flare protons   Cancer treatment   Radium gamma ray   Diameter smallest atom   Diameter largest atom

Frequency

Touch. Whether the stimulus is pressure or pain, heat or cold, the only things we "know" are the *experiences* which occur in various areas of the cerebral cortex. But this is probably the sense which we most readily believe. After all, who ever claimed that "pain" was located in the red-hot coal?

In a word, before the development of sentient creatures on the planet Earth, there were no colors, no sounds, no odors. There were no experiences because there were no experiencers.

OUR SENSES DECEIVE US

8   As a result of such analysis, we may have the uneasy feeling that we are being deceived. We are being led, by our own senses, into believing things which are untrue. The grapefruit may not be yellow, but it surely *looks* yellow; it seems undeniable that the yellowness is in the rind of the fruit itself. Likewise, we would be willing to wager that the sweetness is in the peppermint candy and that the sound of a tree falling came from the bottom of the hill. These are only appearances, however. They are indeed "deceptions."

Furthermore, our *language* is a part of the conspiracy. For I look at the grapefruit and say, "The grapefruit is yellow." The subject of my statement is the noun "grapefruit" and the adjective "yellow" modifies the noun; and the "is" clearly attaches the quality of yellowness to the subject "grapefruit."

It is to be expected that our language would reflect the deception of our senses. Language crystallizes the deception, as it were, and reflects it back to us, reinforcing our belief that the quality yellow does in fact belong to the object.

9   To say that we are being "deceived" seems like a suspicious way of looking at it. After all, none of our senses "intend" to deceive us.

For the sceptic to bewail the fact that we can know nothing but appearance is as silly as it would be to bewail the fact that we have nothing to wear but clothes and nothing to eat but food.

W. P. MONTAGUE

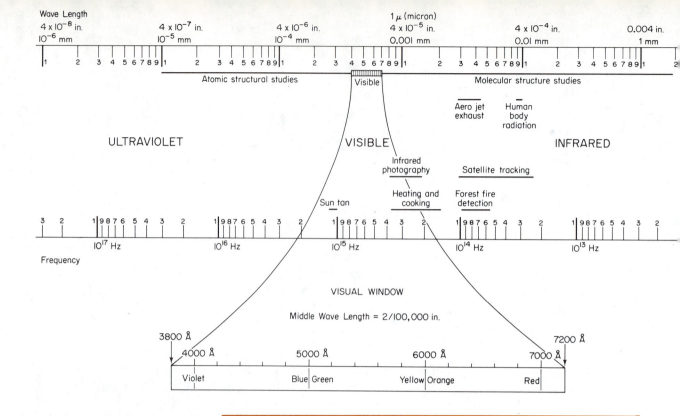

Wave Length

4 x 10⁻⁸ in.	4 x 10⁻⁷ in.	4 x 10⁻⁶ in.	1 μ (micron) 4 x 10⁻⁵ in.	4 x 10⁻⁴ in.	0.004 in.
10⁻⁶ mm	10⁻⁵ mm	10⁻⁴ mm	0.001 mm	0.01 mm	1 mm

Atomic structural studies — Visible — Molecular structure studies

ULTRAVIOLET   VISIBLE   INFRARED

Aero jet exhaust   Human body radiation

Infrared photography   Satellite tracking

Sun tan   Heating and cooking   Forest fire detection

10¹⁷ Hz   10¹⁶ Hz   10¹⁵ Hz   10¹⁴ Hz   10¹³ Hz

Frequency

VISUAL WINDOW

Middle Wave Length = 2/100,000 in.

3800 Å   7200 Å

4000 Å   5000 Å   6000 Å   7000 Å

Violet   Blue | Green   Yellow | Orange   Red

Man is thus his own greatest mystery. He does not understand the vast veiled universe into which he has been cast for the reason that he does not understand himself. He comprehends but little of his organic processes and even less of his unique capacity to perceive the world about him, to reason and to dream. Least of all does he understand his noblest and most mysterious faculty: the ability to transcend himself and perceive himself in the act of perception.

LINCOLN BARNETT

WINDOWS ONTO THE UNIVERSE

A continuous frequency spectrum including both sonic and electromagnetic wavelengths is plotted here on a logarithmic scale. Placed together, the frequency ranges from 6×10^{22} Hz to 5×10^{-4} Hz. This is a range in wavelength from the diameter of an electron to a wave almost two hundred million miles long. Near the long end of the spectrum the "world resonance" (like the vibration of a giant bell) is a single cycle lasting about 20 seconds.

If this frequency spectrum represents two kinds of reality—sonic and electromagnetic—then we have two "windows" open to us onto the universe.

One is the audio window which, with our natural sense, is limited to a range of 20 to 20,000 Hz. The other is the visual window in the electromagnetic spectrum, a very small window ranging from about 3800 to 7200 Å. These windows set the limits to what we can hear and see in the real world.

All the other sonic and electromagnetic realities are there, moving about us; but we are deaf and blind to them, and they are meaningless to us.

When were these windows opened to us? Shall we say, for the audio and visual windows, perhaps a billion years ago? Whenever sentient creatures first began to sense vibrations in the atmosphere and respond to light.

When were the other windows opened to us? Only during the last one hundred years. They were all flung open with breath-taking rapidity.

What reason is there to believe that all the realities have now been discovered, all the spectra plotted, and all the windows opened?

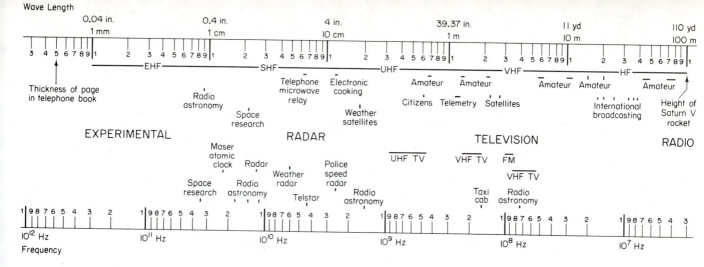

Perhaps the transduction process can be interpreted more positively. For the fact is that all our senses have developed in such a way that they can translate meaningless physical phenomena into meaningful experiences. To use an analogy, at this moment there are probably several television stations transmitting electromagnetic waves through the atmosphere where you are, but if your TV set is not turned on, the waves are meaningless. Turning your TV set on would convert useless phenomena into meaningful information.

This is precisely what our senses do: They turn on to the physical phenomena of the real world and render our environment meaningful. They translate the events going on around us into useful information.

They have given us the kind of information we need in order to survive. What more can we ask of them?

> Knowledge, if it be taken without the true corrective, hath in it some nature of venom or malignity.
>
> *FRANCIS BACON*

SENSORY LIMITATIONS AND THE REAL WORLD

10   Let's look once again at the drastic sensory limitations we operate under. The electromagnetic spectrum is a good example. If we arbitrarily divide the range of all electromagnetic waves into sixty "octaves," then visually we can perceive only a single octave, from about 3800 to 7200 angstrom units. But the waves extend away to great distances on either side of that visual octave.

Below the blue end of the visual spectrum the waves grow shorter into the ultraviolet rays, X-rays, and gamma rays. Above the red end of the spectrum the wavelengths grow longer into the infrared, the microwaves, short radio and long radio waves. We have developed instruments, of course, which are extensions of our senses and can reach out on either side of the visual octave.

Still, without the aid of our instruments, we are limited in per-

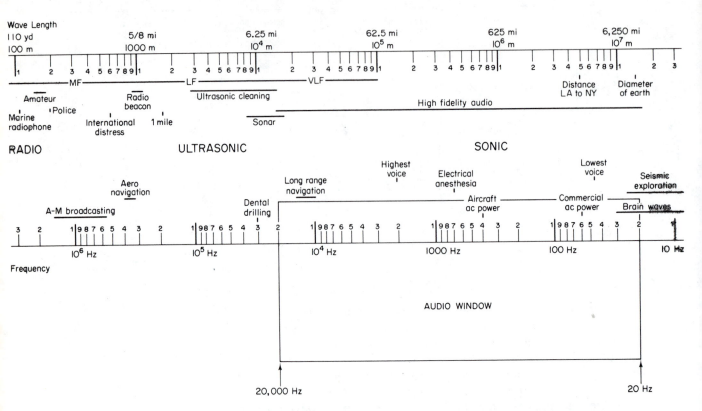

ception to that single octave. It is a bit unnerving to realize how little physical reality we perceive, and how much more there really is.

11   No creature ever has enough senses; it could always use more. Why, then, in the long course of evolution, did we not develop other senses? We believe the answer is fairly simple: given the time we had to evolve and the conditions our ancestors had to cope with, they developed the particular sensors needed most. But if other conditions had prevailed, our sense-systems would have been different in countless ways.

12   We share existence on our planet with millions of species of sentient creatures, many of which have senses we might well envy. (In fact, we do envy them, for we imitate every sense we possibly can with scientific instruments.)

Many animals, of course, possess the same senses we have, but they have intensified their sensitivity beyond our range of sensory pickup. Many animals can hear high-pitched sounds beyond our range. Bats emit high-pitched sounds and then listen to their echo to locate objects ("echolocation," the principle used in radar). Porpoises and fish have an underwater counterpart of the bat's "radar"—a "sonar" system. The "lateral-line" sense in fishes is what we might think of as a combined touch-hear sense, for in the water these senses merge. Fishes living at great depths where no light can penetrate have developed hypersensitive lateral-lines; a preying fish can take a fix on its quarry and zero in with pinpoint accuracy.

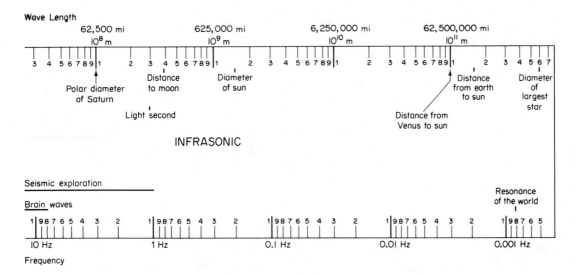

Ants and other insects have delicate chemical senses (combining touch, taste, and smell?) by which they communicate and establish food trails. Moths both smell and hear with their antennae. Bees navigate to their honey sources by reckoning the sun's position.

Then there are still other senses which remain mysteries. At this point we can only admire and wonder about them: the senses by which birds migrate (perhaps partly by star navigation), the "homing sense" of dogs and cats and many wild animals, the senses which enable the Sargasso eels to return to the St. Lawrence and European rivers which their ancestors knew, but which they themselves have never seen.

·And then there are fireflies. Hundreds of tiny sparks in the night: one wonders how they perceive their flashing world.

What a piece of bread looks like depends on whether you are hungry or not.

JALLALUDIN RUMI

LESS THAN A MILLIONTH

"There has been a complete changeover in human affairs. Where man has always been after *things,* after *reality*—reality being everything you can see, touch, taste, smell and hear—suddenly we're in a completely new kind of reality. The reality of the great electromagnetic spectrum which is part of this communications revolution. And we now know that what man can hear, smell, touch, taste and see is less than a millionth of reality."

BUCKMINSTER FULLER

COMPLAINT—

"Tell me," says Micromegas, an inhabitant of one of the planets of the Dog Star, to the secretary of the Academy of Sciences in the planet Saturn, at which he had recently arrived in a journey through the heavens—"Tell me, how many senses have the men on your globe?" . . .

"We have seventy-two senses," answered the academician, "and we are every day complaining of the smallness of the number. . . . "

"I can very well believe," says Micromegas, "for, in our globe, we have very near one thousand senses, and yet, with all these, we feel continually a sort of listless inquietude and vague desire, which are forever telling us that we are nothing, and that there are beings infinitely nearer perfection."

VOLTAIRE

EPISTEMIC LONELINESS

13   At about this point, a feeling of loneliness may begin to overtake us—an "epistemic loneliness." For the egocentric predicament is really an epistemological condition: isolation within a world of our own making. We live in a shell, so to speak, a private, personal shell inside which takes place an immense variety of experiences, *all ours.* And when we try to break out of our shells to make contact with the world and other creatures, we only rediscover the depth of our predicament. We live in an epistemological shell with no doors. None may enter and none may share.

Mankind's common instinct for reality . . . has always held the world to be essentially a theatre for heroism.

WILLIAM JAMES

14   Since certain aspects of our epistemological condition appear to be inescapable, we must learn to live with them.

(1) *The fallacy of objectification is an ever-present danger.* Our experiencing system conspires to make us think that a variety of private experiences are in some way real, that they are events occurring in the real world of objects/events. (The tragic consequences of this fallacy will be felt especially when we try to untangle our value-experiences.)

(2) *Accordingly, we have all lived (unwittingly) in a state of confusion regarding the location of the occurrence of events.* Our subjective and objective worlds are interwoven: events we thought to be private may turn out to be objective, while many supposedly objective events often prove to be experiences only.

(3) *We are restless with our evolutionary limitations and deceptions.* While we can be grateful that our sensory and information-processing systems have rendered our physical environment meaningful, we have reached a point in our quest for reality when we want to go beyond our limitations and to know what the world is really like. We want to

"*The topic for today is: What is reality?*"

By Henry Martin, from *Saturday Review,* May 29, 1971. Copyright © 1971. Reprinted by permission of *Saturday Review* and Henry Martin.

make whatever corrections are necessary in our perception, so we can move out of our shells and come to know our universe and its principles of operation.

THE PRAGMATIC NATURE OF KNOWING

15   From this vantage point, the central problem of Western epistemology may be more intelligible. *If we know only our experiences, how can we be sure that we know anything about the real world?* More precisely, if objective physical phenomena are all converted *before we can experience them* into different kinds of energy, how can we know anything about the original phenomena? Can we ever know what those phenomena are?

If we experience only the subjective side of our interface with reality, can we ever know anything about the objective side of that interface-boundary?

16   In a moment of refreshing honesty, David Hume composed a confession which speaks for many great thinkers, from Socrates to the eighties, whose lifeblood is spent wrestling with abstract and unobservable entities, but who still possess the great gift of keeping their philosophical reflections in perspective. Hume wrote:

> Should it be asked me whether I sincerely assent to this argument which I have been to such pains to inculcate, and whether I be really one of those skeptics who hold that all is uncertain, . . . I should reply . . . that neither I nor any other person was ever sincerely and constantly of that opinion. . . . I dine, I play backgammon, I converse and am merry with my friends; and when, after three or four hours' amusement, I would return to these speculations, they appear so cold and strained and ridiculous that I cannot find in my heart to enter into them any further. . . . Thus the skeptic still continues to reason and believe, though he asserts that he cannot defend his reason by reason; and by the same rule he must assent to the principle concerning the existence of body, though he cannot pretend, by any arguments of philosophy, to maintain its veracity.

17   Let's take seriously what David Hume implies in this moment of truth. Here is our Scottish skeptic whose reason tells him one set of facts (we know nothing certain of the real world), but whose experience seems to contradict his reason (''I dine, I play backgammon, I converse. . . .''). When such conflict exists between theory and experience, then a solution must be sought. (Remember that infamous bumblebee which, according to aerodynamics, can't fly—but does?)

What Hume implies is: (1) it is very impracticable *not* to assume that the real world exists, and (2) day-to-day living is very difficult if one tries to operate on the assumption that he knows *nothing* about the real world.

We can never arrive at the real nature of things from the outside. However much we investigate, we can never reach anything but images and names. We are like a man who goes round a castle seeking in vain for an entrance and sometimes sketching the façades.

SCHOPENHAUER

"George, it's impossible to correct a defective reality-orientation overnight."

URSULA K. LEGUIN
The Lathe of Heaven

Occasionally an epistemolog is found who is capable of smiling, like Bradley or William James; occasionally one is found who understands that his 'ology is only a game, and, therefore, plays it with a worldly twinkle in his eye, like David Hume.

WILL DURANT

There are few philosophers of the modern world who would *not* question, to some extent, the conclusions of Berkeley and Hume. After more than two centuries of debate, we now have adequate reason *to assume* (1) that the real world exists and (2) that we have at least a working knowledge of that world. It is the *nature* of that working knowledge which is still cause for concern.

Truth is a property of beliefs, and derivatively of sentences which express beliefs.

BERTRAND RUSSELL

18   If these conclusions are comforting, our philosophers have made three points which may seem less so. The following arguments seem basically sound and still stand today as starting points for an understanding of the nature of knowledge.

(1) We know only our subjective experience, which begins with sensory reaction and ends with the fabrication of knowledge. This appears to be an inescapable limitation.

(2) Accordingly, we cannot experience directly the real world of objects/events. Neither matter nor the principles of motion are directly perceivable.

(3) Our knowledge of the real world consists solely, therefore, of inferences which we make on the basis of our experience.

**The disputants I ween
Rail on in utter ignorance
Of what each other mean,
And prate about an Elephant
Not one of them has seen.**

JOHN G. SAXE

19   In summary, what is the nature of our knowledge about the real world of objects/events?

Our knowledge of reality is composed of ideas our minds have *created* on the basis of our sensory experience. It is a fabric of knowledge woven by the mind. Knowledge is not given to the mind; nothing is "poured" into it. Rather, the mind manufactures perceptions, concepts, ideas, beliefs, etc., and holds them as *working hypotheses* about external reality. Every idea is a (subjective) working model which enables us to handle real objects/events with some degree of efficiency.

But ideas in our heads are not realities; they are but tools which enable us to deal with reality.

It is as though we drew nondimensional maps to help us understand four-dimensional territory. The semanticists have long reminded us to beware about confusing any sort of map with the real landscape. "The map is not the territory."

Dr. Willard Geer, the inventor of the three-gun color television picture-tube, had an accident in the kitchen of his home in June, 1930, while blowing glass for an experiment in physics. The glass shattered and a splinter embedded itself in his right eye. The injury altered his perception. Dr. Geer can now see, with that eye, a considerable way into the ultraviolet range of the spectrum. When asked to describe what he sees, he cannot. He only replies, "I just see things occasionally which other people can't."

REFLECTIONS—

1 Note the anecdote of the philosopher who "was looking at a half of twenty sheep" (p. 165–QM). Everybody knows that a half of 20 is 10, so what's his problem? How would you suggest that he go about finding a solution?

2 Gaze at, then reflect upon, the painting on p. 165—*Current* by Bridget Riley. (1) What do you see? How much of what you "see" is on the page? (2) How much of what you see is brought to the seeing by your perceptual system? (3) Do you see motion? Are you sure there is no motion on the page itself? If you say yes, then how can you be sure?

3 "Each of our senses is a living transducer" (Sec. 3). What is meant by this? What are the epistemological implications of our realizing that our senses are in fact transducers?

4 Secs. 6 and 7 make a single point: Numerous phenomena which appear to be a part of the real world turn out to be experiences only and have no real status. Do you personally have any trouble accepting these fact-claims as true? Why?

5 What is meant by "the conspiracy of language"? What causes this deception? Give some examples of how we are thus deceived by our language.

6 From this point on it is imperative that you understand the philosophic usage of the terms *real* and *reality*. (See glossary.) Which of the following events would be real and which would be solely experiential? (Be wary: Definitions are crucial, and in some cases it is not an either/or decision.)

an idea	Mr. Spock (of *Star Trek*)
a feeling of loneliness	the state of Arizona
an itch	the state of euphoria
your car	the sound of music
an atom	the Pythagorean
a toothache (in your	Theorem (see p. 420)
wisdom tooth)	Pythagoras
a heartache	the office of the president of
a beautiful painting	the United States
a dirty picture	the president of the
a poem	United States
a mirage	the state
the planet Mars	a sunset
the god Mars	

7 After studying the human "visual window" through which we see reality, how would you describe the real world to: (1) a person who has been blind from birth? (2) a highly intelligent alien from another planet who "sees" wavelengths only in the infrared region of the electromagnetic spectrum? (3) a fellow epistemologist who is acutely aware, as you are, of our severe human perceptual limitations?

8 This chapter speaks of "epistemic loneliness." Are these words meaningful to you? Can you feel this condition personally or does it not apply to you?

9 Review Secs. 16 and 17, read Sec. 14 on pp. 176f., and then reflect: Does it trouble you that the more we know about the "realities beyond appear-

ances" the farther we are moving away from the world of everyday experience? Does this imply that our experiential world is, in some fundamental way, suspect, invalid, erroneous, and/or worthless? Yes or no—and why?

10 In the final analysis, what do we "know" about the real world and how do we know it?

Furthermore . . .

ARNER, DOUGLAS G. (ed.), *Perception, Reason, and Knowledge: An Introduction to Epistemology.* Scott, Foresman, 1972.

CHAPPELL, V. C. (ed), *Hume: A Collection of Critical Essays.* University of Notre Dame Press, 1968.

The Empiricists. Doubleday, ND. (Readings from major works of Locke, Berkeley, and Hume.)

JONES, W. T., *A History of Western Philosophy,* 2nd ed. Harcourt, 1969. (See Vol. III, Locke, Berkeley, and Hume.)

MARTIN, C. B., and D. M. ARMSTRONG (eds.), *Locke and Berkeley: A Collection of Critical Essays.* University of Notre Dame Press, 1968.

MUELLER, CONRAD G., and MAE RUDOLPH, et al., *Light and Vision.* Life Science Library. Time Inc., 1966.

Perception: Mechanisms and Models. Readings from *Scientific American.* W. H. Freeman, 1972.

RUSSELL, BERTRAND, *Our Knowledge of the External World.* Mentor, 1960.

RUSSELL, BERTRAND, *The Analysis of Matter.* Dover, 1954.

STEINKRAUS, WARREN E. (ed.), *New Studies in Berkeley's Philosophy.* Holt, Rinehart and Winston, 1966.

STEVENS, S.S., and FRED WARSHOFSKY, et al., *Sound and Hearing.* Life Science Library. Time Inc., 1967.

SWARTZ, ROBERT J. (ed.), *Perceiving, Sensing, and Knowing: A Book of Readings from Twentieth-Century Sources in the Philosophy of Perception.* Anchor, 1965.

WEINBERG, JULIUS R., and KEITH E. YANDELL, *Theory of Knowledge.* Holt, Rinehart and Winston, 1971.

Data Processing

Have You Ever Wondered . . .

- What an idea is?

- What God's real name is?

- Whether a pig is a pig because we say it's a pig or because it really is a pig?

- Whether a Buddhist could also be a Baptist?

- Whether a Christian could also be a Democrat?

- Whether an animal could also be a plant?

- Whether only you exist?

- Whether Shakespeare was right when he made Hamlet say, "There are more things in heaven and earth, Horatio, than are dreamt of in your philosophy"?

THE PRAGMATIC MIND

1   In its attempt to make sense of the energy-environment in which we live, the mind proves to be a versatile, creative instrument. It translates events of the real world into experiences we can use in living. The mind is not at all the "blank tablet," the *tabula rasa*, which some earlier thinkers thought it to be.

We have a fairly clear understanding now of the general nature of knowledge. Human knowledge is a collection of constructs created by the mind from the raw materials of sensation; it is a series of scaled-down maps which we use to find our way in the full-scale territory of the real world.

Concepts without percepts are empty. Percepts without concepts are blind.

IMMANUEL KANT

WHY WE THINK IN ABSTRACTIONS

2   One of the basic functions of the human mind is to create *abstractions*.

What if we had to have a separate name for every object we ever knew: for each candle, coin, animal, bell, seashell, cloud, and penguin? And a separate word for every single event we ever experienced: the strumming of a guitar, the meteor trail through the sky, the smell of a summer rain? If we were forced to have a different symbol for each object and each event, clearly we would be in trouble. In no time we would run out of words and our minds could not handle the clutter of separate items.

What do we do then? We place such singular items in groups. All the objects/events which have common qualities we group together into a single package with a single label. Once we have so packaged them, we no longer have to deal with the individual objects; we deal only with the whole package.

This is why we create abstractions. Abstractions *are* packages.

3   An abstraction, by definition, is an idea created by the mind to refer to all objects which, possessing certain characteristics in common, are thought of in the same class. The number of objects in the class can range from two to infinity. We can refer to *all* men, *all* hurricanes, *all* books, *all* energy-forms . . . *all* everything.

Abstractions are formed at various levels of generalization. For instance, if we begin with an orange—a particular object as yet unclassified and unlabeled—then the first level of abstraction might be "Valencia orange," grouping together the qualities shared by all Valencia oranges. A next level might include all oranges (Valencia, the navels, sour oranges, etc.); next might come all "citrus fruit" (including oranges, grapefruit, lemons, kumquats, etc.). Still higher would come the whole basket of fruit (citrus fruit, figs, apples, apricots, breadfruit, etc.). Above this level we might class together all "edible things," and more general still, a very-high-level abstraction, "material objects."

Notice how far we have come in the breadth of generalization: from a single orange to an all-inclusive class labeled "material objects." At each higher level of abstraction the objects have less and less in common. Yet such broad, general abstractions dominate our thinking and communicating. We think of fruits and vegetables, or food; we class together medicines, drugs, pollutants; we speak of nations, races of people, Hindus, Easterners, Eskimos, and so on.

While abstraction-building is an inescapable mental process—in fact it is the first step in the organization of our knowledge of objects/events—a serious problem is inherent in the process. At high levels of abstraction we tend to group together objects which have but a few qualities in common, and our abstractions may be almost meaningless, without our knowing it. We fall into the habit of using familiar abstractions and fail to realize how empty they are. For example, what do the

Probably a crab would be filled with a sense of personal outrage if it could hear us class it without ado or apology as a crustacean, and thus dispose of it. "I am no such thing," it would say; "I am *myself, myself* alone."

WILLIAM JAMES

Jean Piaget tells of a little girl who was asked whether one might call the sun the moon and the moon the sun. She explained impatiently that no one could confuse the sun and the moon because the sun shines so brightly.

objects in the following abstractions have in common? All atheists, all Western imperialists, all blacks or all whites (and if you think it's skin color, think twice), all conservatives, all trees, all Frenchmen, all Christians. When we think with such high-level abstractions, it is often the case that we are communicating nothing meaningful at all.

CLASSIFYING AND LABELING

4 The mind has another technique to enable it to assimilate information. *It classifies abstractions and labels them.* This is our mental filing system.

In *Language in Thought and Action*, Dr. S. I. Hayakawa imagines a primitive village—your village—in which a variety of animals scamper about. Some of the animals have small bodies, some large. Some have round heads, while others have square heads. Some have curly tails, others straight tails. And such distinguishing marks are very important.

S. I. Hayakawa

CREDIBILITY GAP?

As a conscious being I am involved in a story. The perceiving part of my mind tells me a story of a world around me. The story tells of familiar objects. It tells of colours, sounds, scents belonging to these objects; of boundless space in which they have their existence, and of an ever-rolling stream of time bringing change and incident. It tells of other life than mine busy about its own purposes.

As a scientist I have become mistrustful of this story. In many instances it has become clear that things are not what they seem to be. According to the story teller I have now in front of me a substantial desk; but I have learned from physics that the desk is not at all the continuous substance that it is supposed to be in the story. It is a host of tiny electric charges darting hither and thither with inconceivable velocity. Instead of being solid substance my desk is more like a swarm of gnats.

So I have come to realise that I must not put overmuch confidence in the story teller who lives in my mind.

SIR ARTHUR EDDINGTON
New Pathways in Science

THE RABBLE OF THE SENSES

In trying to distinguish appearance from reality and lay bare the fundamental structure of the universe, science has had to transcend the "rabble of the senses." But its highest edifices, Einstein has pointed out, have been "purchased at the price of emptiness of content." A theoretical concept is emptied of content to the very degree that it is divorced from sensory experience. For the only world man can truly know is the world created for him by his senses. If he expunges all the impressions which they translate and memory stores, nothing is left. That is what the philosopher Hegel meant by his cryptic remark: "Pure Being and Nothing are the same." A state of existence devoid of associations has no meaning. So paradoxically what the scientist and the philosopher call the world of appearance—the world of light and color, of blue skies and green leaves, of sighing wind and murmuring water, the world designed by the physiology of human sense organs—is the world in which finite man is incarcerated by his essential nature. And what the scientist and the philosopher call the world of reality—the colorless, soundless, impalpable cosmos which lies like an iceberg beneath the place of man's perceptions—is a skeleton structure of symbols.

LINCOLN BARNETT
The Universe and Dr. Einstein

For you have discovered through experience that the animals with small bodies eat your grain, while those with large bodies don't. The small-bodied animals you have labeled "gogo" and you shoo them away; and when you call to a neighbor, "Quick, chase the gogo out of your garden!" he knows what you mean. The large-bodied animals (labeled "gigi") are harmless, so you allow them to wander where they will.

However, a visitor from another village has had a different experience. He has found that animals with square heads bite, while those with round heads don't. Since he has no gardens, their biting is a more noticeable characteristic than their habit of eating grain. The square-heads that bite he calls "daba" and he scares them away. He generally ignores the round-headed "dobos."

Still another man, a relative from a distant village, has found that the animals with curly tails kill snakes. Such animals are valuable; he calls them "busa" and breeds them for protection. But those with straight tails (which he calls "busana") are merely a nuisance, and he's quite indifferent to them.

Now, one day villagers from far and near meet to trade and talk. You are sitting in on a barter-session when one of the animals runs by (let's say the animal marked "C" in the diagram below). You spot the animal headed for your garden, so you call down the path for someone to chase the "gogo" away. A visitor, however, looks at you with disdain, for he knows that the animal is a "dobo." It has a round head. It doesn't bite, and he is surprised that you don't know this. A third visitor scornfully tells the both of you that the animal is clearly a "busana," as everyone knows; it doesn't kill snakes or have any other redeeming qualities.

A heated discussion ensues as to what the animal really is. Is it a "gogo," a "dobo," or a "busana"? A quarrel is brewing as to what the animal *really is*.

It hardly helps when another tribesman, asking what the talk is all about, declares with finality that the animal (still "C") is a "mug-lock" because it is edible and they feast on it every full moon. All the inedible animals in his village he labels "uglocks".

This discussion finally ends where all such discussions finally end.

5   What is the animal *really*? What is *any* object, *really*? In the last analysis, all one can do is point to the object as if to say, "It is what it

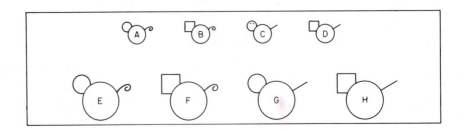

Observers are not led by the same physical evidence to the same picture of the universe unless their linguistic backgrounds are similar or can in some way be calibrated.

BENJAMIN LEE WHORF

is." As Hayakawa puts it, "The individual object or event we are naming, of course, has no name and belongs to no class until we put it in one."

All the objects/events of our experience are classified in this manner: in terms of our experience of them. In the English language, for instance, we have two words that originated in the Middle Ages for the animal *Sus scrofa*. The word "swine" was the term used by the serfs and swineherds who had to tend them; the word "pork" was always employed by those who ate their succulent flesh at the banquet table.

Systems of classification, therefore, are *reflexive*. They inform us about the person who is doing the classifying—they tell us about *his* experience—and they tell us relatively little or nothing about the object classified. Classification never tells us what the classified object *really is*.

Classification systems are *pragmatic*. They are guidelines for operation. They tell us how to think about the object, how to treat it, use it, or relate to it. We classify objects and utilize the classification as long as the system is convenient; the moment it ceases to work, then we reclassify.

6　An understanding of these thought-processes—namely, the nature of classifying and labeling—provides an excellent criterion for distinguishing epistemic naivety from epistemic awareness.

A prescientific thinker has the unshakable belief that his classification tells him what the object really is and that names are by nature attached to the objects they refer to. It was a universal assumption made by the primitive **mind** that there is an intimate and *necessary* connection between the **sym**bol and the object symbolized. Indeed, a mystical power resides in the symbol itself, and words are to be feared or desired in the same way the object/event referred to is to be feared or desired.

To attempt to persuade a primitive thinker that his classifications and labels are merely his mental tools, relative and arbitrary, would be a hopeless task. His own name is "Marika," he will inform you, and it could not be otherwise. His god's name is "Mbwenu" and the deity can be called upon only by using his "right name." And, as everyone knows, a horse is a "horse" and a man is a "man." How could it possibly be otherwise?

7　People are "objects" from the standpoint of classification. If we lived in a small community and knew only a few people, we might find it possible to give each a separate name and deal with him as a singular personality. Our thinking might remain relatively concrete.

But in our modern world where we contact millions of people (personally and via various media) the temptation to move at high-level abstractions is enormous. As stated earlier, we do this because it simplifies our handling of vast amounts of data (or people). The bigger the bundles the better.

Geological eras, periods, and epochs are human inventions; they are man's attempt to put huge stretches of time in their place and make them seem reasonably comprehensible. Nature was indifferent to such fine distinctions. Time flowed on continuously with one phase changing imperceptibly into another without dividing itself neatly into segments.

PHILIP VAN DOREN STERN

The human brain craves understanding. It cannot understand without simplifying, that is, without reducing things to a common element. However, all simplifications are arbitrary and lead us to drift insensibly away from reality.

LECOMTE DU NOÜY

"Everyone must have a label."

A big wild animal of the antelope family and known as the "Nehil Gae" was causing extensive damage to crops in the field. But the farmers would not harm it because "Nehil Gae" means "Blue Cow," and the cow is sacred to the Hindu. So the Indian Government has changed the name to "Nehil Goa"—which means "Blue Horse." Horses are not sacred, and so now the beast can be killed to protect the crops.

Associated Press

Therefore, we move very far from the individual person, just as we moved very far from the single orange we held in our hand. We package people into ever larger groups with fewer characteristics in common and refer to them under a single label: Arabs, liberals, dopers, doctors, rightists, leftists, Catholics, Jews, Germans, Japanese, Gooks, Republicans, politicians, capitalists, feminists, chauvinists, Chicanos, Latins, jetsetters, Bantu, managers and workers, teachers, teamsters, police, astronauts. . . .

Not a single label listed above tells us about the object/person classified. It merely serves as a means of organizing our information about them and clues us in on how we should think about and relate to the individual so classified.

8   Do we need to be reminded that classification alone—arbitrary, unscientific classification—often means the difference between life and death?

Villagers from southeastern Laos were burned out of their homes as the war moved into their area; they escaped over the border into Vietnam. There they became a serious classification problem for Vietnamese officials: Were they "escapees" or "refugees"? The difference? "Refugees" were permitted to remain in Vietnam, while "escapees" were forced to return. Which were they *really*?

In Nazi Germany, to be classified a "Jew" meant extermination. The classification was a fallacy: In Hitler's mind "Jewish" meant "Jewish race." There is no "Jewish race," of course. To be a "Jew" is to belong to a religion—Judaism. Hitler, however is not the first or the last classifier to make such a mistake.

Ashley Montagu, among other anthropologists and ethnologists, has long reminded us that the concept of race is a fallacious myth—"our most dangerous myth." Physiological characteristics which we classify as "racial" are merely the result of environmental adaptation which took place as our presapient ancestors migrated in search of food and hospitable living conditions. If we could trace our genetic history, each and every one of us would find that we possess

The subtlest and most pervasive of all influences are those which create and maintain the repertory of stereotypes. We are *told* about the world before we see it. We imagine most things before we experience them.

WALTER LIPPMAN

By permission of Dennis Renault.

"I forget, are we mesozoic or are we cenozoic?"

If the doors of perception were cleansed, everything would appear to man as it is, infinite. For man has closed himself up till he sees all things through the narrow chinks of his cavern.

WILLIAM BLAKE

various blends of gene stock. A careful historical look will show only an ever-changing series of gene pools.

Still, race remains one of our most pragmatic classifications, although it completely lacks scientific support. While it says nothing of the person classified, it makes quite clear how we are to think about him, treat him, deal with him, and use him. Could one expect a myth to be more useful than that?

9 It might be argued that some classification systems, such as scientific taxonomy, tell us much more precisely what the classified object really is. Such a claim would probably not be made, however, by either (1) a knowledgeable scientist, or (2) the object classified.

Scientists are quite aware that they have merely agreed on the criteria they will use for their system, namely, evolutionary kinship. When sufficient data are available, lines of evolutionary development can be traced, and the common characteristics of species, genera, families, orders, etc. serve as workable criteria for ordering our knowledge. Scientific systems sometimes reveal facts about the classified objects: they tell us how they may relate (those of the same species can mate, those of different species can't—except that this is not always the case); it tells us who might have been the ancestor of some animal or plant; it sometimes tells us (in the words themselves) about the physiology of the object ("vertebrate," "bony fishes," "mammals"). But such information lies in the labels we have chosen to use for the common characteristics we have selected for classifying. Again, as Hayak-

Henri Bergson (1859–1941)

ohm	millimeter
ampere	kilometer
watt	millisecond
erg	second
gauss	minute
oersted	hour
coulomb	day
volt	year
lumen	cosmic year
hertz	percent
acre	cycles per second
section	miles per hour
grain	parts per million
gram	Richter scale
pound	equator
ton	radian
kilogram	cubic inch
angstrom	flux units
horsepower	farad
bar	rod
decibel	peck
magnitude	dram
psi	acre feet
carat	caliber
degree F	jigger
degree C	mach number
degree K	barrell
degree	furlong
micron	knot
meter	joule
inch	atmosphere
foot	century
cubit	millennium
yard	octave
mile	homer
fathom	ephah
parsec	mina
light-year	cord
ounce	darwin
pint	rpm
fifth	megaton
quart	frames per second
liter	week
gallon	dyne
bushel	newton
electronvolt	decade
BTU	hands
calorie	smidgen

awa has said, no animal is a "vertebrate" until we put it in that "vertebrate" class.

It might be worth noting that for the animal classified, the scientific system probably means very little. If a queen conch is gliding through the sand at dusk in search of a meal, the classification "edible" holds more significance for a clam than its proper taxonomic status as "Chione undatella (Sowerby)."

OUR MENTAL GRIDS

10   The French philosopher Henri Bergson describes another way in which the mind handles its knowledge of reality.

The human intellect, notes Bergson, has one habit which stands in the way of its perceiving reality accurately: its propensity for chopping reality into fragments.

For example, the mind takes "time" and cuts it into discrete units: seconds, minutes, hours, days, weeks, seasons, years, decades, centuries, cosmic years, and so on. But time is a continuum, with no breaks, rhythms, or cycles. Our minds create *units of measurement* for the time-continuum so that we can conceive it in usable "lengths"; then we label these units and proceed to think in "units of time"; we may also begin to believe that such "units of time" are real. But where do "hours" exist? or "days"? or "years"? We have *defined* a year as the time it takes the earth to revolve once around the sun; but the earth would have gone on swinging in orbit for millions of "years" without being affected by our definition of its motion—as though the earth ripped off its December sheet as it passed a certain point in space.

11   And what about space and objects in space? We measure them. We have devised units without end to quantify distance and volume. For spatial distances: millimeters, inches, yards, meters, fathoms, miles, parsecs, light-years, and so on. Mass or volume we measure with grams, ounces, pounds, tons, tablespoons, cubic centimeters, acre-feet, a "pinch" of salt and a "dash" of pepper.

Such units are created by our minds to help us reduce the environment to usable proportions; they enable us to conceive small bits of reality at a time (the mind can't possibly think of *all* matter at once).

But after reflection, could any of us believe that such "units of measurement" exist as part of the real world? Just ask: "Please give me eighteen millimeters." Eighteen millimeters of what? "I need five minutes. Can you get it for me?" Five minutes of what? "Time," of course, but once measured, what exactly do you have?

One must conclude that such units exist in the mind, and only in the mind. Such mental units serve to parcel out our environment into practicable quantities.

12   Look at a globe of the earth and note the lines that criss-cross it. There are pole-to-pole lines we *call* meridians, and lines parallel to the "equator" which we *call* latitudinal lines; then there are anomalous lines dividing colored areas. Thus, with a marked globe we have *organized* the earth so that our minds can think about it. ("Where is Bolivia?" "Point out the Arctic circle." "Locate the magnetic pole.") How else could the intellect deal with the earth except in pieces?

In a planetarium, it is of great help to have a celestial grid overlaying the stars on the dome, or to have a projected image linking together the stars in a constellation. When such grids are not used, the thousands of patternless points of light are scattered at random and we cannot remember or make sense of them. Since the mind must organize the points of light, it "draws" connecting lines. So a small square is seen in Hercules, a triangle in Aquarius; or we see several stars whose pattern reminds us of some known object (Aquila the Eagle, Delphinus the Dolphin). In just this way the ancient skywatchers organized the random bits of light which they saw nightly.

It seems that the human mind has first to construct forms independently before we can find them in things . . . knowledge cannot spring from experience alone but only from this comparison of the inventions of the intellect with observed fact.

ALBERT EINSTEIN

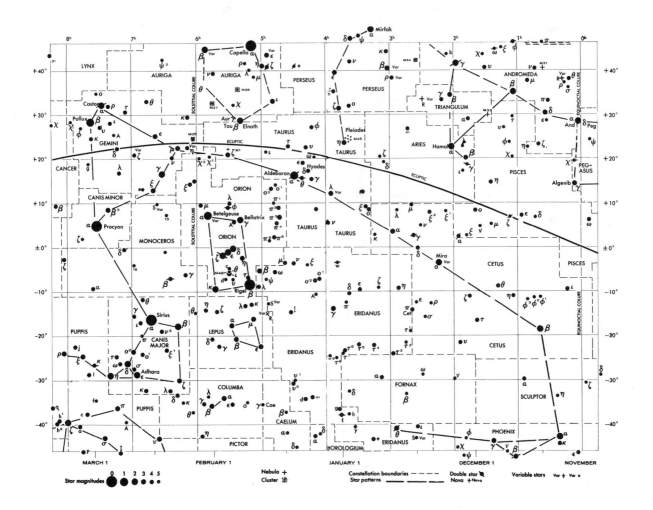

The theater of my mind has a seating capacity of just one, and it's sold out for all performances.

HENRY WINKLER
Tribute to Richard Rodgers

With clarity and quiet, I look upon the world and say: All that I see, hear, taste, smell, and touch are the creations of my mind.

NIKOS KAZANTZAKIS
The Saviours of God

In the planetarium, the grid lights can be turned off, reminding us that the grid is only a mental tool for organizing our experience. In no way could one mistake the grid as a part of the real sky.

In this manner, however, the mind places grids on all that it perceives.

13   What remains when all the mind's "grids" are turned off? Reality—unmeasured, undivided. A continuum of matter in motion and a consciousness of time undisturbed. No days or weeks; no miles or parsecs. To be sure, there do exist in the real world a multitude of rhythms and cycles, and we attempt to coordinate our mental "units of measurement" with these natural rhythms.

Our minds, says Bergson, can indeed "move through" all the pragmatic grids and intuit the nature of reality itself. By a sort of "intellectual empathy" we can come to know the ever-changing, endlessly moving continuum which *is* reality. But to do this we almost have to tell the intellect to cease and desist in its persistent habit of reducing the universe to discrete, manageable units.

To know what the real world is like, therefore, we must turn off the grid lights and let the stars shine. Reality *is*, and that is all.

REFLECTIONS—

1 What do you think of the drawing by Abner Dean on p. 186: "Everyone must have a label"? Is this really true?

2 What is the point that Walter Lippman is making about the way we maintain our habit of stereotyping (p. 186–QM)? Do you agree? How might we cease and desist in this way of thinking?

3 What is an *abstraction?* How many single objects belonging to a class must you experience before you can develop an abstraction? Then what is the relationship of the abstraction to the particular objects? Can you go as far as Plato in holding that abstractions have a real status quite apart from our minds? If you can, where are the real ideas located? If you can't, then what exactly is the relationship between any two objects in the same class? (That is, two warblers that belong to different species but belong to the same family *are* related, aren't they? What relates them?)

4 What is a muglock? How does it differ from a dobo and a busana?

5 When an object is classified, what does the classification tell us about the object, and what does it tell us about the classifier?

6 Discuss with your self (and other selves, if available) the QM on p. 186 regarding the "Nehil Gae." Now reflect very thoroughly on Sec. 8 on the problem of stereotypes. Critique. Insights? Comments?

7 Could we do away entirely with our habit of classifying? What benefits would we gain by eliminating the habit? What would we lose? What's the answer to the problem?

8 Summarize in your words the point Bergson is making when he tells us that our minds have a habit of "chopping reality into fragments." Is this meaningful to you personally? Could Bergson's insights lead you to change your way of seeing and thinking about reality?

Furthermore . . .

A Guide to the Natural World. Life Nature Library. Time Inc., 1965. (Gives an interesting overview of our systems of classification.)

BARZUN, JACQUES, *Race: A Study in Superstition.* Harper, 1965.

BERGSON, HENRI, *A Study in Metaphysics.* Littlefield, 1965.

HAYAKAWA, S. I., *Language in Thought and Action.* Harcourt, 1964.

LOUX, MICHAEL J. (ed.), *Universals and Particulars: Readings in Ontology.* Anchor, 1971.

MONTAGU, ASHLEY, *Man's Most Dangerous Myth: The Fallacy of Race.* Harper, 1952.

WHEELWRIGHT, PHILIP, *The Burning Fountain: A Study in the Language of Symbolism,* Indiana University Press, 1968.

Truth

Have You Ever Wondered . . .

- Whether, if you believe something with all your heart, that makes it true?

- Whether an idea that works has to be true . . . *because* it works?

- Whether an idea could be true today but false tomorrow?

- Whether God exists—and how you could be sure?

- Whether Napoleon existed—and how you could be sure?

- Whether Australia exists—and how you could be sure?

- Whether an idea might be true *and* false at the same time?

- What "truth" really is? and how you can tell if a statement is true or false?

TRUTH-TESTS

No one is so wrong as the man who knows all the answers.

THOMAS MERTON

1   The word *truth* is a delicate and thoughtful symbol, to be used sparingly. But few words are more desecrated. We like its sound: it has that authoritative, virtuous ring, like "freedom" and "rights"; and it serves our aristocentric purposes so well.

Truth-tests are used for checking and double checking the things people say so that we can decide if their statements are true or false. With such tests we can verify or falsify the fact-claims which they make.

There are three truth-tests, and only three, so far as we know.

THE CORRESPONDENCE-TEST

2   One method of checking fact-claims is by *the correspondence-test,* whose development is attributed to Bertrand Russell. This test requires one to check a mental concept against a real object/event, and if the subjective concept "corresponds to" the real object/event, then the concept is considered to be true.

Quite simply, if someone tells you there is a solar eclipse in progress in your area, you can look at the sun; and he is either right or wrong. If you can observe a crescent sun, then his statement can be accepted; if you cannot, his statement is false. You have checked it personally and established to your satisfaction the accuracy of the statement. If there was indeed a correspondence between the mental concept of an eclipse and an actual event taking place, then the fact-claim has become a fact.

A whole class of fact-claims are easily checked this way. "The book you are after is in Section B-16 in the bookstore." *Go look.* "On this side of the tape are selections from Puccini's *Madame Butterfly." Play the tape and listen.* "Some prankster mixed salt and sugar in the sugarbowl." *Taste and find out.* "His pulse is very slow." *Feel it and count.* "The coals are ready for the steak." *Look at them glow red and feel the heat.* "This watermelon is ripe and ready." *Feel it, thump it and listen to the thump, plug it, smell it, and taste it.* All the senses can't be wrong—can they?

3   In order to apply the correspondence-test, two things are involved: (1) a subjective mental concept, and (2) a real object/event to which the mental concept corresponds. The following precautions must be taken seriously when checking fact-claims with the correspondence-test.

(1) We have already noted some of the mind's imaginative operations and the way it creates concepts. No created concept is ever an exact replica of any external object/event. The mind selects a few elements of any object/event to assimilate into the model which it will use for thinking. Furthermore, we have seen that all the physical events which exist in the real world are translated by our transducers into quite different experiential phenomena.

Remembering all this, we must conclude that no mental concept can ever correspond 100 percent with objects/events. Rather, we have only a degree of correspondence between the two. If the degree of correspondence is high, we hold the fact-claim to be true; if it is not, we decide it is false. Where the breakoff point is along that scale of correspondence would be the subject of endless debate.

(2) Since, in the last analysis, we are limited to our own subjective experiencing world, how is it possible for us to harmonize a subjective concept (which we can experience) with a real object/event (which we cannot directly experience)? The answer, of course: we can't. What then does the correspondence-test really do? It compares

What is Truth but to live for an idea? . . . It is a question of discovering a truth which is truth *for me,* of finding the idea for which I am willing to live and die.

KIERKEGAARD

The Jains of India have a doctrine called *syād-vāda*—the "perhaps" method. There are officially 353 different viewpoints that can be held on any problem; and therefore dogmatic closemindedness is unacceptable. To any viewpoint on any issue, the appropriate reply is "perhaps" or, more elaborately, "maybe it is and maybe it isn't."

JLC

Bertrand Russell (1872–1970)

a concept with a set of sensations—the sensations we use when we go about inferring what exists in the real world. Therefore, we are checking a subjective concept with a subjective set of sensations. If they match to some tolerable degree, then we call the concept true; if they don't, we call it false.

This is really not a happy condition to live with, but given our present knowledge of cognitive processes, the predicament seems inescapable. It looks as though—on this test at least—we can never be completely certain of anything.

THE COHERENCE-TEST

4   There is an obvious limitation to the use of the correspondence-test. The real world has to be directly accessible for observation, otherwise there is nothing real against which one can check his concept. In such cases a second checkout method—the coherence-test—might be applicable.

According to *the coherence-test,* a fact-claim can be accepted as true if it harmonizes (coheres) with other facts which one has *already* accepted as true. Like the previous test, this is a routine kind of test we use every day.

"There are sharks in Lake Mead." No, that can't be, and I don't have to go to Lake Mead to check the fact-claim with the correspondence-test; for I already know that sharks can't live in fresh water, and Lake Mead is a fresh-water lake. The fact-claim just can't be made to harmonize with other known facts.°

"When I looked into the mirror, I couldn't see myself. I have lost my reflection!" We would reject such a statement with hardly a second thought. We have read of such fantasies in *Tales of Hoffmann,* and Alice just might be able to manage it. But in the real world of human experience such a fact-claim doesn't harmonize with any experience I know. We will happily keep such "facts" in the world of make-believe.

"Alexander the Great never returned to Rome because he fell in love with Cleopatra and spent the rest of his life in Egypt." No, these fact-claims can't be made to cohere with other previously known data. Alexander died in 323 B.C. and he was certainly no Roman; and Cleopatra died about 30 B.C. Now, it might be possible to substitute Antony for Alexander (with Cleopatra's permission), and the fact-claims would then cohere with one another.

The coherence-test is applicable to large areas of knowledge which are not accessible to personal observation. Two such areas are (1) fact-claims relating to the past ("history"), which is never available for observation, and (2) all contemporary events which we cannot personally witness. This applies to practically all the information we get via television, newspapers, and magazines. A very large percentage of the events which "make news" takes place too far away for us to observe, so we test them by making them cohere with the facts we already know.

5   The coherence-test has a serious weakness. A new fact-claim may fit coherently with a large number of previously accepted "facts" *all of which are untrue*; or, similarly, a new fact which is *true* may be rejected because it can't be made to harmonize with one's set of previously accepted false fact-claims.

In other words, it is about as easy to build an elaborate coherent system that is false as an elaborate coherent system that is true. Unless previously accepted data are well supported by evidence, the truth-status of that new "fact" remains in doubt, no matter how well it fits in.

This point has historical significance. System-building has been the stock-in-trade of philosophers, theologians, political theorists, et al. It has been a common practice to rewrite history from the point of view of some ideology; facts can be selected, interpreted, and squeezed into almost any framework. Resulting systems may be highly coherent, therefore, yet bear little resemblance to anything in the real world.

THE PRAGMATIC-TEST

6   There is a third test which, like the coherent test, is wholly subjective in that it requires nothing immediately accessible in the real world to serve as validating criteria for the mental concept. This is *the pragmatic-test*, and in some ways it is the most complex of the three.

This test was developed by the American philosopher-psychologist William James, but the seminal idea came from Charles S. Peirce. In an article published in 1878, Peirce (pronounced like "purse") attempted to answer the question, "What makes ideas meaningful?" He was interested in clarifying the source and nature of meaning. In his article he concluded that ideas are meaningful if they make some difference in our experience. As Peirce put it, "our idea of anything *is* our idea of its sensible effects. . . ." If we say ice is cold or a match flame is hot, those *ideas* are meaningful only because they relate in a predictive way to what we would experience if we touched the ice or the flame. The ideas have meaning in relation to effects. If we could not touch the ice or the flame, the ideas would be meaningless.

This was a *theory of meaning* only, but William James saw deeper implications in the theory and developed it into a *test of truth*. In 1898, in an address delivered at the University of California at Berkeley, James presented his theory of pragmatism. The truth-value of any idea is to be determined by the results; a "true" idea brings about desired effects. In short—and somewhat more ambiguously—"if an idea works, then it's true."

Peirce had labeled his "theory of meaning" pragmatism, but

> Assume coherence as the test, and you will be driven by the incoherence of your alternatives to the conclusion that it is also the nature of truth.
>
> *BRAND BLANSHARD*

> Begin by believing with all your heart that your belief is true, so that it will work for you; but then face the possibility that it is really false, so that you can accept the consequences of the belief.
>
> *JOHN RESECK*

Charles S. Peirce (1839–1914)

William James

"Truth happens to an idea"

Something happened to truth in April of 1870.

William James read an article by the French philosopher, Charles Renouvier, who held that the most distinctive quality of human beings is the experience of freedom. Like a key piece of a jigsaw puzzle, the idea fell into place.

On April 30, James wrote in his journal:

> I think that yesterday was a crisis in my life. I finished the first part of Renouvier's second "Essais" and see no reason why his definition of Free Will—"The sustaining of a thought *because I choose to* when I might have other thoughts"—need be the definition of an illusion. . . . My first act of free will shall be to believe in free will. . . . Not in maxims, not in *Anschauungen* (contemplations), but in accumulated *acts* of thought lies salvation. . . . Now, I will go a step further with my will, not only act with it, but believe as well; believe in my individual reality and creative power.

This decision to believe in believing marked an about-face in James' life. Heretofore he had been, by his own judgment, "a splintered bundle of fragments in search of consistency." Now he was able to summon strength to reverse the pattern of his past—a lifetime of self-doubt and suffering (he was 28)—and to affirm *the possibility* of taking charge of his life and creating his own future. Renouvier had argued that we possess freedom of the will if we believe that we do, and James believed it.

To those who have sought the origins of William James' condition, the James family remains an enigma—puzzling, haunting, slightly unreal. William's sister Alice suffered from "nervous attacks," fainting spells, and an illusive invalidism all her life; she rejoiced when she contracted cancer because it was, at last, a real physical illness. A brother, Garth Wilkinson, died at 38 of a rheumatic heart. Another younger brother, Robertson, was an alcoholic. And the brother who became a major American writer, Henry James, sustained, as he put it, "an obscure hurt, odious, intimate, horrid"; and he remained celibate all his life.

William shared fully his family's neurasthenia. He was plagued with chronic backache (he dubbed it "this dorsal insanity"), and suffered from digestive disorders, depressions, and acute attacks of diffuse anxiety. He described one such attack: "there fell upon me without warning, just as if it came out of the darkness, a horrible fear of my own existence".

His eye trouble was his one truly somatic ailment.

The father of this troubled family was Henry James, Senior, a brilliant, passionate, and bizarre man whose life seems to have been one long search for spiritual peace, which he eventually succeeded in finding in the teachings of the eighteenth century mystical theologian Swedenborg and his theme of divine love. As a child he suffered a severe burn to his leg which resulted in amputation. Throughout his life he was subject to phobias and hallucinations. He was a gifted thinker who bequeathed his spiritual concerns—as well as his complexities and perplexities—to his children. Table talk and family gatherings were animated, intellectual, wide-ranging, and punctuated by sibling rivalries.

William James was continually tormented by fears and questioned whether life could be worth living at all. He interrupted his medical studies for a year at the health spas in Germany, read widely in psychology and philosophy, and took courses under some of Europe's leading scholars. But his malaise continued—"a paradoxical apathy and restlessness." He wrote home that he spent an entire winter contemplating suicide.

He returned to Harvard and received his M.D. degree in 1869, but lacked the strength and/or will to practice medicine. He continued to withdraw into a state of invalidism, unable to decide what he wanted to do with his life.

At this juncture James read the article by Renouvier. It was a turning-point. Here began his quest for a philosophy that would face up to the stubborn realities of life and, at the same time, provide light for him to live by.

William James was caught in the necessity of believing—his life was at stake—but he could no longer accept the possibility of unthinking (blind) belief. His father could still believe; he could even believe in believing. But blind belief, for William, was fraught with dishonesty and counterproductiveness. He must therefore perform one of man's most delicate psychological maneuvers: Without denying either his own nature or the given realities of the universe, he had to rethink the structure of belief and give it a rationale fully acceptable to the intellect. This he did, and the result was a new way of looking at the dynamics of the ideas we call "true."

What does it mean for an idea to be true? James writes in *Pragmatism*:

> The great assumption of the intellectualists is that truth means essentially an inert static relation. . . .
>
> Pragmatism, on the other hand, asks its usual question. "Grant an idea or belief to be true," it says, "what concrete difference will its being true make in anyone's actual life? . . . What, in short, is the truth's cash value in experiential terms?" . . .
>
> The moment pragmatism asks this question, it sees the answer. *True ideas are those that we can assimilate, validate, corroborate, and verify. False ideas are those that we cannot.* That is the practical difference it makes to us to have true ideas. That therefore is the meaning of truth. . . .
>
> The truth of an idea is not a stagnant property inherent in it. Truth *happens* to an idea. It *becomes* true, is *made* true by events. Its verity is in fact an event, a process. . . .

His belief in free will was probably the most precious truth that James possessed. We can exercise free will, James knows, providing we *believe* that we have free will. My belief makes it true. But when I first start believing it, it may not be *very* true. I may be intellectually convinced of my free will, but the truth of the idea hasn't taken hold of me at a deeper level. It is only slightly true. But if I practice making choices, I can increase my freedom; and the idea becomes *more true*. Freedom is a quality that I have grown. And the statement "I have free will" becomes more and more true. Therefore, the statement "I am free" was true; it had predictive value. But more than that, the truth of the statement *happened to* the idea as I put it into effect.

True ideas, therefore, are the ideas that "work" for us. Does this mean that we can call virtually any fact-claim true providing we can personally validate it by claiming that "It works for me"? Emphatically no. As John McDermott puts it, "James was no subjectivist. And although he sees truth as a function of 'interest,' this position does not encourage predatory action. . . ." James is a relentless empiricist, and he presses the point that our ideas must square with the hard realities of experience. Adjusting our beliefs to the "total push and pressure of the cosmos" is the only way to develop ideas that are pragmatically useful.

James warns: "Woe to him whose beliefs play fast and loose with the order which realities follow in his experience; they will lead him nowhere or else make false connexions."

So James ended by believing, but in a very special way. George Santayana, a Harvard colleague—and one of James' most brilliant pupils—is not wrong when he says that "James didn't really believe. He only believed in one's right to believe that he might be right if he believed."

James took charge of his life with a vengeance, as though making up for lost time. Rather suddenly he was able to put an immense reservoir of stored-up knowledge and ideas to work in a creative way.

In 1873 he became an instructor in Anatomy and Physiology at Harvard, and in 1875 began to teach psychology, at that time a new science. He introduced a course in Physiology and Psychology, the first in America, and established a laboratory of experimental psychology, one of the first in the world. He wrote incessantly. His major works are *Principles of Psychology, The Varieties of Religious Experience,* and *Pragmatism.*

Most significant was his marriage to Alice Gibbens when he was 36. She was 27, lively and intelligent, a teacher in a girls' school. They were married in 1878, though only after some soul-searching on the part of the philosopher.

Something resembling genuine mental and physical health now infused William's whole life. His family and friends were amazed at the change in him. His illnesses disappeared and he found a new zest in living. He became one of the most popular teachers on campus, and for 35 years he delighted generations of students with his informality, sincerity, candor, and anecdotes.

William James was anything but nondescript. Respected by students and colleagues alike, and much-loved for his gentle personality, he was colorful, alert, articulate. He had a slender but sturdy frame, was modestly and neatly bearded, sported a tan, and wore casual tweeds—thus rejecting the stereotype of the Harvard professor. Equally striking were his writing and speaking styles. His conversations were witty, homey, and erudite, his public addresses extemporaneous and substantive. His writing is marked by graphic imagery and simplicity—and it can be understood. His sister Alice once remarked that he could "lend life and charm to a treadmill."

James resigned from teaching in 1907 but continued to write and lecture, both in America and Europe. A European called him the "preeminent ambassador of American thought." The Indian scholar T. K. Mahadevan says simply: "American civilization is what it is because of William James."

During his later years James spent all the time he could at his summer home in New Hampshire, gardening, swimming, and hiking. He loved nature. One day in 1898 he climbed a steep mountain trail with an 18-pound backpack and sustained permanent injury to his heart (a valvular lesion). He maintained a super-active schedule for a decade, however, until the summer of 1910 when his angina attacks became acute. He died in his wife's arms at their summer home in the Adiron cks—August 26, 1910.

when he heard what James had done to his theory by changing it into a test of truth, Peirce was upset. He rechristened his theory of meaning with such an "ugly name," as he said, that no one would ever kidnap his theory again. He called it "pragmaticism." We now associate "pragma*tism*" with William James and John Dewey, and "pragmat*icism*" with Peirce.

7   The pragmatic-test can be used to check out fact-claims in several different areas of knowledge, and we find that the *function* of the test is different in each. This is why the test presents serious problems.

First, let's note our routine use of the pragmatic-test. We use it to check the workability of our ideas and hypotheses, even our guesses and hunches. It is an integral part of our trial-and-error way of solving daily problems.

If, for instance, you turn on your TV set and nothing happens, then you are forced into creating a hypothesis to find out what is wrong. Your first hypothesis may be that the cord is not plugged in. So you check it. It is plugged in, so your hypothesis is wrong. So, since that hypothesis didn't work, you proceed to another one. Perhaps something is wrong inside the TV set. You check the warmup tube and find it cold, so you conclude that electricity is not getting into the set. Now the problem begins to look serious (that is, a solution may cost you time and/or money). You are on your way to the telephone to call a TV repairman when you notice that the nightlight by the telephone is off. You check and find other lights off. So, new hypothesis: a fuse must be tripped. You check. All fuses are in the "ON" position except one. You flip this one to "ON" and power is restored.

By empirical means, you gradually developed a hypothesis which accounted for all the facts. You were forced to collect more and more data before you could develop a workable hypothesis—that is, a hypothesis on the basis of which the TV problem could be corrected. Happily, the hypothesis that finally worked will probably cost you little time and no money.

This illustrates the essential claim of pragmatism: the idea that *works* is the *true* one.

8   Our ideas have a profound effect on how we feel and behave. This fact is fundamental to all of man's religions, and here we discover the rationale for "faith" and "belief."

William James knew from personal experience this pragmatic process he was attempting to formulate into a philosophy. Having been reared in a family distraught with emotional instability, James developed psycholophysical illnesses which plagued him most of his life. He suffered from sleeplessness, digestive disorders, headaches, and depression. He came to believe that there was no escape from his misery, that his suffering had been fatalistically determined for him so that he could do nothing to change his condition. He could easily use his illness as a rationalization for not facing the buffeting which is a part of life.

The falseness of an opinion is not for us any objection to it. . . . The question is how far it is life-furthering, life-preserving, species-preserving, perhaps species-creating.

NIETZSCHE

Better the world should perish than that I , or any other human being, should believe a lie; . . . that is the religion of thought, in whose scorching flames the dross of the world is being burnt away.

BERTRAND RUSSELL

Doubt is an uneasy and dissatisfied state from which we struggle to free ourselves and pass into the state of belief; while the latter is a calm and satisfactory state which we do not wish to avoid, or to change to a belief in anything else. On the contrary, we cling tenaciously, not merely to believing, but to believing just what we do believe.

C. S. PEIRCE

The crisis for James came in 1869–70 when he thought again of ending his life. After a period of deep depression he forcefully rejected suicide as a solution to his problem. He made a commitment which

> marked a decisive break in his attitude toward death and signalized his new belief in the creative dimensions of personal existence. While it cannot be said that the resolution of this crisis ended the pervasiveness of what Perry calls his "morbid traits," it did symbolize for James a new set of possibilities.

About this time he read an essay by Renouvier which convinced him of the reality of personal freedom. His life was not determined irrevocably for him; he really could change the course of his life. *An idea—the idea of personal freedom—had taken hold of him.* On April 30, 1870, James wrote in his notebook: "I think that yesterday was a crisis in my life. . . . My first act of free will shall be to believe in free will." He had committed himself to the affirmation of life; he would not escape from it.

> Having rejected suicide in favor of the possibility of a creative life unsupported by certitude, James developed a doctrine to sustain such a belief. . . . If it can be said that James assented to "The Will to Believe" until the end, we must caution that it was a belief always shot through with irresolution and doubt. Behind the consistent cadences of a rich and future-oriented prose, there lurked a well-controlled but omnipresent sense of despair. James was neither an optimist nor a cynic; he was a man of moral courage, who knew, all too well, the ambiguity and precariousness of the human condition.

9   What about the "truth-value" of a belief powerful enough to prevent one from opting for suicide? Whatever the *rationale* within the belief—that one's time has not yet come, that one has not yet accomplished one's purpose in life, that one should not cause others to suffer, or that taking one's life is morally wrong—whatever the rationale, isn't this belief true? Isn't the truth of ideas to be found in the results they effect? Or, as James so pungently put it, don't we judge the worth of ideas by their "cash value"?

Pragmatism's only test of truth is what works best, wrote James.

> If theological ideas should do this, if the notion of God, in particular, should prove to do it, how could pragmatism possibly deny God's existence? It could see no meaning in treating as "not true" a notion that was pragmatically so successful.

THE PRAGMATIC PARADOX

10   The *pragmatic paradox* may be stated thus: In order for an idea to work pragmatically, one must believe that it is true on other than pragmatic criteria. Now, if we *define* "truth" as an idea that works (that is, that brings about desired results), then we have no serious problem. If

In the whole New Testament, there appears but a solitary figure worthy of honor: Pilate, the Roman Viceroy. . . . The noble scorn of a Roman, before whom the word "truth" was shamelessly mishandled, enriched the New Testament with the only saying in it that has any value—"What is truth?"

NIETZSCHE

an idea works, then it's true; and conversely, if an idea is true, then it works.

But this is not yet the heart of the matter. In order for an idea or belief to work *pragmatically*, we must believe it in terms of *correspondence*. This kind of insight can become a blessing or a bad dream.

For instance, in order for the belief in immortality to become a sustaining belief (that is, *to work*), one must accept that immortality exists in reality; one must believe that there is an objective event which corresponds to the concept. Even though we may not be able to check out the belief with the correspondence-test, if it is not believed on a *correspondence* basis then the belief can have no *pragmatic* results.

What if you should say to yourself: "I have no evidence that souls survive death, but I want to experience the benefits of the belief in immortality (strength, courage, comfort), so I will accept the belief on a pragmatic basis. I will *believe* in immoratlity and make the idea work for me." What are the chances of making the idea "work"? For most of us, very poor indeed. (Incidentally, we see clearly here the role of the authority in our lives, the charismatic figure who can persuade us to believe *on his authority* that an idea is objectively true; this way we can manage to believe, without empirical evidence, what we wanted and needed to believe to begin with but couldn't accomplish on our own.)

One must believe in immortality "with all his heart." With equal conviction one must "know" that a loving Father-God does in fact exist (that is, that God is real); then the belief can be true pragmatically. Likewise, if the devout Muslim knows that Allah endows him with courage in battle, then he will not falter as the Holy War is waged. And the kamikaze pilot could look forward with patriotic fervor to the moment when he could dive his Suisei bomber onto the deck of an aircraft carrier, since he knew beyond doubt that he would return in spirit directly to the Yasukuni Shrine and be visited by family and friends.°

Believing these ideas to be objectively true, they become pragmatically true.

11   A "fact" which is true on one truth-test may be false on another.

For instance, a Muslim would say, "There is no God but Allah" (this fact-claim is a part of the Islamic Creed). Is such a statement true? Check it with the three truth-tests. You can be sure of three things: (1) The Muslim accepts his belief on a pragmatic basis; that is, his faith in Allah works for him. Therefore, *for him*, the statement is true on the pragmatic-test. (2) He also accepts his belief in Allah on the coherence-test; that is, the belief undoubtedly coheres with numerous other accepted data from the Quran and Islamic tradition (the Hadith). Therefore, *for him*, the statement is true on the coherence-test. (3) While it would be extremely difficult or impossible to discover the real object/event referred to as "Allah" so that the correspondence-test could be applied, you can be quite sure that the Muslim *believes* that such a real object/event exists.

Grant an idea or belief to be true, what concrete difference will its being true make in any one's actual life? How will the truth be realized? What experiences will be different from those which would obtain if the belief were false? What, in short, is the truth's cash-value in experiential terms?

WILLIAM JAMES

°*See the letter written by the kamikaze pilot on page 539.*

To say that Newton's law of gravitation is true is to say that it can be applied successfully; so long as that could be done, it *was* true. There is no inconsistency in saying that Newton's law *was* true and that Einstein's law is *at present* true.

HECTOR HAWTON
(describing Pragmatism)

So, is the fact-claim true or false?

Now, if you should reply, "I don't believe your statement is true," what exactly are you saying? (1) Using the pragmatic-test, you are stating that the concept of Allah is not meaningful to you, hence not true *for you.* (2) Using the coherence-test, belief in Allah does not harmonize with facts you have accepted as true. Where can you fit such a fact-claim into the Jewish, Christian, atheistic, or scientific world-view? It is false, therefore, *for you.* (3) Using the correspondence-test, you are stating that you don't think "Allah" is real. If the Muslim claims that Allah is real, we often respond with the challenge, "Prove it"—meaning show us *by the correspondence-test* that there is a real object/event called "Allah." Of course, he cannot.

Therefore, we think we have won our case. Using only the correspondence-test, you retort that the Muslim's fact-claim is untrue. His statement about "Allah" is false. *And yet, on the other two criteria—the pragmatic and coherence—the fact-claim is undeniably true . . . for the Muslim.*

So again we ask: Is the fact-claim true or false?

Society as a whole ultimately gets, on all issues of wide public importance, the classifications it wants, even if it has to wait until all the members of the Supreme Court are dead and an entirely new court is appointed. When the desired decision is handed down, people say, "Truth has triumphed." *In short, society regards as "true" those systems of classification that produce the desired results.*

The scientific test of "truth," like the social test, is strictly practical, except for the fact that the "desired results" are more severely limited. The results desired by society may be irrational, superstitious, selfish, or humane, but the results desired by scientists are only that our systems of classification produce predictable results. Classifications . . . determine our attitudes and behavior toward the object or event classified. When lightning was classified as "evidence of divine wrath," no courses of action other than prayer were suggested to prevent one's being struck by lightning. As soon, however, as it was classified as "electricity," Benjamin Franklin achieved a measure of control over it by his invention of the lightning rod. Certain physical disorders were formerly classified as "demonic possession," and it was suggested that we "drive the demons out" by whatever spells or incantations we could think of. The results were uncertain. But when those disorders were classified as "bacillus infections," courses of actions were suggested that led to more predictable results.

Science seeks only the *most generally useful* systems of classification; these it regards for the time being, until more useful classifications are invented, as "true."

S. I. HAYAKAWA
Language in Thought and Action

In pondering the relativity of truth, Plato pointed out in the *Theatetus* that the relativistic position is a paradox: "The best of the joke is, that Protagoras acknowledges the truth of their opinion who believe his opinion to be false; for in admitting that the opinions of all men are true, in effect he grants that the opinion of his opponents is true."

In their book *Realms of Philosophy*, the Drs. Sahakian summarize the dilemma in the following composed dialogue:

Plato (428–348 B.C.)

PROTAGORAS. Plato, what is true for you, is true for you, and what is true for me, is true for me.
PLATO. Do you mean to say that my personal opinion is true?
PROTAGORAS. Indeed, that is precisely what I mean.
PLATO. But, my dear Protagoras, my opinion is that truth is not relative; truth is not a matter of opinion, but objective and absolute. Furthermore, my opinion is that your belief in the relativity of truth is absolutely false and should be abandoned. Do you still hold that my opinion is true?
PROTAGORAS. Yes, you are quite correct.

The NBC television program *My World and Wel-* *come To It* updated the dilemma in a dialogue between the cartoonist (Monroe, based on Thurber) and the newspaper editor who publishes his cartoons:

EDITOR. I understand your cartoon this time, and it's not funny.
MONROE. You're entitled to your opinion.
EDITOR. It's not an opinion. It's a fact.
MONROE. You can't say that.
EDITOR. Why not? You said I was entitled to my opinion. And in my opinion, it's a fact.

In either case, who is logically correct? Would it be meaningful to ask who is *psychologically* correct?

12   We frequently find ourselves caught in interminable arguments where no meeting of minds takes place—as would undoubtedly happen in the case of the Muslim's claims about Allah. If we can cease to argue long enough to clarify our thinking, we would often find that different truth-tests are being used to support fact-claims.

It is good advice, therefore, to examine carefully the truth-tests being used (or merely assumed). If indeed one individual is using the correspondence-test as the only acceptable criterion for verifying "facts" while another is relying on pragmatic criteria or is caught in the pragmatic paradox, it is no wonder that such discussions end in fruitless stalemates. We are left with frustration because the other person can't accept what is so obviously true to us.

13   Examination of the truth-tests will disclose three points worth noting. (1) All three tests are constantly used by all of us and are indispensable to thinking and communicating. Each has its sphere of legitimate operation.

(2) Each truth-test has intrinsic problems. We cannot be absolutely sure of any "fact" on any test. We are forced to conclude that

At ebb tide I wrote
A line upon the sand
And gave it all my heart
And all my soul.
At flood tide I returned
To read what I had inscribed
And found my ignorance upon the
   shore.

KAHLIL GIBRAN

Truth is the approximation of thought to reality. It is thought on its way home. Its measure is the distance thought has travelled, under guidance of its inner compass, toward that intelligible system which unites its ultimate object with its ultimate end.

BRAND BLANSHARD

"truth" is a probability item, with greater or lesser degrees of likelihood attached to various specific fact-claims.

And (3), this being the case, all truth is tentative. It is always subject to further modification and refinement as new fact-claims are verified and become facts.

REFLECTIONS—

1 Thomas Merton wrote: "No one is so wrong as the man who knows all the answers" (p. 192-QM). This may sound like a pearl or a truism. But is it essentially a true statement? In what sense is it true or untrue? Do you think Socrates would agree? (By the way, "knows all the answers" *to what?*)

2 Contrast the position stated in the quotations from Nietzsche and Russell (p. 199-QMs) by rephrasing their ideas in your own words. Which (if either) do you tend to agree with? Why? Can these extreme statements be reconciled? Or does the problem reduce to a matter of relative values?

3 Describe the use of the correspondence-test. Under what specific conditions can it be used? What are its principal weaknesses? Can you think of any steps we can take to increase the degree of accuracy of the test?

4 Describe the use of the coherence-test. In what specific areas, or under what conditions, does it become the primary truth-test? In what fallacious ways is the coherence-test often used?

5 Describe the use of the pragmatic truth-test as it applies to the development of hypotheses to account for empirical events (such as the nonworking TV set). In what ways must we be wary of its misuse?

6 When applied to nonempirical concepts, the pragmatic test of truth functions in quite a different way than when it is used to explain empirical data. Describe what it is that makes a concept, belief, or doctrine pragmatically true. (You may recall examples from your own experience similar to those of William James.)

7 Can you see a way out of the pragmatic paradox? Is it indeed a paradox in the sense that one must actually deceive himself—that is, that he must believe that an idea is true on the wrong criterion—in order to make an idea work? Would it be better, in your opinion, to hold that some ideas are meaningful even though they are not true? In other words, are we going too far when we call an idea true *because* it is meaningful?

8 Which truth-test(s) would you apply to check out the following fact-claims and, in each case, what degree of certainty would you have?

Black coral grows in the Red Sea.
You can call 411 for Information.
The pious shall prosper.
This postcard was mailed from Madrid.
The Earth is flat.
A UFO just landed in your back yard (but it's an invisible UFO).
Shakespeare wrote *The Merchant of Venice*.
Whirlwinds ("dust devils") are evil spirits in disguise.

This battery is dead.

Dolphins are intelligent animals.

The Whooping Crane is an endangered species.

The World will end on July 14, 1984.

All cats are blue.

Life is meaningless.

As you read this sentence, a solar eclipse is taking place.

"God's in his heaven—All's right with the world!" (Browning)

The Magna Carta was signed June 15, 1215.

All events are predestined.

Transglobal Airlines offers you the lowest fares.

A water molecule is composed of two hydrogen atoms and one oxygen atom.

Allah despises Infidels but loves The Faithful.

Furthermore . . .

AUNE, BRUCE, *Rationalism, Empiricism, and Pragmatism.* Random House, 1970.

AYER, A. J., *Language, Truth and Logic,* 2nd ed., Dover, 1936.

GOULD, JAMES E. (ed.), *Classic Philosophical Questions.* Merrill, 2nd ed., 1975. (See Nos. 23, 24, 25.)

KAPLAN, ABRAHAM, *The Conduct of Inquiry: Methodology for Behavioral Sciences.* Chandler, 1964.

RUSSELL, BERTRAND, *The Problems of Philosophy.* Oxford, 1959.

SCHILPP, PAUL A. (ed.), *The Philosophy of Bertrand Russell* (2 vols.). Harper, 1963.

SUMNER, L. W., and JOHN WOODS (eds.), *Necessary Truths: A Book of Readings.* Random House, 1969.

WHITE, ALAN P., *Truth.* Anchor, 1970.

PART IV

THE INNER WORLD: THE FANTASTIC JOURNEY

With clarity and quiet, I look upon the world and say: All that I see, hear, taste, smell, and touch are the creations of my mind. . . . I create phenomena in swarms, and paint with a full palette a gigantic and gaudy curtain before the abyss. Do not say, "Draw the curtain that I may see the painting." The curtain IS the painting.

NIKOS KAZANTZAKIS

Psyche/Soma

Have You Ever Wondered . . .

- What goes on in your subconscious mind while you're sleeping?

- What the alpha state of mind feels like?

- Whether there is any validity to hypnosis?

- What a "religious experience" is?

- What a "hallucination" is and what it means?

- What a religious "vision" is and what it means?

- Whether there is such an event as "demon possession"?

- Whether "out-of-body experiences" are facts or fictions?

THE EXPLORATION OF INNER SPACE

1 As adults, we have forgotten most of our childhood, not only its contents but its flavor; as men of the world, we hardly know of the existence of the inner world: we barely remember our dreams, and make little sense of them when we do; as for our bodies, we retain just sufficient proprioceptive sensations to coordinate our movements and to ensure the minimal requirements for biosocial survival—to register fatigue, signals for food, sex, defecation, sleep; beyond that, little or nothing. Our capacity to think, except in the service of what we are dangerously deluded in supposing is our self-interest and in conformity with common sense, is pitifully limited: our capacity even to

> What is important is not liberation from the body but liberation from the mind. We are not entangled in our own body but entangled in our own mind.
>
> THOMAS MERTON
> The Asian Journal

see, hear, touch, taste and smell is so shrouded in veils of mystification that an intensive discipline of unlearning is necessary for anyone before one can begin to experience the world afresh, with innocence, truth and love.

R. D. LAING

2   Man's ignorance of his inner world has been an abysmal "darkness of unknowing." Is there, as a matter of fact, anything that we understand less than we understand ourselves? And when we begin to see the facts, how quickly we turn away and refuse to face the truth about our own being. The history of man's exploration of human nature is marked by a singular lack of courage.

In a way, all this is surprising, for there is probably no human adventure more exciting than the exploration of "inner space." To be sure, it can lead us into uncharted country. It can evoke sacred fears and involve unscheduled risks, and not a few may fear that they have strayed into forbidden territory.

And too, it can be a lonely odyssey. No one else can travel with us; they can only call to us, as from a distance.

Yet there can be a feeling of joyous ultimacy in the unique adventure of coming to know one's inner world. Most of us have sensed the mysterious forces—more errant than the winds—that drive and direct our lives. Who among us has not wondered what he would find if he began in earnest to probe the depths of his own being?

3   "Dare I explore my inner world?" The question is rarely stated this directly, but in some form the implicit decision "to explore or not to explore" is forced upon us each day.

And, because human history is in a critical state of change in our understanding of man, the answer, assuredly, must be "yes." The fact is that man has always cast furtive glances inward, but heretofore he has sojourned in his psychic hinterlands without adequate roadmaps. He has groped haphazardly, not knowing where he was going, how to get there, or what he would find. This is no way to begin a journey.

All this is changing. Modern cartographers have begun to do their work and today we have rudimentary but helpful maps to guide us.

4   There is no obvious reason why one should spend his lifetime solely in the two traditional mind-states: the problem-solving conscious state and the "recovery" sleep state. Most of us, in fact, wander off the narrow path and spend time in free-association (woolgathering), browsing through our memories, and enjoying flights of fantasy; we might even tune in a few alpha rhythms. So our reduction of human existence into an alternation of consciousness and unconsciousness—waking and sleeping—is a local (Western) oversimplification.

There are other modes of conscious and subconscious experi-

The exploration of the interior of the human brain will be as dangerous as that of the Antarctic continent or the depths of the oceans, and far more rewarding.

J. B. S. HALDANE

Freud described the therapeutic process as one in which layers of consciousness were gradually removed until the unconscious was reached. [But Allen Wheelis] found that after the layers were peeled, there was often—nothing—a great void that the analyst, though called upon to do so, could not possibly fill.

BERNARD ROSENBERG

How like philosophers! Preening themselves for teaching black-and-white thinkers to see shades of gray and forgetting all about the reds and greens and blues and yellows and. . . .

SUSAN SPARKS

The Buddha
One Who Awakened

The young man sitting under the assattha tree is dressed in a tattered, loose-fitting, yellowish-white garment. He has coal-black hair, long earlobes, fiercely sensitive eyes, and a dark bronzed skin. Under him is a soft bed of kusha-grass. He is seated on the eastern side of the tree trunk, facing eastward toward the Nairanjana river.

For a full night and a full day he has been sitting thus, bolt upright in the lotus position. His eyes are closed. His body is thin, even gaunt, as though he had recently been attacked and mauled by life. By contrast, there is an unmistakable glow of serenity on his face.

This is the man who will be known for centuries to come simply as the Awakened One—the Buddha.

The weight of suffering that goes on in the world—it is unbearable. It is a world that grows old and dies only to be reborn, and grow old and die, again and again, without end. For every living thing in it: birth, suffering, death . . . birth, suffering, death . . . the Wheel turns, endlessly.

If I reveal what I have seen, what would I accomplish? In a world dedicated to lust and hatred, Truth is not easily tolerated.

I have fallen out of love with the world!

Why should I be concerned, O Mara? Why should I be consumed?

Siddhartha was his given name. The only son of a wealthy land-owner named Shuddhodana and his wife Maya, he was born into the Gautama clan of the Shakya tribe in southeastern Nepal. His home was Lumbini, a small town a few hours southwest of the capital city of Kapilavastu. The region was nourished by the icy waters of the Rohini river that cascaded down from the Himalayan peaks.

At 16 he was married to his cousin Yashodara. In sensuous isolation, his years ebbed away, first his teens and then his twenties; his life/time was being used up, uneventfully, in the hideaway world of his father's spacious courts. He knew little and cared less about the outside world. Still, a discontent was stirring. Life was passing; nothing was gained.

At 29 Siddhartha's only son is born and was named Rahula: "Impediment."

The problem is the human condition, nothing less. The human condition is uninhabitable, but we don't know this. We treat life as though it were livable, and we only make things worse. We dream of fame, fortune, and immortality—which we can't achieve. We develop attachments, affections, and loves for people and things—all of which we lose. Our wants and needs are insatiable, and they cause continuous grief.

And worse: we are not really selves at all. The sense of "self" is generated by an ephemeral collection of particles that cohere, enter the world as system, and become conditioned—"I exist!"—and then disintegrate at death—all in the flash of an instant in cosmic time. And that cosmic instant is characterized by a single crushing reality: suffering.

What we need is therapy. A state of mental health could result if we could stop wanting what cannot be. Mental health would consist in the reestablishment of peace of mind and wholeness of being. These qualities can be regained when we understand clearly that (1) the human condition is uninhabitable, and (2) we don't have to live it.

So, Siddhartha was raised in sensuous luxury. Tradition records his saying, "I was delicately nurtured . . . delicately nurtured beyond measure." He had an adoring wife, and the mythical scenario adds countless dancing girls to keep him company. Even his neighbors complained of his riotous indulgences.

But one day Siddhartha ventured outside the confines of his home and visited the city of Kapilavastu. Though he may have "seen" the sights of the world before, now, for the first time, his sensitive eyes *saw*. He saw an old man whose wrinkled body illustrated the degeneration of 80 years of living. Next he saw a man suffering in agony with disease, an affliction of the black plague of the groin. Then he watched a procession of mourners carrying a shrouded corpse to be cremated on the burning ghats by the river's edge.

Still reeling from his confrontation with the realities of life, he beheld a monk in meditation, trying to discover a spiritual path to follow. The contrast shattered him. Siddhartha knew then that he could never retreat to his former life. He wanted to know the truth—the whole truth—about life-in-the-world.

The first truth is that existence *is* suffering.

The second truth is that our pain and suffering are caused by what we perceive to be our human needs and cravings.

The third truth is that our pain and suffering can end if we learn to eliminate our human needs and cravings.

The fourth truth is that continual practice of the eightfold path will lead to the cessation of all suffering and to a life that is serene and free.

He has *seen* the problem; now he *must* find a solution.

Leaving his wife and son—tradition tells how he visited Yashodara and Rahula in the silence of the night, gazed lovingly at them for the last time, felt the urge to embrace them but turned and rode off into the night, leaving this life forever—he flees into a nearby forest, exchanges his fine clothes with a ragged beggar, cuts his long black hair, and sets out to find the answer to life: a solution to suffering. This is the "Great Renunciation." He is 29.

His first move was to find a guru. He came across Uddaka, a Brahmin ascetic living in a cave, and learned from him how to control his breathing and remain motionless while practicing thought-less meditation. He also learned, for the first time in his life, to deny himself and to fast—"like an insect during a bad season." But after a time these brahmanical teachings left him empty and discontent.

He found another yogi, Alara, and learned from him that the answer cannot be found through the control of the senses or bodily pain and fasting. Again dissatisfied, he left.

What he had really learned from the Hindu hermits was that the ways of others were not for him, and that he must seek his own path.

What is this Middle Way between worldly affections and self-torment that leads to a bright awakening—and to Nirvana?

It is an eightfold path.

First comes wisdom, which results from *right perspective* (we cause our own suffering) and *right intention* (a commitment to transcend the world).

Next comes proper conduct, which results from *right speech, right behavior,* and *right living* (ethical purity must become a matter of habit) so that all one says and does will move him toward his spiritual goals.

Thirdly, one must develop proper mental qualities by means of *right effort* (control of the mind through strength of will), *right mindfulness* (keeping the contents of consciousness under perfect control), and *right meditation* (trance states where the world is forgotten and one experiences perfect joy and emptiness).

It is in the practice of right meditation *(samadhi)* that the true spirituality of awakening begins.

Leaving the two gurus, Siddhartha made his way to Uruvela where he was joined by five mendicant ascetics (possibly Jains) who practiced extreme self-mortification and self-denial. The better part of six years he now spent in their company, doing penance and fasting, exploring the ascetic paths which promised control of the senses and the refinement of one's spiritual nature.

He lived on seeds and herbs, finally ate only a single grain of rice or one jujube apple a day. He became wan and emaciated. "If I sought to feel my belly, it was my backbone which I found in my grasp." He weakened to the point of death. One day he sank into unconsciousness and was revived by a bowl of rice cooked in milk given him by a girl from a nearby village. When he regained his strength, he also recovered a clear mind; and asceticism, he now realized, was not the answer.

Stronger now, clothed in a winding sheet borrowed from a tomb, Siddhartha made his way southward to Gaya. At nightfall he came to a fig tree and, after accepting eight armfuls of mowing grass from a helpful farmer, he sat down by the trunk and slipped into meditation. Knowing that he was nearing the end of his search, he pressed forward relentlessly. "Were my skin to dry up, my hand to wither, and my bones to dissolve, until I have attained to supreme and absolute knowledge I shall not stir from this seat."

Endowed with the whole body of noble virtues—sense control, mindfulness and comprehension, and contentment—the truth-seeker chooses a solitary resting place—a forest, the foot of a tree, a hill, a mountain glen, a rocky cave, a charnel place, a heap of straw in the open field. He abandons this world and enters the mind where the Truth can be found.

As I meditate, all desires fade. I eliminate the five hindrances: urges and wants, the need for action, the need to withdraw and sleep, and anxiety and doubt.

When the five hindrances are eliminated, then happiness is born, to happiness joy is added, with his mood joyful his body is relaxed, his relaxed body feels at ease, and as he feels at ease his mind becomes concentrated—he enters *samadhi.*

Deeper in mind I soar upward. Joy and happiness, born of seclusion. Tranquillity. Joy and happiness born of concentration. Happiness of neutrality. Mindfulness. Understanding. Pure neutrality and mindfulness. Sphere of infinite space. Sphere of infinite consciousness. Sphere of nothingness. Sphere of neither thought nor nonthought. Emptiness. Cessation of thought and feeling. Pure consciousness.

Nirvana.

According to Buddhist tradition, on the full moon day in the month of Vaishakha in the year 528 B.C., Siddhartha reached the end of his quest: he attained Enlightenment *(bodhi)* and became the Awakened One, the Buddha. He was 35 years old.

Thinking as a true philosopher, he had faced the realities of experience as he saw them and attempted to understand what he found. And what he had found was that life is brief and painful, birth is evil and death is release; and the best way to live is to fall out of love with life and develop a state of mind which—while you wait it out—will provide an authentic experience of peace and joy. This is the Way of the Buddha.

Siddhartha—now the Buddha—arose

from beneath the Bodhi tree, walked to Sarnath and shared the Truth with his five companions. They saw, and believed. Then he spent the next 45 years preaching and teaching in northeast India. He was immensely successful. The Sangha (order of monks) was organized, and his wife and son both joined. At the age of 80, tradition tells us, the Buddha died under a sal tree at Kushinagara, not far from his birthplace. His last words to his disciples were, "Go now and earnestly seek you own salvation."

ence which can enrich our lives; and on the condition that they do not rob us of our sanity° or endanger others, there is no valid reason why they should not be known.

5   In the Eastern tradition other modes of consciousness such as focused concentration (*samadhi,* leading to *nirvana),* ecstatic trances, and Zen meditation (*zazen,* leading to *satori)* have been considered, for thousands of years, to be higher, more desirable mind-states, valued far above the reality-mode of consciousness. Such outlooks contrast greatly with our Western single-track commitment to just one form of waking experience.

This is not entirely true, however, for even in our Western tradition revered mystics have seen visions and known the rapture of religious ecstasy; and such experiences were invested with ultimate value. They were experiences devoutly to be sought. In these Western cases the *interpretation* of the experience has given them their value. They were understood to be instances of spirit-possession (by the Holy Spirit) and not merely altered psychological states.°

It appears that the West has used a "double standard" in assessing the value of various modes of psychic experience.

6   There is a fundamental condition to the deliberate exploration of human consciousness, a condition which Eastern religions have scrupulously observed. That condition is that the conscious mind not be impaired in its basic functions, which are to mediate reality and to solve problems. Whatever realms of the inner world we decide to explore, we know that we must shortly return to the reality-mode of consciousness and reestablish relations with the real world. The conscious mind must be adequate to the performance of numerous pragmatic functions; it must be able to organize perception, to remember pertinent information, to make operational value-judgments, to engage in rational thinking as needed, and so on.

In some Eastern religions we find acceptable ways of annihilating one's physical organism as well as the "self." Such practices rest on the obvious assumption that the individual will not be required to reenter the reality-mode of consciousness. He may have decided to withdraw into the forest and proceed into the eternal nirvana from which there is no return. But such instances, while permissible, are

°*The words "sane" and "insane" are much-abused layman's terms which cover a multitude of neurotic and psychotic conditions. Don't be disturbed by their general use here; they will be given more precise definition—or rather various possible definitions will be explored—in Chapter 5-3.*

Ful wys is he that can himselven knowe! (Very wise is he that can know himself.)

CHAUCER

°*For more on "spirit possession" as a model for interpreting human behavior, see pages 495ff.*

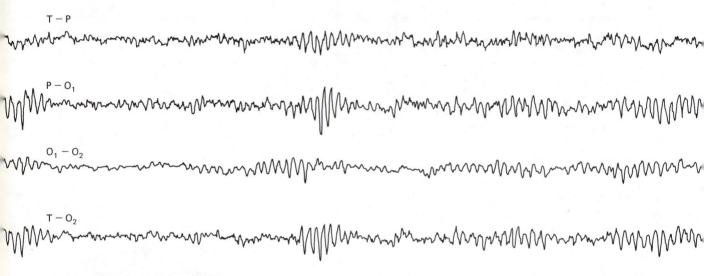

T — P

P — O₁

O₁ — O₂

T — O₂

Gianlorenzo Bernini, *The Ecstasy of St. Theresa*, 1645–52.

Bernini's sculpture (above) in the Cornaro Chapel, Church of Sta. Maria della Vittoria, depicts the moment of sublime consciousness for one of the Western world's renowned mystics, St. Theresa of Avila (1515–1582). At this moment, as she describes it, an angel pierced her heart with a flaming, golden arrow: "The pain was so great that I screamed aloud; but at the same time I felt such infinite sweetness that I wished the pain to last forever. It was not physical but psychic pain, although it affected the body as well to some degree. It was the sweetest caressing of the soul by God."

rare; and the fact of the matter is that, without exception, Eastern religions emphasize the *quality* of the reality-mode of consciousness and look with concern upon Western ("amateur") experiments which endanger conscious functioning. This is precisely the reason why Eastern spiritual leaders are critical of Western use of mind-altering chemicals.

7   The most important aspect of the new worldview is close to the consciousness idea. It is simply that people today, young persons especially, are willing to accept new levels of reality as part of their ordinary experience.

In this, of course, the drug phenomenon has been central. It has made it clear that the spectrum of human experience need not be limited to the ordinary waking state and to a few peripheral ones such as dreaming. It has dramatized that the mind is far richer than most of us ever thought and that the ninety per cent of the mental iceberg that has remained under the water for all but a few great mystics is something that we can all tap.

Drugs were only a catalyst and a raiser of expectations, though, and in a real sense we have entered a post-drug era. I remember picking up a hitchhiker along the California coast some time ago who said that he had dropped acid a hundred and fifty times but now wouldn't even touch aspirin. His search for "natural" highs had led him into some sort of yoga. Others may prefer brain-wave feedback, or transcendental meditation, or encounter, but the quest for life along a wider emotional and mental spectrum underlies them all.

EDWARD B. FISKE

8   Our normal waking consciousness . . . is but one special type of consciousness, whilst all about it, parted from it by the filmiest of screens, there lie potential forms of consciousness entirely different. We may go through life without suspecting their existence; but apply the requisite stimulus, and at a touch they are all there in all their com-

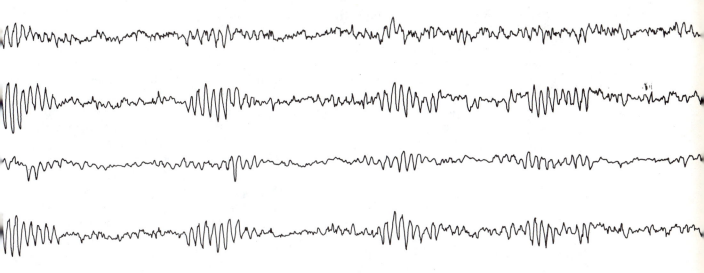

pleteness, definite types of mentality which probably somewhere have their field of application and adaptation. No account of the universe in its totality can be final which leaves these other forms of consciousness quite disregarded. How to regard them is the question—for they are so discontinuous with ordinary consciousness. Yet they may determine attitudes though they cannot furnish formulas, and open a region though they fail to give a map. At any rate, they forbid a premature closing of our accounts with reality.

WILLIAM JAMES

In the province of the mind, what one believes to be true either is true or becomes true within limits to be found experientially and experimentally. These limits are beliefs to be transcended.

JOHN C. LILLY

HUXLEY'S DEEP REFLECTION

9   Aldous Huxley was one of the greatest minds of our century. He had developed, through discipline, a technique for utilizing a high degree of his considerable mental power. At will, Huxley could withdraw into what he called his state of "Deep Reflection" (DR state), a mind-state

marked by physical relaxation with bowed head and closed eyes, a profound progressive psychological withdrawal from externalities but without any actual loss of physical realities nor any amnesias or loss of orientation, a "setting aside" of everything not pertinent, and then a state of complete mental absorption in matters of interest to him.

When Huxley was in such a meditative state it was possible for him to engage in physical activity to some extent—jotting down notes or exchanging pencils—without remembering afterward anything that he had done. As he said, these physical events did not "impinge" on his mental processes. Loud noises could not reach him. He would emerge from his reflective state only when he had finished his self-set creative goals; his emergence was inner-willed.

The last letter of the Tibetan alphabet symbolizes for the Buddhist the fully awakened state of consciousness *(Maha Ati).*

Frequently Huxley began his day's work by entering into his DR state. He would organize his ideas and sort his tasks for that day. One afternoon he was working with total absorption on a particular manuscript when his wife returned from shopping. She inquired whether he had taken down the note she had phoned in to him. Somewhat bewildered, he helped her look for the note, which they found near the phone. He had been in his DR working state when she called, had answered the phone as usual—"I say there, hello!"—listened to the message, jotted it down—all this without remembering a word of the episode. His mind had apparently proceeded to carry on its work without interruption.

The essential point is that this was Huxley's way of working efficiently. His friend Milton Erickson experimented with him in the DR state, and Huxley frequently found himself prepared for work but with nothing to do. He would emerge from his DR state rather puzzled. "There I found myself without anything to do so I came out of it."

His wife commented that when in the state of Deep Reflection, he seemed

like a machine moving precisely and accurately. It is a delightful pleasure to see him get a book out of the bookcase, sit down again, open the book slowly, pick up his reading glass, read a little, and then lay the book and glass aside. Then some time later, maybe a few days, he will notice the book and ask about it. The man just never remembers what he does nor what he thinks about when he sits in that chair. All of a sudden, you just find him in his study working very hard.

10   Religious mystics the world over make a common assertion: no one can understand a profound religious experience until he has himself experienced it. No amount of description with mere symbols can touch its true meaning.

Western mystics—Plotinus, Groot, Eckhart, Tauler, et al.—have consistently stated that there is no experience in daily life that can help one to understand the meaning of the mystical experience, for it is not a mundane experience which is different in degree; rather it is a different *kind* of experience.

The same observation comes from the Eastern mystics: if you think you have achieved an intellectual understanding of nirvana, then you've missed it. Similarly from the Taoist: "The Tao that can be expressed in words is not the true Tao."

MYSTICAL UNITY

11   One of the most valued but ineffable mystical experiences in both East and West is the experience of unity. So profound is it that the mystics thereafter remain silent concerning it. They may indeed

write volumes around the periphery of the experience, but they avow that they could not possibly describe what they have seen.

It is an event in which all experience is somehow seen together. The outer world and the inner merge into one; no distinction is made between subject and object. All knowledge is interwoven; everything is seen in the light of everything else, as though every fragment of knowledge and understanding illuminated every other fragment of knowledge and understanding. There is a coalescence; everything is related; all the contents of the mind become unified. It is all One, and this One may be felt as in some way merging with the cosmos itself; it may be conceived as the uniting of one's essence with Ultimate Reality or Godhead.

By analogy, suppose that you have spent a dozen years devouring knowledge. Imagine that you have carefully read hundreds of books in psychology, history, biology, chemistry, physics; you have studied all the textbooks in higher mathematics, geometry, astronomy, and philosophy; you have memorized the great outpouring of human feeling in music, poetry, literature, and art . . . .

But how do we store and recover such information? Ordinarily our minds move with a pokey, linear motion. They plod along, thinking of one thing at a time. We never read a book at a time, nor even a page at a time: we read only a few words or perhaps a line.

But suppose some psychophysical happening suddenly opened the doors to all your stored information and this vast accumulation of knowledge could flow together into one sustained flash of understanding. Suppose every fact related to every other fact. Suppose that all you had ever learned had somehow bonded into a harmonious whole. In your mind, All was One. Such an experience would indeed be ineffable, so far beyond words that one could never hope to describe what he had seen.

Saint Thomas Aquinas may have had this kind of experience. After producing scores of volumes of systematic theology—the crowning achievement of Western religious thought—Thomas had a vision near the end of his life after which, he said, everything he had previously written was straw. He never attempted to put into mere human words what, at last, he had seen.

ZEN SATORI

12   The state of consciousness sought by the Zen Buddhist is called *satori,* usually translated as "flash of enlightenment." It is a mind-state quite different from a trance or hypnotic condition. It is a state of sharp alertness and wide awareness accompanied, at the same time, by a deep sense of inner calm. We know now that those who practice Zen meditation *(zazen)* are in a specific mental state with a characteristic EEG (electroencephalographic) pattern of brainwaves. Studies show that EEG patterns of experienced Zen meditators are quite different

It seems to me that the greatest lesson of adult life is that one's own consciousness is not enough. What one of us would not like to share the consciousness of half a dozen chosen individuals? What writer would not like to share the consciousness of Shakespeare? What musician that of Beethoven or Mozart? What mathematician that of Gauss? What I would choose would be an evolution of life whereby the essence of each of us becomes welded together into some vastly larger and more potent structure.

FRED HOYLE

A philosopher of imposing stature doesn't think in a vacuum. Even his most abstract ideas are, to some extent, conditioned by what is or is not known in the time when he lives.

WHITEHEAD

from those of beginners. In advanced patterns the alpha waves begin to diminish and a rhythmic "theta train" appears. The typical "advanced" Zen meditation moves through four stages. It begins with initial alpha waves with eyes open (I); then a sharp increase of the alpha (II) followed by a gradual decrease of the alpha (III); and finally there is a sustained period of rhythmic theta waves (IV).

How does *zazen* feel from the standpoint of the meditator? For Western students, Erich Fromm has described the indescribable as well as anyone can.

> If we would try to express enlightenment in psychological terms, I would say that it is a state in which the person is completely tuned to the reality outside and inside of him, a state in which he is fully aware of it and fully grasps it. *He* is aware of it—that is, not his brain, nor any other part of his organism, but *he*, the whole man. He is aware of *it;* not as of an object over there which he grasps with his thought, but *it*, the flower, the dog, the man, in its or his full reality. He who awakes is open and responsive to the world, and he can be open and

The great cause of much psychological illness is the fear of knowledge of oneself—of one's emotions, impulses, memories, capacities, potentialities, of one's destiny.

ABRAHAM MASLOW

responsive because he has given up holding on to himself as a thing, and thus has become empty and ready to receive. To be enlightened means "the full awakening of the total personality to reality."

RELIGIOUS ECSTASY

13   A state of consciousness which a Western religious minority has highly prized is a form of religious ecstasy. Those belonging to the "Pentecostal" tradition—or other traditions which value "spirit possession" (in Christianity, possession by the Holy Spirit)—have sometimes made the ecstatic experience a condition of membership. Within their circles they cultivate an attitude of expectancy in which members may anticipate for years the glorious soul-filling experience.

In religious ecstasy several things occur. The word *ecstasy* derives from the Greek *ek* ("out of") and *stasis* ("standing"), implying that the true person is "standing outside" his body, the assumption being that a "spirit" has taken his place. Thus an "ecstatic" individual is no longer in possession of his own body, and the original "self" is no longer in a reality-mode. An ecstatic individual no longer responds to the realities about him; his behavior has "switched to automatic." Some deeper level of the psyche has taken control while the normal controlling ego has suspended operations.

A typical ecstatic experience is known as *glossolalia*, "speaking in tongues." In this state, one feels he has gradually been overcome or "possessed." He may begin to speak unintelligible words ("babble") to himself or to bystanders. His voice may sound quite different from his own; he may sing beautifully when ordinarily he sings not at all. To the ecstatic individual it feels as though the words and songs are uttered by someone else deep within, and are quite beyond his control. As in cases of hypnosis, some aspect of the personality other than the ego has taken control, and any content originates from the deeper levels of consciousness.

In "Pentecostal" experiences where the ecstatic state is considered to be possession by the Holy Spirit, it not infrequently brings about a fundamental reorientation in the individual's life—a "conversion"or "born again" experience. It is difficult to imagine any experience more meaningful than being possessed by God.

THE WHITE LIGHT

14   I was in the desert, in a very beautiful place I visited frequently last year. Involved in the experience were: the beauty of nature, a strong feeling of my relationship with that Mother Nature, some very loving, very close people putting me physically and mentally in a very comfortable, relaxed physical and emotional setting.

The experience physically was brought on by a cold river and hot springs. Imagine: cold river, hot springs; water of 120 degrees, air of 110, river water somewhere in the 60s.

Le coeur a ses raisons que la raison ne connaît point.
(The heart has its reasons which reason knows nothing of.)

PASCAL

As I see it, such a man, the man who is engaged in a lifetime quest away from encapsulation, moving in the direction of the broadest and deepest possible reality image, has the key to what it means to be and to see. He is thereby representative of man in his deepest and most significant sense. For such an orientation would mean that he was very much alive in the best meaning of the term "existential" and very much aware in the best meaning of the term "philosophical." Such a man would be a man of great compassion, great sensitivity, and great thought. He would, in short, be reaching for ultimate consciousness. And while it is true that such an open approach to life is very risky for the individual man in the short view, it is clearly more creative and productive, and therefore, more viable for all men in the long run.

JOSEPH ROYCE

I began by sitting in the 120-degree water until sweat poured from my face and I could no longer stand the physical feeling of that heat. I jumped out of the hot water, climbed a rock and dove fifteen feet into a three-foot pool of very, very cold water. Now this does quite a number to your body and your mind. I swam across the river to where there was a shaded area and sat in the cold water in the shade until I began shivering and began getting extremely uncomfortable from the shivering, swam back across the river and jumped back into the hot water, feeling absolutely nothing immediately and then an extreme rush. And back and forth nine times.

At the completion of the ninth time I climbed back up on top of the rock to dive back into the cold water, and as I looked down I experienced something that I will call the "white light," the clear light, and as I looked down to see the pool into which I was to dive, my vision was of naught—a complete nothing, of the void. And I can remember thinking, feeling, reacting, something . . . so that the next thing I knew I was sitting down on this large flat rock. And this is very difficult to relate to you because it didn't happen with words— there were no words in my mind then. But I sat down in a position like this, with my heels against my bottom, went back, flat on my back with my arms flat out, feet still touching here, soles of my feet together—and by the way I've never done this before and could never hope to repeat it again, this physical position—still touching here, flat on my back, arms straight out, and allowed myself for the first time in my life to let go of my body. My knees went down and touched the rock, so that I was lying like this, completely flat, released my self from my body. And the next thing I knew I was looking down at that body lying on the rock from a point a little bit higher than the peak of a mountaintop next to the hot springs.

It scared me, and it scared me very much. Part of that fright was because at the time I was into a very heavy, "me-man, you-earth" state of mind, and I wasn't really willing or ready to relate to "me- essence, you-universe." And I snapped real quick, and I was back in my body, and I was hearing my name being called. And I stood up and the experience was gone. And it lasted a total of—from the time I climbed the rock until I was back down—maybe thirty seconds. And yet that experience of only thirty seconds was one of such purity and one of such truth and one of such extreme pure emotion, that I could never possibly hope to forget it. . . .

TERRY ALLEN

15   In the Indian religions, the state of nirvana is a trance-state out- wardly resembling a deep sleep. It is marked by a progressive deep- ening of the trance through religious disciplines that are similar to techniques of self-hypnosis. Gradually, as *samadhi* ("concentration") is practiced, the devotee learns to block out all sensory stimuli from the external world; simultaneously, sensory and emotional input from the inner world are reduced and finally stopped; no bodily sensations or emotions—hunger, pain, fear, loneliness—are registered. Further, however, the mystic enters into a mind-state of zero cognition—no ideas, memories, or rational activity. It is a "contentless" state of consciousness.

This Eastern trance resembles Huxley's "Deep Reflection" in one respect: loud noises or other stimuli are not perceived. But in its central nature, it contrasts with Huxley's DR state. In the latter's mind a high pitch of intellectual activity raced through its plan of operations, while in nirvana there is no mental *content* of any sort. It is *pure consciousness*, a seemingly discarnate, free-floating experience of nothingness.

This is the ultimate achievement of human existence for the Hindu and Buddhist. It is said to be experienced as an indescribable state of tranquility, inner peace, and joy, a timeless state of union with the cosmos itself. In Hindu terms, the self-essence *(atman)* has become one with Ultimate Reality *(Brahman)*.

> All that is comes from the mind.
>
> *DHAMMAPADA 1.1*

THE FANTASTIC JOURNEY

16   The individual who lacks awareness of the depths and facets of his psyche is something less than a whole man, and considerably less than he could be. He is living a single-dimensioned existence in a multidimensional psychic universe. There is no reason not to explore other worlds and—like the Zen monk or religious ecstatic—spend some time living there. The qualifying condition, as emphasized, is that he preserve his autonomy and the integrity of his reality-mode of consciousness.

Of course, our Western methods for accomplishing anything are distinctive: we employ chemistry and physics in everything. It is quite in character that we approach psychic/somatic functions with pills and gadgets, milligrams and voltages. And, typically, we will find faster ways of "getting there" and run the risks so characteristic of our rapid conquest of all known worlds.

> Nirvana is not the blowing out of the candle. It is the extinguishing of the flame because day is come.
>
> *RABINDRANATH TAGORE*

In the eighties we are in process of breaking through archaic traditions regarding the human psyche. We have already come so far that there is now little doubt that we will continue to loosen the confines and, hopefully, move ahead to positive controls and enriching experiences.

But we must take care, for *this* is the "fantastic journey" into the delicate nuclear center of human existence itself—the Mind of Man.

REFLECTIONS—

1 Is Maslow's observation on p. 218-QM meaningful to you? When you read Maslow's comment along with that of R. D. Laing's (Sec. 1), what is your dominant response?

2 Your text makes the opening statement that "there is no obvious reason why one should spend his lifetime solely in the two traditional mind-

states: the problem-solving conscious state and the 'recovery' sleep state" (Sec. 4). Do you tend to agree? Or, in your opinion, are these the only normal and natural modes of consciousness?

3 As you reflect on each of the modes of consciousness described in this chapter (such as Huxley's DR state, mystical unity, Zen satori, ecstatic "spirit possession," the out-of-body projection), are these modes of consciousness that you would like to experience? Do you fear them? If so, are you aware of the source of your fear? Would you want to experience them, do you think, if you could be sure they would turn out to be profoundly meaningful experiences, as others have claimed? In each specific case, what do you think made the experience meaningful to those who knew it?

4 As you ponder Huxley's DR state, would you like to develop this kind of mental technique for work efficiency? Do you think Huxley possessed a special gift or is this a mental skill that many of us could acquire?

5 What is your response to the mystical experience of St. Theresa of Avila (p. 214-QM)? What gave the experience its profound meaning? Would the experience be denigrated or robbed of its significance if it were comprehensible in psychological terms?

6 Do you share Sir Fred Hoyle's feeling that "one's own consciousness is not enough"? If you agree, do you also feel the impulse to transcend your consciousness predicament? How might you achieve such transcendence? Or is the very idea of "transcendence" a vain and futile notion?

7 Reflect upon the statement by Joseph Royce (p. 219-QM), then restate in your own words what you think he is saying. (In this connection, the comment by Colin Wilson on p. 315-QM may be meaningful.) What do you think Royce means by the phrase "reaching for ultimate consciousness"? In what sense might it be "very risky" for the individual man?

Furthermore . . .

Altered States of Consciousness. Readings from *Scientific American.* W. H. Freeman, 1972.

BLOOMFIELD, HAROLD N., et al., *TM.* Delacorte, 1975.

BROWN, BARBARA B., *New Mind, New Body: Biofeedback: New Directions for the Mind.* Harper, 1974.

CASTANEDA, CARLOS, the Don Juan series (4 vols); especially *The Teachings of Don Juan* (Simon & Schuster, 1968) and *Journey to Ixtlan* (Simon & Schuster, 1972).

JOHANSSON, RUNE E. A., *The Psychology of Nirvana.* Anchor, 1970.

NEIHARDT, JOHN G., *Black Elk Speaks.* Pocket Books, 1972.

ORNSTEIN, ROBERT E., *The Psychology of Consciousness.* W. H. Freeman, 1972.

PINES, MAYA, *The Brain Changers: Scientists and the New Brain Control.* Signet, 1976.

WEIL, ANDREW, *The Natural Mind.* Houghton-Mifflin, 1972.

WHITE, JOHN (ed.), *The Highest State of Consciousness.* Anchor, 1972.

WILBER, KEN, *The Spectrum of Consciousness.* Quest Books, 1977.

Past/Present/Future

Have You Ever Wondered . . .

- What time it is?

- What time is? or if time really exists at all?

- How fast time moves (if it moves at all)?

- Why time races by when you're doing something you enjoy but pokes along at a snail's pace when you're bored?

- Whether "the past" exists, and if so, where?

- Whether "the future" might actually exist somewhere? (somewhen?)

- What "the present" (of your experience) is and how long it "lasts"?

- If there is any way for us humans to live time-present more fully?

A PHILOSOPHY OF TIME

1   Time affects us in so many ways. We use it; we abuse it; we enjoy it; we fear it.

     The way we respond to the challenges of time is a test of what we are, of what we are becoming. We grow older day by day, older

The Moving Finger writes; and having writ, Moves on. . .

OMAR KHAYYAM
The Rubaiyat

in the calendar. Does that fact disturb us greatly, little, sometimes, often? How else are we growing in the same time? How much of our time do we enjoy doing what? Do we frequently or seldom feel that the time was really well spent? The answers we would give to these questions reveal our *philosophy of time.* We all acquire one, though we rarely, if ever, venture to spell it out.

R. M. MAC IVER

What is time? If no one asks me, I know. If I try to explain it to someone asking me, I don't know.

ST. AUGUSTINE

2   A "philosophy of *time.*" Time possesses at once, for us all, the *fascinosum* and the *mysterium;* it is intimately familiar *and* ultimately formidable. Time *is* life, and life *is* time; and somehow we know this in the marrow of our bones. But in all of human experience, is there anything which more befuddles our understanding? Is there any concept which, when we try to force open its secrets, betrays the frailty of our thoughts and the ineptness of our language? Whitehead said it all: "It is impossible to meditate on time and the mystery of the creative passage of nature without overwhelming emotion at the limitations of human intelligence."

3   "Time is like an ever-flowing stream." (The *stream* of consciousness, the *flow* of an electric current, the *flow* of words of a great orator?) "Time unrolls like a carpet." (*Unrolls* in the sense of uncovering something which was previously hidden but now lies exposed to view; and will it continue to be displayed or will the carpet begin to re-roll from the other end and thus hide something again?) "Clocks *keep* time." (As we *keep* our possessions, *keep* our moral principles, *keep* a house?) "Time passes." (As we *pass* an automobile on the road, *pass* a course in a university, *pass* from life to the hereafter?) "Time is ever coming into being and passing out of being." (Where was it before it *came into being* and where does it go when it *passes out of being?*) "Time is all-embracing." (If it is all-embracing does it also *embrace time?*) "We tell time." (To whom, in what language, and *what* do we tell about time?) "We expect the future, experience the present, and remember the past." (Is time then merely a subjective image created by our mind, and having no counterpart in the world?) "Time is the relation of before and after." (But *before* and *after* refer *only* to time; hence we are saying literally time is time.) Does this not show that what I have called the straightforward descriptions of time contain metaphors and analogies, ambiguous words, subjective terms, hidden contradictions, and definitions which are purely verbal?

CORNELIUS BENJAMIN

[Time] brings to mind the ideas of corrosion and decay, the knowledge of inexorable and irreversible aging and death. Hence man's efforts to arrest time, to cast off his chronological chains, and to build cities and monuments, pyramids and empires which can resist the teeth of time. Hence, too, his pursuit of a mirage of love which does not wither or fade with time, and his dream of a glory which is outside time. The more man reflects on time, the more his mortality weighs upon him, and the more he realizes that "all our yesterdays have lighted fools the way to dusty death."

JOHN COHEN

One encouraging note can be heard above all our confusion. It has been noted by Friedrich Waismann that, although most of us haven't the foggiest notion what time *is,* our time-language seems to keep on *working.* We understand the meaning of the *word* "time" in various contexts ("What time is it?" "He arrived just in the nick of time." "We all had a great time." Etc.) and thus we continue to function pragmatically without ever knowing what we're talking about.°

Three philosophical questions about time will come into focus here. (1) What is time? How do we experience it? Can we understand it? (2) What is meant exactly by "past," "present," and "future"? In what sense can each of them be said to exist? (3) Where in time do we live? What does time have to do with personal existence?

CLOCK TIME

4   We use the word "time" to refer to at least three different phenomena, all quite distinct, though usually confused in our minds.

One is clock time or chronological time (the latter deriving from the Greek *chronos,* meaning "time"—which doesn't help matters in the least). Clock time probably has nothing whatever to do with time. Clocks measure space. One hour of chronological time is the apparent movement of the sun from, say, its zenith point (12 o'clock noon) to a point 15° westward along its orbital path. The clock on the wall is set to correlate with the sun's motion. While the sun moves 15° in space, one clock hand moves 360° while the other smaller hand moves 30° in space. Both events (sun and clock) are cases of matter-in-motion which we have correlated for practical purposes. We usually say we have "syn*chron*ized" sun and clock, implying our belief that real time is involved in the operation. But this is doubtful. We are correlating events and not synchronizing time.

PSYCHOLOGICAL TIME

5   A second kind of time is subjective time—psychological or experiential time. This is the only temporal phenomenon of which we have any clear conception, and many philosophers are of the conviction that experiential time is the only true time. Psychological time is our individual experience of the continuum of our consciousness. Consciousness *is* time. When we are asleep or unconscious, time is nonexistent for each of us, but it begins again the moment we regain consciousness.

In this context, we can properly speak of the speeding up and slowing down of time, for the metabolic processes which determine our time-consciousness do just that. They vary. To speak of time variability is to describe accurately an experience of consciousness which is a function of the rate of oxygen consumption by the brain.

Henri Bergson preferred the term "duration" when speaking of conscious time. Pure duration is our ongoing experience of the continuum of consciousness. Bergson insisted that our purest intuition of the true nature of all reality is our experience of this duration of our own consciousness.

To say that time is consciousness may be misleading since we (in the Western world) tend to think of consciousness as consciousness *of*

°*The use of the word "time" in this chapter is sufficient evidence of this point. I count at least 30 different definitions of the word in the text of this chapter, most of which, in context, succeed in communicating ideas with some degree of adequacy, but do not necessitate an understanding of what time truly is. What could better illustrate the astounding fact that we can and do communicate with one another continually* without *knowing what we are talking about?!*

The delicious melodies of Purcell or Cimarosa might be disjointed stammerings to a hearer whose partition of time should be a thousand times subtler than ours.

SAMUEL TAYLOR COLERIDGE

We are always the same age inside.

GERTRUDE STEIN

something. Here is one source of confusion about the nature of time. We objectify time and think of it as a sort of fluid medium in which objects/events occur. Just as we find it difficult to conceive of consciousness apart from consciousness of something, so also for time: we have difficulty thinking of time as "pure time" (Bergson's "pure duration") apart from real objects/events. But time and matter-in-motion must be separated in thought. Our ordinary waking consciousness is the time-continuum upon which external objects/events impinge. The telephone rings or someone speaks, and these external stimuli activate sensations which enter directly into consciousness (time) as content. But time and the content are not the same. Time might more easily be conceived as the continuum of consciousness without content.

One important implication of this understanding of time is that if there were no experiencers (no conscious minds), there could be no

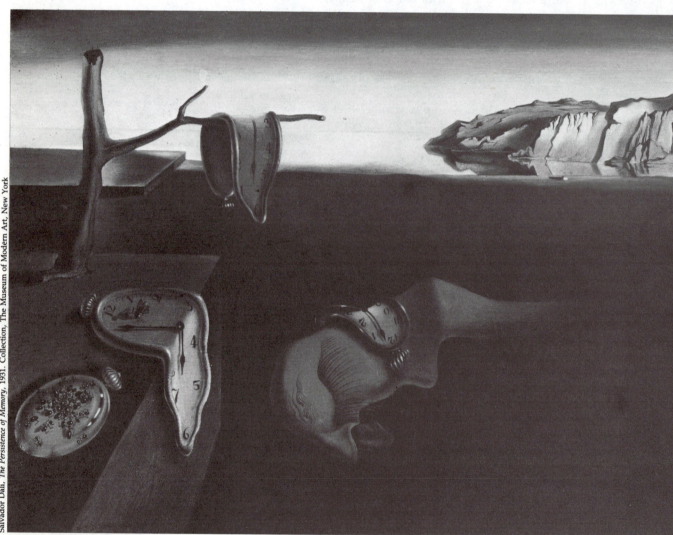

Salvador Dali, *The Persistence of Memory*, 1931. Collection, The Museum of Modern Art, New York

time. Therefore, there was a time (!), perhaps 4.5 billion years ago, before conscious creatures had evolved, when there was no time. Likewise, if all life on earth should cease to exist in the future, time would be no more.

6   As early as 1860 the Austrian physicist Ernst Mach, the first Western thinker to treat time scientifically, concluded that "the time of the physicist does not coincide with the system of time sensations." The physicist can assume an "even flow" of time or, when very great speeds are involved, describe temporal variations ("time dilation") with Einstein's relativistic formulas. His kind of time still behaves with congenial consistency.

The psychologist is not so fortunate: his time is wildly capricious. Psychological time varies with body temperature: if temperature is raised, time passes slower; if lowered, it passes faster. If our metabolic rate is increased, time passes slower; if decreased, it passes faster. Time plods at half a snail's pace in the eager experience of a child; it accelerates like a speed-demon as the adult years pass by.° All these variations are determined by the rate of oxygen consumption by the brain.

°On the variations of time-experience with age, see box on page 137.

Illness and disease can also produce variations in time experience. Among these are Parkinson's disease, some forms of mental/emotional illness, and certain disorders produced by alcoholism.

PURE SPACE AND PURE TIME

In Relativity Theory, the first three purely spatial dimensions have as an attribute perfect reversibility, whereas time, to the extent that it is a physical unwinding, remains irreversible, demonstrating immediately that the parallelism does not go very far. From an epistemological viewpoint, one must say even more: space can be completely abstracted from its content in the measure of pure form and give way to a strictly deductive science of space, which would be pure geometry. By contrast, there is no pure chronometry; there is no science comparable to geometry in the field of time, precisely because time is a coordination of velocities and because when one speaks of velocity, one speaks of a physical entity. *Time* cannot be abstracted from its content as space can. *Temporal order*, in a sense, can be abstracted from its content, in which case, however, it becomes a simple order of succession. But *duration* . . . depends essentially upon velocities. Duration cannot be disassociated from its content psychologically or physically. From the point of view of psychology, Bergson's analyses of pure duration have amply shown the interdependence of time and its psychological content; similarly, from the physical point of view, time depends upon velocities.

JEAN PIAGET
Time Perception in Children

Man's short-term subjective time scale may depend upon the constancy of his internal temperature. For so-called cold-blooded animals this would not hold. For them time would presumably pass slowly on warm days and rapidly on cold days. . . . Time would not appear to flow steadily in the linear sort of way familiar to us mammals.

HUDSON HOAGLAND

Almost all hallucinogens, euphoric drugs such as opium and marijuana, and even some common nonprescription drugs can induce extreme alterations in time experience. Under many conditions, clock time seems to pass incredibly slow.

We say that time "slows down" and "speeds up." But in relation to what? In relation to chronological time—to the ticks of the clock—as well as in relation to our memory of what is for oneself a "normal" experience of time. We are surrounded by clocks by which we constantly gauge our experience of time: clocks and watches proper, the sun in motion, cars going by, traffic signals, jet planes flying overhead, our own heartbeats, the duration required for us to move from one place to another along a familiar route, the time it takes our eggs to fry or toast to burn. These and a thousand other daily events are clocks against which variations in our time experience would be noticed and measured.

REAL TIME

7   A third kind of phenomena which we think of as "time" is matter-in-motion, that is, sequences of events occurring in the real world. The sun rises, dandelion seeds float through the air, clouds gather, rain falls, waves break upon the shore. The majority of time-theorists would hold that all these are *only* sequences of events and do not involve any kind of time per se. However, nothing prevents our using the word "time" to refer to such real events while we measure such events against our calibrated clocks and/or experiential time.

If we ask how long it takes a cannon ball dropped from the top of the leaning Tower of Pisa to hit the ground, then we can time the event with our clocks, in which case we are doing what we did with our clocks and the sun (correlating spatial events); or we can time the event experientially with conscious time as we watch the cannonball fall.

SAINT AUGUSTINE: GOD'S TIME AND OURS

8   At some point in his life, almost every philosopher has become preoccupied with the nature of time. Several developed noteworthy models to explain time and its mysterious operations.

Saint Augustine's concept of time is conditioned by his theological presuppositions. God *created* time, Augustine reasoned, when he created everything else. Since God created time, he existed *before* time, he will exist *after* time, and therefore he exists *outside* time. There was no time before he created it. Judeo-Christian doctrine has consistently held that God created *all* that exists—including time and presumably space—*ex nihilo*, "out of nothing."

In the mind of God, there is no "before" or "after"; there is only

> All the vital problems of philosophy depend for their solutions on the solution of the problem what Space and Time are and more particularly how they are related to each other.
>
> SAMUEL ALEXANDER

a "now." In "God's experience" all events occur simultaneously. To put it another way, all the past and all the future (that is, *our* past and future) exist together in God's present. Thus, when Augustine elaborates on the doctrine that God foresaw the Fall of Man, God really didn't *foresee* anything, as though he were peering ahead through time (as we would have to) and saw what had not yet transpired. In God's all-inclusive present, "future" events are taking place now. God didn't *fore*see; he merely saw. Likewise, he doesn't foreordain an event; he merely ordains (causes) what he sees happening. This, to Augustine, is what is meant for God to be omniscient and omnipotent.

We humans experience the present, remember the past, and anticipate the future; but God is not limited by our human time. It is not correct to say, as some theologians do, that there are really two times, God's and ours. Rather, we are *in* time; God is timeless.

NEWTON: ABSOLUTE TIME

9   Sir Isaac Newton appears to have assumed, somewhat uncritically, that time is real, being an integral part of the operations of nature. But this objective time is not to be *equated with* matter-in-motion, or with objects per se which endure in time. Real time is separate from real objects/events. Newton's oft-repeated description of time—and his critics have had a field day with it—is as follows:

> Absolute, true, and mathematical time, of itself, and from its own nature, flows equably without relation to anything external, and by another name is called duration: relative, apparent, and common time, is some sensible and external (whether accurate or unequable) measure of duration by means of motion, which is commonly used instead of true time; such as an hour, a day, a month, a year.

It was Newton who first introduced into Western thought the notion of an absolute time. This absolute time (whatever it is) is a universal medium which flows smoothly and evenly, unaffected by all the events which occur *inside* it.

Newton's assumption of absolute time dominated the thinking of physicists until the unorthodox reflections of Einstein at the beginning of our century proved it to be an unworkable assumption and rendered it obsolete.

Our real journey in life is interior; it is a matter of growth, deepening, and of an ever greater surrender to the creative action of love and grace in our hearts.

THOMAS MERTON

KANT: TIME IS IN THE MIND

10   Immanuel Kant considered our sense of time to be inherent in the structure of the mind. Our time-sense is not developed through experience; it is rather "a priori," prior to experience. It is a mode of perception, a subjective mental form which the mind employs in its organization of perception. Dr. Cornelius Benjamin has made a succinct summary of the logical arguments which Kant developed to defend his a priori view of time.

In te, anime meus, tempora metior.
(It is in you, O my mind, that I
measure time.)

ST. AUGUSTINE

First, time cannot be an empirical conception since its essential characteristics (coexistence and succession) cannot be perceived by us unless we have some prior notion of time in our minds. In other words, sensations cannot be observed as temporal if we do not already know what is meant by "coexistence" and "succession." Second, we cannot think of phenomena as outside of time, yet we can readily think of empty time. Objects, therefore, can be annihilated from thought, but time cannot. This makes time logically prior to phenomena. Third, only on the supposition that time is a form of intuition can we explain why it is impossible to think of a two-dimensional time or of two coexistent times. This incapacity of our minds is due not to the fact that experience reveals no such notions but to the unthinkable character of the notions. Fourth, time is not a generalization from different times, for different times are merely parts of one and the same time; hence time is an a priori form which interrelates phenomena into a temporal manifold. Fifth, conceptions of time-segments, i.e., limited durations, are possible only on the assumption of an unlimited or infinite time; but this cannot be an empirically derived notion and must consequently be given as a prior form of intuition under which phenomena are perceived.

TIME PAST

11   Many of us find that our ideas about the past, present, and future run together, overlap, or are otherwise blurred.

Ivar Lissner once wrote a book which he entitled *The Living Past.* It's not difficult to infer what he wishes to say with this title, but, for openers, we might logically ask whether, in any sense, the past could be "living" (present tense). Isn't the past dead? And isn't the past, by definition, placed outside the boundary of the present? This is not to say that influences from "past presents" don't linger on and influence us. They do, but their existence is felt only in our living present.

Yet to say the past is "dead" is surely incorrect. To call something "dead" implies that it was once alive, but the past is never "alive." We could just as well speak of a "living future"—which seems to make little sense. Only the present is "alive"—isn't it? Apparently we are having language troubles again.

It is worth remembering that we
never see or experience anything
but the past. The sounds you are
hearing now come from a
thousandth of a second back in
time for every foot they have had
to travel to reach your ears. This is
best demonstrated during a
thunderstorm, when the peal from
a flash twelve miles away will not
be heard for a full minute. If you
ever see a flash and hear the
thunder simultaneously, you will
be lucky to be alive. I have done it
once and do not recommend the
experience.

ARTHUR C. CLARKE

The nature of the past is of primary concern to the historian since "the past" is his sole subject matter. From his standpoint, the past exists only as it is recreated in the historian's mind. The concrete events of the past are forever gone, and they can be recreated again in the historian's imagination only to the extent that records of some kind have survived from those who witnessed the events. The telltale signs left by events are many: words of eyewitnesses who selected what aspects of any event were significant to them, plus their interpretation and valuation; fossil tracks, leaves, bones; geological records in rocks, volcanic layers, seamounts, oceanic trenches, and so on. If an event leaves no record, then it is forever irretrievable; no historian can reconstruct it nor, for that matter, would he have reason to guess that it had ever occurred.

It's a poor sort of memory that
only works backward.

LEWIS CARROLL
Through the Looking-Glass

TIME FUTURE

12   What about the future? Unless we hold to some such theory as Augustine's notion of time, then questions about the existence of the future leave our intellects bewildered.

Can we experience the future? If we can answer "no," then the future can be defined as our expectation that events will continue to occur or that, experientially, we will continue to experience "presents." Our personal future is merely the expectation that our consciousness will continue.

But if, in any way, we can say "yes" to the question "Can we experience the future?", then we must face the most difficult of all philosophical problems and the one with the most far-reaching implications. There is at present ample unexplained time phenomena to prevent our closing the question. Arthur C. Clarke, who, even in his fiction, tries to remain a sound scientist, gives in to the possibility of precognition. "I would be willing to state that seeing into the future . . . [is] impossible, were it not for the impressive amount of evidence to the contrary."

If we can experience the future, then under any theory of time we have now, we must conclude that the future has *already* taken place or is *now* taking place. (Recall that Augustine, in order to allow God fore-knowledge of the future, was compelled to theorize that our past, present, and future are all taking place concurrently in God's mind.)

If the future has happened or is happening, then the very structure of our normal waking experience is destroyed. Gone also are numerous axiomatic assumptions such as cause-and-effect and before-and-after. Causal relations become meaningless: that the seed must be planted before the organism can grow, that the song must be sung before it can be heard, that the fire must be lit before the wood can burn—all such statements are wrong. Experience is shot through with contradictions and illusions.

13   Whether we do experience the future has not been established, but experiences which are difficult to explain on any other basis are not uncommon. J. B. Priestley correctly notes that "if one, just one, precognitive dream could be accepted as something more than a coincidence—bang goes our conventional idea of Time!"

Not only is precognition the most stubborn of all philosophical problems, but (if it exists) it often presents itself as a puzzle within a puzzle. Many instances of precognition, especially of tragic episodes, appear as warnings which make it possible for the person having the experience to take evasive action and prevent the tragedy which was foreseen. But this is a contradiction: to be perceived, the future already exists; but when perceived, it can be altered. Therefore, what has already happened can subsequently be changed. Which makes no sense at all.

Priestley—who accepts precognition as fact—says it well.

Whether the future can be known, even in principle, is one of the subtlest of all philosophical questions.

ARTHUR C. CLARKE

Individual Consciousness is but a shadow; what is permanent is the world.

JOSIAH ROYCE

Let me put it briefly and brutally. The future can be seen, and because it can be seen, it can be changed. But if it can be seen and yet be changed, it is neither solidly there, laid out for us to experience moment after moment, nor is it non-existent, something we are helping to create, moment after moment. If it does not exist, it cannot be seen; if it is solidly set and fixed, then it cannot be changed. What is this future that is sufficiently established to be observed and perhaps experienced, and yet can allow itself to be altered?

(This problem, too, has an interesting theological parallel. A centuries-old controversy turns on whether God's foreknowledge of events necessarily implies predestination. That is, if God "foresees" an event, does that event *have to occur* or can it be altered? In other words, can God be wrong in what he foresees? It would seem that he can be wrong if the hint of human precognition is applicable: prevision does *not* mean predestination.)

At present we have no time-theories which can explain such occurrences. We must either deny that the future can be experienced now, or develop new models regarding the nature of time. Philosophers and scientists have avoided the time problem, partly because of its association with the occult. But those who professionally wonder about the nature of existence should, like foolish angels, rush in—albeit with fear and trembling—and attempt to create comprehension where chaos now reigns.

TIME PRESENT

14   Since Zeno the Eleatic (fl. c. 450 B.C.), analytical thinkers have been bothered by the nature of the present—the "now" of experience. A long-standing tradition has held that the present is a durationless point. This is the theory of the "punctiform present." It seems that the moment we experience the present, it has already become the past, while the very near future keeps rushing across this knife-edge present into the past. The "now" has no duration; it seems like only a timeless boundary between future and past. If this present has any "width," then it must be composed of a series of (durationless) instants. Louise Heath nicely states this line of logic (although she does not herself accept it):

> The nature of time is such that when the present is, the past has been and *is no* longer, the future will be, but *is not* yet, while the present which *is*, turns out on analysis to be not a part of time but only the boundary between past and future.

This leaves us in a quandary. If, on either side, the past and the future sort of squeeze the present into a durationless boundary line, then where does human experience take place? Or might experience be an illusion, after all, as Zeno believed?

Something must be wrong with our reasoning. We don't live in the past or future, so we must live in the present. Is the "now" of our experience really a point? or does it have width? If so, how wide is it? Perhaps our "now" extends a little bit into the future and past, as William James believed:

> The only fact of our immediate experience is what has been called the "specious" present, a sort of saddle-back of time with a certain length of its own, on which we sit perched, and from which we look in two directions into time. The unit of composition of our perception of time is a duration, with a bow and a stern as it were—a rearward- and a forward-looking end. It is only as parts of this duration-block that the relation of succession of one end to the other is perceived. We do not feel first one end and then the other after it, and from the perception of the succession infer an interval of time between, but we seem to feel the interval of time as a whole, with its two ends embedded in it.

15   James is on the right path, we think. What we call the "present" is by its very nature a *psychological* event, rather than a mathematical or physical (real) event.° As a psychological event involving perception and consciousness, it therefore possesses duration. The notion of time as a timeless instant is fallacious. Experiencing takes time; it has width. An experience involving intricate psychophysiological processes "stretches out" and lasts a while and could never occur in a "timeless instant." A French psychologist, Paul Fraisse, describes the present from a modern point of view:

> My present is one "tick-tock" of a clock, the three beats of the rhythm of a waltz, the idea suggested to me, the chirp of a bird flying by. . . . All the rest is already past or still belongs to the future. There is order in this present, there are intervals between its constituent elements, but there is also a form of simultaneity resulting from the very unity of my act of perception. Thus the perceived present is not the paradox which logical analysis would make it seem by splitting time into atoms and reducing the present to the simple passage of time without psychological reality. Even to perceive this passage of time requires an act of apprehension which has an appreciable duration.

Therefore, we can define *time* as the experience of the duration of our consciousness, and *the present* as the perceptual time-span of that duration.

But what is the span of that duration? How long does it last? Its duration is not a constant, but depends rather upon the nature of perceptual events which constitute the perceived present. It depends partly on the number of sense stimuli which are perceived as a unitary event. Any event lasting for more than about two seconds "spills over" into the past, and part of the event is remembered. A series of stimuli (the notes of a melody or the number of spoken sounds) is usually perceived as a unitary event when they last for about one-half to one second. It has been observed that when a clock strikes three or four, we can usually identify the hour without counting the number of consecutive chimes; but beyond four, we have to start counting the number of strikes to identify the hour.

°This would seem to be a fairly obvious conclusion since (1) mathematicians make no claim that mathematical time-points ("instants") are anything other than mental constructs which are useful in solving certain problems; (2) in physics, Einstein's theories have annihilated the notion of simultaneity, that is, that there exists a "universal now"; what is present for one experiencer may be past or future for another experiencer. See the box on page 439.

We are never at home; we are always beyond it. Fear, desire or hope drive us towards the future and deprive us of the feeling and contemplation of what is.

MONTAIGNE

No perception of the present is independent of its content. The duration of the present depends upon the number and nature of the stimuli perceived, the intervals between stimuli, and the organization of the stimuli. The duration of the present also depends upon the state of consciousness of the perceiver and the familiarity and meaningfulness of the organized stimuli. The duration of meaningful sounds in our own language differs from the duration of meaningless sounds in a foreign language. The same is true for a familiar melody in contrast to one never heard before.

In summary, therefore, while in a normal waking mode of consciousness, our perceived present rarely lasts longer than five seconds, and frequently it lasts less than a second. On the average the time-span of our perceived present persists for two to three seconds.

TIME AND PERSONAL EXISTENCE

16   Time and personality are fundamentally related. There is nothing unhealthy about reliving in one's memory the happy moments of one's past or anticipating in imagination the possible happy events of the future. But such movements into past or future can become unhealthy if one is "pushed out of the present" by unbearable conditions and develops the habit, involuntarily, of existing in past or future. In such cases the past becomes not merely a memory of experienced events, but a fabricated blend of actual and imagined events; and likewise the future becomes a confused mélange of possible events and impossible "castles in air." When such intensities prevail, one's temporal horizon has been distorted.

Before such extreme conditions set in, however, "where we live" has already been integrated into our character-structure. If past experiences have been mostly unpleasant we may be oriented toward the future and change. If past experiences have been generally more pleasant and we come to dread future and change, having no grounds for the anticipation of happy events, we may well tend toward the conservation of the conditions of the past which provided the happier experiences.

In a word, those who experience a profound dissatisfaction with the present want change. But whether one seeks better conditions through a future-orientation or a past-orientation will depend upon a fundamental temporal character-structure long since determined by personal experience.

17   The philosophical world-view which goes by the name of existentialism has been immensely popular since World War II. While no two existential philosophers hold quite the same ideas, all share the same attitude toward how we exist in the living present.

Jean-Paul Sartre coined the most famous catch-phrase of modern philosophy: *existence before essence.* To existentialists the word "existence" refers to the concrete "human reality" of experience. Existence is what is—not what should be or might be. By contrast, the word

---

I have always been so afraid of the present and the real in my life. . . .

DE VIGNY

The middle-class man is oriented chiefly toward the future. When he is young he hears repeatedly: "Think of your future," whereas the son of a good family is asked again and again: "What would your grandmother say?" On the other hand, members of the working classes have neither past nor future. What matters to them is to live in the present without concern for a past which inspires or a future which is too uncertain.

PAUL FRAISSE

What it all comes down to is that we just have *to now* harder!

JACK REIDLING

"essence" refers to whatever qualities we deem "essential" to man: "human nature," "original sin," "innate aggression," "rationality," or whatever; but all these are abstractions created after the concrete fact. Minds fabricate essences, and Sartre denied that such notions have any significance for understanding the uniqueness of the individual person.

Satre was thinking only of *human* existence, for objects possess a different *kind* of existence. To see this difference, contrast man's existence with the existence, say, of the *Saturn V* rocket which launched America's lunar missions. Everything about the *Saturn* rocket—its three stages, engine systems, telemetry, payload capacity, engine-out capability, etc.—was conceived *in the minds* of scientists and engineers and elaborated on the design boards long before any single rocket was constructed. The rocket's purpose, conceived in men's minds, determined every element of its design. Once the design had been completed (still in men's minds), then an infinite number of single rockets, produced to perform in a specific way, could be constructed from those master specifications. All the rockets would be identical.

We can speak meaningfully, therefore, of the *essence* of the *Saturn V* rocket: its essence *is* all the elements of structure and function, conceived by its designers, which enables it to accomplish its purpose. For the *Saturn V*, this rocket essence preceded the existence of any single rocket which eventually stood majestically on the launch pad. For created objects, therefore, *essence* precedes *existence*.

Not so for man, argued Sartre. For man *existence* precedes *essence*. Man was not planned out on a drawing board, nor was he preconceived in any mind (divine or otherwise) for a *purpose* and *then* designed to fulfill such a purpose. Man is not created as objects are created. *Man creates himself.* Man even designs himself—*from within*. Each single person is unique since there is no master template which stamps out identical copies of persons, like minted coins. Therefore man has no essence, as does the rocket, which *predetermines* what he shall be and do. For man, and man alone, existence precedes essence.

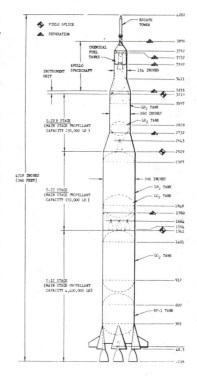

18   Existentialism is a philosophy of time and consciousness. To emphasize existence is to place supreme value upon the quality of one's immediate consciousness. As a philosophy of time, existentialism counsels us to exist as fully as possible in the living "now," to accept and actualize the intense "human reality" of the spontaneous present. For the existentialist, the past is only a repertory of recordings to be used in the service of the present, and the future is but a set of dreams to give the present direction and purpose.

Existentialism asks that we reexamine the way in which we live out our existence within that duration we call the present. Sartre reiterates that the choice is ours as to how we create consciousness. We can hand it over to conditioned responses from our past; we can allow feelings, memories, or habits to impinge upon our present and determine its content and quality. Similarly, we can allow anxieties about future events to impinge upon our present and rob it of its spontaneity and intensity. Thus we can allow our "now" to be deadened.

All animals, large or small, homeothermic or poikilothermic, burn the light of their lives with relative equality. Life, at least on the organismic level, is a democratic process: all of us must die, and the duration of our existence is the same. . . .

ROLAND FISCHER

As a philosophy of time, therefore, existentialism is a way of reevaluating how we use and abuse consciousness. But more than that, it contends that we *can* do something about how time is lived. Within the parameters of our unique personal existence, we can make decisions as to how we shall live the only thing which, in the final analysis, each of us actually possesses—namely, consciousness of time-present.

To *think,* in the highest sense, is to transcend all *natural limits*—such, for example, as national peculiarities, defects in culture, distinctions in Race, habits, and modes of living—to be *universal,* so that one can dissolve away the external hull and seize the substance itself.

WILLIAM TORREY HARRIS

19   The creative person, instead of perceiving in predetermined categories ("trees are green," "college education is a good thing," "modern art is silly") is aware of this existential moment as it *is,* and therefore he is alive to many experiences which fall outside the usual categories (in *this* light this tree is lavender; *this* college education is damaging; *this* modern sculpture has a powerful effect on me).

The creative person is in this way open to his own experiences. It means a lack of rigidity and the permeability of boundaries in concepts, beliefs, perceptions and hypotheses. It means a tolerance of ambiguity where ambiguity exists. It means the ability to receive much conflicting information without forcing closure on the situation.

CARL ROGERS

20   At the end of the spring semester, I packed a few articles and began a four-day trip through the mountains. It was the end of an especially trying school year, and I wanted to make the most of a short vacation before returning to teach summer school.

The countryside was still green and wildflowers gathered in nodding communities along the roadside. I drove alone in my small car, and in a small car one can feel very close to things about him. As I drove, or when I stopped to absorb the landscape, I could almost touch the reddish earth, the striated rocks, the weeds and flowers and grasses. I was one among them.

So I travelled. I saw the trees, the flowers, the animals. The broken clouds sometimes painted blue-green patches on the hillsides. I looked up at tall pines and they looked down at me. I smelled pine fragrance and listened to bird calls.

I began to feel alive again. I was *experiencing* things instead of *doing* things. I was feeling and seeing and hearing rather than thinking about . . . and trying to remember . . . and planning ahead.

Or so I thought.

As I watched cloud-shadows shaping their way across the valleys I caught myself deciding if I should reach for my camera. Would they show up just right in color? And was that lightning-split pine silhouetted in black-and-white against the sky "artistic" enough for a picture?: I saw purple flowers and found myself wondering if they were lupins, wild larkspurs, or what.

I had the right names for few of the beautiful things I beheld: golden poppies, lavender verbenas, sprays of yellow mustard. Also for the pines (I could remember "ponderosa") and cedars (all I could recall was "juniper"). How little I knew! My new-found ignorance bothered me.

But somewhere—and I don't know when or why—I began to realize what I was doing. I was seeing things just to stuff them into my memory *for later use.* I was building a storehouse of pretty details to impress upon others *after I returned.* The mental habits which dominated my days during the year still controlled my brain. I was organizing the events of my journey as though it were another classroom preparation!

I was insane! Quite literally, I was insane! I was allowing myself to pass my hours out of touch with the realities around me. Here I was in the midst of life, and I wasn't seeing it, wasn't hearing it, wasn't feeling it. Rather than experiencing, I was expending my time *processing* experiences!

I became determined, then, to stop my processing habits. When the next cluster of wildflowers appeared beside the road, I didn't say to myself, as to an audience: "I see a cluster of golden poppies. . . ." Rather, I experienced them—saw them, felt them, moved among them, savored them. I refused to let my mind tag them with names or tie them into bundles.

As I tell it now, I find words sufficient to describe my memory of the undulating flight of the mockingbird and the gliding turn of the swallow. I can recount my memories of the smell of pines and fresh rains.

These are things I can do now. But before my short journey ended, I had proved to myself that I could recover the capacity to experience afresh the world about me. I had succeeded in touching reality again.

JUNE HILLMAN

How dull it is to pause, to make an end,
To rust unburnish'd, not to shine in use!
As tho' to breathe were life.

TENNYSON
Ulysses

I don't know what you could say about a day in which you have seen four beautiful sunsets.

ASTRONAUT JOHN GLENN
(in orbit around the earth,
February 20, 1962)

AWARENESS

Awareness means the capacity to see a coffeepot and hear the birds sing in one's own way, and not the way one was taught. It may be assumed on good grounds that seeing and hearing have a different quality for infants than for grownups, and that they are more esthetic and less intellectual in the first years of life. A little boy sees and hears birds with delight. Then the "good father" comes along and feels he should "share" the experience and help his son "develop." He says: "That's a jay, and this is a sparrow." The moment the little boy is concerned with which is a jay and which is a sparrow, he can no longer see the birds or hear them sing. He has to see and hear them the way his father wants him to. Father has good reasons on his side, since few people can afford to go through life listening to the birds sing, and the sooner the little boy starts his "education" the better. Maybe he will be an ornithologist when he grows up. A few people, however, can still see and hear in the old way. But most of the members of the human race have lost the capacity to be painters, poets or musicians, and are not left the option of seeing and hearing directly even if they can afford to; they must get it secondhand. The recovery of this ability is called here "awareness."

ERIC BERNE
Games People Play

REFLECTIONS—

1 The first two sections of this chapter speak of "a philosophy of time." What do you think is meant by such a phrase? What benefits might derive from having a philosophy of time? Has this chapter helped you in developing a philosophy of time or, better, a philosophy of how to use time?

2 Read the following passages synoptically: Sec. 3, including the sidenote on p. 225; pp. 188–190 (Sec. 10-13); p. 445 (Sec. 12). What must we infer regarding the necessities of thought and communication, and the nature of reality? Or, more bluntly, can you actually buy "the astounding fact that we can and do communicate with one another continually *without* knowing *what* we are talking about?!" (p. 225, sidenote)?

3 Summarize in your mind the three "kinds of time" dealt with in this chapter. Can you get a good grasp of each kind of time, and do the concepts sound right to you?

4 Ponder the fact that psychological time is an extreme variable (pp. 225 ff., Secs. 5 and 6; and review the boxed material on p. 137, "What time is it?"). Have you felt the impact of the fact that, as individuals, we actually experience time in quite different ways? Would this insight lead you to revise your attitude toward certain behavior in others that is time-related?

5 How long does "the present" last? Does it have duration or "width"? Do you think you could get the psychologist and the mathematician together on the matter?

6 Does "the past" exist? Where? What are we truly referring to when we speak of the past?

7 Reflect on the quotation from Arthur C. Clarke (p. 230-QM, top) and criticize it. (Here is an interesting case in which *a statement* can be both true and false at the same time, depending upon the interpretation of terms. Can you show how Clarke is both right and wrong?)

8 Can "the future" exist? Is precognition possible, in your opinion? What sort of time model could you develop that would permit the possibility of precognition?

9 The subject that touches us all where we live is our experience of time. After reflecting on Secs. 17-20 and the boxed material on p. 237, what is your personal response to the existential philosophy of experience implied in these passages?

Furthermore . . .

ASIMOV, ISAAC, *The Clock We Live On*. Collier, 1963.

FRAISSE, PAUL, *The Psychology of Time*. Harper, 1963.

FRASER, J. T. (ed.), *The Voices of Time*. Braziller, 1966.

GALE, RICHARD M., *The Philosophy of Time*. Anchor, 1967.

GRÜNBAUM, ADOLF, *Philosophical Problems of Space and Time*, 2nd ed., D. Reidel, 1973. (Only for the bravest.)

PRIESTLEY, J. B., *Man and Time*. Dell, 1968.

REICHENBACH, HANS, *The Direction of Time*. University of California Press, 1971.

Freedom/Choice

Have You Ever Wondered . . .

- Why you do certain things?

- Whether you *can* do anything you really *want* to do?

- Whether we are predestined by God to do the things we do?

- Whether someone under hypnosis can be held responsible for what he does?

- Why you don't *always* will to do what you know you should do?

- Whether you might lose your freedom by simply believing that you're not free?

- Whether you can practice being free and thereby increase your freedom?

- OR whether human beings are merely computer-robots doing what they have been programmed to do?

THE FEELING OF FREEDOM

1 I would like to describe for you a pattern of experience which I have observed, and in which I have participated. . . . It is an experience on which I have placed various labels as I have tried to think about it—becoming a person, freedom to be, courage to be, learning to be free—yet the experience is something broader than, and deeper than, any of its labels. It is quite possible that the words I use in regard to it may miscommunicate. The speculations and ideas I present, based

The Buddha can only tell you the way: it is for you yourself to make the effort.

Dhammapada

239

on this experience, may be erroneous, or partly erroneous. But the experience itself *exists*. It is a deeply compelling phenomenon for any one who has observed it, or who has lived it.

CARL ROGERS

2   But does the experience of freedom, in fact, exist? Or does the *feeling* of freedom mask an illusion?

In one experiment with hypnosis, a man was led into a deep trance and given a simple posthypnotic suggestion. About a month from that date, he was told, after lunch on a certain day, he would sing "America the Beautiful." During the week following this first suggestion, it was reinforced twice during similar deep trances. But at no time was the man informed that any posthypnotic instructions had been given.

When the day for singing arrived, he recalls having the feeling in the morning that he wanted to sing; he did in fact hum or sing a few bars of various tunes. As noontime neared, the impulse to sing unexplainably grew stronger.

Immediately after lunch, he sauntered over to the piano, let his fingers move over the keyboard, and then, on schedule, proceeded to sing "America the Beautiful."

This sort of experiment is common enough in hypnosis. The significant point has to do with *cause:* What *caused* him to sing this specific song at this appointed time. He *felt* free. He felt that it was a *choice* that he had made, and that he could have made other choices. But paradoxically, he also *felt* determined. The impulse to sing the song grew to such proportions that it was difficult or impossible *not* to act it out.

> If a man referred to his brother or to his cat as "an ingenious mechanism," we should know that he was either a fool or a physiologist. No one in practice treats himself or his fellow-man or his pet animals as machines; but scientists who have never made a study of Speculative Philosophy seem often to think it their duty to hold in theory what no one outside a lunatic asylum would accept in practice.
>
> C. D. BROAD

THE DILEMMA OF DETERMINISM

3   This dramatic experiment symbolizes one of our deepest human dilemmas. On the one hand, we feel free; our social lives are founded on the assumption that we and others make genuine choices and should be responsible for them. We blame others for mistakes (that is, they were free *not* to have made them), and we feel guilt at our own mistakes (that is, we ourselves could, and should, have acted differently).

On the other hand, we feel determined. As Saint Paul eloquently put it, "I do not understand what I am doing, for I do not do what I want to do; I do the things that I hate. . . . I do not do the good things that I want to do; I do the wrong things that I do not want to do. But if I do the things that I do not want to do, it is not I that am acting. . . . " Paul's lament rises to a painful crescendo: "What a wretched human being I am!"

Based on experience, we are forced into the conclusion that there are capricious casual forces inside us, directing us to do countless acts against our wills. It was only natural that premodern man inter-

Saint Paul

preted these forces as good/evil spirits thrashing around inside him—"possessing" him—and acting as causal agents behind the thoughts, feelings, and actions over which he felt little control. Today we can better account for the causes of our behavior in empirical terms—in terms of conditioning or with physiological or chemical explanations. Still, the result is the same: we have a dual experience of both freedom and determinism. Both experiences *feel* authentic, and we have never quite understood how to reconcile the apparent contradiction.

4   Western Christian theology has symbolized this experiential dilemma with remarkable accuracy. There is abundant biblical support for two basic beliefs: (1) God is omnipotent and he therefore deter-

---

SAINT THOMAS AQUINAS: THE PARADOX OF DETERMINISM

Man is predestined . . .

It is fitting that God should predestine men. For all things are subject to His Providence. . . . As men are ordained to eternal life through the Providence of God, it likewise is part of that Providence to permit some to fall away from that end; this is called reprobation. . . . As predestination includes the will to confer grace and glory, so also reprobation includes the will to permit a person to fall into sin, and so impose the punishment of damnation on account of that sin.

Summa Theologica, I, 23, 1, 3
Summa contra Gentiles, III, 163

Saint Thomas Aquinas (1225–1274)

Man is free . . .

Man has free choice, or otherwise counsels, exhortations, commands, prohibitions, rewards and punishments would be in vain.

If the will were deprived of freedom . . . no praise would be given to human virtue; since virtue would be of no account if man acted not freely: there would be no justice in rewarding or punishing, if man were not free in acting well or ill: and there would be no prudence in taking advice, which would be of no use if things occurred of necessity . . .

Summa Theologica, I, 83, 1
Summa contra Gentiles, III, 73

Can man be both predestined and free?

The predestined must necessarily be saved, yet by a conditional necessity, which does not do away with the liberty of choice. . . .

Man's turning to God is by free choice; and thus man is bidden to turn himself to God. But free choice can be turned to God only when God turns it. . . . It is the part of man to prepare his soul, since he does this by his free choice. And yet he does not do this without the help of God moving him. . . . And thus even the good movement of free choice, whereby anyone is prepared for receiving the gift of grace, is an act of free choice moved by God. . . . Man's preparation for grace is from God, as mover, and from free choice, as moved.

Summa Theologica, I, 23, 3; I–II, 109,6; I–II, 112, 2, 3.

mines every event in our lives; (2) Man possesses free will and is therefore responsible for his sins; he can justly be condemned to hell for wrong decisions.

In their extreme forms, these two doctrines are logically contradictory; they can't both be true. But Western theology had no alternative but to accept both as absolutely true; they were both given (hence, not debatable) by biblical authority and ecclesiastical tradition. For almost two thousand years now, Christian theologians have wrestled valiantly with these two doctrines, trying to harmonize them so that men could believe both and maintain their intellectual honesty. No two theologians have resolved the problem in exactly the same way—in fact no solution is wholly free of logical difficulties—but there are several general approaches toward a solution. If either doctrine is softened, then they can be reconciled. If God does not predetermine every event of our lives, then we can claim to have some free will; or, if we admit that we are not wholly free, then some predestination can be accepted.

Whatever the solution, however, the striking point is that the theological formulation is an accurate doctrinization of the very real human dilemma. We are *both* determined *and* free; and somehow we must work at the contradiction until we achieve a realistic understanding of how both can be true.

PRIMAL AND SECONDARY LIMITATIONS

5   Without prejudging at this point the relative degrees of human freedom and determinism which we experience, we can speak meaningfully of the limiting factors which diminish our freedom. The point to note is that we confuse primal limitations with secondary limitations: it follows that we also confuse primal freedoms with secondary freedoms. Distinguishing between them is crucial.

Primal freedom is inner freedom, and primal limitations come from within. These limitations may be genetic (sickle-cell anemia, thalidomide deformities), physiological (paralysis from polio or accident), ontological° (fear of death and nonbeing), or conditioned (inability to trust or love). Such limitations are causal; they inhibit us from thinking, feeling, or doing specific things; and as causes, they arise from inside our own psychophysiological organism. Primal freedom, therefore, is freedom *from* such limitations: from conflicts and frustrations, unfounded fears, nail-biting anxieties, lingering hatreds, debilitating habits, and life-negating bitterness. Primal freedom is freedom *for* the full utilization of our abilities, the freedom for each person—considering all the givens of his own unique existence—to be all that he can be.

Primal limitations burden us all. We may want to enjoy a day at the beach but find, while there, that we are reliving the emotional battles of the day; and try as we will, we can only act at having fun.

We are forced to fall back on fatalism as an explanation of irrational events, that is to say, of events the rationality of which we do not understand.

TOLSTOY

°Ontological. *An inherent and inescapable aspect of our being. Ontology is the branch of philosophy which delves into the nature of being. See glossary.*

Or we try to concentrate on reading a book, but in vain, because relentless worries intrude and disturb our will-to-thought. And how often do we undertake a task, knowing full well we have the capabilities to accomplish it, only to find that primal limitations—fears of inadequacy, fears of others' opinions, even fear of success itself—keep us from attaining our goal? Freedom from all these inner limitations is primal freedom.

By contrast, *secondary limitations* originate in our environment. Therefore, we can speak of secondary freedoms as freedom from external limitations. Secondary limitations are placed upon us by nature itself (we can't move backward in time), and by other persons and by our society. We are limited by the customs, common-sense traditions, sociological structures, moral suasions, and civil laws of the society in which we live. We are also limited by the immediate needs and desires of other people. Such secondary limiters impose upon us injunctions *not* to think, feel, and do specific things.

6　　We cause ourselves endless troubles by confusing primal freedom with various secondary freedoms. We often think we are being subjected to external limitations when in fact we are suffering from inner restraints, and vice versa. Primal limitations are undoubtedly more difficult for us to admit and face; recognition of them presupposes some degree of self-knowledge, the ability to empathize with others, and some capacity for abstract thinking. Since secondary limitations appear more concrete, and since we share them with others and can deal with them collectively ("Fight Gun Control," "Legalize Marijuana"), we often expend great amounts of energy in crusades against particular "encroachments upon our freedoms."

We may never realize that such crusades are in fact a struggle against primal limitations. We may accuse others of not liking us when the source of our agony is that we don't like ourselves. We may accuse others of conspiring to harm us when our problem is that we never developed the capacity to trust. In such cases, our desire for freedom is authentic, but we have mislocated the source of the limitation.

This is why it is common for us to spend our lives fighting for causes, only to find later that (to parody a cliché) the causes were won but our freedoms were lost. We may indeed achieve specific freedoms ("The bill finally passed!"), only to find that we are bound with the same primal fetters as before. We do not *experience* an increase of freedom. But having a row of (secondary) freedom awards to point to, we can't quite understand why we don't experience more freedom.

Other things being equal, the greater one's experience of primal freedom, the less he is concerned with secondary freedoms; and conversely, those who are deeply driven to crusade for secondary freedoms are often suffering from excruciating primal limitations.

7　　Few philosophical problems have greater practical implications than the question of freedom versus determinism.

For one thing, if there is no freedom, then there can be no

There is no doubt that Sartre finds it impossible to make a distinction between freedom and free acts. The free man is not distinguished by his beliefs, but by the quality of his actions.

NORMAN N. GREENE

This is one of man's oldest riddles. How can the independence of human volition be harmonized with the fact that we are integral parts of a universe which is subject to the rigid order of Nature's laws?

SIR ARTHUR EDDINGTON

One's ability to move his hand at will is more directly and certainly known than are Newton's laws. If these laws deny one's ability to move his hand at will, the preferable conclusion is that Newton's laws require modification.

ARTHUR COMPTON

moral, legal, or any other kind of responsibility. Yet the fact of personal responsibility is one of our most cherished assumptions. We blame others for their mistakes and give them credit for their achievements. We hold ourselves responsible and feel guilt for our misdoings. We indict alleged lawbreakers, hold trials, and convict or free them. We operate on the assumption that human beings can be morally and legally responsible—that is, free. But if our assumption of freedom is false, then life as we live it is a cruel joke founded upon a tragic illusion. We are playing the game all wrong.

Secondly, we struggle from day to day and year to year, in desperation or joy, and always with hope, to attain our life-goals. But if we are not free, then all our striving is meaningless. We only think we set our own goals whereas in fact they are set for us; and whether or not we attain them is apparently already determined, or at least out of our hands. Life itself, as struggle, is an illusion.

Thirdly, and most deeply, the question of freedom has to do with what we are—or aren't. What can life mean if we have no freedom to make choices, choose lifestyles, set goals? Since we labor under the deepest conviction that, to some extent at least, we are free, then existence itself is a hoax. We think we're free, feel like we're free, act like we're free; we treat ourselves and others as though we were free; we develop monumental moral and legal systems based upon the assumption that we're free—all this fantasized by blind puppets dangling helplessly on black nylon strings?

We are not what we think we are; life is not what we think it is; the rules of the game are not what we thought. Maybe, we discover that we're not playing the game at all: *we are the chessmen and something or someone else is playing the game.*

THE CASE FOR DETERMINISM

8   For almost fifteen years, Dr. Bruno Bettelheim has followed the case of Joey—"the mechanical boy." Joey's loss of freedom was clearly psychogenic rather than genetic or physiological. From birth he had been almost completely ignored; to his mother he hardly existed. Since all that he was as a budding human was bothersome and unacceptable, he quickly got the message; his humanness must be eliminated—repressed. So Joey literally became a machine. He acquainted himself very early with machines and could dismantle and reassemble them with some skill. He also envied the machines and identified with them; they were liked, toyed with; they gave no trouble, were never punished. Gradually he came to think of himself as a machine.

Before he could eat, for instance, he would unroll his imaginary cord and plug it into the outlet, set his switches, and check his bulbs. He could perform routine actions only after he had monitored his circuits, checked his dials, flipped the right switches. He made sure his machine-self was working properly.

All this was more than merely a game of playing like a machine;

Men are freest when they are most unconscious of freedom.

D. H. LAWRENCE

this "game" was deadly serious. He was playing the machine-game to escape the unbearable anguish of further rejection of any of his human qualities.

Bettelheim noted that "Joey's pathological behavior seemed the external expression of an overwhelming effort to remain almost non-existent as a person." Joey had created a world of his own that he could live in, a world that was preferable to the hostile real world. In his fantasy-world he had found a way of life which was at least tolerable. Since he did not need to be human, his human qualities atrophied; more and more Joey *became* a machine.

Machines are not free. Indeed, the word doesn't apply. Machines operate on principles of cause and effect—total determinism. Joey "the mechanical boy" knew no freedom.

9   One of the strongest contemporary cases for determinism has been made by a psychologist-novelist who recently—in *Beyond Freedom and Dignity*—has become a philosopher: Dr. B. F. Skinner of Harvard.

According to Skinner's way of thinking, freedom is a myth, and a dangerous myth because we have invested the myth and its symbol ("freedom") with something close to sacred qualities. It is a fact that many of those who think they disagree with Skinner are eager to make his observations the object of religious and patriotic causes.°

Freedom, Skinner argues, is not a fact of human experience. *All* of our responses—the impulses that lie behind so-called free choices—are the result of unique past contingencies of conditioning and reinforcement that have shaped us into what we are. Skinner's famed laboratory experiments with pigeons and rats have shown that animal behavior can be predicted and controlled, and even produced according to specification. By selecting specific causes (stimuli), desired effects (responses) will result. This is merely the application to the field of animal behavior the scientific assumption of causality. The assumption that every cause produces an effect and every effect is preceded by a cause is the foundation of all science. Whatever made us think that it would *not* apply to the behavioral sciences as well as to the natural sciences?

What we *call* freedom is merely the successful avoidance on the part of any organism of some aversive feature in its environment. All organisms are manipulated and controlled, therefore, by the dynamic features of their environments.

To be sure, when Skinner writes that freedom is an illusion, he is not denying our experience of a rather pleasant *emotion* which we commonly call freedom; but he is saying unequivocally that this emotion is itself a *conditioned* (caused) response. We may label this feeling "freedom" or something else; but whatever we call it, it has been produced by past experience; it was conditioned into us at some prior time and now becomes, in turn, the causal agent of present behavior.

10   Among the illustrations used by Skinner are the accounts of the falling leaf and the buzzing fly.

Give me a dozen healthy infants and I'll guarantee to take any one at random and train him to become any type of specialist I might select—doctor, lawyer, even beggar-man and thief, regardless of his talents, penchants, tendencies, abilities.

JOHN B. WATSON (1925)

°*Skinner's book was still warm from the press when one congressman, in a speech before the House, denounced him for "advancing ideas which threaten the future of our system of government by denigrating the American traditions of individualism, human dignity and self-reliance." As is so often the case, further comments revealed a fundamental misunderstanding of what Skinner is saying.*

B. F. Skinner

Picture a leaf, yellowed from the first frosts, fluttering and suddenly beginning to fall from the top of a tall, red-gold maple tree. In zigzag motions, hovering on the currents of air, it picks a poetic path downward and settles eventually upon a cushion of leaves on the ground.

Now, there isn't a physicist alive who would argue that the leaf is "free." We esthetic onlookers may be mesmerized by the leaf's timeless descent, and even envy the "freedom" of the floating maple leaf wafting to earth. But we have confused our poetic idealism with our physics. The fact is that the leaf follows precisely known laws of physics, laws which can easily be found in any physics textbook.

Yet as the leaf starts its historic fall from the top of the maple tree, what physicist, by applying his formulas, could predict the leaf's trajectory or the spot where it will finally come to rest? The journey is too complex; there are too many variables: air currents, atmospheric density (in terms of elevation above sea level and barometric pressure), humidity, minute photon forces, the mass and volume of the leaf, its configuration, and so on. The number of possible combinations of variables is so great that, although knowing all the applicable laws, predicting the leaf's path or destination is a feat quite beyond the ability of any physicist (or computer) alive today.

So, is the leaf "free" in any proper sense of the word? Not at all. It follows inexorable causal laws.

11   Elsewhere, Skinner ponders a housefly buzzing around a room. In describing the motions of the maple leaf, we were applying physical laws to a passive object. The trajectory of the buzzing fly is infinitely more complex since we are dealing with the active nervous system of a living thing. Our causal factors, to some extent, become internal.

> **If man has once become aware that in his forlornness he imposes values, he can no longer want but one thing, and that is freedom, as the basis of all values. That doesn't mean that he wants it in the abstract. It means simply that the ultimate meaning of the acts of honest men is the quest for freedom as such.**
>
> *JEAN-PAUL SARTRE*

PUPPET THEATER?

We see the puppets dancing on their miniature stage, moving up and down as the strings pull them around, following the prescribed course of their various little parts. We learn to understand the logic of this theater and we find ourselves in its motions. We locate ourselves in society and thus recognize our own position as we hang from its subtle strings. For a moment we see ourselves as puppets indeed. But then we grasp a decisive difference between the puppet theater and our own drama. Unlike the puppets, we have the possibility of stopping in our movements, looking up and perceiving the machinery by which we have been moved. In this act lies the first step towards freedom.

PETER L. BERGER
Invitation to Sociology

If we knew *everything* about the buzzing fly—its previous conditioning, its present chemical states, its "needs," "drives," "goals," or whatever, and all the aerodynamics of a fly's flight—then, according to Skinner, we could predict exactly where the fly will buzz, where it will land, what it will eat, and so on.

Carl Rogers

But we are facing the same paradox with the fly as with the leaf. We might feel that the fly is free as it flies about; it looks free; it even seems to make choices. But such freedom is myth, Skinner contends. There is no more freedom in any buzz of the fly than there was in any flutter of the leaf. Every motion could be predicted if the causal forces were precisely known. More simply, all matter-in-motion obeys the laws of physics, and a fly is matter-in-motion.

These same principles apply to human action, and our complexity, apparently, is no argument against determinism, since the same causal laws apply in every case. Our behavior is more complex than the fly's, just as the fly's behavior is more complex than the leaf's. But freedom is just as much a fallacy for us as it is for the leaf or fly.

12   Rogers says freedom exists. Skinner says it doesn't. Rogers records the following brief exchange between them at a conference at which Skinner had read a paper.

> From what I understood Dr. Skinner to say, it is his understanding that though he might have thought *he chose* to come to this meeting, might have thought he had a purpose in giving this speech, such thoughts are really illusory. He actually made certain marks on paper and emitted certain sounds here simply because his genetic makeup and his past environment had operantly conditioned his behavior in such a way that it was rewarding to make these sounds, and that he as a person doesn't enter into this. In fact if I get his thinking correctly, from his strictly scientific point of view, he, as a person, doesn't exist.

In his reply to Rogers, "Dr. Skinner said that he would not go into the question of whether he had any choice in the matter (presumably because the whole issue is illusory) but stated, 'I do accept your characterization of my own presence here.' "

THE CASE FOR FREEDOM OF CHOICE

13   Human freedom has been stoutly defended by a distinguished line of thinkers in various traditions, East and West. No voice in its defense has been more persuasive than that of the existentialist philosopher Jean-Paul Sartre, whose vehement pronouncements for freedom arose from his own intense experience of human struggle during the Nazi occupation of France in World War II.

The fashionable notion that we are predetermined in our behavior by past experiences—by "operant conditioning"—to the point of

Existentialism's first move is to make every man aware of what he is and to make the full responsibility of his existence rest on him.

JEAN-PAUL SARTRE

Jean-Paul Sartre (1905–1980)

losing our free will—this, for Sartre, is an outrageous fallacy. On the contrary, man is not merely responsible for what he does, but he is even responsible for all that he is.

Sartre is convinced that there is no determinism of any kind. *Nothing* tells me what to do. I myself decide. I cannot blame God, or others, or my past environment. I am—now—what I make myself to be. I have to accept the consequences of my own freedom, take the responsibility for my decisions and face the consequences thereof. For human freedom, as Sartre sees it, is not always a blessing; it is more often a tragedy. Whether we like it or not, man is *condemned to be free.*

But why does Sartre speak of our being "condemned" to freedom? Why such a gloomy term? Shouldn't freedom be a joyous thing? Sartre's position is that freedom carries with it an unavoidable anguish when we fully realize how overwhelming the implications of our freedom can be. It entails tragic choices with formidable consequences. Out of our freedom we do not make decisions for ourselves alone, but for others, and sometimes for all mankind. To realize completely what this means can be a nightmarish insight into the very nature of human existence.

To be free means to be caught in a paradox. We are forever dissatisfied with existence as we know it. But to live means to dream a million dreams and forge ahead to catch the fullness of our being. Indeed, each mortal man wants to be God, but the truer fact is that we are finite and our limitations are crushing. Still, they are unacceptable. So we continue to compete and strive, dreaming our dreams, even though they are futile dreams, and even though we know it.

Why? Why do we do all this? Simply because we cannot do otherwise. For to exist is to be free, and to be free is to act, to take initiative, to make choices and decisions, to dream impossible dreams—however unreachable they are—and to fail. In a word, we *must try to do* what we already know we *cannot* do.

> What is an obstacle for me may not be so for another. There is no obstacle in an absolute sense. . . . Human-reality everywhere encounters resistance and obstacles which it has not created, but these resistances and obstacles have meaning only in and through the free choice which human-reality is.
>
> *JEAN-PAUL SARTRE*

14   Sartre was attempting to get us to see that we exist in an antinomian world without guidelines. Cultural norms are relative, and societies are humorlessly absurd. There is no God and therefore no absolute mandates to give life order. There is no meaning to human life as such. Nor is there any past conditioning which we can blame for making us what we are. There is not even a "human nature" which might help us to define ourselves.

There is nothing to help us—because the moment we become conscious of what we are, then we become responsible for everything we are and do. Of course, we can join the mob and let our passions collectively carry us along, but *we make the decision* to do so, and we are responsible for that decision. We can conform to society's whims, or follow an irrelevant, legalistic ethical code, or accede to peer pressures; but in each instance *we make the decision* to do so, and we must accept the responsibility for that decision.

Whenever we are conscious, therefore, we are responsible. For at the cutting edge of consciousness, we are truly free. At each moment of the living present, we have an infinite number of choices before us, ways of thinking, feeling, and behaving—the options are numberless, so many that to feel them fully is to become overwhelmed by them. It's at this moment of revelation that we frequently retreat into the myths of determinism. We convince ourselves that we move within carefully defined and unbreakable limits, and that we are not really free. Yet, from behind our safe parameters we will *claim* to be free. We are "not supposed" to think, feel, or do certain things, or so we are told by society, church, friends, laws, conscience. But all these excuses are retreats from freedom; and the true fact is that we can do all of them. But since experience of such freedom is fraught with fear, we eagerly accept all the fashionable limitations.

15 Jean-Paul Sartre penned a now-famous passage about the experiences of the French Resistance movement against the Nazis in France.

> We were never more free than during the German occupation. We had lost all our rights, beginning with the right to talk. Every day we were insulted to our faces and had to take it in silence. Under one pretext or another, as workers, Jews, or political prisoners, we were deported *en masse*. Everywhere, on billboards, in the newspapers, on the screen, we encountered the revolting and insipid picture of ourselves that our suppressors wanted us to accept. And because of all this we were free. Because the Nazi venom seeped into our thoughts, every accurate thought was a conquest. Because an all-powerful police tried to force us to hold our tongues, every word took on the value of a declaration of principles. Because we were hunted down, every one of our gestures had the weight of a solemn commitment. . . .
>
> Exile, captivity, and especially death (which we usually shrink from facing at all in happier days) became for us the habitual objects of our concern. We learned that they were neither inevitable accidents, nor even constant and inevitable dangers, but they must be considered as our lot itself, our destiny, the profound source of our reality as men. At every instant we lived up to the full sense of this commonplace little phrase: "Man is mortal!" And the choice that each of us made of his life was an authentic choice because it was made face to face with death, because it could always have been expressed in these terms: "Rather death than . . ." And here I am not speaking of the elite among us who were real Resistants, but of all Frenchmen who, at every hour of the night and day throughout four years, answered *No.*

The essential freedom, the ultimate and final freedom that cannot be taken from a man, is to say No. This is the basic premise in Sartre's view of human freedom: freedom is in its very essence negative, though this negativity is also creative. At a certain moment, perhaps, the drug or the pain inflicted by the torturer may make the victim lose consciousness, and he will confess. But so long as he retains the lucidity of consciousness, however tiny the area of action possible for him, he can still say in his own mind: No. Consciousness and freedom are thus given together. Only if consciousness is blotted out can

Let [the child] believe that he is always in control, though it is always you [the teacher] who really controls. There is no subjugation so perfect as that which keeps the appearance of freedom, for in that way one captures volition itself. . . .

ROUSSEAU

man be deprived of this residual freedom. Where all the avenues of action are blocked for a man, this freedom may seem a tiny and unimportant thing; but it is in fact total and absolute, and Sartre is right to insist upon it as such, for it affords man his final dignity, that of being man.

WILLIAM BARRETT

REFLECTIONS—

1 What do you think of the account of the man who was hypnotized and told he would sing "America the Beautiful"? Does this episode frighten you? What implications do you see in this story regarding the question of human freedom? Would you care to go so far as to liken childhood to a prolonged period of "post-hypnotic suggestions"?

2 In brief, why is the age-old question of free will such a crucial problem? And why is it imperative today that we find a workable solution?

3 Does the description in Sec. 3 of our human predicament as a "feeling dilemma"—We *feel* free and we *feel* determined—sound like an accurate account of your own experience and observation? How would you express the problem?

4 Distinguish between primary and secondary freedoms, and between primary and secondary limitations. Can you think of illustrations from your experience where "we cause ourselves endless troubles by confusing primal freedom with various secondary freedoms"?

5 After reading this chapter, jot down your thoughts regarding the following: (1) Is the question of freedom/determinism an authentic question or does it need to be rephrased in the light of modern knowledge? (2) To what degree can we be truly free? (3) To what degree are we determined, and what determines us? (4) Is the idea of the "growth of freedom" a justifiable concept?

6 After you reach some conclusions (though tentative) about the extent of our determined condition, how much do you think we should be held responsible, morally and legally, for our behavior?

7 Note the boxed excerpts on p. 241. How well do you think Aquinas reconciled the two biblical "givens"—free will and predestination? If you're up to the challenge and would enjoy an exercise in theological logic, try to work out a better reconciliation.

8 Is the question of divine predestination a problem for you personally? Have you, at some time, committed yourself to a predestinarian position? If so, do you have evidence to offer in support of that position? Would you contend that we are *also* free agents? (That is, do you hold yourself responsible for what you do?) How do you reconcile these two positions?

9 What does Jean-Paul Sartre mean when he says that we are "condemned to be free"? Do you share his mood regarding the human condition? Do you agree with him when he insists that we *always* have a choice?

Furthermore . . .

BEROFSKY, BERNARD (ed.), *Free Will and Determinism*. Harper, 1966.

DELGADO, JOSÉ M. R., *Physical Control of the Mind: Toward a Psychocivilized Society*. Harper, 1969.

DOBZHANSKY, THEODOSIUS, *The Biological Basis of Human Freedom*. Columbia University Press, 1956.

HOOK, SIDNEY (ed.), *Determinism and Freedom in the Age of Modern Science*. New York University Press, 1960.

LEHRER, KEITH (ed.), *Freedom and Determinism*. Random House, 1966.

OLSON, ROBERT G., *An Introduction to Existentialism*. Dover, 1962. (See Chapter 2 "The Human Condition"; and Chapter 4 "Freedom.")

SKINNER, B. F., *Science and Human Behavior*. Free Press, 1965.

SKINNER, B. F., *Walden Two*. Free Press, 1962.

STILLMAN, PETER G., "The Limits of Behaviorism." *The American Political Science Review*, Vol. LXIX; March, 1975.

THOMSEN, DIETRICK, "Split Brain and Free Will." *Science News*, April 20, 1974.

4-4

Symbols/ Communication

Have You Ever Wondered . . .

- What a word is?
- What a definition is?
- Why so much of our talk is meaning-less?
- Why you can't use a word to mean anything you want it to mean? (or can you?)
- Why some people talk so much (and say so little)?
- What makes a word or gesture "obscene"?
- Why some people just can't understand what you are saying even though they are trying very hard to hear you?
- Whether mental telepathy might solve some of our communication problems if it exists and could be put to use?

"When I use a word," Humpty-Dumpty said in a rather scornful tone, "it means just what I choose it to mean—neither more nor less."

"The question is," said Alice, "whether you *can* make words mean different things."

"The question is," said Humpty-Dumpty, "which is to be master— that's all!"

LEWIS CARROLL

THE FUNCTIONS OF LANGUAGE

1   Aside from the practical need to transmit survival information, the fundamental goal of all communication is to transcend our egocentric predicament. We are located from birth till death in a space/time predicament which subjects us to limitations we can't accept. Communication between living creatures is a means of transcending this condition. We create symbolic media for transmitting to other beings something of the experience-world going on inside us.

We invent symbols, therefore, which can stimulate the sensors of another person. From this we would like to persuade ourselves that, because we can activate the senses of another organism, we can transfer living experience from one person to another. We want to believe in—and we profoundly long for—a transfer of *content* rather than symbolic transmittals between closed systems.

Man is therefore a symbolic creature *because of* his egocentric predicament. If direct transfer of living experience could somehow be arranged, he would hasten to dispense with all his symbols.

Note that we humans share this condition with all living creatures. The common statement that man is a symbolic creature, while other animals are not, is false. They too must resort to symbolic means of bursting through their egocentric predicaments: the courtship rituals and territorial warnings of birds, the danger barks of baboons, the scent which the female gypsy moth disperses through the night air— these are analogous to man's symbolic communication, and for the same reasons.

Man's ability to use highly abstracted and complex symbols is not to be denigrated, of course. But with all our symbolic sophistication, is our transmittal of *experience* all that great? Are we, as a matter of fact, less lonely?

2 Most of us tacitly assume that the primary function of language is the rational communication of ideas, whereas our everyday experience shows that this isn't so. Happily, our linguistic equipment is designed to serve numerous functions.

In the following list of ten common uses of language, note that usage falls into two categories: whether the primary purpose is to change conditions in ourselves (the subject—S) or in another (the object—O). Equally significant is whether the specific usage is designed to promote emotional results (E) or rational/intellectual results (R). A glance at the list indicates that the primary functions of language are emotional rather than rational and that much use of language is reflexive—designed to alter conditions within ourselves.

3 Language is used to accomplish the following goals.

S (1) *To express emotion* (E). "I love you." "Younger than springtime am I" (from *South Pacific*). "Ouch!" "Damn!" Found here also are the interminable arguments we get into which take the form of idea-exchange but which in fact are prolonged venting of accumulated emotional charges. One of the prime functions of taboo words (obscenities, "four-letter words," etc.) and name calling is to let off emotional steam.

S (2) *To drown out silence* (E). In countless ordinary situations we find silence intolerable: waiting along with others in a doctor's office, sitting beside someone on a bus or plane, passing time with a casual acquaintance. Polite social conversation generally lessens our anxiety. When alone we often turn on TV or radio to ease our loneliness; lacking these, some of us talk with our selves.

The tragedy of our age is the awful incommunicability of souls.

W. O. MARTIN

I know that you believe
you understand
what you think I said,
but
I am not sure
you realize that
what you heard
is not
what I
meant.

ANONYMOUS

I fall *far* short of achieving real communication—person-to-person—all the time, but moving in this direction makes life for me a warm, exciting, upsetting, troubling, satisfying, enriching, and above all a worthwhile venture.

CARL ROGERS

The true meaning of a term is to be found by observing what a man does with it, not by what he says about it.

P. W. BRIDGMAN

I still find that some people imagine that intimacy is only a matter of approximating genitals one to another. . . . Intimacy . . . requires a type of relationship which I call collaboration, by which I mean clearly formulated adjustments of one's behavior to the expressed needs of the other person in the pursuit of increasingly identical—that is, more and more nearly mutual— satisfactions.

HARRY STACK SULLIVAN

"Although humans make sounds with their mouths and occasionally look at each other, there is no solid evidence that they actually communicate with each other."

S   (3)   *To enjoy the sounds of language* (E). Language produces esthetic pleasure, especially familiar phrases with happy associations. This is one purpose of much poetry—"word music." Also, just as there is "mood music" there is "mood language," a fact well known to preachers, hypnotists, playwrights—indeed, to anyone wishing to "set the tone" for an ensuing event. [Incidentally, Littlechap's plaint—"My wife's voice is a symphony"—should probably be classified under (1) above: to express agony!]

S   (4)   *To establish a feeling of belonging* (E). Religious ceremonies in which words are repeated together—unison prayers, litanies, chants; protest chants; cheers led by cheer leaders; war dances. "We shall overcome." Especially effective are hymns, national anthems, and songs recalling a past togetherness—the singing of the alma mater or fraternity/sorority songs.

SO   (5)   *To establish relationships* (E). "Aloha." "Good morning." "How do you do?" "Buenos dias, señor." "How've you been?" "Bonjour, monsieur." "Shalom aleichem." "Hyambo." And polite exploratory conversation: "Looks like it's going to be a nice day." "I'm sure I've seen you somewhere before." Included here also would be ritualized language for severing relationships: "Goodnight." "Adios." "Hasta la vista." "Auf Wiedersehen." "Have a nice day."

O   (6)   *To affect others' emotions* (E). Sermons, patriotic speeches, rallies for causes, TV commercials. "Smile, God loves you." "Oh, I didn't realize you could wear a size sixteen." Popular therapy would be included here: "Don't cry. It's going to be all right." "Don't worry about tomorrow." "The Lord giveth and the Lord taketh away." "You can stand the pain." More professionally: "What are you really feeling—guilt or anger?"

O   (7)   *To affect others' behavior* (E-R). "Don't do that!" "Speed Limit 35." "Vote for Smith." Here must be placed the TV commercials which are designed to make us convince ourselves that we need a

Words, strain,
crack, and sometime break,
under the burden.

T. S. ELIOT

Whenever two or more human beings can communicate with each other, they can, by agreement, make anything stand for anything.

S. I. HAYAKAWA

specific product and to go right out and buy it. Also: "Get hooked." "Think." "THINK BIG." "think small." This is termed "directive language."

O   (8)   *To suggest insights* (R). This is a philosophic and literary usage especially employed by Chinese sages and Indian philosophers. "When a man is in turmoil how shall he find peace / Save by staying patient till the stream clears?" (Lao-tzu). "Does the grass bend when the wind blows upon it?" (Confucius). This is commonly the purpose of parables, anecdotes, proverbs, logia or "sayings" (Jesus said . . . ," "Confucius said . . ."), and maxims of folk-wisdom ("A rolling stone gathers no moss").

O   (9)   *To communicate ideas and facts* (R). "You're overdrawn." "I'd like a hamburger and coffee." "I'm happy to report that it's not malignant." "I regret to inform you. . . . " Here we can classify all media for the transmittal of knowledge: TV newscasts, magazines, books, and technical journals of all sorts, and all our routine daily transfer of information for coping and surviving.

O   (10)   *To effect word-magic* (E-R-?). "Open Sesame!" "Be thou healed in the Name of Isis." "Om" or "Om mani padme hum!" Our language still contains numerous quasi-magical formulas, often disguised: "Well, here goes." "Good luck!" "Gesundheit!" "God bless you." "God damn you." Akin to primitive word-magic are such phrases as "You're stupid!" and "Go on, you can do it" where the words themselves are designed to help bring about the results alluded to. Closely related to word-magic is the "placebo effect": "Two capsules after meals and you'll feel like a new person."

COMMUNICATIONS ANALYSIS

4   At the human stage of sophistication, language (that is, sounds and printed symbols) is our primary symbolic equipment. But our need to communicate is so great that we expect far more of words than they can deliver; we deceive ourselves into believing that our words are accomplishing what is inherently impossible. We are caught in the predicament of having to reduce the fullness of our experience to a few words and gestures. We try, as it were, to encapsulate life in symbolic containers that are hopelessly inadequate for the task.

But we don't want others to hear our symbols: we want them to hear our experience. And others want the same from us.

Success in communication depends not upon the speaker, but upon the hearer. One wishing to communicate his experience to another can try forever, but quite in vain, if the hearer refuses to hear. If for any reason a listener has undergone closure—he may be preoccupied with other problems, he may have developed an ego-defense system to block out pain, or he may have been conditioned against the immediate words or events before him—then his hearing will be symbol-centered, fragmented, incomplete.

Commonly, we are threatened by new or different ideas, and we set up roadblocks so they can't get through. Or if one has devel-

We can never achieve a satisfactory definition of language, for there is no factor common to all our uses of language—describing, joking, praying, commanding, singing, asking, and so on. Wittgenstein asks us to think of the tools in a toolbox: hammer, pliers, a saw, a screw-driver, a ruler, a gluepot, glue, nails and screws. What we do with words is as different as what we do with these objects.

JOSEPH BRENNAN

We have been given two ears and but a single mouth, in order that we may hear more and talk less.

ZENO OF CITIUM

ESP AND THE DREAMER

Most scientists put mental telepathy in the same category as the Ouija board—an entertaining parlor game, but hardly a subject for serious investigation. Yet some, such as Dr. Montague Ullman, remain open-minded about this form of extrasensory perception. The claims about knowledge of tragic events and other messages "transmitted" over long distances, they hold, can't be explained on the basis of coincidence alone. Taking their cue in part from Sigmund Freud—who speculated that such messages might be picked up by

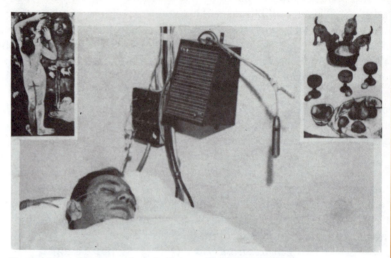

Testing telepathy: Gauguin paintings and wired-up subject.

the unconscious but distorted by the conscious, waking, mind—they have searched for telepathic evidence in the dreaming mind. Ullman, director of psychiatry at Brooklyn's Maimonides Hospital, and psychologist Stanley Krippner have set up a "dream laboratory" at Maimonides, and have carried out studies using the classic techniques of dream investigation devised by Dr. Nathaniel Kleitman at the University of Chicago.

When a person dreams, Kleitman found, his eyes move rapidly from side to side. By watching for these telltale rapid eye movements (REM's) and rousing his subjects during the REM's, Kleitman could elicit dream descriptions in unprecedented detail. In a manner similar to Kleitman's experiments, Ullman put volunteers to bed in an isolated room and attached electroencephalograph electrodes to their heads and sensors to the corner of the eyes to pick up REM's. Aroused at the end of each dream by a researcher watching the EEG and REM tracings in a room nearby, they dictated their dreams into a recorder.

In the Ullman experiment, an "agent" in a third room—usually Ullman or an assistant—fixed his attention on a "target object," such as a painting, and attempted to transmit recognizable impressions to the sleeper.

In one experiment, the target object was "Zapatistas" by José Clemente Orozco, showing followers of the Mexican revolutionary, Zapata, marching along a road with a range of mountains in the background. In a series of separate dream episodes, the volunteer reported dreaming about New Mexico, where he once lived, specifically noting the mountains, the coloring of the landscape, and Indians trooping into Sante Fe at fiesta time.

Gauguin's paintings were used as target objects twice. One was "The Moon and the Earth," portraying a nude, deeply tanned Tahitian girl. The target dreamer, a young secretary, reported dreaming about wearing a bathing suit. In subsequent episodes, she dreamed of a girl with fair skin who wanted to get a tan. The other Gauguin was "Still Life With Three Puppies." The volunteer dreamed of "a couple of dogs making a noise" and saw "dark blue bottles." The Gauguin goblets are blue.

Ullman will claim only that the "striking correlations" between the dream material and the target objects are significant enough to warrant more study and experiments by serious scientists. "The important thing," he says, "is to take the mysticism out of telepathy and study it on a rational basis."

Newsweek, May 24, 1965

oped a rigid conceptual structure, when he listens to another's experience he translates it (and distorts it) to fit into his own inflexible system.

Bertrand Russell once wrote that the stupid person always reduces brilliant concepts to his own level of stupidity since he must oversimplify them to understand them. Something like this takes place in our communicating with one another. Because of our own preestablished conceptual points of view, we "translate" what another is saying into the familiar experiences of our own world. In doing this, we miss the living experience which the other person is in fact attempting to convey.

5   Communications analysis is important in helping us see what is taking place in our conversations, discussions, and dialogues. The purpose of communications analysis is to see and understand the processes by which *meanings* are successfully communicated from one to another; or, if there is a transmission breakdown, to discover what went wrong in our thinking, our symbolizing, or our listening.

Let's join Charlie Brown's baseball game again, and focus this time on the *intended meanings* that move (or fail to move) between individuals.

Frame One. "We're getting slaughtered again. . . ." Charlie Brown's comment (as we noted earlier: page 53) is an expression of frustration. He is using language to express emotion; he is not intending to communicate ideas. Why should he? His catcher knows the score; Schroeder doesn't have to be told. Charlie's third statement

Do you not know I am woman? when I think, I must speak.

SHAKESPEARE
As You Like It, III, ii, 265

"Now that I've established my right to speak, I have nothing to say."

BJC/12-18-78

takes the form of a question—"Why do we have to suffer like this?"—but it's not really a question at all. His statement may look like a question, but it's one more way of expressing his agitation over a (losing) situation. (Here is an example when we can easily be duped by the *structure of language*.) As for Charlie Brown, we may be able to hear, behind his frustrated outburst, a cry for help, a genuine What-can-I-do-now? kind of plea.

Frame Two. "Man is born to trouble. . . ." Schroeder doesn't hear Charlie Brown's meaning at all. His reply is triggered by CB's *words*, not his *meaning*. (CB's "What?" indicates that the catcher didn't catch the intended meaning.)

Frame Three. "He's quoting from the 'Book of Job'. . . ." Linus heard what Schroeder said, but he chooses to give CB the source of the quotation rather than respond to the content of the remark. Linus tried to enlighten CB after his surprised "What?" So both Schroeder and Linus ignore CB's verbalized frustrations. In plain fact, Charlie Brown is the only player who is really in the ball game.

Frame Four. "Actually, the problem of suffering is a very profound one. . . ." Linus continues on Schroeder's wavelength, pondering the suffering that is manifest in the human condition. And Lucy—"If a person has bad luck. . . ."—does she hear what Linus is saying? Obviously not. She didn't even let him finish the idea. Lucy's mind is triggered by words, not by intended meanings. (The word "suffering" leads her, by association, to "bad luck.") Result: communication breakdown.

Frame Five. "That's what Job's friends told him." Did Schroeder hear Lucy? Yes. He heard not her words, but the whole concept of a "moral law." And Schroeder's response is accurate: Job's friends said what Lucy "always says." Did the intended meaning get through? Yes—the first time thus far.

How do we evaluate Lucy's retort to Schroeder: "What about Job's wife. . . ?" Lucy is off on a kick of her own; her comment has no connection to Schroeder's statement. (Job's wife hasn't been mentioned and is only a "bit player" in the drama of Job.) Result: No communication.

Frame Six. Schroeder continues where Linus left off in F-4—with ultimate thoughts. (Lucy is merely an interruption.) "I think the person who never suffers, never matures." Does Lucy hear? No. She hears *the word* "suffer" but not the meaning that Schroeder gives the word. She gives the word a different meaning. Therefore—"Don't be ridiculous!"—she blasts Schroeder for what he didn't say.

On the other side of the pitcher's mound another player tries to confirm the notion that "pain is a part of life, and . . ."—would he have gone on to say, "We must learn to live with it"—or something like that? If so, then he is moving at the ultimate meaning-level with Schroeder and Linus.

What about Linus's comment—"The person who speaks only of the 'patience' of Job . . ."? Is he responding to any previous statement? No. The mention of Job has reminded him of *something else* that he happened to know, something about "the patience of Job." So Linus adds his datum of unconnected information.

Frame Seven. "I don't have a ball team. . . ." Charlie Brown looks just the way most of us feel after we haven't been able to communicate to others or after we have listened to discussions during which no one heard anyone else. "Yes, Charlie Brown, we know. . . ."

6 Good communication is important if effective philosophic dialogue is to take place. Most of us never get around to giving systematic attention to the problems that tend to break down communication in our everyday conversations and relationships. When we are receivers, it is important to develop the habit of listening for intended meanings rather than words; and when speaking, we need to ask ourselves whether our intended meanings are accurately being heard by others.°

There is a distinct difference between Western and Eastern ways of responding to meaning-events. Both ways of interacting are of great value, and we need to be able to recognize each kind and respond appropriately.

A Western philosopher tends to respond to intellectual meanings contained in propositions, fact-claims, value-judgments, and so on, and to work with them analytically and logically. He will take on words and meanings directly. The strength of the Western approach

All words are only so many fingers pointing at Niagara Falls. Some may, like the family's pet dog, look at the finger rather than the rushing waters to which it points. Others on a yet more infantile level may, as Alan Watts puts it, "look at the finger pointing the way and then . . . suck it for comfort." But ultimately the quest for the Ultimate is not to be expressed but experienced. Religion is not to be defined, but explored.

RONALD HUNTINGTON

°*It is often assumed that in the classroom communication is to be held at the rational/intellectual meaning-level, and that analysis is to be primarily critical. The student might find it in order to ask his teacher to clarify the "level(s) of listening" at which discussions are intended to move.*

B.C. by Johnny Hart

By permission of John Hart and Field Enterprises, Inc.

On this planet, anything we think may be held against us. . . .

SPOCK/Star Trek
"Once Upon a Planet"

°Remember how Chuang-tzu answered his visitors (p. 35)?

°See p. 552—QM.

If you believe certain words, you believe their hidden arguments. When you believe something is right or wrong, true or false, you believe the assumptions in the words which express the arguments. Such assumptions are often full of holes, but remain most precious to the convinced.

FRANK HERBERT
Children of Dune

"What must I do, to tame you?" asked the little prince.
"You must be very patient," replied the fox. "First you will sit down at a little distance from me—like this—in the grass. I shall look at you out of the corner of my eye, and you will say nothing. Words are the source of misunderstandings. But you will sit a little closer to me, every day. . . ."

ANTOINE DE SAINT-EXUPÉRY

lies in its rationality. It has given us our sciences and our precisely organized fund of knowledge about the world and ourselves.

The Eastern philosopher tends to respond to levels of meaning that lie quite beyond words; in fact there is frequently a disdain for meanings that can be reduced to symbolic terms. The sage will answer a precise statement with a proverb or a direct question with an anecdote.° Viktor Frankl is quite Eastern when he answers the question "What is the meaning of life?" with another question: "What is the best chess move?"°

7   The Eastern use of language, and the way meaning is dealt with, is nicely described by Edwin Burtt:

> Chinese writers, in philosophy and literature, aim at suggesting fertile insights rather than at achieving analytic precision. . . . The genius of the Chinese mind is revealed most fully, not in its philosophical essays or dialogues, but in its poetry, where the suggestive nuances of thought can be freely expressed, unhampered by any need for meticulous distinctions or for coercion of the reader's thought through logical deduction. . . . One who writes in the fashion of a system-maker thereby shows that he is sure of having attained the essential truth he has sought, and that he is now endeavoring to fasten it upon his reader; his unexpressed attitude is: "You will, of course, take my premises for granted, and I am now going to prove that you must then adopt my conclusions." From the typical Chinese viewpoint such argumentation is not only largely futile (since any keen and determined reader can always find an alternative set of plausible premises); it is unseemly. For if one refuses to take his own convictions too seriously, and approaches his reader with proper respect for the latter's independent integrity, what he will be concerned to do is not to coerce an acceptance of his assertions, but so to express them as to elicit growth toward the reader's own more adequate insight. By its neat exactitude and seeming conclusiveness, logical argument can discourage and even block this growth. Let us think and speak so as to guide constructive progress in the experience and understanding of others, not so as to convert them to some absolute which we have no business to regard as such ourselves.

8   Among many of us, listening is a lost art. How difficult it is for most of us to remain silent in the presence of different or "wrong" ideas. The urge to clobber an alien idea swells within us like a self-righteous demon, and a speaker rarely gets halfway through his sentence before we give way to an impulse to cut him down.

We all know the experience of wanting to be heard by others (or by some one) and not being able to get through. One of our persistent human frustrations is to discover that another person is hearing only words rather than the living experience we feel so deeply and are aching to convey.

Few insights leave one with such a sense of loneliness. To realize suddenly that, no matter how earnestly you try, you can't be heard—this is why there are so many lonely people who belong to the lonely crowd.

The number of individuals who are *word-oriented* rather than *meaning-oriented* indicates the existence of a widespread "normal" neurosis in our society.

DEFINITIONS AND CONTEXTS

9   Semanticists remind us that symbols can be understood intelligibly only within the context of actual usage. The semantic axiom that no word ever has the same meaning twice would appear to be an overstatement, since in practice we seem to use words repeatedly with about the same meaning. But in fact their observation is accurate. *Definitions are predictions of possible meanings which a term may be given in concrete situations.* The precise meaning of any term cannot be known until it occurs in a living context, and then its meaning is inextricably interwoven with the total event and cannot be understood apart from it.

There is a strand of Western tradition going back at least as far as Aristotle that would attempt to give all words exact definitions and insist that they be employed only in this unambiguous way. Within certain academic fields this precise approach has yielded valuable results. But this sort of operation has little relation to our richly varied use of language in daily life.

The individual who is rigidly literal in his use of definitions often fails in the communication of experience. If he has the habit of bringing prefabricated definitions into fluid, living situations, he is apt to miss entirely the nuances and connotations which terms take on in a specific context. Words are "containers" into which we pour the meanings and feelings of the moment, and this personal investment of ourselves in our symbols is intimately tied to the immediate experiences of life.

10   No two persons ever react to any word or symbol in exactly the same manner. How could they? In order to do so, they would have to have the same past experience, the same present environment, the same prospect of the future, the same pattern of thought, the same flow of feelings, the same bodily habits, and the same electro-chemical metabolism. The chances that such multidimensional patterns coincide are practically nil. The surprising thing is not that we often disagree; it is that we ever succeed in achieving some sort of agreement.

SAMUEL BOIS

11   It is surprising how often people still speak of "dirty words" or "obscene language" and believe that *symbols* are *inherently* dirty or obscene. Semanticists keep reminding us that words mean nothing at all until we give meanings to them. There simply is no such thing as a "dirty word"; there are only symbols which individuals and groups have invested with certain (negative) meanings and feelings.

The trouble with speakers who never leave the higher levels of abstraction is not only that they fail to notice when they are saying something and when they are not; they also produce a similar lack of discrimination in their audiences. Never coming down to earth, they frequently chase themselves around in verbal circles, unaware that they are making meaningless noises.

S. I. HAYAKAWA

A man of true science uses but a few hard words . . . whereas the smatterer in science . . . thinks that by mouthing hard words he understands hard things.

HERMAN MELVILLE

Let us not forget that a word hasn't got a meaning given to it, as it were, by a power independent of us, so that there could be a kind of scientific investigation in what the word *really* means. A word has the meaning someone has given to it.

WITTGENSTEIN

The observer can describe the world only in the language available to him. "Fact" has a linguistic constituent. As B. L. Whorf has shown, speakers of languages that do not have a word for "wave" will see not waves but only changing undulating surfaces. The Navahos use one word for blue and green, whereas the Bororó of Brazil have no single word for parrot. In Arabic a wind may be described as *sarsar*, which means both *cold* and *whistling*. The language of Tierra del Fuego has a useful word, *mamihlapinatapai;* it means, roughly, the state of mind in which two people regard each other when both want a certain thing to be done but neither wants to be the first to do it. How many lovely facts are available to them! Of course La Rochefoucauld said a long time ago, *"Il y a des gens qui n'auraient jamais été amoureux, s'ils n'avaient jamais entendu parler d'amour* (There are people who would never have fallen in love if they had not heard love spoken about). Cassirer and Sapir argue that the forms of language predetermine the modes of observation and interpretation; Wittgenstein said that "if we spoke a different language, we would perceive a somewhat different world." Waismann's metaphor is "language is the knife with which we cut out facts."

REUBEN ABEL
Man is the Measure

Nevertheless, the fact that large numbers of individuals are offended by *symbols—quite apart from the experience symbolized*—is a social reality. If one sincerely desires to communicate experience, there is good pragmatic justification for not making unnecessary use of *any* symbols which are apt to produce symbol-centered reactions in others—which can be done with erudite phrases and technical terminology as well as by the use of taboo language. As a general rule, any sort of language that causes us to focus on the symbols rather than the experience symbolized serves to break down the process of communication.

Words have no meaning. Only people have meaning.

AMERICAN RED CROSS
(Radio Commercial)

TELEPATHY AND COMMUNICATION

12   Does telepathic communication exist? There is some evidence that it does, and the widespread popular belief in telepathy is based on actual experiences for which a telepathic hypothesis seems at present the best explanation.

The more plausible fact-claims about telepathy hint at some interesting possibilities. One is that telepathic experiences are less common in cerebral individuals, in "intellectual" and rational people. A domineering intellect stands in the way of nonrational experience in general, including telepathy. Similarly, individuals from less cerebral cultures seem to be more capable of having telepathic experiences.

Not higher sensitivity, not longer memory or even quicker association sets man so far above other animals that he can regard them as denizens of a lower world; no, it is the power of using symbols that makes him lord of the earth.

SUSANNE LANGER

Members of societies which express emotion openly—those that still dance and experience ecstasy, in a word, those who are in touch with the Dionysian side of life—these are more open to supersensory experiences than individuals driven by the Apollonian pursuit of intellect and order.

> **empathize** (em′pȧ-thīz)   To diagnose, that is to recognize and identify the feelings, emotions, passions, sufferings, torments through their symptoms is to *realize intellectually*, to *understand* them, in a remote way to identify oneself with the patient, without ever having personally experienced those feelings,—to *empathize*, as it is known in psychiatry.
>
> On the other hand, to place oneself in the position of the patient, to get into his skin, so to speak, to be able to duplicate, live through, *experience* those feelings in a vicarious way, is closely to identify oneself with another, to *share his feelings with him*, to *sympathize*, from the Greek *syn*, together with, and *páthos*, suffering, passion.
>
> **empathy** (em′pȧ-thē) . . .   Empathy is thus a form of identification; it may be called intellectual identification in contrast to affective identification.
>
> HINSIE AND CAMPBELL
> *Psychiatric Dictionary*

I do desire we may be better strangers.

SHAKESPEARE
As You Like It, III, ii, 276

Another fact is that telepathic experiences appear to have some correlation with physical or psychical abnormalities. They occur more frequently after brain damage, or during alterations of endocrine chemistry, extreme emotional states, or recovery from an illness or accident.

In considering the future capabilities of communication, there is an interesting hint that when we receive telepathic messages from others, the event is not at all a pure transfer of experience. Rather, the content is immediately assimilated into our own fabric of understanding and feeling. That is, we still interpret the telepathic communication in terms of *our* experience, just as we do with all other forms of knowledge which we receive by symbolic means.

Lastly—if telepathy exists—it seems that its base of operation is somewhere deep in the unconscious regions of the psyche. Telepathic channels appear to operate outside the conscious mind and then break in uninvited.

"Why are we going in there again, daddy?"
"Shut up," his father explained.

RING LARDNER

13   In my dream I was driving my car along a road near my home, and quite suddenly, out of nowhere, it seemed to me, a little girl about three years of age appeared right in front of the car. I did all I could but found it impossible to avoid hitting her. On getting out, I was told that she was dead. I looked at her as she lay in the road, and felt completely shattered, though I had never had a chance to save her

If God had said, after Adam named the cats, dogs, and cows, "There is another animal over at the far end of the garden—what name would you give it?" Adam would no doubt have replied petulantly, "How can I give it a name when I can't even see it?"

REUBEN ABEL

Doctor: "How did you happen to call him Harvey?"
Mr. Dowd: "Well, Harvey's his name!"

MARY CHASE
Harvey

Staggering as it may be to contemplate, a life signal may connect all creation. . . .

CLEVE BACKSTER

from what seemed to me to be her inevitable fate. I must stress that feeling I had of inevitability.

When I awoke, I realized with horror that I had to drive down that road that very morning, on my way to lunch with my youngest daughter, and I decided to be more than usually careful. On approaching the spot, I looked round most carefully for any sign of children, and there were none in sight, only about five women standing at a bus stop. Relieved beyond words, I glanced down at my speedometer to check, and on lifting my eyes, was completely horrified to see, standing still in the middle of the road, the little girl of my dream, correct in every detail, even to the dark curly hair and the bright blue cardigan she was wearing. I was afraid to use my horn, in case I startled her and precipitated what I felt was going to be a fatal accident, so I slowly brought the car to a halt, just beside her. She never moved, but stood staring at me.

Meanwhile, the women in the bus queue made no sign of interest, and no one tried to get such a young child off the busy road. In fact, they seemed more interested in the fact that I had stopped. Feeling very shaky, I continued on my way, and looking in the mirror, I saw the child was still standing there, and nobody was bothering about her. By the time I got to my daughter's flat, I was over half an hour late. When she opened the door, she was looking very worried and upset, and said how glad she was to see me safe and sound.

I asked why she had been so worried, as I have been driving for over thirty years, and she looked at me and said, "I know that, Mummie, but you see, last night I had a terribly vivid dream. In this dream you ran over and killed a lovely little girl, dressed in a bright blue cardigan and with lovely dark curly hair!"

14   This dream, which is representative of a very common experience, is recounted by the British author J. B. Priestley. He double checked the facts of the episode with the mother, her husband, and the daughter (but not the little girl!). Priestley comments:

Telepathy, and not any Time effect, was at work here. Whether the daughter took the tragic little-girl-episode from the mother, or the mother from the daughter, we cannot tell. . . . What is certain is that this fascinating double dream is well worth the attention of ESP experts and researchers.

A Soviet parapsychologist, Dr. Pavel Naumov, has concluded that "biological ties between mother and child are incontestable."

In the clinic, mothers are in a distant section, separate from their babies. They cannot possibly hear them. Yet, when her baby cries, a mother exhibits nervousness. Or when an infant is in pain, for instance as a doctor takes a blood specimen, the mother shows signs of anxiety. She has no way of knowing the doctor is at that moment with her child. . . . We found communication in 65 percent of our cases.

Many similar events are noted by Sheila Ostrander and Lynn Schroeder in their book *Psychic Discoveries Behind the Iron Curtain.* They comment that

> such cases open up philosophical, ethical, personal and scientific questions. Across a distance, is mind influencing body? Is body influencing body? Is body influencing mind? As psi moves into the picture, the iron edges of biology and psychology begin to dissolve and mix, pointing to a whole new dynamism underlying both.

15 Dr. Naumov tells of another experiment in telepathy which was conducted aboard a Russian submarine at sea. In this case the subjects were not human beings, but a mother rabbit and her litter of newborn bunnies.

Naumov relates:

> As you know, there's no known way for a submerged submarine to communicate with anyone on land. Radio doesn't work. Scientists placed the baby rabbits aboard the submarine. They kept the mother rabbit in a laboratory on shore where they implanted electrodes deep in her brain. When the sub was deep below the surface of the ocean, assistants killed the young rabbits one by one.
>
> The mother rabbit obviously didn't know what was happening. Even if she could have understood the test, she had no way of knowing at what moment her children died. Yet, at each synchronized instant of death, her brain *reacted. There was communication.* . . . And, our instruments clearly registered these moments of ESP.

Tens of thousands of years have elapsed since we shed our tails, but we are still communicating with a medium developed to meet the needs of arboreal man. . . . We may smile at the linguistic illusions of primitive man, but may we forget that the verbal machinery on which we so readily rely, and with which our metaphysicians still profess to probe the Nature of Existence, was set up by him, and may be responsible for other illusions hardly less gross and not more easily eradicable?

OGDEN AND RICHARDS

REFLECTIONS—

1 Do you sometimes feel overwhelmed by words? What sort of communicative techniques do you think we would resort to or develop or invent if, suddenly, we found ourselves without words?

2 Do you agree with the notion that much of our drive to communicate derives from an "epistemic loneliness"—from a need to transcend a space-time condition which we cannot tolerate? Do you personally feel this condition?

3 Note the following sentence in Sec. 4: "Success in communication depends not upon the speaker, but upon the hearer." Does this sound right to you? Analyze the sequence of "bits" involved in the communication of meaning and explain why this conclusion is or isn't true.

4 What is a "definition"? Is this semantic way of defining definitions helpful to you?

5 Note the many different functions of language (Secs. 2 and 3). If you became aware that much of the language of daily life is not intended to communicate ideas, how might this influence the way you listen to others? How do you think it might affect your relationships?

6 On taboo symbols (Sec. 11): There must be deep psychological needs for such symbols and their surrogates. How would you describe these needs?

7 Everyday life provides ample occasion to practice communications analysis; and our exchanges are never quite the same after we have developed an awareness of the many levels of meaning that move between us. Take advantage of the first opportunities you have .to practice communications analysis in your discussions and dialogues. Review and assess afterwards what you have seen and learned.

8 The Eastern use of language described by Professor Burtt has as long and as rich a tradition as Western analytic thinking; but the Eastern way is designed to achieve an essentially different goal. What kind of insight is the Eastern approach to meaning-events more likely to produce?

9 Do you think telepathic communication exists? If so, what evidence can you offer to support your conclusion? If it does exist, what are some of its philosophic—especially epistemological and ethical—implications? (Note box on p. 256: "ESP and the Dreamer.")

Furthermore . . .

ADLER, RON, and NEIL TOWNE, *Looking Out/Looking In: Interpersonal Communication*. Holt, Rinehart and Winston, 1975.

BOIS, J. SAMUEL, *The Art of Awareness*. William C. Brown, 1973.

CHASE, STUART, *The Tyranny of Words*. Harvest Books, 1938.

FAST, JULIUS, *Body Language*. Pocket Books, 1971.

HALL, EDWARD T., *The Silent Language*. Fawcett, 1961.

HAYAKAWA, S. I. (ed.), *The Use and Misuse of Language*. Fawcett, 1962.

MUNSON, RONALD, *The Way of Words: An Informal Logic*. Houghton-Mifflin, 1976.

ULLMAN, MONTAGUE, *Dream Telepathy*. Macmillan, 1973.

PART V

COEXISTENCE: MAN'S LOVE/HATE CONDITION

The age of cultural innocence is passing; the American is beginning to recognize the patterns to which he conforms.

SNELL AND GAIL PUTNEY

They are playing a game. They are playing at not playing a game. If I show them I see they are, I shall break the rules and they will punish me. I must play their game, of not seeing I see the game.

R. D. LAING

History/Meaning

Have You Ever Wondered . . .

- Whether history has meaning?

- Why—*if* we *can* learn from history—some people never seem to get the message?

- Whether—since "only the fittest survive"—historical "progress" is inevitable and "things are getting better and better"?

- Whether—since man is essentially evil—historical "progress" is a fiction and actually "things are getting worse and worse"?

- Whether Marxism might be a valid interpretation of history?

- Whether our own Western civilization will crumble and vanish like the Greek and Roman civilizations?

- What it would mean to you personally if history has no meaning whatsoever?

THEATER OF THE ABSURD

1   Arnold Toynbee is considered by many to be the greatest of contemporary philosophers of history. His massive twelve-volume *Study of History* stands today as the supreme effort of the human mind to disentangle the complexities of human history in order to see whether there is any large-scale meaning to the whole human enterprise.

Late in 1911 Toynbee left Oxford for a nine-month tour of the Mediterranean lands where he saw for himself the remains of the great civilizations he knew so well from history books. He spent much time walking over the countryside surveying the legacies of these long-dead worlds. He chatted with monks on Mount Athos, examined Etruscan tombs at Cerveteri and Corneto, and mused on the past glory of the Minoan palaces on Crete. Before this visit, the Acropolis had been a page in a book; now its panorama sprawled before him in all its breathtaking reality.

At the same time, he listened to the sounds of the living world. He spent his evenings in Greek cafes and heard talk of world affairs; he visited Greek villages and caught apprehensive conversations among peasants and shepherds about the possibility of war.

He reflected on these two worlds. One was dead, it seemed, the other very much alive. The contrast was a shattering reminder of life, death, and time. Toynbee pondered: What does man's past tell us about the present or future? How dead, really, are past civilizations? If they are dead, what caused them to die? What is their relationship to our own busy world? *Is our civilization also doomed to die like the rest?* If so, why? Could it perhaps be saved? If so, what could save it?

2 These are the essential concerns of the philosopher of history. What, if anything, does history mean? How can we learn from it? Is there any way that our understanding of history can shed light on our own troubled times?

There has been a renewed interest in the philosophy of history due to the maddening chaos of the twentieth century thus far. The "big events" that make and shake history have dominated our time: the Russian pogroms, the Turkish massacre of Armenians, the Nazi

Until philosophers are kings, or the kings and princes of this world have the spirit and power of philosophy, and political greatness and wisdom meet in one, and those commoner natures who pursue either to the exclusion of the other are compelled to stand aside, cities will never have rest from their evils—no, nor the human race. . . .

PLATO

Although a certain amount of hypocrisy exists about it, everyone is fascinated by violence. After all, man is the most remorseless killer who ever stalked the earth. Our interest in violence in part reflects the fact that on the subconscious level we are very little different from our primitive ancestors.

STANLEY KUBRICK

execution of six million Jews; two World Wars initiated by insane racist leaders; an escalating arms race; ongoing guerrilla skirmishes, bush wars, and ideological terrorism; scattered tribal/nationalistic conflicts; plus an all-engulfing global revolution which has only begun.

Such events have sent men back to reexamining their historical experience in an attempt to make sense out of what, in the wake of such enormous tragedies, has seemed absurd and senseless. All too clearly contemporary history sounds like "a tale told by an idiot, full of sound and fury, signifying nothing." Could this assessment actually be true? Or does human history have a deeper meaning which man in his frenzied state has overlooked?

The philosophy of history asks only two central questions, though each leads on logically to countless others. The first-generation questions are: (1) Does human history have meaning? (2) Can we learn from history? These questions may or may not be closely related.

3   The metaphor of the drama is appropriate and helpful when trying to conceptualize the problems of the philosophy of history. "All the world's a stage," wrote Shakespeare, "And all the men and women merely players."

So, think of human history as a long, intricately plotted play, with numerous roles and innumerable characters. If history has meaning, then the drama may be similar to an epic like *Macbeth*. Perhaps it has a playwright who wrote the story and, conceivably, directs the play. (But are we sure the playwright is also the director? And is the playwright also the prop-master?) It has its leading characters—its *dramatis personae*. It has a plot that gives meaning to the lives of the players. It is they who move the plot along. It couldn't develop without them—a play with no players is no play. Every character is essential to the unfolding of the dramatic plot as it moves toward the climax— the dénouement of the play's suspenseful story. To be sure, some characters are more important to the plot than others, but even the spear-carriers have an appointed place in the grand epic.

Now, does this drama metaphor capture the essential truth of human history? Is there in fact a playwright? Is there really a plot? Is there a goal to human history, a final curtain? Is this why our lives are meaningful—because we are all cast in the play? Are we humans really necessary to the working out of the drama? And is the plot a tragedy—as in *Macbeth*—or a comedy—as in *A Midsummer Night's Dream?*

While the stage-play metaphor helps us to formulate questions about the nature of history, the bare fact just may be that history more closely resembles some bizarre act from the Theater of the Absurd—a plotless non-staging of countless non-characters who were never cast but who persist in ad-libbing their lines, interacting with no direction, and moving from scene to scene without purpose. It may indeed be "a tale told by an idiot . . . signifying nothing." There may be no playwright, no director, no plot. There may be no play.

Everyone in Germany is a National Socialist—the few outside the party are either lunatics or idiots.

ADOLF HITLER

The greatest virtue is not to be free, but to struggle ceaselessly for freedom.

KAZANTZAKIS

The notion of a finite and clearly definable goal of progress in history, so often postulated by nineteenth-century thinkers, has proved inapplicable and barren. Belief in progress means belief not in any automatic or inevitable process, but in the progressive development of human potentialities. Progress is an abstract term; and the concrete ends pursued by mankind arise from time to time out of the course of history, not from some source outside it. I profess no belief in the perfectibility of man, or in a future paradise on earth. To this extent I would agree with the theologians and the mystics who assert that perfection is not realizable in history. But I shall be content with the possibility of unlimited progress—or progress subject to no limits that we can need or envisage—towards goals which can be defined only as we advance towards them, and the validity of which can be verified only in a process of attaining them. Nor do I know how, without some such conception of progress, society can survive. Every civilized society imposes sacrifices on the living generation for the sake of generations yet unborn. To justify these sacrifices in the name of a better world in the future is the secular counterpart of justifying them in the name of some divine purpose. In Bury's words, "the principle of duty to posterity is a direct corollary of the idea of progress." Perhaps this duty does not require justification. If it does, I know of no other way to justify it.

EDWARD HALLETT CARR
What Is History?

THE MEANING OF HISTORY

4   In most of man's societies to date, the source of history's meaning has been assumed to be the operation of the supernatural. This was a logical deduction from our inherited theological premises. The causal agents behind the events of human history were the capricious animistic sprites and spirits, the whims of the gods, the will of God, or the cosmic interaction of the Forces of Light battling the Forces of Darkness. In any case, the meaning of history was the preplanned story-line working itself out as man-in-time moved the drama forward from scene to scene.

When it was assumed that supernatural agencies were the source of history's meaning, then human interpretation could move in two directions. It could begin with belief in a preordained plan (God has predestined the minutest details of earth's history from the first appleseed to the last sparrow that falls); and the events of our lives could then be interpreted according to that plan. Or it could look at the events that actually take place and interpret them—and give them meaning—according to these preconceived beliefs ("We won the war because God was on our side"). In Western history it has moved both ways.

If you're looking for a really dangerous and outmoded myth, national sovereignty wins over the papacy hands down.

HARVEY COX

5   One of the first known interpreters of history in the Western world was the so-called Deuteronomic historian who wrote down the stories of various wars carried on by the Hebrew tribes during the twelfth and eleventh centuries B.C. This unknown writer had sufficient records to enable him to describe sporadic battles involving the tribal leaders ("judges") of that time; and because of his theological convictions he perceived a pattern in the wars. He did not—indeed he could not—record history as we know it today; rather he wrote "interpreted history," that is, the historical events *plus* what they meant to him.

The dramatic framework which he placed around each tribal battle was simple but meaningful.

(1) The Israelites do something evil "in the sight of Yahweh" their God.

(2) Yahweh's anger "blazes against Israel." He sends them into battle and "sells them into the power" of the enemy. They are on the point of losing the war.

(3) Then the Israelites repent of their evil ways and "cry unto Yahweh." They ask forgiveness and plead for help.

(4) Yahweh then "raises up a savior" (a leader) who proceeds into battle with "the spirit of Yahweh upon him" and defeats the enemy.

(5) Yahweh has won back his children; he is pleased. So peace "reigns in the land for forty years."

Like a taped replay, this pattern is repeated over and over again throughout the Deuteronomic history. It's the only interpretation the writer knows, and his theological preconviction precludes his seeing the historic events in any other way. This is therefore not history but a meaningful—if one-sided—interpretation of a few significant events. It is a "theology of history."°

This framework can be used to interpret *any* conflict between *any* groups. Consider World War II, for example. The Americans (or British or French, or whoever) did "what was evil in the sight of the Lord." He "was angered and sent them into war" where they are about to lose. But they repent and "he raises up a leader" (Churchill, Stalin, Eisenhower—take your pick) who proceeds to win the war. The Lord is pleased again, so "peace reigns for forty years." (The number 40 is rarely, if ever, an historical figure, but a symbolic number implying the presence and approval of God.) This framework can be used just as well to interpret a World Series baseball game or a presidential election.

This sort of interpretation is too subjective to be of any use to us. We can assume that it was meaningful to the Deuteronomist and subsequent believers, but for those of us who are attempting to discover the realities of the case—the objective patterns of history, if they exist—this writer offers little help.

What the Deuteronomic historian succeeds in doing is to alert us to beware of the ease with which we can let our mind's conceptual habits arrange historical events into subjective patterns of meaning. This is a warning for which we can be grateful.

6 The first great Western philosopher of history was Saint Augustine. He was prompted to write *The City of God* after the fall of the city of Rome to Alaric and his Goths in A.D. 410. This incredible event so shook the Roman world that it had to be interpreted. It was so meaningless there had to be meaning behind it. While the pagan Romans

°Note that a familiar "unexamined assumption" underlies this pattern: the so-called universal moral law expounded by the Book of Job—and Lucy. See pages 60 ff.

were complaining that the tragedy was divine punishment for the abandonment of the old Roman gods, Augustine took up his pen to show that Rome had fallen as a part of a long-range divine plan on the part of the "Christian" God. God had not merely tolerated the degenerate city, but had used the City of Earth to accomplish his ends; for out of that City of Earth there had developed the Church to represent the Kingdom of God on Earth. When that city's task of giving birth to the Church was accomplished, then the City of Earth (Rome) would be replaced by the City of God (the Roman Church).

Therefore, in the fullness of time, the plan of God was manifesting itself on the historical plane. The City of Earth had fallen to give way to the City of God.

Augustine's theological interpretation of the fall of Rome, like the viewpoint of the Deuteronomist, is too arbitrary and subjective. We can be sure that Alaric's Gothic priests didn't perceive the event that way, nor did the majority of Romans. If one does not share the theological assumptions from which Augustine began his interpretation, then his explanation is neither logically sound nor psychologically satisfying.

What we can learn from Saint Augustine is that the temptation to seek meaningful interpretations of life-shattering events can lead us into mythical world-views which have no objective validity. To be sure, they can be comforting, and during times of torment this life-sustaining mode of interpretation is never to be denigrated. But during less stressful periods of life we seek a clearer vision of reality; and the kind of pressures to which Augustine yielded must not persuade us to settle, too soon, for a parochial interpretation of history which, from a synoptic point of view, is of little value.

7   Two influential teleological philosophies of history have dominated modern times: Hegel's dialectical idealism and Marx's dialectical materialism.

Friedrich Hegel was convinced that he had discovered the nature of thought and that he had made a unique discovery. The thought process moves in a three-beat rhythm which he called the "dialectic." It begins with an idea—a thesis—then proceeds to develop into its opposite, the antithesis; after that the mind sees the relatedness of thesis and antithesis and weaves them together into a synthesis. This synthesis, in turn, becomes another thesis, and the dialectic continues. Thus the dialectic effects an ever-expanding comprehension of the connections of the contents of thought.

Hegel was quite sure that this is the way God's mind works. God is pure thought, or, in Hegel's words, the Absolute Mind. Here is no love or compassion (no emotion), just pure thought. The Absolute Mind of God manifests reason through the mind of man and therefore in human history. Whenever men think and act more rationally they are actualizing God's will, and this progressive manifestation of logic is the teleological purpose underlying human history.

Man is a crucial part of this program, and there was reason to

> **Men always love what is good or what they find good; it is in judging what is good that they go wrong.**
>
> *ROUSSEAU*

G. W. F. Hegel (1770–1831)

Karl Marx (1818–1883)

believe, Hegel thought, that man was becoming more reasonable, especially in nineteenth-century Germany. All of this would end in a state which Hegel described as "pure thought thinking about pure thought"—Absolute Mind contemplating itself.

8   Hegel's novel way of interpreting history caught the minds of students in the German universities; but while the idea of the dialectic excited them, the notion of an Absolute Mind behaving like a computer left them cold.

Karl Marx was one of these students. Following the lead of another young philosopher named Ludwig Feuerbach, Marx developed a philosophy of history around the idea of a dialectical movement, operating in terms of the basic material essentials of life. Marx was convinced that *his* vision of the dialectic was real. It is a dialectic of social struggle determined by man's economic needs. Class struggle creates the three-beat rhythm. Marx's interpretation is a "materialistic dialectic" in contrast to Hegel's theistic dialectic.

Thus Marx laid the foundations for a teleological interpretation of history which has come to dominate half the world. All Marxians know that history has purpose; it follows "inexorable law" toward a goal—the Classless Society where equality, justice, and plenty will prevail (which is a down-to-earth version of the Kingdom of God). Each individual is a part of history's drama. As in other teleocosmic dramas, each person must decide whether he will fight on the side of the Righteous (the revolutionaries who actively hasten history toward its appointed end) or on the side of the Wicked (the bourgeois reactionaries who resist change and progress).

9   By now it's clear that each of us, when attempting to make sense of the complexities of the past, must be on guard against projecting our subjective frameworks onto historical events and arranging them to support our own visions and prejudices. We must be equally wary of the hidden *cultural* assumptions of our place and time—the *Zeitgeist* or "time-spirit." Hegel and Marx both fell victim to such an assumption: the idea of "inevitable progress."

The opposing notions that human history is improving (the optimistic view) or degenerating (the pessimistic view) have had a see-saw history in Western thought.

The teleological view of history—the belief that history has meaning and is moving toward a goal—is essentially a Judeo-Christian assumption; and within that teleological point of view a majority report has held that the human lot would continually improve. (In a general way, when times were troubled—during the Roman persecutions, the Islamic conquests, and the twentieth century—the pessimistic viewpoint has prevailed: conditions, it was held, will become progressively worse until God, in his own good time, "breaks in from above" and sets things right. By contrast, when times were relatively peaceful—during the Renaissance, the Enlightenment, and the Victorian era—the optimistic viewpoint has prevailed: history was seen as

> The human being who looks upon his own future as already determined by fate . . . only acknowledges a lack of will power to struggle and win through.
>
> *MAX PLANCK*

a progressive improvement of man's growth and happiness on earth. In either case, however, whether history is going up or down, it never loses its teleological character.)

The nineteenth century was infused with a double dose of optimism. The Industrial Revolution was in full swing. Western nations were moving to all corners of the world, sharing their bounty of material goods and spiritual blessings. And among philosophers of history the mood of the Enlightenment was still waxing. Edward Gibbon sealed his idealism near the end of his great *History of the Decline and Fall of the Roman Empire* (1776–1788) by sharing "the pleasing conclusion that every age of the world has increased, and still increases, the real wealth, the happiness, the knowledge, and perhaps the virtue, of the human race."

To this assessment of human history was added (in 1859) Darwin's massive documentation of the evolutionary theory that, down through aeons of time, it is the fitter species that survive. Nature, too, it turns out, is inherently progressive. So it became clear that both *human* history and *natural* history move together, upwards and onwards; and only the most dismal disbeliever could doubt "the inevitability of progress." Much later Bertrand Russell was to reminisce: "I grew up in the full flood of Victorian optimism, and . . . something remains with me of that hopefulness that then was easy."

Although the philosophies of history constructed by Hegel and Marx can be validly criticized on many other grounds, their optimistic foundations were solely subjective—assumptions that were "in the air" of their times. So we have two more instances when serious thinkers projected their inner visions into the real world and thus failed to give us an accurate account of history's meaning.

Once we have cast another group in the role of the enemy, we know that they are to be distrusted—that they are evil incarnate. We then twist all their communications to fit our belief.

JEROME FRANK

Change is avalanching down upon our heads, and most people are utterly unprepared to cope with it.

ALVIN TOFFLER

A MODERN ATTEMPT: TOYNBEE'S ORGANISMIC INTERPRETATION

10   Arnold Toynbee's *Study of History* is probably the most noteworthy attempt by any modern philosopher of history to make sense of the human drama.

In September of 1921 he was aboard a miserably slow train traveling across Thrace. The rumbling of his train crossing a bridge near Adrianople awakened him before dawn, and during the next few hours, as a countryside haunted with history glided past, his mind began to call up the epochal events of history and legend that had been set in this great theater.

He knew that he was now crossing the westernmost boundaries of the vast empire of the Persian Achaemenids and that when that kingdom had run its course, these rolling hills and lazy pasturelands came under the shield of the young Alexander of Macedon. Three centuries later the astute plans of a Caesar for the conquest of central Europe were shattered when Varus and his legions were lured into the nearby Teutoburg Forest and annihilated by the Germans.

Through here the Goths and the Huns passed, followed in turn by the Crusaders with red crosses flashing on their white tunics and the fire of holy war flashing in their eyes; after encountering the gaily clad Saracens those that returned crept homeward in bloodsoaked rags, and not a few laid their embattled bones beside the little streams in the Thracian woodlands. Much later this countryside, then Rumelia, was drawn into the Ottoman Empire and the Muslims settled the land and made it theirs. Thus it had remained until modern times.

Hour after hour Toynbee stood by the window watching the scenes of history pass by. That night, as the train sped along in the light of the full moon, he jotted down on a half-sheet of notepaper a plan for a comparative study of the civilizations of mankind. He had decided to embark on a research program which would take him on a prolonged journey through all known civilizations in order to determine whether meaningful patterns were discernible in the lifetimes of these civilizations. His primary interest was to discover where we stand today in Western civilization and to glimpse where we are going. He figured that this project would require decades of work, and it did. He completed the last page of his lifelong study on June 15, 1951—thirty years of labor to discover the meaning of history and the current condition of our Western civilization.

11   Toynbee thinks in terms of civilizations, not nations. The latter are but ephemeral and illusory fragments of civilizations. In the wider perspective of man's civilizations, nations are merely ethnocentric tribes which come and go so rapidly that they are quite secondary in importance, though in their short lifetimes they are the source of much narrow internecine bickering within the larger cultural body.

The subject matter of Toynbee's study of history are all the civilizations known to man. He lists twenty-seven civilizations which have been born to date (that includes five arrested civilizations). There were also four abortive civilizations which started out normally but could not make the grade.

Subtracting the arrested civilizations from the total, we have twenty-two that reached maturity. Of those twenty-two civilizations, fifteen are now dead and buried, while only seven are still alive. Of the five arrested civilizations, two are dead and three are still living.

There are, then, a total of seventeen dead and ten living civilizations.

But two of these ten living civilizations are now in their death throes. That leaves only eight, and six of these "bear marks of having already broken down and gone into disintegration," and seven of the eight are presently seriously threatened with annihilation and/or assimilation by Western civilization.

As of the twentieth century, therefore, our own Western civilization stands at the top of the list. From appearances, we are still relatively healthy, and our general prognosis, according to Toynbee, can be one of guarded optimism.

I have a theory that progress is what is left over after one meets an impossible problem.

NORMAN COUSINS

Those who ignore history are doomed to repeat it.

SANTAYANA

Violent revolutions do not so much redistribute wealth as destroy it. . . . The only real revolution is in the enlightenment of the mind and the improvement of character. The only real emancipation is individual. . . .

WILL DURANT

12   As Toynbee studied the lifespans of man's twenty-seven civilizations—rather like drawing lifelines on clear plastic films and making overlays for comparison—what did he discover? Patterns. Consistent, clear patterns of birth, growth, maturity, decline, disintegration, and death—for each and every civilization that had the good fortune (just like individuals) to live a full lifetime. To him the patterns were unmistakable, and he tried to study the movements of civilizations without prior doctrinal commitment. He believed the patterns he saw to be real, not subjective.

Toynbee gave labels to the stages of development in much the same way that Erikson has named the phases of our individual life patterns. A "primitive society" is confronted by a challenge and responds heroically and creatively. It is led out of its primitive condition by a "creative minority" of individuals and becomes a bright, thriving civilization. But the "creative minority" soon loses its vitality and turns into a "dominant minority" that refuses to release its cherished power. Internal power struggles begin as the disintegrating civilization fragments; it is bound together less and less by common values and shared visions. It sinks into a "time of troubles" and becomes vulnerable to dissolving forces from within and without. It unifies briefly into a "universal state"; but it has no vital, creative resources left, and it dies. But from death there is resurrection. From its ashes there arises, Phoenix-like, a second-generation civilization that carries on the great insights and values of the now dead society.

13   Since the larger units (civilizations) behave so much like the smaller units (persons), one can detect an experiential thread running throughout Toynbee's philosophy of history. Outlined in terms of the individual it runs something like this:

An individual experiences a state of

(1) *peace and contentment:* he relaxes his hold on nonmaterial values and becomes more material-minded; he becomes self-satisfied with material things to the point of worshiping himself and his handiwork. This leads to

(2) *disillusionment and suffering:* life has become meaningless as materialism fails to satisfy the needs of human nature; the old gods prove to be false. Man's suffering drives him toward a

(3) *salvaging of values:* his attention is redirected toward the fundamental questions of the nature and value of human life; he seeks meaning once again, and finds it. This question-asking mood stimulates him into a

(4) *period of creativity:* he finds answers to his questions; life takes on new meaning as disillusionment fades away; life becomes livable again, and he is happy. He now enters a state of

(5) *peace and contentment:* and the cycle repeats itself.

This pattern of behavior is typical, but it is not an "inexorable law." It can be broken by innumerable factors, internal and external,

When I come back from war, I discovered that to adjust to the kind of life people lived was simply impossible, after all that I had seen. So many of the things that went on seemed like trivialities.

The World at War
BBC-TV

In the case of most Americans, the internal limitations far outweigh the external ones.

SNELL AND GAIL PUTNEY

and this is true for the civilization as well as the individual. Just as one might learn his lessons vicariously through the sufferings of others and not be compelled to pass through the disillusionment-suffering phase himself, so also a whole civilization might conceivably learn the same lesson and thereby get a new lease on life. If John Dewey has reminded us that we don't get down to the business of thinking until we strike a problem that makes us think, then Toynbee is saying that collective man doesn't get down to the business of assessing life's values until their loss compels him to do so. In short, man learns by suffering, and only by suffering. But he *can* learn—and thereby alter the pattern of his civilization.

Our ignorance of history causes us to slander our own times.

FLAUBERT

THE PLIGHT OF WESTERN CIVILIZATION

14   From this Promethean comparison, what had Toynbee found? Western civilization is probably on the threshold of what Toynbee calls a "universal state," and the appearance of this state in the developmental pattern of a civilization is the unmistakable sign of disintegration. The breakdown of our civilization began in the fifteenth or sixteenth century, probably with the religious wars, and since that time there have been innumerable symptoms of disintegration in the arts, philosophy, religion, and material culture. We recognize these signs from their appearance in corresponding stages in past societies. Since there are only two or three great powers left in the world today serving as rallying points for all the other nations, the universal state cannot be far away.

But at this point a new element has entered the picture: the actual fact of One World. When we ask what sort of universal state we shall see, Toynbee suggests two possibilities. The first kind would have all the characteristics of the universal states of the past. It would be ushered onto the stage of history by the same self-inflicted knock-out blow in which one member-state succeeds in a coup of all the other member-states and itself becomes the universal state. No society has ever been able to recover from this suicidal act, and nothing can turn back the process of dissolution which now sets in. Thoughtfully, Toynbee asks, "Must we, too, purchase our *Pax Oecumenica* at this deadly price?"

The second alternative would be something new in human history: the creation of a new kind of universal state by peaceful means. The entire world is now moving toward homogeneity with unbelievable speed. Momentarily it is dominated by the technology of a materialistic West, but it is clearly, and increasingly, influenced by the non-materialistic values and concepts of the non-Western world. If it does prove to be true that we are on the verge of becoming *one* civilization with *one* culture, this may mean that a new type of political organization could manifest itself. This would be a genuine mutation of the laws of history. If it is possible for Western man to meet the challenge

Arnold Toynbee (1889–1975)

of One World by outgrowing his egocentric illusion—especially as it expresses itself in the nationalism of his parochial states—the doom of Western civilization may be avoided. There could be a new lease on life, and there could be a new world order.

There is the possibility, of course, that man may destroy himself through some nuclear holocaust, but Toynbee does not believe this to be the most probable alternative. But there is always the possibility that man might require a challenge as horrifying as the sufferings of mass destruction before he could learn how to live in peaceful existence with himself.

15   Whichever type of universal state may come, Toynbee is sure that in less than half a century "the whole face of the planet will have been unified politically through the concentration of irresistible military power in some single set of hands." At the present, we don't yet know whose hands these will be, but there is a growing possibility that they will be the hands of the West. Communism may seem to have an advantage from a short-range viewpoint, but in the long view Toynbee does not give communism much hope because, in insisting on shortcuts, it does not answer many of man's deepest needs. "There seems to be in human nature an intractable vein—akin to the temperament of Man's yoke-fellows the camel, mule, and goat—which insists on being allowed a modicum of freedom and which knows how to impose its will when it is goaded beyond endurance. . . . Even the most long-suffering peoples revolt at some point."

Within this coming universal state there will be less physical and material freedom than the peoples of the West have been used to, even in such "sacred" realms as family planning. As he sees it, "in a powerful, healthy, overpopulated world, even the proletarian's freedom to beget children will no longer be his private affair, but will be regulated by the state." He believes, in fact, that the problems of population control and food production will be the critical problems of the near future.

Man cannot live without freedom, however, and "if freedom is suppressed on the material plane, it will break out on the spiritual plane." So in this new world there will be a spiritual freedom superior to that now known by Western man, and this gain will be more than worth the price that man will have to pay for it. "True spiritual freedom is attained when each member of Society has learnt to reconcile a sincere conviction of the truth of his own religious beliefs and practices with a voluntary toleration of the different beliefs and practices of his neighbors.

There will also be an equality among human beings and a respect for human dignity. There will be neither colonialism nor communism to deny these qualities to mankind. The idea of "democracy" as understood by the West to mean self-government will be considerably weakened, and "democracy" as employed by the non-Western peoples to mean social equality will predominate.

And what will be the role of religion? Toynbee clearly sees a

The world revolution, Arnold Toynbee has suggested, has begun. But who will eventually be fighting whom is still not clear.

R. D. LAING

The strongest political force of the day—nationalism—is driving nations to increase their populations rather than to moderate them. This is why I doubt whether action will be taken until the problem has developed from a threat to a disaster.

FRED HOYLE

What's it to me that nobody's guilty and that I know it—I need revenge or I'd kill myself. And revenge not in some far off eternity, somewhere, sometime, but here and now, on earth, so that I can see it myself.

DOSTOEVSKY
The Brothers Karamazov

> So the continuity of history reasserts itself: despite earthquakes, epidemics, famines, eruptive migrations, and catastrophic wars, the essential processes of civilization are not lost; some younger culture takes them up, snatches them from the conflagration, carries them on imitatively, then creatively, until fresh youth and spirit can enter the race. As men are members of one another, and generations are moments in a family line, so civilizations are units in a larger whole whose name is history; they are stages in the life of man. Civilization is polygenetic—it is the co-operative product of many peoples, ranks, and faiths; and no one who studies its history can be a bigot of race or creed. Therefore the scholar, though he belongs to his country through affectionate kinship, feels himself also a citizen of that Country of the Mind which knows no hatreds and no frontiers; he hardly deserves his name if he carries into his study political prejudices, or racial discriminations, or religious animosities; and he accords his grateful homage to any people that has borne the torch and enriched his heritage.
>
> WILL DURANT
> *The Story of Civilization*

What experience and history teach us is this—that people and governments never have learned anything from history, or acted on principles deduced from it.

HEGEL

I think, therefore I am, said Descartes. I am, therefore I am, wrote Augustine. I rebel, therefore we are.

ALBERT CAMUS

resurgence of religion. Just as the nineteenth and the first half of the twentieth century have seen a steady movement away from religion, the twenty-first century will witness a countermovement in which mankind will turn from materialism and technology back to religion and spiritual values. What will this religion be like? A continuing interaction between all existing religions is certain, but for some time to come each of the living religions will maintain its identity and minister to its own adherents. However, there is a strong possibility that, as these great religions find themselves face to face in a shrinking world, a positive tolerance will replace their traditional fanaticism. They will find that all their fellow seekers are engaged in the same quest. In the long run, only a true monotheistic devotion to one Ultimate Reality accepted by all could meet the requirements of men who viewed their world as One World, and who looked upon all other men as brothers.

Can Western civilization survive all this? *Perhaps.* So many new factors have appeared in the modern world that our civilization, if it can come alive and face the challenge of change, can be infused with new vigor and win a reprieve, perhaps even a new chance at growth. If our response includes great leaders—an authentic "creative minority"—who can lead the way by facing realistically the problems of a new era, there is still hope.

Western civilization is not yet dead and buried, not quite.

16   Most philosophers agree that when a civilization becomes materialistic and "sensate" (Pitirim Sorokin's term) in its values, then it is in trouble. In this stage there is usually a universally held belief that this is the "golden age"—a bounteous time of unprecedented prosperity. In reality it is the onset of disintegration. Unless the culture can rediscover its creativity by successfully facing new challenges and recovering its "ethereal" values, it is doomed. What they are saying is that unless a fundamental change takes place in the priority of values of large numbers of people, but above all in the "creative minority" who are the true leaders of men, then the civilization has gone into irrevocable decline.

Another point of agreement among philosophers of history is that nationalism is a necessary but passing phenomenon. Those holding "organismic" theories of history usually liken man's present politico-cultural condition to adolescence, the time when the individual human self is laboring for separation and identity. But once the integrated self has been developed, there is no longer a preoccupation with identity or identity-labels. They suggest that mankind will move collectively through the ethnocentric stage, just as individually we pass (or should pass) through the egocentric stage. While quite normal in the adolescent phase, overconcern with self is hardly becoming to mature adults who have more important things to do than concentrating perpetually on the problem of *who* they are. What philosophers of history agree on is that conditions in the modern world are creating a single world-culture which will, with shattering speed, break down the boundaries of nationalistic consciousness. Indeed, within another thirty years or so, man's survival will be in serious jeopardy if large-scale ethnocentric consciousness still prevails.

A third point on which most philosophers of history agree is that the disintegration of a civilization is not the ultimate tragedy we

As for wars, well, there's only been 268 years out of the last 3421 in which there was no war. So war, too, is in the normal course of events.

WILL DURANT

Picasso, *Guernica*, 1937. Collection, the Museum of Modern Art, New York.

may think it to be. Durant makes this point frequently in his *Story of Civilization.* "We should not be greatly disturbed by the probability that our civilization will die like any other. As Frederick asked his retreating troops at Kolin, 'Would you live forever?' Perhaps it is desirable that life should take fresh forms, that new civilizations and centers should have their turn." Toynbee has similarly noted that the most precious elements of any civilization do not die but become the seeds of a subsequent new civilization. Great inventions, advancements in science, philosophy, art and music, the profoundest insights into nature, and our knowledge of man—these are never lost though the culture that produced them may crumble. "These are the elements of civilization," writes Durant, "and they have been tenaciously maintained through the perilous passage from one civilization to the next. They are the connective tissue of human history."

CAN WE LEARN FROM HISTORY?

17   There has been a recurrent skepticism in our Western thinking as to whether we can learn anything at all from history. Many have said it, but none better than Hegel: The only thing we learn from history is that we never learn from history.

Perhaps we can allow the skeptics their points. Considering all the lessons of history that could be learned, the poverty and pokiness of our learning is nothing less than frightening. As of the twentieth century, we have recovered a vast fund of historical knowledge which ancients never dreamed possible; and yet, with all this wealth of information, we don't seem to be able to read "the lessons of history."

History is *human* history. It is nothing more or less than the record of individual human beings who have lived, loved, fought, dreamed, and (mostly) vanished. Whenever individuals act collectively, then we lump them together with an abstraction and speak of tribes, nations, communities, committees, teams, classes, and so on. And when they create mental systems and subordinate their individuality to the contractual guidelines they have agreed to, then we speak of institutions: governments, armies, churches, monastic movements, industrial complexes, political parties, and the like.

°*On the creation and function of abstractions, see pp. 182f.*

But all such groupings are merely functional abstractions.° In the last analysis, history is the story of single human beings going about the business of living; and in their lives we find exactly what we would expect: the highs and lows, great accomplishments and terrible mistakes, heroic dedication and horrendous cruelty—they're all there. Almost everything we have learned that is worthwhile—that is, wisdom—we have learned by studying the behavior of other human beings. So, who could not learn from all these individuals if he so wished? If they happen to have lived in the past, then, yes, "We can learn from history."

But let's be clear: History *teaches* us nothing. History is dead—it is past; it is silent. The act of learning from history therefore falls to the living, and it becomes a deliberate, aggressive act on our part to search out the lessons that lie quietly in the records, waiting to be brought to life and put to use. So, the question of whether we can learn from history turns around to peer at us: Can we open ourselves to what history has to say to us?

18 Edward Hallett Carr, a historiographer, reminds us that "the axiom that everything has a cause is a condition of our capacity to understand what is going on around us." In daily life we rarely doubt that cause-and-effect patterns exist. We *assume* causality, rightly; and in every realm of experience we want to control events by altering their causes.

Learning from history is analogous to learning from our own experience. We study history, just as we worry through our personal memories, to find out what went wrong, or what *is* wrong. If we can isolate the causes, then, next time, perhaps we can alter those causes and change the outcome. How many science-fiction stories spin out the secretly cherished hope that we might go back in time and alter a single causal event and thereby erase some blackened episode that stains the record of human history?

What caused the great depression? What caused the energy crisis? What caused the discontent of the Sixties? What caused the ecological crisis? What are the principal causes of the second-class status of women in Western history? What will be the effects of the sense of autonomy of the young African nations? What causes "the deaths of the gods"?°

Too often we grasp essential causes only later when discoveries illuminate them. Historic causes are deeply hidden; seeing takes time. Take the Nazi phenomenon, for example. Even today, could we recognize its principal causes so that we could take steps to prevent the recurrence of such a nationalist/racist power state? In the case of Nazi Germany, the Milgram experiments conducted in the early 1960s beamed a flood of light on some of the primal human behavioral traits that permitted such a system to exist and explained how it was possible that "good and decent people" could allow such monstrous cruelties to occur in their midst.°

Thus history provides us with assorted tragedies to work on, and historical analysis never ceases. We try to understand our past in order to provide therapy for our future.

19 There is a special way that we can learn "the lessons of history." The men and women of the past can become our teachers.

From Aristotle we can learn how to unleash our wonderment upon life; to cherish all the understanding yet achieved by the human race; and, with Ulysses, "To follow knowledge like a sinking star/Beyond the utmost bound of human thought."

From Voltaire we can learn how to restoke the fiery furnaces even in "old age"; to rekindle the feeling of outrage at bigotry and

The historian will not mourn because he can see no meaning in human existence except that which man puts into it; let it be our pride that we ourselves may put meaning into our lives, and sometimes a significance that transcends death.

WILL AND ARIEL DURANT

°*The Question is a vital one, and not "merely academic." See pages 420ff.*

°*See pp. 298f.*

injustice; to start the wheels of intellectual action rolling so fast that they shock the conscience of a nation with their clarity and power.

From Nietzsche we can learn about the ironies of having your most eloquent phrases timely ripped from context and misused in order to further the very causes you spent your life fighting.

From Schopenhauer we can learn something of the courage required to face life when your inner machinery has been tangled and twisted, but you know you must continue to live—meaningfully, usefully, and as honestly as possible.

From Augustine of Tagaste and Søren Kierkegaard we can learn how to accept the burning guilt of being human—all-too-human—and how to transmogrify the pain of the human condition into the service of others (Saint Augustine) and the rediscovery of what it means to be an individual human being (Kierkegaard).

From Francis Bacon and Niccolò Machiavelli we can listen to the agony of exile: being severed from your work, your friends, your livelihood; being challenged to cope creatively with years of solitude; being forced to learn to live with yourself.

From Thomas Aquinas and Albertus Magnus we can learn something of the superhuman discipline required to order vast stores of human knowledge; to record, with superhuman strength, all you know as a legacy to your faith and your future.

From Plato and Einstein we can come to appreciate the "adventures of the mind"—the soaring flights into possible worlds that can excite and enthrall but which remain quite beyond the realities of present perception.

From Galileo we can learn something about mustering "the courage of our convictions" against the pressures of conformity; and, with the knowledge that evidence is on our side, winning through to a personal victory by means of our courage and/or stubbornness.

From Wittgenstein we can learn what it means "to think our own thoughts"—not to repeat words heard and phrases memorized, not to resort to clichés, pretending that they are really our own.

From Spinoza we can learn how to live with final and total disapproval by all those we hold dear in order to preserve our integrity; to avoid all vindictiveness; to become more gentle and wise as others call us names and ostracize us from their midst.

All these—just from the ranks of "philosophers"—can teach us. Then there are Francis of Assisi, Thomas More, Abraham Lincoln, Beethoven, Helen Keller, Joan of Arc . . . .

REFLECTIONS—

1 What is the goal of "the philosophy of history"? The question we all want answered is: Does history have meaning? And if so, what is that meaning? If we give an affirmative answer, then we face a prior question: What are the sources of meaning? But prior still: How could we go about gathering evidence to find out if history has meaning? How would you respond to these questions?

After all, when one tries to change institutions without having changed the nature of men, that unchanged nature will soon resurrect those institutions.

WILL DURANT

I am constantly waiting for things to change for the better; amid all the conflicting parties, I have chosen none. I am in the position of someone who hopes to win first prize in a lottery without having bought a ticket.

EUGENE IONESCO

2 What does the word "history" refer to? If the past is "dead," how can there be history? (*Is* the past "dead"?) How does the historian go about "doing history"—does he recall it, read and record it, research it and discover it, invent it, create it, imagine it? Is history better thought of as a science or an art?

3 Having made a comparative study of 27 civilizations, what common patterns did Toynbee find? Do those patterns constitute "the meaning of history"? What was the source of those patterns? In the last analysis, do the patterns described by Toynbee tell us where we are in this ninth decade of the 20th century, and where we are going? (You might enjoy browsing through portions of Toynbee's monumental twelve-volume work, *A Study of History.* You might begin by perusing some of the passages in Vol. X, say pages 213–242, or pages 126–144.)

4 See p. 282-Box. Will Durant makes a fascinating observation about what survives when civilizations finally die—a point also made by many other philosophers of history. Do you believe Durant is right? "Captive Greece has led captive her rude conqueror"—wrote Horace of Rome's "conquest" of Greece. So again: Do civilizations truly die?

5 What do you think of the interpretive framework which the Deuteronomic historian placed upon the tribal stories of the *Book of Judges*? Could this framework be placed on *any* war—World War II, for instance, or the Vietnamese war? Try it.

6 Saint Augustine is considered the first great philosopher of history because he was the first Western thinker who tried to explain in depth the how and the why of history's "meaning." Do you accept his interpretation of the fall of the city of Rome? Could Augustine's basic framework be applied to the fall of Constantinople to the Ottoman Turks in 1453? Or to the fall of Paris to the Nazis in 1940? What human need lies behind Augustine's towering effort *to explain?* Do you and I, today, still *need* such explanations?

7 According to Hegel, whence does history derive meaning? What is the purpose and final goal of human history? What is the role of the individual in the Hegelian view of history? What sort of evidence could be mustered for or against Hegel's interpretation of history?

8 According to Marx, what is the source of the "irrevocable laws" which govern the development of human history? What is the role of the individual in the Marxian view of history? Marx has been linked to the doctrine of "inevitable progress" which was in the air during the latter part of the 19th century. Is there "inevitable progress" in Marx's doctrine? Is inevitable progress inherent in history? (Is inevitable *regress* inherent in history?)

9 Compare and contrast Hegel's "dialectical idealism" with Marx's "dialectical materialism." Both have profoundly influenced the modern world. Which one is right? Could both be right? Is neither right? (Must a doctrine be "right" to be as influential as these doctrines have been?)

10 This chapter summarizes three points of agreement which are shared by most philosophers of history. Note them and ask yourself if you agree.

11 Hegel once said that the only thing that we learn from history is that we

never learn from history. But seriously, *can* we learn from history? If so, what do we learn? And from whom (or what) do we learn it—from individuals, nations, religious societies, institutions, civilizations? Or from individual blunders, or political or military mistakes? Or from examples of courage, heroic transcendence, growth into "greatness," personal achievement? Or what?

Furthermore . . .

CARR, EDWARD HALLETT, *What is History?* Vintage, 1961.

COLLINGWOOD, R. G., *The Idea of History.* Oxford, 1956.

DRAY, WILLIAM H., *Philosophy of History.* Prentice-Hall, 1964.

DURANT, WILL and ARIEL, *The Lessons of History.* Simon and Schuster, 1968.

GUSTAVSON, CARL G., *A Preface to History.* McGraw-Hill, 1955.

HALEY, ALEX, *Roots: The Saga of an American Family.* Doubleday, 1976.

HEGEL, G. W. F., *The Philosophy of History* (1848). Dover, 1966.

JASPERS, KARL, *The Origin and Goal of History.* Yale, 1953.

MACHIAVELLI, NICCOLÒ, *The Prince* (1513). (Available in many paperback editions.)

TOYNBEE, ARNOLD J., *A Study of History*, Vol. 10. Oxford, 1954.

WARD, BARBARA, *Five Ideas That Changed the World.* Norton, 1959.

5-2

Laws/Conscience

Have You Ever Wondered . . .

- Where "being a good citizen" comes in your list of priorities?

- If you are morally obligated, when conscience demands it, to disobey the laws of your government?

- Whether a law-and-order society can tolerate dissent and criticism?

- What a "state" actually is?

- What a "law" in fact is?

- If there is any such thing as a "good criminal"? (For openers, what about Jesus? What about Socrates?)

- What a "conscience" is and how you developed it?

- Whether, maybe, "blind obedience of the masses" is the only way to create a well-regulated, orderly, stable (and just?) society?

THE WESTERN EXPERIENCE: CONFLICTING LOYALTIES

1   All human societies possessing a modicum of individual freedom develop a wide spectrum of strongly held convictions about the structure and power of human society—"strongly held" because it is the human state, after all, which exercises ultimate temporal control over human destiny.

There exists also in such societies a fundamental tension between those who would obey different sets of laws. Men without freedom are spared this condition; those belonging to primitive tribes or rigidly authoritarian states are subject to but a single set of laws. But in freer societies numerous systems of laws burden the individual by claiming to have jurisdiction over him: he *should* obey them *all!*

This predicament is analogous to what we find in ethics. If one is subject to only a single moral code, then he is spared the complex decisions of free men who must make decisions among sundry codes demanding his loyalty.

Our Western experience has been an ongoing conflict of loyalties. Western society derives its deepest commitment from the scriptural concept of covenant which binds the community of the faithful to the laws of God. For well over a thousand years before Christ—indeed, from the time when Moses defied Egyptian law to lead the Children of Israel into a covenant relationship with Yahweh—man has struggled with the tension between obedience to the "laws of God" and the "laws of man." For all those who live under the divine mandate, their final loyalty has been to God; and man's mundane systems of law have, by comparison, only a weak, secondary claim upon their loyalty.

2   This tension between loyalties can be felt in the following passages. First, the case (often implicit) for a higher law.

Martin Luther King, Jr.:

> I think we all have moral obligations to obey just laws. On the other hand, I think that we have moral obligations to disobey unjust laws because non-cooperation with evil is just as much a moral obligation as cooperation with good.

Henry David Thoreau:

> [If the law] is of such a nature that it requires you to be the agent of injustice to another, then, I say, break the law.

Martin Luther:

> When the law impels one against love, it ceases and should *no longer be a law* . . . You have need of the law, that love may be manifested; but if it cannot be kept without injury to the neighbor, God wants us to suspend and ignore the law.

Mark 2:23–24, 27–28 (paraphrased):

> One sabbath while he was walking through the grainfields, his disciples plucked some of the ears of grain and, milling the grain in their hands—which was against the Law of Moses—they ate them.
>   Some of the Pharisees said to him, "Look at them! Why are they doing what is illegal on the sabbath?"

As for adopting the ways which the State has provided for remedying the evil, I know not of such ways. They take too much time, and a man's life will be gone. I have other affairs to attend to. I came into this world, not chiefly to make this a good place to live in, but to live in it, be it good or bad.

HENRY DAVID THOREAU

We must be entirely clear that law is not God. It has always been a basic Christian conviction that there are times when a Christian ought to break the law.

EUGENE CARSON BLAKE

He replied simply, ''The sabbath was made for man, not man for the sabbath.''

But those who knew the Law went away angry.

3   The practical—and pragmatic—side of the dilemma is stated with great clarity in the following passages.

Lewis F. Powell, Jr.:

An ordered society cannot exist if every man may determine which laws he will obey, . . . that only ''just'' laws need be obeyed and that every man is free to determine for himself the question of ''justness.''

Saint Paul (Romans 13:1–2, 5):

Everyone must obey the authorities that are over him, for no authority can exist without the permission of God; the existing authorities have been established by him, so that anyone who resists the authorities sets himself in opposition to what God has ordained, and those who oppose him will bring down judgment upon themselves. The man who does right has nothing to fear from the magistrates. . . . You must obey them, therefore, not only to escape God's wrath, but as a matter of principle, just as you pay your taxes. . . . Pay them all that is due them.

Immanuel Kant:

Resistance on the part of the people to the supreme legislative power of The State is in no case legitimate; for it is only by submission to the universal legislative will, that a condition of law and order is possible. . . . It is the duty of the people to bear any abuse of the supreme power, even though it should be considered to be unbearable. And the reason is that any resistance of the highest legislative authority can never but be contrary to the law, and must even be regarded as tending to destroy the whole legal constitution.

Saint Peter (1 Peter 2:13–15):

Submit to all human authority, for the Master's sake; to the emperor, as supreme, and to governors, as sent by him to punish evil-doers, and to encourage those who do right.°

4   Since this tension is rooted in religion, we would like to be able to turn to a founder of Western religion—to Jesus, for instance—for guidance; but we do so in vain. When forced into comment upon the dilemma, he merely mystifies the question.

Teacher, we know that you are honest and are not swayed by men; for you do not defer to the worldly positions of men, but truly teach the way of God. Tell us then, what you think. Is it lawful to pay taxes to the state, or not?

But sensing their hypocritical intent, he merely said, ''Bring me a coin, and let me look at it.''

The Constitution is the supreme law of our land and it governs our actions as citizens. Only the laws of God, which govern our consciences, are superior to it. . . .

PRES. GERALD FORD
(The Nixon Pardon)

''I was there to follow orders, not to think.''

JOHN DEAN
(Watergate testimony)

''I carried out my orders. . . . Where would we have been if everyone had thought things out in those days?''

ADOLF EICHMANN

°It is the consensus among biblical scholars that the letter called ''The First Letter of Peter'' was not written by the Apostle Simon bar Jonah. For some, this will detract from its authority.

So they brought him a silver denarius.

Then he asked: "Whose picture and inscription is this?"

They said, "Caesar's."

So Jesus replied: "Then render to Caesar what is Caesar's since Caesar's picture is on the coin; and render to God the things that are God's."

Having failed to entrap him as they planned, they went away angry.

Mark 12:14–17 (paraphrased)

GOOD LAWS AND BAD LAWS

5   The case for making a distinction between good and bad laws is well stated by King, Thoreau, Luther, and others. No matter how strongly one advocates lawful obedience to the state and its laws, it is inevitable that some laws will turn out to be bad ones. Lawmakers are not only human—which is sufficient cause for having a few bad laws—but a percentage of them will always be parochial in their interests, shortsighted or dead wrong in their opinion of what constitutes justice, mentally out of touch with reality, and woefully uninformed on the nature of values and value-judgments (and after all, laws are the legislation of human values). These statements can be made with some certainty simply because the leaders of men are not immune to the neurotic problems shared by the populace as a whole

Therefore, *in any legal system*, it is quite possible to point to laws ranging from mildly unjust to callously inhuman, and such laws *should* produce a feeling of outrage in individuals who are victimized by them, or see others hurt by them. More important, perhaps, is the fact that unless laws are periodically challenged—as the authors of the American system recognized°—then they don't get improved. Among mature men criticism is cherished; it is through the assessment of wise criticism that more just laws can be formulated and antiquated laws updated. Also, it is through open criticism that the selfish interests of those in power can be rapidly brought to the attention of enough citizens who can object and, if necessary, dissent before a deeper tyranny sets in.

°*In 1787 Thomas Jefferson said, "God forbid, we should ever be twenty years without such a rebellion." Elsewhere he elaborated: "What country can preserve its liberties, if its rulers are not warned from time to time, that this people preserve the spirit of resistance? Let them take arms. . . . The tree of liberty must be refreshed from time to time, with the blood of patriots and tyrants."*

6   We have another tradition in this country which is in danger of passing away: dissent. The responsibility to object. We might all do well to remember in these days of national distemper the comment of Pastor Niemoeller a quarter of a century ago in Nazi Germany. "They came after the Jews, and I was not a Jew, so I did not object. Then they came after the Catholics, and I was not a Catholic, so I did not object. Then they came after the trade-unionists, and I was not a trade-unionist, so I did not object. And then they came after me, and there was no one left to object."

SENATOR STOWE
The Bold Ones (NBC-TV)

7   Unjust laws exist: shall we be content to obey them, or shall we endeavor to amend them, and obey them until we have succeeded, or shall we transgress them at once? Men generally, under such a government as this, think that they ought to wait until they have persuaded the majority to alter them. They think that, if they should resist, the remedy would be worse than the evil. But it is the fault of the government itself that the remedy *is* worse than the evil. *It* makes it worse. Why is it not more apt to anticipate and provide for reform? Why does it not cherish its wise minority? Why does it cry and resist before it is hurt? Why does it not encourage its citizens to be on the alert to point out its faults, and *do* better than it would have them? Why does it always crucify Christ, and excommunicate Copernicus and Luther, and pronounce Washington and Franklin rebels?

HENRY DAVID THOREAU

For, as among the powers in man's society the greater authority is obeyed in preference to the lesser, so must God above all.

ST. AUGUSTINE

LOYALTY TO HIGHER AUTHORITY

8   Our Western (Judeo-Christian) legal tradition takes the form of a hierarchy of laws—a sort of jurisdictional totem pole—with a clear order of precedence.

Local laws must defer to higher and wider laws. Thus, in case of conflict, the laws of a village or city must give way to state laws. State laws are "higher"; they take precedent. It can be validly argued that in specific areas of concern, only local laws can be truly relevant to local conditions. But populations are mobile; individuals are travelers. If there existed only local laws serving the self-interests of innumerable small jurisdictions, it just wouldn't work. In matters which affect larger populations over larger areas, wider laws must prevail.

By the same principle, federal laws take precedent over state laws. Neither cities nor states can be allowed to enact laws which would nourish their limited interests at the expense of the larger society of which they are but a part. Wider law must prevail if there is to be equal application of law—that is, if there is to be justice.

At this point the covenant principle upon which Western civilization is grounded must come in: that there is a higher and more universal law than that of any sovereign state. For some twenty-seven hundred years now, the Jews of the Dispersion who were carried off from their homeland have considered the Law of Moses to be higher than the laws of any state in which they lived. In the Roman Empire the fierce loyalty of Jews to their monotheistic faith won them exemption from the worship of Caesar; they alone were offically free of obligations to pour libations to the emperor's *genius* and make offerings to him as divine head of state. As Christianity grew in the early empire, some argued that Christians were Jews and should therefore share the exemption; but the majority of Christians declared emphatically that Christianity was not a branch of Judaism. As Christians established themselves to be a separate sect, they were then obliged to pay respects to the divine Caesar.

One dog barks at something, and a hundred bark at the sound.

Chinese Proverb

"You've got to forget the nobler sentiments if you want to live. (Pause . . .) Funny thing—survival."

BRITISH SOLDIER
Play Dirty

It hasn't been done yet, so they haven't got around to prohibiting it.

Destination Moon

But like the Jews, they could not in good conscience do so. The Christians were therefore "disloyal"; they were considered dangerous subversives—"bad citizens." During the years of persecution which followed, the Christians became the main body of conscientious objectors against paying unjust allegiance to Caesar and his state; their highest loyalty was reserved for their God and his laws. For this stand Christians were accused officially of atheism and anarchy: atheism because they refused to worship the state-approved gods, and anarchy because they were "outlaws" who refused to take an oath of allegiance to their government.

It was this refusal to accept "man's laws" that sent Christians into the arena and put them to the sword.

9   In broad terms, the allegiance to a "higher authority" has taken two forms: (1) loyalty to an institution considered to have divine authority over the state; and (2) loyalty to "God's law" as personally understood—by revelation, by "spiritual knowledge" *(gnosis)*, or by conscience.

As the Roman Catholic Church developed and became the universal authority in Europe, the papacy pressed its claim to be the supreme power over all temporal authority; for the pope was the "Vicar of Christ" on earth and the Church was "the City of God."

Since the Emperor Constantine established Christianity as the state religion in A.D. 312, this dual claim upon their loyalty has perplexed Western citizens. Continuing through the Middle Ages, the Renaissance and the Reformation, and into the modern world, there has been a tug-of-war between temporal authorities—who would diminish the Church's power ("God's laws") and increase their own—and the papacy—which would extend its authority and limit worldly governments ("man's laws"). Individuals found themselves caught in this power struggle.

The supreme confrontation between the claimants occurred on January 28, 1077. Pope Gregory VII had stripped all power from Henry IV of Germany with a decree of excommunication. To regain his kingdom Henry crossed the Alps in winter and knelt in the snow before the gate of the castle of Canossa into which the pope had retreated. Henry repented and after waiting penitently for three days, the pope released him from excommunication and restored him to power.

The second form of allegiance to a higher power is allegiance to the word of God as known personally, to one's own conscience, or to a set of ethical ideals or norms by which one judges the quality of actual laws. Such a position can be theistic and/or ethical, but in any case it commands the highest commitment of the individual. Whatever the path by which one arrives at his position, it often *feels* hypocritical to him to obey bad (unjust laws) when he has seen clearly in his ethical reflections the just laws which should prevail.

This stand was epitomized by Martin Luther in 1521 at the Council of Worms where, passionately and sincerely, he cried out,

"My conscience is captive to the Word of God. . . . To go against conscience is neither right nor safe. God help me. Amen."

10   Pope Boniface VIII issued the papal bull *Unam sanctam* in 1302 to define clearly the superiority of God's laws—as embodied here in the Roman papacy—over man's laws—which in this case were represented by the royal heads of England and France. This bull still stands as the most extreme claim of the Church to stand in judgment over the state.

> We are obliged by the faith to believe and hold—and we do firmly believe and sincerely confess—that there is one Holy Catholic and Apostolic Church, and that outside this Church there is neither salvation nor remission of sins. . . .
>
> And we learn from the words of the Gospel that in this Church and in her power are two swords, the spiritual and the temporal. . . . Both are in the power of the Church, the spiritual sword and the material. But the latter is to be used for the Church, the former by her; the former by the priest, the latter by kings and captains but at the will and by the permission of the priest. The one sword, then, should be under the other, and temporal authority subject to spiritual. . . .
>
> Thus, concerning the Church and her power, is the prophecy of Jeremiah fulfilled, "See, I have this day set thee over the nations and over the kingdoms," etc. If, therefore, the earthly power err, it shall be judged by a greater. . . . Furthermore we declare, state, define and pronounce that it is altogether necessary to salvation for every human creature to be subject to the Roman pontiff.

One of the big purposes of the Bill of Rights is to keep the government off our backs.

ARTHUR MILLER

THE SUN AND THE MOON   Pope Innocent III: Church and State

The Creator of the universe set up two great luminaries in the firmament of heaven; the greater light to rule the day, the lesser light to rule the night. In the same way for the firmament of the universal Church, which is spoken of as heaven, he appointed two great dignities; the greater to bear rule over souls (these being, as it were, days), the lesser to bear rule over bodies (these being, as it were, nights). These dignities are the pontifical authority and the royal power. Furthermore, the moon derives her light from the sun, and is in truth inferior to the sun in both size and quality, in position as well as effect. In the same way the royal power derives its dignity from the pontifical authority: and the more closely it cleaves to the sphere of that authority the less is the light with which it is adorned; the further it is removed, the more it increases in splendor.

Sicut universitatis conditor
Ep. i. 401, October, 1198

The true patriot is one who gives his highest loyalty not to his country as it is but to his own best conceptions of what it can and ought to be.

ALBERT CAMUS

OBEDIENCE TO THE RULE OF LAW

Wise men will never do battle over mere symbols, but they may fight to the death for what the symbols stand for.

JLC

The surest way to corrupt a young man is to teach him to esteem more highly those who think alike than those who think differently.

NIETZSCHE

11   Associate Justice Lewis Powell presents persuasively the case for absolute obedience to duly constituted authority: laws must be obeyed, for if each person were permitted to decide which laws were good and which were bad, social chaos would necessarily result. For who is there among us who is able to determine just from unjust laws? And on what criteria could such judgments be made? Wouldn't it be inevitable that every political crank and religious fanatic—not to mention emotionally immature rebels of all ages—would decide that all the laws were "unjust" which didn't cater to his own self-centered interests?

This is precisely the position taken by Socrates when his old and dear friend Crito urged him to escape from prison the day before his execution. Socrates awoke before dawn to find Crito sitting silently beside him in his cell; he has apparently made all necessary arrangements for an escape.

But Socrates has already made up his mind and refuses to flee. He patiently attempts to make Crito understand his reasoning.

Look at it in this way. Suppose that while we were preparing to run away from here (or however one should describe it) the Laws and Constitution of Athens were to come and confront us and ask this question: "Now, Socrates, what are you proposing to do? Can you deny that by this act which you are contemplating you intend, so far as you have the power, to destroy us, the Laws, and the whole State as well? Do you imagine that a city can continue to exist and not be turned upside down, if the legal judgements which are pronounced in it have no force but are nullified and destroyed by private persons?"—how shall we answer this question, Crito, and others of the same kind? . . . Shall we say "Yes, I do intend to destroy the laws, because the State wronged me by passing a faulty judgement at my trial"? Is this to be our answer, or what? . . .

Supposing the Laws say "Was there provision for this in the agreement between you and us, Socrates? Or did you undertake to abide by whatever judgments the State pronounced? . . . Do you not realize . . . that if you cannot persuade your country you must do whatever it orders, and patiently submit to any punishment that it imposes, whether it be flogging or imprisonment? And if it leads you out to war, to be wounded or killed, you must comply, and it is right that you should do so; you must not give way or retreat or abandon your position. Both in war and in the law-courts and everywhere else you must do whatever your city and your country commands, or else persuade it in accordance with universal justice. . . . "—What shall we say to this, Crito?—that what the Laws say is true, or not?

PLATO
Crito

THE PERSONAL DILEMMA

12   The problem of obedience to law might be visualized as an ellipse with two foci. Near one end of the ellipse is the question of human freedom. All of us want freedom, and we want *more* freedom; but as the number of problematic persons in our society increases, the more regulation is required and the less freedom we can enjoy.

The other focus in the ellipse is one's assessment of human nature. If one is basically optimistic about natural man and believes him to be trustworthy, then he will assume we humans can use freedom constructively and will not need punctilious systems of laws to tell us what to do and not to do. But if one distrusts human nature, convinced that it is fundamentally evil, then he must conclude that a complex system of laws is necessary to keep this selfish nature in line and coerce a semblance of order.

Around these two foci—and they *are* inside a single ellipse—turns the question of obedience to all law: to obey or not to obey. The mature, more fully actualized person wants to guide his life solely by a few basic principles; he becomes restive and may chafe bitterly under irrelevant restraints upon his existence. For him they are not needed: he would do what is right anyway! By contrast, however, most human beings appear unable to experience very much freedom without harming others; we are unable to live with one another peacefully without having our behavior guided and restrained by specific regulations touching all aspects of our lives.

13   The dilemma between principles and law has tormented many great souls. Saint Paul, for instance: he tried diligently to follow the 613 precepts of the Jewish Law but only felt more guilty because he could not measure up to its numerous demands. In the end, he found peace only by abandoning the *Law* of Moses and accepting the *principle* of "justification by faith" in Jesus as the Christ.

Similarly, Martin Luther tried to make legalistic Roman Catholic laws work to his benefit, but he found himself caught, like Paul, on a wheel of guilt and ultimately found peace only by following Paul's lead and committing his life to a single principle: "salvation by faith alone."

It is worth noting that Hinduism has provided, within the parameters of acceptable religion, several systems to meet different needs. The "Ways of Liberation" are designed to accomplish this. The "Way of Works" (*Karma Marga*) specifies innumerable rites and duties which the worshiper has only to perform to gain good karma. It makes few intellectual demands. It's a matter of *doing*; one must meticulously perform the actions prescribed by the laws. This is the path chosen by a large majority of Hindus. By contrast, there is the "Way of Knowledge" (*Jnana Marga*). This is philosophical Hinduism, the way of study and meditation which will lead the mind out of the errors

The American advocacy system is a wretched way to determine the innocence or guilt of a man. But no one has yet proposed a better way.

The Bold Ones
NBC-TV

". . . Because politics is the art of the possible, it appeals only to second-rate minds. The *first*-raters, he claimed, were only interested in the *impossible.*"

"SHEIK ABDULLAH"
from Arthur C. Clarke,
The Fountains of Paradise

OBEDIENCE TO AUTHORITY

Sometimes an event occurs during our lifetime that leaves an impression that is both indelible and puzzling. For me that event was the widespread participation of the German people in a system of death camps that destroyed millions of innocent men, women and children. The hapless victims were shot, gassed and burned in ovens.

These deeds were carried out by a people who were as civilized as any people in the world. How was it possible for them to act so cruelly? Did their behavior reveal a potential that is present in all of us? As a social psychologist whose job is to look into the why and how of human behavior, I decided to explore the response of ordinary people to immoral orders.

In order to explore behavior, social psychologists often rely on an important tool, the experiment. Although experiments in chemistry and physics often involve shiny equipment, flasks and electronic gear, an experiment in social psychology smacks much more of dramaturgy or theater. The experimenter carefully constructs a scenario to focus on certain aspects of behavior, a scenario in which the end is unknown and is completed by the experimental subject. The psychologist tries to create circumstances that will allow him to look at the behavior very carefully, note what he observed, and study its causes.

. . .

Imagine you had answered an advertisement to take part in a study of learning. . . . First, you are greeted by a man in a gray technician's coat; he introduces you to a second volunteer and says you are both about to take part in a scientific experiment. He says it is to test whether the use of punishment improves the ability to learn.

You draw lots to see who is to be the teacher and who the learner. You turn out to be the teacher, and the other fellow, the learner. Then you see the learner strapped into a chair and electrodes placed on his wrist. You are told that, when the learner makes a mistake in the lesson, his punishment will be an electric shock.

As teacher, you are seated in front of an impressive-looking instrument, a shock generator. Its essential feature is a line of switches that range from 15 volts to 450 volts, and a set of written labels that goes from slight shock to moderate shock, strong shock, very strong shock, and so on through XXX—danger, severe shock.

Your job, the experimenter explains to you, is to teach the learner (who, unknown to [you] is a confederate and does not actually receive the shocks) a simple word-pair test. You read a list of words to him, such as blue day, nice girl, fat neck, etc., and he has to indicate by means of an answer box which words were originally paired together. If he gets a correct answer, you move on to the next pair. But if he makes a mistake, you are instructed to give him an electric shock, starting with 15 volts. And you are told to increase the shock one step each time he makes an error. In the course of the experiment the "victim" emits cries of pain and demands to be set free, but the experimenter orders you to continue. The question is: how far will you proceed on the shock generator before you turn to the experimenter and refuse to go on?

Before carrying out the experiment, I wanted to know how people thought they would behave in this situation, and so I asked them to predict their own performance. I posed the question to several groups: psychiatrists, psychologists and ordinary workers. They all said virtually the same thing: almost no one would go to the end.

But in reality the results were very different. Despite the fact that many subjects experience stress, and protest to the experimenter, a substantial proportion continue to the last shock on the generator. Many subjects obeyed the experimenter no matter how vehement the pleading of the person being shocked, no matter how painful the shocks seemed to be, and no matter how much the victim pleaded to be let out. This was seen time and again in our studies and has been observed in several universities where the experiment has been repeated.

But there is more to the experiment than this simple demonstration of obedience. Most of our energy went into systematically changing the factors in this situation to see which ones increased obedience and which led to greater defiance. . . . How a person behaves depends not only on his "character" but also on the precise situational pressures acting on him.

When the experiments were published, opinion about them was sharply divided. . . . The experiments that I had hoped would deepen our understanding of how people yield to authority became themselves the focus of controversy.

But the problem of authority remains. We cannot have society without some structure of authority, and every society must inculcate a habit of obedience in its citizens. Yet these experiments show that many people do not have the resources to resist authority, even when they are directed to act inhumanely against an innocent victim. The experiments pose anew the age-old problem: what is the correct balance between individual initiative and social au-

thority? They illuminate in a concrete way what happens when obedience is unrestrained by conscience.

STANLEY MILGRAM
TV Guide, August 21, 1976

which produce human misery. This is the way of liberation for only a few who have the capacity for discipline and abstract reflection.

14 The dilemma between a few guiding principles and numerous laws was carefully explored by Joseph Klausner, an Orthodox Jewish historian, in a scholarly study entitled *Jesus of Nazareth* (1907, English translation 1925). In the squabble between the Pharisees who held firmly to the letter of the Mosaic Law and Jesus who deliberately disregarded Jewish law, Klausner concludes that, in the final analysis, the Pharisees were right. Judaism could never accept such a contemptuous attitude toward the Law.

> For the Jews their religion was more than simple belief and more than simple moral guidance: it was a *way of life*—all life was embraced in their religion. A people does not endure on a foundation of general human faith and morality; it needs a "practical religiousness," a ceremonial form of religion which shall embody religious ideas and also crown every-day life with a halo of sanctity.

By undermining the Law of Moses, Klausner is saying, Jesus would have destroyed the Jewish nation. Jesus' intentions are not to be inpugned, "but it is unquestionable that throughout his entire teaching there is nothing that can serve to the upkeep of the state or serve towards the maintenance of order in the existing world."

There were Jewish scholars long before Jesus who were capable of formulating the *essence* of the Law of Moses in one or two general principles. Hillel, an elder contemporary of Jesus, said: "What is hateful to thyself do not to thy neighbor: this is the whole Law, the rest is commentary: go and learn it." But such rabbis who *saw* the essence never dispensed with the literal requirements of the Law itself: for law regulates collective life and gives it order. People being what they are, Klausner writes that "the nation as a whole could only see in such public ideals as those of Jesus, an abnormal and even dangerous phantasy; the majority, who followed the Pharisees and Scribes (*Tannaim*), the leaders of the popular party in the nation, could *on no account* accept Jesus' teaching."

These illustrations seem to indicate that without firm law, and a sense of obedience to law, a society disintegrates.

15 Socrates sought truth with a rare courage. But he came too close; he was too relevant to be a security risk to Athens. For this he was handed a cup of hemlock in the spring or early summer of 399

When a legal distinction is determined . . . between night and day, childhood and maturity, or any other extremes, a point has to be fixed or a line has to be drawn, or gradually picked out by successive decisions, to mark where the change takes place. Looked at by itself without regard to the necessity behind it, the line or point seems arbitrary. It might as well be a little more to the one side or the other. But when it is seen that a line or point there must be, and that there is no mathematical or logical way of fixing it precisely, the decision of the legislature must be accepted unless we can say that it is very wide of any reasonable mark.

OLIVER WENDELL HOLMES

B.C. Thus ended the career of one of the greatest minds the world has ever known, and the young men who followed Socrates knew then that something deep and terrible was wrong in men, individually and collectively. "This was the end of our comrade," wrote Plato, "a man, as we would say, of all then living we had ever met, the noblest and the wisest and the most just."

These men knew from their own bitter experience that societies persecute and/or execute their *best men* as well as their worst. This fact alone was enough to tell them that something tragic seems built into the human condition; and it was this insight that caused the first philosophers to begin to think deeply about life's problems and to search for solutions.

REFLECTIONS—

1 "Our Western experience has been an ongoing conflict of loyalties." From your point of view, how do you assess this conflict? How much have you been victimized by it? By conviction and temperament, which way do you tend to lean in your allegiance: toward the mandate of personal conscience or the necessities of a lawfully ordered society?

2 Is this conflict of loyalties necessarily a religious conflict, or could one who is not a traditional theist also face the dilemma?

3 If you are convinced that there is a "higher law," on what grounds or under what conditions would you decide to obey that law rather than the laws of the state? How could you be sure that your judgment in such a decision is *right*?

4 Reread Secs. 9 and 10 together. Are you willing to grant the church the right and power to stand in judgment over the state? Or, better, would you grant such right and power to churchmen to stand in judgment over lawmakers?

5 The statement by Associate Justice Lewis F. Powell Jr. (Sec. 3) is a clear, concise summary of this position. How would you respond to this fundamental observation that an ordered society can't endure if every individual is free to pass judgment on which laws are just and which laws are unjust, and proceed to obey only "just laws"? (See Socrates' arguments in Sec. 11.)

6 What is your response to the statement by Camus about "the true patriot" (p. 295–QM)? Does his insight solve some problems for you, or merely produce more?

7 Klausner concluded that Jesus' attack on the Mosaic Law was wrong because the masses need laws to preserve order and maintain consistency in their collective experience; and that without firm law, and a sense of obedience to law, a society disintegrates (Sec. 14). In you opinion, is Klausner essentially correct? Why or why not?

8 See the quotation from Oliver Wendell Holmes on p. 299–QM. Is this an insight worth remembering, or is this judicial opinion merely one more legalism?

Furthermore . . .

ARGYRIS, CHRIS, *Personality and Organization: The Conflict between System and the Individual.* Harper, 1970.

CAHN, EDMOND, *The Sense of Injustice.* Indiana University Press, 1964.

CAHN, EDMOND, *The Moral Decision: Right and Wrong in the Light of American Law.* Indiana University Press, 1955.

MAYER, MILTON, *On Liberty: Man v. The State.* Center for the Study of Democratic Institutions, 1969.

PERELMAN, CHARLES, *Justice.* Random House, 1967.

SHAFFER, JEROME A. (ed.), *Violence.* David McKay, 1971.

THOREAU, HENRY DAVID, "On Civil Disobedience." Paul Kurtz (ed.), *American Thought before 1900.* Macmillan, 1966. (See also Part Two, "Reason and Revolution.")

WALZER, MICHAEL, *Obligations: Essays on Disobedience, War, and Citizenship.* Clarion, 1971.

Lifestyles

Have You Ever Wondered . . .

- What it would be like "to live the meaning of your own life"? or whether this is even an option for you? (or whether you are doing just that?)

- What it would be like to live a quite different lifestyle?

- Whether you can drastically and successfully change your lifestyle?

- Whether your society has "brainwashed" you into obedience to *its* norms quite without your knowing it?

- Whether you can cease being a part of the ethnic group to which you now belong?

- What it means to be sane?

- What it would feel like, experientially, to be genuinely (i.e. pathologically) insane?

- How different you have to be to be classified as "insane"?

- Whether you would prefer to "think like everybody else" and be insane, or be a uniquely sane self and be alienated from society?

We seem to want creativity in the young—but only if it follows all the rules, isn't too noisy, pleases the adults, and doesn't rock the boat.

MC NEIL AND RUBIN
The Psychology of Being Human

AND THERE WAS GREAT REJOICING . . .

1   Once there ruled in the distant city of Wirani a king who was both mighty and wise. And he was feared for his might and loved for his wisdom.

Now, in the heart of that city was a well, whose water was cool and crystalline, from which all the inhabitants drank, even the king and his courtiers; for there was no other well.

One night when all were asleep, a witch entered the city, and poured seven drops of strange liquid into the well, and said, "From this hour he who drinks this water shall become mad."

Next morning all the inhabitants, save the king and his lord chamberlain, drank from the well and became mad, even as the witch had foretold.

And during that day the people in the narrow streets and in the market places did naught but whisper to one another, "The king is mad. Our king and his lord chamberlain have lost their reason. Surely we cannot be ruled by a mad king. We must dethrone him."

That evening the king ordered a golden goblet to be filled from the well. And when it was brought to him he drank deeply, and gave it to his lord chamberlain to drink.

And there was great rejoicing in that distant city of Wirani, because its king and its lord chamberlain had regained their reason.

KAHLIL GIBRAN

> The usual distinction between sanity and insanity is a false one. *We are all insane;* the difference between Napoleon and a madman who believes he is Napoleon is a difference in degree, not in kind; both are acting on a limited set of assumptions.
>
> *COLIN WILSON*

2   The life history of the individual is first and foremost an accommodation to the patterns and standards traditionally handed down in his community. From the moment of his birth the customs into which he is born shape his experience and behavior. By the time he can talk, he is the little creature of his culture, and by the time he is grown and able to take part in its activities, its habits are his habits, its beliefs his beliefs, its impossibilities his impossibilities.

RUTH BENEDICT

> The age of cultural innocence is passing; the American is beginning to recognize the patterns to which he conforms.
>
> *SNELL AND GAIL PUTNEY*

3   Acculturation is a part of the human condition. Throughout recorded time, each individual has been born into, then conditioned into, the roles provided by his culture. They were given. All his roles were carefully *defined* and each individual had "to define" himself into the roles and play out the definition. No alternative to system-acculturation and role-playing existed. His culture's world-view became his, including its values, myths, history, customs, traditions, and—deepest of all—the unexamined assumptions upon which his culture's world-view is grounded.

The result has been universally the same, as Ruth Benedict has aptly phrased it: ". . . its habits are his habits, its beliefs his beliefs, *its impossibilities his impossibilities.*"

> They are playing a game. They are playing at not playing a game. If I show them I see they are, I shall break the rules and they will punish me. I must play their game, of not seeing I see the game.
>
> *R. D. LAING*

4   A frightening experiment in role-playing was conducted by a social psychologist at Stanford University, Philip Zimbardo. It was a simulated-prison experiment scheduled to run for two weeks, but it was halted after six days by a "thoroughly shaken" Professor Zimbardo. It began in the basement of a campus psychology building.

Student volunteers, rated normal and average in psychological tests, had been arbitrarily assigned the roles of guard and prisoner. Prisoners were stripped and deloused—normal procedure in all real prisons. The student guards carried billy clubs, handcuffs, keys, and whistles—all symbols of their authority. Their uniforms were military shirts and reflector sunglasses which made eye contact impossible. The prisoners were made to wear identical smocks and stocking-caps and were only addressed by their number. Keeping order and enforcing the rules were the responsibility of the guards; administering punishment was totally up to them.

At first, the student prisoners did not take the experiment very seriously.

GUARD 1. "Hey, did I say you could laugh, 819? Didn't I tell you that you *could not* laugh? Maybe you didn't hear me right."

GUARD 2. "819, how'd you like to step out of line and do twenty quick pushups for us, huh? OK, come on. Let's go. Sound off. Louder. . . . "

On the morning of the second day the guards met in the corridor to deal with a prison rebellion. During the night they had harassed the prisoners in their windowless cells by constantly waking them for meaningless head counts. The students had stacked their cots against the cell doors and refused to come out for the morning count.

Told only that they must maintain law and order, the guards broke into each cell, stripped the prisoners naked, and confiscated their beds, blankets, and pillows. Eventually the ring-leaders were placed in solitary confinement in a small closet.

Faced with the resistance and hostility of the prisoners, the guards became caught up in their assigned roles. The student guards mixed troublemakers with those who had not rebelled and gave privileges to certain prisoners. This broke prisoner unity, bred distrust among them, and led prisoners to think that the privileges were the result of informing.

The guards stepped up the punishment—a meaningless succession of calisthenics and head counts which often lasted for hours. They even ordered the prisoners to curse each other publicly. Slowly the prisoners became resigned to their fate. They were no longer students. *They had become prisoners*, totally dominated by the guards.

The diary of one student guard shows the day-by-day change in his attitude as his role as guard became more and more real to him.

FIRST DAY: I evolved my strategy, namely, not to smile or it would be admitting it was only a game. I set my voice hard and low. I feel stupid.

SECOND DAY: After lights-out I held a loud conversation so the prisoners could overhear it about going home to my girl friend.

THIRD DAY: Prisoner 817 is being obnoxious and bears watching.

FOURTH DAY: I've been rebuked for handcuffing and blindfolding a prisoner. I resentfully replied it's both necessary security and my business anyway.

FIFTH DAY: I harassed 817. I've singled him out for special abuse because he begs for it, and because I simply don't like him.

By the fourth day of the experiment five student prisoners were emotionally unable to continue and had to be released. Dr. Zimbardo believes that all participants in the experiment, both prisoners and guards, had begun to accept their assigned roles as reality. Prisoners became totally submissive. They depended entirely upon the dominant guards for even their simplest needs. The fact that they were in a simulated environment and could have quit at any time seems somehow to have become lost in the daily experience of their assigned roles.

On the fifth day Prisoner 416 refused to eat. It was the final act of individual rebellion in Stanford prison. The guards failed in every attempt to force him to eat. He was put in "the hole"—the tiny equipment closet used for solitary confinement. At that point Prisoner 416 should have become a hero to the other prisoners. Instead they turned on him. To them he was a troublemaker—a "bad" prisoner.

The demand to give up the illusions about our condition is the demand to give up a condition which needs illusions.

KARL MARX

"Escape into reality"   Copyright © by Abner Dean—1954. From *Cave Drawings for the Future*.

Men in masses are gripped by personal troubles, but they are not aware of their true meaning and source.

C. WRIGHT MILLS

Bloom where you are planted.

Hindu Proverb

The general thrust of the cultural trend throughout both the Western and Communist world is to say that man is not free, that there is no such thing as a free man. We are formed and moved by forces—cultural forces without, and unconscious forces within—which we do not comprehend and which are beyond our control. We will soon be formed more knowingly and more precisely by a scientific technology which will replace the crude way in which we have been molded by partially fortuitous natural events.

CARL ROGERS

Yet we sit there, eyes glued to the set, watching this explication of the obvious in hateful fascination and even find ourselves compelled to stay tuned to whatever follows. . . . Consciously, we despise ourselves, yet we are fascinated . . . as any savage before his totem.

RICHARD SCHICKEL

GUARD. "Now if 416 does not eat all his sausages, then you can give me the blankets and sleep on the bare mattress. Or you can keep your blankets and 416 will stay another day. Now what will it be?"
PRISONER 1. "I'll keep my blankets."
GUARD. "What will it be over here?"
PRISONER 2. "Keep my blankets."
GUARD: "How about 546?"
PRISONER 3. "I'll give you my blankets."
GUARD. "Well, you boys got to come to some kind of decision here."
PRISONER. "We got three who said they'll keep their blankets."
GUARD. "We got three against one. Keep your blankets. 416, you're going to be in there for a while. So just git used to it."

It was no longer an experiment. The basement corridor had become a test-tube prison in which some average, middle-class young men called "prisoners" were actually suffering, and others called "guards" were behaving sadistically. Dr. Zimbardo cancelled the 14-day experiment after only six days.

The Zimbardo prison experiment is not a Doomsday message. It's a warning. It shows us how easily man accepts the impersonal rules of order as substitutes for human understanding, how conditioned he has become to respond to dominant symbols of authority—to a job, a role, to a label in society that forces him into patterns of behavior which dehumanize him and destroy in him the sense of responsibility for his own actions. . . .

Dr. Zimbardo has reminded us that the roles we play are prisons—prisons of our own invention. But we do have the ability to create alternatives based on more human values. To be aware of how easy it is for any of us—for all of us—to fall into the patterned roles of dominance and submission is unique knowledge. Perhaps we will use it to find again the truly human qualities that first appeared almost a hundred thousand years ago in the dark caves of Neanderthal. . . .

Primal Man

AN ALTERNATIVE: TRANSCENDENCE

5   This "prison" condition no longer prevails for increasing numbers of people who discover for themselves that they can re-define their roles. We now have the genuine option of breaking free of the bonds of culture-systems. This can be either a blessing or a curse. The loss of roots which a culture provides can be agonizing, yet the opportunities offered by this new freedom are momentous.

For good or ill, therefore, the freedom is ours. For what is probably the first time in human history, we can pass judgment on our culture and make a more objective assessment of the ways in which it meets or fails to meet our basic needs.

What is asked of us—or *demanded* of us—is no easy path. We are at a crossroads requiring considerable moral courage: the courage to face freedom and seek autonomy *without* the roots and *without* the security which culture has heretofore guaranteed to each of us.

6   The sources of this new freedom are many; three are fairly obvious.

First, from the vast researches of the social scientists, we have come to recognize the cultural patterns which have shaped our existence. From the anthropologists' patient examination of other cultural patterns, we can see more dispassionately the patterns which others have unconsciously followed. After comparing the patterns of numerous societies we have come to understand the function and operation of a culture-system. We find that each culture is an internally coherent structure with its component parts harmonizing into an interdependent working system. Each culture provides a world-view, so that life for each individual in the system has coherence and meaning.

> "I say it is useless to waste your life on one path, especially if that path has no heart."
>
> "But how do you know when a path has no heart, don Juan?"
>
> "Before you embark on it you ask the question: Does this path have a heart? If the answer is no, you will know it, and then you must choose another path."
>
> "But how will I know for sure whether a path has a heart or not?"
>
> "Anybody would know that. The trouble is nobody asks the question; and when a man finally realizes that he has taken a path without a heart, the path is ready to kill him. At that point very few men can stop to deliberate, and leave the path."
>
> "How should I proceed to ask the question properly, don Juan?"
>
> "Just ask it."
>
> CARLOS CASTANEDA
> *The Teachings of Don Juan*

When we apply this knowledge to our own culture, we begin to understand its function and our roles in it. We see how relative some of the patterns and values are. Previously—while living in that small green valley—we took them for granted; we may even have believed them to be universal or absolute. Now we find that they were merely functional. We have discovered that individuals immersed in their cultures, from the primitive to the most civilized, endow their respective patterns with the same ultimacy and finality which we felt. For each, his culture has worked pragmatically for him, and therefore no other culture existed, or could exist. We can now recognize ethnocentrism, wherever it occurs.

The result is that we see ourselves in a larger context, and having seen, we can no longer follow a tacit ethnocentrism. We see through it; we understand its root causes. The egocentric illusion has been found out!

Secondly, in the decade of the eighties we are involved in a cataclysmic increase in cultural interaction. No single major culture stands today as a monolithic, isolated system, as they all once did.

Would it really do to find out that our game is not serious, that enemies are friends, and that the good thrives on the evil? Society as we know it seems to be a tacit conspiracy to keep this hushed up for fear that the contest will otherwise cease.

ALAN WATTS

He who is his own servant cannot be his own master. A mere matter of space in our minds. He will *think* kitchen, bathroom, laundry, garbage, instead of thinking living room and library, conversation and paintings, beautiful clothes and flowers. After a very short time he will become the servant of that servant: earn a living for him.

NICCOLO TUCCI

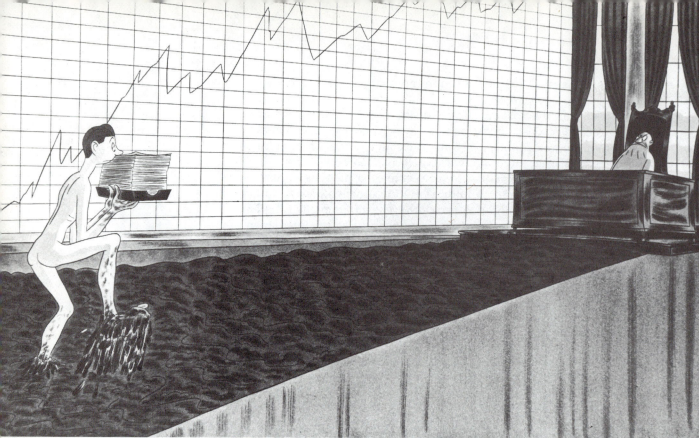

"What am I doing here?"

Few places exist in the world today where one could be born and remain culturally naive. Arnold Toynbee has pointed out that a cultural map of the earth a few centuries ago showed large pure-color patches, distinct from one another and with fairly sharp edges; but by the end of our century the patches will have vanished and the cultural colors will everywhere be woven together—like "shot silk"—with only faint blushes of color remaining in a few isolated enclaves.

Probably the most significant world-fact of our time is the disintegration of cultures as distinct and separate functional systems. This is the fundamental fact that has given us our freedom—and our pain.

A third source of our freedom is new insight into the dynamics of our inner world. We know a great deal now about the processes of psychological conditioning and reinforcement. We know that individuals can be acculturated into any set of customs, beliefs, and values; they can be made to believe, value, and even worship almost anything. If societies can condition us, then we know that we can be *un*conditioned and *re*conditioned.

And so, as we gain a clearer picture of our basic human needs—*which may or may not be fulfilled by the particular culture in which we live*—we feel a new freedom to pursue their fulfillment. *We* can take the initiative. We no longer submit to the doctrine that we *must* remain, unquestioningly, within a particular system; indeed, with our awareness of alternatives, external coercion for us to do so might be interpreted as enslavement. Various cultures, subcultures, and segments of

However romantic it seemed to be a beachcomber, I learned I had to get back to the neurotic society I need in order to function.

ALBERT FINNEY

About then I made a horrible discovery. I didn't want to go back to school, win, lose, or draw. I no longer gave a damn about three-car-garages and swimming pools, nor any other status symbol or "security." There was *no* security in this world and only damn fools and mice thought there could be.

ROBERT HEINLEIN
The Glory Road

308

culture are readily accessible to us. We are free to experiment with them, identify with them; some can even find a home in several systems simultaneously or sequentially.

CULTURAL RELATIVITY

7   In any society, specific BTF-patterns are considered "normal" not merely because the majority adheres to them, but also because they are meaningful and functional. They enable us to predict the behavior of others, and them ours. They create consistency in our experiencing of life together; they provide us with a unifying world-view. "Normal" behavior supports and enhances that unity; "abnormal" behavior does not cohere with the system and tends to destroy it.

As we move from culture to culture we find the same principles. Normal BTF-patterns will differ, but within each society these elements will cohere and interact. The system will provide guidelines for living and a high degree of conformity and security. Therefore, within each culture, these accepted BTF-patterns are normal and right.

The fact of cultural relativism was first recognized, so far as we know, by the Greek Sophist Protagoras. Denying that any belief or custom was absolute, Protagoras declared that "man is the measure of all things" (that is, customs are man-made, not divinely given); and he held that we have an obligation to conform to the cultural patterns of any society we might visit. After all, what right have we, flaunting our ethnocentric arrogance, to subvert a workable system by introducing our alien BTF-patterns?

> The central point in cultural relativism is that in a particular cultural setting, certain traits are right because they work well in that setting, while other traits are wrong because they would clash painfully with parts of that culture. This is but another way of saying that a culture is integrated, and that its various elements must harmonize passably if the culture is to function efficiently in serving human purposes.
>
> HORTON AND HUNT

8   A phenomenon found in every culture is what we sometimes call the "double standard." There are, first, the acceptable BTF-patterns; these are the publicly professed, ideal patterns that everyone is "supposed to" follow. But along with these acceptable norms also exist clearly established, socially sanctioned ways of breaking the ideal norms. That is, *there are acceptable ways of misbehaving.*

Man, it would appear, finds it difficult to live with a single set of BTF-patterns; he must have at least two sets of rules. The first set represents his ideals, the way he believes his society should be. These are projections of what he would like others to think of him and the way he would like to think of himself and others. Many convince themselves that all or most people truly follow such ideal standards of behavior.

The natural tendency to form social in-groups could never be eradicated without a major genetical change in our make-up, and one which would automatically cause our complex social structure to disintegrate.

DESMOND MORRIS

"It just goes to prove that there's nothing you can do with a really dedicated misfit."

"DR. SMITH"
Lost in Space

Ruth Benedict's book *Patterns of Culture* is a well written account of the importance of these cultural differences in the determination of the "normal" personality of three very different peoples, the Pueblo Indians of New Mexico, the Kwakiutls of the Northwest, and the Dobuans of New Guinea. The Pueblos are described as being essentially self-effacing, the Kwakiutls as being concerned with glorification to the point of megalomania, and the Dobuans as being a treacherous, and even murderous, lot.

JOSEPH ROYCE

The unacceptable patterns are just as much a part of a cultural process as the acceptable patterns, and perhaps just as vital. Man seems to need these unacceptable BTF-patterns to express a side of his nature which he is reluctant to admit. They are outlets for taboo feelings—fears, sexual urges, hostilities, prejudices—feelings which he would prefer to repress and not worry about. But since he can't escape the fact that they exist, they are expressed in various cultures in "acceptable unacceptable" ways.

Every known society has a double standard, and the "unacceptable" patterns must be considered an integral part of that culture.

Tension is necessarily involved where individuals are forced to function in line with several BTF-patterns, as in the case of a double standard. After all, we can't be fully open about the repressed patterns no matter how widely they are practiced, for one of the rules is that they not be *openly* accepted. Some amount of deception with others—and perhaps with ourselves—is inevitable.

Such tensions, however, are not usually very destructive. Most individuals learn to accept the fact that conflicting sets of rules are a part of the culture. They proceed to live with them, or by them. Still, one must be most cautious about when and where he admits the existence of the "unacceptable" patterns of behavior.

"SANE" DOES NOT MEAN "NORMAL"

9   There are several reasons why the question of the nature of sanity/insanity could become a major issue in the near future:

1. Political use of psychopathological labels may be frequently used to silence critics and remove nonconformists from the action scene. Those so charged may not be insane by any meaningful definition of the term, but name calling with scientific-sounding diagnoses could continue to accomplish partisan or totalitarian ends.

2. In the light of our growing understanding of various modes of consciousness, mind-states heretofore considered "sane" and "insane" should be revaluated. It could be that some forms of consciousness labeled "insane" may not be so; and some states of mind considered "sane" (and hence "normal") might be better classified as forms of "insanity."

3. Many psychotherapists are presently taking a second look at the function of "insanity" processes. It has long been held by some theorists that psychoses should be thought of as healing processes taking place along with, or subsequent to, the disintegrating processes. To attempt to change psychotic behavior, they say, is merely symptom relief which doesn't touch the root-causes of the malady. If given a chance, or treated effectively, the psyche can reestablish, on its own terms, a "sane" mode of consciousness.

4. From a philosophical standpoint, the most significant question has to do with the nature of reality. Any meaningful definitions of "sane" and "insane" must be developed in relation to what is con-

The American divorce rate has been variously attributed to teenage marriage, delayed marriage, premarital sexual experience, lack of sexual experience, decline of religious influence, residual Puritanism, glamorization of divorce, and even the automobile. But our analysis suggests a different, perhaps a shocking answer: American marriages are unstable because Americans marry for love.

SNELL AND GAIL PUTNEY

Never hope to realize Plato's republic . . . for who can change the opinions of men? And without a change of sentiments what can you make but reluctant slaves and hypocrites?

MARCUS AURELIUS

Man is by nature a social animal; and an unsocial person who is unsocial naturally and not accidentally is either unsatisfactory or superhuman . . . . Society is a natural phenomenon and is prior to the individual. . . . And any one who is unable to live a common life or who is so self-sufficient that he has no need to do so is no member of Society, which means that he is either a beast or a god.

ARISTOTLE

sidered to be "real." But if all we ever know of reality is a mental construct, and if this mental "reality" is not merely a private construct but a social fabric, then any and all psychic states may need redefinition in relation to this "subjective reality."

10   For most of the twentieth century we have viewed mental health as being closely related to accepted behavioral norms. The idea of "normal" has been based on values derived from the culture viewed as a whole, and the bell-shaped curve applied to all BTF-patterns. "Well adjusted" has been a term given to all those individuals who fall within the 68.26% or "average" part of the curve.

Deviation from the norm has been regarded as "abnormal," and psychotherapy has generally concentrated on helping people learn how to function within the boundaries of the "normal"; relatively little attention has been paid to individuals considered to be "successfully adjusted."

Our educational systems have been designed to aid in the acculturation process toward the middle of the curve. Those whose behavior was obviously different soon learned that they were excluded from the privileges of class membership and that they had better "shape up" or face the consequences.

11   Once "normal" and "sane" become synonymous, the door is open to various problems. Henceforth, by definition, the person who is abnormal is also in-sane. Societies are so structured that there is an innate pressure upon the individual to conform to the "norm," the BTF-patterns of the majority. The infinitely varied demands of society are directed against one's designing a life outside the 68.26% of the curve.

Societies always assume the prerogative of demanding a certain amount of conformity, and within limits, of course, this is necessary. "In this society we don't kill each other; neither do we lie, cheat, or swindle." But in the broadest historical perspective, societies don't limit their enforcement to a few general principles; in practice they have coerced a narrow range of values and beliefs upon all their members.

In previous ages the threatening deviants of a society were labeled "heretics" or "infidels" and racked or staked. In the Dark Ages unusual behavior was thought to be witchcraft or the Devil's work and was often rewarded by the stake, either through the heart or being burned at.

But since our age is psychologically oriented, it works best to find psychopathological labels to separate the conformist from the nonconformist, the "sane" from the "insane." Historically, society's critics have been charged with about everything; to charge them with "insanity" to accomplish this end would be a typical modern method of doing things. Indeed "psychoadaptation" has already been widely practiced in the twentieth century in most advanced countries of the world.

> It is hard to avoid the conclusion that we are accepting a definition of sanity which is insane, and that as a result our common human problems are so persistently insoluble that they add up to the perennial and universal "predicament of man," which is attributed to nature, to the Devil, or to God himself.
>
> *ALAN WATTS*

> But my dear Crito, why should we pay so much attention to what 'most people' think? The really reasonable people, who have more claim to be considered, will believe that the facts are exactly as they are.
>
> *PLATO*
> *Crito*

> Insanity in individuals is something rare—but in groups, parties, nations, and epochs, it is the rule.
>
> *NIETZSCHE*

> Once upon a time, I, Chuang-tzu, dreamt I was a butterfly, fluttering hither and thither, to all intents and purposes a butterfly . . . suddenly, I awoke. . . . Now I do not know whether I was then a man dreaming I was a butterfly, or whether I am now a butterfly dreaming that I am a man.
>
> *CHUANG-TZU*

THE SOCIAL CONSTRUCTION OF REALITY

12   "Sanity" may be defined as the ability on the part of an individual to enter into an efficient reality-mode of consciousness and to remain there as long as he wishes to or conditions require it.

It's simple enough to define "sanity" as the ability to conceptualize reality efficiently, but the problem can become stubborn when we press for further clarity about "reality."

We have defined "reality" before as the sum of everything that exists apart from our perception; but this definition is useless when attempting to understand sanity/insanity, since we saw that we cannot know reality as such. The only "reality" we know is a mentally manufactured system of pragmatic constructs about the real world.

In a book entitled *The Social Construction of Reality*, Berger and Luckmann show that "reality" must be thought of, not merely as an individual construct, but as a social construct produced collectively by the members of the same culture. It is a fabric woven from objects/events which have been valued, selected, conceptualized, and articulated by the group. We are individually acculturated into a society and into *its* reality.

Therefore, when each of us "constructs reality" we create it not merely by following ontological processes of the mind, but also according to the guidelines of society. Such realities will differ from one society to another. These are the various world-views (see Chapter 2–1), each equally workable in the society in which it is held.

13   A psychiatrist trying to diagnose an individual whose psychological status is in doubt asks him questions to determine the degree of his "reality-orientedness." This is quite logical; from a psychiatric viewpoint there is obviously something problematic about an individual who does not know what day of the week it is or who readily admits he has talked with departed spirits. Indeed, the term "reality-oriented" itself can be useful in such a context. The sociologist, however, has to ask the additional question, *"Which* reality?" Incidentally, this addition is not irrelevant psychiatrically. The psychiatrist will certainly take it into account, when an individual does not know the day of the week, if he has just arrived by jet plane from another continent. He may not know the day of the week simply because he is still "on another time"—Calcutta time, say, instead of Eastern Standard Time. If the psychiatrist has any sensitivity to the sociocultural context of psychological conditions he will also arrive at different diagnoses of the individual who converses with the dead, depending on whether such an individual comes from, say, New York City or from rural Haiti. The individual could be "on another reality" in the same socially objective sense that the previous one was "on another time." In other words, questions of psychological status cannot be decided without recognizing the reality-definitions that are taken for granted in the social situation of the individual. To put it more sharply, *psychological status is relative to the social definitions of reality in general and is itself socially defined.*

BERGER AND LUCKMANN

14   Schizophrenia, like any other psychotic state, must be defined not only in psychiatric terms but also in social terms. Schizophrenic experience *beyond* a certain threshold would be considered a sickness in any society, since those suffering from it would be unable to function under any social circumstances (unless the schizophrenic is elevated into the status of a god, shaman, saint, priest, etc.). But there are low-grade chronic forms of psychoses which can be shared by millions of people and which—precisely because they do not go beyond a certain threshold—do not prevent these people from functioning socially. As long as they share their sickness with millions of others, they have the satisfactory feeling of not being alone; in other words, they avoid that sense of complete isolation which is so characteristic of full-fledged psychosis. On the contrary, they look at themselves as normal and at those who have not lost the link between heart and mind as being "crazy." In all low-grade forms of psychoses, the definition of sickness depends on the question as to whether the pathology is shared or not. Just as there is low-grade chronic schizophrenia, so there exist also low-grade chronic paranoia and depression. And there is plenty of evidence that among certain strata of the population, particularly on occasions where a war threatens, the paranoid elements increase but are not felt as pathological as long as they are common.

ERICH FROMM

Four paintings by Louis Wain (here and page 312) showing a gradual withdrawal from reality into psychosis. Wain became famed in England for his gentle and beautiful (and realistic) portrayal of cats. At the age of 57 strong signs of paranoid schizophrenia appeared in his behavior and his art; his last fifteen years were spent in mental institutions. These paintings dramatically depict one person's withdrawal from reality and escape into fantasy.

WE ARE ALL INSANE

15   There are occasional philosophers and psychologists who, on their gloomier days, would suggest that insanity is ontological. The psychologist might prefer to say it is endemic to the human species. In any case, they mean that insanity—"misreading reality"—is somehow built into the very structure of human experience. In most of us these "misreading" patterns are relatively weak, but these are the same patterns of experience which, during times of trouble, can be escalated into full-fledged psychoses.

Advocates of this point of view are saying that *all of us* are slightly insane *all the time;* and that we are all potentially more insane if tragic conditions should drive our present incipient states into full-scale conflict.

The age-old belief that those who are classfied "insane" are somehow different in kind from the rest of us is a myth that has had its day. "The insane," as someone put it, "are just like us in every way—only more so."

Freud (1856–1939)

THE UNIVERSAL NEUROSIS OF MANKIND

Thus Freud's first paradox, the existence of a repressed unconscious, necessarily implies the second and even more significant paradox, the universal neurosis of mankind. Here is the *pons asinorum* of psychoanalysis. Neurosis is not an occasional aberration; it is not just in other people; it is in us, and in us all the time. . . . The doctrine of the universal neurosis of mankind is the psychoanalytical analogue of the theological doctrine of original sin. . . .

. . . Man the social animal is by the same token the neurotic animal. Or, as Freud puts it, man's superiority over the other animals is his capacity for neurosis, and his capacity for neurosis is merely the obverse of his capacity for cultural development.

Freud therefore arrives at the same conclusion as Nietzsche. . . . Neurosis is an essential consequence of civilization or culture. . . .

NORMAN O. BROWN
Life Against Death

PERSONAL ALIENATION

16   Is there any quality of "American" thought which distinguishes it from that developed elsewhere?

> If I were asked to define an American in a single phrase I would say "An American is a person who has the right to be different," and I think that right is growing.
>
> WILLIAM MANCHESTER

One peculiar and all-pervasive characteristic is its pluralism. . . . Thought in America has developed in response to external influences and to internal problems and challenges. America has been receptive to many cultures and to a variety of intellectual themes. There is, for example, both a liberal and a conservative tradition throughout American history. There is the America of radical democratic individualism and equalitarianism of Thomas Jefferson, Thomas Paine, Ethan Allen, Benjamin Rush, Henry Thoreau, Abraham Lincoln and John Dewey—an America in which liberal causes are espoused or in which a dominant secular and naturalistic outlook prevails. But there is also a conservative stream in American history, represented in the religious interests of the Puritans, Jonathan Edwards, and Samuel Johnson, in the defense of orthodoxy by the Scottish realists and speculative idealists, and in the conservative politics of Cadwallader Colden, Alexander Hamilton, John C. Calhoun, and even George Santayana. America is thus the meeting place of divergent ideas and movements: Puritanism, deism, materialism, Unitarianism, transcendentalism, idealism, realism, and pragmatism—and most recently of naturalism, positivism, analytic philosophy, Marxism, Thomism, phenomenology, Zen Buddhism, and existentialism. Any simple formulas designed to reduce these diverse elements into a uniform tradition are bound to be distorted.

> Notice the difference between what happens when a man says to himself, "I have failed three times," and what happens when he says, "I am a failure!" It is the difference between sanity and self-destruction.
>
> S. I. HAYAKAWA

PAUL KURTZ

17   Much current anxiety and alienation is the result of the interaction of cultures and their breakdown as functional systems. Since different systems have conflicting BTF-patterns, what happens when they collide and interact? Each system loses its coherence, integrity, and workability. We discover that various BTF-patterns are right *and* wrong, acceptable *and* unacceptable *at the same time,* depending upon which strand of culture one uses as the criterion of valuation.

What happens to you and me as we try to adjust to a cultural eclecticism? We *internalize* that eclecticism. The outer world is a hodge-podge, so our inner worlds become hodge-podges. Our culture is fragmented, so we too become fragmented. We don't know which values to follow, so we attempt to hold conflicting values which reflect our culture. We don't know what behavior is acceptable, so we behave differently in different settings.

Consistent behavior is no longer possible, and the integrity so essential to the harmonious operation of our inner world becomes ever more elusive. Self and sanity are at stake, and, by degrees, both can be lost.

18   When one is in this condition—when his inner world reflects the fragmentation of the outer world—he will feel from within a pressure to find a solution. Several easy and attractive alternatives are at hand; at least momentarily they can provide security and relieve anxiety.

One alternative is to identify with but a single isolated strand of culture where one can feel more at home. In such a group one's BTF-patterns will be shared by others and tensions can therefore diminish. One can feel more at ease with those who share his values. Feelings of alienation and fragmentation may subside. Surrounded by those who are congenial, one can usually ignore the uncongenial patterns which heretofore caused trouble.

The difficulty with this alternative is that it doesn't solve the problem. To be sure, changing the environment can be a step in the right direction, but one must recognize that the *vulnerability* to fragmentation is an inner problem, and it may remain. The wound is in the inner world, not in the environment. Finding congenial surroundings may ease the pain only temporarily unless healing can proceed within.

A similar alternative is to join a truth-group. One can plunge into a subcultural unit which devalues all other BTF-patterns; once devalued, they tend to lose their power over us. Relegating them to an inferior status brings more satisfaction than ignoring or repressing them. One doesn't have to take seriously the experience of any other person or group which differs, since he knows that their BTF-patterns are erroneous or wrong. Truth-groups usually make aristocentrism a condition of membership, and the sense of identity and security they offer is therefore especially rewarding.

This alternative prevents one from discovering effective chan-

At present, the gap between the sane man and the maniac is very small indeed. As William James rightly understood, the "hour" can strike for any of us. Remove a few of the walls of illusion, and the sane man becomes insane.

COLIN WILSON

C'est de quoy j'ay le plus de peur que la peur.
(The thing of which I have most fear is fear.)

MONTAIGNE

Paranoid thinking is characterized by the fact that it can be completely logical, yet lack any guidance by concern of concrete inquiry into reality; in other words, logic does not exclude madness.

ERICH FROMM

Paul Klee, *Senecio*, 1922.

Being crazy and doing crazy things is what keeps me sane.

DEBBIE SHENEFIELD

The main path to health and self-fulfillment for the masses is via basic need gratification rather than via frustration. This contrasts with the suppressive regime, the mistrust, the control, the policing that is necessarily implied by basic evil in human depths.

ABRAHAM MASLOW

Thoreau (1817–1862)

We cannot return to a simpler world. Much of contemporary social criticism is made irrelevant by its refusal to face that fact.

JOHN GARDNER

nels of growth. Genuine identification with a truth-group is possible only while one remains unaware of the implications of the egocentric predicament. Nevertheless, when our cultural confusion becomes too great, such a refuge, for many, may be the only viable alternative.

For others, there is a third path, but it is anything but a choice. This is psychosis. If the real world appears too hellish, it is quite possible to create an inner world that is less threatening. It is never a freely chosen alternative, but rather a condition that takes over when we have lost our freedom of choice.

The majority of us, however, follow the easiest path; we try halfheartedly to conform to many noncoherent patterns of culture at the same time—wearing various masks, playing various roles—whatever the cost to our mental health. Even at the risk of a mild schizophrenia, the expediency is not too costly, we think. The possibility of developing autonomy will be lost, but then, nobody's perfect. . . .

"I LEARNED THIS, AT LEAST . . ."

19   I left the woods for as good a reason as I went there. Perhaps it seemed to me that I had several more lives to live, and could not spare any more time for that one. It is remarkable how easily and insensibly we fall into a particular route, and make a beaten track for ourselves. I had not lived there a week before my feet wore a path from my door to the pond-side; and though it is five or six years since I trod it, it is still quite distinct. It is true, I fear, that others may have fallen into it, and so helped to keep it open. The surface of the earth is soft and impressible by the feet of men; and so with the paths which the mind travels. How worn and dusty, then, must be the highways of the world, how deep the ruts of tradition and conformity! I did not wish to take a cabin passage, but rather to go before the mast and on the deck of the world, for there I could best see the moonlight amid the mountains. I do not wish to go below now.

I learned this, at least, by my experiment: that if one advances confidently in the direction of his dreams, and endeavors to live the life which he has imagined, he will meet with a success unexpected in common hours. He will put some things behind, will pass an invisible boundary; new, universal, and more liberal laws will begin to establish themselves around and within him; or the old laws be expanded, and interpreted in his favor in a more liberal sense, and he will live with the license of a higher order of beings. In proportion as he simplifies his life, the laws of the universe will appear less complex, and solitude will not be solitude, nor poverty poverty, nor weakness weakness. If you have built castles in the air, your work need not be lost; that is where they should be. Now put the foundations under them.

HENRY DAVID THOREAU

after 50,000 years
rapturous in sky
I find you
      living
         in a box

REFLECTIONS—

1 Note the QMs on p. 303 by the Putneys and Laing. Do you agree with the point they are making? What percent of Americans do you think recognize "the patterns" or see "the games"? Or does this apply only to the few who take courses in philosophy? (Shades of aristocentrism?!)

2 Imagine yourself in the position of one of the guards or prisoners in the Zimbardo experiment. What games or gimmicks would you play on yourself, what knowledge, beliefs, or strengths would you remind yourself of to prevent prescribed roles from overwhelming you into losing yourself and *becoming* what the roles *define* you to be? How long do you think you could last in such a "game"? (This is a reminder of the creative mental gymnastics which many prisoners of war engage in to prevent their succumbing to the roles forced upon them.)

3 Sec. 5 contends that freedom has been *imposed* upon us whether we wish it or are ready for it. Do you agree?

4 Ponder the quotation from Laing (p. 303) in relation to that from Watts (p. 307). In what sense might society's BTF-patterns be considered "games" the rules for which we must know to get along? What exactly is a game? Where do the rules come from? What is meant by "playing" a game?

5 Page 316-QM: This observation by Maslow strikes some of us as a profound insight; but to others it might be only a trite truism. What do you think about it?

6 Note the (surprising?) statement by the Putneys (p. 310-QM). Do you understand what they're saying when they write that "American marriages are unstable because Americans marry for love"? What do they mean? Do you agree?

7 What do you think about Hayakawa's comment about failing versus failure on p. 314-QM? In your opinion, is this an insight worth programming into your computer?

8 The aphorism from the Taoist philosopher Chuang-tzu (p. 311-QM) is a delightful poetic fantasy, and we have no idea how seriously Chuang-tzu took the statement. For the sake of thought, assume that it's to be taken seriously. If you had dreamed that you were a butterfly, how could you be sure that you are not now a butterfly dreaming that you are a man or woman still dreaming that you are trying to answer a philosophy question as to whether you are a dreaming butterfly? Can you be *absolutely* sure? How?

9 Study the quotation from Colin Wilson on, p. 304-QM. What does he mean? Is he saying that the sane person, *by definition,* is the individual who has the capacity to order events? In other words, is it this ability which makes a person sane?

10 After reading the caption to the cat paintings by Louis Wain, study the four paintings very carefully and move into them as empathetically as possible. What do you think transpired in Wain's own experience as he became more schizophrenic?

11 In the last analysis, the "sanity" of an individual must be determined, not in terms of society's behavioral norms, but in terms of one's internal personality integration or disintegration, functional capacity or dysfunction. For which of the following conditions might one be well advised to seek therapeutic help?

    spontaneous hallucinations
    persistent emotional need for anesthesias (alcohol, narcotics, etc.)
    pervasive feelings of worthlessness
    racial prejudice
    inability to empathize with any feelings of others
    intense generalized suspicion of others' motives
    inability to perceive the consequences of one's behavior
    political dissention
    deviant sexual behavior
    harboring aspirations of becoming a philosopher
    inability to develop authentic loyalties to any other person or group
    membership in the Democratic party
    wanting to become President
    belonging to a religious cult
    belonging to a minority group
    fighting for unpopular causes
    inability to develop an awareness of social realities

Furthermore . . .

ARONSON, ELIOT, *The Social Animal*. W. H. Freeman, 1972.

BENEDICT, RUTH, *Patterns of Culture*. Mentor, 1948.

BERGER, PETER L., *Invitation to Sociology: A Humanistic Perspective*. Anchor, 1963.

BERGER, PETER L., and THOMAS LUCKMANN, *The Social Construction of Reality*. Anchor, 1967.

BROWN, NORMAN O., *Life against Death*. Vintage, 1959.

FROMM, ERICH, *Beyond the Chains of Illusion: My Encounter with Marx and Freud*. Pocket Books, 1962.

FROMM, ERICH, *The Sane Society*. Holt, Rinehart and Winston, 1955.

HAYAKAWA, S. I., *Symbol, Status, and Personality*. Harcourt, 1953.

LAING, R. D., *The Politics of Experience*. Ballantine, 1967.

LONDON, PERRY, *Behavior Control*. Harper, 1969.

LYND, ROBERT S., and HELEN MERRILL LYND, *Middletown*. Harcourt, 1929. (A classic which can still shatter some of our social myths.)

MORRIS, DESMOND, *The Human Zoo*. Dell, 1971.

SLATER, PHILIP, *The Pursuit of Loneliness*. Beacon, 1970.

SPIEGEL, DON, and PATRICIA KEITH SPIEGEL (eds.), *Outsiders USA*. Holt, Rinehart and Winston, 1973.

STANFORD, NEVITT, and CRAIG COMSTOCK (eds.), *Sanctions for Evil*. Beacon, 1972.

SZASZ, THOMAS S., *Ideology and Insanity: Essays on the Psychiatric Dehumanization of Man*. Doubleday, 1970.

WATTS, ALAN, *The Way of Zen*. Mentor, 1959.

Ethics/Choices

Have You Ever Wondered . . .

● Why we humans argue and fight so much about what is right and what is wrong?

● Why we can't seem to agree on what issues are important? (or what "issues" even are?)

● Whether there is anything in the world that all human beings agree is beautiful?

● Why sex is more obscene than violence (if it is)?

● How we might realistically go about solving our moral dilemmas?

● Whether the deliberate killing of another human being can be morally justified?

● Whether you have moral obligations toward (i. e. should *care about*) your animal pets? Whales and dolphins? Mockingbirds and frogs?

SIN AND/OR VIRTUE

**There is nothing either good or bad,
But thinking makes it so.**

SHAKESPEARE
Hamlet

1   Last night I invented a new pleasure, and as I was giving it the first trial, an angel and a devil came rushing toward my house. They met at my door and fought with each other over my newly created pleasure; the one crying, "It is a sin!"—the other, "It is a virtue!"

KAHLIL GIBRAN

2   It is difficult for most of us to accept that there is a body of fact regarding the nature of value-judgments and ethical codes which might render our convictions in the area of moral behavior shaky, at least, or wrong, at most. In the sphere of morality, *everyone knows* what is right and what is wrong.

"We have a right to expect decent shows on television." "Killing is wrong, for the Commandment says 'Thou shalt not kill.' " "I don't care if it is fun, it is still sinful." "What we need are tighter laws against obscenity." And more—ad infinitum.

Defining our terms doesn't seem to be required in such cases.

> The perfect Way [Tao] is without difficulty,
> Save that it avoids picking and choosing. . . .
> If you want to get the plain truth,
> Be not concerned with right and wrong.
> The conflict between right and wrong
> Is the sickness of the mind.
>
> *SENG-TS'AN*

DEBATABLE AND NONDEBATABLE VALUE-JUDGMENTS

3   There are several varieties of value-judgments, but there is considerable disagreement among value-theorists on how to classify them. For our purposes we can work with two relatively clear-cut kinds of value-statements: (1) those that are statements of personal taste and temperament and are not debatable; and (2) those that lend themselves to rational analysis and empirical investigation and are, therefore, debatable.

I may inform you that "I like liver and onions." This kind of value-judgment is strictly a matter of personal taste, and only an epistemological nitwit would make an issue of the matter. (A vegetarian could rightly want to debate the ethics of my eating meat, but my taste for liver remains undebatable.) In a word, personal values of this kind are not arguable. There are no "shoulds" or "should nots" involved in them. They just are. And in the last analysis, we can't even talk much about them. "I like turnips," I complain, and that's the end of the matter.

Nondebatable value-judgments have to do mostly with our sensory and emotional responses. For describing sensory experience, the following statements are fairly straightforward and accurate: "I like the flavor of real Italian spaghetti" (taste). "I think Susan is beautiful" (vision—although beauty as such is not actually seen but is created from visual perceptions and past experiences). "I enjoy walking in the rain" (touch, plus). "I'm turned on by the fragrance of orange blossoms" (smell). "I prefer the rhythms of Ravel's *Bolero* to Stravinsky's *Rite of Spring*" (sound).

Our emotions are similarly expressed: "I enjoy playing mathematical games." "I hate being embarrassed in public." "I like Susan." "I distrust bureaucracies." "I'm scared of love."

These judgments are all nondebatable. No fact-claims are made

> A cynic is a man who knows the price of everything, and the value of nothing.
>
> *OSCAR WILDE*

> TAYLOR (to Zira): Doctor, I'd like to kiss you goodbye.
> ZIRA (to Taylor, giggling): All right. But you're so damned ugly!
>
> *Planet of the Apes*

> *De gustibus non disputandum est.* Concerning taste there can be no argument.

in any of these statements. Each statement is *a description* of one's experience, sensory or emotional as the case may be. If her boyfriend thinks Susan is beautiful, then—since "beauty is in the eye of the beholder"—Susan *is* beautiful *to him*, and only a fool or a sour-grapes loser would argue with him.

By contrast, a second kind of value-judgment is debatable. If I say that "I favor mercy-killing," then I have made a value-statement which, if carried into action, would affect the lives of other people; and that action is clearly subject to analysis and investigation. We can talk about whether euthanasia is right or wrong when judged in the light of specific ethical criteria. We can discuss the justice of forcing terminally ill patients to suffer against their will. We can debate certain religious doctrines and why their adherents would be for or against the practice. In a word, there are ideas to be analyzed and relevant empirical facts to be gathered.

4   "But surely," it may be said, "people do disagree in their basic moral attitudes, and they do try to persuade other people to agree with them." Indeed they do. People seem to feel more strongly about their moral attitudes than they do about their food preferences (we do not talk, for example, about our "culinary convictions"), and few people appear willing simply to accept differences at this point and let it go at that. But the methods by which anyone can persuade anyone else to change his basic moral attitudes . . . are not those of rational argument but only the methods of non-rational persuasion: name-calling, intimidation, threats, and so on. This is probably why our language has words like "prude," "moral ignoramus," and the like.

Does not this view lead to pessimistic conclusions about the possibility of achieving enough ethical agreement among men to make harmonious life on our planet possible? Not at all. To so conclude would be equivalent to a restaurateur's concluding that, since people's tastes differ, he might as well give up trying to develop a menu that will win the general approval of his customers. Fortunately, people by and large tend to approve and disapprove of the same sorts of things: that is why one seldom finds anyone who will disagree with statements like "The infliction of needless pain is evil," or "It is good to help others who are in need." It is not the alleged objectivity of moral judgments, but the substantial similarity of our basic moral attitudes, that renders possible a reasonably harmonious society.

WILLIAM HALVERSON

THE MORALITY OF ETHICS/THE ETHICS OF MORALITY

5   A young bank employee was indicted for embezzlement, and the evidence all seemed to point to a conviction. But *he* knew he was innocent, and his wife believed him. She was soon informed by another bank employee that he knew the whereabouts of documents which would reveal the real embezzler and prove that her husband

was innocent. But her informant also made it clear he would give out with the evidence only if she made herself sexually available. The couple were devout Catholics, but to clear her husband of almost certain conviction she quickly made the decision to get whatever information at whatever cost. So she spent several nights with the other bank employee. Eventually the documents were forthcoming, her husband was exonerated, and the real embezzler was indicted and convicted.

Question: Was her act moral or immoral?

Question: Was *she* moral or immoral?

6   In a World War II movie called *Manhunt*, the principal figure is a big-game hunter. For the sheer love of stalking his prey, he creeps into the forest high above Hitler's retreat at Berchtesgaden. Lying concealed in a thicket, he aligns the cross-hairs of his telescopic sight on the Führer's heart as he stands on a balcony. He pulls the trigger . . . on an empty chamber. He had stalked his game, and won.

Shortly, however, the hunter is caught by the Nazis and repeatedly tortured between escapes. In the beginning it never occurred to him to *kill* Hitler; but at the end of the story, having seen the bestial cruelty of the Nazis, he parachutes by night into the German forest, this time to hunt his game with live ammunition.

(This story is not far-fetched. Many attempts were made on Hitler's life by "good and decent men who wanted to put an end to the tyranny of this maniac." One such man was Dietrich Bonhoeffer, a devout Christian leader, who was executed for attempting to do what he believed to be a Christian duty: to murder Hitler. And recently a leader of the Jewish Defense League, Meir Kahane, has stated his conviction that "if an American Nazi Party leader posed a clear and present danger to American Jews, then not to assassinate such a person would be one of the most immoral courses I could imagine.")

Question: Is it ever *right* to kill another human being deliberately and "with malice aforethought"?

7   The story is told of a tragic incident that occurred when a frontier village was raided by Indians. Several members of the village hid where they could not be found. One woman had a very small baby in her arms. As some Indians drew close, she smothered the baby rather than risk giving away their hiding place and thereby ensuring death for them all. Some time after the raid, she was punished by both church and community for committing murder.

8   From George Bernard Shaw (via *Playboy*): A girl was asked by a rich man if she would spend the night with him. She responded with a righteous "No!" When he asked if she would for a hundred thousand dollars, she uttered an exultant "Yes!" "Then what about ten thousand dollars?" he asked. With some hesitation: "Yes, I guess I would." "Then what about five hundred dollars?" She replied angrily, "No, what do you think I am?" To which his final words were: "We have already established that. Now we're merely haggling over the price."

The truly adequate personality has the capacity for identification with his fellows. The feeling of identification seems to produce a deep sensitivity to the feelings and attitudes of others.

One learns to identify with others, depending upon the nature of his contacts with the important people in his life.

ARTHUR W. COMBS

An intelligence that is not humane is the most dangerous thing in the world.

ASHLEY MONTAGU

Nature and history do not agree with our conceptions of good and bad; they define good as that which survives, and bad as that which goes under; and the universe has no prejudice in favor of Christ as against Genghis Khan.

WILL AND ARIEL DURANT

9   Joseph Fletcher recounts an episode involving the ship *William Brown* which struck an iceberg off Newfoundland and sank in 1841. Seven crewmen and thirty-two passengers crowded into a lifeboat, but this was almost double the number the lifeboat could hold. Winds and heavy seas would have capsized the whole lot in a very short time. So the first mate ordered the men in the company out of the boat, but no one moved. One of the crewmen—a man named Holmes—therefore tossed the men into the ocean. The rest in the boat survived and were eventually rescued. In Philadelphia, Holmes was tried and convicted of murder, though the jury recommended clemency.°

10   Near the turn of the century a young couple in a small Arkansas town were still childless after several years of marriage. When they went to their doctor to find out why, tests showed the man to be sterile. After talking over their problem, they went together to their local pastor and asked him if he would make the wife pregnant. In due time, he obliged, and she conceived. The child was fully accepted by the man and his wife and was loved and raised as their own. The minister, however, was forced to surrender his orders and leave the ministry.

THREE ETHICAL QUESTIONS

11   There are three questions which, if asked sincerely and explored carefully, will carry one a long way toward understanding ethical problems and deciding what moral action to take in the very human dilemmas in which we find ourselves caught. Three questions. That may sound simple; and authentic morality may indeed be simpler than our tangled intellectual analyses often indicate. However, our previous exploration of value-judgments should remind us that ethical problems can be very complex.

The three questions: (1) *Who* actually makes an ethical decision? (2) What criteria should I use in making a relevant and meaningful ethical decision? (3) To whom (or what) do my moral obligations apply?

There is a fourth question which might logically follow these three: Can I in fact *do* what I decide is right? That is, having decided what is right, can I *will* it and then *do* what I will? We need not belabor the question further at this point, since the problems of autonomy and freedom around which this question turns have been covered in previous chapters.° The more mature the self has become, the better are the chances that one will be able to will into action what he knows to be right. There is a close correlation between personal autonomy and ethical behavior.

WHO REALLY MAKES DECISIONS?

12   The first question we must answer is: *Who is to make the ethical decision?* We can assume that only the individual can make moral choices and act them out, but determining *what* action is moral may

°*This incident has received some legal attention. The issue is whether such a "crime" can be excused or justified because of the circumstances. To date, a defense argument based on "necessity" (that is, a greater harm would have occurred if the defendant hadn't acted as he did) is not allowed in capital crimes such as homicide. "However, there is some authority which would justify even the taking of an innocent human life, if absolutely necessary for the preservation of the lives of others . . . providing some lottery or other arbitrary means is designated for selecting which life is to be taken. [E.g., the 'shipwreck' cases; U.S. v. Holmes, 26 Fed.Cas.No. 360] . . . And, the presence of such facts may be enough to reduce the homicide from murder to manslaughter . . . although this is a minority view." William A. Rutter, Criminal Law, Harcourt Brace Jovanovich, 1976, §§213–218.*

There are no ethical truths; there are just clarifications of particular ethical problems. Take advantage of these clarifications and work out your own existence. You are mistaken to think that anyone ever had the answers. There are no answers. Be brave and face up to it.

DONALD KALISH

°*The material in this chapter presupposes that the problem of human freedom versus determinism (Chapter 4-3) has been resolved, to some extent at least, in favor of the conclusion that freedom is an authentic human experience. If you have concluded otherwise, then skip this chapter: the ethical problems discussed herein will necessarily be illusory and meaningless.*

not have been decided by him at all. On this question regarding decision, there are two schools of thought, for we can speak of (1) authoritarian decisions and (2) autonomous decisions.

In authoritarian ethics, decisions about right and wrong are given. They originate objectively and are not the product of one's personal experience. That is, the decisions of what is right and what is wrong have *already* been made, perhaps by an authority of a society— but often by a deity who subsequently revealed his decisions at some point to man. It was assumed by different peoples, for instance, that the decision had been made by Yahweh (and revealed in the Torah or the Decalogue); or by Allah (and revealed in the Quran); or by Shamash (and revealed to Hammurabi); or by Ahura Mazda (and revealed to Zoroaster). In the case of the Decalogue, an absolute decision had already been made: killing, lying, stealing, etc. are wrong, and any further debate is out of the question.

What is man's task? To obey these laws. Our first responsibility is to know the rules and then to resolve the ethical problems of our daily lives by the faithful application of these laws. We also have an obligation to cultivate the moral life *so that we will be able to act morally* when forced to make moral choices.

Hence, these are authoritarian ethics. The individual takes no part in the first-order decision-making on what constitutes moral/ immoral behavior. The given laws are immutable and final.

13   Autonomous ethics arise from inside oneself, for the individual himself has been in on the decision-making regarding what constitutes moral/immoral action. As the word *autonomy* implies, the individual is self-determined; his actions are manifestations of his own decisions.

We can contrast these two forms of ethics. The first is behavior

> To have a purpose for which one will do almost anything *except betray a friend,*—that is the final patent of nobility, the last formula of the superman.
>
> *NIETZSCHE*

> Teilhard de Chardin emphasized that the more evolved human being is one who, on the one hand, becomes more highly individualized, and who achieves, on the other hand, a high degree of conscious integration with other men. The evolution of man thus reveals two simultaneous and complementary trends: one toward keener awareness of self, and the other toward more intensive cooperation and participation.
>
> *RENÉ DUBOS*

ABORTION AND THE COURTS

I would like to respond to Robert J. Trotter's fine article on "Abortion laws still in ferment" by saying that I think it behooves the scientific community (physicians, biologists, et al) to come forth with a viable definition of exactly what constitutes a Person whom the 14th Amendment proscribes against depriving "of life, liberty or property without due process of law." Such definition is particularly crucial insofar as the anti-abortion forces rest their case on the assumption that any human homunculus from the moment of conception onward is a "person."

It would seem to me that this involves addressing ourselves to the question of whether a fetus in utero, by virtue of its total dependency on the body of its hostmother, is closer to the status of an *internal organ* than it is to that of a separate and discrete individual.

Perhaps there is a clear-cut biological line of demarcation or threshold in utero beyond which the fetus would be capable of independent survival if born—and this may perhaps provide the much-needed distinction between surgery and murder. In any event, I believe that it is along these lines that a useful definition will one day emerge. Meanwhile I'd hate to think that a decision so vital to the human condition and to the ultimate quality of life on this planet might, by sheer apathy on the part of the scientific community, be left entirely up to the courts.

BRADFORD WILSON
Science News, April 8, 1972

that conforms to given codes and social customs; the second is autonomous—ethical behavior which is inner-motivated and grounded in geniune moral interest in the well-being of others. Autonomous ethics is largely the product of one's own experience; in this sense it is deeply personal, reflecting one's own sensibilities and values. Furthermore, in this perspective, "morality" is not merely *what one does*; it is rather the inevitable expression of *what one is*. It is sincere goodwill and never empty conformity to prevailing customs. In a word, it is autonomous.

14   Jean-Paul Sartre has stated his conviction, based on his belief in human freedom, that *all* ethical decisions are autonomous, that in the final analysis there are no authoritarian ethics. Sartre is saying that although we may adhere to given customs and codes—from parents, peers, society, church—when making ethical decisions each of us still decides which codes we will use in resolving our problems. If we decide to seek answers to our ethical questions by applying the Decalogue rather than our parents' values, or by appealing to our church's teaching rather than to peer values, then it is still we who make such decisions.

Ultimately, therefore, we can never escape personal responsibility for the ethical decisions that *we* make; and we are likewise responsible for the moral/immoral actions which *we* perform.

Sartre's position is a sort of half-truth. He is surely correct when speaking of persons who, to use his phrase, "have become conscious"—that is, those who have become aware of alternatives. The ethically informed individual *knows* that there are many criteria for making decisions; knowing this, his decisions rest upon his own shoulders, and he must assume responsibility for them.

But for the majority of us, such options don't exist. We are convinced that there is but a single set of rights-and-wrongs: how could it be otherwise? If one believes with all his heart that the decision of right/wrong has been wholly settled, and that this settlement is embodied in a single set of customs or codes, then he cannot justly be held responsible for *not* making ethical decisions based on other codes which (in our opinion, perhaps) would have been superior decisions. For this individual, it is not possible, as Sartre would have it, for him to say "No!" to his own given code.

Perhaps the truer half of Sartre's argument needs to be emphasized: Once we become aware that there are many criteria for making ethical decisions, then the full responsibility for our own decisions rests squarely and heavily upon our shoulders.

WHAT MAKES A DECISION RIGHT OR WRONG?

15   The second question we must answer is: *What criteria should I use in making a relevant and meaningful ethical decision?* Or put differently: What is the source of the data which I should take into account in

In the new age, the dominant note in the corporate consciousness of communities is a sense of being parts of some larger universe, whereas, in the age which is now over, the dominant note in their consciousness was an aspiration to be universes in themselves.

ARNOLD TOYNBEE

Love thy neighbor as thyself. First of all: where is my neighbor? I commute: he is not in the office, not in the elevator, not at the station, not at home. All the people I meet in those different places are looking for their neighbor as I do. Some of their children, perhaps mine, may drop a bomb, not indeed on their neighbors, but on this tired search for one.

NICCOLÒ TUCCI

making an ethical judgment? Three different answers to this question come from (1) the formalist, (2) the relativist, and (3) the contextualist.

(1) Formalism

The formalist believes that the criteria to be used in making ethical decisions are universal laws which apply to all men. Man's responsibility is to be informed on these rules *ahead of time*—that is, before we find ourselves caught up in life's ethical complexities. By analogy, one should know the laws in the state motor-vehicle code *before* he gets behind the wheel and takes to the streets. Likewise, we should be taught the laws of the moral life before taking to the highways. Our personal task, in both cases, is to be thoroughly acquainted with the rules so that we can apply them to concrete situations as we come to them. Whether approaching a red light or being tempted to cheat, we should know to *stop*, since we have studied the codebook. (Our first obligation, of course, is to try to avoid situations where weighty ethical decisions have to be made, but daily life rarely permits us so easy an out.)

16   There are several kinds of formal ethical codes. One kind is represented by the Decalogue, written on Mount Sinai "by the finger of God." These are apodictic laws—absolute and incontestable. In actual practice they don't work and must be continually redefined and modified. The commandment "Thou shalt not kill" is hardly practicable if a tribe is fighting for its survival against other invading tribes. So "to kill" was understood to mean "to murder"; hence, by redefinition, it became applicable only to fellow citizens in good standing.°

The German philosopher Immanuel Kant concluded that universal moral laws do exist, but that they are to be found within the structure of the human mind. Just as 7 + 5 is always 12—it is a priori knowledge yet applies to the real world—there are, Kant holds, moral "rules of thought" which are a priori and therefore universal (like 7 + 5 = 12). Kant writes that ethical rules "must not be sought in human nature or in the circumstances of the world . . . but [must be sought] a priori simply in the concepts of reason." Kant formulated his famous "categorical imperative" to be such an a priori rule. It categorically applies to all rational men and is imperative as an absolute "ought" that binds men to the moral law. His formula (in part) is: "Act only on the maxim whereby thou canst at the same time will it should become a universal law." This resembles our concept of natural law as described by modern physics. Kant was contending that if any kind of action can be universalized, then it is ethical. For instance, can I universalize lying? Hardly. I may think lying expediently justifiable in some particular case, but can I therefore recommend telling lies as a universal form of behavior? Obviously not. Human interaction would be rendered chaotic if we couldn't depend upon one another. Therefore, telling the truth is a "categorical imperative."

A more recent attempt to develop a system of universal formal

It ain't so much a question
of not knowin' what to do.
I've known what's right and wrong
since I been ten.

ADO ANNIE
Oklahoma!

The simple-minded use of the notions "right or wrong" is one of the chief obstacles to the progress of understanding.

ALFRED NORTH WHITEHEAD

°*Actually, this is not a redefinition, since the Commandment was never intended to have general application. It is for this reason that the reported killing of some 3000 Israelites by Moses and the Levites in a single day (Ex 32:26–29) is not at all a violation of the Commandment against killing (Ex 20:13). To the ancient Hebrew the Sixth Commandment implicitly meant, "Thou shalt not kill a fellow Hebrew as long as he is a faithful follower of the god Yahweh." If this interpretation seems puzzling, read Deut 13:6–11.*

Immanuel Kant (1724–1804)

laws was undertaken by the American philosopher Edgar Brightman. For example, the Law of Autonomy: "All persons ought to recognize themselves as obligated to choose in accordance with the ideals which they acknowledge." The Law of Consequences: "All persons ought to consider and, on the whole, approve the foreseeable consequences of each of their choices." The Law of Altruism: "Each person ought to respect all other persons as ends in themselves, and, as far as possible, to co-operate with others in the production and enjoyment of shared values." These are normative laws; they state what we ought to do. Because of their logical and axiomatic nature, they are meant to apply universally to all ethical decisions made by man.

(2) Relativism

17   Another answer to our second question comes from the relativist. The relativist begins with the empirical fact that there are numerous systems of customs and codes to be found in various societies. The Greek Sophist Protagoras (481–411 B. C.) was one of the first philosophers to observe in his travels that different societies do in fact have different customs which are morally binding upon their respective inhabitants. Protagoras thus began to understand the function of customs and codes: they serve to regulate and give cohesion to a society. He therefore concluded that within any particular society, its own set of customs and codes is right *for it* since they perform the very pragmatic function of enabling that society to operate with a greater degree of internal harmony. What is "right" is therefore what works in a society, and whatever "works" in a society is therefore right. Notions of right and wrong are therefore relative to a particular society, and they differ from one society to another.

Protagoras also noted a corollary to his relativism. If one is to spend time in other societies (as he and his fellow Sophists did), then one is morally obligated to obey the vital customs and codes of the societies they visit. "Who are we," he would ask, "to come as visitors to some society other than our own, bringing with us our own social customs and moral convictions which may be quite alien to that society, and then have the effrontery to claim that *our* customs and codes are the ones that are really right? Wouldn't such behavior serve to destroy the integrated system which that society has working for it? And wouldn't our actions therefore be immoral in the truest sense?" And isn't Protagoras right?

Relativists hold that one can make meaningful ethical decisions only in the social context in which an ethical problem occurs. In other words, what is right in one place or time may be wrong in another place or time. Infanticide may have been right in Caesar's time, but is not in twentieth-century Rome. Polygamy (but with not more than four wives) may be right in Cairo, but not in Tel Aviv. Sharing one's wife with an overnight guest may be right in an Eskimo igloo, but not in Middletown, U.S.A.

Ethical relativism may mean something else: that what is right for one person may be wrong for another. This, again, is merely the recognition of the fact that different people have different convictions and follow different customs. It is wrong for Jews and Muslims to eat pork; it is wrong for Jains to eat any animal flesh at all. But such restrictions do not apply to Christians, Shintos, or others outside the faith.

(3) Contextualism

18   A third answer comes from the contextualist. He believes, first, that moral laws of the kind held by the formalist don't exist. There are no rules that one can memorize ahead of time and apply meaningfully to a particular situation. Nor will the contextualist go along with the relativist. He will readily agree that societies do in fact possess different customs and codes, and that these perform the pragmatic function which the relativist claims they do. Granted: Romans practiced infanticide, Greeks practiced slavery, Cypriots practiced sacred prostitution, modern societies disenfranchise minorities, whole nations generate hate toward other nations—societies indeed do such things, but that doesn't make such practices ethically right. The fact that a practice exists doesn't make it moral. What societies actually do, therefore, is no guideline for deciding what is ethically right.

The contextualist holds that relevant criteria for making a meaningful ethical decision can be found only within the context of each concrete ethical problem. Every ethical situation is in fact unique, and a truly ethical solution to a problem can be arrived at only when *all the factors of the unique situation* can be weighed *by those involved in the problem*. Each person makes the best decision he can, using the best knowledge which he possesses at that time of decision. Such a meaningful ethical judgment can be made only *after the problem situation exists*, not before.

Such ideas as "don't kill," "don't steal," etc., can be used as guidelines, but they must be abandoned if the specific situation calls for it. Dietrich Bonhoeffer phrased it eloquently: "Principles are only tools in God's hands soon to be thrown away as unserviceable." The same applies to formalistic rules which may prove irrelevant to a particular set of conditions. In fact, the contextualist contends that moral predicaments constantly make it necessary for us to kill, steal, lie, or whatever, *in order to be moral*.

19   Implied in all this is one single guideline which the contextualist uses in making all ethical decisions. That guideline is one's concern for the well-being of others. This principle can be developed in several ways. In *Situation Ethics*, Joseph Fletcher formulates it in terms of *agape*, the "ethical love" or "empathetic concern" which is the foundation of Christian ethics. Fletcher submits that only love is good, and rules are made to serve love, not the other way around. When one is truly involved in the well-being of another, he may be called upon to kill, to tell lies, or more, in order to carry through in authentic action

SCHILLER (Nazi colonel):
"Ours was a conflict of moralities, wasn't it? Each thought his own morality the greater. But, as Napoleon said, morality is on the side of the one with the heaviest artillery."
EVANS (American conductor):
"By the way, what ever happened to Napoleon?"

Counterpoint

Principles are only tools in God's hands, soon to be thrown away as unserviceable.

DIETRICH BONHOEFFER

It must not be forgotten that although a high standard of morality gives a slight or no advantage to each individual man and his children over the other men of the same tribe, yet an advancement in the standard of morality will certainly give an immense advantage to one tribe over another.

CHARLES DARWIN

Confucius

*The Dreamer-Who-Talks-Talks**

I had never seen Master Kung change from mood to mood this way, as though possessed by raging river spirits. We all sensed that something extraordinary was happening, and my report, apparently, had upset the balance.

It was only mid-afternoon, but we had made a very long journey. After overnighting in the village of Hu the ten of us traveled along the high road westward until mounted troops swirled dust into our faces and drove us off the roadway. We followed a path alongside the rice fields and down to the river. As we reached the river crossing I heard my name called.

"Tze-lu! Hey! What a surprise. Why here?"

Two men were perched on the grassy bank, dipping yellow poles into a murky pool. I recognized them as old acquaintances from a neighboring village. I stepped aside to return their greetings while Master Kung and his company of scholars continued across the footbridge to the other side of the river.

Then, in a scornful voice, Li Chou hissed at me: "Why are you still chasing after this dreamer-who-talks-talks? Disorder is spreading over the empire like a rising flood over a rice paddy. Does Kung still believe he can really change anything? Instead of following this man who continually escapes from one place to another, why not join those of us who withdraw altogether from this silly world? Why, Tze-lu? And why not?"

Shortly I said goodbye to the Taoist fishers. I found Master Kung and his company seated by the water's edge where the tall canes could shield the sun's heat. I recounted to Master Kung what Li Chou had said. He smiled at first; then his perpetual frown swelled into subdued laughter. Minutes later this laughter dissolved into weeping, as though torrents of wind were shaking his enormous frame and blowing his soul over the tombstones of his past.

He stilled again. How sensitive, I thought, and how brilliant. His mind is a storehouse and his memory is an inscription on stone. As he sits thus he is an impressive figure; and when he walks he is stately—tall, with broad chest and round back, like a tortoise. His large stern face—which he presents

*Through the eyes of Tze-lu, one of Confucius' disciples.

to outsiders—softens into humorous affection for those of us who love him.

Master Kung looked at me: "Tze-lu, why did you not tell your friend that you follow a man who longs to change the world, but who, in truth, cannot even coax a magpie to alight on his shoulder?"

His words recalled to me an earlier reproach from his lips. The Duke of Shi had questioned me about Kung's teaching, and, to be on the safe side, I revealed nothing. Later Master Kung chided me: "Why didn't you say to him, 'The truth about Master Kung is that he is so intent upon teaching those who hunger after knowledge that he forgets to eat, and that he is so happy in his work that he forgets his sorrows and ignores the fact that old age is creeping up on him?'" This scolding was followed by a sting when he added, "Your zithern has no right to play in my house at all. You've apparently arrived at the front door but have yet to enter into any of the inner rooms."

Master Kung's eyes drifted slowly over his other disciples, as if taking their measure. Then he settled back.

"At fifteen I was eager to learn. At thirty I could walk firmly on the ground. At forty all my doubts had cleared up. At fifty I understood what Heaven wanted of me. At sixty I could securely obey the dictates of mind and heart. But now—?"

We listened apprehensively.

"But now? No statesman has emerged who will honor this sage and listen to the wisdom that would bring peace to the world."

Then Master Kung softly sing-songed the lines of a poem he often returned to of late:

The great mountain must crumble,
The strong beam must break,
And the wise man wither away like a
    plant.

I have followed Master Kung for 15 years, and truly these last months have been the most difficult. He rose to the pinnacle of his public career a dozen years ago when he was appointed Minister of Justice in his home state of Lu by Duke Ting. His greatness was immediately apparent. Deceit and loose living hid their heads in shame. Theft and burglary ceased. Citizens could venture out safely and children slept in peace. Master Kung's fame spread to other states, and he became a hero to his people.

But Duke Ting fell from Heaven and Master Kung fell from favor. Rumors were about that he was in danger, so I went to him and said, "It's time to leave." He glared at me, but turned and walked straight out of the palace and out of the state of Lu.

Since then we have visited the towns and villages of four provinces. We are usually met with open arms, but too often we find ourselves among enemies. On two occasions we were attacked and beaten by hoodlums. Hunger has frequently plagued us, and once we feared we would starve. For three seasons we have encountered troops along the highways, and there is talk of war between Duke Ting and the Duke of Tsi. Even I began to complain about our hardships—"For *this* did we become Wise Men?"—and I made it more burdensome for the Master.

I pondered.

Our times are in disarray. Men kill, plunder, rape, and cheat. Our leaders steal from us and make wars. Husbands beat their wives, wives disobey their husbands, sons mock their fathers. Common decency is hardly to be found anywhere in the land.

Master Kung recognizes that all our ills have resulted from a breakdown in the fundamental morality of human nature. Man has fallen away from the Tao and no longer knows himself or understands others; hence, he is no longer in touch with the natural, normal way of behaving.

Master Kung has taught us how to behave in all our relationships. But he sees that we must feel right in order to behave right. We should not behave right just for the sake of be-having right—as empty men do. Rather, we must behave right in order to reawaken within ourselves the feelings of rightness; then we will behave right because right behavior will feel natural and normal again.

Master Kung believes that if these principles were taught throughout the land, then there would be peace again. If leaders could show the people how to behave, then, just as surely as the grass bends with the winds that blow over them, so the masses would follow their leaders into justice, good will, and peace.

Master Kung teaches it this way:

The wise leaders of ancient times wanted their kingdoms to be peaceful. But how did they go about achieving this?

They began by restoring the proper relationships within the family, since it is the family that produces mature individuals who can lead wisely.

But to produce well-ordered families, they first had to look to themselves, since happy families begin with mature individuals.

So you start by setting your heart right—by learning to behave toward others with respect and good will. It is thus that one becomes a good and decent human being.

But how does one set one's heart right? By being absolutely honest with yourself. This means being sincere in your thoughts and avoiding rationalizations, defensive lies, and self-deceptions. The true self is naturally good, but you have to learn to be your true self.

But how does one develop this honesty with one's self? By becoming knowledgeable about one's self and others and thus arriving at an understanding of our true natures.

But how does one obtain such knowledge? By studying everything in the world about you and seeing things as they really are.

Thus does Master Kung believe that each of us could become a Superior Man.

See the world, and knowledge grows;
As knowledge grows, thoughts are honest;

As thoughts are honest, the heart is good;
As the heart is good, the self is whole;
As the self is whole, the family is content;
As the family is content, the state is governed;
As the state is governed, the world is at peace.

I stirred from my thoughts to find that Master Kung had been speaking quietly for some time. The waters of the river had turned gray and hummingbirds were dipping into the flame flowers for their evening feeding. I presumed we would camp here for the night. The day is lately spend, and . . .

. . . Then I realized that Master Kung had spoken in my mind's reverie: "The day is lately spent," he had said. "Our leaders prefer war to wisdom and poverty to peace."

The journey of life has been difficult for Master Kung: To see so much, to be heard so little. What a waste! How utterly mad for the world to turn its back on such wealth!

His mood was quiet now as he reflected on his life's work and shared with us his developing decisions about the future.

"I wish to return home to Lu. There the libraries are rich with records of the past. I have long wanted to write the history of our people from the Golden Age to present times and to recount the story of the Superior Men of old and tell of their wisdom. It is my wish now—the years consenting—to collect these materials and leave them to you, my patient, faithful, weatherbeaten friends.

"War ravages our land, but war is like summer clouds that come and go each day. Foolish leaders rise and fall. If we cannot revitalize the present, then we shall dream a better future. Wise men will arise again. We shall work for them. When Superior Men draw close to Heaven once more, peace will return to the Middle Kingdom."

his loving concern for that other person. Again, the *rules* serve *love*. There are no laws which the contextualist will not finally break, if forced to, to manifest his ethical love for another. Just as Thoreau could say of civil law that if it "requires you to be the agent of injustice to another," then "break the law," the contextualist would say that if so-called moral laws require you to act unlovingly toward others, then break the "moral laws."

Contextualism can also be formulated in pragmatic terms. It is only our ethical concern for the well-being of others that produces a positive environment in which all of us can more fully actualize our lives. Qualities are contagious. Compassion and concern generate compassion and concern, just as hate generates hate and distrust generates distrust. Such basically human qualities as love, concern, and trust are the only qualities upon which a fulfilling collective existence can be grounded.

To summarize, therefore, the contextualist holds the following: (1) there are no universal moral laws; (2) ethical decisions can be made only in the context of concrete situations; and (3) there is a fundamental ethical guideline for all ethical behavior—one's authentic concern for the well-being of others.

20   Contextualism has significant implications. It recognizes accurately the nature of our moral predicaments. Our most agonizing ethical decisions must be made in situations where only *bad* alternatives are open to us. If daily life always set up situations so that we had to choose between a good option and a bad option, then moral existence would be simple. But actual life-situations continually force us into predicaments in which only various degrees of bad-consequence alternatives are open to choice. We may have to kill in order to save oneself, a friend, an innocent victim; we may have to lie, to pretend, to play games in order to protect someone from serious damage.

Contextual ethics says that if, out of one's concern for the well-being of others, he makes the *best decision* he possibly can, then he is unequivocally moral. If one must tell lies to save another, he has acted morally; *not* to have lied—to have allowed irreparable harm to come to another person—would have been immoral. Since this is the way that life forces us to make decisions, there is no justification for holding a person morally guilty if he has made the best decision possible in any given predicament.

By contrast, formalism and most forms of relativism have admitted that we often have to take bad action in a situation because good alternatives don't exist, but they also contend that this doesn't make the bad action right. *Having to do what is wrong doesn't make it right*. And having done wrong, we *should* feel guilt, and we may justly be subject to moral or civil recriminations. Contextualism responds that such a person is morally innocent and is, in fact, morally commendable. Having chosen the best options available, why should anyone be considered immoral?

"Don't be silly, Ninety-nine. We have to shoot, kill, and destroy. We represent everything that's wholesome and good in the world."

"MAXWELL SMART"
Get Smart

MORALITY VERSUS ETHICS

21   Each society has its own code of ethics, including the American West of the nineteenth century. The following scene from the NBC series *High Chaparral* is an instance when that code was deliberately broken. The question is how—or if—such action can be ethically justified.

In this case a gunman, Tulsa, has extorted five thousand dollars from John Cannon by threatening to kill Cannon's brother Buck. Since Buck is hot-tempered, Tulsa knows he can needle Buck into a shootout in which he could easily outdraw him. John Cannon feels he has no choice but to pay, which he does. But Buck "steals" back the money and proceeds to the local saloon, thereby ensuring a confrontation with Tulsa.

It's at this point that Buck decides to change the rules of the game. Buck is hunched over the bar when Tulsa comes to get him in the Tucson saloon.

[When asked if he had but a single gift to bequeath to the next generation, Ray Bradbury replied:] . . . The gift to see that not all Republicans are evil, that not all Democrats are evil, that not all Communists are evil, that not all Negroes are evil, that not all whites are evil, that not all anything is evil. The ability to see the paradox in every person.

RAY BRADBURY

Become what thou art.

FICHTE

TULSA. Turn around, Buck.
BUCK. Well, I tell you, Tulsa. If you wish to admit that *you* had made a mistake, and if *you* wish to crawl on out of here, I just might forget the whole thing.
TULSA. I don't make mistakes. Turn around.
BUCK. You sure?
TULSA. (*Kicking back the chairs and screaming at Buck.*) Turn around!
    (*Buck turns slowly . . . with a derringer in his hand.*) What are you doin'?
BUCK. Turnin' around, like you said.
TULSA. That's murder, Buck.
BARTENDER. Well, I think I'll go in the back room and check the stock. What I don't see I can't testify to.
BUCK. All right, Mr. Tulsa. It is now your play.
TULSA. It's murder, Buck. You gotta give me a chance.
BUCK. I don' have to give you anything.
TULSA. This ain't a fair fight!
BUCK. Fair. Hey, that's a good word. I bet you'd like for them to cut it on my tombstone, wouldn't you. "Here lies Buck Cannon, a *fair* man." But you know, I'd sooner end up standin' over your grave, and people whisperin' behind their hands, "That's Buck Cannon. He don' fight fair."
TULSA. Never figured you for a coward.
BUCK. Well, you live and you learn. I jus' don' want to die. That's the thing about a man like you. You're so ready to kill, you must be ready to die too. It's jus' the other side o' the coin, isn't it?
TULSA. You gotta give me an even chance.
BUCK. Who's gonna say it wasn't a *fair* fight. There's only you and me, and you'll be dead.
TULSA. Buck, I don't believe you'd do it.
    (*A shot, from the derringer in Buck's hand. Tulsa is wounded in his right shoulder.*)
BUCK. Aim must be off. Now it's a fair fight. Draw. Whenever you're ready.

TULSA. *(His gun arm is half-paralyzed and trembling.)* No! This ain't fair!

BUCK. Tough.

TULSA. *(Throws gun down.)* You kill an unarmed man and that's murder.

JOHN CANNON. *(From background.)* He's right, Buck.

BUCK. Well, then, get out.

TULSA. It ain't over, Buck.

BUCK. Sure it is, Tulsa. For now anyways.

TULSA. We'll meet again, I promise you.

BUCK. It might happen. But jus' remember, I'm not as fast as you. I won't draw against you. So I just might have to back-shoot you next time.

TULSA. I believe you would, too.

BUCK. Try me.

> *(Tulsa backs out and leaves saloon. Others crowd in.*
> *John comes over and leans on the bar beside Buck.)*

You know what, John? I don' fight fair.

JOHN. You know what, Buck? Nobody's goin' to hold it against you. He *would* have killed you.

BUCK. C'mon, I'll ride back to Chaparral with you. All of a sudden, I feel . . . tired.

WHOM (AND WHAT) SHOULD I CARE ABOUT?

22   The third question that one must answer is: *To whom (or what) do my moral obligations apply?* We must ask ourselves how large we are obligated to draw our circle of ethical concern. Should our ethical actions apply only to ourselves and to our primary groups such as family, clan, sect, or firm? Or do they extend to all the members of our tribe, nation, religion, or race? Do they extend to one's antagonist, attacker, enemy? Do they extend to all human beings? to all higher forms of life? to all organisms that share the impulse-to-life?

Historically, men have rather universally applied their codes of ethics only to their in-groups. Since groups are forever engaged in attempts to annihilate one another, survival demands that ethical niceties be suspended during wartime. Applied to one's own group, ethical obligations produce social cohesion, predictable and orderly behavior; they reduce internecine discord of all kinds and make it possible for a united group to fight other groups with greater efficiency. Hence—as Protagoras saw so clearly—ethical codes are pragmatic necessities.

Quite simply, ethical obligations practiced in the in-group don't apply to those outside; the out-group (historically, anyway) has never been the object of serious ethical concern. This distinction between out-group and in-group, with a code governing behavior in the in-group, is merely one aspect of the whole evolutionary arrangement. From prairie dogs and baboons to man, in-group behavior is clearly prescribed, while behavior toward all out-groups is a matter of expediency: whatever aids survival is good/moral/right/just/virtuous—and necessary!

Perhaps your conscience is colored by your skin. . . .

JOSEPH CONRAD
Lord Jim

There slowly grew up in me an unshakable conviction that we have no right to inflict suffering and death on another living creature unless there is some unavoidable necessity for it, and that we ought all of us to feel what a horrible thing it is to cause suffering and death out of mere thoughtlessness.

ALBERT SCHWEITZER

23   Since conditions on "spaceship earth" are rapidly changing, this question needs continual reexploration. Although in-group consciousness continues, and will continue, in countless forms, we need to ask whether, in a shrinking world, one's circle of obligations must be extended for purely pragmatic reasons. In the world of the seventies, traditional in-groups are being broken down and their constituents constantly rearranged.

Increasing numbers of people are thinking of the whole human species as a single in-group. If we should be attacked by extraterrestrial LGMs, the feeling of humanity's oneness would immediately surface, and for the same old reason: unite to survive. But lacking an obvious antagonist, the unity of the human species is not yet a world-fact, though sought by some and intuited by many more.

The belief that all men comprise a single *ethical* community is not new. The Stoics taught that all men are subject to the same natural and moral laws, and that they should therefore be subject to the same civil laws. All men should belong to a *cosmopolis*—a "world-city"—and should not be artifically broken up into tribes and states with different laws. Some branches of Christianity and Islam have developed similar concepts, and Jesus' mandate that we love even our enemies would, in effect, annihilate all boundaries between men.

Do our ethical obligations extend further yet? Do they extend to the higher animals? (Do they extend to our pets?) Do they extend to all animal life? The Hindus and Jains have always believed so. Do we have moral obligations to plants? to all of nature? The American Indians believe that we do.°

Exactly how does one finally decide how wide his circle of ethical concern should extend?

24   Ethical affirmation of life is the intellectual act by which man ceases simply to live at random and begins to concern himself reverently with his own life, so that he may realize its true value. And the first step in the evolution of ethics is a sense of solidarity with other human beings.

To the primitive, this solidarity has narrow limits. It is confined, first to his blood relations, then to the members of his tribe, who represent to him the family enlarged. I have such primitives in my hospital. If I ask an ambulatory patient to undertake some small service for a patient who must stay in bed, he will do it only if the bed-ridden patient belongs to his tribe. If that is not the case, he will answer me with wide-eyed innocence: "This man is not brother of me." Neither rewards nor threats will induce him to perform a service for such a stranger.

But as soon as man begins to reflect upon himself and his relationship to others, he becomes aware that men as such are his equals and his neighbors. Gradually he sees the circle of his responsibilities widening until it includes all human beings with whom he has dealings. . . . The idea of the brotherhood of all human beings is inherent in the metaphysics of most of the great religious systems. Moreover, since antiquity, philosophy has presented the case for humanitarianism as a concept recommended by reason.

> **The need for love characterizes every human being that is born. No psychological health is possible unless the "inner nature" of the person is fundamentally accepted, loved and respected by others.**
>
> *ABRAHAM MASLOW*

> °*See the words of the old Wintu holy woman on page 382.*

> **I remember on the trip home on Apollo 11 it suddenly struck me that that tiny pea, pretty and blue, was the earth. I put up my thumb and shut one eye, and my thumb blotted out the planet earth. I didn't feel like a giant. I felt very, very small.**
>
> *NEIL ARMSTRONG*

"Chi Wen Tzu used to think thrice before acting. The master hearing of it said, 'Twice is quite enough.'"

Analects of Confucius

Throughout history, however, the insight that we have a wider duty toward human beings has never attained the dominance to which it is entitled. Down to our own times it has been undermined by differences of race, religion and nationality.

Man belongs to man.

ALBERT SCHWEITZER

REFLECTIONS—

1 What is the difference between a fact-claim and a value-judgment? By way of review, how do you go about checking out the truth of a fact-claim? (See Chapter 3-4). How do you go about checking out value-judgments?

2 The most significant ethical choice that we make is deciding if we will approach a problem as a formalist, a relativist, or a contextualist. All our ethical problems are seen, interpreted, and resolved from one of these positions, or combinations of them. So, before proceeding further, think about how each of these schools analyzes an ethical problem. Work on each until it is succinct and clear.

3 Return to the case studies (Sec. 5 through 10) and zero in on each problem. How would the formalist, relativist, and contextualist analyze and resolve the problem in each case?

4 Summarize in your words the basic tenets of the formalist, relativist, and contextual approaches. What are the strengths and the weaknesses of each system? In which school of ethics do you personally feel most comfortable?

5 After working through the case studies (as suggested in No. 3, above), what are your most significant ethical conclusions? Can killing, stealing, lying, etc., be ethically and/or morally justified? Are your solutions ones that you can live with and practice—at least for now?

6 What is your personal answer to the first ethical question (Secs. 12–14): "Who is to make the ethical decision"? Do you accept Sartre's contention

that *all* ethical decisions are autonomous since only *persons* make decisions?

7 Buck Cannon believes that he broke an ethical code which he *should* have obeyed. "I don' fight fair," he grumbled. Yet we can be sure he felt a sense of justice about what he had done. How can you reconcile these two feelings? Can you justify ethically and/or morally what Buck Cannon did? In this episode there is a distinct difference between *being ethical* and *being moral.* What is that difference? *Who* was ethical and *who* was moral?

8 To the question, "To whom (or what) do my moral obligations apply?" (Secs. 22–24), what is your personal answer? Do they apply to your pet animals? to wild animals? to all living things? Does Schweitzer's "Reverence for Life" appeal to you as a solution to this problem? (See Sec. 24 and p. 328-QM.)

9 Return to the first page of this chapter and spend some leisurely thought on Seng Ts'an's counsel that we "be not concerned with right and wrong." What is Seng Ts'an trying to say to us?

Furthermore . . .

CAWS, PETER, *Science and the Theory of Value.* Random House, 1967.

COX, HARVEY (ed.), *The Situation Ethics Debate.* Westminster, 1968.

DOMMEYER, FREDERICK C., et al. (eds.), *In Quest of Value.* Chandler, N.D.

EMMET, E. R., *Learning To Philosophize.* Penguin, 1968. (See Chapter 5 on value-judgments.)

FEINBERG, JOEL (ed.), *The Problem of Abortion.* Wadsworth, 1973.

FLETCHER, JOSEPH. *Situation Ethics: The New Morality.* Westminster, 1966.

KOHL, MARVIN (ed.), *Beneficent Euthanasia.* Prometheus, 1975.

LEISER, BURTON M., *Liberty, Justice and Morals: Contemporary Value Conflicts.* Macmillan, 1973.

LICKONA, THOMAS (ed.), *Moral Development and Behavior: Theory, Research, and Social Issues.* Holt, Rinehart and Winston, 1976.

LIPMAN, MATTHEW, *What Happens in Art.* Appleton, 1967.

MAYEROFF, MILTON, *On Caring.* Harper, 1971.

NEWMEYER, SARAH, *Enjoying Modern Art.* Mentor, 1957.

PERRY, WILLIAM G., Jr., *Forms of Intellectual and Ethical Development in the College Years.* Holt, Rinehart and Winston, 1970.

SCHWEITZER, ALBERT, *The Teaching of Reverence for Life.* Holt, Rinehart and Winston, 1965.

WARD, HILEY H., *Religion 2101 A.D.* Doubleday, 1975.

WEINBERG, JULIUS R., and KEITH E. YANDELL, *Ethics.* Holt, Rinehart and Winston, 1971.

WELLMAN, CARL, *Morals and Ethics.* Scott, Foresman, 1975.

PART VI

THE PROTOPLASMIC VENTURE

"Are you happy? Why did you do all this, why did you struggle so hard . . . ?"

"Why! For what!" Nikolaiev leaned forward and one sensed a sort of heraldic thunder rumbling in him. "Why, to *be* more. What else is life for? To develop all your possibilities. That is *happiness*, to love what you're doing, to keep expanding, to keep turning into something more."

OSTRANDER AND SCHROEDER

6-1

Life

Have You Ever Wondered . . .

- What "life" is and where it came from?

- What "matter" is and where it came from?

- Whether life may exist all over the universe?

- How many species of living things have existed on Earth since life began?

- Whether the theory of evolution is a scientifically adequate hypothesis?

- Where evolution is "going" (if it's going anywhere)?

- Whether evolution is still in operation?

- What human beings might be like—in physical appearance as well as in intellectual and emotional qualities—in, say, a million more years?

THE FOUR GREAT ETIOLOGICAL QUESTIONS

1   During the past three decades scientists working in the field of biochemical evolution have made a quantum-leap breakthrough: They have succeeded in laying the empirical foundations for answering one of the persistent questions raised by the mind of man: *What is the origin of life?* And, as so often happens after the mind is fortified with facts, we look back and say, "Of course! Now the answer is beginning to make sense. *I understand!*"

It has taken the planet Earth 4.5 billion years to discover it is 4.5 billion years old. . . .

GEORGE WALD

This sort of philosophic question is not one of the common garden variety. It's one of the four great etiological questions that have baffled and irritated man's understanding. These four questions are: What is the origin of *life,* of *man,* of *matter,* and of *the universe?* These problems have appeared, from the beginning, to be Gordian knots that the human intellect could not cut.

We had good reason to feel stymied. None of these questions could be answered until enormous amounts of scientific knowledge had been gathered and correlated. Before Western science had reached the stages of intense specialization and, subsequently, interdisciplinary synthesis, any answers to these etiological questions had to be mythical. Man was caught in the perennial human predicament. He couldn't stop asking the questions, yet he possessed no factual knowledge that would lead him to the understanding that his psyche demanded.

So these questions were dispatched with celebrated pragmatic myths. *Whence man?* He was created from white, red, and brown clay; or he was sculpted from rock, or carved from wood, or assembled from pine bark, turquoise chips, and crow feathers. He was created by Tiki, Juok, i Kombengi, Yahweh, or one of a thousand other anthropomorphic man-makers.°

And *whence matter? Whence the universe?* On these two etiological puzzles little could be said. Matter apparently exists eternally, shaped

According to one of the most fundamental laws of physics, the universal tendency in the world of matter is for everything to run downhill, to fall to the lowest possible level of tension, with constant loss of potential energy and of organization. In contrast, life constantly creates and maintains order out of the randomness of matter. To apprehend the deep significance of this fact one need only think what happens to any living organism—the very smallest as well as the largest and most evolved—when finally it dies.

RENÉ DUBOS

°*See pages 366–369. Note also the technical use of the word "myth." See pages 497f and glossary.*

ON DEFINING LIFE

One's definition of life may then lead one to accept a particular level of organization of matter as a "living" state but not any level below it, whereas another may accept one or more levels lower or consider one or more levels higher as "living." What is important is not an exact definition of life at the borderline on which we can all agree, but rather the recognition of the existence of increasing levels of organization of matter and the understanding of the mechanisms which operate to bring these about. In other words, it would appear more sensible to approach the problem of the origin of life not as an attempt to discover the precise point at which lifeless matter gave rise to the "first living thing," but rather as an examination of the mechanisms operating in the transition of matter on this earth to higher and higher levels of organization. Then the first level of organization which can be considered "alive" will still be a matter of personal preference, but at least we will all be talking about the same thing. Thus, as others have pointed out, attempts at an exact definition of life are not only fruitless, at least for the present, but meaningless.

JOHN KEOSIAN
The Origin of Life

into familiar forms by a Demiurge; or a supernatural X-factor created everything in the universe *ex nihilo*, out of nothing. Even when critical minds tried to think carefully about the cosmos, there was still very nearly nothing to be thought. Aristotle is typical. His notion of an Unmoved Mover—the First Domino in an infinite series—was the only near-logical answer to the problem that he could come up with.° Virtually no progress was made on any of these problems until the twentieth century.

As of 1980, however, two of these wild dragons—the origins of life and of man—have been domesticated: the rough outlines of an empirical answer are now clear. And the other two—the origins of matter and the universe—have been tamed: viable questions and empirical models are beginning to be developed.

BIOCHEMICAL EVOLUTION

2   The beginnings of the science of biochemical evolution are associated with the work of three men.

In 1922 a Russian biochemist, Alexander Oparin, delivered before a group of scientists in Moscow a paper outlining his theory of biogenesis. Two years later he published his thoughts in a booklet entitled *The Origin of Life*. In 1928 the English biologist J. B. S. Haldane published a technical paper with a similar line of thinking. Both men developed coherent theoretical models from their knowledge of physics and biochemistry, but there was as yet no empirical evidence to support their speculations. Then in 1953 The American biochemist Stanley Miller performed experiments that began to lay empirical foundations for an understanding of how life evolves.

Oparin had theorized that in the earth's early stages a variety of organic compounds had already developed out of inorganic materials. He described theoretically how these compounds could develop into the first prevital organisms and then into living things. As the crust of the earth began to form and the temperature of the atmosphere dropped below a thousand degrees centigrade, a variety of chemical reactions took place. Torrential rains poured down upon the young planet, accompanied by constant discharges of lightning. Hot pools of water formed containing organic compounds that washed down from the atmosphere. Most important, Oparin thought, were the carbon bonds that formed in ever-larger molecular chains. Fatty acids, sugars, and tannins could have formed in this way. Eventually amino acids could have been naturally synthesized, and amino acids are the basic constituents of proteins.

Thus, during the first phase of earth's history—perhaps a billion years long—mixtures of hydrocarbons, nitrogen, hydrogen, and ammonia were continually producing an endless variety of organic compounds that formed complex molecules that became the building-blocks of living cells. At this stage the earth was covered with what Haldane called a "hot dilute soup" in which these prebiotic reactions

°See pages 517ff.

It is mere rubbish, thinking at present of the origin of life; one might as well think of the origin of matter.

CHARLES DARWIN

Life is not one of the fundamental categories of the universe, like matter, energy, and time, but is a manifestation of certain molecular combinations. These combinations cannot have existed forever, since even the elements of which they are composed have not always existed. Therefore life must have had a beginning.

Biology and the Future of Man

Alexander Oparin

were taking place. With the synthesis of proteins the first steps had been taken toward the development of life.

3   The first empirical evidence that Oparin's theory might be correct came from Miller's experiments at the University of Chicago. Into a simple glass apparatus Miller introduced methane, ammonia, and hydrogen. The one essential ingredient of life—carbon—was there in the methane (CH_4). As these chemicals mixed with vapor from boiling water and passed through glass tubes, they flowed across two tungsten electrodes generating a continuous electric spark. All this was de-

Dr. Stanley Miller

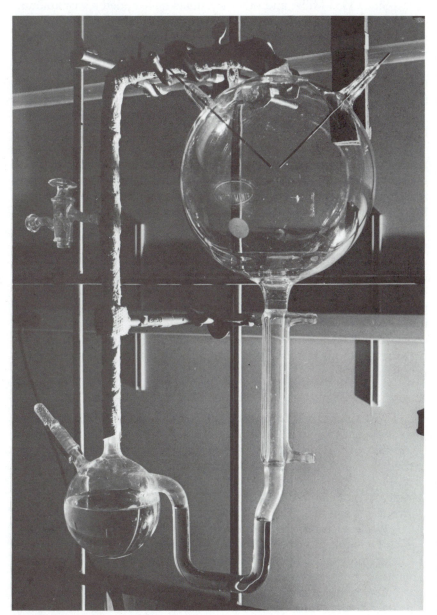

It was in this glass apparatus that Dr. Stanley Miller produced the first empirical evidence supporting the theory that living organisms may have resulted from the combination of various chemical compounds.

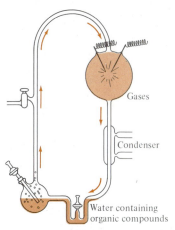

Steam from the boiling water in the lower left chamber circulates upward through a mixture of ammonia, methane, and hydrogen; then over and down into the larger chamber containing electrodes. After a week of electrical sparking the water in the tube at bottom had accumulated a variety of amino acids and other organic compounds.

People used to think that the primeval elements had to sit around in the ocean for millions of years before something happened. We now know that once the right molecules accumulated at the right time and in the right arrangement, life could begin almost instantaneously. Evolution is what takes time.

CYRIL PONNAMPERUMA

The alphabet of life is obviously extremely simple—a handful of chemicals are responsible for the vast variety we see in the entire biosphere.

CYRIL PONNAMPERUMA

All the biologicals are converting chaos to beautiful order. All biology is antientropic. Of all the disorder to order converters, the human mind is by far the most impressive. The human's most powerful metaphysical drive is to understand, to order, to sort out, and rearrange in ever more orderly and understandably constructive ways. You find then that man's true function is metaphysical.

BUCKMINSTER FULLER

signed to simulate hypothetical primitive-earth conditions—the circulating gases represented the early atmosphere, the flask of boiling liquids represented the young oceans. The experiment ran continuously for a week. At the end of that time, the gases were pumped out and the brownish liquids were analyzed. He found that a variety of organic compounds had formed along with several amino acids. Miller notes that one of the unexpected results was that "the major products were not themselves a random selection of organic compounds but included a surprising number of substances that occur in living organisms."

Since 1953 Miller and other scientists have added a vast amount of supporting data. Various gaseous mixtures have been tried along with other forms of energy, and in every case biochemically significant molecules were synthesized.

Many specific ingredients essential to living things have now been formed in the laboratory under possible primitive-earth conditions. These include the creation of carbon chains, polypeptides, and ATP, a catalytic enzyme that supplies the basic source of metabolic energy in living systems.

Significant also is the laboratory creation of porphyrins, molecules that function like plants in being able to utilize light to store energy—a primitive kind of photosynthesis. Miller believes that "almost certainly they became important for the metabolic processes leading to ATP synthesis early in the evolution of life." This supports the suggestion that photosynthesizing cells were among the earliest forms of life.

Another significant achievement has been the synthesis of the purines and pyrimidines. The five strategic nucleuic acid bases have been formed: adenine and guanine, cytosine, uracil, and thymine. In turn these purines and pyrimidines have been joined with sugars and phosphates to create nucleotides, the basic links in the DNA gene codes for all living things on earth. Furthermore, it has been shown that these molecules could have formed with comparative ease on the primitive earth.

4   In 1975 the first laboratory synthesis of a complete mammalian gene was accomplished. It was a relatively simple hemoglobin gene composed of 650 nucleotides. The report of the event in *Science News* carried the comment: "It's hard to believe that in a swift quarter-century, biologists have made the quantum leap from the identification of hereditary material to its synthesis. Yet that is precisely what has happened."

While such phrases sound like descriptions of living organisms, it must be emphasized that they are not living—yet. All these achievements are only stepping-stones toward the complexity required for the laboratory synthesis of true living organisms.

One of the world's foremost biochemists, Cyril Ponnamperuma, is at once hopeful and realistic in assessing the future of biochemical

THE MURCHISON METEORITE

Just before noon on September 28, 1969, a bright flash was seen in the sky near Murchison, a small town about 85 miles north of Melbourne, Australia. An object exploded in the sky, and 180 pounds of meteorite fragments fell to the ground. Not long after, [Dr. Cyril] Ponnamperuma received a telegram from the Smithsonian's Center for Short-lived Phenomena notifying him of the meteorite's fall. He had worked with meteorites years before but had given up because of the contamination problem. Now, because of the precise and contamination-proof techniques developed by him for analyzing the moon rocks and a freshly fallen sample, Ponnamperuma was anxious to tackle meteorites again.

A number of stones were soon on their way to him at Ames Research Center near San Francisco. Analyzing a core sample from a stone having the fewest cracks and the least exterior contamination, he detected 18 amino acids. Twelve are not found in proteins made on Earth, so their presence indicates they must be of extraterrestrial origin.

The other six amino acids are commonly found on Earth—with a slight, but very important difference. Waves of natural light, which radiate in many planes, can be polarized into one plane by passing them through a prism. When polarized light is passed through amino acids, it is rotated slightly to the right or left. With extremely rare exceptions (the cell walls of certain bacteria), amino acids found in the proteins of living organisms rotate light only to the left. Outside the living world, all molecules showing optical activity consist of equal amounts of left-handed and right-handed forms, which are mirror images of each other. But life on Earth uses only one form, and that is the left-handed form. Ponnamperuma explains: "A large, sound and sturdy protein molecule just couldn't be made by using both forms— it's like trying to put a right foot into a left shoe. We don't know why nature chose left."

In contrast to the one form found in proteins, the Murchison meteorite's protein amino acids are almost equally divided between left-handed and right-handed, additional evidence that the amino acids are not the results of earthly contamination. Ponnamperuma believes that the mixture was formed in one of the steps of chemical evolution, and he terms his findings "probably the first conclusive evidence of chemical evolution occurring elsewhere in the universe."

IRENE KIEFER
The Smithsonian, May, 1972

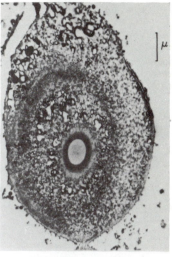

Under laboratory conditions, cell-like microspheres develop which possess many of the properties of naturally occurring living cells.
At the University of Miami's Institute for Molecular and Cellular Evolution, Dr. Sidney Fox has synthesized microspheres, which he named "proteinoids" because they looked and behaved so much like living protein cells. They possessed a double-layered surface analogous to a membrane, and they carried on a kind of internal enzyme activity. Like living cells, they were sufficiently stable to permit sectioning and staining for microscopic examination. Most significantly, they performed a sort of reproduction. When left standing for a week in liquid the spheres formed small attached minispheres or "buds" that could be split off from the parent-spheres. These would proceed to grow to the size of the original cells by the ingestion of selected substances, and then stop growing. In a few days these "offspring" would produce their own "buds" and replication would continue.

evolution. "There is no reason to doubt that we shall rediscover, one by one, the essential conditions which once determined, and directed, the course of chemical evolution. We may even reproduce the intermediate steps in the laboratory. Looking back on the biochemical understanding gained during the span of one human generation, we have the right to be quite optimistic. In contrast to unconscious nature,

Empedocles
Survival of the Fittest

(The tale is told [by Diogenes Laertius who is quoting Heraclides Ponticus who was endowed with a fanciful memory] that the philosopher/physician Empedocles ended his illustrious life by leaping into the bubbling lava of Mount Aetna to prove that he was a god. Doubtless this is just another volcano story. However . . .)

Empedocles moved about the amphitheater from one group to another, helping to settle his followers after their tiring journey from Leontini. Daybreak was still hours away and the stars were brightening in the thin morning air.

So many of his friends were here, especially from Selinus and his home city of Akragas. Corax and Tisias were here, resting on their laurels, as was his sister, whom he had never quite forgiven for burning two of his best poems. Plus his favorite pupils: Gorgias, a promising young skeptic, and dear Pausanius—both already asleep on the hard ground.

More than two hundred young men and maidens accompanied their Master on this trek without rest, and the ascent up the steep slopes of Aetna had been exhausting. During the final hours they climbed blindly through night-mists that obscured the path and enshrouded the tall pines. On reaching the crest they dropped with fatigue and proceeded to gather what sleep they could from the night hours that remained to them.

All who were here followed Empedocles with abiding faith, though why they were at this place at this hour was not altogether clear. Some had heard rumors that Empedocles planned to plunge himself into the molten lava to dispel any doubt that he was divine. Most accepted the journey as a pilgrimage to the sacred precincts of Demeter; for she had lit her torches from the fires of Aetna before setting out in search of her daughter Persephone who had been kidnapped by Pluto and taken to his lair in Hades.

Empedocles looked with affection at the huddled sleepers. He was a tall, broad-shouldered man with a luxuriant growth of black hair and beard, streaked with silver and crowned with a Delphic wreath. He was clothed this night in a purple robe with golden sash and wore bronze-colored shoes.

The tripworn travelers slept.

Far out on the ledge overlooking the cauldron Empedocles listened to sounds echoing from below. Then with his feet planted firmly on the rock, he folded his arms across his chest and closed his eyes.

He drifted. A delicious warmth moved through the whole of his being, making him feel lightheaded—spinning, giddy, like too much Sardinian wine was taking his brain apart, setting each brain-seed adrift in its own gentle vortex.

Residual images fluttered through his mind. He felt himself falling through steaming winds till the fury of the reddish clouds faded to a soft glow.

He was in a pine forest blanketed by mist. Through the trees he caught glimpses of roaring fires rising from the earth and illuminating the fog.

He recognized instantly where he was: in the Mists of Creation. Shocked into belief, he wandered about, groping.

He stepped on something soft. Looking down he found himself standing on a human toe, a great toe, quite still and lifeless. With a feeling of revulsion, he backed away through the mists.

Bewildered, he found a log and sat down to think himself through his nightmare.

A hand touched his shoulder. He jerked back, scurried over the log, and crouched looking at a hand and arm . . . and nothing more. Where there should have been a shoulder and torso there was nothing. The hand turned back on itself and pointed to its upper arm, and, like a puppy chasing its tail, continued motioning to the stump of the upper arm. Empedocles stared as the hand-arm stopped pointing, drooped, and floated away.

A head drifted toward him out of the haze, only a head, with one ear downside up.

"Can you help me find a body, please? I'm beginning to grow cold and cannot last much longer. Please . . . a body, or just a neck with, perhaps, a shoulder--?"

Empedocles stood helpless. "I saw a hand-arm assembly a short ways back," he replied, angry that his words were neither coherent nor comforting.

"Which way?" the head asked hopefully. "We could share life if only for a while. As soon as our fire goes out we die."

Empedocles was aware of a rising sense of outrage. Nothing about all this seemed right or fair or the-way-it-was-supposed-to-be.

"Wait here. I'll go to find it." Empedocles moved back along the path to the log, but the hand-arm had disappeared. He listened, heard nothing, peered through the fog, saw nothing.

When he returned, the head was lying on the ground, its fire gone. By itself it could not survive.

Empedocles felt sick. He was witnessing a tragedy beyond all imagining. Each living thing was using its few fiery hours in a desperate attempt to find some other life with which to share its warmth. Suffering and death were the order of things. He wondered: What were the odds of these innumerable pieces of life—the arms and eyes and ears and limbs and torsos—finding one another and fitting themselves together into some configuration that could survive and reproduce? None, he concluded with growing depression, none at all.

An orange glow flickered through the mists. As he approached he beheld a broad abyss of pure fire exploding into emanations from the bowels of the nether world. It was in the depths of raging forges such as this that each piece of living matter was generated. Air and water were combining with just enough earth to be activated by the abyssal fire. Fire-earth-air-water, energized by the forces of Philotês/Love and Neikos/Strife, churned into being the million billion things that are, thenceforth to struggle, to survive, to reproduce its kind. Fingers, ears, feet, heads, whole torsos were being born, full of fire, eager to complete themselves and begin life.

He turned away and retreated into the cooler mists. For a time he lost himself in mindless wandering. Parts of bodies drifted past him, sometimes singly, sometimes joined in hideous fashion. He wished he could have done with the Mists of Creation.

Something humanlike stirred on the path ahead. It uttered a long cry. Empedocles jumped forward and raised the figure to a sitting position. It was a man, almost complete— he had not seen any living thing nearly so well put together; but the man was barely warm and was rapidly losing his fire. He was missing only an arm and generative organs.

Empedocles wondered if he could find the glowing fire again, and, if he could find it, what the chances were of his finding the vital parts for this man.

No chance at all. He eased the rag-limp corpse back to the ground, its fire gone.

Time vanished, for a time. When he next opened his mind he heard voices. He listened, not quite sure it was not the wind. Two figures approached along the path: a man, seemingly perfect, and a woman, seemingly perfect. Empedocles trembled with fear that he would discover malformities as they drew near. Talking animatedly the man and woman walked past him and gradually disappeared from view. The couple were perfect human beings—fiery shoots from the realm of night and wellsprings of all future generations of mortal men.

The philosopher sat down again and wept for joy.

Empedocles aroused himself from his distraught dream to find the Eastern sky faintly backlighted with threads of silver. A few of his followers were stretching their muscles awake. The rolling mists had overtaken them and were quietly swathing the trespassers in a milky haze.

Empedocles turned to speak.

"What we have accomplished, we have accomplished. What we have left undone, we leave undone. Come awake, my friends, this is the end of our journey."

He lifted his voice as the mists rose over the crater rim.

"This world is not my home. I wept and mourned when I discovered myself in this un-familiar land. The life of mortals is so nebulous that it resembles non-life. Oblivion is swift, and we are blown away and vanish like smoke.

"From time to time there appear on earth certain men who are prophets, bards, physicians, and princes; and these men are indeed transmogrified into gods, to be extolled in honor, and are destined to share hearth and table with other immortals, freed, finally, from the evils of human suffering.

"Thus, I speak to you no longer as a mortal but as an immortal divine, and your honors are not misplaced; for hereafter you will remember this hour and say: 'There walked among us a man of rare knowledge, a man endowed with wisdom, a man who, when he reached out with all his mind, encompassed all knowledge so far attained by the human race.'

"I shall tell you one thing more: There is no birth and there is no death. There is only the co-mingling and separation of the elements."

Like bundles of woolen fleece pushed by the wind, the mists swirled through the amphitheater and spilled into the caldera. The world of sight and sound dissolved.

The listeners waited.

After an eternity the mists thinned away and the reddish glow of the cauldron reappeared.

Except for a pair of bronze-colored sandals, the ledge was empty.

Postnote. Empedocles lived for about 60 years, from *c.* 492 B.C. to *c.* 432 B.C. His famous cosmobiology was the first elaborate concept of evolution and natural selection—"the survival of the fittest."

There are two other versions of Empedocles' death: (1) that he was banished from Akragas and died in exile in Greece; and (2) that he simply disappeared from the earth after celebrating a feast during which he wrought miracles. The Aetna account derives from Diogenes Laertius, who is a generally untrustworthy source.

which had to spend billions of years for the creation of life, conscious nature has a purpose and knows the outcome."

5   Many of the sequential steps in the development of living organisms are not yet known. Much more work will be necessary to close the gaps in our knowledge.

We would like to know more about the time-scale for the origin of life during the period from the earth's beginning to those first known microscopic organisms which lived some 3.5 billion years ago. During that one-billion-year gap, how long did it take for living cells to develop? Did it happen once or many times? Is the creation of life in such a manner still taking place today? We would also like to know something about the rates of evolution of these primitive organisms. How long did the blue-green algae float around in the "hot thin soup" before complex life-forms developed?

The most complex problem still facing biogenetic theorists is to reconstruct the evolution of the *genetic mechanics* by which cells replicate themselves. During the eighties, scientists will be working to show how the DNA code was synthesized from nucleic acids.

In 1957 Dr. George Wald, a Harvard biologist, stated that he was sure that we will have produced life in the laboratory within fifty years. Today most scientists would reduce such an estimate.

THE BEGINNING OF LIFE ON EARTH

6   When did life begin on the planet earth?

The solar system was born about 5 billion years ago, and about a half-billion years later our planet had become a dense, round, hot ball, still inhospitable, angry, and forbidding.

From the fossil record we know that the first hard-shelled animals emerged in the late Precambrian era about 700 million years ago and continued to diversify in an explosion of species throughout the Cambrian period (beginning about 600 million years ago). Traces of these life-forms are easily found since they had reached an advanced stage of evolution when their hard shells could leave a fossil record. Soft parts dissolved, of course, and left no trace.

We can be quite sure that soft-bodied animals, including countless species of single-celled organisms, had by this time passed through a long history of evolutionary development. But they have successfully eluded fossil hunters.

The oldest known forms of life are algalike cells which lived some 3.5 billion years ago. These cells were capable of green-plant photosynthesis. Chances are that this process had been going on for some time, but no earlier record has been found.

When, then, did life begin? All we can say for sure is that life developed sometime between 4.5 billion years ago—when the earth was formed—and 3.5 billion years ago—with our earliest record of microfossil life. During that one-billion-year period, some wonderful and incredible events were taking place.

Cyril Ponnamperuma

The raw materials of life are assumed to have been hydrogen, helium, carbon, nitrogen, and oxygen, the same elements now found in the sun and the stars. . . . Dr. Ponnamperuma observes that "the aphorism that we are the stuff of which stars are made is more than rhetoric."

IRENE KIEFER

The universality of the genetic code and the related fact that the nucleic acids and proteins of all species are built out of the same building blocks lead to the conclusion that all known organisms are fundamentally the same. Despite appearances, there is only one form of life on the earth.

Biology and the Future of Man

Creatures extremely low in the intellectual scale may have conception. All that is required is that they should recognize the same experience again. A polyp would be a conceptual thinker if a feeling of "Hello! thingumbob again!" ever flitted through its mind.

WILLIAM JAMES

We have sufficient knowledge now to make informed guesses about some of those events, and here begins one of the exciting stories in the history of human knowledge.

EARTH'S LIFE-FORMS: AN INVENTORY

7   Since the time that living organisms first emerged from the "hot thin soup," the proliferation of species on our planet staggers the imagination. Taxonomists—those ever-patient classifiers—have so far discovered, ordered, and described about 1½ million species of living organisms, and some ten thousand new species are added annually to the list.

To date they have recognized some eighty-six hundred species of birds and one hundred fifty thousand species of marine organisms, including nearly twenty-five thousand species of fishes. Yet at least a third of the planet's fishes are still unknown to science. Some three-quarters of a million species of insects are recorded and six to seven thousand new ones are added yearly. The higher vertebrates are mostly accounted for, but the invertebrates are relatively unknown, especially the mites, nematods, worms, and parasites which total hundreds of thousands.

About a half-million higher plants have been classified, but taxonomists estimate that a quarter-million species are still unknown, especially in the tropical climates. Lower plants, such as fungi, have hardly been touched.

It is estimated that on our planet perhaps 10 million species of organisms exist today, yet this number is less than 1 percent of all the species that have existed on earth since life began.

Almost all animal phyla with preservable hard parts are represented in the fossil record from late Precambrian times onward, but millions of soft-bodied species doubtless lived before this but left no trace. Scientists guess that perhaps one out of five thousand to ten thousand extinct species show up in the fossil record.

All told, then, how many species has evolution produced on earth since the planet's beginning? The staggering figure is in the vicinity of 10 billion.

BIOGENETIC THEORIES

8   Several other theories about the origin of life have not been disproved or abandoned. Although the biogenetic model outlined above is shaping up as a sound scientific hypothesis, another theory—*panspermia*—may *also* be valid. This theory suggests that life may exist throughout the universe and that living substances journeyed to our planet from some other location, most likely embedded in meteorites. While panspermia may prove to be true, it is often pointed out that it doesn't solve the problem of how life began. It only pushes the problem light-years away to some unknown location.

This secret spoke Life herself unto me: "Behold," said she, "I am that which must ever surpass itself."

NIETZSCHE

The theory of *spontaneous generation* was believed for thousands of years until the experiments of Louis Pasteur proved it false. "Never will the doctrine of spontaneous generation recover from this mortal blow," Pasteur told the French Academy—and it hasn't. This theory held that fully developed species are generated out of nonliving materials: maggots from decaying meat, for example, or frogs from mud, mice from old rags, or fireflies from early morning dew. Our knowledge of microscopic life-forms renders this notion worthless.

Hylozoism is the belief that *all* matter is alive. It was held by the earliest Greek philosophers and has been championed by occasional theorists ever since. The idea that matter itself might be alive, or in some way might involve "mental" activity, has intrigued philosophers. The more dematerialized our concept of matter becomes, the more we may be tempted to consider mystical or panpsychic theories of ultimate reality.

Creationism is the belief that life can originate only by a touch of the supernatural, and *vitalism* is the hypothesis that a special "life-force" must infuse nonliving matter before it can come alive. Both theories are still widely held, but their viability depends partly upon whether it can be shown that living organisms can develop from inorganic matter. If this can be demonstrated, then hypotheses involving creationism or vitalism will be unnecessary.

CAN "LIFE" BE DEFINED?

9 What is "life"? Can the word be defined? Can the reality be conceived? Long lists of defining characteristics have been proposed, yet accurate, workable definitions are still lacking.

At present, it appears that "life" can be defined with two qualities: self-replication and mutability. Any organism possessing these two qualities can be considered alive. In these two characteristics is contained the essential processes of evolution: continuity and adaptation.

An organism must be able to replicate itself (unless it's immortal—that is, deathless—and hence not a part of the process of evolution). If it can produce a likeness of itself, then it possesses the power to assure continuity of its species. But mutability—the ability to effect changes from one generation to another and adapt to a fluid environment—is essential. Without the ability to change and adapt no species could long survive. Environmental conditions are forever changing; species must be able to change along with their environments.

So far as we know, only living organisms have these two qualities, and an organism must possess both qualities to be considered alive. It has been noted that mineral crystals and flames of fire can reproduce; they both effect replication of their own kind without affecting themselves. In addition, flames display a sort of metabolism: they ingest material, digest it, and excrete wastes. However, neither crystals nor flames have adaptive mutability.

Life is an offensive directed against the repetitious mechanism of the universe.

WHITEHEAD

Life is the life of life.

Bhagavata Purana

Several other qualities are often suggested as essential to a definition of what it means to be alive.

Motility —the ability to move about: to wiggle, crawl, run, fly, dart, bore through, swim. *Metabolism*—the ability to ingest materials, digest them (separate usable components from the unusable), and excrete wastes. *Growth*—the ability to proceed through some sort of life-cycle, beginning with seeds or embryos and moving through various stages of adulthood and beyond. *Irritability*—the ability to react to external stimuli, a first step in adaptation. *Dynamic Equilibrium*—the ability to maintain a stable internal condition within changing external conditions (such as adjusting to temperature, conserving a balance in the flow of food and liquids through the body of the organism, etc.).

10   When we say an organism possesses the ability to reproduce and mutate, we are not really defining *life* at all. In fact, we are not even thinking of life. We are only talking about the external motions ("behavioral patterns") of we-know-not-what. We are merely saying: *If an organism can *do* these things, then we will classify it as "alive." But what is *life?* Apparently we don't know. Or, is life *nothing but* the ability *to do* certain things?

Somehow, as we continue pondering life and living things, this isn't very satisfying. Our dissatisfaction can become sharper as we subjectively feel our own existence. We feel that life is not merely the ability *to do* something, but rather *is* something—a process, a flow, a flame, a special energy—something that persists through time inside us.

EVOLUTION AS A FIELD THEORY

11   When Charles Darwin finally got around to publishing the *Origin of Species* in 1859—after more than twenty years of procrastination—he had formulated a coherent theory about the development of all living things and documented his theory so massively that it swept the field. No other theory of evolution could hold its ground when compared with the concept of natural selection.

Darwin had not developed his notions out of nothing, of course. It had been noted that trait-changes take place from parent to offspring and that these variations are often inherited. Selective breeding of domestic animals and plants had long been practiced. And even the ideas of "the struggle for survival" and "natural selection" were hardly new, going back at least to the Greek philosopher Empedocles (c. 450 B.C.).

Darwin's genius was (1) his ability to bring a synoptic mind to these disparate elements and fit them all together, and (2) his meticulous gathering of scientific data to support his theory.

12   Following Darwin's development of the theory of natural selection from the struggle for survival, there were two large gaps in man's understanding of how evolution works.

First, heredity was not understood. But with the rediscovery in 1900 of Gregor Mendel's work, light began to dawn. Mendel's experiments had been forgotten since 1865; when they were recovered they fell into place in Darwin's theory. The transmission of specific characteristics from parents to offspring was by means of what Mendel called "genes" and followed predictable patterns.

The second information gap was knowledge of how trait-changes occur between parent and offspring. Understanding this process has come only during the last few years as scientists have penetrated the genetic code itself and found it to be a template determined by the arrangement of nucleotides in the helix-shaped DNA (deoxyribonucleic acid) molecule.

Today we have a general understanding of the three basic processes of evolution: (1) the laws of heredity, (2) mutations produced by changes in the DNA code, and (3) the dynamics of natural selection.

NAME: (Unknown)
ALIAS: Shanidar I
NICKNAME: "Nandy"
ADDRESS: Shanidar Cave, Iraq
TRIBE: Neanderthalers
CAUSE OF DEATH: Rockfall
DATE OF DEATH: 46,000 B.C.
NEXT OF KIN: Man

Creatures extremely low in the intellectual scale may have conception. All that is required is that they should recognize the same experience again. A polyp would be a conceptual thinker if a feeling of "Hello! thingumbob again!" ever flitted through its mind.

WILLIAM JAMES

The theory of evolution has become one of man's great unifying "field theories," bringing many areas of knowledge together into a single formula and providing us with a fundamental understanding of the nature of life on our planet.

PHILOSOPHIC IMPLICATIONS

13   Why does it mean so much that we can now say, "We *understand* how life evolves"?

The theory of chemical biogenesis will become a first-magnitude *field theory*. It will be comparable in its effects to the Pythagorean discovery that mathematics is the key to understanding physics, to Darwin's theory of biological evolution, and to Freud's conceptualization of a subconscious inner world.

The critical consequences of discoveries in biochemical evolution will lie in the almost unlimited control that man will possess in laboratory experiments as well as in real-life conditions. The manipulation of gene codes will permit a far more fundamental kind of scientific activity than has previously existed. In all probability we will soon know precisely what arrangements of nucleotides produce specific characteristics; this knowledge in turn will enable scientists to synthesize DNA linkages to produce any desired replicating template. Science fiction will again become fact: man will bring to life creatures that he had designed on the drawing board.

Ethical considerations raised by the creation and control of life will be complex. Having to face new kinds of ultimate concern will stretch our moral tolerances to their limit and, hopefully, force us onto new planes of ethical awareness. The beneficial consequences for life will be enormous, but our wariness is justified. Although the statement is largely a play on words, in the minds of some, man will have become a god—the designer and creator of life. Will he be a wise and competent draftsman, or might he be by nature a caricaturist? If the demonic in his subconscious splashes out onto the drawing board, then we have reason to fear. In any case, we will be compelled to monitor biogenetic activities and set parameters within which the "life designer" must work.

The cosmic implications of the theory of chemical biogenesis are revolutionary. The fact that life will evolve anywhere in the entire universe where congenial conditions exist will eventually become the nucleus of a new world-view. Yet at present the discoveries of biochemical evolution have not made a profound impact. "This tremendous event is still on its way, still wandering"—to misquote Nietzsche. "It has not yet reached the ears of man."

14   What will it mean philosophically when life is created in a glass tube by a scientist?

Man's creation of life is a predictable next step in his unraveling of life's secrets. It is an event in a continuing series: the use of fire, the

---

We now believe with confidence, that the whole of reality is one gigantic process of evolution. This produces increased novelty and variety, and ever higher types of organization; in a few spots it has produced life; and, in a few of those spots of life, it has produced mind and consciousness.

SIR JULIAN HUXLEY

In one form or another, the concept that life entails the operation of some principle of nature which is as yet ill defined seems to be gaining ground at the present time; and there is reason to believe that it is the fear of entrenched scientific orthodoxy which stills the voice of many who believe that life involves something more subtle than the latest chemical formulae for nucleic acids.

RENÉ DUBOS

wheel, weapons; harnessing steam power, nuclear power, and solar power for his energy needs; the control of weather; the use of chemicals to control emotions, explore psychopathological conditions, and eradicate disease. In kind, it is nothing new; but the door it will open is so momentous that in effect it will be as though a door had been opened onto a new world.

Man's entrance into the creation of life is one of the giant steps which puts man in control of his own destiny. This step, along with another momentous event—taking over his own evolution—is part of the grand transition man is now undergoing, the transition from being a *passively produced organism* to being the *active controller* of life and destiny.

With each step taken by man to control events in his two worlds, many are constrained to cry doom and declare the area off-limits. This response results both from theological conviction and from a deep distrust of man's ability to use his knowledge constructively, a distrust which can be supported with too much evidence. But historically, warnings of this sort have had little affect. Man proceeds to establish control over all that he can, and, following his deepest impulses, will undoubtedly continue to do so.

Life defies our phrases . . . it is infinitely continuous and subtle and shaded, whilst our verbal terms are discrete, rude, and few. . . .

WILLIAM JAMES

PHILOSOPHIC PROBLEMS

(1) Irreversibility

15   The theory of evolution has made us face numerous philosophical problems, partly because the evolutionary "field theory" is so comprehensive.

One problem is the enigma of irreversibility. We have no difficulty accepting the fact that a single organism can't move from adulthood back through adolescence into childhood, or that a butterfly can't move from its adult flying stage back through the chrysalid into its larval stage. Such notions are absurd, and we know it. But in just the same way, evolution can't move backward from complex to simpler life-forms.

The famed aphorism, *Ontogeny recapitulates phylogeny*, summarizes a well-documented fact. The long evolutionary journey of each species has left its imprint upon the embryo of the individual organism. In other words, as each embryo develops from fertilization to birth, it retraces the path of the organism's evolutionary history. For example, the human embryo at one stage exhibits a "tail" and gill-like slits which make it almost indistiguishable from the embryos of fishes or other animals which, at some point in man's dim evolutionary past, emerged from the sea.

Scientists have noted that it is not necessarily the adult stage of an ancestor which the embryo resembles. Rather the embryo mimics immature phases of its ancestors; the embryo's growth stages seem to

imply that "ancestral plans of structure" may be retained in the organism's later stage of evolutionary development.

(2) *Evolutionary Convergence*

16   Evolutionary convergence, with similar selective pressures driving unrelated and rather different genotypes into similar ecological niches, is another exciting but inadequately investigated phenomenon. The "cactus" growth form has appeared in several distinct families of plants, and some of these succulents are so similar in appearance that a non-specialist has difficulty in identifying the family. Old World tree frogs and New World tree frogs are so similar in adaptation to life in trees that it is necessary to examine the skeleton to determine which is which, yet they have originated as independent radiations within separate families. In Australia, where ordinary frogs (ranids) are virtually absent, a tree frog has evolved habits, body size, and even shape and appearance of our common leopard frog (a ranid). These and many other examples of convergence imply that there is a finite number of ways in which an organism of a given basic genotype can "make a living."

Biology and the Future of Man

(3) *Altruism and Competition*

17   The relative roles of competition and cooperation in natural selection pose another problem. Which, we wonder, has played the dominant role in the game of survival?

Competition between species seems most obvious. Species prey upon species. We watch the bloody food-chain—the "deadly feast of life"—as it operates among both animals and plants. But with a close look, we also find countless cases of cooperation, from simple symbiosis to a higher altruism in which a single individual voluntarily suffers self-deprivation or death for the welfare of its group.

Evolution clearly employs both of these seemingly contradictory mechanisms. Evolution appears to be opportunistic, caring nothing about technique. Perhaps ideas like "cooperation" and "competition" are mere human valuations which we misapply to a system that operates outside the boundaries of such anthropomorphic notions. Evolution is seemingly pragmatic—cooperating or competing, protecting or destroying, aiding or eating—whatever will increase chances of survival. The only success *is* survival, and the only criterion is whatever helps each species survive.

The long-term problem is not merely which pattern has been dominant. Once man has taken over this planet's evolution and must deal with the complex interrelationships of all living things—*the* Ecosystem—the problem man must face is whether competition and interspecific destruction can be replaced—or *should* be replaced—by patterns of mutual cooperation.

Both competition and cooperation are observed in nature. Natural selection is neither egotistic nor altruistic. It is, rather, opportunistic.

THEODOSIUS DOBZHANSKY

Nature is not made in the image of man's compassion.

TENNESSEE WILLIAMS
Suddenly Last Summer

EVOLUTIONARY TELEOLOGY: A QUESTION MARK

18   Perhaps the most difficult issue in evolution has been the problem of teleology. Is the evolutionary process one of sheer chance and opportunism, or in some way is it guided teleologically by some force, extrinsic or intrinsic, so that evolution is, in fact, "going somewhere"? Does it unfold according to a plan? Is it directed? Does it have a goal? Is its purpose to develop new and ever-more-complex forms of life? That it moves inexorably from simpler to more complex life-forms is undeniable; but does it do so "purposefully" or "opportunistically"? And even if its mode of operations is opportunistic, we still wonder *why* it moves toward ever-increased complexity.

Despite the tone of many biologists, the problem is not settled, and it is a very complicated one. It's helpful to remember that science fought its way free of religious establishments which employed harsh measures to enforce belief in ideas which were shown to be false by empirical facts. Western theology pronounced that history *is* a divine teleological plan, the plot of which is the unfolding story of God's cosmic struggle with the forces of evil for the salvation of the souls of men.

Since science freed itself from this teleocosmic myth, the word *teleology* has left a bitter taste in the mouths of scientists. Furthermore, when the theory of evolution became widely known after 1859, those inclined toward teleological thinking were quick to see in the idea of the "survival of the fittest" positive proof of a natural (as opposed to

> For the first time since the beginning of its history, humanity has become master of its destiny. . . . In order to grow afresh, it is forced to make itself anew. And it cannot make itself anew without pain, for it is both the marble and the sculptor. Out of its own substance it must send the splinters flying with great hammer-strokes, in order to recover its true face.
>
> *ALEXIS CARREL*

> Teleology, it is often said, is like an attractive woman of easy virtue, without whom a biologist cannot function happily, but with whom he does not want to be seen in public.
>
> *RENÉ DUBOS*

EVOLUTION AND ALTRUISM

On the matter of the survival of altruism during evolution, I believe we should note Darwin's group theory. In *The Descent of Man,* he wrote:

> "When two tribes of primeval man, living in the same country came into competition, if (other circumstances being equal) the one tribe included a great number of courageous, sympathetic and faithful members, who were always ready to warn each other of danger, to aid and defend each other, this tribe would succeed better and conquer the others."

And again:

> "Obscure as is the problem of the advance of civilization, we can at least see that the nation which produced, during a lengthened period, the greatest number of highly intellectual, energetic, brave, patriotic, and benevolent men, would generally prevail over less favored nations."

As to the survival of the altruistic individuals within the group, Darwin's theory is that devoted people propagate their own kind of personalities, not through their physical children, but through their ethical children, those who imitate the actions of the altruistic ones. The disciples that an altruistic person can create, even in a short lifetime, are a much larger number, Darwin says, than the children that a selfish man can father. (References: Charles Darwin, *The Origin of Species* and *The Descent of Man.* The Modern Library, pp. 490, 498–500.)

SPENCER D. POLLARD
Science News, April 8, 1972

The whole order of things fills me with terrible anguish, from the tiny gnat to the mysteries of incarnation. All is entirely unintelligible to me—particularly myself. Great is my sorrow, without limits. None knows my sorrow except God in Heaven, and He cannot have pity.

KIERKEGAARD

To put the matter in a nutshell: the capacity of living substance for reproduction is the expansive driving force of evolution; mutation provides its raw material; but natural selection determines its direction.

SIR JULIAN HUXLEY

supernatural) teleological movement: if only the fitter survive, then we can conclude, on purely scientific grounds, that life will climb forever toward unimaginable heights. The superior organism will always win over the inferior. Eternal progress is assured. Thus "social Darwinism" colored much late nineteenth- and early twentieth-century thought.

The myth of "inevitable progress" became a religious tenet to those wanting to believe that history has meaning. It ceased to be a scientific hypothesis and was transformed into dogma. It is against such doctrinaire teleology that biologists have struggled; it is but natural that occasional hostilities linger on.

19   Two positions have been taken on the questions of purpose and direction in evolution.

Some thinkers have explicitly affirmed the teleological concept of evolution. Writing in the 1880s, Friedrich Nietzsche was one of the first philosophers to develop some of the possible implications of the idea of natural selection. In several brilliant books—most notably *Thus Spake Zarathustra*—Nietzsche envisioned evolutionary history as a grand surge of life upward toward a superior being (Nietzsche called him *Übermensch*—"Overman" or "Superman"). History's intrinsic goal, argued Nietzsche, is to produce a man who has such greatness that he would be, in essence, a new species. He would possess new qualities only dimly presaged by the greatest now living among us. While he would be nothing less than ruthless in his mission of aiding evolution in its purpose, he would also display magnanimity and compassion, even gentleness, when called for.

Nietzsche's teleological interpretation of evolution also implied an ethic (which was immediately perverted by unscrupulous followers). The criterion for deciding between virtue and evil is whether any given human activity supports or thwarts evolution's fundamental purpose of producing the superior race of men. Any human act that improves man's genetic stock is moral in the fullest sense; any act that preserves inferior qualities is immoral in the same final sense. Evolution's sublime destiny is to produce superior man. Nothing must be allowed to stand in its way.

20   One of the most influential evolutionary thinkers of the twentieth century was the French philosopher Henri Bergson, whose masterpiece, *Creative Evolution*, was published in 1907. It was Bergson's conviction that what we observe in evolution cannot be explained adequately by the mechanics of natural selection. Something more profound is taking place in evolution, and natural selection has missed it. Some further insight must be added to the idea of natural selection before it can answer the question of why higher forms of life continue to emerge. Bergson postulated the existence of an *élan vital*, a "vital life-force" or "impulse-to-life." He reflected that if adaptation and change were all that was required, then the ants had it made millions of years ago. They have been able to survive, almost unchanged, since long before the beginning of "the ascent of man." This being the case, why should evolution have bothered to evolve more complex forms of life? Something else, Bergson insisted, is at work in the forces of evolvement.

The élan vital is unpredictable and opportunistic, pushing ahead in every species of animal and plant in order to create greater complexity and higher life-forms. It has no goal as such; its only purpose is to exploit every opportunity in the struggle of an organism with its environment to advance the quality of life.

21   In contrast to such teleologies, the majority of biologists hold an opportunist interpretation of evolution. They adhere to the principle that everything can be explained solely by physical, chemical, biological, or ecological principles; there is no need to introduce mysterious factors such as an élan vital or some far-off goal toward which evolution is laboriously winding its way.

Nietzsche (1844–1900)

Philosophy has not yet digested the biologist's way of looking at living nature, free of all vitalistic and finalistic ideas; but in the wake of the spectacular advances of chemical and evolutionary biology, one day there must emerge a new philosophy of science, based largely on the findings of biology rather than those of physics.

Biology and the Future of Man

To endure life remains, when all is said, the first duty of all living beings. Illusion can have no value if it makes this more difficult for us. . . .

SIGMUND FREUD

REPUBLIQUE FRANÇAISE

POSTES

50F

HENRI BERGSON
PHILOSOPHE FRANCAIS
1859 — 1941

At first sight the biological sector seems full of purpose. Organisms are built as if purposefully designed, and work as if in purposeful pursuit of a conscious aim. But the truth lies in those two words "as if." As the genius of Darwin showed, the purpose is only an apparent one. However, this at least implies prospective significance. Natural selection operates in relation to the future—the future survival of the individual and the species. And its products, in the shape of actual animals and plants, are correspondingly oriented toward the future, in their structure, their mode of working, and their behavior. A few of the later products of evolution, notably the higher mammals, do show true purpose, in the sense of the awareness of a goal. But the purpose is confined to individuals and their actions. It does not enter into the basic machinery of the evolutionary process, although it helps the realization of its results. Evolution in the biological phase is still impelled from behind; but the process is now structured so as to be directed forward.

SIR JULIAN HUXLEY

WHERE IS EVOLUTION "GOING"?

An unlearned carpenter of my acquaintance once said in my hearing: "there is very little difference between one man and another; but what little there is, is very important." This seems to me to go to the root of the matter.

WILLIAM JAMES

22   A similar position—but with a fine distinction—is held by the microbiologist René Dubos. Dubos agrees that chance and opportunism undoubtedly operate in the adaptation of a species to a specific environment. But he observes that while most biologists disown the notion of teleology, they nonetheless *operate* on the tacit assumption that evolution does involve a kind of "purpose" or movement toward a functional complexity.

Organisms diversify into literally millions of species, then the vast majority of those species perish and other millions take their place for an aeon until they, too, are replaced. Species evolve exactly as if they were adapting as best they could to a changing world, and not at all as if they were moving toward a set goal.

GEORGE GAYLORD SIMPSON

As we know it today, life operates as if most of its structures and functions were designed to fulfill some ultimate end, for the good of the individual and of the progeny. Life has its roots in the past, and its activities are projected into the future. Furthermore, it is a creative process, elaborating and maintaining order out of the randomness of matter, endlessly generating new and unexpected structures and properties by undergoing spontaneous changes, and by building up associations which qualitatively transcend their constituent parts. Clearly then, living things cannot be differentiated from the inanimate world only in terms of structures and properties. Their unique characteristic resides in the fact that their behavior is determined by their past and conditioned by the future, a property as yet mysterious but real nevertheless.

RENÉ DUBOS

23   The question, "Where is evolution going?" remains unresolved. Without the assumption of any life-essence, divine plan, or evolutionary goal, the very fact that evolution is future-oriented and that it does indeed advance toward increasing complexity and qualitatively higher levels of life means that *we can still wonder what evolution might eventually produce.*

Such a question also applies to branches of evolution other than man. Let's remind ourselves that it might not be through the humanoid line that evolution may actualize such wonderful possibilities. I seem to remember a story—supposedly science fiction—in which a colony of ants on a south Pacific island have just arrived at a higher stage of intelligence and, from their anthill, are carefully watching a busy group of scientists—and planning their next move.

In broad terms, the destiny of man on earth has been made clear by evolutionary biology. It is to be the agent of the world process of evolution, the sole agent capable of leading it to new heights, and enabling it to realize new possibilities.

JULIAN HUXLEY

WHY SEX?

Mendelian genetics has provided an incisive answer to the old question of the biological value of sexual reproduction. Biparental reproduction and Mendelian assortment provide a means of shuffling the genes so that they can be tried out in various combinations. Then those that work best in the most combinations are retained by the population. In an asexual population, the only way that two favorable mutant genes can get into the same individual is if the second mutant gene occurs in the same individual or one of its descendants. In a sexual population mutant genes that arise in different individuals can be combined in the same one. In this way evolution can proceed much faster. The biological value of sexual reproduction, then, is that it greatly increases the speed of evolution. In this way the population has a far better chance of keeping up with a constantly changing environment.

PHILIP HANDLER (ed.)
Biology and the Future of Man

Could there possibly be some validity to Nietzsche's vision that higher forms of humanity will develop if evolution has its way? Dr. Harry Overstreet of Harvard has proposed the idea that man is evolving a new form of consciousness, and that "we have every reason to believe that a further form of our conscious life is already observable among us—a high degree among certain rare individuals, in lesser degree among most of us." Overstreet has in mind the sort of "cosmic consciousness" found in some of the world's religious leaders (Gautama, Jesus), mystics (Plotinus, Swedenborg, William Blake), ecstatic intellectuals (Socrates, Descartes, Shakespeare, Einstein), and visionaries (Dante, Whitman, Fuller). Overstreet adds that such manifestations of a high order of consciousness are regarded by most of us "as signs either of supernatural power or of psychic disorder. Is it not possible, on the other hand, to regard these occurrences as signs simply of a higher stage of the very same typical development through which all of us are passing?"

What indeed is evolution's potential? Are there inherent limitations in evolution, or is it unlimited? What undreamed-of life-qualities are possible and, with a little luck, might become realities?

Dr. Thomas Gold of Cornell suggests that our earth may have been visited in the distant past by extraterrestrial passersby. Finding conditions inhospitable, they journeyed on, leaving their picnic trash behind. In a billion years or so, life-forms from this debris had evolved to the point where we call them *Homo sapiens.*

REFLECTIONS—

1 Note the four great etiological questions that the mind of man has bumped against since the beginning of philosophic thought. In your opinion, after reading Sec. 1 how far have we progressed by this ninth decade of the twentieth century toward sound empirical answers to each of these questions?

2 What do you think are the most far-reaching philosophic implications of the biochemical theory of the origin of life? Do you feel a sense of relief that foundations have been laid for an empirical answer to this question? Why or why not?

3 Page 357: Ponder the suggestion that man is now undergoing a "grand transition" from a passively produced organism to the active controller of life and destiny. What evidence can you think of that supports this conclusion? What evidence can you muster against it? Speculate: If this "grand transition" is actually taking place, what are its philosophic implications? What lies ahead?

4 "The aphorism that we are the stuff of which stars are made is more than rhetoric," writes Dr. Ponnamperuma. Is this insight meaningful to you?

5 Note the biological inventory in Sec 7. Comment?

6 Look at the illustration on p. 355. It is difficult to study this photograph of "Nandy" without having some response. What is your response? Is this photograph a metaphor?

7 What is your thinking (at present) regarding the problem of teleology in evolution? Gather evidence and develop arguments, as best you can, first in support of the notion, and then against it.

8 What scientific data can you draw upon to help resolve the question of competition versus cooperation in evolution? Which has played the more important role, do you think? (Or do you feel there may be something wrong with the way we are asking the question?)

9 How can you account for "evolutionary convergence"? Is this properly a philosophic problem, or is there a satisfactory biological answer?

10 As an answer to one of the great etiological questions, this chapter contends that the theory of evolution has become one of man's great unifying field theories (Secs. 11–12). Is this a fair and accurate evaluation of the evolutionary model? Why or why not?

11 René Dubos believes (see Sec. 22) that evolution is at least "future oriented" and that we can validly ask "What might evolution eventually produce?" Speculate then: What *might* it produce? Is Overstreet's suggestion (Sec. 23) about "higher stages of consciousness" a probable (and congenial) eventuality? (What is meant by "higher stages of consciousness"?)

Furthermore . . .

ADLER, IRVING, *How Life Began*. Signet, 1957.
ASIMOV, ISAAC, *Is Anyone There?* Ace, 1967.
BERGSON, HENRI, *Creative Evolution*. Holt, Rinehart and Winston, 1911.

CARR, DONALD E., *The Deadly Feast of Life*. Doubleday, 1971.

DUBOS, RENÉ, *The Torch of Life*. Pocket Books, 1962.

HUXLEY, JULIAN, *Evolution in Action*. Mentor, 1953.

KEOSIAN, JOHN, *The Origin of Life*, 2nd ed. Van Nostrand, 1968.

LILLY, JOHN C., *The Mind of the Dolphin*. Doubleday, 1967.

LURIA, S. E., *Life: The Unfinished Experiment*. Scribner's, 1973.

MILLER, STANLEY L., and LESLIE E. ORGEL, *The Origins of Life on the Earth*. Prentice-Hall, 1974.

MOORE, RUTH, et al., *Evolution*. Life Nature Library. Time Inc., 1962.

OPARIN, A. I., *The Origin of Life on Earth*. Macmillan, 1938.

PONNAMPERUMA, CYRIL, *The Origins of Life*. Dutton, 1972.

SIMPSON, GEORGE GAYLORD, *The Meaning of Evolution*. Mentor, 1951.

SULLIVAN, WALTER, *We Are Not Alone*. McGraw-Hill, 1966.

TEMERLIN, MAURICE K., *Growing Up Human, A Chimpanzee Daughter in a Psychotherapist's Family*. Science and Behavior Books, 1975.

von KOENIGSWALD, G. H. R., *The Evolution of Man*. Michigan University Press, 1976.

WATSON, JAMES D., *The Double Helix*. New American Library, 1969.

MAN

Have You Ever Wondered . . .

- What need in man moves him to fantasize such a variety of creation stories?

- Whether "man" (i.e. the word "man" or the "essence of man") can be defined?

- If there are any qualities that make human beings unique among the animals?

- Whether animals can "think"? Whether animals can "feel"—i.e. have emotions?

- Whether "human nature" is essentially good or bad (or whether "human nature" exists at all)?

- Whether man—as is often claimed—descended from "the killer apes"?

- What the future might hold if man actually begins to control his own evolution?

- Whether the whole human species might actually come to an end some day?

THE SCULPTOR-GODS

An average human life/time has a duration of about 10^9 seconds.

1   The Maoris of New Zealand say that a certain god, variously named Tu, Tiki, and Tane, took red riverside clay, kneaded it with his own blood into a likeness or image of himself, with eyes, legs, arms, and all complete, in fact, an exact copy of the deity; and having perfected the model, he animated it by breathing into its mouth and nostrils,

whereupon the clay effigy at once came to life and sneezed. So like himself was the man whom the Maori Creator Tiki fashioned that he called him *Tiki-ahua*, that is, Tiki's likeness.

2   Until modern times man lived close to the soil. One thing he knew how to do well—a skill universally found at a specific stage of culture—was to scoop clay from the river bank and shape it into vessels—cooking pots, water jars, urns, amphorae, lamps. Shards of pottery have been found wherever men have lit their fires and lived together.

Besides practical items, man also made figurines, miniatures molded from imagination and clay—images of men and earth mothers, of barques and scarabs, of animals and gods. Some of the earthen images he used to lure bears into his trap, to placate the gods, to grow green stalks heavy with corn, to weaken his enemies.

Some of the clay figurines he made just for fun. He molded them in his own likeness. He toyed with them, pondered them, and doubtless joked and laughed at them as he sculpted head and torso and limbs from the damp clay.

This universal experience becomes the archetypal pattern for mankind's creation stories. What was more natural and more obvious than to know, deep in his blood and bones, that he had been shaped by an unknown Sculptor from the clay of the earth? After all, was he not a clay figurine brought to life?

3   The Ewe-speaking tribes of Togo-land, in West Africa, think that God still makes men out of clay. When a little of the water with which he moistens the clay remains over, he pours it on the ground, and out of that he makes the bad and disobedient people. When he wishes to make a good man he makes him out of good clay; but when he wishes to make a bad man, he employs only bad clay for the purpose. In the beginning God fashioned a man and set him on the earth; after that he fashioned a woman. The two looked at each other and began to laugh, whereupon God sent them into the world.

4   Thus, creation myths explain to man's satisfaction far more than mere physical origins. They also tell us why he must die and return to the earth, why he is only partly immortal, and why his soul can sometimes return to heaven; they explain why there are many colors of men and many languages, why some men are good and some bad, and why there are two sexes. Almost every fact of life that puzzled early man eventually called forth some sort of mythical explanation.

The Toradjas of the Celebes tell how

i Lai, the god of the upper world, and i Ndara, the goddess of the under world, resolved to make men. They committed the task to i Kombengi, who made two models, one of a man and the other of a woman, out of stone or, according to others, out of wood. When he had done his work, he set up his models by the side of the road which leads from the upper to the under world, so that all spirits

Kingdom	Animalia (Animals)
Phylum	Chordata (Chordates)
Class	Mammalia (Mammals)
Order	Primates (Primates)
Super-family	Hominoidea (Hominoids)
Family	Hominidae (Hominids)
Sub-family	Homininae (Hominines)
Genus	*Homo* (Man)
Species	*sapiens* (Modern Man)

It is the large brain capacity which allows man to live as a human being, enjoying taxes, canned salmon, television, and the atomic bomb.

G. H. R. VON KOENIGSWALD

passing by might see and criticize his workmanship. In the evening the gods talked it over, and agreed that the calves of the legs of the two figures were not round enough. So Kombengi went to work again, and constructed another pair of models which he again submitted to the divine criticism. This time the gods observed that the figures were too pot-bellied, so Kombengi produced a third pair of models, which the gods approved of, after the maker had made a slight change in the anatomy of the figures, transferring a portion of the male to the female figure. It now only remained to make the figures live. So the god Lai returned to his celestial mansion to fetch eternal breath for the man and woman; but in the meantime the Creator himself, whether from thoughtlessness or haste, had allowed the common wind to blow on the figures, and they drew their breath and life from it. That is why the breath returns to the wind when a man dies.

5   In the earliest Hebrew account of creation, it is said that the god Yahweh moulded the first man out of clay, just as a potter might do, or as a child moulds a doll out of mud; and that having kneaded and patted the clay into the proper shape, the deity animated it by breathing into the mouth and nostrils of the figure, exactly as the prophet Elisha is said to have restored to life the dead child of the Shunammite by lying on him, and putting his eyes to the child's eyes and his mouth to the child's mouth, no doubt to impart his breath to the corpse; after which the child sneezed seven times and opened its eyes. To the Hebrews this derivation of our species from the dust of the ground suggested itself all the more naturally because, in their language, the word for "ground" (*adamah)* is in form the feminine of the word for "man" (*adam*).

> **Hockett and Ascher remind us that our ancestral proto-hominids "were not striving to become human; they were . . . trying to stay alive."**
>
> *PHILIP VAN DOREN STERN*

EXPERIMENTAL MODEL

So there he stands, our vertical, hunting, weapon-toting, territorial, neotenous, brainy, Naked Ape, a primate by ancestry and a carnivore by adoption, ready to conquer the world. But he is a very new and experimental departure, and new models frequently have imperfections. For him the main troubles will stem from the fact that his culturally operated advances will race ahead of any further genetic ones. His genes will lag behind, and he will be constantly reminded that, for all his environment-moulding achievements, he is still at heart a very naked ape.

DESMOND MORRIS
The Naked Ape

Thus, both in language and myth, *ha-adam*, "the Man" (masculine), is created from *ha-adamah*, "the Earth" (feminine). And divine spirit/breath (in Hebrew *ruah* means "spirit," "breath," "wind" and "soul"°) is breathed by Yahweh himself into the Man's nostrils and pumped into his lungs. The Man's body is from the earth, but his spirit/breath is from Yahweh.

°The Greek word pneuma *carries similar meanings. See box on page 495.*

6   The Shilluks of the White Nile

ingeniously explain the different complexions of the various races by the differently coloured clays out of which they were fashioned. They say that the creator Juok moulded all men out of the earth, and that while he was engaged in the work of creation he wandered about the world. In the land of the whites he found a pure white earth or sand, and out of it he shaped white men. Then he came to the land of Egypt and out of the mud of the Nile he made red or brown men. Lastly, he came to the land of the Shilluks, and finding there black earth he created men out of it.

Before man possessed an evolutionary context in which to see himself, he observed that lions produce lions, turtles produce turtles, bluejays produce bluejays—and man produces man. The logic of this was overwhelming. But a piece of the puzzle is obviously missing. There had to be a beginning: something had to create man in his full sapient form so he could stand in his flesh and be half-god, half-clay. And logically the first creator of man had to be like man. Doesn't man produce man?

STILL TRYING TO DEFINE "MAN"

7   An adequate understanding of man must begin—but not end— with man's place in the program of evolution. He belongs to the animal kingdom, but he is something more than an animal.

Defining man so that he knows that he differs from his animal kin has been a bothersome problem. Men have passionately and religiously guarded their lists of distinctions.

Man's origins, it was supposed, could be discerned in the fossil records by his use of fire or weapons; or it was held that only a fully human creature could make or use tools. "Man alone is a toolmaker," wrote early anthropologists.

Special physical characteristics clearly mark man as a superior being. His upright posture allows mobility, agility, and better chances of survival. His larger brain capacity (averaging about 1300 cc, at least double the volume of the closest living primate) implies greater intelligence, as does the weight ratio of the brain to body. His complex nervous system permits subtle operations. Furthermore, he is free from the instincts that so bind the lower animals within predetermined behavioral limits. Man is said to be the only animal with true freedom of choice, perhaps the only creature ever to have lived on our planet that must make agonizing decisions because of that freedom.

Man's greatly expanded "new brain" provides him with the capacity for abstract thought and reason. Greek thinkers pointed out that it is man's faculty for reason—the ability to use known facts to arrive at new facts—that makes him human and gives him a clue to his reason-for-being: to cultivate his rational mind. This faculty alone, they believed, distinguishes man from the animals. Apart from reason, they reasoned, man *is* an animal.

Neglect of an effective birth control policy is a never-failing source of poverty which, in turn, is the parent of revolution and crime.

ARISTOTLE

The nature of man is not what he is born as, but what he is born for.

ARISTOTLE

"The way to do things is neither the way of Heaven nor that of Earth but that of Man."

HSÜN TZU

Along with abstract thought goes self-consciousness, man's power to reflect upon his self, his nature, his knowledge, and the meaning of his existence. Man is surely the only animal that can philosophize.

We must not fall into the error of supposing that the early progenitor of the whole simian stock, including man, was identical with or even closely resembled an existing ape or monkey.

CHARLES DARWIN

8   Three rather more ethereal qualities—man's ethical, esthetic, and religious feelings—are frequently considered to be distinctive features separating man from other animals. Only man, it is held, has a moral sense, feelings of justice and injustice, and only man develops behavioral codes to live by. Only man responds to beauty and creates objects for no other reason than to enjoy them. Only man can conceive a supernatural order of reality, believe in deities, develop a soteriology of history, and feel "ultimate concern" about the meaning of his own existence.

There is an obvious omission from all these lists: *soul*. This singular quality finally distinguishes man from all other animals. Man's soul-essence (Greek *psyche*) survives death, and no other animal is supposed to have a psyche. Considerable debate has taken place as men have tried to decide at what point along the evolutionary line prepsychic man developed (or was given) a soul.

There are 180 billion cells in the human body. Each of these little factories is carrying out hundreds of chemical processes at a speed that astounds the mind.

JOAN AREHART-TREICHEL

9   Recent scientific discoveries have initiated a redefinition of man. The Naked Ape is presently undergoing agonizing reappraisal of himself vis-à-vis the animal world.

> Jane Goodall's discovery that chimps not only use but manufacture tools, significantly changed the scientific definition of man. He could no longer be classified as the only maker of tools. Their achievement is a simple one by human standards, but it elevates them far above all other animals save one. *This one girl has forced the scientists and psychologists of the world to redefine man.* Her chimps have helped remove man from some remote pedestal and return him to the natural world of the animal kingdom. She sees in her chimpanzees basic recognizable emotions and a need to communicate their feelings. Though physically incapable of forming the sounds of human speech, there is an unmistakable natural language that any human being can understand, signs of recognition, affection, and reassurance. . . .
>
> Three generations of chimpanzees are now part of Jane Goodall's life. It took years to do what no one else had done: win their trust and confidence. From her understanding of these animals has come unexpected insight and increased appreciation of mankind. These chimpanzees are a source of growing wonder, a reminder of how far humanity has really come in the evolution of man's intellect and language, his ability to love unselfishly, to appreciate and create beauty. Perhaps the narrowing chasm between man and apes will not be spanned by science alone, but by understanding and compassion.

NATIONAL GEOGRAPHIC—CBS-TV
Monkeys, Apes and Men

THE KILLER-APE DEBATE

10   In the process of redefining man a controversy has arisen. It appears that man's propensity for violence far exceeds any possible evolutionary demands; man's intense cruelty toward members of his own species is unique in the animal kingdom. He kills not merely for food but is vicious for ideological and symbolic reasons: he will kill "on principle." In the name of mental abstractions he kills other men, whereas other animals battle members of their own species only into submission. Together, all man's religious constraints, moral codes, legal systems, and rationality seem barely able, under ideal conditions, to keep his viciousness within bounds.

The question is whether man's aggressive behavior is inherited or learned. Is it possible that man is a killer because he descended directly from a line of "killer-apes"? This is the position held by the zoologists Konrad Lorenz *(On Aggression)* and Desmond Morris *(The Naked Ape),* and the playwright Robert Ardrey *(African Genesis, Territorial Imperative).*

The suggestion has been made by Dr. L. S. B. Leakey and other paleontologists that different branches of African australopithecines pursued different evolutionary paths of development. While some remained peaceful vegetarians, at least one branch became aggressive carnivores; and it is quite possible that it is from this latter line that modern man has developed. Man's killer instinct is set deep in his genes.

Man's trouble, Lorenz believes,

> arises from his being a basically harmless omnivorous creature, lacking in natural weapons with which to kill big prey, and, therefore, also devoid of the built-in safety devices which prevent "professional" carnivores from abusing their killing power to destroy fellow members of their own species. A lion or a wolf may, on extremely rare occasions, kill another by one angry stroke, but . . . all heavily armed carnivores possess sufficiently reliable inhibitions which prevent the self-destruction of the species.

11   It is a curious paradox that the greatest gifts of man, the unique faculties of conceptual thought and verbal speech which have raised him to a level high above all other creatures and given him mastery over the globe, are not altogether blessings, or at least are blessings that have to be paid for very dearly indeed. All the great dangers threatening humanity with extinction are direct consequences of conceptual thought and verbal speech. They drove man out of the paradise in which he could follow his instincts with impunity and do or not do whatever he pleased. There is much truth in the parable of the tree of knowledge and its fruit, though I want to make an addition to it to make it fit into my own picture of Adam: that apple was thoroughly unripe! Knowledge springing from conceptual thought robbed man of the security provided by his well-adapted instincts long, long

Just as we do not know what life is, yet can distinguish between an inanimate object and a living animal or plant, similarly we cannot give a scientific definition of man, yet we have no difficulty in differentiating him from even the most manlike monkey. One of the gross deficiencies of science is that it has not yet defined what sets man apart from other animals.

RENÉ DUBOS

MAN   A biodegradable but nonrecyclable animal blessed with opposable thumbs capable of grasping at straws.

BERNARD ROSENBERG

A self-balancing, 28-jointed adapter-base biped; an electrochemical reduction plant, integral with segregated stowages of special energy extracts in storage batteries for subsequent actuation of thousands of hydraulic and pneumatic pumps with motors attached; 62,000 miles of capillaries. . . . The whole, extraordinary complex mechanism guided with exquisite precision from a turret in which are located telescopic and microscopic self-registering and recording range finders, a spectroscope, etc.; the turret control being closely allied with an air-conditioning intake-and-exhaust, and a main fuel intake. . . .

BUCKMINSTER FULLER

Man is a biped without feathers.

PLATO

Man is the only animal that walks upright and carries a slanted point of view.

ANONYMOUS

Man is the only creature that spends its entire life trying to become what it already is.

ANONYMOUS

Man is the only creature that keeps trying to define himself.

JIM WODACH

Man is star-stuff that has taken over its own destiny.

CARL SAGAN
"Cosmos"

DELL
6266

95c

THE SENSATIONAL WORLDWIDE BESTSELLER BY
DESMOND MORRIS
THE
NAKED
APE

before it was sufficient to provide him with an equally safe adaptation. Man is, as Arnold Gehlen has so truly said, by nature a jeopardized creature.

KONRAD LORENZ

12   The killer-ape notion has brought angry rebuttal from other life-scientists and from psychologists. They all counter that there is no significant evidence that man's aggression is inherited, but there is strong evidence that it is learned. Man's entire range of bitter emotions and cruel behavior can be causally explained by early conditioning within a hostile environment. If cruel and violent actions are "programmed" into us as acceptable forms of behavior, and if we ourselves are treated cruelly and violently so that we store up an explosive reservoir of bitterness, then we have become, in the very core of our being, killer-apes. But all this is learned, and easily learned. We don't have to look far—only as far as the nearest TV set—to discover how acceptable "man's inhumanity to man" can become.

Dr. Ashley Montagu considers the killer-ape theory absurd and takes an opposing stand: any human being's aggressive cruelty results from the frustration of his more basic need to love and be loved. "His combativeness and competitiveness arise primarily from the frustration of his need to cooperate." The most basic drive of human nature—strictly from the standpoint of evolutionary survival—is love and cooperation.

> The organism is born with an innate need for love, with a need to respond to love, to be good, cooperative. This is, I believe, now established beyond any shadow of doubt. Whatever is opposed to love, to goodness, and to cooperation is disharmonic, unviable, unstable, and malfunctional—evil. . . . All of man's natural inclinations are toward the development of goodness, toward the continuance of states of goodness and the discontinuance of unpleasant states. . . . Where hatreds exist in any persons within any society we may be sure that they, too, are due to love, for hatred is love frustrated. Aggression is but a technique or mode of seeking love.

13   The question is perpetually raised: "Is man *inherently* evil or good?" "Is man *genetically* a killer-ape or fallen angel?"

Something is probably wrong with the question. (Most either/or questions generate more problems than they solve.) Surely, man is *inherently* neither good nor bad. Even a cursory observation indicates that man possesses the capacity for cooperation and love as well as the capacity for aggressive and hostile behavior. Which traits develop in an individual and grow to dominate his relationships depends upon the demands of his environment. He develops his stance toward life out of life's stance toward him. It depends, for each individual, on conditioning—on whether, for him, "things go right" or "things go wrong."

A better question might be: How does man differ from his animal kin in his feelings of aggression? Probably in no significant way *except in his complexity*. With man's advanced cerebral cortex and his faculty for abstract thought, he possesses a capacity for infinitely complex responses. He has almost unlimited choice. It is his complex perception of threat and the variety of his responses to it that makes man different.

Contrary to popular belief, man has long since ceased to evolve. . . .

JEAN ROSTAND

"I made this."

In the rest of the animal kingdom, response tends to be simple and direct: flight, fight, or submission. In human beings the basic emotional response patterns are the same, but they are obscured by endless maneuvers of each individual according to his potential for indirect response.

But where there is no threat, man is no more hostile than any of his animal relatives. To those who have lived with animals and trained and loved them, it is clear that when you take away threat, you eliminate violence; but when the environment threatens, violence results. It is more than likely that the same simple principle applies as well to man.

14   What, then, distinguishes man from the other animals? At the present time, we cannot with any certainty point to a single *human* quality which cannot be found, *to some degree*, in other animals.

The deep chasm that separates man from his animal kin reflects differences in degree. No one questions the fact that man possesses mental powers that dramatically outdistance his closest primate kin: logical reason, creative imagination, self-consciousness. It is also a fact, however, that numerous animals possess abilities that far outdistance man: highly developed sensing organs, for instance, and the ability to "intuit" subtle relationships that are missed by man.

It is probably true that every empirically observable characteris-

To regard man, the most ephemeral and rapidly evolving of all species, as the final and unsurpassable achievement of creation, especially at his present-day particularly dangerous and disagreeable stage of development, is certainly the most arrogant and dangerous of all untenable doctrines.

KONRAD LORENZ

374

tic hypothesized to distinguish man from other fauna can be found, in some degree, somewhere in the animal kingdom.

PRIMUS INTER PARES

Man's view of himself has undergone many changes. From a unique position in the universe, the Copernican revolution reduced him to an inhabitant of one of many planets. From a unique position among organisms, the Darwinian revolution assigned him a place among the millions of other species which evolved from one another. Yet, *Homo sapiens* has overcome the limitations of his origin. He controls the vast energies of the atomic nucleus, moves across his planet at speeds barely below escape velocity, and can escape when he so wills. He communicates with his fellows at the speed of light, extends the powers of his brain with those of the digital computer, and influences the numbers and genetic constitution of virtually all other living species. Now he can guide his own evolution. In him, Nature has reached beyond the hard regularities of physical phenomena. *Homo sapiens*, the creation of Nature, has transcended her. From a product of circumstances, he has risen to responsibility. At last, he is Man. May he behave so!

PHILIP HANDLER (ed.)
Biology and the Future of Man

Out of the dreaming past, with its legends of steaming seas and gleaming glaciers, mountains that moved and suns that glared, emerges this creature, man—the latest phase in a continuing process that stretches back to the beginning of life. His is the heritage of all that has lived; he still carries the vestiges of snout and fangs and claws of species long since vanished; he is the ancestor of all that is yet to come.

Do not regard him lightly—he is you.

DON FABUN

THE IMMENSE JOURNEY

15   Science has two functions: control and comprehension. The comprehension may be of the universe in which we live; or of ourselves; or of the relations between ourselves and our world. Evolutionary science has only been in existence, as a special branch of scientific knowledge, for less than a century. During that time its primary contribution has been to comprehension—first to that of the world around us, and then to that of our own nature. The last few decades have added an increasing comprehension of our position in the universe and our relations with it; and with this evolutionary science is certainly destined to make an important and increasing contribution to control; its practical application in the affairs of human life is about to begin. (1952)

SIR JULIAN HUXLEY

Far from seeing in man the irrevocable and unsurpassable image of God, I assert—more modestly and, I believe, in greater awe of the Creation and its infinite possibilities—that the long-sought missing link between animals and the really humane being is ourselves!

KONRAD LORENZ

16   This stage in "the immense journey" has already begun. Man is now in process of taking control of his own evolutionary destiny and, by default, the destiny of all other living creatures on his planet. While man was produced by processes of which he had no understanding and no control, it looks as though he is moving rapidly to a point of

There is no doubt that human survival will continue to depend more and more on human intellect and technology. It is idle to argue whether this is good or bad. The point of no return was passed long ago, before anyone knew it was happening.

THEODOSIUS DOBZHANSKY

no return when there is but one choice left to him: to take on his shoulders the full burden of his future.

Two events have made this inevitable. First, man has made such rapid progress in science/technology that the selective function of the environment has been radically altered. Many detrimental or lethal inheritable characteristics are now being preserved; under natural conditions they would die out. Among such genetic disorders are hemophilia, retinal blastoma, sickle-cell anemia, and susceptibility to a host of physical and emotional dysfunctions. Many of these defects are now being corrected or rendered tolerable through surgery, chemistry, and psychiatry. Carriers of such genes produce offspring, and the defective genes multiply. This has now happened in the case of so many genetic traits that the "fittest" are not the individuals who survive. Natural selectivity is no longer the primary mechanism in evolution.

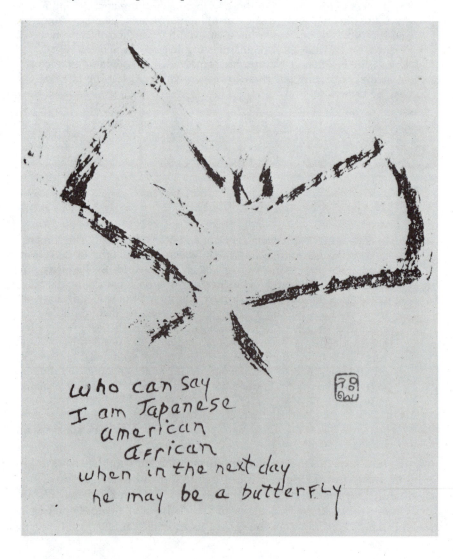

who can say
I am Japanese
american
african
when in the next day
he may be a butterfly

17   The second event forcing man to take over his own evolution is the destruction of his natural environment. Man developed through selective competition with and in a natural environment: *it* produced *him* according to *its* criteria. Man, not the environment, did the adapting. Environment is the creator; man is the creature. The ever-changing ecosystem "decided" which traits this evolving organism would possess.

But this trait-selecting environment no longer exists. Man's scientific/technological applications, along with the proliferation of his species, has altered the environment so much that it has lost the power to select specific adaptive traits. No known forces are presently operating to determine that "fitter" traits survive and weaker traits perish.

Symbolically, the offspring has annihilated the parent that produced it.

18   It is humbling to realize that man is, in this sense, only one part of nature, just as a consideration of the size of the universe makes him realize his own relative smallness. But evolutionary biology has also shown us the central role that man is destined to play in evolution from now on—unless, of course, he engineers his own extinction. Although man arose out of an evolutionary process that he didn't understand and over which he had no control, he must now realize that he is unique in the living world in the realization that the responsibility for continuance of this process is his. . . .

The capacity of biologists to develop ways by which man can determine his future evolution is undoubted. The more difficult question is whether he will choose to make such decisions, *and with what wisdom.*

Biology and the Future of Man

> Man is a rational animal who always loses his temper when he is called upon to act in accordance with the dictates of reason.
>
> *OSCAR WILDE*

> Man differs from the animal only by a little; most men throw that little away.
>
> *CONFUCIUS*

REFLECTIONS—

1 Ponder the drawing by Abner Dean on p. 374: "I made this." Is this an indictment of man for his egocentric needs? Or is it a compliment that man can accomplish something more than hauling heavy loads (in slavish obedience to the "Puritan" work ethic) along the path of life? Or does the drawing say something else entirely?

2 Read for a synoptic overview the various creation stories at the beginning of this chapter. What do they all have in common? What are the major differences? What are the ultimate questions that these creation myths seem designed to explain? (Refer to your glossary for a definition of "myth," if needed.)

3 What is your candid response to the various creation stories? (Remember these are but a few of thousands of such myths.) Do these accounts help to clarify for you the functions of myths?

4 In your opinion, what qualities separate man from the other animals? Make a list of all such separating qualities that you can think of; then

proceed down the list and argue off each characteristic which current evidence shows man may share with one or more of his animal kin. What characteristics do you have left on your list?

5 Make an attempt to define "Man." How would you describe "essential Man"? What are some of the problems we must face in developing a definition?

6 What is your own inclination regarding the aggression debate? Can you develop a strong case that man is genetically aggressive? Can you make an equally strong case that his aggression is learned? Where must you go for hard data to resolve the controversy?

7 How much do you agree or disagree with the sentence in Sec. 13: "Surely, man is *inherently* neither good nor bad. He develops his stance toward life out of life's stance toward him"—? What data can you offer to support your assessment?

8 Our attitudes toward "human nature" are so basic that they shape our politics and economics, our religions, our judgment of history and our stance toward the future, and our relationships with others and ourselves. What is your assessment of human nature? Are you essentially optimistic and trusting or pessimistic and wary? What facts do you possess that would support your general attitudes? (Be careful. Perhaps the question is not phrased right. Maybe there is no such thing as "human nature," in which case how should the question be stated?)

Furthermore . . .

ARDREY, ROBERT, *African Genesis*. Delta, 1961.

BLEIBTREU, JOHN N., *The Parable of the Beast*. Collier, 1969.

DUBOS, RENÉ, *Beast or Angel?: Choices That Make Us Human*. Scribner's, 1974.

EISELEY, LOREN, *The Immense Journey*. Vintage, 1957.

HALACY, D. S., Jr., *Genetic Revolution: Shaping Life for Tomorrow*. Mentor, 1976.

HARDIN, GARRETT, *Nature and Man's Fate*. Mentor, 1961.

HOWELL, F. CLARK, *Early Man*. Life Nature Library. Time Inc., 1965.

LORENZ, KONRAD, *On Aggression*. Bantam, 1967.

MONTAGU, ASHLEY, *On Being Human*. Hawthorn, 1966.

MORRIS, DESMOND, *The Naked Ape*. Dell, 1967.

NANCE, JOHN, *The Gentle Tasaday*. Harcourt, 1977.

TURNBULL, COLIN, *The Mountain People*. Simon & Schuster, 1972.

van LAWICK-GOODALL, JANE, *In the Shadow of Man*. Dell, 1971.

6-3

Earth

Have You Ever Wondered . . .

- Whether men have the right to kill dolphins?

- Whether dolphins have the right to kill men?

- Since all living creatures share equally in living on planet earth, then precisely who has a right to do what to whom and who says so and why?

- Whether plants and trees have rights?

- Why people of different cultures and religions have different attitudes toward animals and plants and what difference it makes?

- Why man kills for pleasure?

- Whether the science-fiction scenarios of a "dead earth" might actually happen?

MAN'S PLACE IN THE SCHEME OF THINGS

And the wind shall say: "Here were decent godless people Their only monument the asphalt road And a thousand lost golf balls."

T. S. ELIOT

1 The idea of Reverence for Life offers itself as the realistic answer to the realistic question of how man and the world are related to each other. Of the world man knows only that everything which exists is, like himself, a manifestation of the Will-to-Live. . . .

Let a man once begin to think about the mystery of his life and the links which connect him with the life that fills the world, and he cannot but bring to bear upon his own life and all other life that comes within his reach the principle of Reverence for Life. . . . Ex-

Stranger by the roadside, do not
smile
When you see this grave, though
it is only a dog's.
My master wept when I died,
and his own hand
Laid me in earth and wrote these
lines on my tomb.

ANONYMOUS
Greek epitaph for a dog

Man has survived, hitherto, by
virtue of ignorance and
inefficiency.

BERTRAND RUSSELL

istence will thereby become harder for him in every respect than it
would be if he lived for himself, but at the same time it will be richer,
more beautiful, and happier. It will become, instead of mere living, a
real experience of life.

ALBERT SCHWEITZER

2   Man has never sought knowledge of his world merely to understand it with his intellect. His driving concern has been his relationship to it and his place in it. All our rational inquiries are merely a
prelude to the establishment of a more meaningful relationship. The
implicit question for man has always been, "What is my place in the
scheme of things?"

Man evolved in a world that is at once friendly and hostile.
With one hand it gives him life, while with the other it inflicts pain
and death. He has always felt like a stranger in a strange land. But he
had to make it his home even while it felt to him like enemy territory.

The story of *general evolution* is an account of how species search
for a suitable niche in their environment. The story of *man's evolution*
is the account of his transcendence of that evolutionary niche. And the
story of *man's civilization* is the account of his gradual conquest and
control of his environment.

3   Man's relationship to his natural environment seems to have
moved through three stages.

Man first experienced nature in a parent-child relationship. Nature produced him; he was its offspring. He was never sure how to
conceptualize the forces that generated life, but he could not doubt
that they were everywhere—in his crops, his herds and flocks, in his
human family. So his myths helped him conceive the inconceivable.
Nature's life-giving forces were, naturally, male and female. The prime
source of life was Mother Earth personified as Magna Mater, or Gaia,
or Demeter—each was in some way the Earth-Mother. (We still habitually think of "her" as Mother Nature, and the very idea of "Father
Nature" *feels* wrong even to us!) There must be masculine forces too,
of course, so there was Jupiter (Dyaus Pitar or Zeus Pater, "Father
Zeus"); and the Semitic tribal gods—Yahweh, Chemosh, Milcom, Allah—are all male figures. Generally the dynamic forces of nature such
as storms, earthquakes, thunder, and lightning were conceived as
masculine in potency; while the more passive aspects of nature—the
quiet earth which absorbs the rain and brings forth new sprouts of
corn—were thought of as feminine potencies.

These personified forces are man's parents. The characteristic
response on man's part in this state is fear and awe, acceptance and
obedience. He has no control over nature's forces; *they* condition *his*
behavior. Like authoritarian parents, they nurture him; but they also
punish him. His dependence is almost absolute. He stands helpless
before the storm, the flood, the drought, the mortal pain. He is a child
who knows nothing of the motives of the forces which rule him. They

cut some humans from their stems
tie them in a bunch
pull a few out
stick them in a vase
look at them

throw
the
rest
away

Human arrangement
by Flowers

We have come [to the oceans] as aliens from another world. . . . The time has come to recognize that the sea and the creatures in it have their needs and their rights to exist. An ocean ethic is needed which will combine wisdom, sensitivity, and forethought; an ethic which will not betray the dream which began our long, deep journey.

Mysteries of the Sea

possess secrets he cannot understand. Yet he does his best to relate to them and please them, to discover the ''desires'' of these personified forces and accede to their wills. Thus, he makes every attempt—as he would with human parents—to keep them as favorably inclined as he can.

You can always tell when it's autumn in Hollywood. They put away the green plastic plants and bring out the brown plastic plants.

JOHNNY CARSON

4   The second stage—man as conqueror—is found in a rudimentary way in all man's cultures, but its successful development belongs to the West. It began with the discovery by Pythagoras of nature's greatest secret: that she speaks the language of mathematics. Foundations were thus laid for scientific control, but time dallied for two more millennia before this knowledge was used. Physics and mechanics were finally born in the seventeenth century, followed shortly by chemistry and biology and, belatedly, by the social and behavioral sciences. Communication and transportation technologies belong to our own century. Controls have now spread to almost every area of human experience. Lagging behind, of course, is control of man himself, but this appears to be the arena wherein the next giant steps will be taken.

A weed is a plant whose virtues have not yet been discovered.

EMERSON

This rapid conquest and control of our dynamic environment is sapient man's greatest success story, and it is basically a story of a

---

THE EARTH IS SORE

The white people never cared for land or deer or bear. When we Indians kill meat, we eat it all up. When we dig roots we make little holes. When we build houses, we make little holes. When we burn grass for grasshoppers, we don't ruin things. We shake down acorns and pinenuts. We don't chop down the trees. We only use dead wood. But the White people plow up the ground, pull down the trees, kill everything. The tree says, "Don't. I am sore. Don't hurt me." But they chop it down and cut it up. The spirit of the land hates them. They blast out trees and stir it up to its depths. They saw up the trees. That hurts them. The Indians never hurt anything, but the White people destroy all. They blast rocks and scatter them on the ground. The rock says, "Don't. You are hurting me." But the White people pay no attention. When the Indians use rocks, they take little round ones for their cooking. . . . How can the spirit of the earth like the White man? . . . Everywhere the White man has touched it, it is sore.

(The words of an old holy woman of the Wintu Indians of California.)

DOROTHY LEE
Freedom and Culture

---

love/hate relationship. Man has loved his earth; it nourished him. But he has also hated it for its relentless attempt to annihilate him. It was a life/death struggle between man and nature; and as in any love/hate relationship, the question has been *which* would win out: love or hate. *Who* would win: Man or Nature?

Man has won—or is winning. Man is on the threshold of setting controls over ever-larger forces of nature—climate and earthquakes, for instance. The control of life and evolution is near. There are repeated hints in futuristic literature that man may eventually establish control on a cosmological scale. We might alter the orbit or the tilt of the earth, for example, or capture small asteroids to serve as scientific stations or to provide transportation to remote outposts. Such comprehensive controlling power would be merely a large-scale extension of man's present capacities, and we are moving rapidly in this direction. On the condition that man doesn't destroy himself first, such controls are probably inevitable.

5   A third stage, beginning in our time, is a protective feeling toward nature. If man no longer fears nature because he understands her ways, and if he has established control over the more threatening elements of his environment, then fear can give way to other feelings: kinship, appreciation, protection. Man will become nature's advocate; then—if he is a wise landlord—he might justly be called Lord of the

If our numbers continue to increase at the present frightening rate, it will eventually become a matter of choosing between us and them [other animal species]. No matter how valuable they are to us symbolically, scientifically or aesthetically, the economics of the situation will shift against them. The blunt fact is that when our own species density reaches a certain pitch, there will be no space left for other animals.

DESMOND MORRIS

Earth. Man is only beginning to feel a new awareness of an environment from which, until now, he has had to wrest a living in frustration and pain.

This has been the Western experience. Other branches of the human story exhibit different responses toward nature. Western man's achievements bring mixed feelings, of course. We wonder whether his compassionate concerns have surfaced in time to salvage his spaceship. It is Western man's problem not merely because it is his controls that have caused our environmental problems; it is probably the case that only Western man has the techniques for solving the problems he has created.

AN ECOSPHERIC ETHIC

6   Through a continuing process of self-discovery, man has had to reassess his place "in the scheme of things" and learn how to behave responsibly within his newly perceived relationships. Having discovered that he exists as part-and-parcel of all Earth's living things, the vital question has become: *Who has a right to do what to whom and why?*

Ecology, therefore, is not only a scientific discipline, but more basically it is a matter of ethics. How should man relate to other fauna and flora with whom he shares a planet? How should he treat the ecosphere, including the earth, oceans, and atmosphere? Is man the only creature with "rights" or do animals also have "rights"? Do trees have "rights"? Does man have a "right" to kill any animal—harmless wild animals, predators, dogs and cats and other "pets"? Does man have a "right" to kill only "food" animals? or only "dangerous" animals? Does man have a "right" to kill gorillas? or dolphins? Do lions have a "right" to kill and eat zebras and antelope? Do dolphins have a "right" to kill men? Etcetera. . . .

In a word, on what criteria can all these questions be given factually sound answers? And, as a final question, "Who says so?"

Since man has now dominated his planet, ethical responsibilities rest on his shoulders. But even then the question persists: Who (or what) gives man the right to make these life-or-death decisions?

7   Professor George Sessions, an ecophilosopher, has given an excellent description of our ecological plight and analyzed some of the ethical puzzlements inherent in it. He reminds us that we are in ecological trouble because of the traditional Western world-views we have inherited. "Ethical beliefs and attitudes do not exist in a vacuum." How we treat other creatures that share our world is dictated to us by the cosmology within which "we live and move and have our being." "When these cosmologies are no longer viable or believable, the entire ethical system or attitude becomes irrelevant and inappropriate." This has now happened to us. Sessions writes:

> In contrast with the earliest animisms and pantheisms of the West, and the pre-industrial nature orientations of the East, a perva-

In wildness is the preservation of the world.

THOREAU
Sunday Morning (CBS-TV)

In my opinion, the greatest scandal of philosophy is that, while all around us the world of nature perishes—and not the world of nature alone—philosophers continue to talk, sometimes cleverly and sometimes not, about the question of whether this world exists.

KARL POPPER

sive cultural feature of the more recent West has been its anthropocentric cosmologies together with a correspondingly anthropocentric ethical orientation. From the Judeo-Christian account of man's separation from, and transcendence over, Nature, and the rise of man-centered philosophical systems and ethics in classical Greece, to the Cartesian mind-body dualism which became the cornerstone of early modern European philosophy, these essentially dualistic views of man and nature have provided the metaphysical basis for an outlook which sees *Homo sapiens* as the exclusive focus of ethical interest and concern.

The science of ecology is only the most recent and perhaps the most dramatic and subversive manifestation of the impact of modern science upon Western man's largely distorted sense of self-importance in the cosmos.

GEORGE SESSIONS

By 1960 the dark clouds hovering over Earth's delicate ecology had become obvious to field specialists, but the threat hadn't yet been seen by other specialists or by political/industrial agents who could initiate change. They were still caught up in other concerns. Marston Bates, an ecologist, scolded philosophers for "dallying in their academic groves" at the very moment when a new ethical perspective was desperately needed.

The appearance of Rachel Carson's attack on the indiscriminate use of pesticides (*Silent Spring*, 1962) and then Paul Ehrlich's *The Population Bomb* (1968) "marked the beginning of the end of an era of almost total ecological naiveté in the modern Western world. Belief in the omnipotence and omnicompetence of man through his scientific technology received a tremendous jolt from a wholly new quarter. It was now evident that Nature was not totally manipulable for the 'good' of human societies, nor was it 'meant' to be."

Another fundamental error [is] . . . the unnatural distinction Christianity makes between man and the animal world to which he really belongs. It sets up man as all-important, and looks upon animals as merely things. . . . Christianity contains in fact a great and essential imperfection in limiting its precepts to man, and in refusing rights to the entire animal world.

SCHOPENHAUER

8   There was another turning-point in our ecological awareness, according to Sessions: the publication of an article by Lynn White dealing with the religious roots of the developing crisis.

> White's message was quite simple: Christian anthropocentrism was the root cause of the environmental crisis. The paper was reprinted in innumerable ecological anthologies which were just beginning to flood the book market. Controversies raged. Conscience-stricken Christian theologians, preachers, and scientists denounced his views, or reexamined their religious beliefs and attitudes. Conferences with titles such as the "theology of survival" were hurriedly called. By one stroke White subsequently claimed (with justification) to have created "the theology of ecology."
>
> White pointed to the drastic attitudinal change towards Nature which occurred when Christianity replaced ancient forms of pantheism and animism, calling it "the greatest psychic revolution in the history of our culture." An animistic metaphysics, which saw spirit in nature, resulted in attitudes of respect and veneration for natural objects and thus helped protect Nature from man's unthinking exploitation. Christianity's desacralization of Western man's world encouraged an attitude of "indifference to the feelings of natural objects."

In a typical ocean food-chain, tuna eats mackerel, mackerel eats smelt, smelt eats copepods, and copepods eat diatoms. "Or, stated in the reverse, 10,000 lb. of diatoms will make 1,000 lb. of copepods; 1,000 lb. of copepods will make 100 lb. of smelt; 100 lb. of smelt will make 10 lb. of mackerel; 10 lb. of mackerel will make 1 lb. of tuna; 1 lb. of tuna will make 0.1 lb. of man. It takes 10 lb. of food to make 1 lb. of the animal that feeds upon it. . . ."

MAC GINITIE AND MAC GINITIE

In order to restore some bit of intrinsic value to nature, White suggested that the modern world might be well advised to return to the medieval world-view of Saint Francis of Assisi whose "view of nature and man rested on a unique sort of pan-psychism of all things animate and inanimate, designed for the glorification of their transcendent Creator." All things are revered by God and therefore they should also be revered by man. "Francis tried to depose man from his monarchy over creation and set up a democracy of all God's creatures."

Sessions considers the Franciscan world-view to be an ethical improvement upon both of the traditional Judeo-Christian models of the man-nature relationship: the exploitation model and the stewardship model.

> But a closer look at the Franciscan ethic reveals that it contains difficulties which stem from an ecologically naive view of the world. For on this view, each individual entity (whether man, chipmunk, or rock) is apparently envisioned to be of equal worth "in the sight of God." It provides no basis for an adjudication of the conflicts which inevitably arise—for example, who or what has a "right" to eat whom, and upon what basis this is to be decided. Predation is an inevitable fact of biological life. If all individuals are to be accorded equal worth, the problem of predation is left unsolved (for humans: other animals appear to be largely unencumbered with these kinds of "problems").
>
> Furthermore, it is not made clear how rocks and the "less articulate" forms of life are to participate, either directly or indirectly, in the universal democratic process.
>
> But most seriously, this solution misleadingly focuses attention on the "rights" of individual entities (a distinctively Western humanistic preoccupation), thus obscuring the crucial ecological point that the environmental crisis is not primarily the result of a threat to the continued existence of *individual entities* as such, but to the *species diversity* so essential to the continued viable functioning of the earth's fragile *ecosystems*. In a very fundamental sense, the unit of ecological meaningfulness is the entire functioning interdependent ecosystem—or more generally, the ecosphere.

9   Other recent attempts have been made by philosophers and theologians to establish criteria for solving the ethical problem of "who may eat whom."

Professor Charles Hartshorne tackles the problem of the relative value of the inhabitants of our ecosphere by picturing a God who looks upon all his creation with "impartial delight." Hartshorne contends that "the ultimate value of human life, or of anything else, consists *entirely* in the contribution it makes to the divine life." Since God created all that exists, then everything is of some value to "the divine life"; but since God is essentially rational, then the more rational the creature is, the more valued it would be in God's eyes. The relative value of organisms and species is therefore established. Creatures that are very low on the sentient-rational scale are also very low in value; man is of greatest value because he is highest on the sentient-rational scale. Nothing possesses intrinsic value, according to Hartshorne; something gains the quality of value only because God values it.

A contemporary theologian, Professor John Cobb, has at-

> The more difficult and complex the undertaking, the more likely it is that knowledge will be gained that can be applied more fruitfully far beyond the undertaking itself.
>
> *NORMAN COUSINS*

> [Lamarck] formulated a number of very modern ideas: that you cannot attribute to any creature psychological capacities for which it has no organs: that mental processes must always have physical representation; and that the complexity of a nervous system is related to the complexity of mind.
>
> *GREGORY BATESON*

> Pythagoras and Empedocles . . . assert that there is a single status of justice belonging to all living creatures. . . . that everlasting punishment awaits those who have wronged anything that lives.
>
> *CICERO*

tempted to establish *intrinsic* criteria by which various creatures in the ecosphere could be judged to be of relative value. Cobb suggests that "experiential states"—such as sensitivity, capacities for pleasure, abstract reasoning, and creativity—establish such a hierarchy of worth. Used with caution—since we aren't yet certain about the "experimential states" of all Earth's creatures—man appears to be at the top of the scale. On such a quality-of-experience scale, those creatures at the top of the ladder would possess "rights" over the life and destiny of those creatures lower on the scale.

This analysis by Dr. Cobb seems to reflect with some accuracy the actual state of things in nature. Still it may be risky to elevate evolution's apparent hierarchy into a normative ethical system and conclude this is the way the value-system *ought* to be. Cobb acknowledges the anthropocentric nature of the scale but suggests that this is inescapable since, after all, we humans are the ones engaged in the task of trying to make sense of the whole ecological/ethical problem.

Attempts such as these to establish a hierarchy for "the world of an individual or species" has drawn angry criticism from some eco-philosophers. Stuart Hampshire, for instance, believes all attempts to discern *intrinsic* qualities are off the mark because such attempts will always be designed to fulfill our own aristocentric needs. Such scales of value implicitly say that the creatures of earth are to be cherished to the degree they are most like humans and can minister to our needs. This utilitarian viewpoint, Hampshire writes, "places men at the very center of the universe, with their states of feeling as the source of value in the world." Then he asks a difficult question: "Is the destruction, for instance, of a species of animal to be avoided, as a great evil, only or principally because of the loss of pleasure that human beings may derive from the species? May the natural order be farmed by human beings for their comfort and pleasure without any restriction other than the comfort and pleasure of future human beings?"

10   George Sessions writes:

> An ecological world-view has been unbelievably slow to dawn on modern Western man. Such a view of man and Nature has been intuitively obvious to ancient cultures, but modern Western man, even with all of his recent scientific sophistication, still seems to resist the full implications of the Copernican and Darwinian revolutions and an ecological view of man as continuous with, and fully dependent upon, the rest of Nature.
>
> It is difficult to envision an adequate, or metaphysically appropriate, environmental ethics which does not *begin* by taking the *natural system* as ethically ultimate.
>
> But "conventional wisdom" continues to view science primarily as a means of gaining control over a "hostile and alien" Nature. Nature is seen as a backdrop for society's ever-expanding ecologically suicidal way of life.
>
> The attempt to "mine" Nature in order to satisfy apparently insatiable desires for material goods has objective limits—natural limits set by the delicate homeostatic equilibriums of ecosystem functioning.

When I'm near that animal, I know I'm in the presence of an intelligence. Namu, I wish I could understand your language, and your mind. I don't know, maybe one day we'll find a way. Maybe . . . maybe it'll be something more direct than words, maybe something as simple as touch—language of mutual trust.

Namu, the Killer Whale
NBC-TV

If we spoke a different language, we would perceive a somewhat different world.

WITTGENSTEIN

What is to be feared is that we have already surpassed these limits in some cases with future consequences we can only begin to guess.

11   Those who feel deeply about Spaceship Earth with all its sentient creatures are fortunate to have had a champion whose stature approaches that of a patron saint: Aldo Leopold, a forester who loved all forms of living things, cared for them, and—incredibly—foresaw the ecological consequences of our callous unconcern for the world we live in. His testament—"a powerful plea for a land ethic"—was published posthumously after his death in 1948.

In *A Sand County Almanac* Leopold pointed out that no viable ecospheric ethic could work "without love, respect, and admiration for the land, and a high regard for its value." Then he added, lest he be misunderstood, "I mean value in the philosophical sense." For an ethic, he wrote, is "a process in ecological evolution."

> An ethic, ecologically, is a limitation on freedom of action in the struggle for existence. An ethic, philosophically, is a differentiation of social from anti-social conduct. These are two definitions of one thing. The thing has its origin in the tendency of interdependent individuals or groups to evolve modes of co-operation. The ecologist calls these symbioses. Politics and economics are advanced symbioses in which the original free-for-all competition has been replaced, in part, by co-operation mechanisms with an ethical content. . . .

There is as yet no ethic dealing with man's relation to land and to the animals and plants which grow upon it. . . . The land-relation is still strictly economic, entailing privileges but not obligations.

All ethics so far evolved rest upon a single premise: that the individual is a member of a community of interdependent parts. . . . The land ethic simply enlarges the boundaries of the community to include soils, waters, plants, and animals, or collectively: the land. . . . In short, a land ethic changes the role of *Homo sapiens* from conqueror of the land-community to plain member and citizen of it.

COEXISTENCE—IN LIFE AND DEATH

12   Man used to regard himself as somehow apart from the animals and plants, following a set of rules that were different from those followed by the rest of nature. Then the study of comparative anatomy made him realize that he is similar in many structural ways to the other animals. The study of physiology showed similar mechanisms of blood circulation, of muscle contraction, of digestion, and of other body functions. Comparative biochemistry demonstrated the basic similarity of chemical mechanisms, reaction sequences, and metabolic patterns in all living organisms. The study of evolution revealed that all these similarities were the consequences of a common origin.

The interrelatedness of all life is now regarded as a part of the beauty and excitement of nature.

Biology and the Future of Man

Man will not merely survive—he will prevail.

WILLIAM FAULKNER

In sober truth, nearly all the things which men are hanged or imprisoned for doing to one another are nature's everyday performances. . . . All human action whatever consists in altering, and all useful action in improving, the spontaneous course of nature.

JOHN STUART MILL (1884)

In human history, we have learned (I hope) that the conqueror role is eventually self-defeating. Why? Because it is implicit in such a role that the conqueror knows, *ex cathedra,* just what makes the community clock tick, and just what and who is valuable, and what and who is worthless, in community life. It always turns out that he knows neither.

ALDO LEOPOLD (1948)

13   Man has had deep, ambivalent feelings about his kinship with the other animals. He has grudgingly accepted coexistence with them.

On the one hand, man is aware of striking similarities. Skeletal systems are structurally similar, even down to single bone-shapes. The flesh that we carry is too much alike, and when cut we bleed red whether we be bird, beast, or man. Facial configurations are alike and sometimes appear like parodies on one another. We look into the eyes of animals and feel that we recognize. We know their inner worlds in the same way we know the inner worlds of other men. We empathize with their behavior, from the pain of a wounded deer to the playfulness of bear cubs and sea otters. We identify with the hunting instinct of a mother lioness as well as the fear-flight of the hunted antelope. We feel guilt when we have hurt an animal, just as we do if we have hurt another human being. All this gives us a queasy feeling. We do what we can to suppress it, yet the feeling of kinship remains.

It is precisely because the kinship was so obvious that we have protested so loudly that there is no kinship. Man resents it, feeling that he is endowed with vastly superior qualities which make him unique and special. As evolutionary man advanced he has felt the distance increasing between himself and the other animals.

So, our kinship with animals has been an uncomfortable one. On the one hand we intuit the kinship and confess our commonality; on the other, we deny it vehemently and demean the animal world.

14   An awareness is just dawning in our brains of the *physical*/ecological relationships with the animals of our planet, but the *psychological*/ecological relationships are probably of equal importance, though to date they have been but little explored.

From the standpoint of other animals, man is a killer to be feared. Early in his hominid evolution man learned to use weapons to kill for food. Although he is basically omnivorous, his appetites place him in a class with other killer-carnivores. But man has one behavioral pattern rarely found in the animal world: he kills for pleasure—for "sport"—even when his stomach is full. For this reason the animals of the world are realistic in their fear-response to man. This combination of pleasure-killing and advanced killing technique renders man extremely dangerous.

But all this goes without saying; today we are all aware of it. But the question persists as to *why* man kills *for pleasure*. What is meant by "pleasure" in this context? How can one experience pleasure from the act of killing something? It's a question that needs an answer, and no trite appeal to "sportsmanship" or "stalking instinct" is quite sufficient.

Man kills because there is something ultimate in what he is doing. When man kills he has in his hands the essence of life and death. Much of man's killing is done to affirm his own existence; it is a confirmation of his own still-being-alive. Man is the only animal that can reflect upon his own life *and death*; he alone can philosophize

---

Mental health and the ultimate happiness of man consists in his active striving to understand his place in Nature through a scientific understanding of the interrelatedness of all aspects of the Universe.

GEORGE SESSIONS

Don't take man too seriously, even when orienting him among the animals and plants on this local planet; and certainly not when comparing him with possibilities elsewhere in the richly endowed Metagalaxy.

HARLOW SHAPLEY

Short then is the time which every man lives, and small the nook of the earth where he lives. . . .

MARCUS AURELIUS
Things Written to Himself

about it, question its meaning, and fear it ahead of time. Life and death are both mysteries, but while we have life it is death that haunts our living.

When one holds in his hand a pheasant, or kneels beside a bear or antelope, each of which, a few moments before, shared the impulse-to-live which is the essence of existence, he can feel for a moment that he has conquered life and in so doing has also conquered death. At that moment one becomes God: although he didn't give life, he has been able to take it away—as though "it" existed as an item of personal property—like a cherished memento or trinket—which the creature "owned." Indeed, to hold a dead animal *from which* one has taken life is to *possess* life. Primitive men often believed that they could accumulate more life by collecting life from those creatures they killed. Perhaps some of this feeling lingers in us; for by contrast, as a hunter stands holding a no-longer-living animal, he often uses the phrase that he "feels alive."

15   Not too long ago, human sacrifice was practiced in most of man's religions, great and small. Sometimes members of other tribes, especially captured warriors, were sacrificed ritually to the god of the conquering tribe. Often this was a contractual obligation: the deity had helped them win in battle, so they offered a gift in return. Many tribes, however, sacrificed their own members. Instances of ritual killing are the Babylonian sacrifice of a surrogate king; the Canaanite primitial sacrifice of one's firstborn by bloodletting or "passing through fire"; the Egyptian, Assyrian, and Chinese practice of killing scores of attendants to serve the spirits of their royal masters in the next life. Abraham's near-sacrifice of his son Isaac presupposes the existence of the institution of ritual sacrifice. In one form or another, human sacrifice has been practiced in almost every ancient culture known to man.

At some point, however, sensitivity to suffering deepens, and ways are devised to avoid human sacrifice. Historically, the story of the sacrifice of Isaac by Abraham was understood by ancient Hebrews to be the origin of the ransom system. Make no mistake, one's firstborn belonged to the god Yahweh, but henceforth he could be "ransomed" with an ox, a ram, or perhaps a pair of doves. Similar animal substitutes are found elsewhere.

Eventually, in almost every tradition, ritual killing comes to an end, accompanied by appropriate theological rationale. In the Christian tradition, the sacrifice of God's only son was interpreted to be the final, complete sacrifice which replaced the Judaic sacrificial system; and the sacrifice of God's only son—which is parallel to the sacrifice of Abraham's only son—recurs eternally in the "Sacrifice of the Mass." In other religions, live sacrifices were replaced by figurines which were ritually broken, or by wood or paper substitutes bearing names which were buried or burned.

Few places in the world today still witness bloody sacrifices carried on for religious reasons.

Our climb to the top has been a get-rich-quick story, and, like all *nouveaux riches,* we are very sensitive about our background.

DESMOND MORRIS

Of the domestic animals man has attempted to corrupt with his bribes for affection and his anthropomorphic entreaties, the cat retains its magnificent autonomy. In the presence of such authenticity our façades become transparent. The cat *assumes* a peer relationship. If you do not, the problem's yours.

BARBARA CHRISTIAN

It was quite incomprehensible to me—this was before I began going to school—why in my evening prayers I should pray for human beings only. So when my mother had prayed with me and had kissed me good night, I used to add silently a prayer that I had composed myself for all living creatures. It ran thus: "O, heavenly Father, protect and bless all things that have breath; guard them from all evil, and let them sleep in peace."

ALBERT SCHWEITZER

Slowly in our European thought comes the notion that ethics has not only to do with mankind but with the animal creation as well. This begins with St. Francis of Assisi. The explanation which applies only to man must be given up. Thus we shall arrive at saying that ethics is reverence for *all* life.

ALBERT SCHWEITZER

16 Ordinary ethics seeks to find limits within the sphere of human life and relationships. But the absolute ethics of the will-to-live must reverence every form of life, seeking so far as possible to refrain from destroying any life, regardless of its particular type. It says of no instance of life, "This has no value." It cannot make any such exceptions, for it is built upon reverence for life as such. It knows that the mystery of life is always too profound for us, and that its value is beyond our capacity to estimate. . . . True, in practice we are forced to choose. At times we have to decide arbitrarily which forms of life, and even which particular individuals, we shall save, and which we shall destroy. But the principle of reverence for life is none the less universal.

ALBERT SCHWEITZER

17 Dostoevsky's psychology rests on a fundamental belief in the deep, ineradicable humanity of men. A logical, officially sanctioned decision to spill blood is reversible and remedial, if deep in a person's heart there is still a small spark of compassion. Sometimes a man is driven to things; he finds that he has to be inflexible. But it is important that he should keep the feeling that the circumstances that forced him to cruelty are themselves unnatural.

Permission to kill with the approval of one's conscience destroys the humanity of man.

PAVEL SIMONOV

18 One of the most interesting things we humans do is to anthropomorphize all our animal kin, and we did this long before Walt Disney institutionalized the technique. We project our human qualities into the lives of nonhuman creatures; we think of them as though they have the same experiences we do. We endow them with our fears, angers, jealousies. In animated cartoons every animal we know—from mice to roadrunners, from dumb dogs to stammering pigs and elephants with outsized ears—feels human feelings.

We anthropomorphize (the word means "to make into human form," from the Greek *anthropos*, "man," and *morphos*, "form") for at least two reasons. (1) We can't help it. Since we experience only human experiences, it is inevitable that we would project our experience onto other creatures. (2) We want other creatures to be like us. The more humanoid they are the better we feel about them and can relate to them.

Look at the matter in another way: How could we *not* project our experiences into our fellow creatures? If we look into the eyes of a baby seal or hear the cry of a dog in pain—even though we can't know for sure what the animal is experiencing—it's difficult not to respond as though the animals feel what we would be feeling were we in their place. We empathize through our own experience to theirs, and in fact it may be that our intuition here is closer to the truth than our solipsistic skepticism.

"NO MAN IS AN ILAND"

19   Man has always been a part—but only a part—of the evolutionary/ecological system. Man may soon be the controller of all our planet's life and the determiner of its destiny, but what he will control will be a complex system of interrelationships, and man will remain a part of the system.

It is easy for one to feel lonely in the midst of a crowd; it is easy to feel alienated in a world to which one is deeply related. We may never realize the existence of the multitudinous tie-lines that connect us to the world we live in.

"No man is an Iland, intire of itself," wrote John Donne. Each man is a part of the whole. He is subject to the same physical forces that move the atoms and the planets. He is composed of the same five-score elements that make up the seas and rocks, trees and stars. He is subject to the same protoplasmic processes found throughout the animal kingdom. The same neural events explode in all our brains and our physical being is determined by a DNA code system identical to that which guides the replication of all animals and plants. Most profoundly, we share the will-to-live with every living creature.

We are part of an awesome protoplasmic venture.

Reverence for life, therefore, is applied to natural life and spiritual life alike. In the parable of Jesus, the shepherd saves not merely the soul of the lost sheep but the whole animal.

ALBERT SCHWEITZER

Death also provides a challenge and a test, particularly to men who must prove to themselves that they can face death and not run or flinch—the essence of bravery. Perhaps a person feels that he must conquer death through flaunting it, or at least through looking straight into its hollow eye sockets before he can feel man enough to live.

THEODORE LIDZ

REFLECTIONS—

1 What are your thoughts on our recent recognition that man is a part of the whole evolutionary/protoplasmic venture, and that, in a sense, man can claim "to be one" with plants, animals, and perhaps larger processes? Do you have a philosophic response to this concept?

2 See Sec. 13: Do you agree that we humans harbor a deep ambivalence about our kinship with other animals, perhaps because we feel that close tie and fear it?

3 Sec. 18 contains an important realization—that we anthropomorphize our animal kin. What does it mean to say that we "anthropomorphize" other beings? Why do we engage in anthropomorphic imaging since, after all, it involves a fallacy?

4 The question persists as to why man kills for pleasure. What would be your answer to this "strange and dangerous quality" which *Homo sapiens* appears to possess? What do you think is meant by "pleasure" in this context? Is there a better name for it?

5 This chapter suggests (pp. 388f) that much of man's killing is done to affirm his own existence; it is a confirmation of his still-being-alive. Do you agree? How would you put it?

6 Read the pungent description of Dostoevsky's psychology by Pavel Simonov (Sec. 17). Listen carefully to his meaning, then decide whether you agree with it.

7 Think about Schweitzer's Reverence for Life—a concept which he believed to be "the realistic answer to the realistic question of how man and the

world are related to each other" (Sec. 1). How do you feel about this all-inclusive ethic?

Furthermore . . .

FARB, PETER, et al., *Ecology*. Life Nature Library. Time Inc., 1969.

FORSTNER, L.J., and J.H. TODD (eds.), *The Everlasting Universe*. Heath, 1971.

FULLER, BUCKMINSTER, *Operating Manual for Spaceship Earth*. Pocket Books, 1970.

LEOPOLD, ALDO, *A Sand County Almanac*. Sierra Club/Ballantine, 1970.

LIVINGSTON, JOHN, *One Cosmic Instant*. Houghton-Mifflin, 1973.

PASSMORE, JOHN, *Man's Responsibility for Nature*. Scribner's, 1974.

SCOTT, JOHN PAUL, *Animal Behavior*. Anchor, 1963.

SINGER, PETER, and TOM REGAN (eds.), *Animal Rights and Human Obligations*. Prentice-Hall, 1976.

STEINBECK, JOHN, *The Log of the Sea of Cortez*. Viking, 1962.

STONE, CHRISTOPHER, *Should Trees Have Standing?* W. Kaufmann, 1974.

Future

- Whether the future "exists"?

- What the earth and the human race will be like in, say, 500 years? ten thousand years? a million years?

- Whether World War III will take place? or World War IV? or VII? or XVIII? or XLIV?

- Whether the human race will succeed in annihilating itself?

- Whether we will achieve permanent peace between nations?

- Whether the human races will become one race?

- Whether the future will see—
space colonies? floating cities? underground cities? a world government? creatures designed on drawing boards? people birthed from jars? communication with aliens from distant planets? travel between the stars? cloning of human beings? the eradication of all disease? the annihilation of death?

THE THEORETICAL LIFE

It's a poor sort of memory that only works backward.

LEWIS CARROLL
Through the Looking-Glass

1   Plato once made the distinction between the practical life *(praktikos bios)* and the theoretical life *(theoretikos bios)*, but he was not saying at all what modern usage of these terms might lead us to think.

By the practical life Plato meant a life that is lived in terms of short-range goals, while the theoretical life is lived in terms of long-range goals. The theoretical life is in every way as "practical" (in the modern sense) as the platonic practical life, but it is planned and guided in terms of our deeper and more ultimate requirements rather than in terms of the immediate and often too-pressing needs and desires of today. The theoretical life is to be planned so that the future will be fulfilling when its time comes.

It was the task of philosophers, Plato believed, to think further ahead in order to envision realistically the distant problems and goals which are as inevitable as tomorrow and which, in our prevision of them, determine profoundly the quality of the life we live today.

Is it a puerile truism or a refreshened insight to be reminded that the future will arrive—for us, for our children, for their children? Few of us would disagree with the notion that a life lived exclusively in terms of the next twenty-four hours would leave each of us in a pickle the following day. Wisely, therefore, we plan ahead—for hours, days, months (vaguely), and years (more vaguely). But we do plan. Only a fool would not plan for the good life, providing future-planning is a viable possibility.

Plato's point is that the better we envision wise and fulfilling futures for ourselves and our children, the better the chance of our dreams becoming realities. This same point is now being made by contemporary future-thinkers, including the veteran futurist Fred Polak: "In the act of searching out the road into the future, man crosses the frontiers of the unknown and raises homo sapiens to a new level: the level of foresight and purposefulness. . . . In taking thought for tomorrow, man begins to create tomorrow."

2   Our histories are created for us by historians. Past events are resurrected from the record of past presents, selected because of their meaning and value, and summarized for us in history books. We can then see ourselves in the long perspective of our past.

Creation of our past is but one side of the story: our futures can be created in similar fashion. "Humans are time travelers, who chart their courses through time with maps of the future," writes Robert Bundy. Without the creation of our futures we can't know where we are going. We need to perceive ourselves in the light of optional futures fully as much as we need to know our pasts.

Heretofore, our futures have been created by our religions, by visionaries, utopians and anti-utopians, and by science-fiction writers. Only recently has futurism come into its own.

RESEARCH INTO THE FUTURE

3   Until a few years ago "research into the future" was not a thinkable thought. Conceptually its time had not yet arrived. Of course, this did not prevent human imagination from giving substance to our futures. Dreaming has always been a part of being human.

> Anyone who wishes to cope with the future should travel back in imagination a single lifetime—say to 1900—and ask himself just how much of today's technology would be, not merely incredible, but *incomprehensible* to the keenest scientific brains of that time.
>
> ARTHUR C. CLARKE

> The world's biggest problems today are really infinitesimal: the atom, the ovum, and a bit of pigment.
>
> HERB CAEN

B.C. by Johnny Hart

Man cannot live without hope, or face an empty future. Man's great religions all envision a future time when the tragedy of earthly history will be replaced by, or be consummated in, a Reign of God, a Messianic Age, a Golden Age, a New Jerusalem. A blank future is intolerable. Even a frightening future is preferable to nothingness.

"We create our literary myths, legends, and epics of the future, not so that we will find our golden age, but because in the creation of utopian standards, we have created forms which make present action possible" (Hugh Duncan). The Garden of Eden in Western doctrine remains the archetype of the perfect human condition to which we will return . . . someday.

Another kind of inhabitable fantasy-world has entered the scene: literary utopias. Among them are Plato's *Republic*, Thomas More's *Utopia* (More coined the word from two Greek words, *ou-topos*, meaning "no-where"), Voltaire's *Candide*, Campanella's *City of the Sun*, and H. G. Wells' *Modern Utopia*. These utopias were motivated in part by the perception of this world as essentially uninhabitable by sensitive spirits. If Racine is right that life is a comedy for the thinker, but a tragedy for one who feels, then utopias are attempts on the part of some sensitive thinkers to create in their minds, if not in this world, a place where life would be worth living.

In recent decades anti-utopias have largely replaced the utopias in our consciousness: Huxley's *Brave New World*, Orwell's *1984*, Bradbury's *Fahrenheit 451*, Ayn Rand's *Anthem*. These visions fell upon us with a shattering impact. Their shrill warning was heard by many because they warned of the totalitarian dangers. Much of their success was due to the fact that we recognized them to be future versions of conditions that we could already observe around us. These anti-utopias were fiction-worlds born from the minds of gifted seers who passed their scenarios on to us.

There is today—in a time when old beliefs are withering—a kind of philosophical hunger, a need to know who we are and how we got here. There is an ongoing search, often unconscious, for a cosmic perspective for humanity.

CARL SAGAN

4   Serious research into the future began only some twenty years ago, and as a discipline and worldwide movement it is only about a dozen years old. In 1964 a project called "Mankind 2000" attempted to sensitize the European populace to rapidly approaching global problems. The first World Future Research Conference was convened in Oslo in 1967. The Soviets have several prestigious futures programs in operation. The Club of Rome was organized in 1968 for the purpose of alerting world leaders to the coming collision between the soaring human population and economic growth.

In America a large number of future research organizations have been launched: the RAND Corporation, the Hudson Institute, The Commission on the Year 2000, the American Institute of Planners, and the World Future Society. Today most governments and large private industries have futures groups that carry on forecasting in special interest fields.

Four things have conspired to bring about the rapid birth of the futures research movement. (1) Techniques for forecasting developed almost overnight, largely because of the progress of science and technology. Compared to human behavior, technology is relatively predictable. Coupled with the burgeoning, microminiaturized computers, trend projections and correlations not previously possible suddenly became quick and easy. "Given his present state of knowledge, social as well as scientific and technological, man now has an enormously enhanced capacity to choose his future, both collectively and individually" (McHale).

(2) A series of global events has scared us into thinking about the real possibility of world catastrophe: uncontrolled weapons escalation; polluted lakes, rivers, and skies; blackouts and brownouts; oil spills and the killing of the oceans; near extinction of many animals; defoliation, droughts, and possible ozone depletion; the hunger-zones of the world with growing populations and food shortages. Add to all this unstable governments, wobbly international currencies, economic troubles, global power struggles, and world leaders who command little or no confidence—put all this together and there is little wonder that, in the minds of many, a spectre of doom hovers over a shrinking world.

(3) There has developed a rapid realization that all the countries of the world are now so interdependent in fundamental ways that problems can only be understood and dealt with in terms of world systems. Energy problems are global. Pollution obeys no political checkpoints. The world is one system economically. Any war now affects all nations. Movements that flare up in remote corners rapidly ignite tensions around the world. Communications are global and instant. In a word there will no longer be any really significant local problems. The serious challenges of the next fifty years will all be global in nature, and localistic or nationalistic mobilization cannot hope to change the course of such worldwide threats.

(4) It has become clear that we are still thinking within frameworks from the past, and they no longer work. The idea that any one

nation can go it alone for its food, energy, and basic materials is not true any more. The belief that wars can be won is a myth; in nuclear wars there are no winners. The idea of "manifest destiny" is history. And the "rugged individualism" that once moved men and mountains and bred pioneers who held themselves beholden to no one—all this is gone.

5   This, then, is the goal of futures research: to establish organizations—political, economic, industrial, academic, and more—that will prevision the nature of these problems and have on the drawing boards contingency plans for facing them; and to have on a stand-by basis international organizations ready to give counsel and guidance to the power-movers when the time comes that world leaders can no longer ignore the problems.

So futurists and futurism were born. In 1945 Arthur C. Clarke began to describe in detail specific upcoming technological events. In 1958 Robert Jungk began talking about "early warning systems" that would study the long-range consequences of uncontrolled technologies. By 1960 Fred Polak had begun to clarify how our visions of the future help us to achieve the futures we envision; and Herman Kahn had begun to develop complex "scenarios" of alternative futures and to analyze systematically the events that might actually bring them about. In 1963 Dennis Gabor wrote of "inventing" our futures and then creating means of arriving at our inventions.

In 1963 Buckminster Fuller began to make us dream with a colorful stream of futuristic images, holistic programs, and novel hardware—the boldest display of concrete previsions since Leonardo da Vinci, with whom he is often compared. By 1965 Bertrand de Jouvenel was turning out treatises on humanistic elements in future planning ("the intellectual construction of a likely future is a work of art"). By 1966 Marshall McLuhan, with cryptic phrases and lilting puns, was warning us that new communications media—the media themselves, that is, quite apart from their content—would revolutionize our world-views and lifestylves. By 1968 Erich Jantsch was engaged in "integrative forecasting" to determine the technological impact on social and human institutions.

Also in 1968 Paul Ehrlich jolted a complacent society by pointing out the inevitable consequences of unchecked population growth. And in 1970 Alvin Toffler described the "future shock" that awaits us: "We cannot create a sane social system until technology is tamed, the educational system revolutionized, and future-consciousness injected into our political lives."

6   Just because the problems are so new and our thinking is so outdated, it is the consensus among futurists that mankind now stands at the threshold of the most critical period of human history. There is a near-unanimous feeling that the next fifty years will constitute a transition period that will write the future of man, one way or the other. Their deepest fear derives from the fact that the dangerous problems

The military mind will be the curse of the race so long as there is a military . . . . or will it be the salvation?

CHRISTOPHER ANVIL

Our world is now future-oriented, you see, in the sense that the rate of change has become so rapid that we can no longer wait until a problem is upon us to work out the solution. If we do, then there is no real solution, for by the time one has been worked out and applied, change has progressed still further and our solution no longer makes sense at all. The change must be anticipated *before* it happens.

ISAAC ASIMOV

The psychologist Abraham Maslow divided human needs into five sequential levels:

1 *Physiological needs:* the basic needs for food, shelter, rest. Only when these are obtained can an individual proceed to . . .

2 *Safety/security needs:* protection of self, family, property; plans for the future. Once these are secured, the individual can move on to . . .

3 *Social/belonging needs:* sharing-in-community, establishing relationships, friendships; meeting love and sex needs. Having met these needs, one can then concentrate on . . .

4 *Self-needs:* developing independence, self-confidence, self-respect; achieving self-worth in the eyes of oneself and others. Only now can one begin to work toward . . .

5 *Self-actualizing needs:* personal growth, fulfillment, expressing one's special talent—realizing one's human potential to the fullest possible degree.

To some extent these need-levels overlap, but in general the sequence is fairly rigid: one can't turn his attention to higher needs until the lower-level needs have been met. On an "intensity scale" each of us is dominated by these need-levels in a sort of wave pattern:

Maslow intended his "need hierarchy" to apply to the psychological development of individuals, but social psychologists and culture theorists suggest that it also applies to larger groups that share a common condition. In the following world-model, the divisions are based on "shared commonality of major problems which will eventually be encountered by these nations."

Question: Does Maslow's need-scale apply to the developed and developing nations of the world? Will the future be shaped largely by "the emerging nations" as they gradually (and rapidly?) move through the need hierarchy from Step 1 to Step 5?

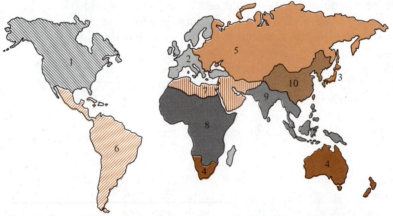

(1) North America; (2) Western Europe; (3) Japan; (4) Australia, South Africa, and the market-economy developed world; (5) Eastern Europe and the Soviet Union; (6) Latin America; (7) North Africa and the Middle East; (8) Tropical Africa; (9) the Indian subcontinent and Southeast Asia; (10) China.

are all global while humankind's mental machinery is still fueled by past ideas that no longer burn. Our concepts remain essentially local, regional, tribal, and nationalistic. This is not a matter of irrelevant patriotism, for realistic loyalties promote cohesive bonds and foster shared visions and goals. It is rather that aristocentric myths prevent an accurate understanding of the nature of the global problems which threaten us and make it impossible to set in motion the forces that could be effective against these large-scale problems.

The most recent report of the Club of Rome was issued in a volume entitled *Mankind at the Turning Point* (1974). Derived from a massive accumulation of data, conclusions were clear: We face an urgent need for a thoroughgoing restructuring of our conceptual frameworks, basic assumptions, and a reorientation of values—if we are to survive the next fifty years.

(1) A *world consciousness* must be developed through which every individual realizes his role as a member of the world community.

(2) A *new ethic in the use of material resources* must be developed which will result in a style of life compatible with the oncoming age of scarcity. One should be proud of saving and conserving rather than of spending and discarding.

(3) An *attitude toward nature must be developed based on harmony rather than conquest*. Only in this way can man apply in practice what is already accepted in theory—that is, that man is an integral part of nature.

(4) If the human species is to survive, man must develop a *sense of indentification with future generations* and be ready to trade benefits to the next generations for the benefits to himself. If each generation aims at the maximum good for itself, Homo sapiens is as good as doomed. One futurist commentator, Howard Didsbury, summarized the mood of the report: "Enlightened self-interest dictated by necessity may tend to make clear mankind's ultimate choices: cooperation or destruction. If cooperation is chosen it may 'lead to the creation of a new mankind.' Should mankind choose the alternative, all is silence."

OPTIONAL FUTURES

7   Looking ahead for decades and centuries, there is no single world-picture on which all futurists agree, although there is remarkable agreement on many points. A futurist's vision will depend partly upon his specialty and partly upon his personal feelings of optimism or pessimism about the operations of "human nature" past and present. Moreover, whether a futurist is essentially negative or positive depends somewhat on whether his picture of the future is a short-range or long-range vision. In general, the short-range futurists concentrate on the looming problems that could engulf us and tend to be less cheery about the decades immediately ahead. The middle- and long-range futurists tend to be far more optimistic because of that

Europe 10,000 BC

526 AD

1519 AD

1914 AD

Europe 2035 AD

Once we have cast another group in the role of the enemy, we know that they are to be distrusted—that they are evil incarnate. We then twist all their communications to fit our belief.

JEROME FRANK

We live now on a satellite adrift in space—why would man not make more satellites to his taste if it came within his means?

RON BRACEWELL

In so far as mathematics is about reality, it is not certain, and in so far as it is certain, it is not about reality.

ALBERT EINSTEIN

Man will not ultimately be content to be parasitic on the stars but will invade them and organize them for his own purposes.

J. D. BERNAL

The earth's population is not increasing *exactly* at a geometrical rate. Actually it is a bit faster; the rate of population increase is itself proportional to the population. If this rate could continue, the population would become infinite in a finite time. The present growth formula leads to an infinite population in 2026 A.D.—in fact, on Friday, November 13, a day dubbed "doomsday."

GEORGE O. ABELL

widely held intuition that *if* mankind can make it through the next fifty years then the more distant future is practically unlimited in its promise of progress, human growth, and personal fulfillment.

8   *Herman Kahn.* In the early 1960s Herman Kahn gained wide attention for his analyses of the consequences of possible thermonuclear war. In 1961 he published *On Thermonuclear War*—and became the prototype for Stanley Kubrick's Dr. Strangelove. He followed in 1962 with *Thinking About the Unthinkable*. In 1967 he co-authored *The Year 2000*. Kahn is essentially a short-range analyst who specialized first in politico-military scenarios involving weapons, resources, logistics, and the like; but in the late sixties he turned to the analysis of the world's not-too-distant socioeconomic and political leadership problems.

During his first "think tank" period as an expert in military strategy and weapons design, Kahn's logic went like this: There is strong probability that thermonuclear war will occur *at some time* in the future since it is difficult to believe that war can be successfully evaded *forever* by such erratic plays as bargaining talks, diplomatic trade-offs, détentes, summit maneuvers, arms sales, power balancing, treaties, or whatever. Therefore, Kahn asks what exactly would happen if war should occur. He projected detailed "scenarios" of possible results. In actual wars, there would be "degrees of awfulness" depending upon the weapons used, strategies employed, and states of preparedness. Kahn's conclusions were largely responsible for America's emphasis upon civilian defense programs during the early sixties.

Kahn's blunt realism provoked outraged responses, especially from church groups, and he was criticized by laymen and experts alike for his heartless, inhuman analyses of "the unthinkable."

It is therefore significant that the hardminded realist of the sixties has now become optimistic about the prospects for world peace and prosperity for the era that lies ahead: "I think there are good prospects for what the Europeans would call *la belle époque* . . . a worldwide period of growth, trade, peace, and prosperity on the whole, and a time, generally speaking, of optimism about the future."

Kahn, working with the Hudson Institute which he founded, has analyzed in depth the economic resources of the world today, and he is adamant about what he sees: "Are we running out of energy? The answer is absolutely no. No way. Are we running out of resources? Absolutely not. No way. Are we running out of the ability to feed people from a technological and economic point of view? Absolutely not. No way. Can we retain clear air and clear water and a reasonably esthetic landscape? Absolutely."

Kahn points out that our water and air are far cleaner today than a decade ago. We Americans, however, love to worry. Our environmental and pollution problems are essentially solved. We have cleaned up the Willamette River and Lake Erie, and many species of fish, long gone, have returned to the Hudson and the Thames. "Many mistakes and setbacks will certainly occur. But 10 or 15 years from now, almost certainly by the year 2000, it is very likely that we will

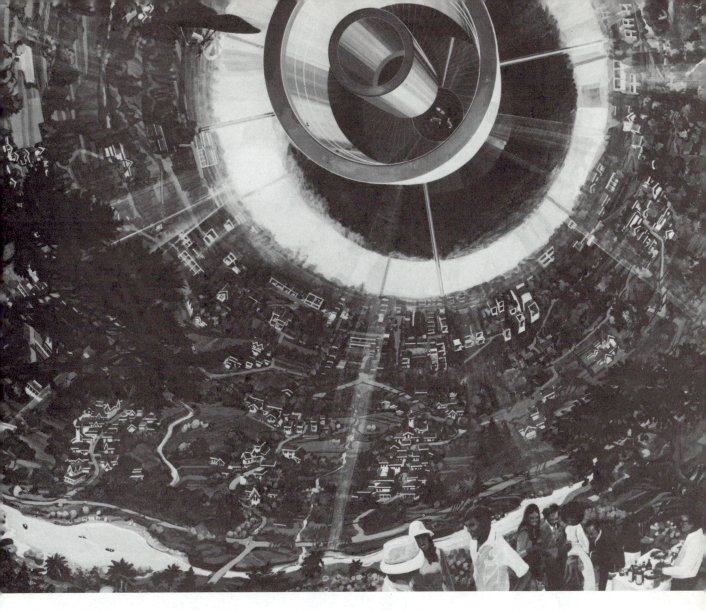

look back with great pride on our accomplishments. We will breathe the clean air, drink directly from the rivers, and smile with pleasure at the aesthetic landscape. . . . In any reasonable historical perspective, that outcome will be termed a clear win for environmental protection."

Furthermore, our energy problems are best thought of as passing socioeconomic adjustments rather than as portents of major cataclysms. We may well go through seasons of energy conservation or be forced to modify our lifestyles. But in the long run the promise is hopeful: the use of solar energy will increase; with safeguards nuclear fission will continue to meet our needs; and nuclear fusion "has never appeared more promising."

After exhaustive analysis of the world's present condition in terms of population, food, energy, and materials resources, Kahn summarizes: "All in all, we remain optimistic about the potential of man's future. We can only hope that he does not throw away this potential

Politics is no longer the art of the possible. It is now more the art of attempting to avoid the inevitable.

JOHN MCHALE

401

through foolish political behavior or misplaced concern about non-existent or badly formulated growth issues." In general, "things are going rather well."

9   *Alvin Toffler.* With the publication of *Future Shock* in 1971 Alvin Toffler reached international prominence as a futurist. Since then he has edited *The Futurists* (1972) and written *The Eco-Spasm Report* (1975). He is essentially a short-range futurist (relatively, that is) who is especially knowledgeable about socioeconomic trends.

As a futurist Toffler is acutely aware of two essentially human problems which threaten all global economic and political processes during the next few decades.

> First: *Lack of future-consciousness.* Instead of anticipating the problems and opportunities of the future, we lurch from crisis to crisis. The energy shortage, runaway inflation, ecological troubles—all reflect the failure of our political leaders at federal, state, and local levels to look beyond the next election. Our political system is "future-blind." With but few exceptions, the same failure of foresight marks our corporations, trade unions, schools, hospitals, voluntary organizations, and communities as well. The result is political and social future shock.
>
> Second: *Lack of participation.* Our government and other institutions have grown so large and complicated that most people feel powerless. They complain of being "planned upon." They are seldom consulted or asked for ideas about their own future. On the rare occasions when they are, it is ritualistic rather than real consultation. Blue-collar workers, poor people, the elderly, the youth, even the affluent among us, feel frozen out of the decision process. And as more and more millions feel powerless, the danger of violence and authoritarianism increases. Moreover, if this is true within this country, it is even more true of the world situation in which the previously powerless are demanding the right to participate in shaping the global future.

In *Future Shock* Toffler massively documented his thesis that world economic conditions are out of control, are accelerating, and are being faced only with outmoded myths and methods. He pointed out that, almost without exception, those dealing with these gigantic "economic" problems know nothing but economics; whereas the actual problems are interdisciplinary by nature and can't even be understood, let alone solved, by narrow-range economics specialists.

The giant economic forces of our time have become tails wagging the dogs. Many economic systems, especially the multinational corporations, are more powerful than the nations they use as bases of operation. Such nations are, in effect, "colonies" of such transnational powers. And all these economic processes are moving faster than we can understand or cope with.

Toffler therefore suggests alternative approaches for facing a world that has "gone random" and is running out of control. One solution is long-range planning. We need to think big and to think boldly.

There is a vast difference between letting changes occur under the impact of technological advances and choosing the changes we want to bring about by our technological means.

BERTRAND DE JOUVENEL

Futurism differs from planning, if one wishes to make that distinction, by reaching beyond economics to embrace culture, beyond transportation to include in its concerns family life and sex roles, beyond physical and environmental concerns to include mental health and many other dimensions of reality. It reaches beyond the conventional time frame of the industrial style planner toward longer, 10-, 20-, or 30-year speculative horizons, without which the short-range plans make little sense. Furthermore, it seeks radical new ways to democratize the process—not merely because that is good, just, or altruistic, but because it is necessary: without broad-scale citizen involvement, even the most conscientious and expertly drawn plans are likely to blow up in our faces.

These accelerating out-of-control global economic movements are scary, to be sure, but, Toffler adds, we are faced with "an awesome but exhilarating task that few generations in human history have ever faced: the design of a new civilization."

10   *Arthur C. Clarke.* Serious scientific forecasting had its first futurist in Arthur C. Clarke, a scientist writer equally renowned for his science fiction. In 1945 he presented a remarkably accurate and detailed description of radio and television communications satellites (and has regretted ever since not attempting to patent "an idea whose time had come"—and he didn't recognize it!). Another futurist, John McHale, makes the significant comment that "Clarke has been consistently more accurate in his prophecies than many of his fellow scientists and science-fiction writers." His major futurist writings are *Profiles of the Future* (1963), *Voices from the Sky* (1965), and *The Promise of Space* (1967). Whether his science-fiction classic *Childhood's End* should also be included among his prophetic visions remains a tantalizing question.

Clarke contends that there are two good reasons for believing that the future will not much resemble the present. One is that known trends are accelerating on all fronts and in a relatively short time the world will be almost unrecognizable to those of us living today.

But there is a stronger reason: the pace of *unpredictable breakthroughs* is also accelerating, and these are the true causes of the quantum leaps in man's progress. A few of man's past unforeseen discoveries are: X-rays, nuclear energy, radio, television, photography, sound recording, quantum mechanics, relativity, transisters, and lasers. There can be little doubt that such unpredictables will continue, and these unexpected jumps will propel us into unexpected worlds.

What about the foreseeable events of the future?

For the 1980s Clarke foresees manned exploration of Mars and other planets; a fairly complete understanding of the links in life's chain; and the first knowledge of gravity waves. During the 1990s will come the practical use of nuclear fusion, the application of bionics, and true artificial intelligence.

During the first quarter of the 21st century, Clarke envisions our colonizing the planets and their satellites; breaking the secret of matter at the subparticle level and understanding the fundamental nature of

When a distinguished but elderly scientist states that something is possible, he is almost certainly right. When he states that something is impossible, he is very probably wrong.

ARTHUR C. CLARKE
("Clarke's Law")

The dangers that face the world can, every one of them, be traced back to science. The salvations that may save the world will, every one of them, be traced back to science.

ISAAC ASIMOV

matter and energy; storing man's vast accumulation of knowledge in a world library; and the practical use of robots, for home or office. Weather control will be advanced and interstellar probes will have been sent on their way.

Before mid-century is reached, Clarke believes that electronic contact will have been made with extraterrestrial intelligences (ETIs); and in human society genetic engineering will be generally practiced.

Clarke declines to peer beyond the year 2100, but during the second half of the 21st century some of the more auspicious realities will be the control of gravity and planetary engineering (the greening of Mars, the cooling of Venus); the design and creation of life-forms in the laboratory. As for space travel, we will have achieved velocities near the speed of light, and interstellar voyages will have begun. Near the end of the 21st century two world-shattering events are likely: direct contact with ETIs and the achievement of virtual immortality for mankind.

Of all these achievements, three will probably be more future-transforming than the rest: gravity control, immortality, and exchanges with ETIs.°

°See Chapter 7-4 on contact with ETIs.

On gravity: Clarke-the-scientist is not sure that gravity control can be accomplished, but he has an intuition that there has to be some way. He elaborates in detail on the benefits of gravity control if it could be achieved, but then he demurs: "It may seem a little premature to speculate about the uses of a device which may not even be possible, and is certainly beyond the present horizon of science. But it is a general rule that whenever there is a technical need, something always comes along to satisfy it—or to bypass it. For this reason, I feel sure that eventually we will have some means of either neutralizing gravity or overpowering it by brute force."

On immortality: "Death—like sleep—does not appear to be biologically inevitable. . . . Because biological immortality and the preservation of youth are such potent lures, men will never cease to search for them. . . . It would be foolish to imagine that this search will never be successful, down all the ages that lie ahead."

Clarke notes that traditionally—for very good reasons—we think of the mind, the brain, and the body as "going together," necessarily. But this natural "triad" may not be indivisible. It just may be that the entire human body—*except the brain*—can be bionically replaced, so that the brain could continue to live on in the fullness of personality for hundreds of years. Beyond this bionic stage, however, Clarke has envisioned the theoretical means by which *the mind alone* could exist without brain. That is, the mind—with all its capacities, its perceptions, memories, and awareness—may then exist independent of the physical encumbrance of brain-matter.°

°For the fictionalized version of how this may be possible, read Clarke's novel, The City and the Stars (and note Chapter 2). Also, do you recall the finale to the motion picture 2001: A Space Odyssey?

11   *Sir Fred Hoyle.* There has never been a time during his adult lifetime when Fred Hoyle did not "think big." The universe, nothing less, has constituted his thought-world since his professional life began. When he turned his attention to man's unholy condition, it was inevitable that his viewpoint would be cosmic. Hoyle's best-known writings are in astrophysics and cosmology. His principal futurist work is *Encounter with the Future* (1965).

Hoyle describes and diagrams the general time-line which he believes most likely for the next five thousand years. He assumes the inevitability of thermonuclear war. Hoyle's model is planned around mathematical probabilities regarding population expansions and depletions of various raw materials. He considers it nearly impossible at this late date for us to harness our reproductive energies and reduce birthrates to the level of deathrates. On the contrary, he believes, birthrates will continue almost exponentially and deathrates will diminish. But a point will be reached at which the world population will have neither living room nor adequate food; the world's organizational systems will suddenly disintegrate, followed by a sharp decrease in populations. Famines and plagues might play a part in this process, but Hoyle is fairly sure that nuclear wars will be the primary instrument of depopulation.

The ultimate outcome of this series of population growths and collapses will be the emergence of superior qualities in man, including an average I.Q. of perhaps 150. He will in fact be a new species of man wise enough, finally, to stop the oscillations and stabilize human existence at a more mature level. But only through a continuing experience of consummate tragedies can man prepare his fundamental nature for a more civilized phase of human (or posthuman) existence.°

Let me then outline in a few words, by way of conclusion, what the broad history of our species is going to be over the next five thousand years, give or take a millennium.

°Time and again we come across the "Law of Pathei Mathos" in the thinking of some philosopher as he ponders a specific subject. Here we encounter it again as Hoyle applies it to future man: only further suffering, it seems, can produce sufficient maturity for man to live in peace with other men. See pages 127f.

Incidentally, there is a remarkably similar (and equally horrifying) projection of a future "dark ages" in the SF classic by Walter M. Miller Jr., A Canticle for Leibowitz.

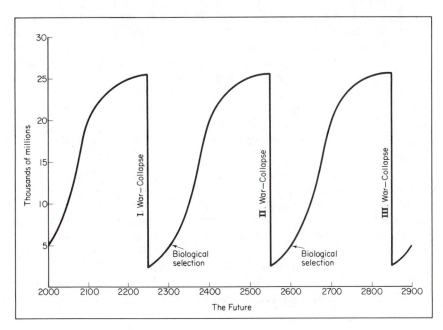

I think that at present we are in the first big expansion phase. This first phase is specially important. It possesses assets—coal, oil, etc—that will not be repeated again. In return for the consumption of these assets it must establish a body of knowledge around which future civilizations will be able to build themselves. Without the establishment of this body of knowledge I do not believe our species will have more than a few centuries of existence ahead of it.

I think there will be a series of organizational breakdowns, or catastrophes, occasioned by overpopulation. This will lead to the saw-tooth-shaped population curve [in the diagram]. During the beginnings of the reexpansion phases there will be selection for greater sociability and for higher intelligence. The degree of selection in any one cycle need not be dramatically large because the effects of the repeated cycles are cumulative. Indeed, I expect the number of cycles—the number that occurs before they are damped away—to be determined by how much selection occurs per cycle. If this is large, the number of cycles will be small—and vice versa, the net effect being the same.

The ultimate outcome I believe will be a highly sociable, highly intelligent creature. With this, I would consider a new species to have arrived. It will have its own problems, no doubt, but they will not be as elementary as those with which we are faced today.

SIR FRED HOYLE

The only certainty in [the] remote future is that radically new things will be happening.

FREEMAN DYSON

12   *Ray Bradbury.*   The more distant future of Mankind, we assume, cannot be foreseen; but a poet's vision, touched with inspiration, might intuit futures far beyond the point where trends fade away.

A "sense of the future" permeates the pages of about everything Ray Bradbury has written. As a reader enjoys his way through the novels, plays, poems, and 350 short stories that Bradbury has penned during the last thirty years, he has a picture-filled memory of having visited the future: fiery starbound rockets, wispy gold-coin-eyed Martians, the moldy drizzle of a rainy Venus, other strange people and stranger planets. From *The Martian Chronicles* to "Christus Apollo," Bradbury paints our futures in fresh metaphors. He thinks of science fiction as the conceptualization of ideas whose time has not yet come, and it is in this sense that a science-fiction writer can fantasize our futures long before they can become reality—long before they can be *real*-ized.

As a futurist, Bradbury has never attempted to become an "early warning system" for specific dangers. He is at heart a raconteur, a teller of future tales, a spinner of far-out fantasies. Still, scattered through his writings are warnings of what the future might hold if things should go wrong. For instance, in *Fahrenheit 451* we have a prevision of a world gone awry, a society in which reading is banned and literature is burned. It is therefore a world without ideas, peopled with wax-tablet brains on which a Big Brotherly television can easily write its own embalmed image. No ideas, no creativity, no growth. The End.

There also runs through Bradbury's writings an ever-present theme of machines-gone-astray. A robot police car patrols a darkened city watching intently for any hint of nonconformist behavior. A nursery, activated by the thought-wishes of the playing children, runs amuck and takes on a horrifying life of its own. Bradbury was an articulate critic of Stanley Kubrick's motion picture *2001: A Space Odyssey* not merely because the mellow-voiced HAL-9000, the spaceship computer, became paranoid and destructive, but because the men and women of the entire space venture, as conceived by Kubrick, were already exactly that: computerlike non-humans in deceptively human form.

On the condition that a modicum of pragmatic imagination is applied to Mankind's painful transition during the near future, then Bradbury is far more a harbinger of the great things that are in store for the human race. He thinks not in terms of decades or centuries—the "practical life"—but in terms of thousands and even millions of years—the truly "theoretical life"; and a joyous optimism infuses all that he sees. There are sophisticated machineries, for example, that allow one to face death, and then to die, over and over again, as often as needed, until at last one can accept life. There is a robot foster mother created in the perfect image of the children's needs who comes into their lives with just the right amount of caring. There is a Mister-George-Bernard-Shaw-Robot that will forever carry on learned dialogues about the Universe and its multifarious contents, and discourse on their meaning. And there is a very special banquet:

> . . . a Future Room with forty men and women seated with alternately empty chairs between. Eighty chairs in all, but only forty occupied. It is a robot's banquet in the year 1999, and I have been invited.
>
> I enter and am greeted with a chorus of voices. The men and women at the tables raise their glasses and call out:
>
> "Here, sit here, no here, here!"
>
> And I sit now with Aristotle, now with Emily Dickinson, now with Schopenhauer, in a great feasting of thoughts and a banqueting of words.
>
> "Dear Mr. Bradbury!"
>
> Plato seizes my hand.
>
> "Sir," I say. "How goes it with your 'Republic'?"
>
> "Superb! Fine. Except—"
>
> And he tells me. And I listen.
>
> And I rise to change seats and speak to Sara Teasdale or Albert Camus. I rise and go now with William Butler Yeats. I take tiffin with the somewhat darker philosophies of Shakespeare or the lighter but still deep philosophies of Shaw.
>
> So you move around the endless table, breaking your fast with splendid works, meeting and basking with talented people reborn in robots to outlast time.
>
> Sit with Kazantzakis and he might shout: God cries out to be saved. We shall save Him. And in symbiotic cries of relief, He will then save us. For we are One.

We are free to choose which elements we wish to apply in the construction of physical reality. The justification of our choice lies exclusively in our success.

ALBERT EINSTEIN

Think? Why think! We have computers to do that for us.

JEAN ROSTAND
(describing the computer age of the future)

Behind every man now alive stand thirty ghosts, for that is the ratio by which the dead outnumber the living. Since the dawn of time, roughly a hundred billion human beings have walked the planet Earth.

ARTHUR C. CLARKE

Make up your own table, guest list, menu.

Sit Gerard Manley Hopkins there and he will perhaps doodle on the linen napkin: What I do is me. For *that* I came.

Bradbury's previsions of Man's journey—on which he has just embarked—are magnificent dreams, filled with the excitement of discovery and the adventure of the unknown. A million years, a billion years, and more—until man is immortal and he has graced the stars.

"The thing that I have against the negative futurists of the last thirty years is that they're all changing their minds now. And what you want to say to them is 'Dammit, why did you depress us in the first place? Where were you when we needed you? You almost destroyed us during the Flower Period a few years ago. I believe in being negative in the instant of negativity. I believe in kicking people and saying, 'Here, this way! Get up, come with me, and we'll do it right.' Of course, some of them wanted to scare the devil out of us, and they did. But too often they scare all hope out of us and no one does anything."

"My philosophy is "Don't confuse me with facts if they're going to paralyze me!' I'm reminded of Nietzsche's old saying, 'We have art that we do not die of the truth.' There's a certain point where the facts, if you're not careful, can make you stop doing anything. And then you have to look for new facts. The negativists keep saying that these other facts aren't there, and I always know they are there if you look for them. Our minds select facts congenial to our temperaments and moods."

Bradbury is aware that we are shaped by the machineries that we invent: we shape the technology that in turn shapes us. He sides with McLuhan: the medium has drowned out the message. Television, for instance, makes us think small. We have built skyscraper rockets and gone to the Moon and Mars, but by the time we witness our greatness on TV—with lens zoomed-in and videotape timely spliced—"it's the wrong kind of space and time." Television diminishes everything it touches—"the esthetic of size"; it telescopes light-years into fifty-minute segments—"the esthetic of time." "It takes a rocket that is 300 feet high and crushes it down to a 14-inch image. And everything we are larger than, we have contempt for. When the screen gets larger, we can see the Universe again."

And what of Man—"this strange, weeping, laughing animal who wakens from monkey dreams to find himself almost Man? What is this remarkable thing that we are?"

In phrases reminiscent of Shaw: "We are something that's becoming itself. We are matter and force that does not know itself, changing ourselves, during the long night of the universe, into imagination and will. Willing ourselves to survive." That's what man has been doing for millions of years and will continue to do for more millions of years. "Man will not die . . . ever. Hate as we often hate ourselves, yet we love ourselves more and the gift given us to live one

---

To put finally to rest our Newtonian delusions, to renew our conception of nature as living, and so to see ourselves once more as living beings in a world of living beings, still constitutes the major task of philosophy in the twentieth century.

MARJORIE GRENE

In the coming world the capacity to face the new appropriately is more important than the ability to know and repeat the old.

CARL ROGERS

Man, the sentient species of a small planet circling a small sun in a dim backwater of the galaxy, is about to undertake the breath-taking adventure of re-creating himself. By tinkering with the mechanisms of his heredity, he plans to improve on nature's designs. He believes he can learn to change any part of his body's engineering: his susceptibility to disease, his height and intelligence and beauty, the very span of his life. After two billion years of evolution by trial and error, we now stand at the beginning of human-kind's next phase: the Second Genesis.

MAX GUNTHER

time in a Universe as brutal, stunning, and nightmarish as it is beautiful. Oh, then again beautiful beyond our powers to say."

The life-force, still mysterious, works within us; and our task is to work with it creatively. . . .

> And in genetics' marrow
> Seek God's will, to find lost man
> And send him up the hill of stars;
> To change the dreadful dates of 1984,
>   and send them up with shouts
> To make a score man could not dream or hope
>   or care to do.
> Make Orwell laugh in year 2002.
> Grand Things To Come? Yes. . . .
> And star-blown winds then echo endlessly,
> Which shall it be?
> Oh wandering man, which shall,
>   which shall it be?

13   The most important question we would ask about the future is simple: *Will life be worth living?* The answer is equally simple: Yes, of course. Life in any age will be just as "worth living" as now.

If the worst should happen then (1) some who have known happier circumstances might find life practically unendurable; but (2) such conditions will be within tolerable limits to those who know no other way. If war and mass annihilation should occur, then for those still living life would probably not differ greatly from that of ancient men who had but a few simple tools and weapons and hunted for a living. Doubtless life was just as precious to primitive man as to us; he fought just as hard to stay alive. So, our ancestors survived, and life for them was "worth-living."

For those who know but a single world-view, life is almost always worthwhile, precisely because no one is aware of alternative modes of existence. Living hell is reserved for the person confined to prison after experiencing freedom, for the person frustrated by perpetual danger after experiencing peace and security, for the person forced to the lowest level of physical survival after experiencing a lifestyle of personal fulfillment.

The *contrast* is the hell of it, and thus it would be in the future, whatever conditions prevail. Defeat would be less likely from life's realities as from the contrasts which we might remember or which we conjure in our imaginations.

However, if man succeeds in muddling through and avoids the tragic world-paths, then the advances which must come should provide him with promising conditions *within which* he can *pursue* fulfillment. In the goods and services which society will offer, life will be unimaginably richer.

But there's the splinter. After all is said, it's what happens in man's inner world that determines whether life is "worth living," and

We plant trees to benefit another generation.

CAECILIUS STATIUS

life is always in the singular, never the plural. Men are frequently tormented to the point of insanity or suicide in the midst of plenty.

MANY FUTURES/A COMMON VISION

14   Images of the future serve many purposes. The images so far described have been employed primarily to forecast threatening global problems and set up the machinery through which they may be effectively met and solved. This is one function of future-images. But there is another.

Today's world has come unglued, unraveled. The old loyalties no longer bind, and the countless collectivities have fragmented, traveled, intermixed, interwoven. Out of this new mixture is emerging a new world. It isn't born yet, and it may remain in labor for another fifty years, perhaps a hundred. Barring catastrophe, however, it will be born. We can be fairly sure of that, for lack of alternatives.

There is a pressing need for a sense of global identity and a shared vision of the future—a reason to exist. It is this profoundly human need that futurists have been watching and diagnosing, like physicians. The illness is clear enough, but the prescription is not at all clear as yet.

15   Robert Bundy writes:

> The West has lost any reason for being. Simply to further develop scientific and technological tools for their own sake, or to increase our mastery over nature, or to further expand the consumptive society, with its hedonistic license, cannot provide the motive power for a civilization. Some deeper spiritual center and transcendent values are required.
>
> This loss of a reason to go on means we have no inspiring image of the future, no dominant vision within whose embrace different ex-

**Someday is
too far away. . . .**

Master Charge TV Commercial (1976)

**Someday may be too
late. . . .**

Kodak TV Commercial (1976)

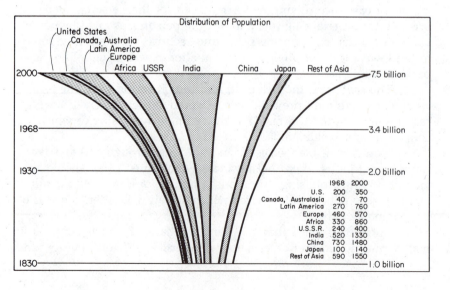

Distribution of Population

	1968	2000
U.S.	200	350
Canada, Australasia	40	70
Latin America	270	760
Europe	460	570
Africa	330	860
U.S.S.R.	240	400
India	520	1330
China	730	1480
Japan	100	140
Rest of Asia	590	1550

pectations can survive and draw strength, no overarching dream capable of infusing all of us with hope and giving us courage to confront and cope with our awesome problems.

A shared vision of our common future is therefore enormously important. Bundy notes that "positive images tell of another and better world in a coming time. They infuse people with the foreknowledge of a destiny of happiness, and thus engender the courage to confront and solve the problems facing a civilization. Negative, pessimistic images work in the opposite way and may forecast a period of cultural decline and breakdown. . . . Without a living image of the future a society can become doomed to a rootless vacuum" and "condemned to disappear."

Bundy concludes:

> Western civilization is passing away. So be it. This does not mean that our total inheritance from the past or our leadership potential for the future are lost. It does mean that many of the central dogmas and visions that drove Western civilization forward do not have a prominent place in the future. What does have a place in the future are: (1) the shared conviction that new magnetic images of the future can be born, (2) people who are united by common beliefs necessary for survival and development within a global perspective, and (3) groups that share across their boundaries while, as always, they remain separated by particular visions they are free to follow as long as others may also follow their visions.

Most intellectual problems are, ultimately, problems of classification and nomenclature.

S. I. HAYAKAWA

REFLECTIONS—

1 Recall the statement that opens this chapter: That we create the past and can also create alternative futures; and that we need both past and future to see ourselves in perspective. How much value is there in this way of looking at ourselves and our place in time?

2 Of the various alternative futures which are suggested here as real possibilities, which one(s) do you think are most likely to transpire? Why?

3 As you ponder the future, are you personally trusting and optimistic or wary and pessimistic? Do your own experiences and feelings tend to color the optional futures which you can imagine? (Do you think personal experiences may have colored the views of professional historians and professional futurists?)

4 What is your response to some of the specific events enumerated in this chapter as virtual certainties for the future? Are you eager to see some of these events and conditions materialize? Are there some that you fear? Would you want to live with them? Do you think that our great-grandchildren will be able to accept and live with them?

5 Ponder the sequence of maps on p. 399. Do you think this is a likely prediction of what will happen? (Apologies to Herr Rorschach, but *what is it* that's going to happen?)

6 What is your response to Sir Fred Hoyle's projection of the future? Can you

see what his long-range optimism is based on? (See sidenote on p. 405 on the "Law of Pathei Mathos.") Do you think there is a probability that Hoyle's vision will actually happen?

7 After reading pp. 409f, how would you respond to the question, "Will life be worth living?" In general do you agree with the speculations in this chapter?

8 Would you like to live in a space colony? What kind of a life do you think you would live there? Would you enjoy it more or less than living on Spaceship Earth? Can you tell why?

Furthermore . . .

BERRY, ADRIAN, *The Next Ten Thousand Years*. Saturday Review/Dutton, 1974.

BUNDY, ROBERT (ed.), *Images of the Future: The Twenty-first Century and Beyond*. Prometheus, 1976.

CLARKE, ARTHUR C., *Profiles of the Future*. Bantam, 1964.

CLARKE, ARTHUR C., *Imperial Earth*. Ballantine, 1976.

EHRLICH, PAUL, *The Population Bomb*. Sierra, 1972.

FERKISS, VICTOR, *The Future of Technological Civilization*. Braziller, 1974.

HEILBRONER, ROBERT L., *The Future as History*. Grove, 1961.

HUXLEY, ALDOUS, *Brave New World*. Harper, 1969.

KAHN, HERMAN, *The Year 2000*. Macmillan, 1967.

KOTHARI, RAJNI, *Footsteps into the Future: Diagnosis of the Present World and a Design for an Alternative*. Free Press, 1974.

LACONTE, RONALD T., with ELLEN LACONTE, *Teaching Tomorrow Today: A Guide to Futuristics*. Bantam, 1975.

MCHALE, JOHN, *The Future of the Future*. Ballantine, 1971.

MEAD, SHEPHERD, *How to Get to the Future before It Gets to You*. Hawthorn, 1974.

MESAROVIC, MIHAJLO, and EDUARD PESTEL, *Mankind at the Turning Point*. Dutton/Reader's Digest Press, 1974. (The second report of the Club of Rome.)

ORWELL, GEORGE, *Nineteen Eighty-four*. Signet, 1951.

STAVRIANOS, L. S. *The Promise of the Coming Dark Age*. Freeman, 1976.

TOFFLER, ALVIN, *The Eco-Spasm Report*. Bantam, 1975.

TOFFLER, ALVIN, (ed.), *The Futurists*. Random House, 1972.

TUCCILLE, JEROME, *Who's Afraid of 1984? The Case for Optimism in Looking Ahead to the 1980s*. Arlington House, 1975.

PART VII

MICROCOSM/ MACROCOSM/ COSMOS

There is today—in a time when old beliefs are withering—a kind of philosophic hunger, a need to know who we are and how we got here. There is an ongoing search, often unconscious, for a cosmic perspective for humanity.

CARL SAGAN

Nature

Have You Ever Wondered . . .

- Why "Nature speaks the language of mathematics"?

- Why 7 + 5 = 12?

- Whether there might be other universes in which $7 + 5 = 14\frac{1}{4}$?

- Why snowflakes always take the form of six-pointed crystals (if they do)?

- What "matter" is?

- What the forces are that drive the universe?

- If time really exists?

- If space really exists?

- If time exists, then what it exists in?

- If space exists, then what it exists in?

- What was the origin of matter?

This is a world of pure mathematics, and when we penetrate to the bottom of it, that's all it will be.

JOHN A. WHEELER

MAY 28, 585 B.C.

1   Philosophy and science were born together in 585 B.C.—on May 28 at 6:13 p.m. (Milesian Standard Time); for at that instant an eclipse began in the Ionian city of Miletus, a solar eclipse which had been *predicted* by a philosopher named Thales. We have no evidence that

Thales established the exact time of the event. This precise date has been calculated by modern astronomers, and if Thales had even come close—within a day or a week—he would have done well. But the significant point is that he had become aware of the regularities of nature on the basis of which he had made a prediction. However elementary this may seem, it is the dim recognition of what we now know as "natural law."

THE NATURE OF EMPIRICAL KNOWLEDGE

2   Our knowledge of nature and her "laws" derive from two distinct kinds of epistemic operations: empirical observation and rational system-building. Thus we have empirical knowledge and rational (or "a priori") knowledge. Both present problems not yet solved.

Suppose you took a Jovian philosopher to a baseball game. He is a handsome humanoid with shining eyes. Having recently arrived from Jupiter, and being ever-alert to adventures of the mind, he watches the game with eager awareness. Since he has never seen a baseball game, you begin to explain the rules to him. He declines the offer and tells you he would prefer to figure out the rules for himself. And so, through all nine innings, you let him watch the action.

As he observes the players, he notes their patterns of movement; they perform the same motions over and over again. A player walks up to a particular spot and tries to hit a small round object which another man throws at him (no, it's always thrown past him). If the man with the stick swings and misses three times, the hand of the man dressed in black goes up and the man with the stick walks away looking either sad or angry. But if he hits the round object with the stick, he starts running, always in the same direction, toward another man.

And so, little by little, the "rules of the game" are inferred and reconstructed as he watches the players' consistent, repeated patterns of behavior.

The "rules of the game" exist in the players' heads, and they play by them. The players know the rules because they have read them or have grown up with them, but our extraterrestrial epistemologist must *infer* the rules by watching behavior—that is, by watching matter-in-motion.

By the end of the second inning, he has some rough ideas of a few rules. By the fifth, he has added several more consistencies to his mental list and refined some previous observations. By the end of the game—Jovian genius that he is—he has been able to understand and jot down a set of rules which describes much of the players' actions.

After the game, the Jovian checks his list of inferred rules with you, and you find that he has indeed discovered most of the rules which you know about baseball.

Thales (fl c. 585 B.C.)

Philosophy is written in the vast book which stands open before our eyes, I mean the universe; but it cannot be read until we have learnt the language and become familiar with the characters in which it is written.

GALILEO

Now, he never *saw* the rules; he *created* the rules *in his mind* because they seemed to describe consistently the behavior of the players. All that he actually observed, of course, were players-in-motion.

3   Our minds operate in similar fashion to formulate "scientific laws." They are the "rules of the game" which we have inferred. We often deceive ourselves by thinking that we have observed the rules, whereas the fact is that we created them to account for consistencies *which we remembered* while watching matter-in-motion. We never observe the "law of gravity" or the "inverse-square law" which describes the propagation of light or the "laws" of mass-energy transformation. All the "laws" of physics are created in our minds; all this is *empirical* knowledge.

Scientists who work with submicroscopic entities are at a special disadvantage since they never even get to see matter-in-motion. They must create the "rules of the game" by observing only secondary traces (streaks on photographic plates, for example) left by particles of matter. In other words, particle physicists must create in their minds pictures of the matter as well as the principles of motion which describe the behavior of such matter.

4   All empirical knowledge is hypothetical and merely probable. That is, it consists of operational hypotheses which we continue to use as long as they are consistent with our observations.

Plants need sunlight to grow. Gray whales migrate in March. Robins lay blue eggs. Norwegians have blond hair. Water will conduct electricity if salt is dissolved in it. Light travels at 186,000 miles per second. Water cannot flow uphill. A lunar month is 27 days, 7 hours, 43 minutes. Tornadoes never occur in December. A fire will not burn without oxygen. Whale sharks are harmless to man.

All these things we know from repeated experience. But do we know them for sure? *All* robins' eggs are blue, someone might argue; he has investigated countless nests and noted thousands of robins' eggs—all pale blue. That seems to settle the matter. Still, can one be absolutely positive that some berserk robin hasn't laid a bright purple egg in a nest somewhere?

No empirical knowledge is ever certain. *To every statement one can imagine an exception.* One can easily imagine a gray whale deciding not to migrate in March, or a tornado tearing across Kansas in December, or a whale shark mistaking a man for a rather large tidbit of plankton. If one can imagine an exception to the statement, then it is obviously not *necessary* knowledge; it is only *contingent* knowledge with a probability of being correct. This is true of all the "natural laws" of physics which we have formulated to describe matter-in-motion.

This is also why, in the social sciences, we must employ statistics to establish the "coefficient of correlation," that is, so we can figure the probability of correctness of any hypothesis. What we determine is the number of cases out of 100 in which the hypothesis would hold true.

Metaphysicians are musicians without musical talent.

RUDOLF CARNAP

The laws of mathematics and logic are true simply by virtue of our conceptual scheme.

W. V. QUINE

Sense-perception, for all its practical importance, is very superficial in its disclosure of the nature of things. . . . My quarrel with modern epistemology concerns its exclusive stress upon sense-perception for the provision of data respecting Nature. Sense perception does not provide the data in terms of which we interpret it.

ALFRED NORTH WHITEHEAD

THE NATURE OF A PRIORI KNOWLEDGE

5   A second kind of knowledge about the natural world is rational or "a priori" knowledge. It has baffled philosophers from the beginning and still puzzles us to the point of irritation.

We know certain *necessary* truths, it seems, to which *we cannot imagine exceptions*. Seven plus five equals twelve—now, always, and everywhere. Parallel lines in the same plane will never intersect. The area of a circle can be determined with the formula πr^2. The angles of a triangle always add up to 180°.

Now, are these truly universal truths? The rationalist answers yes. Can one conceive, in his wildest imagination, any exception to these statements? Can we imagine two parallel lines intersecting? or 7 + 5 ≠ 12? or a triangle's angles not totaling 180°? No, we can't.

Here, then, lie the foundations of the "exact sciences": all known systems of mathematics, geometry, and logic.

6   How many robins' eggs would we have to examine to be sure that *all* robins' eggs are blue? Obviously, all of them: every egg ever laid. How many triangles do we have to investigate to be sure that they all contain angles totaling 180°? One or two, or just a few. The rationalist argues that once we understand the nature of the knowledge we are dealing with, then we don't have to ponder any more triangles at all. We know a priori (that is, without further empirical observation) that the angles of *all* triangles will total 180°. And what about 7 + 5 = 12? Is this true for this and all imaginable universes? It would seem to be.

If an ornithologist reported the discovery of a clutch of bright purple robins' eggs, we might believe him. We would have no *logical* reason to disbelieve him. But if a geometrician reported that he had spotted a circle somewhere in Antarctica whose diameter was greater than its circumference, we might think he had stayed out in the snow too long. We would disbelieve him on *logical* grounds.

Therefore, it is clear that we are dealing with two distinctly different kinds of knowledge about nature, and the way they apply to the external world is different.

Nature's modus operandi—her most prized secret—was discovered by a single man, one of the giants in the history of human thought. Pythagoras (fl. 500 B.C.) laid the foundations of mathematics and geometry and therefore made possible the development of physics. Russell comments that Pythagoras was "intellectually one of the most important men that ever lived, both when he was wise and when he was unwise."

Pythagoras was both mathematician and mystic, and in a strange way this combination of qualities may have been responsible for his insight into nature. According to Aristotle, Pythagoras recognized that in a particular mathematical or geometrical construct, when it is clearly understood, one knows a universal truth. The famous "Py-

Consider the way in which a great deal of mathematical thinking is actually done. The mathematician does not ask whether his constructions are applicable, whether they correspond to any constructions in the natural world. He simply goes ahead and *invents* mathematical forms, asking only that they be consistent with themselves, with their own postulates. But every now and then it subsequently turns out that these forms can be correlated, like clocks, with other natural processes.

ALAN WATTS

Pythagoras (c. 580–c. 500 B.C.)

thagorean theorem" is a perfect example: the sum of the squares of the sides of a right triangle is *always* equal to the square of the hypotenuse.

From this realization that absolute truths are not actual but merely mental, he was led to the position that the realities of the universe are nonmaterial. They are abstract mathematical principles, or, in his words, "the whole heaven or visible universe is a musical scale or number."

There is a story (though probably a legend) that Pythagoras was passing by a blacksmith shop when he heard the rings of the hammers pounding on the anvils inside. He listened to the varied pitches of sound which the hammers made, and when he went in to watch he discovered that the lower notes were being made by heavier hammers and higher notes by lighter hammers. Since Pythagoras had already experimented with measurements of weights, he quickly saw that there is a relationship between weight and sound, that is, a relationship between mathematical measurement and musical intervals. He had already studied the vibration of strings and knew that the harmonic intervals were determined precisely by the length of the vibrating string.

Through observations such as these, Pythagoras discovered (as Galileo later phrased it) that "the book of nature is written in the language of mathematics." All the operations of nature can be thus described. This momentous discovery gave Western man his first great insight into the natural world.

The problem with empirical knowledge is that we can never be absolutely sure of anything. Sometimes we can't even be sure how uncertain we should be! We must always ask: Do we have sufficient experience of an event to be reasonably (operationally) sure? Most of our "scientific laws" continue to work, but then we are reminded of some "laws" which have recently become extinct.

The more theoretical problem of a priori knowledge haunts our intellects. Why is it that mathematical knowledge describes so accurately the operations of nature? Why does $7 + 5 = 12$? Could it be that we can develop a coherent mathematical system in our minds which, by some sort of coincidence, applies to the natural world? Or does nature really operate on inherently perfect mathematical principles? How do we know there are not exceptions to nature's mathematical system?

We are still mystified at the relationship between our magnificent mental system and the equally magnificent natural system—both of which seem to be perfect mathematical systems in harmony with one another.

Or is our problem defined incorrectly? Why does two plus two equal four? Is it because we say so? Is this formula—$2 + 2 = 4$—an eternal truth because we have constructed a logical system which is internally coherent? Or is it because this operation describes real operations in nature? The pragmatist contends that we keep on using the formula only because it keeps on working; but the rationalist is not satisfied with such an answer. He argues that two plus two *must* equal

Reason is the *substance* of the universe. . . . The design of the world is absolutely rational.

HEGEL

four, anywhere in the universe; it is a cosmic truth, not a pragmatic model.

OTHER WAYS OF KNOWING?

7   When it is said that there are two ways of knowing the natural world, this claim has a decidedly Western sound. It is a Western assumption that the subject is the knower and that nature is the object known. If the relationship is *defined* this way, then the foregoing elucidation of the problems involved between subject and object should be fairly accurate and not without meaning.

But we might wonder whether there are other ways of knowing. Is it a true and final fact that man is the experiencing subject and the real world is the experienced object, and that the two are distinct, separate entities? Or might there be a "field interaction" that would render false the subject-object dichotomy? Perhaps man's knowing is more immersed in the "object" than he thinks and his separateness is merely an illusion. Perhaps the processes of knowing are but part of a larger process. Or perhaps there are other *ways* of knowing realities.

A Western philosopher who was convinced there is a better way was Henri Bergson. He contended that the only true method of "doing metaphysics"—knowing the real world as it actually is—is through "intuition," a kind of "intellectual empathy." The rational mind is far too occupied with static concepts and mental filing systems to be able to perceive the ever-changing *process* we call "nature." Nature is pure duration, with no stops and starts, absolutes, or quantification. Man can only know nature by putting aside the intellect and intuiting directly the flowing reality of which he is a part.

Those familiar with Eastern modes of experience are aware that this is a meaningful way of knowing reality. Buddhism, for instance, explicitly rejects the subject-object dichotomy as dangerously false. The goal of Zen meditation is satori, a sort of "flash of realization" that man is one with reality and not separate from it. It is a sensitive, totalic awareness of being a part of nature. Subject and object merge into one, or better, they are at last perceived as always having been one.

REALITIES BEYOND APPEARANCES

8   Man has been disturbed by the natural world into which he is born and in which he has to live. It is clear to him that things are not quite what they seem.

There are life-giving forces that make things grow, and all living things are in a condition of constant change. There are forces which shake the ground and belch up cinders and ash from the mountaintops. There are forces which rumble in a rainstorm and crackle across the sky in streaks of light. There are insidious forces which make one hurt inside and burn with heat and die. There are roots and insects and animals and seeds which give off juices which can kill.

Science is an attempt to read the cryptogram of experience; it sets in order the facts of sensory experience of human beings.

SIR ARTHUR EDDINGTON

Some of the ablest men in the world at present regard matter as merely a special type of undulatory disturbance.

J. B. S. HALDANE

MATHEMATICS AND ETERNAL TRUTHS

Mathematics is, I believe, the chief source of the belief in eternal and exact truth, as well as in a supersensible intelligible world. Geometry deals with exact circles, but no sensible object is *exactly* circular; however carefully we may use our compasses, there will be some imperfections and irregularities. This suggests the view that all exact reasoning applies to ideal as opposed to sensible objects; it is natural to go further, and to argue that thought is nobler than sense, and the objects of thought more real than those of sense-perception. Mystical doctrines as to the relation of time to eternity are also reinforced by pure mathematics, for mathematical objects, such as numbers, if real at all, are eternal and not in time. Such eternal objects can be conceived as God's thoughts. Hence Plato's doctrine that God is a geometer, and Sir James Jeans' belief that He is addicted to arithmetic. Rationalistic as opposed to apocalyptic religion has been, ever since Pythagoras, and notably ever since Plato, very completely dominated by mathematics and mathematical method.

The combination of mathematics and theology, which began with Pythagoras, characterized religious philosophy in Greece, in the Middle Ages, and in modern times down to Kant. . . . I do not know of any other man who has been as influential as he was in the sphere of thought. . . . The whole conception of an eternal world, revealed to the intellect but not to the senses, is derived from him. . . .

BERTRAND RUSSELL

MATHEMATICS AND THE PHYSICAL WORLD

Dr. ROBERT H. DICKE: There's a structure to mathematics that has no obvious inherent relation to the structure of the physical world. . . . It's not clear that there should be any connection at all. It's true that when you look at the structure of mathematics you find a game, like chess, played with rules, a formal structure. Yet, you reason and think about the external world in relation to the mathematical structure of physical theory. Like moves on the chessboard, you play with the formal mathematical structure of the physical theory and gain some understanding of the physical world itself, with no direct observation. (Of course, the theory originated in a host of observational results.) Later you make an observation to see whether you're off the track or not. This observation is the essential part—without this there can be no science.

Dr. REMO J. RUFFINI: How a mathematical structure can correspond to nature is a mystery. One way out is just to say that the language in which nature speaks is the language of mathematics. This begs the question. Often we are both shocked and surprised by the correspondence between mathematics and nature, especially when the experiment confirms that our mathematical model describes nature perfectly.

Intellectual Digest, June 1973

Ancient man wondered about these things. Obviously there were all sorts of *realities beyond appearances*. They could be felt. They could be benevolent, but more often they were hostile and harmful. What were these forces—these invisible, capricious powers?

Today, of course, we know that the ancient intuition was correct: There are indeed forces beyond appearances. We must admire ancient men for making as much sense of their world as they did.

9   Sir Arthur Eddington illustrates the difference between macrocosmic reality as we experience it and some of the "realities beyond appearances."

The learned physicist and the man in the street were standing together on the threshold about to enter a room.

The man in the street moved forward without trouble, planted his foot on a solid unyielding plank at rest before him, and entered.

The physicist was faced with an intricate problem. To make any movement he must shove against the atmosphere, which presses with a force of fourteen pounds on every square inch of his body. He must land on a plank travelling at twenty miles a second round the sun—a fraction of a second earlier or later the plank would be miles away from the chosen spot. He must do this whilst hanging from a round planet head outward into space, and with a wind of ether blowing at no one knows how many miles a second through every interstice of his body. He reflects too that the plank is not what it appears to be—a continuous support for his weight. The plank is mostly emptiness; very sparsely scattered in that emptiness are myriads of electric charges dashing about at great speeds but occupying at any moment less than a billionth part of the volume which the plank seems to fill continuously. It is like stepping on a swarm of flies. . . .

Happily even a learned physicist has usually some sense of proportion; and it is probable that for this occasion he put out of mind scientific truths about astronomical motions, the constitution of planks and the laws of probability, and was content to follow the same crude conception of his task that presented itself to the mind of his unscientific colleague.

THIS WORLD OF OURS—WHAT IS IT?

10   The very first Greek philosophers asked questions, not about man, but about the world in which they lived. They knew nothing of the basic elements (hydrogen, oxygen, etc.) or natural law ("physics"—the science of matter-in-motion) as we do. But sensing man's perilous (mis)understanding of his world, they asked questions, and asked them in a new way.

What is this "matter" of which everything is made? Is everything made of some single substance which we know (like water, air, or fire)? Or is it made of some unknown substance which under certain conditions, turns into the water, air, and fire of experience?

And what are the forces which activate matter into motion? The winds blow, lightning fells the giant pine, crops grow and die. What are the forces behind all this? Is it a single force or many? Could the force be "divine" or "mental"? Could it be alive? Is it *outside* matter (Zeus doesn't really hurl the thunderbolt of lightning) or *inside* matter? (Thales pondered magnets and decided their forces were internal; he concluded that they must have "souls.")

These first philosopher-scientists phrased such questions as best they could. In all, they were asking but two fundamental questions: (1) What is everything made of? (2) What are the forces that cause motion? There must be a lesson in all this. Our present accumulation of scientific knowledge about the natural world is nothing less than staggering, yet what are the fundamental questions we are asking today? *(1) What is everything made of? (2) What are the forces that cause motion?*

Still, we mustn't leave the matter here. We have truly traveled a long journey in our understanding of the substances that make up the realm of the real. We may still use the same sentences, but we

Sir Arthur Eddington has calculated that the number of particles in the universe is 2.36216×10^{79}, or, in round numbers, 2^{264}.

"The Master said, 'Yu, shall I teach you what knowledge is? When you know a thing, to recognize that you know it, and when you do not know a thing, to recognize that you do not know it. That is knowledge.'"

Analects of Confucius

This alone I know, that I know nothing.

SOCRATES

I cannot know even whether I know or not.

ARCESILAUS

The deeper science probes toward reality, the more clearly it appears that the universe is not like a machine at all.

LINCOLN BARNETT

So far as quantum theory can say at present, atoms might as well be possessed of free will, limited, however, to one of several possible choices.

BERTRAND RUSSELL

At the moment man's investigation of the ultra-small ends in mystery and his investigation of the ultra-large ends in mystery. It is not a very far-fetched hope that the two mysteries will turn out to be closely connected.

FRED HOYLE

There are no whole truths; all truths are half-truths. It is trying to treat them as whole truths that plays the devil.

WHITEHEAD

aren't asking the same questions. Today, when we ask ''What is every-thing made of?'' our minds jump to a vast accumulation of exciting information to shape possible answers. The stuff-of-the-world is composed of 105 basic atoms or elements; or it's composed of molecules, an infinite variety of compounds, chemicals; or it's made up of protons, neutrons, and electrons; or it's all put together with 30 to 200 particles, some with mass and some without mass; or deeper still: the world is a swirl of energy, vibrations, or (maybe) quarks.

So the grammar remains, but the meanings have been reincarnated many times over.

11   Take an ordinary piece of matter of any sort—a car key, a piece of chalk, a piece of candy, or a piece of paper—and suppose we were somehow able to divide it into finer and finer and even finer pieces. What would we eventually find? What, in short, are the ultimate constituents of matter?

All matter is made up of *molecules*, a specific molecule in a specific arrangement for each specific substance. Thus there are an enormous, almost incomprehensibly large, number of physically (and chemically) distinct molecules corresponding to the enormous variety of substances we see about us. The first great simplification in the description of nature came with the realization that every one of these vast assortments of molecules is composed of relatively few more elementary objects called *atoms*. About one hundred different atoms are known, ranging from the lightest and simplest, hydrogen, to the highly complex and unstable atoms that have only recently been synthesized and observed.

It was long believed that atoms were absolutely indivisible and immutable. Atoms were thought to be the basic and fundamental building blocks, mysteriously presented to us by nature, describable but intrinsically unexplainable. The next great step came when it was learned, at the turn of the century, that atoms are made up of still more fundamental objects. How many different kinds of such objects or, as the physicist calls them, *elementary particles*, are required to make up the one hundred or so different atomic species and therefore all of matter? The staggeringly simple answer is three. In short, the ultimate constituents of all ordinary matter are just three distinct and different elementary particles called the *electron*, the *proton*, and the *neutron*. . . . Reflect for a moment on the fact that all matter, everywhere in the universe, no matter its appearance, form, or properties, is made up of electrons, protons and neutrons appropriately arranged. . . .

[This] description is adequate as far as it goes. However, as the physicist began to study the elementary particles more closely, he rather quickly began to discover that the universe, at its most fundamental level, cannot be characterized by these three constituents of ordinary matter alone. Indeed, he now realized that there are at least thirty entities (some would say as many as two hundred or more), which can be thought of as elementary particles. It is almost as if a new kind of periodic table has appeared at this subatomic level, a table that no one understands very well. It has been suggested that each of the elementary particles in this uncomfortably large array is

ZENO'S PARADOXES OF MOTION

Zeno of Elea (fl. c. 450 B.C.) left a legacy of logical paradoxes that philosophers have wrestled with for some 2,400 years, often in vain. Zeno's contribution was to show that many of our common assumptions about motion and time appear to lead us into contradictions.

His most famous argument is the story of a handicap race between Achilles and a tortoise. If the tortoise begins the race some distance ahead of Achilles, then by the time Achilles reaches the point where the tortoise *was*, the tortoise, however pokey, will have moved ahead a ways. Again, when Achilles reaches the point where the tortoise *was*, the tortoise will still be ahead, though the distance between them is closing. And so on, ad infinitum. Therefore, since the distance between them is forever closing, Achilles can never overtake the tortoise.

Another paradox involves the racetrack. A runner cannot reach the end of the raceway until he has reached the half-way mark; but he can't reach the half-way mark until he has first reached the half-way mark to the half-way mark (the "quarter-way" mark), and so on, ad infinitum. Conclusion: the runner can never even begin the race, and motion is an illusion.

A similar point is made with the paradox of the arrow. At any instant, argued Zeno, the arrow in flight occupies a space equal to itself, and, therefore, is at rest. And the same holds true of the arrow at any instant of its alleged flight through the air. At *every* instant it is at rest, and therefore motion doesn't exist.

Zeno was one of the truly great Greek minds. He invented arguments, notes Russell, "all immeasurably subtle and profound, to prove that motion is impossible. . . . From him to our own day, the finest intellects of each generation in turn attacked the problems, but achieved, broadly speaking, nothing." Although his paradoxes have now been solved, mathematically and logically, they remain so intriguing that new volumes about them appear almost annually.

some combination of three still more elementary objects called *quarks*°. However, such objects have not yet been discovered. . . . "

SAXON AND FRETTER

°NOTE: *Evidence for the existence of several quarks has been greatly strengthened in the ten years since these words were written. (Fretter, 12/80)*

THE DEMATERIALIZATION OF MATTER

12   The present particle picture remains confused; no semblance of order has yet emerged from studies of the atomic nucleus. The search for "quarks" is continuing. But a simple description of "ultimate reality" has yet to be found.

A nuclear physicist, Walter Scott Houston, observes that "in many respects the physics of elementary particles today is at a very

real crossroads," partly because discoveries have progressed so rapidly. "Curiously, although many people call physics an 'exact science,' there is more confusion than certainty in the nuclear particle field today."

About all that we can say is that all the elementary particles discovered in the atom are forces of energy. As they interact with one another according to what appears to be mathematical principles, they produce (or become) "matter." It is questionable whether the particles themselves are matter in any proper sense of the word; but matter as we know it is in some way dependent upon the combinations or configurations which the particles assume.

But what is "energy"? The honest fact is that we don't know, but we are beginning to suspect that it is not matter. "Energy" is *something* in motion which exerts force, but we don't know yet what that something is, and it looks more and more as though "ultimate reality," which we in the West have always assumed to be "substance" or "matter," may turn out to be nonmaterial, perhaps not unlike a set of mathematical principles in action.

> Nature loves to hide.
>
> HERACLITUS

13   "What is everything made of?"
Werner Heisenberg has written that, to such a question,

> the final answer will more closely approximate the views expressed in Plato's *Timaeus* than those of the ancient materialists. . . . The elemental particles of present-day physics are more closely related to the Platonic bodies than they are to the atoms of Democritus.
>
> The elemental particles of modern physics, like the regular bodies of Plato's philosophy, are defined by the requirements of mathematical symmetry. They are not eternal and unchanging, and they can hardly, therefore, strictly be termed real. Rather, they are simple expressions of fundamental mathematical constructions which one comes upon in striving to break down matter ever further, and which provide the content for the underlying laws of nature. In the beginning, therefore, for modern science, was the form, the mathematical pattern, not the material thing. And since the mathematical pattern is, in the final analysis, an intellectual concept, one can say in the words of Faust, *"Am Anfang war der Sinn"*—"In the beginning was the meaning."

> **The notion that matter is something inert and uninteresting is surely the veriest nonsense. If there is anything more wonderful than matter in the sheer versatility of its behaviour, I have yet to hear tell of it.**
>
> FRED HOYLE

14   Matter has been dematerialized, not just as a concept of the philosophically real, but now as an idea of modern physics. Matter can be analyzed down to the level of fundamental particles. But at that depth the direction of the analysis changes, and this constitutes a major conceptual surprise in the history of science. The things which for Newton typified matter—e.g., an exactly determinable state, a point shape, absolute solidity—these are now the properties electrons do not, because theoretically they cannot, have. . . .

The dematerialization of matter encountered in this century . . . has rocked mechanics at its foundations. . . . The 20th

The Periodic Table of Elements (left).

1	2	3	4	5	6	7	8	9	10	11	12	13	14	15	16	17	18
Hydrogen 1 H 1.008																	Helium 2 He 4.003
Lithium 3 Li 6.939	Beryllium 4 Be 9.012											Boron 5 B 10.81	Carbon 6 C 12.01	Nitrogen 7 N 14.01	Oxygen 8 O 16.00	Fluorine 9 F 18.99	Neon 10 Ne 20.18
Sodium 11 Na 22.99	Magnesium 12 Mg 24.31											Aluminum 13 Al 26.98	Silicon 14 Si 28.09	Phosphorus 15 P 30.97	Sulfur 16 S 32.06	Chlorine 17 Cl 35.45	Argon 18 Ar 39.95
Potassium 19 K 39.10	Calcium 20 Ca 40.08	Scandium 21 Sc 44.96	Titanium 22 Ti 47.90	Vanadium 23 V 50.94	Chromium 24 Cr 52.00	Manganese 25 Mn 54.94	Iron 26 Fe 55.85	Cobalt 27 Co 58.93	Nickel 28 Ni 58.71	Copper 29 Cu 63.55	Zinc 30 Zn 65.37	Gallium 31 Ga 69.72	Germanium 32 Ge 72.59	Arsenic 33 As 74.92	Selenium 34 Se 78.96	Bromine 35 Br 79.90	Krypton 36 Kr 83.80
Rubidium 37 Rb 85.47	Strontium 38 Sr 87.62	Yttrium 39 Y 88.91	Zirconium 40 Zr 91.22	Niobium 41 Nb 92.91	Molybdenum 42 Mo 95.94	Technetium 43 Tc (99)	Ruthenium 44 Ru 101.1	Rhodium 45 Rh 102.9	Palladium 46 Pd 106.4	Silver 47 Ag 107.9	Cadmium 48 Cd 112.4	Indium 49 In 114.8	Tin 50 Sn 118.7	Antimony 51 Sb 121.8	Tellurium 52 Te 127.6	Iodine 53 I 126.9	Xenon 54 Xe 131.3
Cesium 55 Cs 132.9	Barium 56 Ba 137.3	Lanthanide series 57–71	Hafnium 72 Hf 178.5	Tantalum 73 Ta 180.9	Tungsten 74 W 183.9	Rhenium 75 Re 186.2	Osmium 76 Os 190.2	Iridium 77 Ir 192.2	Platinum 78 Pt 195.1	Gold 79 Au 197.0	Mercury 80 Hg 200.6	Thallium 81 Tl 204.4	Lead 82 Pb 207.2	Bismuth 83 Bi 209.0	Polonium 84 Po (210)	Astatine 85 At (210)	Radon 86 Rn (222)
Francium 87 Fr (223)	Radium 88 Ra (226)	Actinide series 89–103	Rutherfordium 104 Rf (260)														

Lanthanide series

Lanthanum 57 La 138.9	Cerium 58 Ce 140.1	Praseodymium 59 Pr 140.9	Neodymium 60 Nd 144.2	Promethium 61 Pm (145)	Samarium 62 Sm 150.4	Europium 63 Eu 152.0	Gadolinium 64 Gd 157.3	Terbium 65 Tb 158.9	Dysprosium 66 Dy 162.5	Holmium 67 Ho 164.9	Erbium 68 Er 167.3	Thulium 69 Tm 168.9	Ytterbium 70 Yb 173.0	Lutetium 71 Lu 175.0

Actinide series

Actinium 89 Ac (227)	Thorium 90 Th (232.05)	Protactinium 91 Pa (231)	Uranium 92 U 238.0	Neptunium 93 Np (237)	Plutonium 94 Pu (242)	Americium 95 Am (243)	Curium 96 Cm (247)	Berkelium 97 Bk (247)	Californium 98 Cf (249)	Einsteinium 99 Es (254)	Fermium 100 Fm (253)	Mendelevium 101 Md (256)	Nobelium 102 No (256)	Lawrencium 103 Lr (257)

"What is the world made of?" This question has bothered man since the beginning of human inquiry. Thales thought the world was nothing but water. Anaximenes reasoned that it was all air. Heraclitus said it was fire. Empedocles and Aristotle decided it was a blend of Fire, Earth, Air, and Water.

At the atomic level, we now know what "the world" is made of. The entire universe and everything in it—including ourselves—is composed of about a hundred basic elements. When the "Periodic Table of Elements" was devised by Dmitri Mendeleev in 1871, even in its incomplete form it began to reveal numerous secrets regarding the orderly relationships within Nature. Today the philosophic implications are staggering.

Each element is determined solely by the number of protons it contains in its nucleus (carbon has six protons, for example; gold has 79). As the elements were arranged in the Table according to the number of each element's protons, then groups of elements with strikingly similar characteristics were seen. The columns to the left of the zigzag line tend to be metals; those to the right are nonmetals. The helium group (vertical column at right) consists of inert gases that refuse to react with other elements; but the volatile elements of the fluorine group react with almost any element they touch. The way all these elements combine to produce other substances is determined by the number of electrons that swirl in shells around the nucleus.

Today it's fashionable to take all this knowledge for granted, but this is the kind of understanding that would have made the first philosopher/scientists jubilant with excitement.

century's dematerialization of matter has made it conceptually impossible to accept a Newtonian picture of the properties of matter and still do consistent physics.

NORWOOD RUSSELL HANSON

THE FOUR KNOWN FORCES

The knowledge of science fails in the face of all ultimate questions.

KARL JASPERS

Mathematics may be defined as the science in which we never know what we are talking about nor whether what we say is true

BERTRAND RUSSELL

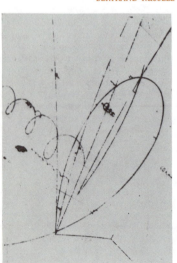

15   If ultimate reality turns out to be a series of waves or vibrations, then we can turn to our other fundamental question: "What are the forces that cause motion?" We have traveled far since Thales first asked the question, but we are far from the end of the journey. Today there are four known forces which cause motion.

One is gravity. When we lift an arm, walk, or stumble and fall, we discover our conditioning to the earth's gravity field. Enough is known about its operation to enable us to orbit satellites, calculate the trajectory of lunar missions, and describe the orbits of the planets. In fact, gravitational interaction is the best understood of the known forces. It seems to be simply described by the inverse-square law.

However, the nature of gravity remains a mystery. Current experiments are beginning to indicate that gravity takes wave form, and strong sources of gravity waves appear to be coming from the center of our galaxy. Also it is of interest to note that gravity seems to be the only known force that is irreversible: it always attracts and never repels. Once gravity waves are better understood, it will be interesting to know whether our notions about anti-gravity forces are science or fiction.

16   A second force is the electromagnetic, and this, like gravity, is familiar at the experiential level of reality. The interaction of magnets and iron, the combining of atoms into molecules, and the transmission of signals along a neural pathway to the brain, through the air to a TV set, or along a wire to a videophone—all these are electromagnetic interactions. Because it manifests itself in so many forms at the macrocosmic level, and because of its great versatility, this is the force we have been able to put to practical use serving man's needs.

Two other forces are found at the subatomic level, and little is known about either of them. One force—the so-called strong interaction—holds together the nucleus of the atom. Since the nuclear protons are positively charged (while neutrons are uncharged), they would strongly repel each other electrically. Despite this, the nucleus holds together. Some force, therefore, incredibly strong, acts to overcome the electromagnetic repulsion and binds from a few to several hundred protons and neutrons together into an ordered nucleus. Whatever its nature, this strong interaction is about a hundred times stronger than electromagnetic forces.

The second subatomic force—the "weak interaction"—operates only on specific atomic particles and is always associated with their disintegration. Its behavior in relation to a variety of particles is known, but its basic function is not understood.

PHILOSOPHIC INTERESTS

17   Several philosophic problems come to mind in relation to our present understanding of physics.

(1) Are these the only forces at work in our universe or might there be more, perhaps of a different kind? (2) Have our notions of reality been affected by our deeper knowledge of nature? (3) Can we make any meaningful inquiries at this point into the origins of matter/ motion?

Admittedly, dealing with such questions may be quite beyond our present capacities. Our fragmentary understanding leaves much to be desired. However, in the larger perspective of man's quest for knowledge, we have been approaching reality objectively for only a short time. Our questions are really just beginning, and we may have to wait for answers.

18   Are these physical forces the only activating principles at work in our world? Do these four known sources, interacting with energy/ matter, account for all of the objects/events in the cosmos? Or must we postulate other forces? What about the order and "design" of nature? or the aggregates of matter which constitute living cells? or complex life systems? or the delicate operations of mind and consciousness? Can *all* these things be accounted for by the four known physical interactions?

As one scans the panorama of human experience, it appears that there are at least three other forces which men have believed existed. In order to think of them as causative forces parallel to the physical forces, we might call them (1) mind-force, (2) spirit-force, and (3) god-force.

Many would contend that there is sufficient evidence in experience to warrant the hypothesis of some sort of mind-force. Evidence might come from telepathy, psychokinesis, or clairvoyance. If such events are actual—and present evidence is highly inconclusive—all attempts to reduce such events to known physical forces (for example, very short electromagnetic wavelengths) have failed. Of course, this might be the result of inadequate scientific technique. Those who have had experiences which they have interpreted as ESP events are convinced that mind-force is real.

Spirit-force has been postulated by men from the beginning to account for a multitude of experiences, from the blowing wind (*pneuma* in Greek and *ruah* in Hebrew mean both "wind" and "spirit") to emotional disturbances. We are convinced now that most of these events experienced by prescientific man can be accounted for on physical or psychological principles. Still, when one hears reports of poltergeists

The true lover of knowledge is always striving after *being.* . . . He will not rest at those multitudinous phenomena whose existence is appearance only.

PLATO

Physics today is not all clear-cut understanding and superefficient mathematics. The old view of its simple discrete particles and precise planetary orbits is gone. The physicist now prefers to view the atom as a ball of energetic and uncertain fluff. The wonder is that the more clouded its structure has become, the better has been the view into its heart.

RALPH E. LAPP

There is a famous anecdote about Laplace's submitting to the Emperor Napoleon a copy of his *System of the World.* Napoleon asked him what was the place of God in the system. Laplace answered: "Sir, I do not need this hypothesis." It is interesting to note that Laplace, who did not need the hypothesis of God in his book on astronomy, needed a Superior Intelligence in his formulation of the principle of causality. . . .

PHILIPP FRANK

What has been thought of as a particle will have to be thought of as a series of events. The series of events that replaces the particle has certain important physical properties, and therefore demands our attention; but it has no more substantiality than any other series of events that we might arbitrarily single out. Thus "matter" is not a part of the ultimate material of the world, but merely a convenient way of collecting events into bundles. . . .

BERTRAND RUSSELL

At the basis of the whole modern view of the world lies the illusion that the so-called laws of nature are the explanations of natural phenomena.

WITTGENSTEIN

that bang on doors and knock vases off shelves, one may be tempted to give second thought to the idea of a spirit-force.

Apart from religious belief derived from authority, is there any evidence for the existence of a god-force? In all of man's religions there have been mystics who claim that their lives have been touched by a god-force; they have seen the supernatural in visions or had their bodies healed by the divine. A large number of these experiences can be explained psychologically, so the problem would be to determine whether there are events which cannot be so explained and which necessitate the hypothesis of a god-force.

In man's experience, these forces—if they exist—have never been neatly separated, nor can they be now. (It has only been in our century, of course, that the four physical interactions have been distinguished as separate forces.) Whether such metaphysical forces exist remains an open question. Care must be used to apply "Occam's razor": the principle which calls for the simplest explanation and precludes hypothesizing any force which the evidence does not demand.

19   How have our notions of reality been affected by current concepts of matter/motion?

There has been a strong temptation on the part of some philosophers—especially those inclined to make their philosophy a religion—to think of reality in degrees. That is, they considered some object/events to be "more real" than others. Precisely what the terms "more real" or "less real" could mean is not always made clear. Generally, this world—the macrocosmic world of experience—was considered unreal; therefore, it was not to be valued. Plato was convinced that this world of particular things is an imperfect reflection of the perfect abstract "forms"; qualitatively it is not up to standard and therefore should not be taken too seriously. This world is made of matter, and matter is always imperfect. It resists shaping, like thick clay resists sculpturing. Only the eternal verities of mathematics or the "forms" of Goodness, Truth, and Beauty are truly real.

Similar concepts are to be found in the philosophies of the Gnostics, Neoplatonists, and Thomas Aquinas. The Hindu system of Shankara is even less equivocal: *everything* in this world is maya ("illusion"); it is merely a mirage and only Brahman is real.

20   Unless—for religious reasons—one has a need to declare this world "unreal," current thought tends to accept all levels of existence as equally real. We are gradually moving away from two extremes which have prevailed in the past: the idealism which considered macrocosmic experience as more real than, say, atomic interactions; and the overreaction of a scientism that held that physics provides the only true picture of reality.

There seems to be no good reason not to accept all objects/events in the external world as equally real, and this must include the full range from "point-events" of energy—whatever they are—to the grandest cosmological operations involving billions of galaxies.

There may be one qualification to all this. As indicated earlier, it is too soon to tell for sure what "matter" is. When physicists write that particles cannot "strictly be termed real" and may turn out to be something like "mathematical principles," then we may have to rethink the nature of ultimate reality at this particle or subparticle level.

Or is the problem merely semantic? "Ultimate reality" may eventually turn out to be nonmaterial, but would that necessarily mean that it is "less real"?

WHAT IS THE ORIGIN OF MATTER?

21   In the history of ideas, certain questions have to wait before they can be asked. One such question (the most obvious of all) was so overwhelming that it was asked and immediately tucked away, never to be taken seriously again. There is, however, a strong likelihood that during the eighties the question is going to be reopened and treated empirically. The question: What is the origin of matter?

The problem has been ignored because it seemed insoluble; a simple creationist answer appeared the only one possible. When did the universe begin? What created matter? Or from what was matter created? "God created the universe and set matter in motion." And the little girl who persisted—"Then who made God?"—we brushed aside.

Her question is legitimate. Philosophers have long pointed out that the creationist answer is no answer at all. It was merely a deus ex machina like that employed by Greek tragedians to unravel a tangled plot. The deity dropped in from above the stage and, by divine fiat, set everything right. To say that *X* created *Y*—or *G* created *M*—*ex nihilo*, "out of nothing," is merely to *define* the question as being off-limits to serious inquiry.

22   At this early stage of inquiry into the origin of matter only a few promising lines of thought have been developed. In his "steady-state" theory of the universe, Dr. Fred Hoyle assumed that matter is being created continually in space out of nothing, but he never attempted a serious explanation of how this might happen. Hoyle did little more than pose the problem.

> Matter is capable of exerting several types of influence—or fields as they are usually called. There is the nuclear field that binds together the atomic nuclei. There is the electro-magnetic field that enables atoms to absorb light. There is the gravitational field that holds the stars and galaxies together. And according to the new theory there is also a creation field that causes matter to originate.

To this last statement, Hoyle adds: "Matter originates in response to the influence of other matter."

Matter-in-motion can create other matter; for matter-in-motion is energy, and energy can be transformed into more matter. Therefore,

Physical things are those series of appearances whose matter obeys the laws of physics.

BERTRAND RUSSELL

Scientists have narrowed down the mystery of creation. All that seems to be necessary is some hydrogen gas at the beginning. We understand how the hydrogen condenses into a first generation of stars, how these stars cook heavier elements in their interiors, how these heavy elements are spewed out in supernova and other explosions to enrich the interstellar medium, and how subsequent generations of stars and planets form from the hydrogen and heavier elements. . . . And yet there's the beguiling problem: Where did the original hydrogen come from?

CARL SAGAN
The Violent Universe

Rationalism is an adventure in the clarification of thought.

WHITEHEAD

in theory, if we can imagine the universe beginning with even a very small amount of matter—perhaps just a few atoms—in a state of acceleration, then we can logically describe how all the matter in the universe might have come into existence. Each bit of matter traveling at high speeds can be transformed into more matter.

23 Today we can (almost) create matter in our laboratories. In a phenomenon known as "pair-creation," physicists can create electrons in the vacuum of the accelerator, that is, out of nothing. They have also succeeded in creating pairs of positive and negative protons out of nothing. Weisskopf states that, in his opinion, this represents the actual creation of matter.

Electrons can also be created from photons of light. The interesting point is that light does not have mass, while electrons have. Photons (with a rest mass of zero) are massless energy; at the speed of light the photons can be transformed into mass according to the mass-energy transformation equation: $E = mc^2$.

What does all this mean? One implication seems to be that questions about the origin of matter are not wholly out of order. Nevertheless, at the present time really convincing answers are lacking. In all cases physicists began their experiments with something (not "nothing"), and they had at their disposal sophisticated scientific equipment with which they could accelerate particles into higher energy states. Theoretically, we can imagine a universe empty of all mass but a single, lonely electron, plus some force that can push that electron into relativistic speeds, then we can logically account for all the rest of the matter in the entire universe. But what that "prime mover" might be still bothers us.°

The best we can do at present is to hold on to the question and not be lured into thinking it has been answered. We will probably have to rephrase the question numerous times before an answer begins to come. Indeed, it might be found in some different frame of reference altogether.

We believe in the possibility of a theory which is able to give a complete description of reality, the laws of which establish relations between the things themselves and not merely between their probabilities.

ALBERT EINSTEIN

°*This is the problem which generated the "cosmological argument" for the existence of God as Prime Mover. See page 517.*

REFLECTIONS—

1 Reflect on the snowflakes and other illustrations of natural objects/events throughout the chapter. What can you infer about "nature" from their common patterns?

2 Why was Thales' prediction of the eclipse so important that we date the beginnings of philosophy and science from this event? (Recall earlier comments about Thales on pp. 21f., Sec. 4)

3 We possess two clear-cut kinds of knowledge about the real world—empirical knowledge and a priori knowledge. Clarify the working of each and then go to the question raised in Sec. 7: Can you think of any further *ways* of knowing reality? Might Bergson's notion of intuitive knowledge be correct?

4 Summarize—briefly, and very carefully, in your own words—exactly what the Jovian philosopher saw and did as he watched the baseball game. In fact, did he *see* the baseball game at all? What is the role of memory in the construction of knowledge? Now, how does this analogy apply to our knowledge of (a) the natural world, (b) human behavior, and (c) the personality of another individual?

5 Now, when all is said and over with, isn't it true that all robins' eggs are blue? What's the hassle all about? Why make such a big deal of something that everyone knows?

6 Note the comment in Sec. 6: The "theoretical problem of a priori knowledge haunts our intellects. Why is it that mathematical knowledge describes so accurately the operations of nature?" What is the best answer you can give to this puzzle?

7 Whether or not you have ever studied physics or chemistry, spend some time pondering and just enjoying the Periodic Table of Elements (p. 427). This table shows how incredibly far we have come since the first philosopher-scientists began to inquire into the nature of the "world-stuff"—matter. Note the many varieties of order evident in the Periodic Table. What is your philosophic response to the varieties of relationships and patterns to be found here—that is, in "nature"? Do you think you can share Sir Fred Hoyle's feeling (p. 426-QM) about the fascination of pure matter?

8 Ponder Heisenberg's statement in Sec. 13 along with Hanson's in Sec. 14 (See also Russell's remark on p. 425-QM). Can you restate in your words what you think they mean when they all contend that, in the twentieth century, "matter has been dematerialized"? What might be some of the philosophic consequences of this achievement?

9 Note the four known physical forces, the forces that "perform the work" of the universe by keeping "matter in motion." Besides these basic four, do you have any evidence that there are any forces at work in the universe?

10 Spend some time—perhaps a lot of time—reflecting on Zeno's paradoxes on motion. Take any one and analyze the argument to the point where you understand his logical errors (if there are any).

11 Criticize the argument that God must have created matter because the assumption that matter has existed through all eternity is an illogical assumption. Therefore, there *must* have been a "first cause"—which is God (Sec. 21). Refer to the "cosmological argument" for God on pp. 517.

12 Have you personally speculated on the problem of the origin of matter? Are you willing to do so now? What questions can you think of to initiate inquiry? To whom might we turn for hard data that would help us phrase our questions in an intelligible fashion?

Furthermore . . .

ASIMOV, ISAAC, *Asimov on Physics*. Doubleday, 1976.
ASIMOV, ISAAC, *The Search for the Elements*. Fawcett, 1966.

ASIMOV, ISAAC, *View from a Height*. Lancer, 1963.

BURTT, E. A., *Metaphysical Foundations of Modern Science*. Anchor, 1955.

COLLINGWOOD, R. G., *The Idea of Nature*. Oxford, 1960.

DURBIN, PAUL R., *Philosophy of Science: An Introduction*. McGraw-Hill, 1968.

FRANK, PHILIPP, *Philosophy of Science: The Link between Science and Philosophy*. Prentice-Hall, 1957.

LAPP, RALPH E., et al., *Matter*. Life Science Library. Time Inc., 1965.

REICHENBACH, HANS, *The Philosophy of Space and Time*. Dover, 1957.

RUSSELL, BERTRAND, *The Problems of Philosophy* (1912). Oxford, 1959.

SALMON, WESLEY C. (ed.), *Zeno's Paradoxes*. Bobbs-Merrill, 1970.

SAXON, DAVID S., and WILLIAM B. FRETTER, *Physics for the Liberal Arts Student*. Holt, Rinehart and Winston, 1971.

SHAPERE, DUDLEY, *Philosophical Problems of Natural Science*. Macmillan, 1965.

STEIN, SHERMAN K., *Mathematics: The Man-Made Universe: An Introduction to the Spirit of Mathematics*, 3rd ed. W. H. Freeman, 1976.

TOULMIN, STEPHEN (ed.), *Physical Reality*. Harper, 1970.

WATSON, W. H., *On Understanding Physics: An Analysis of the Philosophy of Physics*. Harper, 1959.

WILSON, MITCHELL, et al., *Energy*. Life Science Library. Time Inc., 1967.

Time/Space

Have You Ever Wondered . . .

- What Einstein's theory of relativity really means?

- Whether astronauts might travel into the future and/or the past?

- Whether anything at all exists "outside" space and time?

- What might be meant by such a phrase as "empty space"? (Think about it for a moment.)

- Whether the science-fiction notion of parallel universes has any validity?

- What's happening right now—at this very instant—on some other planet orbiting some other star in some other galaxy?

- What quasars are?

- Whether it means anything to you personally to be told that you're living in a relativistic universe?

WE LIVE IN A RELATIVISTIC UNIVERSE

1   We live in a relativistic universe. The Newtonian universe which existed till the beginning of the twentieth century was one in which conventional physics adequately described matter-in-motion.

I cannot believe that God plays dice with the cosmos.

ALBERT EINSTEIN

But a relativistic universe is one in which matter is in motion at very great speeds. When velocities are sharply increased some strange things begin to happen. Such high velocities, we now know, are the general rule at both the microscopic and cosmological scales of physical reality. It is primarily at the macroscopic level of experience that Newtonian theories still operate.

Since Albert Einstein published his paper on special relativity in 1905, our understanding of our universe and our place in it has undergone continual revision. It may not seem at first glance that relativistic notions affect our routine behavior, but the fact is that we are immersed in relativistic events. For instance, light photons striking our retinas can be described only in relativistic terms, and the very atoms that compose our bodies are themselves in motion at these high velocities.

Beyond all this, the significant fact is that a new world-view was born with special relativity. It has gradually become part of our consciousness.

2   Relativistic phenomena astound the layman, excite the physicist, and boggle the mind of the philosopher. In fact, the physicists don't even pretend to understand much of what they describe; they go their way developing pragmatic equations without worrying very much whether their formulas describe realities presently accessible to experience.

At the microscopic level, common sense is offended. "Almost all the 'great principles' of traditional physics turn out to be like the 'great law' that there are always three feet to a yard; others turn out to be downright false." So observes Bertrand Russell.

Particles can be accelerated so as to increase their energy and when "smashed" each resulting particle will weigh as much as the original particle. Also there is discontinuity: a particle observed at one place will be subsequently observed at another place without having moved through any point to get there. Even the concept of time-reversal is used by some physicists to explain particle behavior.

3   Equally strange events are occurring at the cosmological level. Einstein's equations predict that as objects move at very high speeds (near the speed of light), time slows down, mass increases, and length decreases (at least, that's the way we would observe and measure them). Also the universe may be curved (positively or negatively, but as yet we don't know which), and Einstein thought in terms of "curved space."

If time is real, there may indeed be time anomalies; and if space is real, there could be space anomalies. This is, events have been observed for which hypotheses of time/space anomalies would be workable explanations.

Other unbelievable goings-on have been observed for some time. Quasars, for instance, generate far more energy than present physical theory can explain, and pulsars are probably the long-pre-

If space *is,* it will be in something; for everything that *is* is in something; and to be in something is to be in space. Space then will be in space, and so on *(ad infinitum).* Therefore space does not exist.

                    ZENO OF ELEA

There are more things in heaven and earth, Horatio,
Than are dreamt of in your philosophy.

                    SHAKESPEARE
                    Hamlet

dicted neutron stars—stars in the throes of death—whose matter weighs billions of tons per cubic inch. Now astronomers are developing models of "black holes" where the gravitational attraction of a collapsing neutron star would be so great that no light could escape from it.

Another incredible fact is that our relativistic world-view was developed within the mind of one man.

4   What Einstein did was not a formal accomplishment. He did not approach the problem from the standpoint of finding some mathematical equation which will describe a certain group of phenomena. Something much more fundamental was at stake, namely, the critical evaluation of the cultural foundation of theoretical physics. Certain things which were always taken for granted, were put under scrutiny and their falseness proved. This was no longer mere physics and mathematics . . . . Here started that dogged uphill fight of Einstein which lasted ten years and which is perhaps unparalleled in the entire history of the human mind; a fight which did not arise from any experimental puzzle of the mind.

CORNELIUS LANCZOS

> **I maintain . . . that the transient now with respect to which the distinction between the past and the future of common sense and psychological time acquires meaning has no relevance at all apart from the egocentric perspectives of a conscious (human) organism and from the immediate experiences of that organism.**
>
> *ADOLF GRÜNBAUM*

THE SPECIAL THEORY OF RELATIVITY

5   According to Einstein's theory, no material object can travel faster than the speed of light (which is about 186,000 miles per second). Relativistic phenomena begin to occur around 10 percent of the speed of light.

At these velocities, three significant things begin to happen to all objects in motion, including human beings: (1) time slows down; (2) the mass of objects increases; and (3) the length of objects (measured parallel to the plane of motion) decreases.

Take, for instance, the phenomenon known as "time dilation." The measurement of time—and perhaps the actual "flow" of time—is strictly relative—relative, that is, to the standpoint of the observer. Two travelers moving in different reference systems at high speeds relative to each other would *measure* time differently, and both would be right.

The "twin paradox" apparently illustrates actual realities. Imagine twin brothers twenty years old, one of whom becomes an astronaut. He takes a journey through space to a planet orbiting the star Rigil Kent (which is also known as Alpha Centauri, the nearest star to us after the sun), which is about 4 light-years distance. His spaceship travels at 148,000 mps (miles per second). At that speed (which is $^4/_5$ the speed of light), according to all the clocks on this spaceship—calendars, wristwatches, atomic clocks, heartbeats—his experience of time would slow to $^3/_5$ its normal rate *as observed and measured by his twin brother on earth*. He would therefore make the journey to Rigil

> **The idea that time can vary from place to place is a difficult one, but it is the idea Einstein used, and it is correct—believe it or not.**
>
> *RICHARD FEYNMAN*

Kent in 3 years and the return trip in 3 years, the entire roundtrip taking 6 years. But while he was on the 6-year journey his twin brother on earth would age 10 years. From his earthbound viewpoint, he would measure his space-traveling brother's journey taking 5 years out and 5 years back—10 years according to his calendars and clocks.

And both measurements are correct. There is no suggestion that one measurement is the real one and the other is distorted or illusory. Both are true. The astronaut would experience the passing of only 6 years and he would age only 6 years. But according to his stay-at-home brother, the space journey would have taken 10 years and he himself would have aged a full 10 years.

Time, therefore, is relative. It looks as though it's not merely a matter of the way we observe objects in motion. It appears that these phenomena are real. They take place within the objects themselves.

6 The relativity of time-measurement was a cornerstone of Einstein's system. In 1905 it was only theory, but we now have evidence

THE MESSAGE FROM PLANET X

There is no absolute time throughout the universe by which absolute simultaneity can be measured. Absolute simultaneity of distant events is a meaningless concept.

How radical this notion is can be seen by a thought experiment in which vast distances and enormous speeds are involved. Suppose that someone on Planet X, in another part of our galaxy, is trying to communicate with the earth. He sends out a radio message. This is, of course, an electromagnetic wave that travels through space with the speed of light. Assume that the earth and Planet X are 10 light-years apart, which means that it takes 10 years for the message to travel to the earth. Twelve years before a radio astronomer on earth receives the message, the astronomer had received a Nobel Prize. The special theory permits us to say, without qualification, that he received this prize *before* the message was sent from Planet X.

Ten minutes after receiving the message, the astronomer sneezes. The special theory also permits us to say, without qualification, and for all observers in any frame of reference, that the astronomer sneezed *after* the message was sent from Planet X.

Now suppose that sometime during the 10-year period, while the radio message was on its way to the earth (say, 3 years before the message was received), the astronomer fell off his radio telescope and broke a leg. The special theory does *not* permit us to say without qualification that he broke his leg before or after the sending of the message from Planet X.

The reason is this. One observer, leaving Planet X at the time the message is sent and traveling to the earth with a speed judged from the earth to be slow, will find (according to his measurements of the passing of time) that the astronomer broke his leg *after* the message was sent. Of course he will arrive on earth long after the message is received, perhaps centuries after. But when he calculates the date on which the message was sent, according to his clock, it will be earlier than the date on which the astronomer broke his leg. On the other hand, another observer, who also leaves Planet X at the time the message is sent, but who travels very close to the speed of light, will find that the astronomer broke his leg *before* the message was sent. Instead of taking centuries to make the trip, he will make it in, say, only a trifle more than 10 years as calculated on the earth. But because of the slowing down of time on the fast-moving spaceship, it will seem to the ship's astronaut that he made the trip in only a few months. He will be told on the earth that the astronomer broke his leg a little more than 3 years ago. According to the astronaut's clock, the message was sent a few months ago. He will conclude that the leg was broken years before the message left Planet X.

If the astronaut traveled as fast as light (of course this is purely hypothetical; not possible in fact), his clock would stop completely. It would seem to him that he made the trip in zero time. From his point of view the two events, the sending of the message and its reception, would be simultaneous. *All* events on earth during the 10-year period would appear to him to have occurred before the message was sent. Now, according to the special theory there is no "preferred" frame of reference: no reason to prefer the point of view of one observer rather than another. The calculations made by the fast-moving astronaut are just as legitimate, just as "true," as the calculations made by the slow-moving astronaut. There is no universal, absolute time that can be appealed to for settling the differences between them.

MARTIN GARDNER
The Relativity Explosion

to support it. According to predictions, all physical, chemical, and biological processes would begin to slow down when achieving relativistic speeds, and this is exactly what we find. In the accelerators, atomic particles (pions and others) have been pushed to high speeds and then subjected to high-energy collisions with other particles. When thus "smashed" these particles disintegrate at known rates. At high velocities, however, these particles disintegrate considerably more slowly, and the rate of disintegration is in exact agreement with

It is estimated there may be 135,000,000,000 stars in the Galaxy, and there may be as many as 100,000,000,000 other galaxies distributed through space. Astronomers are generally convinced that there are unnumerable worlds on which life might develop.

ISAAC ASIMOV

TIME DILATION AND SPACE TRAVEL		
Speed of spaceship relative to earth in terms of the speed of light *(c)*	Factor by which crew's time slows down compared to earth time	Number of years of crew time required for round-trip journey to a star 100 light-years away
0.9999	70.712	2.8
0.98	5.025	40.6
0.95	3.203	65.7
0.90	2.294	96.9
0.75	1.512	176.4
0.50	1.155	346.4
0.10	1.005	1990.0

Einstein's predictions. This means the "time experience" of the particle has slowed down to a fraction of what it was at rest.

The fact of time dilation is also supported by more recent observations of naturally occurring (nonlaboratory) phenomena. Cosmic rays from outer space continually collide with the gaseous molecules in the earth's upper atmosphere and break those molecules into component particles. One such particle, the mu-meson or muon, has a lifetime of only two microseconds (two millionths of a second). Should a muon be knocked from an atom and continue to travel near the speed of light, it could cover a distance of only a few hundred feet. Yet large quantities of muons are detected on the surface of the earth more than six miles from their collision points. But how can muons travel six miles in two microseconds? Only two answers seem possible. One is that the muons are traveling faster than the speed of light. But according to relativity theory this is impossible; nothing in the universe can travel faster than the speed of light. The other answer is that the muons do in fact disintegrate in two microseconds according to *their* time scales, but they have a longer lifetime (and can therefore travel farther) according to *our* time measurements. Just as in the "twin paradox," the muon's time-experience (two microseconds) remains unchanged; but to an outside observer its time appears to have slowed down, and therefore it is observed to travel immense distances in its short two-microsecond lifetime.

Saxon and Fretter comment that it took forty years for scientists to find direct empirical confirmation of the Special Theory of Relativity formulated by Einstein in 1905, "but physicists believed it implicitly from the outset because of its internal consistency and because a very substantial body of indirect evidence was gradually amassed."

A good deal of current science fiction involving space travel (*Planet of the Apes*, for example, in which the astronauts jump ahead in time some two thousand years) embodies principles that are not at all fictional, but plausible science. According to present understanding

One of our problems is trying to figure which is up and which is down.

JOHN YOUNG
(From Apollo X spacecraft)

it is quite possible to move forward in time. How far forward one might travel depends solely on the speed one can attain. (Note figures in box on page 440.)

There may be some semantic confusion in the phrase "we can move into the future." No object—astronaut, particle, or whatever—can move into *its own future.* The personal experience of time always remains constant. The "future" that we can "move into" is the future of the other reference system (the earth's, that of the twin who stayed at home, that of the scientist who measures the muon), simply because your time has slowed down and, relatively, their time has speeded up. Experientially, no matter what relativistic speeds we may attain, each singular life/time is lived in the same old way.

7   Special relativity also predicts that mass will increase and length will decrease. These two ideas have also been accepted from the beginning by most physicists, and the former has been empirically verified. Again, in the accelerators, the mass of high-speed particles increases so much that adjustments must be made in the magnetic fields which drive and guide the particles. The increase in mass would otherwise fling them outside the magnetic holding field.

To date no empirical evidence has been found to substantiate the prediction about decrease in length, yet there seems to be no reason to doubt it as part of the relativistic package.

8   There is disagreement among physicists as to the philosophic implications of such relative measurements. The problem is whether these phenomena are real—that is, whether the object actually undergoes these changes—or whether the changes are merely observational phenomena.

One school of thought holds that these phenomena take place only from the standpoint of an observer in one reference system who is watching objects in another system moving at high speeds. In other words, they are observational, and the thought-experiment involving the light-clock appears to imply that they are perceptual only.

In the diagram, the light-clocks are on two spaceships moving at high speeds relative to one another, speeds not far short of the speed of light. What would a passenger on each spaceship see if he could observe the light-clock on the other spacecraft?

Light-clock *A*, on your ship, just sits there, blinking. The top bulb sends a beam of light down to the photoelectric cell which in turn triggers the bottom bulb which sends a beam of light to the cell at the top; so down and up the light-beams go.

There is an identical light-clock *(B)* on the other spaceship. As it passes, what would you see? You would perceive a much longer beam of light than is emitted by your own clock which (to you) is at rest. So the light-beam on the other spaceship travels farther *in the same period of time* as your light-beam. This could have two explanations: either the light of the other light-clock is moving faster or time has slowed down. The former is impossible, according to relativity, since the speed of

Quasar 3c 273

Hitherto people have looked upon the Principle of Causality as a proposition which would in the course of years admit of experimental proof with an ever-increasing exactitude. . . .
   Now Heisenberg has discovered a flaw in the proposition. . . . The principle of causality loses its significance as an empirical proposition.
   Causality is thus only conceivable as a *Form of the theoretical system.*

ALBERT EINSTEIN

Perhaps the most majestic feature of our whole existence is that while our intelligences are powerful enough to penetrate deeply into the evolution of this quite incredible Universe, we still have not the smallest clue to our own fate.

FRED HOYLE

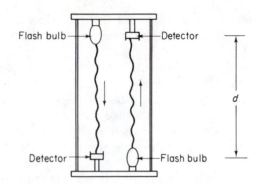

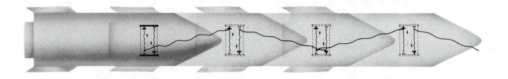

light is a constant; it always travels at 186,000 mps. Therefore, what you are witnessing is a slower movement of time on the other spaceship compared with the movement of time according to your clock.

But ask: What would the passengers on the other spaceship see as they watch your clock pass by? They would see precisely what you see, only reversed. To you, *his* time has slowed down; to him, *your* time has slowed down.

This sort of thought-experiment seems to indicate that the whole matter of relativity is merely perceptual. Einstein's equations describe nothing more than the way we would measure things that move very fast relative to our point of observation.

But other physicists are not so sure. Some are convinced such phenomena are not perceptual, but real, that they really happen to objects. It would seem that the increase in particle mass in the accelerators and the slowdown of decay time in the disintegration of pions is not merely a matter of measurement, but is an event which the particle actually undergoes. If this is not the case, then why the adjustments which are necessary in the magnetic fields?

The same dilemma applies to time. Saxon and Fretter candidly write that to understand relativistic phenomena, "we must realize that time dilation is a property of time itself, not of any particular clock."

At present the puzzle does not appear to be soluble.

TIME IN PHYSICAL THEORY

9   Is time real? Does time exist in the real world, or is time merely an experience? The majority of philosophers and psychologists (as opposed to physicists) have held that time is an experience only. It is our

The objective world simply *is*, it does not *happen*. Only to the gaze of consciousness, crawling upward along the life-line of my body, does a section of this world come to life as a fleeting image in space which continuously changes in time.

HERMANN WEYL

The exciting discovery of quasars by astronomer Maarten Schmidt, and the subsequent development of the black hole theory, was the subject of a TV documentary on the Public *Broadcasting System. The event was narrated by Robert MacNeil, PBS host, and Carl Sagan, an astronomer from Cornell University.*

MAC NEIL. Six years ago such a spectrum [as in the photograph above] was a turning point in astronomy. Schmidt obtained it from a quasar. . . . Schmidt puzzled over the spectrum for six weeks. It made no sense. Then on February 5, 1963, he understood. He recognized a group of lines, but they were completely shifted to the red end of the spectrum.

SCHMIDT. That night I went home in a state of disbelief. I said to my wife, "It's horrible! Something incredible happened today!"

SAGAN. Let's see, roughly, why Schmidt was so shocked and what his spectrum meant. Imagine a bright source of light which is moving rapidly away from you. The light waves that it emits are "stretched out"—they are moved toward longer (and therefore redder) wave lengths. The faster the thing is moving away from you the more red-shifted its spectral lines become. Astronomers are by now used to the conclusion that galaxies with the biggest red-shifts—that is, those which are moving fastest away from us—are also the most distant galaxies. . . .

Schmidt recognized a pattern of three lines due to atomic hydrogen, but these three lines were not in their usual place in the spectrum. . . . They had been red-shifted by this very large distance. The amount of the red-shift corresponds to a velocity of about 30,000 miles per second, and such an enormous velocity means that the quasar must be very far away, in fact that it must be about a billion light years from the earth.

Now, how is it possible that an object which appears to us so bright could be so far away? A huge mass of gas or stars falling together might conceivably produce such a large amount of energy, enough to drive a quasar. But there's a problem with this idea: it's that gravity is, in a sense, too strong. There's nothing to stop the collapse of such a mass of gas or stars. It would continue to collapse. It would pass through the neutron star stage. . . . and eventually its gravity would become so intense that even light would be unable to escape from the object.

Therefore the object would "turn off"—it would disappear. It would vanish from the universe, leaving behind only a sort of "black hole" of gravity, a little like the grin on the Cheshire cat. The universe may in fact be riddled with such black holes.

Imagine a spaceship wandering around, minding its own business, encountering such a black hole. What happens to it? Well, it must vanish. It must disappear from the universe.

There are some who believe that matter which disappears down such a black hole must reemerge at some other point in space, at some other epoch in time. This may be just a sort of highbrow science fiction, or it may really be true.

The quasars are such a puzzling phenomenon that they may really lead us to revise our notions of the laws of nature.

The Violent Universe
PBS-TV, April 1969

experiencing of the continuum of our flow of consciousness. If there were no consciousness there would be no experience of time, and therefore there would be no time. Time, they have contended, is in no sense a property of the real world.

To be sure, there are sequences of events in the real world, and it appears that certain events must happen before other events. The concept of causality has meaning as these events take place in sequence. There is a "before" and "after" which is real. But these are merely events, and events are matter-in-motion; and there is no ingredient called "time" involved in such processes.

If this is the case, then before consciousness came into being, events took place over the billions of years. Atoms interacted and the forces of the universe moved matter about, but no time was involved in these events.

On the other hand, physicists are almost equally split on the reality of time. There are many who hold—and Einstein himself held—that time is in some sense a feature of the real world. Clocks and relativistic physics do not merely measure the flow of our conscious experience; they measure time itself.

10　　Will man ever be able to move back and forth in time? Any answer to this depends in part on the reality of time. Our popular notions of "time travel" have been derived largely from science fiction and TV programs, and a recent book entitled *Psychic Visits to the Past* states:

> Commonly we think of ourselves as captives of time, caged in the present, moving toward the future at a set speed, with the past forever behind us. But this illusion swiftly fades as we begin to investigate the experiences of those with the psychic ability to move back and forth through time with seeming ease.

> There is no need for these hypotheses to be true, or even to be at all like the truth; rather, one thing is sufficient for them—that they should yield calculations which agree with observations.
>
> ANDREAS OSLANDER (1543)

What exactly a dematerialized psyche can do cannot at present be described by a scientist, but if we remain in the realm of matter-in-motion, we can get some tentative answers. Our best knowledge at present indicates that we can move forward in time, but never backward in time. If we could travel just short of the speed of light—say, at a speed of 185,000 mps—it would be quite possible in one lifetime to move millions of years ahead in time. But moving backward in time appears to be an impossibility. The heros of science fiction can move up and down the corridors of time, with or without a time-machine, tampering with historic events along the way; but it looks at present as though any "journey into the past" will be confined to fantasy.

SPACE IN PHYSICAL THEORY

11　　Is space real? Does space exist in the real world or is space only in our heads? Immanuel Kant was one of the first epistemologists to make the unequivocal statement that both time and space are aspects of the mind. They are "modes of perception," that is, structures of consciousness through which we experience the real world. They are a priori and develop in minds through experience, but they are not derived from any experience of real time or space. Kant contended that it is impossible for us to do any thinking about real objects without the *concepts* of time and space. We can think of nothing in the real world without the idea of a space in which we can relate objects; mentally, objects "occupy" space: they are so many feet apart or they move at a certain speed through space. But space exists only in our concepts.

The same view can be taken of time. We cannot experience an object without having it "endure" in our consciousness. As we watch an object its existence persists "in time"; that is, it endures in our consciousness. Obviously, we could not perceive an object if this experience of duration were not so structured. Therefore, time and space are both in our minds as perceptual necessities. They are in no way a part of the external world.°

°*They are not a part of the real world, that is, unless we choose to define them as such. See page 228.*

12   How far does space extend? For hundreds of years man has puzzled over this question. We want to know how big the universe really is. If our universe curves back on itself and is therefore a finite universe, we want to know what lies "beyond" or "outside" this universe. How far *can* space extend?

If "space" is defined as the absence of everything, then it is "nothing." We are therefore asking how far "nothing" extends, and this turns out to be a false question. Our thinking about the "extension of the universe" becomes a conceptual problem and not a problem about anything real.

Can we use such expressions as "empty space" or "objects in space"? According to Einstein himself (and he seems to be agreeing with Kant) such concepts are essential to our thinking. Mathematicians are aware that they must use symbolic concepts even though they refer to nothing real: irrational numbers, imaginary numbers, the square root of minus one, etc. The idea of "empty space" is such a necessary concept.

We can think of an "empty box" which means that "nothing" is in the box. But how can *nothing* be *in* a box? If we are interested in knowing how much matter (e.g., three bushels of grain) we might place in the box, then the question is meaningful. Space is a potential. Similarly, we can think of the universe as a large box and ask how much matter could be placed in this hypothetical "empty space." How much space is there between the universes and is it empty? Such concepts, Einstein has written, are mental tools, but necessities nevertheless.

It would appear at present that space is indeed "nothing." If we say there is space between any two objects, then we are saying that there is "nothing" between them. It is doubtful that space has any real status. The question, however, is not closed.

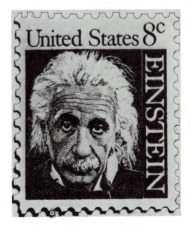

13   Is it possible for anything to exist "outside" space and time? Apart from theological assumptions, it is difficult to give meaning to such a question. Since we exist *in* space and time (or space and time exist *in* us), it is questionable whether we could know if anything exists "beyond" space and time. It is conceivable that there might be

Does the harmony which human intelligence thinks it discovers in Nature exist apart from such intelligence? Assuredly no. A reality completely independent of the spirit that conceives it, sees it or feels it, is an impossibility. A world so external as that, even if it existed, would be for ever inaccessible to us. What we call "objective reality" is, strictly speaking, that which is common to several thinking beings and might be common to all; this common part . . . can only be the harmony expressed by mathematical laws.

POINCARÉ

space anomalies—"holes in space"—or time anomalies—"time warps." Such ideas, however, are meaningless unless one assumes that time and space are real.

To conclude that anything, including deity, could exist outside of time would be a problematic concept. If time is merely an experience (which it most likely is), then to state that something can exist outside time is to say that it can exist outside of consciousness. This, of course, is a truism (except for Bishop Berkeley). To say that God existed before time is to say he existed before consciousness which, again, is quite possible. So we arrive at a theological statement which cannot be proved or disproved: that God alone existed and therefore (providing he is conscious) time existed only in the consciousness of God. This is a standard orthodox concept of Western theology. It is not an empirical statement and rests upon numerous unexaminable presuppositions.

REFLECTIONS—

1 Sec. I of this chapter begins, "We live in a relativistic universe." What is meant by this?

2 Einstein's work has been hailed as a landmark accomplishment by the human mind. How so? What is so important about the *way* Einstein went about developing his theories?

3 The "twin paradox" is the most famous prediction of Einstein's Special Theory of Relativity and has been imaginatively explored by science-fiction writers: "time travelers," "time tunnel," *The Time Machine, Planet of the Apes,* and countless others. If Einstein's calculation is in fact true, do you understand what it predicts and—since it batters down our "common sense"—can you accept it and live with it?

4 Analyze and enjoy the story of "The Message from Planet X" (p.439). Do you understand how simultaneity is a fallacy when applied to reference systems moving at high speeds relative to one another? What philosophic implications do you see in this relativistic concept?

5 When you reflect on the nature of time—such as moving backward and forward in time, or wondering how many dimensions time has—is it possible that you may be engaging in "the fallacy of the spatialization of time"—that is, thinking of time in terms of space? Can you think of de-spatialized time—pure time?

6 Old Zeno again! Ponder his argument (p.436-QM) that space doesn't exist. Could he be right? If space *does* exist, does that make his argument wrong? If space *doesn't* exist, does that make his argument right?

7 Ancients and moderns alike have asked, "What is beyond space?" or "How far does space extend?" After reading Secs. 12 and 13, how would you answer such questions?

8 By way of summarizing, is time real (Sec. 9)? Is space real (Sec. 11)?

9 In the story of the discovery of quasars (p.443), Dr. Maarten Schmidt remarked, "It's horrible! Something incredible happened today!" What had

he seen that produced such disbelief? What are some of the implications—
which Schmidt himself immediately began to see—of his discovery?

Furthermore . . .

BARNETT, LINCOLN, *The Universe and Dr. Einstein*. Mentor, 1950.

BERGAMINI, DAVID, et al., *The Universe*. Life Nature Library. Time Inc., 1967.

CLARK, RONALD W., *Einstein: The Life and Times*. Avon, 1972.

GARDNER, MARTIN, *The Relativity Explosion*. Vintage, 1976.

KAUFMANN, WILLIAM J., III, *Relativity and Cosmology*. Harper, 1973.

SCHILPP, PAUL A. (ed.), *Albert Einstein: Philosopher-Scientist* (2 vols.). Harper, 1959.

Cosmos

Have You Ever Wondered . . .

- What the word "universe" refers to?

- How big the universe is?

- What exists beyond the "edges" of the universe?

- Whether space can "go on forever"?

- How many stars there are?

- What is really "out there" in the universe—: star clusters, galaxies, dust clouds light-years across, exploding stars, infrared stars, colliding galaxies, black holes, time warps (maybe), space warps (maybe), bridges from one universe to another (?)—and what else that we haven't dreamed of?

- What might happen if Atlas got tired of holding up the earth and decided to set it down and walk away?

ANCIENT COSMOLOGIES

1   Ancient man lived very close under the stars. His life was much affected by them, especially by the steady points of light that wandered through the star-fields as though they were alive. They might in fact be the bright bodies of the gods themselves playing beneath the blue-black firmament, gods such as Jupiter, Venus, and Mars.

Men felt themselves enclosed in a finite container of some sort:

The Universe is not only queerer than we imagine—it is queerer than we *can* imagine.

J. B. S. HALDANE

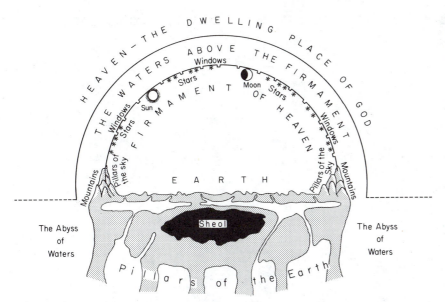

a box, or a valley with an inverted clay bowl arching overhead, or a flat disk under a giant crystalline dome. When men tried to make sense of their cosmos they saw different things.

Egyptians thought of their flat earth as the floor of a rectangular box. Some saw also a flat sky that extended away to the distant corners of the box; but others saw a bowl-shaped sky supported around the rim by a range of mountains surrounding the world like a great wall. The stars were burning lamps suspended high above from the roof or dome.

2   Babylonians knew their flat earth to be a round disk of land floating in a vast sea. Beyond this sea mountains rose to support the dome holding aloft the heavens. These heavens were the dwelling place of the gods and were strictly off-limits to mortals; man's sole domain was his circular disk of earth. He could neither visit the outer corners of earth nor gaze upon the abode of the immortal gods.

The ancient Hebrews saw above them a gigantic bowl of beaten metal (like the "brazen heaven" of Homer's *Iliad*) which separated the lower from the upper waters. This "firmament" was everywhere pitted with small holes through which the light of Heaven could be seen. The sun and moon were attached to the vaulted firmament and appeared to roll across it each day. The firmament was held up around the edge by a great range of mountains ("pillars of the sky"). An ocean of water extended around the sides of the inverted bowl and down under the earth. High above the water dwelt God and the Host of Heaven. Beneath the flat surface on which man lived "roots of earth" plunged deep into the abysmal waters. Also under the earth, near its center, there existed an enormous cavern called *sheol* where (some said) the ghost-shades of men slept after death.

"One ought not to grumble at Heaven that things happen according to its Way (Tao). . . . When stars fall or the sacred tree groans, the people of the whole state are afraid. They ask, 'Why is it?' I answer: There is no reason. This is due to a modification of Heaven and Earth, to the mutation of *Yin* and *Yang*. . . . If people pray for rain and get rain, why is that? I answer: There is no reason for it. If people do not pray for rain, it will nevertheless rain."

HSŬN TZU
(c. 250 B.C.)

Egyptian cosmos, showing the goddess Nut, her body dotted with stars, bending in a giant arch over the earth, represented by a reclining figure wearing a skin of leaves. The sun moves across the sky above the goddess in a heavenly barge.

The deflation of some of our more common conceits is one of the practical applications of astronomy.

CARL SAGAN

3   The night could be quiet, but it was the raging, blinding fireball by day which dominated the lives of men.

To Egyptians the sundisk which scorched the desert and brought green life to the meandering Nile was the god Amon-Ra, floating across the liquid sky in a barge. He passed into the Valley of the Gods at sunset and emerged from the valley at dawn.

Mesopotamians saw the eastern gates opening each morning and Shamash the sun god racing out in a great chariot drawn by wild asses. The sun was one of the chariot's burning orange-bright wheels. At sunset Shamash exited through the western gates and all through the night drove his chariot along a dark tunnel under the mountainous edge of the universe, emerging again from the eastern gates at dawn.

To early Greeks, Helios arose daily out of the eastern sea in a quadriga drawn by four white stallions. As he lifted his fiery chariot into the sky the stars were scattered and dove into the sea. In late afternoon he approached the western boundaries of the earth, and far-away peoples living too near the edge would be singed by the heat of his chariot.

To ancient men the universe was closed, and they felt a kind of security in knowing that. There was continuous interaction among the gods, the evil spirits, and men who wandered the flat earth. Generally, good things went on above, bad things went on below, and man knew that his place was somewhere in the middle.

This woodcut depicts man's restless curiosity to know what "the heavens" are really like. Here a man has traveled to the edge of the universe and poked his head through the firmament; he beholds the machinery that moves the heavenly bodies. This is precisely what Homo scientificus has succeeded in doing.

TODAY'S UNIVERSE

4   As the twentieth century wanes, what do you and I see when we look up at the stars?

We know, first and last, that we are looking *out into space* and *back in time*. Whenever we look at any object in space we are also looking into the past: about $1\frac{1}{4}$ seconds into the past when looking at the nearest natural object (our moon); about 9 minutes back in time to the nearest star (our sun); about 4 years back in time to the second nearest star (Alpha Centauri); about 2 million years into the past when gazing at our nearest neighbor galaxy (Andromeda). And with the aid of telescopes we can peer into time past some 10 billion years. The farther we look out in space, the farther we are looking back in time.

Astronomers today share a unique kind of excitement because there exists a real possibility that we may be looking far enough into the past to see events which took place near the time of origins—the creation of our universe. Evidence indicates that such a beginning occurred between 12 and 25 billion years ago, and some of the objects we are now seeing (notably the quasars) are probably phenomena which happened shortly after that beginning.

In the thousands of years for which men have wondered about the meaning of what goes on in the sky, there has never before been such a dramatic period as this. . . . All over the world astronomers have spotted events of breath-taking violence, scarcely explicable in the known forces of nature. They are also on the brink of establishing for the first time the history and fate of the universe we live in.

The Violent Universe
PBS-TV

A medieval diagram of the geocentric (Ptolemaic) universe. With earth at the center, the other members of the solar system move in concentric orbits. Diagram from Peter Appian's *Cosmographia* (1539).

5   Conceptualizing the size of the universe as we know it today strains our imaginations. Indeed, one may have to live with incredible concepts for a time before they can become believable.

Our solar system is composed of our star/sun and nine orbiting planets, plus assorted planetoids, asteroids, and comets. If we take the orbit of the planet Pluto as the outside limit of our solar system, then it is about 7½ billion miles (or 11 light-hours) in diameter. This local system is our home, our "front yard," incredibly small on a cosmic scale. The nearest star to our sun is a little more than 4 light-years away (about 26 trillion miles). Our Milky Way galaxy is about a hundred thousand light-years across, and our solar system moves within one spiral arm of our galaxy, some thirty thousand light-years from its center. We are really quite far out and not even in the central plane.

Furthermore, our galaxy is a part of a larger system. Some two dozen galaxies move together in what is known as the "local group." These include the Andromeda galaxies and the Magellanic clouds.

Photographs taken with very long exposures through giant telescopes reveal billions of galaxies extending in all directions. Many are

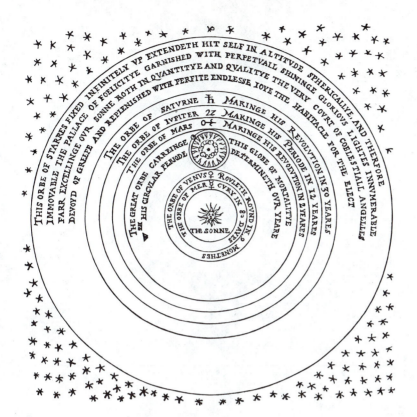

The heliocentric (Copernican) cosmos as drawn by Thomas Digges in 1576. In the center of the system is "the sonne," and the other heavenly bodies—though, strangely, not the stars—revolve in circular orbits around the sun. Notice, however, that the moon revolves around the earth.

spiral-shaped like our Milky Way, but they also come in many other shapes and sizes. Sometimes as many as several hundred galaxies appear together on a single photographic plate spanning but a few minutes of arc across the sky. The largest radiotelescopes now reach out more than 10 billion light-years—and the galaxies keep on going.

It is not impossible that we may be part of a "metagalaxy," a cluster of hundreds or thousands of galaxies spiraling together in what might look like our own Milky Way magnified a million times.

THE EXPANDING UNIVERSE

6   Modern cosmology is based on a single discovery made by Dr. Edwin Hubble in 1929. That discovery was that the universe is expanding. With refined photographic equipment we can see literally billions of galaxies—"island universes"—and judging from the "red shift" (the Doppler effect) in their spectra, they all appear to be moving away from us at constant speeds. This expansion is the fundamental fact which any and all cosmological theories are obliged to explain.

In your mind's eye draw an imaginary sphere 1 mile in diameter and fill it with quarters and half-dollars floating about a foot apart. These coin-disks are the galaxies of our perceptual universe. If we locate ourselves at the center of this imaginary sphere, then what we observe is that all of these coin-galaxies are receding from us. Those

NEXT PAGE: In contrast with the fanciful ancient cosmologies, here is the universe as we know it today. These dust clouds, stars, star clusters, and much more are merely a fraction of our own Milky Way galaxy. The smaller, dark globules in the photograph are dense masses of gas and dust which are contracting into stars; that is, new stars are continually being born out of such interstellar and intergalactic matter.

Everything indeed, everything
visible in nature or established in
theory, suggests that the universe
is implacably progressing toward
final darkness and decay.

LINCOLN BARNETT

nearer to us are moving slower; the farther away they are the greater
their speed of recession from us. Out near the edge of the sphere their
velocities are nearing the speed of light. When, all around the inside
surface of the sphere, the galaxies reach that speed, they become invisible. Each galaxy emitting light in our direction at 186,000 miles per
second, but moving away from us at 186,000 mps, would cross over
the threshold of perception. Light would require infinite time to reach
us; hence, it becomes invisible. This is the edge of our "perceptual
universe." All galaxies reaching the speed of light would vanish from
sight.

These perceptual limits we must accept, but we can't avoid
wondering what lies beyond perception. If we exist in a pulsating universe, then we wonder how far the galaxies continue beyond that perceptual threshold before they begin their long journey back to the center. How much of the pulsating bubble can we actually see? Are there
other bubble-universes? If so, how many? Could they possibly extend
to infinity? How much space exists between the bubble-universes?

At present we can do little more than develop models which are
coherent extensions of our theories about the closer parts of the universe which lie within our range of perception.

THREE COSMOLOGIES

For myself, I find it hard to accept
the big-bang theory. I would like
to reject it. How can I believe such
a naive theory that says there was
a finite time only twice as long as
the age of our earth, [when] the
universe was vastly different from
its present state—a red hot ball? I
much prefer Mr. Hoyle's more
subtle steady-state. But I have to
face the facts, as a working
physicist. The evidence mounts
up, experiment after experiment,
[and] at least suggests that the
clear predictions of the most naive
theory—the big-bang—are coming
true.

PHILIP MORRISON

7   There are three cosmologies widely held at present: (1) the "big-
bang" theory, (2) the "steady-state" theory, and (3) the "pulsating-
cosmos" theory.

(1) The Big-bang Theory

The big-bang theory holds that all of the matter in the universe
was pulled together by gravity into one huge, hot ball—a "primordial
atom"—several hundreds of light-years in diameter. As gravitational
forces increased, the ball became ever more condensed. Pressure and
temperature reached enormous levels. As contraction continued, there
occurred a gravitational collapse amounting to an implosion. The outer
layers rushed inward until they reached a critical point at which the
massive cosmic ball exploded. This is the "big bang."

Matter was flung outward in all directions. Great clouds of gases
and dust formed. Stars condensed from the dust clouds and pulled
one another closer into clusters; great accumulations of matter began
swirling as galaxies. This vast hodge-podge of exploded matter continued—and still continues—to journey outward from the scene of the
explosion.

According to this picture, there was but a single explosion and
since that time the universe has been "running down." From the time
of the explosion the second law of thermodynamics (entropy) operates
to dissipate energy. Living things exist only during this interim period

while the fires are still burning. After that all the galaxies, stars, and planets will grow cold and die; they will float outward forever into the distant reaches of space. There will be no more heat and no more light.

(2) *The Steady-state Theory*

8   The steady-state theory was developed by Sir Fred Hoyle of Cambridge University. Hoyle attempted to account for the expanding universe by suggesting that matter is continually being created out of nothing in interstellar and intergalactic space. Hoyle couldn't accept the theory of a "big-bang" beginning; a one-time explosion seemed too arbitrary, too "accidental"; *unique* occurrences feel not-quite-right to scientists since they develop theories from repeated observations of regularities.

Sir Fred Hoyle

Hoyle reasoned that if matter is being continually created in space, then the "expanding universe" can be explained. The expansion is merely displacement by newly created matter.

Hoyle calculated that if one hydrogen atom is created in each cubic mile of space every hundred years, then sufficient matter is coming into existence to account for the displacement of existing matter. The creation of all other elements can also be accounted for as the hydrogen atoms combine into ever-larger accumulations of matter and develop high temperatures and pressures within star systems.

One problem with Hoyle's theory is explaining how matter can be created (create itself?) *out of nothing*. Hoyle himself avoided the problem. He wrote:

> There is an impulse to ask where originated matter comes from. But such a question is entirely meaningless within the terms of reference of science. Why is there gravitation? Why do electric fields exist? Why is the universe? These queries are on a par with asking where newly created matter comes from, and they are just as meaningless and unprofitable.

Hoyle reiterates that science asks *how* things operate the way they do, but not *why*. "We must not go on to ask why," he says. (This is a fallacious argument, incidentally, and Hoyle, like the rest of us, wants very much to ask "Why?" for elsewhere he writes: "For myself there is a great deal more about the Universe that I should like to know. Why is the universe as it is and not something else? Why is the universe here at all? . . . Throughout the history of science, people have been asserting that such and such an issue is inherently beyond the scope of reasoned inquiry, and time after time they have been proved wrong.")

In any case, Hoyle abandoned his steady-state cosmology a few years ago. He concluded that new evidence (especially from quasars) lent strong support to some sort of explosion theory. But in admitting that his own theory was probably wrong, Hoyle proved his adherence to the highest principles of scientific objectivity.

When the pulsars turned up [in 1968] the Cambridge radio-astronomers who discovered them were so astonished that they labelled their first records of these regular pulsars "LGM." That stood for "Little Green Men." It seemed at first less incredible to think that intelligent beings elsewhere in the universe were trying to get in touch with us, than to imagine that a star could produce this jazzy rhythm.

"The Violent Universe"
PBS-TV

(3) *The Pulsating-universe Theory*

9   A third theory—the "pulsating cosmos"—is increasingly accepted as the most coherent hypothesis.

This theory concurs with the big-bang theory that matter was shot outward in every direction by a cosmic explosion. However, the total gravitational attraction of all the mass in the universe is so great that the universe cannot "escape from itself." That is, the gravitational pull of the universe's mass is greater than the force of the explosion. Galaxies traveling outward will gradually slow down—as though there were an elastic net around the entire universe—and reverse their direction, moving back toward the center from which they were exploded. As all mass converges, it becomes again a primordial hot ball. The dynamics repeat themselves and another big bang sends matter on its way through space. Calculations indicate that explosions occur at intervals of about 80 billion years. After each explosion galaxies, stars, and planets are born and life emerges, perhaps throughout the universe. But ultimately the stars grow cold, life dies, and all matter contracts again into a hot ball.

Thus, the universe "pulsates," from explosion to explosion. A pulsating universe is anything but dead; it is a live, eternal universe, building up energy and dissipating it randomly only to build up energy again, losing nothing. Its perpetual processes are inherent and irrevocable.

We are now at a point in time about 20 billion years after the last big bang. The universe is still rapidly expanding. Some 20 billion years from now most of the galaxies will have stopped receding and begun their return journey. In 60 billion years another explosion will start the cycle again, and, perhaps, some 80 billion years hence, countless living beings will look up at the stars at night and wonder what it's all about.

10   It is interesting how closely the pulsating-cosmos theory resembles the teleocosmologies of some of man's religions. According to Hindu mythology, the god Shiva spins out the universe while he dances; when the Lord of the Dance tires, his creative activity wanes, the universe runs down, all life vanishes, and there is quiescence until Shiva revives and begins dancing again. This cosmic cycle, billions of years long, eternally repeats itself.

Similar also is the Norse cycle which ends in the Doom of the Gods (the *Götterdämmerung*), when the forces of chaos will inaugurate the final battle. In stunning contrast to most of man's religious teleocosmologies, the battle will be fought in vain. The valiant warriors of Valhalla, and even the gods themselves, will be crushed, and all life will be extinguished. Earth and cosmos will be consumed by fire. Then, after a long while, a new earth will be born, and order will be restored by the sons of Odin and Thor. Mankind too will be generated again from a human couple who will have survived the conflagration. Thus, after a fiery end, the cycle of life begins again.

I think the universe is slowing down. In fact, it is slowing down so fast that sometime in the future the expansion of the galaxies will cease and contraction begin. . . . The galaxies will coalesce with one another and finally merge once again into a primeval fireball.

ALLEN SANDAGE

When you understand all about the sun . . . and all about the rotation of the earth you may still miss the radiance of the sunset.

ALFRED NORTH WHITEHEAD
Science and the Modern World

A torrent of new insights into the nature of the Universe is almost upon us. It is now possible to perform relatively precise calculations on the natures of astronomical objects. The instrumentation for ground-based observations has reached a high state of sophistication. Large space telescopes (LSTs) can be placed above the Earth's atmosphere, where images are steadier, more distant objects can be detected and much finer detail can be resolved. There are new windows in the electromagnetic spectrum: Gamma ray, X-ray, ultraviolet, and certain kinds of infrared and radio astronomy are possible for the first time. In the next few decades we will have explored completely the electromagnetic spectrum. It is likely that the enigmas of such mysterious objects as pulsars, quasars, X-ray sources, galactic nuclei and black holes—all of whose most important properties are indetectable in visible light—will be solved.

Astronomy is no longer merely an inferential science, studying light waves emitted or reflected from elsewhere. The advent of space-vehicle exploration permits us to examine the neighboring celestial bodies directly. In the next few decades we should see the nearly complete reconnaissance of the nine planets, 33 moons and miscellaneous comets and asteroids of our solar system. We may see the first solar probe—a spaceship shot into the fiery inferno of the nearest star. And just possibly we may witness the launching of the first space vehicles designed to explore other solar systems.

CARL SAGAN
Other Worlds

A MULTIBUBBLE UNIVERSE—?

11   Recent cosmologists are beginning to envision the possibility that the universe may consist not merely of a single pulsating bubble, but several bubbles or perhaps an infinite number. All that we can perceive is a portion of our own bubble-universe, but if there is one pulsating bubble, then why not more? If matter should extend infinitely, then the dynamics of pulsation must operate everywhere in similar fashion.

This multibubble universe is more gigantic than anything the human mind has heretofore tried to comprehend. Yet the more knowledge we obtain the more credible a multibubble cosmology becomes. The fact of the matter is that there is a feeling of aristocentrism about the notion that there is but a single bubble-universe—namely *ours*.

We feel as though we've been displaced. Again. How absurd! Why must man continue to insist upon *positioning* himself? We are precisely where we have always been. *Here*.

BARBARA CHRISTIAN

DO WE LIVE IN A CURVED UNIVERSE?

12   One aspect of the theory of relativity is that space is "curved" and that therefore we live in a "curved universe." Einstein suggested that the total gravitational force of all mass produces a universe which must be understood in terms of "curved space geometry." All objects moving in such a universe—from massive pulsars to massless photons—would follow curved trajectories. Whether the universe is curved positively or negatively (or not curved at all) has not yet been established. If negatively curved, it is an "open" universe; mass moving along gravitational lines of force would exit from our universe and vanish. But if positively curved—and there seems to be increasing in-

direct evidence that it is—then it is a "closed" universe curving back on itself. Mass (and photons of light) would curve in great circles through the gestalt gravitational fields.

    If positive curvature is real, then visual displacement of distant objects may be far greater than we have thought. Nothing in the heavens would be where we presently "see" it. Light emitted by objects will have been bent in its journey to us. Out near the edge of our perceptual universe where galaxies are receding from us at great speeds, the objects we observe may now exist in some other part of the universe altogether; indeed, they may not now exist at all. Moreover, the speeds we observe may represent their velocities billions of years ago. Where such objects are located now, and what their veloci-

I always felt that man is a stranger on this planet, a total stranger. I always played with the fancy: maybe a contagion from outer space is the seed of man. Hence, our prior occupation with heaven—with the sky, with the stars, the gods—somewhere out there in outer space. It is a kind of homing impulse. We are drawn to where we come from.

ERIC HOFFER

ties are, we cannot be sure. We find ourselves caught in a frustrating but exciting quandary.

We are beginning to get an idea of man's place in the cosmic picture, but undoubtedly some shattering discoveries—always the unexpected—are still in store for us.

AND THEN WHAT HAPPENED?

There is an amusing short tale by the Irish writer Lord Dunsany (in his book *The Man Who Ate the Phoenix*) in which Atlas explains to Dunsany what happened on the day when science made it no longer possible for mortals to believe in the old Greek model of the universe. Atlas admits that he had found his task rather dull and unpleasant. He was cold, because he had the earth's South Pole on the back of his neck, and his hands were always wet from the two oceans. But he remained at his task as long as people believed in him.

Then the world, Atlas says sadly, began to get "too scientific." He decided he was no longer needed. So he just put down the world and walked away.

"Yes," Atlas says. "Not without reflection, not without considerable reflection. But when I did it, I must say I was profoundly astonished; utterly astonished at what happened."

"And what did happen?"

"Simply nothing. Simply nothing at all."

MARTIN GARDNER
The Relativity Explosion

REFLECTIONS—

1 There is one single idea which, if we could assimilate it deep into our consciousness, can change the way we perceive the universe. When looking at all heavenly objects, "we know, first and last, that we are looking *out into space* and *back in time*" (Sec. 4). Next time you have a clear sky and a little time, recall this fact as you gaze at each star or planet with new space/time eyes.

2 Reflect on, and just appreciate, the ancient cosmologies. In general, what do you think of the accomplishments of these prescientific minds in ordering their perceptions of their universe?

3 Browse through the pages of this and the following chapter and gaze empathetically into the photographs of the stars, galaxies, and other deep-space objects which populate our universe. Move *into* the pictures . . . and *out into* the universe. Can you comprehend its vastness? What do you feel as you ponder a universe of such dimensions?

4 "Modern cosmology is based on a single discovery"—that we live in an expanding universe (Sec. 6). What does that mean? What is expanding? Where are we located in this expanding model?

5 Review each of the cosmologies currently considered viable. Do you understand the general dynamics of the big-bang, steady-state, and pulsating theories? Do you understand what kind of evidence astronomers are now seeking that would make possible a final determination of which theory is correct?

6 As you think of the three cosmologies most widely held by scientists to-

day, which would you prefer to believe in? Or live in? Which would be the most comforting and most secure?

7 If we are living in a pulsating universe, then the probability is very high that life develops throughout the universe and exists for lengthy durations after each big bang. What does this possibility do to your thinking about the nature of life? about God? about the universe? about yourself? about the purpose of life?

8 What is meant by Einstein's phrase that "space is curved"? If, by definition, space is "nothing," then how can "nothing" be curved? (See Sec. 12.)

9 Martin Gardner's account (from Lord Dunsany) of how Atlas "just put down the world and walked away" is a charming parable; and, as with all parables, the meaning remains implicit. Make explicit what the story says to you.

Furthermore . . .

ASIMOV, ISAAC, *The Universe: From Flat Earth to Quasar*. Avon, 1965.

GAMOW, GEORGE, *The Creation of the Universe*. Bantam, 1965.

HODGE, PAUL W., *Concepts of the Universe*. McGraw-Hill, 1969.

HOYLE, FRED, *Astronomy and Cosmology*. W. H. Freeman, 1975.

HOYLE, FRED, *The Nature of the Universe*. Signet, 1960.

NEEDLEMAN, JACOB, *A Sense of the Cosmos: The Encounter of Modern Science with Ancient Truth*. Doubleday, 1975.

SHIPMAN, HARRY L., *Black Holes, Quasars, and the Universe*. Houghton Mifflin, 1976.

TOULMIN, STEPHEN, *The Fabric of the Heavens*. Harper, 1965.

Biocosmos

Have You Ever Wondered . . .

- As you stand under the stars at night, whether the heavens are alive with life?

- OR what it might feel like if it is actually true that we humans are *totally alone* in the universe?

- How many civilizations there may be in our Milky Way galaxy?

- How we humans would *feel about ourselves* if we find that we belong to a vast, cosmic community of advanced intelligent beings?

- When a "close encounter of the third kind" might actually take place?

- What extraterrestrials might look like?

- Whether we and extraterrestrial beings would share *experiences* in common?

WE ARE NOT ALONE

1   Only a few years ago the attitude of the scientific community toward the existence of life on other worlds was an unyielding skepticism. In 1934 the British astrophysicist Sir Arthur Eddington could summarize the scientific consensus this way:

> Within our galaxy alone there are perhaps a thousand million stars as large and as luminous as the sun; and this galaxy is one of many

In our time this search [for extraterrestrial life] will eventually change our laws, our religions, our philosophies, our arts, our recreations, as well as our sciences. Space, the mirror, waits for life to come look for itself there.

RAY BRADBURY

millions which formed part of the same creation but are now scattering apart. Amid this profusion of worlds there are perhaps other globes that are or have been inhabited by beings as highly developed as Man; but we do not think they are at all common. The present indications seem to be that it is very long odds against a particular star undergoing the kind of accident which gave birth to the solar system.

During the 1950s several renowned astronomers were giving serious thought to the possibility that life is a common cosmic occurrence. It was no longer believed that the creation of our solar system was a once-in-a-billion accident resulting from a near-collision with a passing star. The accident theory of Sir James Jeans was rapidly replaced by the hypothesis that solar systems condense from the same "nebula" of gaseous and dusty cloud-matter from which the star condenses, and at the same time. This model—the "nebular hypothesis"—is almost universally accepted today. The conclusion, therefore, is that planetary systems similar to our own are scattered throughout the universe and orbit their home stars in the same way that Sol's nine planets swirl around their sun. Other worlds exist on which life might well evolve and develop.

One of the first astronomers to conclude that other-worldly life must exist was Harlow Shapley. In 1957 Shapley wrote that he was convinced that

> sentient organisms, the product of biochemical evolution, must be a common occurrence in the universe. From general considerations of planetary origins and the evolution of chemical compounds on a cooling planet's surface, we concluded first that not less than a hundred million "high life" locations exist, and the number is probably more like a hundred trillion. Secondly, that there is no reason not to believe that the biochemical evolution on, let us say, one half of the suitable planets has equalled or attained much greater development than here. Thus, in answer to an earlier question, we have decided that *we are not alone* in this universe. . . .

Harlow Shapley

2   There are good grounds for believing that the development of life-forms through an evolutionary process is a universal operation. Assuming this to be so, Shapley attempted to calculate the probabilities of evolvement of intelligent life.

Life *on* stars seems to be out of the question because of their high temperatures, so life would most likely arise in planetary systems associated with stars. Such planets would have to move in stable, near-circular orbits which would avoid great temperature extremes. Some sort of atmosphere, the presence of some free water, and somewhat constant radiation levels might also be requisites. Within these broad parameters for tolerable conditions, it appears likely that some form of life will inevitably develop.

Shapley makes the conservative guess that perhaps one star in a thousand has a planetary system; and that perhaps one in a thousand systems has a planet with just the right temperature tolerances for life; then of these planets perhaps only one in a thousand has sufficient quantities of air and water to transform organic molecules into protoplasm.

Using these figures Shapley estimated that only one star in a trillion (10^{12}) has a planet that meets all the requirements. The odds against life-supporting environments seem overwhelming. Still, if the total number of stars in our universe is about a hundred billion billion (10^{20}), then the number of planets with conditions suitable for the growth of life comes out to be a hundred million ($10^{20} \div 10^{12} = 10^{8}$). And "this is a minimum," Shapley concluded, not too happily: "Personally I would recommend . . . its multiplication by at least a thousand times, possibly by a million."

$$N = R_* f_p n_e f_l f_i f_c L$$

3   Since Harlow Shapley completed his calculations, significant advances have been made in many of the sciences relevant to the question of extraterrestrial life—in biochemical evolution, microbiology and genetics, radioastronomy, communications theory and technology, and many others. An enormous amount of thought has been given to the subject, and estimates have been refined.

Two astronomers from Cornell University, Frank Drake and Carl Sagan, developed an equation for calculating the number of communicating civilizations which may exist in our Milky Way galaxy at the present moment in time. (After all, if we want to communicate, we want to communicate now!) Here is their formula:

$$N = R_* f_p n_e f_l f_i f_c L$$

In this equation, the number of such advanced civilizations (*N*) is assumed to be the function of seven variables:

R_* = the number of stars that are born each year in our Milky Way galaxy (a good estimate: ten per year)

f_p = the average number of planets orbiting each star (on the average: about one)

n_e = the number of such planets that have a life-sustaining environment (again, probably about one per planetary system)

f_l = the number of such congenial planets on which life actually evolves (again: probably one. The consensus among biologists is that life will eventually evolve in just about any congenial site, given enough time.)

f_i = the number of these life-bearing planets which evolve intelligent life (the probable number: one. The reasoning is the same as for f_l: given sufficient time, intelligence will almost always evolve.)

f_c = the number of intelligent life-forms that develop a communications technology (a conservative guess: perhaps one percent)

Civilizations in space may have contacted each other with strong, directed radio beams and formed a club talking back and forth. Consequently, the better the club, the more members are in it. So each member looks around for stars with worlds having indications of advanced technology. When they see a promising star, they cast their beam toward it. It is like waving a flashlight. They may have been waving it for thousands of years.

RAY BRADBURY

A one-planet deity has for me little appeal.

HARLOW SHAPLEY

Our first astronauts then must be the wisest and most temperate men, slow to revulsion, quick to sympathy. . . .

RAY BRADBURY

L = the average lifetime of such a communicating civilization. (Here we're stumped and can make only feeble guesstimates. We know of only one such civilization: our own. If *we* make it through the next couple of centuries, how long will *our* "communicating civilization" last?)

Substituting these figures for the symbols in the Drake/Sagan equation, we get:

$$N = 10 \times 1 \times 1 \times 1 \times 1 \times 1/100 \times L$$

or

$$N = 1/10 \times L$$

The conclusion, therefore, is that the number of civilizations in our galaxy with whom we could communicate at the present time is one-tenth the mean lifetime of such a technological civilization. If scientific societies such as ours last, say, 200 years after they reach the technological stage, then one-tenth × 200 is only 20. There are only twenty possible contacts in our galaxy of over a hundred billion stars. We might as well give up hope of finding other intelligent life in the biocosmos and learn to live with our loneliness.

But *if* civilizations survive their crisis transitions and last for millions of years—and a plausible argument can be made that, having

survived a technological infancy (rather like a three-year-old child playing with a hand-grenade), then civilizations continue to exist almost forever—then there exist thousands or millions of extraterrestrial societies right now. The figure could be one-tenth of a million or one-tenth of a billion; but in any case, our attempt to make contact across the light-years of space would not be undertaken in vain.

Man has probably reached a point in his relationship to the biocosmos from which there is no turning back. Peter Angeles makes the point: "If extraterrestrial intelligence is never found at any time in the universe, the quest will still go on: there will always remain a possibility in an infinite universe that extraterrestrial intelligence exists *somewhere*, or did exist *somewhere*, or will come into existence *somewhere*. In an infinite universe the biocosmic belief cannot be eradicated."

A COSMIC CONTEXT FOR MANKIND

4   Carl Sagan reminds us that all human societies, like human infants, begin their lives in an egocentric condition. "A human infant begins to achieve maturity by the experimental discovery that he is not the whole of the universe. The same is true of societies engaged in the exploration of their surroundings." Maturity must include the continuing reassessment of oneself in relation to one's world and to the component parts of that world.

The need to understand our place in the scheme of things has taken on a special meaning because of man's problematic future on this world and the probable existence of life on other worlds. In the words of Nobel laureate George Wald, "We need some widely shared view of the place of Man in the Universe."

The search for extraterrestrial life should be seen as a natural, normal next step in the "reality adjustments" we make in our relationships. Such adjustments continue on all fronts: in man's relationship to man, in our ecological ties with other fauna and flora that share our planet, and with the life-sustaining physical elements of our environment. We live in times of change; vital information about ourselves and our world is acquired faster than we can process it. We urgently need to know where we stand so that we can make sound survival judgments and behave appropriately.

"There is today," notes Sagan, "—in a time when old beliefs are withering—a kind of philosophical hunger, a need to know who we are and how we got here. There is an ongoing search, often unconscious, for a cosmic perspective for humanity."

From the time of their joint beginnings, philosophy and science have worked together to achieve a more realistic picture of man—of his origins, his nature, and his destiny.

Sagan: "We are aware of our deep connection, both in form and in matter, with the rest of the universe. The cosmos revealed to us by the new advances in astronomy and biology is far grander and more awesome than the tidy world of our ancestors. And we are becoming a part of it, the cosmos as it is, not the cosmos of our desires."

The APCD predicts no smog again tomorrow. . . . Birmingham, Alabama, has had an air pollution crisis this week. . . . The planet Mars today had a violent dust storm, and it'll take at least 10 days to clear. . . . On the moon the low tonite will drop to 307 degrees below zero, and tomorrow it'll climb all the way up to an afternoon high of 273 degrees above zero. . . . The astronauts will stir up some more dust tomorrow cruising around in the moon buggy, so there'll be light to moderate eye irritation on the moon.

KELLY LANGE
KNBC News

Sagan

E.S. Munson II '80

Carl Sagan

The Spaceship of the Imagination

I

He stands on a rocky cliff by the sea. Waves churn below and seagulls skim the breakers. He wears an orange windbreaker.

"The Cosmos is all there is or ever was or ever will be. Our feeblest contemplations of the Cosmos stir us . . . we know we are approaching the greatest of mysteries."

He plucks a dandelion seed from a crevice in the rock and lets it dance away in the wind.

"Come with me," he beckons.

For years to come, Carl Sagan will be known as the eloquent tourguide who lectured us and dreamed us through the light-years of space and time in his 13-part television series *Cosmos.* Backed by a gifted team of film-makers and scientists, and with dazzling special effects, the dandelion seed is transformed into "the spaceship of the imagination," and Sagan shows us the wonders of the universe.

"In the last few millennia we have made the most astonishing and unexpected discoveries about the Cosmos and our place within it. . . ."

Sagan invites us to share his knowledge and excitement; and this "personal voyage" truly becomes the grandest of adventures. Before it is over he shows us supernovas, pulsars, black holes, star clusters, exploding galaxies, the Big-bang, other worlds where intelligent life might be found—and countless other cosmic and historical events.

"They remind us that humans have evolved to wonder, that understanding is a joy, that knowledge is prerequisite to survival."

II

Sagan leans against a STOP sign, watching a police officer give out a ticket, listening to rail-cars roaring past. He wears the same orange windbreaker.

"I lived here . . . in Brooklyn . . . . I knew my immediate neighborhood intimately—every candy store, front stoop, back yard, empty lot, and wall for playing Chinese handball. It was my whole world."

In winter, he recalls, he could see the stars. "I looked up at them and wondered what they were." His friends told him "they were lights in the sky." Since he already knew that, he went to the library and found a book on stars. "I opened the book breathlessly right there in the library and the book said something astonishing—a very big thought. Stars, it said, were suns, but very far away. The sun was a star, but close up.

"I was ignorant . . . but I could tell that if the stars were suns they had to be awfully far away, farther away than 86th street, farther away than Manhattan, farther away, probably, than New Jersey.

"This just blew my mind. Until then, my universe had been my neighborhood. Now I tried to imagine how far away I'd have to move the sun to make it as faint as a star. I got my first sense of the immensity of the universe. I was hooked."

Sagan decided then and there that he would become an astronomer.

"But," his worried grandfather asked, "how will you make a living?"

Carl Sagan was born in Brooklyn in 1934, of an American-born mother and an emigrant Russian father, a cloth-cutter in the garment industry. His parents expected their son to follow the family vocation, but they had the wisdom to support his own gifts and intellectual interests. "As a child it was my immense good fortune to have parents and a few good teachers who encouraged my curiosity." So he grew up under the city lights, playing handball, devouring science-fiction, and dreaming of other worlds "fabulously unlike Brooklyn."

After high school, Sagan headed directly for a career in science. In 1951, at 16, he entered the University of Chicago on a scholarship. Nine years later he emerged with four degrees in science, including a Ph.D. in astronomy and astrophysics. He was 26.

While in graduate school at Berkeley and Stanford, Sagan sensed the far-ranging implications of the work of the biochemists. At 22 he wrote his first technical paper on "Radiation and the Origin of the Gene"; and this has been followed by more than 300 articles and a dozen books, most of them related to the biochemistry of life-origins. Sagan is preeminently an exobiologist.

"Science is a joy," says Sagan, and it belongs to everyone. "It is not just something for an isolated, remote elite. It is our birthright."

III

In tropical southern India, inside a temple dedicated to Shiva, Sagan walks among some very old bronze statues of Hindu gods.

"The most elegant and sublime of these bronzes is a representation of the creation of the universe at the beginning of each cosmic cycle, a motif known as the Cosmic Dance of Shiva."

Sagan describes the blackened-bronze figure standing in a circle of flame: Shiva as Nataraja, dancing the Cosmic Dance of creation and destruction. His right hand holds a drum, symbolizing creation; his left hand holds a torch of flame, representing the conflagration that will finally destroy the universe. "Creation and Destruction."

Sagan emerges from the dark interior of the temple and sits in the warm sun. In a niche in the temple wall above him is a gray stone statue of the ever-popular Ganesha, the elephant-headed god of prosperity and enlightenment.

"The most sophisticated cosmological ideas came from Asia, and particularly from India," Sagan ponders aloud. "Most cultures imagine the world to be only a few hundred human generations old. Hardly anyone guessed that the cosmos might be far older. But the ancient Hindus did." The Hindu cosmic cycle of 8.64 billion years—about half the actual age of our universe—is "a kind of premonition of modern astronomical ideas"—

especially the theory of the oscillating universe.

Music from a village festival drifts through the palm trees.

"The Big-bang," he notes, "is modern scientific myth. It comes from the same human need to solve the cosmological question."

The philosophic enterprise that Sagan is conducting is a part of what he calls "cosmic consciousness-raising." For our era, science—or more exactly, the scientific way of thinking—is the source of the fundamental data of consciousness. It alone can give us an understanding of the realities of our universe. After millennia of mythology, it is now possible for the mind of man to enter realistically into the fabric of the universe and to involve itself, in a liberating way, with the events of the cosmos.

Intelligibility becomes a function of the interaction between the self and the world. In his work, Sagan is facilitating this interaction of selves with a newly discovered cosmos. He is guiding us through an odyssey which can resurrect all our rationalities and all our sentiments. "In *Cosmos*, we have tried to speak not just to the mind but also to the heart." From physics and chemistry to the music of the spheres and the poetry of our souls, *nothing is to be left out*. Our total humanness is to be expressed and reaffirmed.

IV

Sagan walks to the helm of "the spaceship of the imagination." At the console he reaches upper left and punches up a monitor showing the Milky Way galaxy; at upper right is a readout screen for displaying information on each world and its life-forms.

"Advanced technological civilizations would know about many worlds," he explains. A great blue-white spiral galaxy comes up on the screen at the front of the spaceship.

"Perhaps they would share their find-ings, assembling some vast repository of the knowledge of countless worlds. They might compile an Encyclopaedia Galactica.

"Perhaps someday there will be an entry in the Encyclopaedia Galactica for our planet or perhaps, even now, there exists a planetary dossier . . . a listing for 'Earth.' What do they know about us?"

WORLD: 806.4615.0110
Civilization Type: 1.0 J
Society Code: 4G4, "Humanity". . . .
Technology: Exponentiating
  Fossil fuels / nuclear weapons
  Organized warfare
  Environmental pollution. . . .
  Probability of survival (per 100 yr): 40%

The Encyclopaedia Galactica is Sagan's way of imaging "a cosmic context for mankind." We have an essential longing to know where we fit into the scheme of things.

Meanwhile, until such evidence is obtained, we must think in cosmic terms. The truth, notes Sagan, is that we have moved in a cosmic perspective since our presapient beginnings. "The deepest cosmological questions are embedded in human folklore and myth, superstition and religion." We have *assumed* that a relationship with heavenly beings exists.

"We have always watched the stars and mused about whether there are other beings who think and wonder. In a cosmic setting vast and old beyond ordinary human understanding, we are a little lonely."

The search for a cosmic context for mankind has begun and cannot end until that context is known.

"In the deepest sense," writes Sagan, "the search for extraterrestrial intelligence is a search for who we are."

Our religious myths reveal that we humans want desperately to be participants in a meaningful biocosmic program. The chances are strong that we are in fact participants, and always have been. In the not too distant future, we may at last discover what that "scheme of things" might be.

OUR EXPANDING CONSCIOUSNESS

5   Isaac Asimov has drawn up a short history of cosmic measurements showing "the successive enlargement of man's picture of the universe."

> 500 B.C.: 5,000 miles (the distance across the known universe: a flat disc-shaped earth with a vaulted dome. The calculator: Hecataeus of Miletus)
>
> 225 B.C.: 8,000 miles in diameter (a spherical earth. The calculator: Eratosthenes of Cyrene)
>
> 150 B.C.: 480,000 miles (an imaginary sphere including the moon. The calculator: Hipparchus of Nicaea)
>
> 1671: 1,800,000 miles (diameter of the known universe: the solar system as far out as Saturn. The calculator: Giovanni Cassini)
>
> 1704: 6,000,000,000 miles (diameter of the known universe derived from the orbit of Halley's Comet. The calculator: Edmund Halley)
>
> 1840: 320 trillion miles or 54 light-years (diameter based on the known distance to the star Vega. The calculator: Friedrich von Struve)
>
> 1906: 55,000 light-years (diameter of hypothetical disc-like galaxy. The calculator: Jacobus Kapteyn)
>
> 1920: 330,000 light-years (diameter of Milky Way galaxy. The calculator: Harlow Shapley)
>
> 1923: 5,400,000 light-years (a spherical universe including the newly recognized Andromeda galaxy. The calculator: Edwin Hubble)
>
> 1940: 400 million light-years (the known universe including galaxies observed to be 200 million light-years away from us. The calculator: Milton Humason)
>
> 1963: 2 billion light-years (after discovery of the first quasar by: Maarten Schmidt)
>
> 1973: 24 billion light-years (based on measurement of the most distant object observed in the universe as of this date, a quasar known as OH471).

This list is more than a compendium of figures. It is a metaphor for the expansion of our consciousness. As our world-view has grown so has our perception of the parts—religious, ethical, esthetic, epistemological, etc.—that make up that world-view.

Larry Niven hits the mark when he points out that planet dwellers riding along on a cosmic pinpoint tend to think small. We can't deny our history: tunnel-vision has plagued our perceptions. Today we are challenged *to see* the universe as it really is. This gigantic bubble-cosmos is there and it undoubtedly contains all forms of life, and

---

Understanding man and his place in the universe is perhaps the central problem of all science.

DUNN AND DOBZHANSKY

If we establish contact with extraterrestrial life it will reveal to us our true place in the universe, and with that will come the beginning of wisdom.

ISAAC ASIMOV

*That I am mortal I know and do confess
My span of a day:
        but when I gaze upon
The thousandfold circling gyre of the stars,
No longer do I walk on earth
                but rise
The peer of God himself to take my fill
At the ambrosial banquet of the Undying.*

PTOLEMAIOS THE ASTRONOMER

The trouble with living on a planet is that it tends to make most of the inhabitants think small.

LARRY NIVEN

Ozma radiotelescope.

The General Theory of Relativity allows for the existence of other universes which may be connected to our own universe by bridges in space-time. When these bridges were first discovered by Drs. Einstein and Rosen . . . it was thought that it would be completely impossible to get from one universe to another. Recent calculations, however, have shown that this is not the case. The recently discovered Kerr Solution to Einstein's equations does indeed allow for the possibility of space travel to other universes as well as space travel backward and forward in time in our own universe!

WILLIAM J. KAUFMANN

SIX SEARCHES FOR EXTRATERRESTRIAL CIVILIZATIONS

One of the best-attended sessions at the sprawling annual meeting of the American Association for the Advancement of Science in Boston last week was a self-confessed ado about nothing—negative results. It is only because of the staggering significance of a "something," should it ever appear, that six research teams in three countries have been listening for signs of intelligent communication attempts from extraterrestrial civilizations: messages from the stars. Last week's session was the first meeting presenting results from a range of observational searches.

The quest began in 1959 when Frank Drake used the antenna of the National Radio Astronomy Observatory in Green Bank, W. Va., in a small but pioneering venture to listen to two stars, at a single frequency, for a period of a few weeks. He named the effort Project Ozma, after the princess of the idyllic but hard-to-reach kingdom of Oz. Now there is Ozma II, as well as a number of other searches on a larger scale capable of covering Ozma's original territory in as little as 0.01 second. But now, as then, the leading question is where to search, and how. And why.

The odds against success are ridiculous. Our galaxy has perhaps 250 billion stars. There are approximately 100 billion other galaxies. Every step in trying to conceive a manageable hunt requires fundamental decisions based on limited data, educated guesswork and sheer speculation. How many stars have planets? How many of those have life? How many of that number have suitably advanced technical civilizations? And even of that final, eligible bunch, how many happened to be around at just the right time to be sending messages so that earthlings would be receiving them today? Carl Sagan, director of the Laboratory for Planetary Studies at Cornell University, who has been playing with the numbers for as long as many and longer than most, guesstimates that all but 0.00001 percent of the stars would be weeded out by such an accounting, yet the remainder in our galaxy alone is still an imposing million. Other factors suggest that 100,000 stars must be examined for a statistical chance of finding even one.

If the inhabitants could actually send messages, would they do so? What if no one is listening at the right time? Or at the right frequency?

This last point is a major question. Both Project Ozmas have concentrated on the 21-centimeter wavelength that results from the 1420-megahertz emission frequency of hydrogen, in hopes that an extraterrestrial civilization, knowing that hydrogen is the most abundant element in the universe, would pick it as a logical choice. But there are other logical choices. Between the hydrogen and hydroxyl (OH) bands, for example, lies the "water hole," the emission frequency of H_2O, which is not only a basic constituent of life as even most exobiologists can envision it, but also offers a frequency less drowned in deep-space static, or "sky noise."

Project Ozma II is largely the work of Patrick Palmer of the University of Chicago and Ben M. Zuckerman of the University of Maryland. Again at Green Bank they have the advantages over Ozma I of a much larger antenna (300 feet vs. 85), a more noise-free receiver and a filter system capable of breaking down the general 1420-MHz frequency into 384 separate parts to dig out possible messages that might otherwise be masked in the broader bandwidth. Before even beginning, they eliminated some stars as too old (or post-catastrophic) for life, others as too young for life to have yet developed, others as chemically deficient and still others whose planets would have to be so close for adequate warmth that they would be bathed in lethal radiation. Once started, they studied 659 star systems, laboriously checking their early results by hand ("I guess we were too old-fashioned to trust the computer," says Palmer) and ultimately examining nearly 20 million data points in some 51,700 individual radio spectra. Results: negative.

The reasons for deciding how and where to search are, of course, largely speculative. In the words of a previous searcher, who was in the AAAS session's audience and who gave up the idea years ago, "It's like looking for a needle in a haystack and then giving a scientific rationalization for which side of the haystack to start looking in." But the difficulties, Sagan points out, are only half of an equation that must also include the import of success—that man is not alone.

Sagan and Drake, in fact, are engaged in one of the largest of the searches, using the huge, 1,000-foot radio dish at Arecibo in Puerto Rico to study whole galaxies of stars. Drake estimates that such signals would have to be sent with a million times Arecibo's power to be detectable, but extraterrestrial transmitters could be far advanced over those of the earth, which are in only the earliest stages of stellar conversion attempts. Using four different frequencies—1420 MHz, 1667 MHz (hydroxyl), 1652 MHz (the water hole) and 2380 MHz (Arecibo's radar frequency)—the giant ear has monitored the galaxies Leo 1, Leo 2, Messier 33 and Messier 49. On one occasion, "phone lines crackled," says Drake, when a small peak appeared on the broader 1420-MHz signal from Leo 1, but disappointment followed when the same peak showed up from a slightly different direction. This implied that the signal source was far too broad for a point-source transmitter, and was probably a cold gas cloud. So far, nary a message.

Two Canadian researchers, Alan H. Bridle of Queens University in Kingston, Ontario, and P. A. Feldman of the National Research Council, Downsview, Ontario, have auditioned the master frequency of water for 28 stars, with another 250 in mind, using the 150-foot telescope of the Algonquin Park Radio Observatory. The results again have been negative, but such sky-watches often have unexpected payoffs. Other researchers at Algonquin, says Feldman, have just verified the detection of the heaviest interstellar molecule yet announced, cyanodiacetylene, HC_5N. Sagan points out the parallel with cyanoacetylene, one of the basic components in living systems—at least on earth.

A much broader survey, albeit a modest one, is being carried out by Robert S. Dixon and colleagues at Ohio State University. Using a variety of equipment cobbled from a variety of sources and running on a shoestring budget, often completely unattended, the hydrogen-line survey is nonetheless free to operate almost 24 hours a day, 365 days a year. The antenna system is the equivalent of a 175-foot-diameter dish, and although results are so far the same as everyone else's, the value of such a broad mapping effort is obvious. Two other wide-ranging experiments are being conducted in the Soviet Union, using arrays of radio telescopes spanning the country under the auspices of the Institute of Cosmological Research in Moscow and of Gorky University. Both, says Sagan, use a "coincidence-count" system, in which a signal must appear on at least two receivers to be registered.

With all this listening going on and more to come, Philip Morrison of Massachusetts Institute of Technology took advantage of the AAAS session to call for order. A journal, he suggested (with a broad hint at Sagan's ICARUS), or some central clearing house ought to keep track of who has looked where, when and at what frequencies. . . .

Science News, February 28, 1976

An interstellar dust cloud with stars and planets in process of formation.

The universe is not a machine, but an organism, with an indwelling principle of life. It was not made, but it has grown.

JOHN FISKE

Arecibo listening to distant galaxies.

when we discover our cosmic context then our primitive world-views will turn into new visions. Then we will belong to a biocosmos.

PHILOSOPHIC CONSEQUENCES

6   What will it mean if we establish contact with extraterrestrial intelligences (ETIs)? Since we have misgivings about our own future on earth, perhaps the realization that *they exist* will be the most significant message. George Abell, an astronomer, suggests that we should be jubilant if we "discover even *one* other civilization that has endured for tens of thousands of years; at least if those fellows made it, perhaps there is hope for us!"

Psychological impact upon us will be deep. Of special importance is how we think and feel about ourselves. In terms of evolution, it was probably inevitable that one single species would win out over all others on earth in the survival game; and for man the evolvement of the capacity for abstract reasoning gave him the edge. But it's lonely at the top!—far lonelier than we now admit to ourselves; and this "ontological loneliness" is surely the motivating drive behind much human behavior for which we commonly give other facile explanations: the destructive competition within our own species (wouldn't this competitive animosity be redirected if we were having to relate with several different kinds of peer-intelligent life-forms?); our cruelty to other forms of life (that is, our general lack of empathy and respect for other living things); our preoccupation with the noise of communication (words, speeches, dialogues, and other "silence breakers") as over against communication itself; and a variety of problems in our relationships with one another (for instance, individual alienation and the resulting pressures we place on others "to end our loneliness"). If we were forced to relate to peers or superiors—forced to understand, empathize, tolerate, respect—then our individual and collective self-images would probably undergo rapid change.

7   Religious ideas would also change. In a biocosmos of populated planets with varied rotation times ("days") and revolution periods ("years"), severe strain would be placed on doctrines and dogmas that tie Ultimate Reality to earth-functions. For instance: *sacred space* (geography: "holy ground," holy cities: Mecca, Jerusalem, Benares; temples, shrines, the "Holy of Holies"); *sacred time* (sabbaths, Holy Days, Holy Weeks, sacred festivals); *sacred languages* (Sanskrit, Arabic, Hebrew, or "King James English"); *sacred foods* (corn in the Eleusinian and Osirian mysteries, Eucharistic bread and wine, "kosher" foods); *sacred teleocosmic dramas* that depend upon earth-history ("Adam and Eve and the Snake," Faithful Remnants and Chosen People, the New Jerusalem, the "End of the World"); and *our anthropomorphic images* of the deities (note Michelangelo's frescoes on the ceiling of the Sistine Chapel).

8   Our ethical and esthetic notions will be threatened. We will be forced into asking new kinds of questions. Would ETIs be "persons" or "selves"? Would they have a serious "right to life"? On what criteria might they be defined as worthy of our moral concern? What is the role of empathy in moral considerations? Could we empathize with them? What if—because of their appearance—we couldn't empathize with them? What if—because of *our* appearance—they couldn't empathize with us? (Is empathy learned or inherent?)

Imagine ETIs engaging in behavior that, to our way of thinking, is clearly immoral: ritual flagellation of themselves to develop "moral qualities"; indiscriminate sex with countless variations on a theme by de Sade; the practice of "emotional violence" to maintain "survival readiness"; and so on. The more humanoid they appeared to us, the more easily we would become offended by behavior that, if *we* indulged in it, would be defined and felt as immoral.

Given such ethical situations, what are our capacities for rapid redefinition of "right" and "wrong"? What might be their capacities for rapid redefinition? Could we develop a calculus of "minimal reaction" that would guide human behavior toward ETIs so that, as with other life-forms on earth, we would inflict the least possible harm? Could we communicate such a calculus to them? Would a biocosmic perspective serve to clarify the pragmatic character of moral codes? How might humans respond to a truly advanced morality? (What is "a truly advanced morality"?)

9   On one point there is universal agreement among scientists: whatever ETIs look like, they will *not* look like us. They will not be humanoid. "The biology on other planets is of course expected to be different from our own because of the statistical nature of the evolutionary process and the adaptability of life." This conclusion, written by Frank Drake and Carl Sagan, opens the door to every plausible organismic configuration imaginable to the human mind.

In hundreds of his stories, Ray Bradbury has described scenarios in which man and ETIs confront each other and find themselves caught in sundry dilemmas. His science-fiction settings can serve as thought-experiments that prevision the ethical and esthetic problems of actual encounter.

In a *Life* magazine article Bradbury painted verbal pictures of how extraterrestrials might appear. Among the beings that he conjured were creatures that live in very thick atmospheres and have extremely small bodily openings to cut down on intake; and creatures that live in very thin atmospheres and have "mouths and nose vents like barn doors."

Bradbury warns:

> To the lonely space man, an alien woman with the above features would hardly be attractive. Right here, the entire field of esthetics looms before us. Astronautical history may depend on those concepts

The earth is the cradle of mankind, but one cannot live in the cradle forever.

TSIOLKOVSKY

For the first time in the history of our species, we have devised the tools—unmanned space vehicles and large radio telescopes—to search for extraterrestrial life. I would be very ashamed of my civilization if, with these tools at hand, we turned away from the cosmos.

CARL SAGAN

Ray Bradbury

Martian landscape from Viking 1 Lander. Meteorology boom, which supports Viking's miniature weather station, cuts through the picture's center.

of beauty and utility our men take along as unacknowledged cargo to the stars. Countless books will have to be written under the general title: *Esthetics and Etiquette for Other Worlds.* Otherwise, we are in danger of mistaking a rough skin for a rough mind, a third eye for an evil eye, a cold hand for a cold and hostile heart.

MAN AND COSMOS: ADJUSTING OUR RELATIONSHIPS

10   What is man's place in the cosmos? As a better understanding of our universe has been growing, old perspectives have become obsolete. New answers are more realistic, but they are sometimes more painful.

Man has undergone three agonizing decentralizations. He has waged a steady struggle *against* decentralization, but at the same time—paradoxically—his accumulating knowledge has gradually forced him to abandon all illusions about his centrality.

(1) The Cosmological Decentralization

11   The *cosmological decentralization* was man's first painful reassessment of his place in the scheme of things. The evidence began to mount that the geocentric picture of our solar system was in error and that the earth is not the center of all Creation as men had hoped and religion had held. Early in the seventeenth century the Copernican theory gained ground with the observations of Galileo and the mathematical calculations of Kepler and Brahe. The battle raged between those who would defend man's right to be the center of the cosmos and those who, consenting to fact, were beginning to consider the heliocentric theory. The latter theory—that the earth orbits around the sun—had been known since ancient times, and when Copernicus (1473–1543) reintroduced it there was little stir. But as evidence in support of it mounted, bitterness increased.

It seems always great to me when God's world gets a little bigger and when I get a somewhat more true view of my place and my smallness in that universe. The growing awareness of cosmic cohabitation is enormously important for me, and it fits well into a growing knowledge of God's world.

KRISTER STENDAHL

480

It was Galileo Galilei, a teacher of geometry and astronomy at the University of Padua, who suffered the wounds of battle. With a naive optimism, Galileo published his theories and invited scholars and churchmen to check his evidence supporting the heliocentric theory. He did not foresee the hostile reaction he received. When he invited a certain professor of philosophy to look through his telescope and see for himself the moons of Jupiter, the professor merely laughed and declined. He knew, from logic alone, that Jupiter could not have moons, and he knew on theological grounds that the earth was the center of the universe.

A similar argument was put forth by a Florentine astronomer named Francesco Sizzi. In a famous polemical passage he reasoned:

Galileo (1564–1642)

> There are seven windows in the head: two nostrils, two eyes, two ears, and a mouth. So also in the heavens there are two favorable stars, two unfavorable, two luminaries, and Mercury alone undecided and indifferent. From all this, and from other such natural phenomena, such as the seven metals, etc., all too pointless to enumerate, we can conclude that the number of planets is necessarily seven.
>
> Furthermore, the [alleged] satellites [of Jupiter] are invisible to the naked eye, and therefore can have no influence on the earth, and therefore would be useless, and therefore do not exist.
>
> Besides all this, the Jews and other ancient peoples as well as modern Europeans have always divided the week into seven days and have named them after the seven planets. Now if we [like Galileo] increase the number of planets, this whole and beautiful system falls to the ground.

Sometimes I think we're alone. Sometimes I think we're not. In either case, the thought is staggering.

BUCKMINSTER FULLER

12 Following this first cosmological displacement, three others have taken place, all minor by comparison.

The second occurred early in this century when it was discovered by astronomers that our solar system is not central in our Milky Way galaxy. Rather, it is located in a spiral arm, and this is indeed the periphery—the "south forty"—of our island universe.

The third displacement took place during the thirties when it was established that the Milky Way galaxy is only one of many island universes. We are but one of a local cluster of some two dozen galaxies; and we are an infinitesimal part of a universe composed of billions of galaxies. Our Milky Way is not central in any way that we can see, except to us.

In theory, there could be a fourth cosmological displacement: the discovery that our bubble-universe is only one of many. While much can be said for the theory, whether other pulsating universes exist is quite beyond our knowing. However, there seems to be no good reason *not* to believe that there are pulsating bubbles scattered in all directions through the Universe. To cling to the belief that there is but a single bubble-universe rings now like another aristocentric claim. Cosmologically, we are part of the universe, which undoubtedly extends farther than we can ever know.

(2) *The Biological Decentralization*

13   Man has also undergone a *biological decentralization*. We have considered ourselves superior to all other living creatures and believed we possessed a divine mandate to conquer, domesticate, or kill the "lower" animals. Moreover, there was a qualitative difference between man and the animals: the former had a soul, while the latter did not.

Charles Darwin brought the simmer to a boil. Shortly after his publication in 1859 of *Origin of Species*, the battlelines were drawn. The notion that man was not created as man—in distinctive Homo sapient form—and placed in the Garden by God himself; the idea that he might have developed over great spans of time from primitive animal creatures that were distinctly unhuman—this was an insult comparable to the cosmological decentralization.

The climax of the battle might be thought of as the "monkey-trial" in Dayton, Tennessee, in 1925. The young science teacher, John Scopes, was indicted in a test case for teaching evolution in the local high school. By the time defense attorney Clarence Darrow had shown the fallacy of the arguments against evolution and had placed William Jennings Bryan, the prosecuting attorney, on the stand, the trial had become a worldwide spectacle. Darrow lost the case, legally; but time has shown that the principle of intellectual freedom was the real victor. Since the Scopes trial we have been less disturbed that our remote ancestors might have been something less than "human."

We are now undergoing another phase of the biological decentralization: it is a reassessment of our ecological status. Although our pride seems less involved in this process, we are realizing that man is but part of a system. By some criteria, we can claim to be a superior part of the system. We are having to admit, however, that we can't exist without the system, nor can we proceed to do whatever we wish to the fauna and flora around us. To survive we must bow to the balancing mechanisms at work within the ecosystem. Man is *not* the system; he did not *make* the system. He *belongs* to it.

It is enough for me to contemplate the mystery of conscious life perpetuating itself through all eternity, to reflect upon the marvelous structure of the universe which we can dimly perceive, and to try humbly to comprehend even an infinitesimal part of the intelligence manifested in nature.

ALBERT EINSTEIN

Consider the question of whether earth is the only haven for intelligent life in the universe. It is very unlikely that such is the case. On the contrary, the number of planets in the universe capable of sustaining life is believed to be enormous, perhaps as many as 10^{22}, which is about a million times greater than the total number of individual cells in the human body.

SAXON AND FRETTER

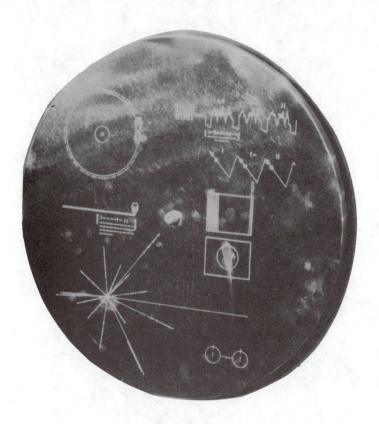

The two Voyager spacecraft that left Earth in 1977 and sent back photographs of the Jupiter and Saturn systems in 1979 and 1980 have attached to them two records carrying messages for any intelligent beings that might intercept the space machines. Each record contains 116 coded pictures of Earth's life-forms, greetings in 54 languages, and selections of Earth sounds.

The gold-coated cover displays directions for playing the record and reconstructing the pictures (upper quadrants, left and right), a pulsar map showing the precise location of our solar system ("starburst" at lower left), and a drawing of the hydrogen atom (lower right) indicating the unit of time to be used in playing the record and decoding the pictures.

(3) *The Psychological Decentralization*

14   Man is also undergoing a *psychological decentralization*. It is probably just beginning.

Until the present time nothing has challenged man's *intellectual* superiority: his capacities for abstract reasoning, communicating, knowledge-storage, and culture. These were clearly supreme. But if man must confront other intelligent forms of life, this could turn out to be the most painful "rite of passage" he will ever face. (The only greater ego-pain I can imagine would be the utterly shattering realization that the human race is irrevocably bound for extinction.)

There is some likelihood that we are nearing such a confrontation. We are beginning to consider the possibility that other forms of intelligent life may exist on earth. Many of the higher primates have greater intellectual skills than we thought. Dolphins, of course, come to mind. They may possess an intelligence as great as man's but so different that we underestimate it because we don't understand it. It may turn out to be a complex intelligence deserving our sincere respect.

Man's most severe reassessment of himself will come if and when we confront extraterrestrial intelligence. Almost inevitably, *they* will contact *us*, which means that they will be far advanced compared to us. Their intelligence may be superior to man's—perhaps an I.Q. of

What is the ultimate truth about ourselves? Various answers suggest themselves. We are a bit of stellar matter gone wrong. We are physical machinery—puppets that strut and talk and laugh and die as the hand of time pulls the strings beneath. But there is one elementary inescapable answer. *We are that which asks the question.* Whatever else there may be in our nature, responsibility towards truth is one of its attributes.

SIR ARTHUR EDDINGTON

250 is merely bright normal to them. By comparison—however much it may hurt—the only appropriate stance for man may be one of humility.

It is often noted that science-fiction writers have prepared us, for more than a half-century now, for "future shock." Perhaps they have extended our horizons in preparation for a confrontation with intelligence so it might be less of a shock. One cannot but wonder when/if this rather ultimate "decentralization" will occur and how severe its affects may be upon man's opinions of himself.

The *Pioneer* and *Voyager* planetary probes, mankind's first interstellar travellers, carry plaques and records indicating the planet of their origin and bearing pictures of the beings that created it. The striking fact is *the explicit assumption* that other intelligent creatures might someday intercept the probe and wonder who sent it hurtling through space.

15   All these decentralizing crises which man has experienced are religious in nature, for they deal with the ultimate question of man's place in the universe and his relationships within it.

It has heretofore been a role of Western religion to affirm man's worth. Man feels inferior enough as it is. The preservation by religious institutions of the convictions that man is only just lower than the angels and that he is, in fact, a child of God has undoubtedly been both comforting and healing. Man might not have survived the struggle without the sense of worth and purpose such beliefs have given him.

Nevertheless, as a child grows he realizes that he must compromise his ego-centered nature if he is to live in the world of men. Man's decentralizations are part of his growth as a cultured species; it is a part of his humanization. To face realistically one's place in the scheme of existence offers us yet another chance to adjust to "the world as it is." For some, accepting realities is more fulfilling than defending therapeutic beliefs. We can feel better about ourselves and others when we no longer have a need for aristocentric myth.

The latter half of the twentieth century might well be marked as the day of the Image Makers. The faster the pace of the technological explosion, the more the cipher-citizen seems to worry about his identity. What will be the role of the Image Makers when Earth is just one star system among many?

JOHN JAKES

REFLECTIONS—

1 In only a couple of decades scientists have done a remarkable about-face on the question of the existence of life on other planets. Carl Sagan, an exobiologist and philosopher, has written extensively on man's need of, and search for, a "cosmic context" within which we could better understand ourselves. (See Sec. 4.) Are you in essential agreement with Sagan's assessment of this human venture?

2 What do you think of Larry Niven's sage-like comment (p. 475-QM) that the trouble with people who live on planets is that they "tend to think small"? Is this a truism, or an adage you could store for later use?

3 The Florentine philosopher, Francesco Sizzi, has become famous (or infamous) for his reply to Galileo. After your first chuckle, what did you think of his stand and the way he rationalized it?

4 What do you think of the intent of the Drake/Sagan formula (Sec. 3)?

Although some of the quantities are not yet known with precision, what is the general message of the equation itself? On reflection, what do you think of "the L-factor"?

5 Reflect on the impact upon our thinking and feeling of the discovery of the existence of extraterrestrial life and intelligence (Secs. 6–9). What is your evaluation of the implications suggested in this chapter? Can you think of other eventual changes in the way we think and feel if we do live in a true biocosmos?

6 Phrase in your own personal way your response to the question, "What is man's place in the cosmos?" (Maybe you can be specific by focusing on man's relationships to component elements of the universe—such as his earth, other human beings, other living creatures, extraterrestrial intelligence, etc.—and then formulating a general answer.)

7 Put into your own words the three decentralizations that Western man has experienced. If taken seriously, how do you think these new perspectives would affect (1) our self-image as individuals? and (2) mankind's collective image of itself?

8 Note the statement in Sec. 15: "All these decentralizing crises which man has experienced are religious in nature. . . ." Is this meaningful? Do you agree? Why or why not?

9 What do you think of the afterthoughts by Astronauts Mitchell and Schweickart on how their space voyages changed their lives (p. 478-QM)?

10 What do you think of the proverb-like saying by Tsiolkovsky (p. 479-QM)?

Furthermore . . .

BERENDZEN, RICHARD (ed.), *Life beyond Earth and the Mind of Man.* NASA, 1973.

BRADBURY, RAY, "Christus Apollo." *I Sing the Body Electric!* Bantam, 1971.

BRACEWELL, RONALD N., *The Galactic Club: Intelligent Life in Outer Space.* W. H. Freeman, 1974.

CHRISTIAN, JAMES L. (ed.), *Extra-Terrestrial Intelligence: The First Encounter.* Prometheus, 1976.

MARUYAMA, MAGOROH, and ARTHUR HARKINS (eds.), *Cultures beyond Earth: The Role of Anthropology in Outer Space.* Vintage, 1975.

PONNAMPERUMA, CYRIL, and A. G. W. CAMERON (eds.), *Interstellar Communication: Scientific Perspectives.* Houghton-Mifflin, 1974.

SAGAN, CARL (ed.), *Communications with Extraterrestrial Intelligence (CETI).* MIT Press, 1973.

SAGAN, CARL, *The Cosmic Connection.* Anchor, 1973.

SAGAN, CARL, and I. S. SHKLOVSKII, *Intelligent Life in the Universe.* Dell, 1966.

SHAPLEY, HARLOW, *Of Stars and Men.* Washington Square, 1960.

PART VIII

OF ULTIMATE CONCERN

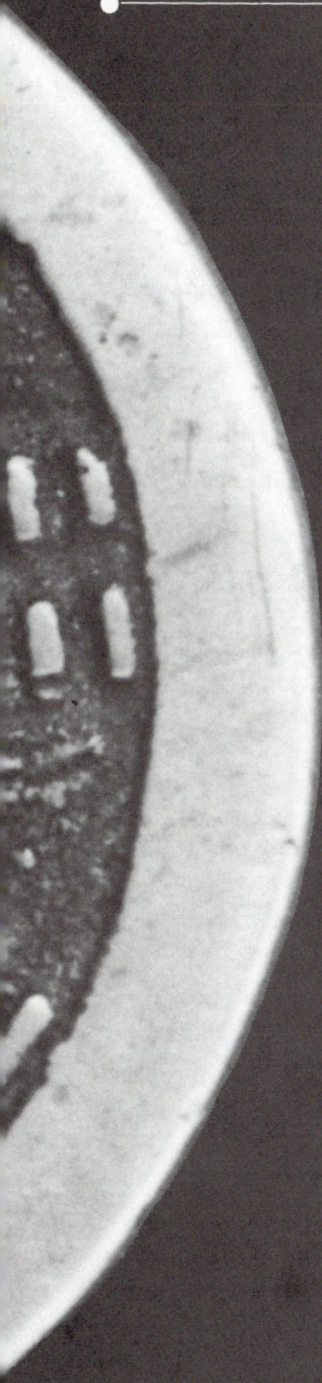

We have seen the highest circle of spiraling powers. We have named this circle God. We might have given it any other name we wished: Abyss, Mystery, Absolute Darkness, Absolute Light, Matter, Spirit, Ultimate Hope, Ultimate Despair, Silence.

NIKOS KAZANTZAKIS

We are all children in a vast kindergarten trying to spell God's name with the wrong alphabet blocks.

TENNESSEE WILLIAMS

Of Ultimate Concern

Have You Ever Wondered . . .

- What religion is and does?

- Whether human beings can live without religion?

- Whether there is One True Religion and which one it is?

- Why mankind's gods and goddesses look so much like us?

- Whether God is the cause of the tragic events in our lives?

- Why some people believe the world will end (soon!) and others don't?

- When the world will end according to Hinduism? Zoroastrianism? Islam? Buddhism? Judaism? Christianity?

- Why "Heaven" has to be *up* and "Hell" has to be *down?*

- What mankind's great religions will be like in, say, a thousand years?

RELIGION AS A SEARCH FOR MEANING

There are many paths to God, my son. I hope yours will not be too difficult.

LEW WALLACE
Ben Hur

1   Religion is man's involvement in the meaning of his existence, and the depth of one's involvement is the depth of his religion. It is participation in life in a special way for a special purpose. Religion is our attempt to find a meaningful relatedness to all the significant

events of human experience. It is, as Paul Tillich phrased it, "our ultimate concern for the Ultimate."

Sometimes one finds definitions of religion which take into account only a particular set of answers to man's ultimate questions. Accordingly, religion is defined as belief in the supernatural, belief in spirits, or belief in One God; or an anthropologist might define religion as man's ritualistic expression of socially accepted beliefs and values.

But such definitions of religion miss the point. Religion is not to be defined in terms of the *answers* which men give—for they are legion—but rather in terms of the *questions* men ask. The particular local and cultural answers to which a single religious society commits itself tells us much about that group; but it is in our agonized questioning that we discover the universal religious condition of all men.

Indeed, the atheist who feels no necessity to hypothesize an Omnipotent Deity to account for the machinations of the universe is making an observation fully as ultimate, and fully as religious, as the theist who protests that the universe cannot be understood apart from belief in God.

2   Religion is not to be confused with the various forms of intellectualization which follow religious experience.

As time passes and people find that they share similar convictions, doctrines develop. A *doctrine* is a formal interpretation of religious experience. Its purpose is to crystallize and preserve the fundamental elements of an experience, and to make it possible for those within the group to communicate concerning the nature of the experience. A doctrine is a social phenomenon. Those with similar beliefs are saying they belong together as part of the believing group; more than that, they are attempting to participate in the religious experience which the doctrine refers to.

As a religious institution develops, leaders emerge who are empowered to distinguish between true and false doctrines. Thus, they proclaim dogmas. A *dogma* is a doctrine which is supposed to have universal acceptance by all believers. It is a closed issue. It must be accepted as true if the particular benefits offered by the religion are to be attained.

A *creed* also is a formalization arising from religious experience. The term *creed* is from the Latin *credo*, "I believe," and a creed thus functions to distinguish believers from nonbelievers. Creeds in the form of short, capsule statements of essential beliefs are often used as membership cards and passwords.

Lastly, *theology* is the intellectualization of the totality of one's religion. Traditionally, the theologian belongs to a particular religion. He is not a "philosopher of religion" who studies, with an eye to objectivity, the religious experience of all mankind; rather he is a believer who stands within the "circle of faith," attempting to update and reinterpret the meaning of the faith for the people of his own time. Thus a Muslim theologian speaks to Muslims, a Catholic theologian speaks to Catholics, and so on.

All phases of becoming are subject to arrest. . . . Infantilism in religion results in an arrest due to the immediate needs for comfort and security of self-esteem. . . . We find many personalities who deal zealously and effectively with all phases of becoming except the final task of relating themselves meaningfully to creation. For some reason their curiosity stops at this point.

GORDON ALLPORT

All religions pronounce the name of God in their particular language. As a rule it is better for a man to name God in his native tongue rather than in one that is foreign to him.

SIMONE WEIL

CAN RELIGION BE DEFINED?

"Religion is one's attitude toward whatever he considers to be the determiner of destiny." [James Bissett Pratt]

"Religion is man's ultimate concern for the Ultimate." [Paul Tillich]

"Religion is the ritual cultivation of socially accepted values." [John Fischer]

"Religion, as a minimum, is the belief in spiritual beings." [E. B. Tylor]

"Religion is a propitiation of, and dependency on, superior powers which are believed to control and direct the course of nature and human life." [Sir James G. Frazer]

"Religion is *concern* about experiences which are regarded as of supreme value; *devotion* towards a power or powers believed to originate, increase, and conserve these values; and some *suitable expression* of this concern and devotion, whether through symbolic rites or through other individual and social conduct." [Edgar S. Brightman]

"Religion consists in the perception of the infinite under such manifestations as are able to influence the moral character of man." [Max Müller]

"A religion, on its doctrinal sides, can thus be described as a system of general truths which have the effect of transforming character when they are sincerely held and vividly apprehended." [Alfred North Whitehead]

"Religion is a belief in an ultimate meaning of the universe." [Alfred R. Wallace]

"Religion is a theory of man's relation to the universe." [S. P. Haynes]

"Religion is our feeling about the highest forces that govern human destiny." [John Morely]

"Religion is a sense of the sacred." [Sir Julian Huxley]

"Religion is (subjectively regarded) the organization of all duties as divine commands." [Immanuel Kant]

"The essence of religion is the feeling of utter dependence upon the infinite reality, that is, upon God." [F. Schleiermacher]

"Any activity pursued in behalf of an ideal and against obstacles and in spite of threats of personal loss because of conviction of its general and enduring value is religious in quality." [John Dewey]

"Captain Pike has his illusions, and you, Captain Kirk, have your realities. May you find your way as pleasant."

"The Menagerie"
Star Trek

This traditional role, however, is presently being broken and broadened. Many of today's theologians are making statements of ultimate concern which apply to all men and not merely to the members of a particular group. This change contains profound implications for the future of parochial religion.

THE ANTHROPOMORPHIC SPIRITS

3 Primitive man lived out his life in a world of aggressive natural forces: rainstorms, floods, forest and veld fires, locusts and famine, illness, pain and death. Most of these forces were hostile—they were "evil." But there were friendly forces, too: rain for crops, life-generating energies which brought new lambs to his flocks and new children to his family and clan, sun to make his corn grow, good winds to sail his outrigger, good conditions which filled his nets with fish. These forces were aggressive; they took the initiative; the storms, floods, and forest fires came whether he liked it or not.

These are impersonal, illusive, inconceivable forces. What caused them? What are the causal energies behind the raging hurricane or the silent, burning disease?

As we have seen, all that man can know is his own experience. He experiences his consciousness, his feelings, his will, his ideas. He also experiences a self which he does not identify with his body, so he concludes that his essence is not body but "soul."

Therefore, of necessity, the universe about him is conceived within the limits of his own experience. He cannot negotiate with unseen forces; he cannot even think about the inconceivable. Yet conceive them he must, for he cannot escape negotiating with them.

Therefore, in order to understand and negotiate with the forces that be, he thinks of them as consciousnesses with minds, wills, ap-

In a maritime community depending on the products of the sea there is never magic connected with the collecting of shellfish or with fishing by poison, weirs, and fish traps, so long as these are completely reliable. On the other hand, any dangerous, hazardous, and uncertain type of fishing is surrounded by ritual. . . . Coastal sailing as long as it is perfectly safe and easy commands no magic. Overseas expeditions are invariably bound up with ceremonies and ritual.

E. B. TYLOR

In Kathmandu, Nepal, the jet age has been introduced. Nepal has bought itself a Boeing 707. In the inaugural ceremony two goats were slaughtered and the blood smeared around the cockpit to keep away the evil spirits.

CHARLES OSGOOD
CBS News

petites, and emotions. Through a complex linguistic history, we have come to call them "spirits," and they come in many forms: demons, evil spirits, ancestral ghosts, angels, gods and goddesses, kami, jinn, and so on.

These spirits are like man, enough like him so that he can talk with them. He can cajole, threaten, complain, and bargain with them. He can understand why at times they behave with consistency (for he does) or become capricious and unpredictable (he is occasionally that way with members of his family). He can bribe them into doing him favors; he can offer them gifts of varying worth. More sophisticated spirits are believed to respond to higher, subtler forms of sacrifice: the sacrifice of one's will in obedience, or of earthly pleasures, or of one's ego.

The AMA [American Medical Association] urges you to let the faith that nourishes you grow strong, for faith is a physician. . . .

TV Commercial

In the nineteenth century the problem was that *God is dead;* in the twentieth century the problem is that *man is dead.* Man is surely at least on the critical list.

ERICH FROMM

The priest smiled. "What man who has lived for more than a score of years desires justice, warrior? For my part, I find mercy infinitely more attractive. Give me a forgiving deity any day."

ROGER ZELAZNY
Lord of Light

4   These are profound processes, developed over long periods of time. They arise from man's deepest needs to survive the onslaught of the aggressive forces of nature and society. During more peaceful times, though, these personified forces can help man achieve fulfilling goals; they enable him to "grow in spirit" and become more stable, confident, and loving—a man at peace with himself.

What motivates man to colonize his universe with spirits like himself? *Survival.* The whole purpose of religion is to work out a "saving" relationship. In Judeo-Christian terms this relationship is known as "justification"—getting into a "right relationship with God." But it can be universalized: The goal of religion is to get into a right relationship with Shiva, with Allah, with Isis, with Christ, with Mithras, with Amitabha Buddha—all so that the desired end might be attained. And that end is to survive—that is, to find "salvation."

5   An interesting phenomenon often overtakes the spirits if they live a long while. They frequently become a part of a "theological complex," a system so grandiose that they are no longer accessible to the masses of men and cannot meet their daily needs. In the Greek and Roman religions the gods became so engrossed with the affairs of state that they were no longer meaningful to the common man. During the empire the great gods of the Roman pantheon were functionaries of state ceremonies, to be worshiped by emperors and other dignitaries. So distant had they become that the farmer and merchant had long since forgotten them.

And so, the great gods were replaced by godlets, by the lares and penates who still had plenty of time to take care of man's mundane affairs. Pomona would look after his fruit trees, Mellona his beehives, Epona his horses, Juventa his children; and two-faced Janus still had time to act as sentinel over his door, looking after all who went in or came out of the house.

This is a common development. Whenever the deities become too great, too important—too distant in their transcendent glory—to take care of man's immediate concerns, then lesser spirits inevitably replace them and carry on their ministrations. They may be called an-

πνεῦμα, ατος, τό, (πνέω) *a blowing*, πνεύματα ἀνέμων Hdt., Aesch.: alone, *a wind, blast*, Trag., etc.   **2.** metaph., θαλερωτέρῳ πν. with more genial *breeze* or *influence*, Aesch.; λύσσης πν. μάργῳ Id.; πν. ταύτης οὔποτ' ἐν ἀνδράσιν φίλοις βέβηκεν *the wind* is constantly changing even among friends, Soph.   **II.** like Lat. *spiritus* or *anima, breathed air, breath*, Aesch.; πν. βίου *the breath* of life, Id.; πν. ἀθροίζειν to collect *breath*, Eur.; πν. ἀφιέναι, ἀνιέναι, μεθιέναι to give up *the ghost*, Id.; πνεύματος διαρροαί the wind-pipe, Id.   **2.** *that is breathed forth, odour, scent*, Id.   **III.** *spirit*, Lat. *afflatus*, Anth.: *inspiration*, N.T.   **IV.** *the spirit* of man, Ib.   **V.** *a spirit*; in N.T. of *the Holy Spirit*, τὸ Πνεῦμα, Πν. ἅγιον:— also of *angels*, Ib.:—of *evil spirits*, Ib.   Hence
πνευμᾰτικός, ή, όν, *of spirit, spiritual*, N.T.
πνεύμων, in later Att. πλεύμων, ονος, ὁ, (πνέω) *the organ of* breathing, *the lungs*, Lat. *pulmo*, Il., Plat.: mostly in pl., Trag.; πνεύμ' ἀνεὶς ἐκ πλευμόνων Eur.
πνεῦν, Dor. poët. for ἔπνεον, impf. of πνέω.
πνευστιάω, *to breathe hard, pant*, Arist.; Ep. part. πνευστιόων, Anth.
ΠΝΕ'Ω, Ep. πνείω, Ion. impf. πνείεσκον: f. πνεύσομαι, Dor. πνευσοῦμαι: aor. 1 ἔπνευσα: pf. πέπνευκα:— Like other dissyll. Verbs in -έω, this Verb only contracts εε, εει:—*to blow*, of wind and air, Od., Hdt., Att.; ἡ πνέουσα (sc. αὔρα) *the breeze*, N.T.   **II.** *to breathe, send forth an odour*, Od.:—c. gen. *to breathe* or *smell of* a thing, Anth.   **III.** of animals, *to breathe hard, pant, gasp*, Il., Aesch.   **IV.** generally, *to draw breath, breathe*, and so *to live*, Hom.; οἱ πνέοντες = οἱ ζῶντες, Soph.   **V.** metaph., c. acc. cogn. *to breathe forth, breathe*, μένεα πνείοντες *breathing* spirit, of warriors, Il.; so, πῦρ πν. Hes.; φόνον, κότον 'Άρη Aesch.; so, πνέοντας δόρυ καὶ λόγχας Ar.; Ἀλφειὸν πνέων, of a swift runner, Id.   **2.** μέγα πνεῖν *to be of* a high *spirit, give oneself airs*, Eur.; τοσόνδ' ἔπνευσας Id.:—also, with a nom., as if it were the wind, μέγας πνέων Id.; πολὺς ἔπνει καὶ λαμπρὸς ἦν Dem.

---

gels, guardian spirits, genii, lares and penates, saints, bodhisattvas, or avatars of Vishnu or Shiva. But in all cases, they are concerned, responsive, and available in time of need.

SPIRIT POSSESSION

6   Spirits "possess" or "inhabit" people. Man has always been quite sure of this since he intuits himself to be a "spirit inside a body." If his own being is a dualism of essence and matter—soul and body—then it is only reasonable that other spirits, too, might inhabit his body.

This phenomenon—"spirit possession"—has been the universal means of accounting for the complexities of human behavior. Not only does possession explain the various forms of "insanity" and certain symptoms of illness (epileptic attacks, for instance) which we observe in others; it also accounts for the strange feelings we find inside ourselves: dizziness, fevers, pains, convulsions. And almost all states of religious consciousness can be thus explained: ecstatic trances, visions,

---

If God did not exist it would be necessary to invent him.

VOLTAIRE

If there were not a Devil, we would have to invent him.

OSCAR WILDE

Note the variety of different, but *associated*, meanings attached to the Greek word "pneuma" and its related forms.

News item: This is the first step in the investigation into the bridge disaster. A public hearing will be held . . . next week. The cause may never be learned, but as Assemblyman ["Smith"] put it, "This bridge collapse was not an act of God. Someone is responsible."

KNBC News

°*Was Scipio's prayer answered? He
shortly destroyed two great armies of
Carthaginians and Numidians and
went on to a decisive defeat of Hannibal
in a battle near Zama on October 19,
202 B.C. There was a tradition that
Scipio was a favorite of the Gods and
was therefore in intimate
communication with them. How does
one determine whether prayers are
answered if not in terms of results?*

In the year 204 B.C. Scipio Africanus sailed from Sicily to attack Hannibal's forces at Carthage. Just before the great expedition sailed, Scipio stood on his flagship at dawn and, after the herald had ordered silence, offered this prayer.

> Ye gods and goddesses, who inhabit the seas and the lands, I supplicate and beseech you that whatever has been done under my command, or is being done, or will later be done, may turn out to my advantage and to the advantage of the people and the commons of Rome, the allies, and the Latins who by land or sea or on rivers follow me, [accepting] the leadership, the authority, and the auspices of the Roman people; that you will support them and aid them with your help; that you will grant that, preserved in safety and victorious over the enemy, arrayed in booty and laden with spoils, you will bring them back with me in triumph to our homes; that you will grant us the power to take revenge upon our enemies and foes; and that you will grant to me and the Roman people the power to enforce upon the Carthaginians what they have planned to do against our city, as an example of [divine] punishment.°

"conversions," "speaking in tongues," oracular prophecies, and so on. Negatively, if possessed by a bad spirit (by a demon, a witch, a jinn, or by "sin"), we can point to the cause of the evil things we do. On the other hand, when possessed by helpful spirits (Vohu Manah, the Holy Spirit, the Spirit of Allah), then we can do good things and even accomplish feats which otherwise would have been quite beyond our capability.

From earliest times special techniques have been known for exorcizing demons—for depossessing one of a bad spirit. Likewise, techniques have been used for inducing possession by good spirits. To be possessed by the "Holy Spirit" is the most valued of human experiences according to Zoroastrians, Christians, and Muslims. In some groups such a blessing would be proven by intense emotion (the "strange warming of the heart" described by John Wesley), "speaking in tongues" (among Pentecostals), or an egoless consciousness (among Catholic mystics).

Spirit of this place, we give thee
tobacco; so help us, save us from
the enemy, bring us wealth, bring
us back safely.

Iroquois Indian Prayer

7   Men have always had experiences which they invest with ultimate significance, and often such events—from acts of courage and moments of love to visions and esthetic "highs"—effect drastic changes in our lives.

We preserve the essence of an experience by reflecting on it, conceptualizing and labeling it. As time passes, the mind "processes" the experience; it interprets it. Interpretations necessarily make use of available theological ideas and linguistic tools. What the experience "means" is therefore culturally relative, though we are not usually aware of this fact.

When attempting to understand a religious experience, there are two *kinds* of interpretations to be taken into account. One is given to the event by the experiencer himself. It will develop within the framework of his personal religious beliefs, and it is this interpretation which gives the experience meaning and affects his life.

Another interpretation, equally valid, must be made by a knowledgeable analyst or scientist. The experience may be explained in terms of motivations, emotional needs, or altered physiological states and body chemistry. Although the objective account does not pretend to include the meaning which the experience holds for the experiencer, it provides a valuable perspective for understanding one aspect of the event.

THE FUNCTION OF MYTH

8   The word *myth* is a technical term in religious anthropology and carries none of the popular implication that it is historically false or mere imagination. By definition a "myth" is a story circulated and accepted within some social group (a clan, religious community, a tribe, a nation) which gives ultimate significance and meaning to an event or explains some ultimate problem.° For example, the "Four Passing Sights" (during which Siddhartha discovered the true nature of existence by witnessing old age, disease, death, and a monk's search for the secret of life) is a myth. It "explains" to Buddhists how it happened that the man Siddhartha was drawn into the profound depths of human suffering from which he was to emerge triumphant as the "Enlightened One" (that is, as the Buddha) who had found the secret. Similarly, the Genesis account of the Tower of Babel explains in simple fashion the multiplicity of languages which the Amorites (later to be the Hebrews) encountered in their travels.

A "myth" is no more and no less than that: an explanatory account (which may or may not be historically accurate) which gives ultimate significance to some event. Myths are the product of man's unceasing effort to interpret meaningfully the world around him. This is further evidence for the contention that man cannot live for very long without meaning.

9   Viktor Frankl recounts a conversation between himself and a rabbi.

> He had lost his first wife and their six children in the concentration camp of Auschwitz where they were gassed, and now it turned out that his second wife was sterile. I observed that procreation is not the only meaning of life, for then life in itself would become meaningless, and something that in itself is meaningless cannot be rendered meaningful merely by its perpetuation. However, the rabbi evaluated his plight as an orthodox Jew in terms of despair that there was no son of his own who would ever say *Kaddish* [prayer for the dead] for him after his death.
>
> But I would not give up. I made a last attempt to help him by inquiring whether he did not hope to see his children again in Heaven. However, my question was followed by an outburst of tears, and now the true reason of his despair came to the fore: he explained

O millet, thou hast grown well for us; we thank thee, we eat thee.

Ainu Prayer

°*In the history of religions a myth is a social phenomenon. However, if a story performs the same functions for a single individual, then the word "myth" is quite in order; and here, too, it does not carry any implication of being false or "merely imagination."*

It seems as though the conception of a human soul . . . served as a type of model on which [man] framed not only his ideas of other souls of lower grade, but also his ideas of spiritual beings in general, from the tiniest elf that sports in the long grass up to the heavenly Creator and Ruler of the world, the Great Spirit.

E. B. TYLOR

We must respect the other fellow's religion, but only in the same sense and to the extent that we respect his theory that his wife is beautiful and his children smart.

H. L. MENCKEN

Let the one who put a jinx on the village die. Let him die, he who thought evil thoughts against us. Also give us fish.

Wapokomo Prayer

"O, Great Motage, Protector of humble men, Descendant of the Great Fish, Father of the Most Terrible Volcano and Devourer of All Enemies, we humbly beg your leave to join with the Methodists."

Great Quahootze! Let me live, not be sick, find the enemy, not be afraid of him, find him asleep, and kill many of him.

Nootka Indian Prayer

that his children, since they died as innocent martyrs, were found worthy of the highest place in Heaven, but as for himself he could not expect, as an old sinful man, to be assigned the same place. I did not give up but retorted, "Is it not conceivable, Rabbi, that precisely this was the meaning of your surviving your children; that you may be purified through these years of suffering, so that finally you, too, though not innocent like your children, may *become* worthy of joining them in Heaven? Is it not written in the Psalms that God preserves all your tears? So, perhaps none of your sufferings were in vain." For the first time in many years he found relief from his suffering, through the new point of view that I was able to open up to him.

10   When the *Apollo XIII* spacecraft was some fifty-six hours into its flight to the moon, an explosion in an oxygen tank blew open quad 4 of the service module.

APOLLO. OK, Houston, we've had a problem here. . . . We've had a main-B buss interval.

HOUSTON. Roger, main-B interval. OK, stand by Thirteen. We're looking at it.

APOLLO. OK, right now, Houston, the voltage is looking good. And we had a pretty large bang associated with the caution and warning there. . . . And we've got a main buss-A interval, too, showing. . . .

HOUSTON. Stand by, Jim. . . . Thirteen, Houston, We'd like you to attempt to reconnect fuel cell one to main-A and fuel cell three to main-B. Verify that quad-delta is open.

APOLLO. OK, Houston. . . . I tried to reset, the fuel cells one and three are both showing gray flags. But they're both showing zip on the flows.

HOUSTON. We copy. Thirteen, Houston, we'd like you to open circuit [to] fuel cell one. Leave two and three as is.

APOLLO. OK, I'll get to work on that.

A day later, after the spacecraft had looped around the moon and was limping homeward to earth, a course correction was necessary.

HOUSTON. Apollo Thirteen now 5,426 nautical miles out from the moon, traveling at a speed of 4,552 feet per second. . . . Less than thirty seconds away. . . . The engine is on. Stand by. . . . Ground confirms ignition.

APOLLO. We're burning. Forty percent.

HOUSTON. Houston copies. Attitude looks good at this point. . . . One minute now into the burn. . . . We've gained 451 feet per second at this time. . . . All systems are looking good. Coming up on three minutes. . . . The on-board display shows less than a minute to go in the burn now. . . . Coming up on four minutes into the burn. . . . Ten seconds to go.

APOLLO. Shut-down.

HOUSTON. Roger, shut down. . . . The engine is off. We are at 79 hours 32 minutes into the flight. . . . 5,707 nautical miles out from the moon at this time.

APOLLO. I'd say that was a good burn.

The President proclaimed Sunday, April 19, a national Day of Thanksgiving for the safe return of the astronauts. Earlier in the week the California state senate had swiftly passed a resolution urging citizens to join in praying for the safe return of the *Apollo XIII* crew. Senator Murphy said he had learned that when you're in trouble it is wise not only to look around but to look up as well.

Frank Reynolds reported on ABC television: "In Rome the pope prayed, for which we are grateful; and in South Africa a witch doctor did the same thing, and we are grateful for that too."

The dean of a major metropolitian cathedral prayed: "We give thanks to Almighty God for the safe return of our astronauts. . . . We praise Thy Holy Name that Thou hast conducted in safety through the vast vistas of space, Thy servants James, Frederick, and John, and to return them to this good Earth, our home, where Thy children dwell."

Much later a newsman asked the astronauts if they were aware of the Infinite which was looking over them. Jack Swigert replied: "If you're asking me if I prayed, I certainly did. And I have no doubt that perhaps my prayers and the prayers of the rest of the people contributed an awful lot to us getting back."

The religion of Ted Serios: **His relationship with God, which has always sustained him in the rough spots, is both intensely intimate and rather original. "God," he says, "understands me; he knows I'm human." Atheism is absolutely incomprehensible to him. "What do them guys do when they're in a tight spot," he asks, "like when the cops are layin' for them?"**

DR. JULE EISENBUD

The world is now without mysteries.

PIERRE BERTHELOT (1885)

> We would be a lot safer if the Government would take its money out of science and put it into astrology and the reading of palms. I used to think that science would save us. But only in superstition is there hope. I beg you to believe in the most ridiculous superstition of all: that humanity is at the center of the universe, the fulfiller or the frustrater of the grandest dreams of God Almighty. If you can believe that and make others believe it, human beings might stop treating each other like garbage.
>
> KURT VONNEGUT JR.

TELEOCOSMIC DRAMAS

11   Men have rarely been able to shake the feeling that they are participants in a sweeping drama or a teleological universe, and that their lives are a vital part of its plot and program. After all, our macroscosmic existence has a sort of story line: we are born and proceed psychophysiologically through a series of "dramatic" developmental phases—childhood, adolescence, the stages of adulthood, and so on. All living things around us seem to share this developmental sequence and even "nature" goes through a birth-life-death cycle: spring-summer-winter, dawn-day-night, the lunar phases. "Everything has a pattern"; it must also have meaning.

Of even greater significance is the fact that man is not alone. He exists in a universe filled with supernatural spirits with perhaps a Supreme Spirit, and these beings have human characteristics: they play, they fight, they needle one another and us with prankster-jokes, they scheme (note the Greek Olympians). They carry on a colorful social life with human beings (note, for instance, the love life of the shepherd god Krishna), and thus we humans become a part of their plans. We may even become the central concern or the principal characters in the ongoing cosmic drama.

Our search for meaning is so intense that we are always more than willing to be cast in whatever teleocosmic dramas may exist.

> The lonelier I am, the more of a recluse I become, the greater is my love for myths.
>
> ARISTOTLE

12   Teleocosmic programs have existed in all of man's religions, from the simplest to the most sophisticated; and they have been developed in infinite detail by the Riddle-challenging minds of theologians and philosophers. Since our need *to interpret* everything is irrepressible, our selective interpretation of the events of life commonly take on a teleological structure. Somewhere we will find the basis for a story-line, a plot, a plan, an apocalyptic drama, a goal-directed scheme, even a conspiracy (recall the Book of Job, for instance).

By merely being born we have been cast in the play, and our roles are to be taken seriously, for how well we perform our given roles affects the quality of our lives and determines our destiny. Little wonder, then, that we attempt again and again to clarify the teleocosmic plot so that we can better understand and play our roles.

> We have art that we do not die of the truth.
>
> NIETZSCHE

The teleocosmic dramas most familiar to us are theological and have their origins in the Western religions: Zoroastrianism, Judaism, Christianity, and Islam. These Western dramas are *linear* and *historical*.

APOCALYPTIC DRAMAS

13   We saw in an earlier chapter (5-1) that the metaphor of the drama has been used by philosophers of history to try to interpret the meaning and goal of human history (if either in fact exist). Just as a drama may move from the opening curtain through three or four acts that are subdivided into several scenes, and with a named *dramatis personae* who move the suspenseful plot through its tangles to the dénouement, the unraveling of the plot, and a final curtain—this way of interpreting history provides us with a teleocosmic story-line in which we can participate, individually and collectively.

This metaphorical interpretation of history-as-drama has been developed to its highest point in the Western family of religions. The metaphor called for a moment in time for the opening curtain—such as 4004 B.C. (Archbishop Ussher's calculation) or 5737 B.C.E. (the Judaic calculation)—and a set moment for the descent of the final curtain—A.D. 156, 732, 1946, 1984, 2001, or 2026. Various elements of the plot along the way have been mapped out. Therefore one's role in the drama should, in principle, be knowable; and if we can understand the plot, determine which scene we are currently playing, and read the signs of the times, then we'll know what is expected by the Playwright. By a correct reading of the plot (especially if we have a script) we'll know when the dénouement is destined to occur.

These are personal linear-historical dramas, directed from above. They are, in the fullest sense, apocalyptic dramas since much of the program—the background scenario, the props, the stagehands, as well as the Director—are offstage, *above* space and time, carrying on the drama; while we humans are *in* space and time, moving along from scene to scene, playing out the story.

14   The teleocosmic drama held in common by the Western family of religions has its origins, as we would expect, in the world-view of the parent: Zoroastrianism.

Here the battlefield metaphor is first developed by the founder, Zoroaster (c. 660 B.C.), and the teleocosmic drama—not unlike *Macbeth* or *Richard III*—is the account of a great battle. When this world was created by the Divine Mind, hosts of heavenly creatures of light also came into being: a Holy Spirit through whom the God of Light works his will; plus the Amesha Spentas (Immortal Holy Ones) and Yazatas (Angels), all led by Ahura Mazda, the Creator and Wise Lord of this world and the final judge and redeemer of history.

The evil counterparts are the daevas led by the supreme evil spirit, Angra Mainyu, the Lord of Darkness. Human history is a battlefield confrontation of the evil forces and heavenly forces, led by the "generals" Spenta Mainyu and Angra Mainyu. In this aeons-long struggle man is caught up in a cosmic conflagration and must decide, of his own free will, on which side he will take his stand.

For man, just as for the spiritual forces, the war is essentially a moral struggle. Man has but one chance—one lifetime—during which he can determine his destiny. Professor Robert Smith describes the scene in this fashion:

> The cardinal Zoroastrian moral principle that each man's soul is the seat of the war between good and evil sets the stage for man's plight. This war in the breast is of critical importance as the supreme Ahura Mazda is not unopposed in creation. Over against Asha (the Truth) is Druj (the Lie). Truth is confronted with Falsehood, Life with Death. The Good Spirit is opposed by the Bad Spirit. On this earthly battle-

There is an old story that John Knox was interrupted by his wife in a midnight prayer for Scotland. The wife pleaded with her husband to seek rest from a terrible agony of intercession. Knox rebuked her with the reply that through his prayer he already had won half of Scotland and that, if she had not broken in upon him, he would have won it all by daybreak.

FRANCIS J. MC CONNELL

Saint Augustine was asked by a scoffer what God was doing before He created the world. Replied the great theologian: "He was busy creating hell for people who ask foolish questions."

The Buddha's right hand points downward to touch the earth; the other hand supports a begging bowl—symbolizing acceptance of the gift—grace. . . . An *active* attitude toward the world and a *passive* attitude toward heaven. The ignorant man does the opposite: he passively accepts the world and resists grace, gift, and heaven.

THOMAS MERTON

"IT WAS A GOOD PLAY . . ."

Finding Dr. Faustus in his study, Mephistopheles recounted to him the story of creation.

The endless praises of the choirs of angels had begun to grow wearisome; for, after all, did he not deserve their praise? Had he not given them endless joy? Would it not be more amusing to obtain undeserved praise, to be worshipped by beings whom he tortured? He smiled inwardly, and resolved that the great drama should be performed.

For countless ages the hot nebula whirled aimlessly through space. At length it began to take shape, the central mass threw off planets, the planets cooled, boiling seas and burning mountains heaved and tossed, from black masses of cloud hot sheets of rain deluged the barely solid crust. And now the first germ of life grew in the depths of the ocean, and developed rapidly in the fructifying warmth into vast forest trees, huge ferns springing from the damp mould, sea monsters breeding, fighting, devouring, and passing away. And from the monsters, as the play unfolded itself, Man was born, with the power of thought, the knowledge of good and evil, and the cruel thirst for worship. And Man saw that all is passing in this mad monstrous world, that all is struggling to snatch, at any cost, a few brief moments of life before Death's inexorable decree. And man said: "There is a hidden purpose, could we but fathom it, and the purpose is good; for we must reverence something, and in the visible world there is nothing worthy of reverence." And Man stood aside from the struggle, resolving that God intended harmony to come out of chaos by human efforts. And when he followed the instincts which God has transmitted to him from his ancestry of beasts of prey, he called it Sin, and asked God to forgive him. But he doubted whether he could be justly forgiven, until he invented a divine Plan by which God's wrath was to have been appeased. And seeing the present was bad, he made it yet worse, that thereby the future might be better. And he gave God thanks for the strength that enabled him to forgo even the joys that were possible. And God smiled; and when he saw that Man had become perfect in renunciation and worship, he sent another sun through the sky, which crashed into Man's sun; and all returned again to nebula.

"Yes," he murmured, "it was a good play; I will have it performed again."

---

field, Angra Mainyu is set over against Spenta Mainyu in dualistic fashion. One must feel that they are co-equals in his earthly battle. However, the capacity of Angra Mainyu for mischief is boundless and the evil power he possesses is many times multiplied by the demons he creates to assist him. Without man's active participation on the side of Ahura Mazda, the world will not be a "brighter place to live" and man will not "be like God." Consequently, even in the working out of the Zoroastrian doctrine that the ultimate victory will be Ahura Mazda's, the first duty of every right-thinking man is to oppose and win the battle here and now.

And so, the battle progresses down through human history, man's only weapons being Truth and Righteousness, assisted by Good Thoughts, Good Words, and Good Deeds. Each man is to "fight all the enemies of Good Mind as though they were his own enemies and as if he were the only warrior upon the battlefield."

All battles come to an end eventually, and the victorious vanquish the losers. Whole armies win and lose battles, but in the final analysis, all armies are composed only of individual soldiers. So, prior to any battle's final outcome, each soldier carries on his own personal struggle to the death, or life. So also for Zoroaster's spiritual warriors.

For the first time in world religion, the concept of eschatology dominates. The drama of individual judgment—a single scene, perhaps, in the great cosmic battle—occurs. If a warrior falls in battle, then his judgment takes place on the fourth day after his death. For three nights the soul of the dead sits at the head of its former body, meditating on its past deeds, words, and thoughts. During this time the soul is comforted (if it has been a righteous soul) by good angels, or tormented (if it has been wicked) by demons.

On the fourth day the soul makes its way to the Chinvat Bridge. There the soul stands in judgment before its judges: Truth, Conscience, and Justice. The last holds the scales for the final weighing of merits and demerits. Judgment is rendered and sentence passed, the soul then walks onto the Bridge. The Zoroastrian text called the *Bundahishn* describes what then takes place in the center of the Bridge.

Detail from Lucas Cranach the Elder, *Adam and Eve.*

Imagine how the Christian conscience would react to the idea that, behind the scenes, God and the Devil were the closest friends but had taken opposite sides in order to stage a great cosmic game. Yet this is rather much how things stood when the Book of Job was written, for here Satan is simply the counsel for the prosecution in the court of Heaven, as faithful a servant of the court as the *advocatus diaboli* at the Vatican.

ALAN WATTS

> There is a sharp edge which stands like a sword; . . . and Hell is below the Bridge. Then the soul is carried to where stands the sharp edge. Then, if it be righteous, the sharp edge presents its broad side. . . . If the soul be wicked, that sharp edge continues to stand edgewise, and does not give a passage. . . . With three steps which it (the soul) takes forward (evil thoughts, evil words, evil deeds) it is cut down from the head of the Bridge, and falls headlong into Hell.
>
> When (the righteous soul) takes a step over the Chinvat Bridge, there comes to it a fragrant wind from Paradise, which smells of musk and ambergris, and that fragrance is more pleasant to it than any other pleasure.
>
> When it reaches the middle of the Bridge, it beholds an apparition of such beauty that it hath never seen a figure of greater beauty. . . . And when the apparition appears to the soul, (the soul) speaks thus: "Who art thou with such beauty that a figure of greater beauty I have never seen?"
>
> The apparition speaks (thus): "I am thine own good actions. I myself was good, but thine actions have made me better."
>
> And the apparition embraces the soul, and they both depart with complete joy and ease into Paradise.
>
> But if the soul be that of a wicked man . . . there blows to him an exceedingly foul wind from Hell [and] it sees an apparition of such extreme ugliness and frightfulness that it hath never seen one uglier and more unseemingly. . . .
>
> She speaks (thus): "I am thine own bad actions. I myself was ugly, and thou madest me worse day after day, and now thou hast

thrown me and thine own self into misery and damnation, and we shall suffer punishment till the day of Resurrection.''

And the apparition embraces it, and both fall headlong from the middle of the Chinvat Bridge and descend to Hell.

15   The cosmological structure of the Zoroastrian drama was adopted by its offspring. Many elements were revised, but most remained intact just as they came from Zoroastrianism. In late Judaic theology, the archangels and angels fought on behalf of Yahweh and constituted the Forces of Light; while demons and evil spirits led by Satan made up the Forces of Darkness.

Hebrew religion had its own heritage before it was infused (after the sixth century B.C.) with Zoroastrian elements. That drama was now combined with the battlefield metaphor.

The Judaic telecosmos began in the Garden of Eden. This was paradise and the tenants were perfect, companions and children of God. This is the opening scene of the drama, and the final scene is a return to Eden—to paradise and perfection. By the time the concept had been filled out with details the Hebrews had ceased to be a wandering tribe and had become a nation. The final scene of the plot was therefore envisioned as a ''messianic age'' in which the nation Israel, or at least a faithful Remnant, would reign supreme over all the earth. Truly it would be a paradise, for peace would be forever and prosperity would surpass belief. As one fragment of late Jewish literature put it, every grapevine would bear a thousand clusters, and every cluster would bear a thousand grapes, and every grape would yield a gallon of wine.

Between these opening and closing scenes lies human existence as we know it, with suffering and death. It is only too likely that this is the only condition evolutionary man has ever known; but we find profound satisfaction in the conviction that there was a time when everything was all right and that we can anticipate a future setting in which all will be made right again.

16   Being a child of Judaism and a grandchild of Zoroastrianism, Christianity adopted about the same beginning to the teleocosmic drama—the garden paradise of Eden—and developed further the metaphor of the cosmic battlefield. Christians, however, added a new element. Along the time-line of human existence, there came a moment when life was suddenly given meaning by the intervention of the Creator deity himself. Until the advent of the redeemer god, the Christ, human suffering had been pointless; it counted for nothing. But after his appearance, human suffering became a ''trial by fire'' to create spiritually worthy souls who, collectively, would compose a ''communion of saints'' to bear witness until they could join together in the Kingdom of God. Nevertheless, human suffering will continue until the final act of the drama, when the Reign of God begins with the Parousia, the Return of the Messiah. ''For the Lord himself, at the summons, when the archangel calls and God's trumpet sounds, will come down from heaven, and first those who died in union with Christ will rise; then those of us who are still living will be caught up with them on clouds into the air to meet the Lord, and so we shall be with the Lord forever" (I Thess. 4:16f.).

For early Christians (and adventist groups of any century) this is the joyous fulfillment of God's plan. With a climactic crescendo—full orchestra and chorus—it closes out the tragic drama and opens the Reign of God.

17   The cosmology of the New Testament is essentially mythical in character. The world is viewed as a three-storied structure, with the earth in the centre, the heaven above, and the underworld beneath. Heaven is the abode of God and of celestial beings—the angels. The underworld is hell, the place of torment. Even the earth is more than the scene of natural, everyday events, of the trivial round and common task. It is the scene of the supernatural activity of God and his angels on the one hand, and of Satan and his daemons on the other. These supernatural forces intervene in the course of nature and in all that men think and will and do. Miracles are by no means rare. Man is not in control of his own life. Evil spirits may take possession of him. Satan may inspire him with evil thoughts. Alternatively, God may inspire his thought and guide his purposes. He may grant him heavenly visions. He may allow him to hear his word of succour or demand. He may give him the supernatural power of his Spirit. History does not follow a smooth unbroken course; it is set in motion and controlled by these supernatural powers. This aeon is held in bondage by Satan, sin, and death (for "power" is precisely what they are), and hastens towards its end. That end will come very soon, and will take the form of a cosmic catastrophe. It will be inaugurated by the "woes" of the last time. Then the Judge will come from heaven, the dead will rise, the last judgment will take place, and men will enter into eternal salvation or damnation.

This then is the mythical view of the world which the New Testament presupposes.

RUDOLF BULTMANN

18   *The Eschaton.*   In linear-historical plots, we find that believers almost universally conclude that they are living near the end of the play. Their hope is that the dramatic last scene will be acted out during their lifetime. The history of apocalyptic thinking suggests that there are clearly identifiable psychological factors which make us want to live at the climax of the historical drama. We want to know, deep in our bones, that the bloody period of man's agony is about over; that peace, justice, and goodwill are about to prevail; that in our own lifetimes we can enjoy a modicum of happiness. To live prior to the dénouement of the drama leaves one in a suspended state—like leaving an exciting motion picture before the ending.

And when you hear of wars and rumors of wars, do not be disturbed . . . the end is not yet.

Mark 13:7

"Yes," he murmured, "it was a good play; I will have it performed again."

Thomas Merton
The Other Side of Kanchenjunga

On October 15, 1968, Thomas Merton, an American Catholic monk from a Trappist monastery in Kentucky, began a spiritual journey. "I am going home," he wrote in his journal, "to a home where I have never been in this body . . . ."

In actual fact, he was sitting in a Pan American jet on the runway of the San Francisco International Airport waiting for take-off. He was flying to the Orient. It was early morning, with the taxiing planes performing a "slow ballet of big tail fins in the sun."

> The moment of take-off was ecstatic. We left the ground—I with Christian mantras and a great sense of destiny, of being at last on my true way after years of waiting and wondering and fooling around. May I not come back without having settled the great affair.

This trip would carry him—while still "in the body"—through unscheduled adventures in India, Sri Lanka, and Thailand. In Bangkok the great affair would be settled.

The world first knew of Thomas Merton in 1948 when his autobiographical novel, *The Seven Storey Mountain*, revealed who he was and how he became a Trappist.

His parents were artists—strong-willed, independent, avant garde; and they shaped their son's inner world before their early deaths: his mother when he was six, his father when he was fifteen. From both came a Dionysian drive "for work and vision and enjoyment and expression." His mother was filled with "insatiable dreams" and a "great ambition after perfection"; she was "worried, precise, quick, critical of me, her son," and intellectually demanding. She kept a detailed diary in which she chronicled her son's every move.

Merton's youth was disturbed and unhappy. Out of a loneliness that was to haunt him all his life, he very early began to write down his thoughts and feelings. By the time he was eight he had written three "novels."

His late teens took an Augustinian turn: wild revelries and continuous affairs. While he was attending Cambridge, a young woman bore him a son; Merton abandoned both, and they were later killed in an air raid in London. He had a penchant for erotica, contributed bawdy sketches to school papers, and once became a barker for a sleazy sideshow.

By his early twenties, Merton's psyche was a raging fire. Driven by enormous guilt, confusion, and loneliness; fueled by boundless energies, creative urges, and an intense longing for love, beauty, and perfection—Merton had arrived at the classical psychological spiritual condition for the making of a monk. Although he converted to Catholicism at 23, much of the next two years seem to have been spent in confession. Still, the love affairs and wild parties continued, with miserable hangovers.

The turning point came in December, 1941—the week the world exploded at Pearl Harbor. Thomas Merton renounced this world and entered the Trappist abbey of Our Lady of Gethsemani.

The Trappists were (and still are) one of the world's severely ascetic communities. Their days are lived in terms of prayer, work, and silence. They arise at 2 A.M. for prayer, meditate or read till 5:30; offer more prayers at 7:45 and 11:00, vespers at 4:30; listen to a reading at 6:10, and retreat to bed at 7:00 P.M. They subsist on a meager vegetarian diet. Labor consists of hoeing, cutting, threshing in the monastery's orchards and fields, tending livestock, making repairs. They live in silence; all communication is managed with some 400 basic gestures in sign language.

Merton's first years at Gethsemani were relatively happy, even though the physical labor, fasting, and scanty diet often left him weak. Separated from the world, his spirit found a modicum of peace and began the long process of healing. He was allowed to live in a "hermit hatch" a half-mile from the monastery.

He wrote continually, and passionately; and in his seventh year as a monk he published *The Seven Storey Mountain*. To everyone's surprise, it soared upward on best-seller lists and the author was hailed as a new Augustine—"the most significant spiritual leader in America"—and more. Overnight, fame and admiration came from the world to this world-renouncing monk. Soul-mates, would-be disciples, and notables ferreted out the path to the "hermit hatch," and Merton's solitude was lost. Still, he continued producing poetry, essays, and novels, and carried on a voluminous correspondence. His writings would eventually be collected into more than 40 volumes.

In the summer of 1968, Merton was invited to attend an interfaith conference in Bangkok. For a decade he had been studying Eastern literature and religion and had long felt a kinship with other "contemplatives" who had withdrawn from the world to give their spiritual lives highest priority. (It was a Hindu monk who first persuaded him to read St. Augustine's *Confessions*.) He corresponded with Theravada monks, Tibetan rimpoches ("spiritual masters"), Hindu swamis, Taoist and Confucian priests. He developed a warm friendship with Daisetz Suzuki, the famed Zen master, and felt especially close to Zen. In 1965 he published *The Way of Chuang Tzu*, an interpretation of the Chinese sage whose teachings struck a responsive chord in him.

His flight from San Francisco carried him first to Bangkok, where he experienced firsthand the "other world" he knew so well from books and letters; and then to Calcutta—"the big, beat-up, teeming, incredible city. People!" Next to Dharamsala to meet with the Dalai Lama, the Tibetan leader now in exile. His time with the Dalai Lama was immensely rewarding; of special value was their exchange of ideas on methods of meditation. Easily and naturally, Merton moved into the Buddhist experience. The Dalai Lama called him a *geshe*, a "learned lama."

In Sri Lanka Merton talked with hermits living in caves near Kandy, then journeyed to Polonnaruwa. Here, at last, there was a gathering together of all the parts, the scattered pieces, in the spiritual vision of this Western trespasser. In a tree-lined, rock-cut canyon were open caves containing statues of the Buddha. "Polonnaruwa was such an experience that I could not write hastily of it and cannot write now, or not at all adequately."

I am able to approach the Buddhas barefoot and undisturbed, my feet in wet grass, wet sand. Then the silence of the extraordinary faces . . .

questioning nothing, knowing everything, rejecting nothing, the peace . . . that has seen through every question without trying to discredit anyone or anything—*without refutation*—without establishing some other argument. For the doctrinaire, the mind that needs well-established positions, such peace, such silence, can be frightening. . . . I don't know when in my life I have ever had such a sense of beauty and spiritual validity running together in one aesthetic illumination. . . . I know and have seen what I was obscurely looking for. I don't know what else remains, but I have now seen and have pierced through the surface and have got beyond the shadow and the disguise.

Thomas Merton represents for the modern world a new stage of maturity in religious understanding—a new spirit in dialogue and a new way of listening.

It is characteristic of Merton's approach to Eastern thought that he did not so much reach out for contact with other traditions, but rather went so deeply into his own that he could not help discovering the common roots. A strange journey indeed: the traveler, instead of going abroad, digs into the ground on which he stands, but digs so deep that he comes out in China

DAVID STEINDL-RAST.

What Merton gradually came to see is not uncommon in the lives of seekers: that experience opens the avenues of communication, while rigid belief closes them off. That experience encourages dialogue where belief encourages pronouncement. And that whereas experience leads to empathy and appreciation, commitment to doctrinal formulas produces antipathy and disparagement.

Merton found that those who enter into a "dialogue of experience" can share and learn from one another.

This inclusive view made it impossible for him to deny any authentic scripture or any man of faith. Indeed, he discovered new aspects of truth in Hinduism, in the Madhyamika system, which stood halfway between Hinduism and Buddhism, in Zen, and in Sufi mysticism. His lifelong search for meditative silence and prayer was found not only in his monastic experience but also in his late Tibetan inspiration.

AMIYA CHAKRAVARTY
in the Preface to *The Asian Journal*, vii

From Sri Lanka Merton flew on to Bangkok. On the morning of December 10, 1968, he spoke to a gathering of monks and clerics on "Marxism and Monastic Perspectives." He spoke casually and with humor, noting that both monk and Marxist believe that "the claims of the world are fraudulent," and his speech concluded with a call for empathy for other religions and an openness to the "painfulness of inner change."

Shortly after lunch Merton returned to his guest cottage to rest. When he failed to reappear his friends went to his cottage and found him lying on the floor, with an electric fan, still spinning, lying across his chest. He had been accidentally electrocuted.

That night his friends kept vigil. His body was returned to its present resting place at Gethsemani.

A few weeks earlier, during a visit to the forested tea country of northeastern India, Merton stood looking at the snow-covered Himalayan peak of Kanchenjunga. He wrote in his journal:

Last night I had a curious dream about Kanchenjunga. I was looking at the mountain and it was pure white, absolutely white, especially the peaks that lie to the west. And I saw the pure beauty of their shape and outline, all in white. And I heard a voice saying—or got the clear idea of: "There is another side to the mountain!"

Thomas Merton had climbed the peak alone, as all must. And the seeker—whether he be Buddhist, Christian, Hindu, Jew, Muslim, Jain—must find his own path. It takes enormous courage and, perhaps, a special grace to see that *there is* another side. "There is another side of Kanchenjunga and of every mountain . . . ."

FINAL CURTAIN/END OF DRAMA

19   Man is a creature of hope, and his teleocosmic dreams almost always foresee a future time when life will be good again and there will be no more fear, pain, loneliness, and death. It is here that man reveals his deepest pessimism. He intuits that he cannot bring about such conditions by himself, so he envisions supernatural beings who will appear on earth at their appointed times to call a drumroll for the last act of the teleocosmic drama.

Judaism looks forward to the coming of the *Messiah* (the "Anointed One"). According to one interpretation, the nation Israel will be established by God as the Chosen Light to the gentiles to rule over them forever. According to another interpretation, the Son of Man will appear to usher in a spiritual Messianic Age.

Christians came to believe that *Jesus the Christ* (again, the specially "Anointed One") will return and supervise the Last Judgment, the separation of the righteous from the wicked. He will represent God himself when the Reign of God begins.

In Buddhism, *Maitreya* is at present a Buddha-in-the-making, waiting to come to earth in due time to inaugurate the final age and bring peace. In Hinduism, a messiah named *Kalki* will make his appearance riding a white horse and brandishing a flaming sword. This savior, the tenth avatar of Vishnu, will save the righteous and destroy the wicked at the end of the fourth (hopelessly depraved) world period.

In Zoroastrianism, a messiah called *Soshyans* will appear in the final days and preside over a general resurrection. A flood of molten metal will pour across the earth, purging the wicked of their evil but bathing the righteous in soothing balm. Ahura Mazda will hurl the Evil One, Ahriman, into a lake of fire, and the saved will then dwell together in a new heaven and a new earth, enjoying eternal peace. (Incidentally, in this particular drama, adults will remain forever at the age of forty and and children at fifteen.)

In Islam, the Shi'ites await a messianic figure entitled the *Mahdi* to complete the task, begun by Muhammad, of carrying the message of salvation to all mankind. This "Divinely Guided One" will usher in a period of peace before the end of the world and the onset of the Last Judgment.

In the long run men give their supreme loyalties to overall patterns of life, to those ideas and attitudes concerning the nature of the world and of life, which provide them with incentive and direction for living. These patterns of thought and action commonly have gone by the name of religion. Their importance is evidenced by the fact that no human society of any size is long without them, and by the fact that they outlive nations and governments.

ARTHUR E. MORGAN

UNITY IN DIVERSITY: ALL RELIGION IS ONE

20   There is a minority report within man's religions that contends that all religions are one. Most have said this because they wanted it to be so, but some of these claims are the result of personal experience with many religious faiths.

We are not today at the point of knowing whether "all religions are one." Certainly the various Gods are thought to possess different characteristics. They behave differently and demand different responses from their worshipers.

Yet when men have experienced a religious odyssey, they commonly emerge with a feeling of oneness. It could be that our ultimate experiences are similar but become distorted in the process of interpretation. It might also be that certain universal psychophysical processes operate to produce similar experiences. Among these may be alpha rhythms and methods of self-hypnosis.

It may also be that one finds what he looks for. If he wishes to find the differences in the many religions of man, they can be found; but if one searches for the similarities which underlie man's religious approaches to the Riddle of Life, they too are there and can be found.

21   One of the most successful attempts to clarify the "highest common factors" contained in Man's great religions has been called "the Perennial Philosophy." Aldous Huxley described four such elements from which we might infer that, however varied the paths we travel, Man's religious quest is quintessentially One.

(1) This world as we conceptualize and experience it is a manifestation of a greater reality, a "Divine Ground of Being." All the realities of experience, both mental and material, are merely "bits and fragments" of that Ultimate Reality. They constitute only limited, angular glimpses of that Divine Ground.

(2) Human beings can acquire knowledge *about* that Divine Ground, but such knowledge is relatively unimportant. Of greater significance is the fact that we can enter into a direct intuitive knowledge of it, a knowledge involving our whole being and not merely our conceptualizing intellects. This is a mystical knowing which unites the knower with the Known, or the known with the Knower.

(3) In his very nature, man is a duality. We are composed of ephemeral elements (body, ego-self, data bits, memory) and eternal essence (soul, atman, "divine spark"). The ephemeral elements are temporal and temporary, but the eternal essence can become One with the Divine Ground of Being.

(4) The singular goal of human existence on earth is for each individual to come to know the eternal essence of his being and to identify it more and more closely with the Divine Ground of all Being.

Huxley considered the Perennial Philosophy to be one of the great insights in the history of human understanding, and his judgment is still shared by many present-day philosophers of religion. Huxley's previsions are clear and strong.

> In existing circumstances there is not the slightest chance that any of the traditional religions will obtain universal acceptance. Europeans and Americans will see no reason for being converted to Hinduism, say, or Buddhism. And the people of Asia can hardly be expected to renounce their own traditions for the Christianity professed, often sincerely, by the imperialists who, for four hundred years and more, have been systematically attacking, exploiting and oppressing, and are now trying to finish off the work of destruction by "educating" them. But happily there is the Highest Common Factor of all reli-

gions, the Perennial Philosophy which has always and everywhere been the metaphysical system of the prophets, saints and sages. It is perfectly possible for people to remain good Christians, Hindus, Buddhists or Moslems and yet to be united in full agreement on the basic doctrines of the Perennial Philosophy.

22　There was a man who worshiped Shiva but hated all other deities. One day Shiva appeared to him and said, "I shall not be pleased with thee so long as thou hatest the other gods." The man was inexorable. After a few days Shiva again appeared to him and said, "I shall never be pleased with thee so long as thou hatest." The man kept silent. After a few days Shiva again appeared to him. This time he appeared as Hari-har, namely, one side of his body was that of Shiva, and the other side that of Vishnu. The man was half pleased and half displeased. He laid his offerings on the side representing Shiva, and did not offer anything to the side representing Vishnu. Then Shiva said, "Thy bigotry is unconquerable. I, by assuming this dual aspect, tried to convince thee that all gods and goddesses are but various aspects of the one Absolute Brahman."

RAMAKRISHNA

Ramakrishna (1836–1886)

23　The Muslim mystic Ibn Arabi is quoted as saying:

There was a time when I took it amiss in my companion if his religion was not like mine, but now my heart admits every form. It is a pasture for gazelles, a cloister for monks, a temple for idols, a Ka'aba for the pilgrim, the tables of the Law, and the sacred book of the Quran. Love alone is my religion, and whithersoever man's camels turn, it is *my* religion and *my* faith.

> Indeed, I do not forget that my voice is but one voice, my experience a mere drop in the sea, my knowledge no greater than the visual field in a microscope, my mind's eye a mirror that reflects a small corner of the world, and my ideas—a subjective confession.
>
> *CARL G. JUNG*

REFLECTIONS—

1　This chapter offers a working definition of "religion" as "man's involvement in the meaning of his existence." After reflection on this definition along with others on p. 492, develop the best definition you can of religion as you personally understand it. Can you defend, rationally and empirically, each part of your definition?

2　Note the anthropologist Tylor's observation of the use of ceremonies and ritual by maritime communities (p. 493-QM). What inference can you make from such religious practice?

3　How would you respond to the question asked in the sidenote on p. 496: "How does one determine whether prayers are answered if not in terms of results?" Was Scipio's prayer answered?

4　Recall your reflections upon the story of the Indian physicist/priest (pp. 2–3) who described the eclipse in terms of celestial mechanics and then proceeded to chant to the goddess Kali to make the eclipse go away. Is there a similar incompatibility of world-views in the story of the Apollo XIII explosion and the subsequent behavior of astronauts and others (Sec. 10)? Can you apply the conclusions you reached regarding the Indian's dilemma to the Apollo incident?

5　Study the many varied meanings attached to the Greek word *pneuma* in

> Without God, we cannot. Without us, God will not.
>
> *SAINT AUGUSTINE*

ancient times (p. 495-Box). What can you conclude from a comparison of the multiple English translations of this one word?

6 What is the function of the concept of "spirit possession"? (See Sec. 6.)

7 Understanding the more technical usage of the word "myth" is important. So, what psychological and epistemic function does "myth" refer to? What about the beliefs held by the rabbi described by Frankl in Sec. 9—would you call these beliefs myths? What exactly are you saying about his beliefs?

8 Examine the Angola bank note on p. 493. What is your response to the scene depicted here?

9 Rudolf Bultmann, a contemporary German theologian, paints a vivid picture of the three-storied cosmology of the early Christians. This is essentially a "battlefield" analogy with origins in Zoroastrianism. What religious needs are met by this particular mythical version of the universe? (Incidentally, can this sort of teleocosmology survive in the "space age"?)

10 What are your thoughts and second-thoughts after reading the list of future saviors (Sec. 19)?

11 After your first startled reaction to Kurt Vonnegut's plea on p. 500-QM, can you bring yourself to agree with him? Can you at least build a hypothetical case for what he is saying?

12 List some of the human needs that are met by teleocosmic dramas. Could we live without such dramas? Would our lives be richer without them or impoverished without them?

Furthermore . . .

ALTIZER, THOMAS J. J., et al. (eds.), *Truth, Myth, and Symbol*. Prentice-Hall, 1962.

BARTSCH, HANS WERNER (ed.), *Kerygma and Myth*. Harper, 1961.

CAMPBELL, JOSEPH, *Myths To Live By*. Bantam, 1973.

CASSIRER, ERNST, *Language and Myth*. Dover, 1946.

CLARK, ELMER T., *The Small Sects in America*. Abingdon, 1949.

de VRIES, JAN, *The Study of Religion*. Harcourt, 1967.

di NOLA, ALFONSO M., *The Prayers of Man*. Heinemann, 1962.

ELIADE, MIRCEA, *Myth and Reality*. Harper, 1968.

ELIADE, MIRCEA, *Patterns in Comparative Religion*. Sheed, 1958.

ELIADE, MIRCEA, *The Two and the One*. Harper, 1965.

FRAZER, JAMES G., *The Golden Bough* (1922). Macmillan, 1960.

MAVRODES, GEORGE I., *Belief in God: A Study in the Epistemology of Religion*. Random House, 1970.

MILLER, ED. L., *God and Reason: A Historical Approach to Philosophical Theology*. Macmillan, 1972.

MURRAY, HENRY A., (ed.), *Myth and Mythmaking*. Beacon, 1968.

SWANSON, GUY E., *The Birth of the Gods*. Ann Arbor, 1964.

TREMMEL, WILLIAM CALLOLEY, *Religion: What Is It?* Holt, Rinehart and Winston, 1976.

WATTS, ALAN, *Myth and Ritual in Christianity*. Grove, 1960.

WEINBERG, JULIUS R., and KEITH E. YANDELL, *Philosophy of Religion*. Holt, Rinehart and Winston, 1971.

Ultimate Reality

Have You Ever Wondered . . .

- How you could find out for sure whether God exists?

- Whether there is any empirical evidence for God's existence?

- What God is like (if He/She does in fact exist)?

- Whether you *can* think of God at all if He/She doesn't possess (human) sexual characteristics?

- Whether Zeus might truly have existed during the lifetime of Greek civilization?

- Whether gods can die?

- Whether one can have a "religious experience" if he doesn't believe in God?

- Whether one can believe in God without having a "religious experience"?

ULTIMATE QUESTIONS

1   The Ethiopians make their gods black-skinned and snub-nosed; the Thracians say theirs have blue eyes and red hair. If oxen and horses had hands and could draw with their hands and make works of art just as men do, then horses would draw their gods to look like horses, and oxen like oxen—each would make their bodies in the image of their own.

XENOPHANES

Non ridere, non lugere, neque detestari, sed intelligere.
Not to laugh, not to lament, not to curse, but to understand.

SPINOZA

2   The questions which we ask about Ultimate Reality are always
phrased in terms of our own particular world-view, of course; and the
questions which have meaning to a Hindu or Buddhist may be meaningless to a Christian or Muslim. Problems about Ultimate Reality cannot be made intelligible apart from the thought-framework within
which they are posed.

The questions which we in the West ask are deceptively simple:
Does God exist? What is he like? How can we know what he wants
of us?

In Eastern religion, the Hindu might ask: What is the true nature of the Ultimate Reality that lies beyond the gods? Is the world of
physical matter merely illusion? How can I attain liberation from the
round of rebirths? The Buddhist might ask: Is it really true, as the
Buddha claimed, that to exist is to suffer? If so, how can I escape suffering and attain enlightenment?

Other, Far Eastern worshipers might ask: What is the true way
of life—the Tao? How can I best seek the Tao so that my life may be
peaceful and full? What does Heaven want of me?

3   Philosophy is neither theology—which attempts to make religion intellectually meaningful—nor evangelism—which attempts to
persuade others to believe. Rather, philosophy's concerns are primarily metaphysical and epistemological. *Metaphysical:* What is Ultimate
Reality? How many orders of reality exist? Is there a supernatural order of reality? Do deities and spirits exist? Does God exist? In fact,
what exactly is meant by such terms? *Epistemological:* Can we humans
who belong to the natural order know that which belongs to the supernatural order? If so, how? Does God (or do the gods) "reveal"?
Does he reveal a person (as some Christian theologians claim) or a
data content? How can we be sure about the source of supernatural
fact-claims mediated through human beings?

THE PROBLEM OF DIVINE KNOWLEDGE

4   The images of deity which men hold are largely the product of
particular circumstances of time and place. Western religions of Near
Eastern origin conceive deity as male. We ask if *he* exists and we speak
of a *father*-god. The majority of men, however, have imagined their
deities to be feminine, and to these goddesses they have prayed for
intercession, tender care, love, and life-generating energies.

The Judeo-Christian God is necessarily masculine since our god-
concepts originated in the Bedouin sheikdoms that wandered out of
the Arabian desert into the Fertile Crescent. The gods of these no-
madic clans were modeled after the sheik chieftain. They were
strongly masculine deities, associated with the aggressive forces of nature—volcanoes, earthquakes, storms—and with intertribal battles.

Rarely, if ever, does the concept of a female deity evolve in a Bedouin society with patriarchal dominance. The early Hebrew god Yahweh exhibits the characteristics of the sheik chieftain. He is authoritarian in monitoring the loyalty pledged to him by his followers. He is stern, demanding, and quick to punish backsliding. He is a "jealous God" who will tolerate no competition from other gods. This early Hebraic world was patriarchal and the survival qualities necessary in a deity were authority and firmness; he must be quick to anger and of mighty power in battle. The blood-covenant binding the deity to his tribe (Exodus 24:4–8) is basically Bedouin: he will be their leader and protector as long as they obey and "keep the covenant."

By contrast, where sprawling vineyards cover the hillsides and the valleys shelter fields of grain and fruit trees, here we are more likely to find the goddesses and their consorts. In gentler climes and social settings, the qualities associated with feminine roles—love, fertility, nurturance—are more valued than the fearsome, bellicose qualities of the desert deities. These female deities are at once Earth-mothers, fertility-goddesses, and sacred virgins. As Earth-mothers they generate the life-giving forces that underlie the birth and growth of all living things. As fertility goddesses they symbolize conception, and by means of mystery rites, temple prostitution, and spring festivals, they can be persuaded to stimulate fertility in man's clans, flocks, and crops. As eternal virgin-goddesses their primary purpose is to symbolize purity and to merit the devotion of mortal men.

5   When deities are considered to be male, then they frequently mate with mortal women. Zeus was forever entangled in amorous affairs, and the shepherd-god Krishna spent much of his time in the company of beautiful milkmaids. In Zoroastrian myth, the seed of Zoraster, preserved for thousands of years in a crystal-pure lake, will impregnate three virgins who are to appear at intervals of three thousand years; they will give birth to the savior-gods for each period of human history, the last being Soshyans, who will inaugurate the Last Judgment.

In Buddhist myth, a male Bodhisattva (savior-being) placed his reflection in the womb of Queen Maya. In her tenth month of pregnancy she gave birth to the Buddha from her right side. Her case was both a virgin-conception and a virgin-birth. We can follow the sequence of historical development by inverting this order of thinking: Buddhist apologists began with the undeniable facts of the Buddha's existence and his birth from a mortal mother. Since the Buddha's paternity was known (from doctrinal tradition) to have been divine, the supernatural parent must, of course, be male. This is a rather obvious line of logic. In similar fashion, the Holy Spirit which impregnated the Virgin Mary must be conceived in human minds as an aspect of the masculine Father-God.°

This enigma—the virgin-conception by Mary—has produced more doctrines and convened more councils than any other event in

> **Christ for Black Africa must be seen as black.**
>
> *The Long Search*
> BBC/TIME-LIFE TV

> **What is the God of a mortal but a mortal magnified?**
>
> *MARY BAKER EDDY*

°I have heard it argued that the Holy Spirit is not masculine, but neuter (the Greek word for "spirit," pneuma, is neuter); but such rationales only emphasize the uneasiness we feel about the problem of anthropomorphism and the difficulty we humans have in conceiving our deities in any way other than as male and female. (I choose to ignore for the present Aristophanes' famous eulogy of the hermaphroditic condition in Plato's Symposium)

Western history. The idea of a male deity mating with a mortal maiden to produce what would logically be a God-man—half-God, half-man—is a common enough motif in man's religions, but the soteriological complexities of the Christian version required centuries of analysis and debate. Is this "son of God" himself man or God or both? Throughout the first four centuries of Christianity there were churchmen who held that he was *solely* God or *solely* man, but the doctrine that he was both God and man finally prevailed. This conclusion, however, merely posed further problems. If he was both, then how did his divine nature relate to his human nature? And what was the relationship of the divine nature in Jesus to the divine nature in the Father? (The Council of Nicea settled these questions in A.D. 325; the churchmen reaffirmed his dual nature and concluded that the divine nature in the Son and the Father were "in essence" the same.) What about will? If he was both God and man, did he have two distinct wills? (This problem—the "monothelite" controversy—was settled at a council in Constantinople in A.D. 681: Jesus has two wills, the divine and the human, but the human will was subservient in all things to his divine will.) And what of Mary? If Jesus was wholly God as well as wholly man, does this not mean that Mary was the mother of God? (The Council of Ephesus in A.D. 431 answered yes. She is properly designated *Theotokos*, "the bearer of God."°)

°*St. Jerome, who is best known for his translation of the Scriptures into Latin (the* Vulgate*), had a friend named Paula whose daughter Eustochium took the vows of a nun and thus became "a bride of Christ." Jerome considered Mary to be the Mother of God, and he habitually addressed Paula as the mother-in-law of God. This is not the only case, however, where a god had a mother-in-law. Demeter, for instance, was Pluto's mother-in-law after Persephone became the bride of the king of Hades.*

°*Note also our habit of anthropomorphizing our animal friends. See page 390.*

In the multiplicity of his gods man does not merely behold the outward divinity of natural objects and forces but also perceives himself in the concrete diversity and distinction of his functions. . . . Over and over again we thus find confirmation of the fact than man can apprehend his own being only insofar as he can make it visible in the image of his gods. . . .

ERNST CASSIRER

6   When we find ourselves theologically entangled in mundane human relationships such as these, it is easy to lose our philosophical perspective. But if we can survive the subtleties of such debates, we may feel that our anthropomorphizing has gone too far. Xenophanes observed very early that "mortals suppose that the gods have been born, that they have voices and bodies and wear clothing like men"; he complained that "Homer and Hesiod attributed to the gods all sorts of actions which when done by men are disreputable and deserving of blame—such lawless deeds as theft, adultery, and mutual deception."

The supernatural figures of our great living religions may be ethically and spiritually nobler, but their anthropomorphic qualities are just as human as those shared by the Olympian gods and goddesses.°

7   Much thought has been given to the problem of divine knowledge by other Western philosophers who were aware of our anthropomorphic manner of thinking.

Philo of Alexandria (fl. c. A.D. 40) contended that *no* qualities conceivable by the human mind can be attributed to God. God, that is, cannot be *thought* about. Whenever we think we are thinking about God, we are merely "deifying" human qualities. All we can do, Philo concluded, is to say what God is not.

Around the year A.D. 500 an anonymous writer called Pseudo-Dionysius (his writings were for a time attributed to a certain Dionysius mentioned by Saint Paul) decided that there are two ways of knowing God. Following the positive way, we can collect the qualitative concepts which we apply to man—man is good, wise, loving, alive, etc.—and attribute these qualities in their ultimate form to the divine nature. That is, God is perfect goodness, wisdom, love, being, and so on. Since God is perfect, we can be sure that we are correct in attributing perfect qualities to God even though we cannot ourselves *conceive* these perfect qualities. (What exactly is "perfect wisdom" or "perfect being"?) But there is a second way of knowing—the negative way. We can collect in our minds all the qualities which we are sure God cannot possess: God is not corporeal matter; he is not evil; he cannot hate, cheat, deceive, etc. By a process of "remotion" all these qualities are removed from our thinking about God. Thus, as we proceed to subtract all qualities which God cannot possess, we are left with an increasingly accurate nonconcept of God. By the "darkness of unknowing" we can arrive at a mystical notion of what God in fact is.

ARGUMENTS FOR THE EXISTENCE OF GOD

(1) The Cosmological Argument

8   In our Western philosophical tradition, there have been several attempts to prove, rationally or empirically, that God exists. At least three are noteworthy. These are the cosmological, ontological, and teleological arguments for the existence of God.

The *cosmological argument* was first stated by Aristotle and further developed by Thomas Aquinas (1225–1274). The argument attempts to prove logically that there must be an "unmoved mover" and that such a force is in fact what we have thought of as God.

We live in a world of matter-in-motion. This is an obvious empirical fact. Aquinas observed that if an object is at rest, then it is not in motion; but any object at rest is potentially in motion. Motion is the actualized potential of a particular object. All objects at rest are potentially in motion, but no object will be activated into motion unless it is caused to move by something that is actually moving. No object at rest can be activated by another object at rest, nor can an object at rest set itself in motion. This means simply that every object in motion was set in motion by something else; but that something else must have been set in motion by something before it, and so on. Therefore we are confronted with an infinite series of objects, each of which actualizes the potential motion of the next in the series. But if we attempt to account for motion by going back in our minds in an infinite regression, we find ourselves in a logical contradiction—a dead end. Something *must* start the series, and this something, from a purely logical standpoint, must be something without an antecedent activator. Such an activator must necessarily be pure actuality and not potential. Whatever this pure actuality is, it is the "unmoved mover" which, writes Thomas, "everyone understands to be God."

The rash assertion that "God made man in His own image" is ticking like a time bomb at the foundations of many faiths, and as the hierarchy of the universe is disclosed to us, we may have to recognize this chilling truth: if there are any gods whose chief concern is man, they cannot be very important gods.

ARTHUR C. CLARKE

THE ONTOLOGICAL ARGUMENT

I. Anything that can be coherently conceived is either actual or an unactualized potentiality.
   A. Meaningful statements are statements with a referent.
   B. A referent is either actual or an unactualized potentiality.
   C. Hence meaningful statements are statements referring to an actuality or an unactualized potentiality.
   D. That which is meaningful is coherently conceivable; it refers to an actuality or an unactualized potentiality.
II. God is coherently conceivable.
III. Therefore God is either actual or an unactualized potentiality.
IV. God is not an unactualized potentiality.
   A. Nothing unactualized can be actualized unless an adequate cause exists.
   B. Hence, God or Unsurpassable Being cannot be actualized unless an adequate cause exists.
   C. An adequate cause must surpass that which it causes.
   D. God as unsurpassable Being is unsurpassable.
   E. Therefore, God can have no adequate cause.
   F. Hence, God is not an unactualized potentiality.
V. Therefore God is Actual.

JAMES L. CATANZARO, Ph.D.
California State University
Fullerton, California

---

(2) The Ontological Argument

9   The *ontological argument* was developed by Anselm of Canterbury (1033–1109). Anselm is sometimes called the father of Scholastic philosophy, that movement of the twelfth and thirteenth centuries which rekindled intellectual activity in the West after the Dark Ages. Saint Anselm was a devoutly religious Benedictine monk whose writings, debates, and pastoral leadership greatly influenced his time.

While Thomas's cosmological argument for God is founded upon an empirical observation of matter-in-motion, Anselm's argument has no such empirical referent. It attempts to prove God's existence from the nature of thought alone. For several weeks Anselm had been convinced that such a proof might be possible. He devoted much thought and prayer to it and finally, late one night during vigils, his proof of God's existence stood clearly before his mind. Anselm was sure that he knew, by thought alone, that God exists—indeed, that God *has* to exist. Here is his argument.

The mind has a concept of a Being than which nothing greater can be conceived. This Being, than which nothing greater can be conceived, must exist in reality as well as in thought. For if it existed only in thought (subjectively), then it would be possible for the mind to conceive of an even greater being who exists in reality (objectively) as well as in thought, and this being would be greater. But this is impossible. Therefore, this Being, than which nothing greater can be conceived, must exist in reality as well as in thought. And this Being is God.

Anselm was elated that he could prove rationally what he already knew to be true. He appends a thankful prayer to God "because

"Do you believe in God?"
"No."
"Then everything's more dangerous."

Bobby Deerfield

through your divine illumination I now so understand that which, through your generous gift, I formerly believed. . . . " He continues: "So truly dost thou exist, O Lord God, both in thought and in fact, that it is impossible for the minds of Thy creatures not to know of Thine existence."

(3) *The Teleological Argument*

10   The *teleological argument* for the existence of God is based on the apparent order and design of nature and cosmos, and on the purposive nature of evolution.

From earliest times man has wondered about the cyclical motions of the stars and planets, the endless rounds of days and seasons, the consistency of nature's operations, and the rhythmic patterns of order in the world about him. Greek thinkers used the word *logos* (literally "word") to account for this order. This logos might be thought of as a kind of "world reason," an organizing force, possibly emanating from a divine mind, which binds all the dynamic elements of nature into a working order.

Today, of course, we know that the cosmos has more order than the ancients could have imagined, an order that can be described in terms of mathematical equations, physical and chemical formulas, and psychobiological processes. Living organisms have distinctive metabolic and life-cycle rhythms, largely determined for each by an incredibly complicated DNA code. Subatomic studies have revealed the complex configurations of energy patterns. We also know that cosmic processes—involving suns, galaxies, and perhaps even the pulsating universe itself—run through ordered sequences resembling birth, life, and death.

The question: Can all this beautiful harmony exist apart from an ordering intelligence, a mind which would be the creator and sustainer of this order? The Stoics, among others, drew a simple analogy. The human mind is fundamentally an organizer: it orders, systematizes, labels, and stores bits of experience for later use. Our minds order our experiences of reality. Likewise, there must be a Cosmic Mind pervading reality itself and operating toward similar ends. The ordered world as we know it cannot be accounted for apart from the ordering of a Cosmic Intelligence.

The teleological argument—as the word "teleology" indicates—has to do with direction or destiny; and it was the development of life and the movement of evolution that seemed to demonstrate most clearly the possibility of a directive intelligence.

This argument was given careful scrutiny by the biologist Lecomte du Noüy in his book *Human Destiny*. Du Noüy calculated that according to the laws of probability the emergence of living organisms from inorganic molecules would have been less than one in a hundred billion. He concludes that life could only begin through an act of a purposive intelligence, and that the movement of evolution is, in his word, "telefinalistic."

Man has never been the same
   since God died,
He has taken it very hard.
Why, you'd think it was only yes-
   terday
The way he takes it.

EDNA ST. VINCENT MILLAY
"Conversation at Midnight"

Every saint has a past and every sinner a future.

OSCAR WILDE

Faith is best defined as expecting the best until the worst has been proved.

GERALD ENSLEY

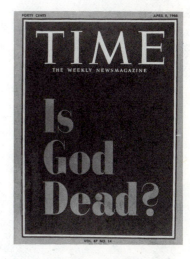

Telefinality orients the march of evolution as a whole and has acted, ever since the appearance of life on earth, as a distant directing force tending to develop a being endowed with a conscience, a spiritually and morally perfect being. To attain its goal, this force acts on the laws of the inorganized world in such a way that the normal play of the second law of thermodynamics is always deflected in the same direction, a direction forbidden to inert matter and leading to ever greater dissymmetries, ever more "improbable" states.°

°For the teleological argument as it applies to evolution, see pages 359ff.

THE DEATH(S) OF GOD(S)

11   *Is God dead?* Friedrich Nietzsche believed so.

> The God-complex is the focus around which other symbols gather, and from it comes the energic force with which they may be vitalized into a "lived" religion. . . . No constellation of symbols can function as a religion in the psyche unless its particular symbol for God is "alive."
>
> IRA PROGOFF

Have you not heard of that madman who lit a lantern in the bright morning hours, ran to the market place, and cried incessantly, "I seek God! I seek God!" As many of those who do not believe in God were standing around just then, he provoked much laughter. Why, did he get lost? said one. Did he lose his way like a child? said another. Or is he hiding? Is he afraid of us? Has he gone on a voyage? or emigrated? Thus they yelled and laughed. The madman jumped into their midst and pierced them with his glances.

"Whither is God" he cried. "I shall tell you. *We have killed him—* you and I. All of us are his murderers. . . . God is dead. God remains dead. And we have killed him. How shall we, the murderers of all murderers, comfort ourselves? What was holiest and most powerful of all that the world has yet owned has bled to death under our knives. Who will wipe this blood off us? What water is there for us to clean ourselves? What festivals of atonement, what sacred games shall we have to invent? Is not the greatness of this deed too great for

With superb craftsmanship, a worker in a porcelain factory in Canton (Peoples Republic of China) sculpts crucifixes for export to Western nations.

us? Must not we ourselves become gods simply to seem worthy of it? There has never been a greater deed; and whoever will be born after us—for the sake of this deed he will be part of a higher history than all history hitherto.''

Here the madman fell silent and looked again at his listeners; and they too were silent and stared at him in astonishment. At last he threw his lantern on the ground, and it broke and went out. "I come too early," he said then; "my time has not come yet. This tremendous event is still on its way, still wandering—it has not yet reached the ears of man. . . ."

It has been related further than on that same day the madman entered divers churches and there sang his *requiem aeternam deo.* Led out and called to account, he is said to have replied each time, "What are these churches now if they are not the tombs and sepulchers of God?"

12 Nietzsche and others have presaged the death of God. But what does such a statement mean? A modern death-of-God theologian, William Hamilton, rhetorically asks, "Is there really an event properly called 'the death of God'? Or is the current chatter enveloping the phrase simply another of the many non-events afflicting our time?" He answers: "No. The death of God has happened. To those of us with gods, and to those without. To the indifferent, the cynical and the fanatical. God is dead, whatever that means."

To Nietzsche it meant that the very concept of God as traditionally conceived in Western thought no longer has the power, as it once did, to transform human life. Belief in a God is still held by individuals, and countless others pay lip service to god-doctrines. But these beliefs no longer do what beliefs are supposed to do: to grip one's very existence with ultimate truths; to establish one firmly in a meaningful teleocosmic plan; to transform character and hence the quality of one's whole life; to make one feel special and of infinite worth; to provide secure and final answers to questions about living and dying.

World-views have changed. Spirits and demons have died: we now account for human behavior in terms of operant conditioning and motivation. The Devil has died: a "devil" is nothing more than a mental abstraction which we have personified and objectified. And a capricious, all-too-human deity can no longer command our devotion. We have seen too many gods; our anthropomorphic habits are too obvious to be brushed aside. God, too, is dead.

13 If we scan the pantheon of man's divinities, we discover deicides without end. Sooner or later, it seems, all the gods of men die.

There was a time when Egyptian fellahin knew that King Osiris weighed the hearts of men before they could enter into his kingdom, and Isis the Queen was a benefactress to all—revealing laws, rendering justice, calming the sea, timing the harvests, and persuading men and women to love each other.

The sky-god Varuna was able to see into the hearts of his Aryan worshipers and cast away their sins. The redeemer-god Balder re-

Politics and religion are obsolete; the time has come for science and spirituality.

VINOBE BHAVE

The progress of religion is defined by the denunciation of gods. The keynote of idolatry is contentment with the prevalent gods.

WHITEHEAD

THE DEATH OF GOD

What does the phrase "the death of God" mean to the theologians who use it? One such theologian is the Rev. William Hamilton who notes that there are at least ten ways in which the phrase is used today.

1. It might mean that there is no God and that there never has been. This position is traditional atheism of the old-fashioned kind, and it does seem hard to see how it could be combined, except very unstably, with Christianity or any of the Western religions.

2. It might mean that there once was a God to whom adoration, praise and trust were appropriate, possible and even necessary, but that there is now no such God. This is the position of the death-of-God or radical theology. It is an atheist position, but with a difference. If there was a God, and if there now isn't, it should be possible to indicate why this change took place, when it took place and who was responsible for it.

3. It might mean that the idea of God and the word God itself both are in need of radical reformulation. Perhaps totally new words are needed: perhaps a decent silence about God should be observed; but ultimately, a new treatment of the idea and the word can be expected, however unexpected and surprising it may turn out to be.

4. It might mean that our traditional liturgical and theological language needs a thorough overhaul: the reality abides, but classical modes of thought and forms of language may well have had it.

5. It might mean that the Christian story is no longer a saving or a healing story. It may manage to stay on as merely illuminating or instructing or guiding, but it no longer performs its classical functions of salvation or redemption. In this new form, it might help us cope with the demons, but it cannot abolish them.

6. It might mean that certain concepts of God, often in the past confused with the classical Christian doctrine of God, must be destroyed: for example, God as problem solver, absolute power, necessary being, the object of ultimate concern.

7. It might mean that men do not today experience God except as hidden, absent, silent. We live, so to speak, in the time of the death of God, though that time will doubtless pass.

8. It might mean that the gods men make, in their thought and action (false gods or idols, in other words), must always die so that the true object of thought and action, the true God, might emerge, come to life, be born anew.

9. It might have a mystical meaning: God must die in the world so that he can be born in us. In many forms of mysticisms the death of Jesus on the cross is the time of that worldly death. This is a medieval idea that influenced Martin Luther, and it is probably this complex of ideas that lies behind the German chorale *God Himself Is Dead* that may well be the historical source for our modern use of "death of God."

10. Finally, it might mean that our language about God is always inadequate and imperfect.

WILLIAM HAMILTON
Playboy, August 1966

turned each spring to the snow-laden northland and brought with him light and warmth. The mystery-gods Dionysus, Orpheus, and Mithras promised immortality to all who pledged their loyalty and performed the proper rites. From his temple on the slopes of Mount Parnassus the bright sun-god Apollo offered divine wisdom and worldly counsel to faithful pilgrims.

The beautiful virgin-goddess Artemis protected wandering children and assuaged the pain of women in childbirth. Persephone brought health and prosperity to her devotees, and then led them down to the nether realm where she was queen. The virgin Athena, proud and protective, was close to the hearts of her Athenian worshipers.

The virgin-born Quetzalcoatl who, in Nahuatl mysteries, was a man become god, presented himself as an example of man's purest aspiration, having burned himself in a fire to purge away his sin. Lord Mazda proffered aid and eternal life to righteous Zoroastrians who believed in Spenta Mainyu (the Holy Spirit) and in the Amesha Spentas (the Immortal Ones—angel-like beings and divine messengers).

As long as there were followers who believed in them, all these gods and goddesses could transform lives. But when, with the passing of the centuries, there were no longer any believers, then no more lives were transformed, no more guilt forgiven, no more souls saved.

In the pantheon of deceased gods and goddesses are enshrined the most awesome names ever uttered by the suppliant voices of mortal men and women: Adonis, Aphrodite, Apollo, Aton, Bacchus, Balder, Cybele, Demeter, Diana, Dionysus, El, Fortuna, Gaia, Hel, Hercules, Indra, Ishtar, Isis, Janus, Jupiter, Marduk, Mars, Nanna, Orpheus, Osiris, Persephone, Quetzalcoatl, Rudra, Saturnus, Shamash, Tammuz, Thor, Uranus, Varuna, Venus, Wotan, Xochipilli, Zagreus, Zeus . . . .

14   One of the tasks of a theologian is to update the faith and make it intelligible to his contemporaries. Numerous attempts have been made to deal with the problem of God-knowledge in modern terms. A notable example is that of Dr. Paul Tillich.

Tillich contended that we cannot *know* anything about God, but this limitation does not prevent God's working in our lives. Knowing about him and experiencing him are hardly the same. God is "the ground of our being." We exist, and objects exist; but "existence" is a human category of thought, and God is beyond existence. He is pure being itself.

But, Tillich notes, we are caught in a human predicament which it were best we accept. It is true that we cannot conceive the inconceivable or speak the unspeakable. But if we think or speak at all, then we must think in concepts and speak with language symbols. Therefore, we must continue to do just this, but with the full understanding that our thoughts and words refer to nothing whatever that is real. There is nothing to be gained by fighting our predicament, says Tillich. Rather, we must accept it and live within its confines. Let's continue to speak of God as "he" (or in other traditions as "she" or "it"); we

"Now that Starglider has effectively destroyed all traditional religions, we can at last pay serious attention to the concept of God."

"Dr. Choam Goldberg"
ARTHUR C. CLARKE
The Fountains of Paradise

Even for a god there is a point of no return. . . .

Star Trek
NBC-TV

"Yes, there is a God . . . yes, there is a God . . . yes, there is a God. . ."

Almost all philosophers have confused ideas of things. They speak of material things in spiritual terms, and of spiritual things in material terms.

PASCAL

All words are only so many fingers pointing at Niagara Falls. Some may, like the family's pet dog, look at the finger rather than the rushing waters to which it points. Others on a yet more infantile level may, as Alan Watts puts it, "look at the finger pointing the way and then . . . suck it for comfort." But ultimately the quest for the Ultimate is not to be expressed but experienced. Religion is not to be defined, but explored.

RONALD HUNTINGTON

can continue to think of God as "knowing," "seeing," "hearing," "loving," and so on. These are pragmatic modes of thinking and feeling. Man is a symbolic creature, and we can live with our condition providing we don't confuse symbol and reality. Such words as "God" and "he" are indispensable as symbols, but we must never mistake them for realities.

The only "God" that "exists" is beyond the gods of man. Since all our thinking ultimately is symbolic, Christians can continue to think of the Christ as the "new man" described by Paul, the whole man whose existence and essence have become one. He symbolizes the ultimate possibilities for each of us. It is only by accepting these symbols for what they truly are—as ontological aspects of the human condition—that we can come to terms with our existence and express our "ultimate concern for the Ultimate."

15   Religious experience is absolute. It is indisputable. You can only say that you have never had such an experience and your opponent will say: "Sorry, I have." And there your discussion will come to an end. No matter what the world thinks about religious experience, the one who has it possesses the great treasure of a thing that has provided him with a source of life, meaning and beauty and that has given a new splendor to the world and to mankind. He has pistis [faith] and peace. Where is the criterium by which you could say that such a life is not legitimate, that such experience is not valid and that such pistis

Carl Gustav Jung (1875–1961)

"CLEARLY I MISS HIM . . ."

"But if I live later, I will try to live in such a way, doing no harm to any one, that it will be forgiven."

"By whom?"

"Who knows? Since we do not have God here any more, neither His Son nor the Holy Ghost, who forgives? I do not know."

"You have not God any more?"

"No. Man. Certainly not. If there were God, never would He have permitted what I have seen with my eyes. Let *them* have God."

"They claim Him."

"Clearly I miss Him, having been brought up in religion. But now a man must be responsible to himself."

"Then it is thyself who will forgive thee for killing."

"I believe so," Anselmo said.

ERNEST HEMINGWAY
For Whom the Bell Tolls

is mere illusion? Is there, as a matter of fact, any better truth about ultimate things than the one that helps you to live?

CARL G. JUNG

REFLECTIONS—

1 How do philosophical concerns with religion differ from theological and evangelical concerns (Sec. 3)?

2 We could analyze ad infinitum "the problem of divine knowledge" and the way we anthropomorphize our deities. We have created literally millions of gods and goddesses "in the image of man" (and woman). No thinker has expressed the problem better than the Greek philosopher Xenophanes (Sec. 1). Is the human habit of anthropomorphizing a new insight for you, or have you previously worked through the problem? Do you still accept a deity-image with anthropomorphic qualities? If you answer Yes, then how do you reconcile your imagery with our anthropomorphic predicament?

3 Analyze critically the cosmological argument developed by Aristotle and Aquinas (pp. 517 ff.). What are the basic assumptions upon which the argument rests? What are its logical fallacies, if any? After analysis, does it remain to you a persuasive argument for the existence of God?

4 Analyze critically the ontological argument of St. Anselm (pp. 518–519) or Dr. Catanzaro's formal arrangement of the steps in the argument (p. 518). What implicit assumptions are behind the argument? What are its major fallacies? In the final analysis, what is its persuasion power to you personally?

5 Analyze critically the teleological argument for God's existence (pp. 519–520). What fallacies are involved in this argument, if any? Where

would you go for hard data to help clarify the question and to answer it? Is the argument convincing?

6 On the subject of "the death of God," read again Secs. 11-13 and the summary by Dr. William Hamilton on p. 522-Box. What are the death-of-God theologians saying to us? (Try to avoid easy, simplistic answers.) Are they correct, in your opinion? How could you check their fact-claims or value-judgments to decide if they are correct?

7 What is your assessment of the conviction of Dr. Carl Jung, the Swiss depth-psychologist (Sec. 15), that "religious experience is absolute. It is indisputable"—?

8 To the best of your knowledge, and after pondering this chapter, what is the nature of Ultimate Reality? Can it be described in mere human words? Is it material? Is it natural but nonmaterial? Is it personal (that is, person-like)? Does it take the form of deity? If so, do you think this deity has particular characteristics such as masculinity or femininity? What kinds of *human experiences* might be interpreted as indicators of the existence and/ or nature of this Ultimate Reality? (Take care, all along the way, to offer rational arguments or empirical evidence in support of your ideas; or, if this is not possible, then label carefully which ideas are personal beliefs.)

Furthermore . . .

ANGELES, PETER A. (ed.), *Critiques of God.* Prometheus, 1976.
ANGELES, PETER A., *The Problem of God.* Merrill, 1974.
ALTIZER, THOMAS J. J. (ed.), *Toward a New Christianity: Readings in the Death of God Theology.* Harcourt, 1967.
SMITH, WILFRID CANTRELL, *The Meaning and End of Religion.* Mentor, 1964.
CHENEY, SHELDON, *Men Who Have Walked with God.* Delta, 1974.
HAPPOLD, F. C., *Mysticism.* Penguin, 1963.
HICK, JOHN, *God and the Universe of Faiths.* St. Martin's, 1973.
HUXLEY, ALDOUS, *The Perennial Philosophy.* Harper, 1945.
JAMES, WILLIAM, *Varieties of Religious Experience* (1902). Mentor, 1958.
STRENG, FREDERICK J., et al., *Ways of Being Religious.* Prentice-Hall, 1973.

8-3

Death/ Immortality

Have You Ever Wondered . . .

- ● Whether there is any scientific evidence for the survival of "souls" after death?

- ● Whether there exists such an entity as a "soul"?

- ● Why we fear death (if, in fact, we do fear it)?

- ● How your feelings about your life would change if you expected to live, say, three hundred years?

- ● Whether there might be living creatures in the universe who are virtually immortal?

- ● What the experience of death might actually be like? or whether one can in fact experience his own death?

- ● How one can prepare himself for the best possible "experiencing" of his own death-event?

ALL GRAVES ARE WRONG—

1 "You been up to the grave yet?" asked the hunter, as if he knew I would answer yes.
"No," I said.
That really surprised him. He tried not to show it.

Death is the true inspiring genius, or the muse of philosophy. . . . Indeed, without death men could scarcely philosophize.

SCHOPENHAUER

527

O great Nzambi, what thou hast made is good, but thou hast brought a great sorrow to us with death. Thou shouldst have planned in some way that we would not be subject to death. O Nzambi, we are afflicted with great sadness.

Congo Funeral Chant

Time is but the stream I go a-fishing in. I drink at it; but while I drink I see the sandy bottom and detect how shallow it is. Its thin current slides away, but eternity remains.

HENRY DAVID THOREAU

"They all go up to the grave," he said.

"Not this one."

He explored around in his mind for a polite way of asking. "I mean . . ." he said. "Why *not?*"

"Because it's the wrong grave," I said.

"All graves are wrong graves when you come down to it," he said.

"No," I said. "There are right graves and wrong ones, just as there are good times to die and bad times."

He nodded at this. I had come back to something he knew, or at least smelled was right.

"Sure, I knew men," he said, "died just perfect. You always felt, yes, that was good. One man I knew, sitting at the table waiting for supper, his wife in the kitchen, when she came in with a big bowl of soup there he was sitting dead and neat at the table. Bad for her, but, I mean, wasn't that a good way for him? No sickness. No nothing but sitting there waiting for supper to come and never knowing if it came or not. Like another friend. Had an old dog. Fourteen years old. Dog was going blind and tired. Decided at last to take the dog to the pound and have him put to sleep. Loaded the old blind tired dog on the front seat of his car. The dog licked his hand, once. The man felt awful. He drove toward the pound. On the way there, with not one sound, the dog passed away, died on the front seat, as if he knew and, knowing, picked the better way, just handed over his ghost, and there you are. That's what you're talking about, right?"

I nodded.

"So you think that grave up on the hill is a wrong grave for a right man, do you?"

"That's about it," I said.

"You think there are all kinds of graves along the road for all of us?"

"Could be," I said.

"And if we could see all our life one way or another, we'd choose better? At the end, looking back," said the hunter, "we'd say, hell, *that* was the year and the place, not the *other* year and the other place, but that one year, that one place. Would we say that?"

"Since we have to choose or be pushed finally," I said, "yes."

"That's a nice idea," said the hunter. "But how many of us have that much sense? Most of us don't have brains enough to leave a party when the gin runs out. We hang around."

"We hang around," I said, "and what a shame."

We ordered some more beer.

RAY BRADBURY
"The Kilimanjaro Device"

2   Our feelings about death are the subtlest of all motivators, but also the strongest. No problem in the human condition has been subject to man's creative imagination more than the prospect of his own cessation. Ernest Becker writes that "the idea of death, the fear of it, haunts the human animal like nothing else; it is the mainspring of human activity—activity designed largely to avoid the fatality of death,

to overcome it by denying in some way that it is the final destiny for man."

There is no experience that so forces even the most unphilosophic among us into philosophizing. Plato viewed the philosophic life as a rehearsal for death. "To philosophize," wrote Montaigne, "is to learn to die." Schopenhauer summarized it all: "Death is the true inspiring genius, or the muse of philosophy. . . . Indeed, without death men could scarcely philosophize at all."

There is significant variation in how far each of us will go to avoid facing the fact that we must die. The evidence for postmortem consciousness is ambiguous, which only adds to our need to relieve anxiety about nonexistence and to mitigate the agony we associate with dying. Our minds create elaborate myths to allay our anguish over this event. Yet it is a universal event and a basic function of the cosmos.

3   It is difficult to define "death" except in arbitrary terms. "A person is dead when his heart stops"—we have long believed. But this age-old criterion is obsolete now that medical science can sustain a body's physical processes, including a beating heart, for months or years by artificial means. If the machines are shut down, the heart stops. Was the individual alive while the heart was beating?

Brainwaves are a better indicator, for to exist as a human person is to have a mind. Without the possibility of consciousness, there is no person; there exists only a physical organism which has lost its potential as a person. Therefore, when all the brainwaves are flat on the electroencephalograph, we conclude the person is dead.

Yet even this is not accurate. Cases are known in which brainwaves were nonexistent for many hours (that is, the person-potential apparently ceased to exist), but the individuals were ultimately restored to full health, physically and mentally.

Another test of life/death is the brain's utilization of oxygen. If no oxygen is being used, brain cells are dying. When sufficient cells die (and this occurs within minutes of the onset of oxygen depriva-

While we are reasoning concerning life, life is gone; and death, though perhaps they receive him differently, yet treats alike the fool and the philosopher.

DAVID HUME

tion), then the brain reaches a point of irreversibility. At that point in time the person can be pronounced "dead."

How arbitrary and loose are our definitions, yet how crucial! At present, we can agree upon certain working definitions of "life" and "death" without having the foggiest notion of what *life* (and its absence, *death*) really is.

DEATH—A NON-EXPERIENCE

4   We cannot experience death, although in our fear and confusion we may not know this to be so. Death can never be experienced because death is the *cessation* of experience. Wittgenstein's pungent logic helps: "Death is not an event in life. Death is not lived through." We may be able to experience *dying* to some degree. If one believes he is dying and indeed he is, he may be able to experience a progression of dying-events. But if one is convinced he is dying, but in fact he is not (that is, he recovers), then he has not experienced dying. One can be sure he is experiencing dying only if he dies; hence—from a strictly logical point of view—no one can ever be sure that he is having such an experience.

"We know what fear is. We live with it all of our lives. Only the dead are without fear."

The Magnificent Seven

Phoenix Arizona
                    Jan 2.nd 1946
this is my first and only will
and is dated the second day in
January 1946. I have no. heir's
have not been married in my life,
an after all my funeral expenses
have been paid and $100. one hundred
dollars to some preacher of the
gospital to say farewell at my
grave sell all my property which
is all in cash and stocks with
E F Hutton Co Phoenix some in
safety box, and have this balance
money to go in a research or some
scientific proof of a soul of the
human body which leaves at death
I think in time their can be a
Photograph of soul leaving the
human at death,

                              James Kidd

(dated 2nd
January 1946)

some cash in Valley
bank some in Bank America LA Cal

In a certain sense the whole of mythical thought may be interpreted as a constant and obstinate negation of the phenomenon of death. By virtue of this conviction of the unbroken unity and continuity of life myth has to clear away this phenomenon. Primitive religion is perhaps the strongest and most energetic affirmation of life that we find in human culture.

ERNST CASSIRER

All of the significant issues regarding life and death are brought into focus by the question of life's meaning. But how we look at life is in large measure shaped by our perspective on death.

RICHARD DOSS

MINER'S REQUEST: FIND PROOF OF MAN'S SOUL

PHOENIX (UPI)—An obscure Arizona miner named James Kidd was a man concerned with the human soul.

In a handwritten will dated in 1946 he said:

"After my funeral expenses have been paid and $100 (given) to some preacher of the Gospel to say farewell at my grave, sell all my property, which is all in cash and stocks and have this balance money go into a research or some scientific proof of a soul of the human body which leaves at death."

Monday a Phoenix court begins hearings to determine how to dispose of Kidd's estate, now valued at $200,000. There are many claimants to the money, including some who assert they can fulfill Kidd's strange last request.

Kidd was last seen in 1949 when he apparently left to work on two mining claims. He was 70 and a year after his disappearance he was declared legally dead. His will was filed for probate in 1964.

He left a checking account of $4,100.66 at the time of his disappearance, and he owned stocks worth more than $100,000 which have nearly doubled because of dividends and other earnings.

A Miami man who knew Kidd said the miner had always talked about the supernatural and, despite the fact he never went to church, believed in the existence of a human soul which could be photographed as it left the body.

The court hearings on the will begin here before Maricopa County Superior Court Judge Robert L. Myers.

UPDATE: The case of the James Kidd will was closed on January 30, 1973, and the estate was awarded to the American Society for Psychical Research. Since that time ASPR research has concentrated on two hypotheses: "that some part of the human personality is capable of operating outside the living body on rare occasions"—that is, a temporary out-of-body experience (OBE); and "that it may continue to exist after the brain processes have ceased and the organism is decayed"—that is, permanent immortality.

Six OBE projects have been conducted. An OBE "fly-in" and an attempt to correlate OBEs and apparitions both supported the OBE hypothesis, but other interpretations (e.g. ESP) are possible. Perceptual experiments with OBEs and psychophysiological studies of subjects gave similar results: evidence in harmony with OBE hypothesis but other explanations possible. Instrumental recordings (i.e. photos) and a test of mediums gave negative results.

As for the second hypothesis, deathbed studies of apparitions, visions, hallucinations, etc. (reported by attending doctors and nurses) supported the conclusion that "some of the dying patients indeed appeared to be already experiencing glimpses of ecsomatic existence." But again, other interpretations can't be ruled out; so these results "should not be taken as a final balance of evidence for or against survival." Masses of data are still being processed.

ASPR Newsletter, Numbers 22, 24, and July 1976.

Thanatologists—that is, philosophers of the death-event—make a helpful distinction between the unique inner experience—the cessation of consciousness—and the outer experience—the termination of physiological processes. The latter we obtain through observation of the death-events of others. We can watch the gradual deterioration of life-processes and then their actual termination, and we say *this* is the end of life: *this* is death.

Within ourselves, all we experience is the onset of the cessation of consciousness. This is often a gradual process, beginning long before the termination of our physiological processes. Most individuals subside into an unconscious state or coma at some point before death occurs, so they don't experience the later (and possibly eventful) stages leading to the death-event.

5   Which of these events do we fear and so desperately try to avoid? Or do we fear both? Would we really care about the termination of our physiological processes if we could be assured that the cessation of our consciousness would *not* follow?

We do not fear death itself, and death—the cessation of consciousness—is nothing to be feared. Each night when we enter sleep we experience the cessation of consciousness; this is an experience which probably resembles the final cessation followed by death. Each night we die, literally. (But we awaken again. There is no wonder that sleep has become a synonym for death and that we universally picture ourselves waking from it.)

Three distinct kinds of fear are associated with death, and one of them—fear of suffering—is realistic. One does not live for very long before learning that pain and grief are companions of death. As children we see animals in pain before they die; throughout life we witness the agony of individuals caught in war, accidents, and disease. The constant association of pain and death never ceases. It becomes difficult for us to *think* of death without *feeling* the fears we have been conditioned to associate with it.

Another kind of fear, less common, results from confusion. For instance, a teen-age girl awoke repeatedly with nightmares about death, and her terror became so intense it dominated her waking hours as well. When her ideas of death were explored with a therapist, it was discovered that what she really feared was being buried alive. That is, the body in her dreams would in fact be dead, but she was unable to separate the idea of consciousness from the buried corpse. Well-known stories by Edgar Allen Poe and others supply ideas which can grow into such nightmares. When the fallacy of identification was recognized, the girl's "fear of death" gradually diminished.

FEAR OF NONBEING

6   Another kind of death-anxiety is all-pervasive. This is the universal fear: the fear of nonexistence. It is not fear of possible punishment in some hell or purgatory; nor is it merely a fear of the unknown.

> We come from a dark abyss, we end in a dark abyss, and we call the luminous interval life.
>
> *NIKOS KAZANTZAKIS*

Rather, we experience a relentless anguish about nonexistence itself.
We fear the *experience* of *nonbeing*, not recognizing that this is a contradiction in terms. However, a rational response to a nonrational fear is
no solution.

   We can remind ourselves that we already know "the experience
of nonexistence." Most of us were not alive, say, two hundred years
ago, but it didn't bother us then, nor does it concern us now. And,
barring a scientific breakthrough, most of us will not be alive two
hundred years hence. But *this* bothers us. The possibility of nonexistence in the future can disturb us, while nonexistence in the past
doesn't.

   Why?

7   *Valhalla* (Norse): the great hall of immortality where warriors
await the call of Odin to join in the final battle (the
Götterdämmerung). *Elysium* (Greek): a place at the end of the earth on
the banks of the river Oceanus where perfect happiness rewards those
favored by the gods. *Paradise* (Persian): a lush, green park which
serves as a temporary resting place for righteous souls awaiting the
final resurrection. *Gardens of Delight* (Islamic): a place of reward for the
faithful of Allah where, robed in silk and brocade, they are given all
earthly delights imaginable. *Heaven* (Christian): the abode of God
where the righteous dead will dwell together in perfect happiness in
God's presence after the Last Judgment. *Isatpragbhara* (Jain): the
heaven at the very top of the universe whither the pure consciousnesses of the righteous will rise and enjoy perfect bliss. *Isles of the Blest*
(Orphic): the mystic Greek isles where the purified, now free from
rebirth, will be rewarded with eternal happiness. *Kingdom of Osiris*
(Egyptian): an oasis in the western desert with lush vegetation where
the souls of the blessed will forever rest under spreading shade trees.
House of Song (Zoroastrian): a place somewhere among the stars beyond the Chinvat Bridge where the righteous will enjoy perfect happiness in their companionship with one another.

8   Our endless contemplation of various heavens and hells reflects
the conviction that we do not really die. Deep within we intuit that we
are immortal. Actually, we are split by an ambivalence about the mystery of death. On the one hand, we know we will die, and as a social
convention we confess this to others; but on the other hand, each of
us has an instinctlike resistance: "It can't actually happen *to me*."

   Generally, man does not identify his self/essence with his physical body. When we look at others, we see bodies, of course; we perceive physical organisms. But when we look into another's eyes, we
see not merely the working parts of a transducer (cornea, iris, etc.);
we "see" a person. As we watch facial expressions, we "see" in others
what we feel in ourselves: a self or soul which dwells in the body but
which is not part of it. Our experience of consciousness feels like a
"spirit" which dwells inside a "house," and in various religious traditions man speaks of the coming and going of his "spirit" into and out

of his body. It "inhabits" his body. Indeed, several spirits may inhabit his body, simultaneously or in turn.

9   The Greeks developed the belief that the spirit of man is free and of great value, while the body, quite a separate entity, is of little importance. The spirit can leave the body and wander where it wills. Some of the Greek philosophers held that the soul can be truly free only when the body-prison dies and releases it. The Greeks, therefore, had no strong feelings about mutilation or cremation. They felt concern if the corpse could not be given proper rites without which the soul could not find release; and it was especially tragic when Greek sailors were lost at sea and could never be given proper burial. Nevertheless, the body as such was of little worth.

Our Judeo-Christian psyche-ology ("soul-ology") has been less dualistic. Jews and Christians distinguished between spirit and body, but they could never think of them as separable entities; therefore, after death reassembly of bodily materials is necessary for survival. The Hebrew could not imagine spirit wandering about without a body. For him, as for the Egyptians, Sumerians, and others, mutilation of the body is a tragic misfortune, for we must carry into the next life whatever scars we acquire in this life.

Jesus uttered words to the effect that if your eye or hand causes you to sin, then destroy it, for "it is better for you to get into the

When one has lived as long as I have, it's a serious matter to die. Every year one puts out new roots.

DAVID LINDSAY
Voyage to Arcturus

Fresco on wall of the tomb of a nobleman, Menena, at Royal Thebes. The fresco retains its vivid colors after 3,500 years. Note that the faces and parts of the bodies of Menena and his family have been chiseled away, thus ensuring that the "soul" of each would enter the next life faceless and maimed.

Kingdom of God with but one eye than to be thrown into Gehenna with both eyes . . ." (Mark 9:47). These words were not meant symbolically; they reflect the late Judaic notion that we take into the next life whatever scars we sustain in this one. When Jesus reappeared to his disciples after the discovery of the empty tomb, he was seen to bear on his spirit-body the wounds of the crucifixion.

In the Egyptian tomb of Menena, some culprit regained entrance to the burial chamber of this nobleman and mutilated the freshly painted frescoes. The faces of Menena and his family were chiseled away in order in ensure they would go faceless into the next life.

You bury only my body, not me.

SOCRATES

"THE DENIAL OF DEATH"

10   In Western thought we have strong religious reassurance that we will survive physical death. Orthodox doctrine denies that we die. The recorded fact-claim that Jesus awakened after physical death and promised us that we shall do the same is part of our Western theology of history. We have inherited a specific interpretation of the death-event: there is no death of the self, and physical death is merely an event in a continuing drama.

Since these various antideath concepts are part of our own teleocosmic world-view, it is easy to avoid the feeling of certainty that death, in fact, awaits each of us. The idea of total oblivion has not been widely held or seriously faced.

Well, really, Crito, it would be hardly suitable for a man of my age to resent having to die.

SOCRATES

11   Our difficulty in accepting the finality of death can be seen in a simple analysis of our linguistic utterances. Our talk about death generally occurs in two ways: we speak of our own death as "my death" and of the death of others as "your death." As I sit behind by typewriter thinking about death, it is rather easy to contemplate "your death." I read about the death of others in the morning newspaper; I saw it on the late news on television; it was vividly portrayed in a recent film I saw. Occasionally I see the death of others on the highway as I hurriedly drive by on the other side of the road. Perhaps I am one of those rare persons who has been with someone who died. In such an instant I observe "your death" as the cessation of respiration and heartbeat, in short, the termination of bodily processes. But "my death" is a completely different matter. Not only is it impossible for me to observe, I have great difficulty thinking about it and imagining what it is like. How does one contemplate one's own nonbeing? It was this question that led Freud to postulate that every person, in his unconscious mind, is convinced of his own immortality. In observing his patients Freud discovered that denial functions as a coping mechanism enabling patients to handle their anxiety about their own death. Every time we attempt to contemplate our own death, Freud noted, we do so as spectators, that is, we are unable to think about or imagine our own nonbeing. What Freud described clinically was the overwhelming difficulty we have in thinking about death as a personal experience, death in its interiority.

The starting point is to investigate the nature of our experience as we think about and attempt to contemplate our own death. What is involved in my own experience (and I assume your own experience as well)? The first thing I am aware of is ambiguity. When I recognize my own mortality and finitude and the fact that my death is a reality, I feel helpless, even frustrated, that I can do nothing about it. I feel trapped by some power, some force I do not fully understand and cannot avoid. In her clinical experience Elisabeth Kübler-Ross has found that many of her terminally ill patients think of death as an uncontrollable, powerful force that comes upon them and about which they can do nothing. One patient said, "Right now I feel strong and well, but I know I have something growing inside of me that is beyond my control." It is this sense of "no exit," no way out of an existence in which death is the end, that gives rise to the basic ambiguity regarding the human condition.

RICHARD DOSS

12   When attempting to face the fact of death, the ever-present television screen is no help. It blurs the distinction between the living and the dead by holding before us an illusion of immortality. Television has been called "the great immortalizer." Each day we watch innumerable figures who, we have been told, are no longer alive. Yet obviously they live. They are alive before our eyes. The (alleged) fact that some physical organism no longer exists in space/time seems to make little difference.

From the time we enter formal education the great men of history live on in our books and our minds. They are as alive as others we read about who may or may not be alive. We don't (and can't) make any clear distinction between the living and the no-longer-living. Is George Washington dead? Not to millions of schoolchildren. Is Martin Luther King dead? John Kennedy? Dwight Eisenhower? Spencer Tracy? Marilyn Monroe? Clark Gable? Nikita Khrushchev? We see them all on TV occasionally.

We see Robert Kennedy's victory speech at the Ambassador Hotel, over and over again. . . .

13   For those who can't believe in the true survival of consciousness the human mind has rationalized a variety of comforting alternatives. They allow us to retain the feeling that *something of us* is left after we cease to exist.

Biological immortality stresses the continuity of germ-plasm from parent to offspring. *Social immortality* reminds us that we will linger in the memories of others for the good we do. *Moral immortality* holds that while we may be forgotten, we can add our small contribution to the continuing moral development of the human species. *Life-cycle immortality* suggests that energy is never lost but is conserved in other living things: from life to dust and to life again.

In the genre of science fiction, we can comfort ourselves with quasi-immortal states such as *cryonic suspension* ("freeze now, thaw

The bullfight is a miniature of life. Death is a part of life, and it is an integral part of the bullfight. As in life, death hovers; it is inevitable, if not for the man, certainly for the bull. And in life, each of us must eventually die. One of the things the matador is saying when he fights bravely is that the way we die is important, or, that what is really important is how we live.

JOSEPH ROYCE

LAST FLIGHT

The following letter is by Flying Petty Officer First Class Isao Matsuo of the 701st Air Group. It was written just before he sortied for a kamikaze attack. His home was in Nagasaki Prefecture.

28 October 1944

Dear Parents:

Please congratulate me. I have been given a splendid opportunity to die. This is my last day. The destiny of our homeland hinges on the decisive battle in the seas to the south where I shall fall like a blossom from a radiant cherry tree.

I shall be a shield for His Majesty and die cleanly along with my squadron leader and other friends. I wish that I could be born seven times, each time to smite the enemy.

How I appreciate this chance to die like a man! I am grateful from the depths of my heart to the parents who have reared me with their constant prayers and tender love. And I am grateful as well to my squadron leader and superior officers who have looked after me as if I were their own son and given me such careful training.

Thank you, my parents, for the 23 years during which you have cared for me and inspired me. I hope that my present deed will in some small way repay what you have done for me. Think well of me and know that your Isao died for our country. This is my last wish, and there is nothing else that I desire.

I shall return in spirit and look forward to your visit at the Yasukuni Shrine. Please take good care of yourselves.

How glorious is the Special Attack Corps' Giretsu Unit whose *Suisei* bombers will attack the enemy. Movie cameramen have been here to take our pictures. It is possible that you may see us in newsreels at the theater.

We are 16 warriors manning the bombers. May our death be as sudden and clean as the shattering of crystal.

Written at Manila on the eve of our sortie.

Isao

Soaring into the sky of the southern seas, it is our glorious mission to die as the shields of His Majesty. Cherry blossoms glisten as they open and fall.

INOGUCHI AND NAKAJIMA
The Divine Wind

I sent my Soul through the Invisible,
Some letter of that After-life to spell:
And by and by my Soul return'd to me,
And answer'd "I Myself am Heav'n and Hell."

OMAR KHAYYAM
The Rubaiyat

If I were given the choice of how long I should like to live with my present physical and mental equipment, I should decide on a good deal more than 70 years. But I doubt whether I should be wise to decide on more than 300 years. Already I am very much aware of my own limitations, and I think that 300 years is as long as I should like to put up with them.

FRED HOYLE

later" or, in Alan Harrington's phrase, "freeze-wait-reanimate") or *total transplants* whereby a continually renewed physical organism can sustain indefinitely an individual consciousness. Scientists are also researching the mechanics of *regeneration* which operate so well for some lower creatures such as starfish and lobsters.

But all such notions are consolation prizes rather than immor-

Judgment scene before King Osiris. The dog-headed god Anubis is weighing the heart of the deceased—Princess Entiu-ny—against a symbol for Truth; if judged worthy, her spirit can pass on into the western paradise, the Kingdom of Osiris. The goddess Isis, sister of Osiris and compassionate interceder, stands behind the princess.

talities. They are designed to ease the pain of loss—the loss of conviction that consciousness survives death.

Does true immortality—the survival of a conscious self—really exist? Is there any conceivable way that there could be a continuity of conscious experience after the termination of our physical processes? What arguments—rational or empirical—might convince us that such continuity does indeed take place?

ARGUMENTS FOR IMMORTALITY

With respect to immortality many men in the western world today are in the position of the church-warden who, when buttonholed by F. W. H. Myers . . . and asked what he thought would happen to him after death, after vainly trying to evade the question, burst out with "Well, I suppose I shall enter into everlasting bliss, but I do wish you would not talk about such depressing subjects."

ASHLEY MONTAGU

14   The strongest *rational argument for immortality* is based on belief in the goodness of God. This is an "if . . . then" kind of argument: *If God exists and if he is good, then* immortality must necessarily exist.

According to this reasoning, it is unthinkable that God would create purposive beings who dream dreams and have the capacity for unlimited growth, only to let all this come to nothing. Could a good God *not* make provision for the fulfillment of these dreams and the actualization of this potential? The fact is that man barely begins to understand life and grow during his short lifetime. Most of us just begin to touch our dreams and solve some problems—and it's over. This would surely be an agonizing joke for a compassionate God to play on his children.

Therefore, there must exist an afterlife where man's self/essence can continue to grow. How great such a growth potential would be, especially if released from the impediments of the physical body, we can only imagine.

The American Personalist philosopher, Edgar Brightman, considered this to be the strongest argument for immortality. To his way of thinking there is no strong argument for immortality apart from the existence of God; but granting God's existence, then there exists no weighty argument *against* immortality.

Death plays an important part in each day of my life. I have worked half in shadow, half in sun all of my life. When I put my new book *The Halloween Tree* (a history of Death in the world, really) in the mail 8 weeks ago, I cried half-aloud: "There you are, Death, one up on you again!" My books are victories against darkness, if only for a small while. Each story I write is a candle lit for my own burial plot which it may take some few years to blow out. More than many writers, I have known this fact about myself since I was a child. It puts me to work each day with a special sad-sweet-happy urgency.

RAY BRADBURY

---

15   The strongest *empirical evidence for immortality*—and it may seem strange to some—is from seances during which contact is allegedly established with discarnate spirits.

It would not be far wrong to say that "special effects" and/or hypnosis is involved in 95 percent of all mediumistic activity; and therefore perhaps 5 percent of seances are free of fraud and demonstrate authentic phenomena. Now, within this 5 percent, the great majority of happenings can be accounted for with known psychological principles or telepathic hypotheses. This leaves only a small part of 1 percent which necessitate hypotheses assuming something like discarnate spirits. Within this very small percentage of cases, interesting but problematic events occur. For instance, the "discarnate spirits" frequently reveal information which no one present could possibly know. It has been suggested that there is a "collective subconscious" or a "superconsciousness" which is tapped by the mind of the medium; and while such a theory is not beyond the realm of possibility, the hypothesis of the existence of discarnate spirits seems at present a simpler and better explanation.

It is somewhere within this small percentage of spiritualistic phenomena that empirical data might be found to support the idea of a continued consciousness after physical death. At present we have no verified data in this area, and much more research is needed.

Je m'en vay chercher un grand Peut-être. **(I am going to seek a great Perhaps.)**

RABELAIS
(from his deathbed)

ARGUMENTS AGAINST IMMORTALITY

Much as I love truth in abstract I love my sense of immortality still more; and if the final outcome of all the boasted discoveries of modern science is to disclose to men that they are more evanescent than the shadow of the swallow's wing upon the lake . . . if this, after all, is the best that science can give one, give me then, I pray, no more science. I will live on in my simple ignorance, as my father did before me; and when I shall at length be sent to my final repose, let me . . . lie down to pleasant, even though they may be deceitful, dreams.

FREDERICK BARNARD

16   The strongest *rational argument against immortality* derives from empirical observations that man has a profound "instinct" to stay alive. He is terrorized by this final unknown, this "great Perhaps," as Rabelais put it; and along with this ultimate fear goes man's incredible power of imagination. He can create an endless variety of concepts to meet his emotional needs. Therefore, with a simple formula—man's intense need plus his ever-fertile imagination—we may be able to explain to our satisfaction all of man's dreams of immortality: subtle imagery of blissful spirits, teleocosmic schemes of reincarnation, myths without end about heavens and hells and how we can get there, or stay out. As one surveys the range of man's fantasies about postmortem life, it seems that they just might be man's most lavish creative productions. Man dreams of a paradise, but this life is anything but a paradise. There must be a paradise somewhere . . . .

This is a rational argument, but it is founded upon empirical observation and possesses considerable coherence; while it *proves* nothing, as an inductive hypothesis it is formidable.

My death does not belong to me— it is the outer limit of my consciousness, the last of my possibles. The meaninglessness of death for me is summed up in the phrase that "my death is the one moment of my life which I do not have to live." My death is not for me but for others; it is not my concern, but the concern of others who will notice it and need to deal with it. . . .

JOSEPH MIHALICH

17   The strongest *empirical evidence against immortality* is the observation—apparently without exception—that the termination of physical processes is soon followed by the cessation of consciousness as measured on EEGs and other instruments. That is, our bodies die and we have no evidence—unless the "discarnate spirits" are real—that consciousness continues in any form. We have no scientific knowledge at present which would be compatible with the continuation of consciousness; just the reverse, in fact: our best scientific knowledge is only compatible with the cessation of consciousness.

We could argue that, from the cessation of brainwaves on an electroencephalograph, we cannot validly infer that consciousness ceases. This is strictly true. Yet no alternative inference seems better. We can *think of* such things as "organized electromagnetic fields" or "vibration patterns" that somehow sustain themselves without underlying physical systems, but do we have any dependable evidence at present which would lead us to believe such concepts refer to anything real? Since there appears to be a one-to-one causal relationship between brainwaves and consciousness, there is logical justification for inferring the end of experience from the termination of the brain's electrical activity.

Que acreditó su ventura,
Morir cuerdo y vivir loco.
(For if he like a madman lived,
At least he like a wise one died.)

CERVANTES
Don Quixote's Epitaph

THE FUTURE OF DEATH

18   How we perceive "the problem of death" depends partly upon the attitude-options open to us at any particular time and place. Mankind's general stance toward death has wavered between a stubborn denial and a grudging submission. Our religious myths deny the death of the personal self while confirming the intolerable anxiety and pain of physical death.

Western man has long attempted to see death in new ways, and, thanks to recent investigations, death is now perceived as the terribly complex and ambiguous event that it is. From the nihilistic angle, the shriek of Ivan Ilytch° paints the horror of facing one's own death at the end of a meaningless life. But Albert Camus goes further: "Because of death, human existence has no meaning. All the crimes that man could commit are nothing in comparison with that fundamental crime which is death."

°*See pages 148f.*

By contrast, a more positive feeling is expressed by those who see death as the singular event that puts one's life in perspective and acts as the ultimate source of its meaning. Without death, they contend, our lives would be meaningless. The length of one's lifetime is irrelevant. If one lives a life filled with good experiences, then fifty years of meaningfulness is a full measure; but if one's life is meaningless, then five hundred years would be hell.

19   A brand new kind of vision has recently emerged: a prolongation of life that borders on immortality. For as long as we humans defined ourselves as "mortal men" condemned to a death-condition with "no exit," it was impossible for us to dream of alternatives. We could not allow ourselves to think that there might be an "exit." When we want very, very much something that is wholly beyond our reach, it is too painful to dream of possessing it; but given the remotest chance of grasping it, then we dream. *More* life—in quality perhaps, but certainly in quantity—may be (*may* be) within reach.

Science has extended the life expectancy of an individual in the Western world by about 25 years during the last century; and there is every reason to expect this trend to continue. How long might a lifetime become if we could solve the secret of aging? Or if we could learn how to transplant all man's vital organs or replace them with synthetic surrogates? Or discover a chemistry that will prevent senility and loss of memory? Or develop a eugenics technology that would pair genetic factors that sharply increase human longevity? Recent trends in microbiology and related fields enable us to take some of these possibilities seriously for the first time.

O my soul, do not aspire to immortal life, but exhaust the limits of the possible.

PINDAR

A blunt defiance of death is now coming from some quarters. Alan Harrington, author of *The Immortalist*, takes an unequivocal stand: "Death is an imposition on the human race, and no longer acceptable. Man has all but lost his ability to accommodate himself to personal extinction; he must now proceed physically to overcome it. In short, to kill death: to put an end to his own mortality as a certain consequence of being born."

20   Current reassessment of man's place in a biocosmos of living creatures is another helpful perspective. Whether or not we succeed in the near future in making contact with extraterrestrial intelligences (ETIs), this "cosmic context for man" has become a coherent worldview within which we can rethink the nature and destiny of man. In this perspective we are faced with *a new kind of question* about death.

This is the great error of our day in the treatment of the human body that physicians separate the soul from the body.

PLATO

THE HEART OF HELLAS: EPITAPHS

My name is—What does it matter?—*My*
Country was—Why speak of it?—*I*
Was of noble birth—Indeed? And if
You had been the lowest?—*Moreover, my life*
Was decorous—And if it had not been so,
What then?
          —and I lie here now beneath you—
Who are you that speak?
To whom do you speak?

                    PAULUS SILENTIARIUS

Epitaph of an Abstainer

Remember Euboulos the sober, you who pass by,
And drink: there is one Hadês for all men.

                    LEONIDAS OF TARENTUM

Epitaph of a Slave

Alive, this man was Manês the slave: but dead,
He is the peer of Dareios, that great King.

                    ANYTE

Epitaph of a Young Man

Hail me Diogenês underground, O stranger, and pass by:
Go where you will, and fairest fortune go with you.
In my nineteenth year the darkness drew me down—
And ah, the sweet sun!

                    ANONYMOUS

Epitaph of a Sailor

Tomorrow the wind will have fallen
Tomorrow I shall be safe in harbor
Tomorrow
        I said:
           and Death
Spoke in that little word:
The sea was Death.
           O Stranger
This is the Némesis of the spoken word:
Bite back the daring tongue that would say
  Tomorrow!

                    ANTIPHILOS OF BYZANTIUM

                    Dudley Fitts (translator)
                    Poems from the Greek Anthology

Q Suppose we should discover that ETIs actually exist who enjoy life-spans of three hundred years, or five hundred years, or a thousand. Might we then come to feel that man's life-span of three score years and ten is wholly intolerable?

Q How might we humans feel if ETIs are enabled to fulfill their plans and dreams to a degree that has heretofore seemed unthinkable to us? Could we continue to accept docilely the early and frustrating curtailment of our dreams?

Q In terms of our self-esteem, could we continue to tolerate a seventy- to eighty-year life-span? Wouldn't all our deaths then be viewed as premature?

Q How long might we want to live *under present conditions* if we discover that some ETIs live for hundreds or thousands of our earth years?

Q What grounds do we have for assuming that death-events as we know them are cosmic universals? Perhaps our notions are based solely on local and contingent examples.

Q Is it remotely conceivable that there may be forms of "process termination" other than death as we know it?

Q Wouldn't higher life-forms at least attempt to establish control over both the time and the conditions of life-termination?

Q Wouldn't such control in fact be merely an extension of scientific and medical goals now on our human drawing boards?

Q If such control could be accomplished by man, how might it affect the whole intent and meaning of human existence?

Q If we could live for two thousand years, would our present profound need for immortality be assuaged? What would we want *then?*

21   In a science-fiction classic, *Time Enough for Love,* Robert Heinlein has successfully captured the painful contrast between the near-immortal members of the Howard families and the short-lived "ephemerals"—that is, us. The Howards are normal earthlings who find that they live for centuries as a result of a natural genetic mutation. The oldest member of the clan, Lazarus Long, reminisces about one short period of his long life, a very happy time spent with a short-lived ephemeral, Dora.

> I have just returned from a party of which I was the life and soul; wit poured from my lips, everyone laughed and admired me—but I went away—and the dash should be as long as the earth's orbit--------
> ---
> -----and wanted to shoot myself.
>
> *KIERKEGAARD*

Dora is the only woman I ever loved unreservedly. I don't know that I can explain why. I did not love her that way when I married her; she had not had a chance as yet to teach me what love can be. Oh, I did love her, but it was the love of a doting father for a favorite child or somewhat like the love one can lavish on a pet.

I decided to marry her not through love in any deepest sense but simply because this adorable child who had given me so many hours of happiness wanted something very badly—my child—and there was only one way I could give her what she wanted and still please my own self-love. So, almost coldly, I calculated the cost and decided that the price was low enough that I could let her have what she wanted. It could not cost me much; she was an ephemeral. Fifty,

When my time comes, I hope no one drains my veins of their sustaining fluid and fills them with formaldehyde, then wastes me by putting me in a concrete box in the ground for eternity.

Rather, just a simple pine box with an acorn on top of it. Find a place where a tree is needed and return me to nature. When the acorn grows, I can nourish it and give back in some measure what I've taken. Maybe someday kids can crawl in my branches or a raccoon might curl up in my trunk or the larks can sing out from my leaves. At any rate, I would rather let an oak tree be my epitaph than a marble slab be my tombstone.

MIKE ROYKO

sixty, seventy, at the most eighty years, and she would be dead. I could afford to spend that trivial amount of time to make my adopted daughter's pitifully short life happy—that's how I figured it. It wasn't much, and I could afford it. So be it.

* * *

I decided that the husband of an ephemeral had to *be* an ephemeral, in every way possible to him. The corollaries to that decision caused us to wind up in Happy Valley.

Happy Valley—The happiest of all my lives. The longer I was privileged to live with Dora, the more I loved her. She taught me to love by loving me, and I learned—rather slowly; I wasn't too good a pupil, being set in my ways and lacking her natural talent. But I did learn. Learned that supreme happiness lies in wanting to keep another person safe and warm and happy, and being privileged to try.

And saddest, too. The more thoroughly I learned this—through living day on day with Dora—the happier I was . . . and the more I ached in one corner of my mind with certain knowledge that this could be only a brief time too soon over—and when it *was* over, I did not marry again for almost a hundred years. Then I did, for Dora taught me to face up to death, too. She was as aware of her own death, of the certain briefness of her life, as I was. But she taught me to live *now,* not to let anything sully *today* . . . until at last I got over the sadness of being condemned to live.

DEATH—VERSUS LIFE

There are many forms of life in space. Many forms of death, too.

Space: 1999

Whoe'er can know,
As the long days go,
That *to live is happy*
Hath found his heaven.

EURIPIDES

22   Clearly, *how* one dies is very important—while one is still alive. We want assurance that our death will be dignified; that the conditions of termination will be surrounded by respect and honor; that it will not be degrading to ourselves or loved ones; that it will not be an unplanned, messy kind of death. We want to feel sure that it will not result from ignominious causes; from cowardice, foolish anger, or stupidity. And certainly not least, we want the assurance that our last experience of consciousness will not be dominated by physical pain or emotional anguish.

23   There are two central questions involved in facing our own death: the questions of what we can leave behind and what we can take with us. It has been written that we must develop convictions and feelings about each of these questions if we are to face our own cessation with any sense of peace.

But some say that the better question is: What can I do with the days I have left to make life really worthwhile?

REFLECTIONS—

1 "All graves are wrong when you come right down to it" (Sec. 1). How do you respond to the point Bradbury is making?

2 How would you answer the question: "Would we really care about the termination of our physiological processes if we could be assured that the cessation of our consciousness would *not* follow?" (Sec. 5.)

3 "The possibility of nonexistence in the future can disturb us, while nonexistence in the past doesn't. Why?" (Sec. 6).

4 This "fear of nonexistence" is widely dealt with in existential literature, and many philosophers are convinced that this fear is one of the powerful driving forces behind much human behavior. So, what exactly is meant by the "fear of nonexistence" (or "nonbeing")? Is the concept meaningful to you personally?

5 Three kinds of fear commonly associated with death are described in Secs. 5 and 6 of this chapter. Are these descriptions accurate, in your judgment? Have any of these fears (or others) been a significant part of your experience? How have you dealt with them?

6 Think awhile about the James Kidd will (p. 530, plus the UPI report on the will, p. 532). Do you think there is any empirical evidence for the existence of a "soul"? Do you think there could be? If so, what kind of evidence? How would you go about gathering evidence? That is, what path might you follow if you really wanted to "show cause" why you should receive the James Kidd estate?

7 Review and clarify in your own mind the empirical and rational arguments presented in this chapter for and against immortality (Secs. 14–17). Which of these arguments are most persuasive? On the basis of these four arguments, what is your conclusion regarding the existence of personal immortality?

8 Answer the following question as precisely as you can, but first give careful attention to the definition of each term in the question: "Where do you think we will go after we die?" (If you think that fallacious or meaningless words are used here, then rephrase the question until you get it to produce results.)

9 Evidence would seem to indicate that the preponderance of human beings can't face death without myth. Myths that attend upon death, its meaning, and its aftermath are legion in all religions. In your opinion, could man face death without myth? (What is meant by "myth" in such a question?) What do you think the experiential consequences might be?

Furthermore . . .

BECKER, ERNEST, *The Denial of Death*. Free Press, 1973.

CHORON, JACQUES, *Death in Western Thought*. Collier, 1963.

DOSS, RICHARD W., *The Last Enemy*. Harper, 1974.

FEIFEL, HERMAN (ed.), *The Meaning of Death*. McGraw-Hill, 1965.

HARRINGTON, ALAN, *The Immortalist*. Avon, 1969.

HEINLEIN, ROBERT, *Time Enough for Love*. Berkley, 1974.

INOGUCHI, RIKIHEI, and TADASHI NAKAJIMA, *The Divine Wind*. Bantam, 1960. (Story of the kamikaze pilots in World War II.)

KÜBLER-ROSS, ELISABETH, *On Death and Dying*. Macmillan, 1969.

MONTAGU, ASHLEY, *Immortality*. Grove, 1955.

ROSENFELD, ALBERT, *Prolongevity*. Knopf, 1976. (On the lengthening life-span and the future of death.)

TOLSTOY, LEO, "The Death of Ivan Ilytch." (Available in most collections of Tolstoy's works.)

Meaning/ Existence

Have You Ever Wondered . . .

- What you're doing here?!

- What you want out of life?

- Whether there really is a key to happiness?

- What you want to be when you grow up?

- What the answer is to the World-Riddle?

- How you can avoid getting bogged down in the trivialities of life (especially the trivialities of *others'* lives)?

- How you can decide what is important in your life and what is unimportant?

- What the next chess move is for you?

- What you might find on the far shore (*if* there is a far shore, and *if* there is a raft, and *if* there is a river . . .)?

THE KNOWLEDGE WHICH HURTS MOST

1   Once there lived in the ancient city of Afkar two learned men who hated and belittled each other's learning. For one of them denied the existence of the gods and the other was a believer.

One day the two met in the market-place, and amidst their fol-

Ever look at a male lion in a zoo? Fresh meat on time, females supplied, no hunter to worry about—he's got it made, hasn't he? Then why does he look bored?

ROBERT HEINLEIN
The Glory Road

lowers they began to dispute and to argue about the existence or the non-existence of the gods. And after hours of contention they parted.

That evening the unbeliever went to the temple and prostrated himself before the altar and prayed the gods to forgive his wayward past.

And the same hour the other learned man, he who had upheld the gods, burned his sacred books. For he had become an unbeliever.

KAHLIL GIBRAN

It is extremely important to grasp the notion that *man does not yet exist.*

COLIN WILSON

2 The Don Juan of the Mind: no philosopher or poet has yet discovered him. What he lacks is the love of the things he knows, what he possesses is *esprit*, the itch and delight in the chase and intrigue of knowledge—knowledge as far and high as the most distant stars. Until in the end there is nothing left for him to chase except the knowledge which hurts most, just as a drunkard in the end drinks absinthe and methylated spirits. And in the very end he craves for Hell—it is the only knowledge which can still seduce him. Perhaps it too will disappoint, as everything that he knows. And if so, he will have to stand transfixed through all eternity, nailed to disillusion, having himself become the Guest of Stone, longing for a last supper of knowledge which he will never receive. For in the whole world of things there is nothing left to feed his hunger.

FRIEDRICH NIETZSCHE

Does the grass bend when the wind blows upon it?

CONFUCIUS

WHAT *DID* I WANT?

" . . . in New Orleans. On Bourbon Street."
"No, that's your dream. It's not mine."
"Well, then, what is yours?"
"I have no dream."
"How terrible for you!"

TENNESSEE WILLIAMS
This Property Is Condemned

3 New Zealand, maybe. The *Herald-Trib* had had the usual headlines, only more so. It looked as if the boys (just big playful boys!) who run this planet were about to hold that major war, the one with ICBMs and H-bombs, any time now.

If a man went as far south as New Zealand there might be something left after the fallout fell out.

New Zealand is supposed to be very pretty and they say that a fisherman there regards a five-pound trout as too small to take home.

I had caught a two-pound trout once.

About then I made a horrible discovery. I didn't want to go back to school, win, lose, or draw. I no longer gave a damn about three-car garages and swimming pools, nor any other status symbol or "security." There was *no* security in this world and only damn fools and mice thought there could be.

Somewhere back in the jungle I had shucked off all ambition of that sort. I had been shot at too many times and had lost interest in supermarkets and exurban sub-divisions and tonight is the PTA supper don't forget dear you promised.

Oh, I wasn't about to hole up in a monastery. I still wanted—
What *did* I want?

I wanted a Roc's egg. I wanted a harem loaded with lovely odalisques less than the dust beneath my chariot wheels, the rust that never stained my sword. I wanted raw red gold in nuggets the size of your fist and feed that lousy claim jumper to the huskies! I wanted

"You missed life."

to get up feeling brisk and go out and break some lances, then pick a likely wench for my *droit du seigneur*—I wanted to stand up to the Baron and *dare* him to touch my wench. I wanted to hear the purple water chuckling against the skin of the *Nancy Lee* in the cool of the morning watch and not another sound, nor any movement save the slow tilting of the wings of the albatross that had been pacing us the last thousand miles.

I wanted the hurtling moons of Barsoom. I wanted Storisende and Poictesme, and Holmes shaking me awake to tell me, "The game's afoot!" I wanted to float down the Mississippi on a raft and elude a mob in company with the Duke of Bilgewater and the Lost Dauphin.

I wanted Prester John, and Excalibur held by a moon-white arm out of a silent lake. I wanted to sail with Ulysses and with Tros of Samothrace and eat the lotus in a land that seemed always afternoon. I wanted the feeling of romance and the sense of wonder I had known as a kid. I wanted the world to be what they had promised me it was going to be—instead of the tawdry, lousy, fouled-up mess it is. . . .

Maybe one chance is all you ever get.

ROBERT HEINLEIN
The Glory Road

4   Who has not asked, "What am I doing here?" But what is the answer?

Socrates believed we are here to be happy, and the path of happiness is through knowledge which leads to virtue which leads to happiness. *Epicurus* taught that we are here to cultivate the pleasures of the mind—wisdom and understanding—but the Cyrenaic philosopher *Aristippus* became famous for teaching that we are here to cultivate pleasures, and the more the merrier (and those of the mind only as a last resort). A prophet from Nazareth, *Yeshua bar Yoseph*, suggested we are here to learn the qualities of faith and love toward one another so that we will merit membership in the Reign of God when it begins. Shortly after that, *Paul of Tarsus* preached that we are here to have

> If I had my life to live over again, I would have made it a rule to read some poetry and listen to some music at least every week. . . . The loss of these tastes is a loss of happiness, and may possibly be injurious to the intellect, and more probably to the moral character, by enfeebling the emotional part of our nature.
>
> *CHARLES DARWIN*

> Man is by nature a purposive creature, who develops neuroses when purpose is denied him.
>
> *COLIN WILSON*

551

faith in the Messiah so that our original sin could be washed away and we would be ready for the return of the Christ.

Lao-tzu apparently believed that we are here to seek the Tao and know the inner harmony of Nature's Way; but *Confucius* disagreed, declaring that we are here to discover the proper way to behave in our relationships with others. *The Buddha* taught that we are here to transcend tanha—the selfish craving which is the cause of human suffering—and enter the state of nirvana. *Shankara*, a Hindu mystic, was convinced that we are here to discover that this world is only maya ("illusion") and to realize that each of us is already one with Ultimate Reality.

Muhammad believed that we are here to render faithful obedience to Allah as revealed in the Quran. *John Calvin* told the Genevans that we are here solely to love God and so live a life of faith and discipline that we will "enjoy Him forever." But *Hegel*, being a philosopher on the rational side, wrote to persuade us that we are here to develop our capacity for reason and, in so doing, manifest the logic of the Absolute Mind in the movement of human (especially German) history.

EXISTENCE AND THE REAL: PERSISTENT CONFUSION

5 It is impossible to define the purpose of life in a general way. "Life" does not mean something vague, but something very real and concrete, just as life's tasks are very real and concrete. They form man's destiny, which is different and unique for each individual. No situation repeats itself and each situation calls for a different response. Sometimes the situation in which a man finds himself may require him to shape his own destiny by action. Sometimes a man may be required simply to accept fate, to bear his cross.

When a man finds that it is his destiny to suffer, he will have to accept suffering as his task; his single and unique task. He will have to struggle for the realization that even in suffering he is unique and alone in the universe. No man can relieve him of his suffering, or suffer in his place. His unique opportunity lies in the way in which he bears his burden.

VIKTOR FRANKL

6 The central character of *Nausea*, Antoine Roquentin, enunciates Jean-Paul Sartre's reflections on the meaning of human existence.

Prior to these past few days, I had really never felt what it means "to exist." . . . Ordinarily, existence hides itself. It is here, round about us, within us: we are it, and we cannot speak two words without speaking of it, but in the end we never grasp it. . . . Existence is not something which can be thought from a distance: it overwhelms you brusquely. . . .

[Existence means nothing more than] to be here; existents ap-

If a patient [should ask] Frankl, "What is the meaning of life for me?" he is likely to get a Socratic answer: "What is the best chess move?"

AARON UNGERSMA

How terrifying and glorious the role of man if, indeed, without guidance and without consolation he must create from his own vitals the meaning for his existence and write the rules whereby he lives.

THORNTON WILDER
Julius Caesar

The sweetest optimism springs from an inability to face despair.

TODD GITLIN

pear, they are encountered, but they can never be inferentially deduced. I believe there are people who have understood this, but they have been trying to overcome this contingency by inventing a Necessary Being who causes himself (a *causa sui*). No Necessary Being, however, can explain existence. . . . There is not the least reason for our "being-there." . . . And I, too, am *"de trop"* [superfluous, unnecessary, absurd]. And yet people are trying to hide themselves behind the idea of law and necessity. In vain: every existent is born without reason, prolongs its existence owing to the weakness of inertia, and dies fortuitously.

7   That Man is the product of causes which had no prevision of the end they were achieving; that his origin, his growth, his hopes and fears, his loves and his beliefs, are but the outcome of accidental collocations of atoms; that no fire, no heroism, no intensity of thought and feeling, can preserve an individual life beyond the grave; that all the labours of the ages, all the devotion, all the inspiration, all the noonday brightness of human genius, are destined to extinction in the vast death of the solar system, and that the whole temple of Man's achievement must inevitably be buried beneath the debris of a universe in ruins—all these things, if not quite beyond dispute, are yet so nearly certain, that no philosophy which rejects them can hope to stand. Only within the scaffolding of these truths, only on the firm foundation of unyielding despair, can the soul's habitation henceforth be safely built.

BERTRAND RUSSELL

Those who have suffered much become very bitter or very gentle.

WILL DURANT

When the universe has crushed him man will still be nobler than that which kills him, because he knows that he is dying, and of its victory the universe knows nothing.

PASCAL

NOTHINGS

Even as a child I could never understand why certain things that were important to me appeared to older people to be nothing. My dreams were nothing. What I "made up" to delight or terrify myself was nothing. Certain queer feelings, coming out of the blue, were nothing. I can remember, though it must be all of 65 years ago, sitting in the sun on a tiny hillock at the back of our house, and feeling, not lightly but to the very depths of my being, that I was close to some secret about a wonderful treasure, which had no size, no shape, no substance, but all the same was somewhere just behind the sunlight and the buttercups and daisies and the grass and the warm earth. And this too, it seemed, was nothing. I was surrounded and often enchanted, it appeared, by nothings.

J. B. PRIESTLEY
Man and Time

TRIVIALITIES

8   But wherein do such pronouncements about the absurdity of existence become statements about the real world? Are they not more on the order of reflexive value-judgments which betray the inner

world of the individuals who make them? After all, to say the world is meaningless is merely to say, "I find no meaning in it." Value-judgments are personal responses, not scientific descriptions.

Much modern Western philosophy has contended that there are no real values and that, by a sort of hopeless *tour de force*, we each must inject meaning into his own life. Existentialists such as Heidegger and Sartre have held that only a personal confrontation with death itself puts our lives in perspective but that this "flash of authenticity" cannot be made a part of our everyday consciousness. But this is questionable, for "there are states of consciousness that are not 'everyday consciousness' and which are not 'transcendental' either. These produce a definite sense of values and purpose." In saying this, perhaps Colin Wilson is closer to the truth, and he goes on:

"Peak experiences" all seem to have the same "content": that the chief mistake of human beings is to pay too much attention to everyday trivialities. We are strangely inefficient machines, utilizing only a frac-

paper flower
paper bird
paper moon
who walks
the wild earth
any more?

tion of our powers, and the reason for this is our short sightedness. Koestler's "mystical" insight made him feel that even the threat of death was a triviality that should be ignored; "So what? . . . Have you nothing more serious to worry about?" Greene's whisky priest: "It seemed to him, at that moment, that it would have been quite easy to be a saint." Death reveals to us that our lives have been one long miscalculation, based on a triviality.

9

A painter who is painting a large canvas has to work with his nose to the canvas; but periodically he stands back to see the effect of the whole. These over-all glimpses renew his sense of purpose.

Man's evolution depends upon a renewal of the sense of over-all

THE CREATIONS OF MY MIND

1. With clarity and quiet, I look upon the world and say: All that I see, hear, taste, smell, and touch are the creations of my mind.

2. The sun comes up and the sun goes down in my skull. Out of one of my temples the sun rises, and into the other the sun sets.

3. The stars shine in my brain; ideas, men, animals browse in my temporal head; songs and weeping fill the twisted shells of my ears and storm the air for a moment.

4. My brain blots out, and all, the heavens and the earth, vanish.

5. The mind shouts: "Only I exist!

6. "Deep in my subterranean cells my five senses labor; they weave and unweave space and time, joy and sorrow, matter and spirit. . . .

10. "I impose order on disorder and give a face—my face—to chaos.

11. "I do not know whether behind appearances there lives and moves a secret essence superior to me. Nor do I ask; I do not care. I create phenomena in swarms, and paint with a full palette a gigantic and gaudy curtain before the abyss. Do not say, 'Draw the curtain that I may see the painting.' The curtain IS the painting. . . .

13. "I am the worker of the abyss. I am the spectator of the abyss. I am both theory and practice. I am the law. Nothing beyond me exists."

NIKOS KAZANTZAKIS
The Saviours of God

purpose. For several centuries now, the direction of our culture has been a concentration upon the minute, the particular. In the field of science, this has produced our present high level of technological achievement. In the field of culture, we have less reason for self-congratulation, for the concentration upon the particular—to the exclusion of wider meanings—has led us into a *cul de sac*. Yeats described the result as "fish gasping on the strand"—a minute realism that has lost all drive and purpose.

COLIN WILSON

"My dear Rikki," Karellen retorted, "it's only by *not* taking the human race seriously that I retain what fragments of my once considerable mental powers I still possess."

ARTHUR C. CLARKE
Childhood's End

WORK, WORK . . . TO KILL THE FLOWERS

10   In subjecting these views to the critical questioning that constitutes one important side of the philosophical task, we are, therefore, engaging in an experiment that is both very personal and at the same time "vicarious." We are not only taking the personal risk of having our views exposed as inadequate, but, since most of our views are also those of the vast majority of the rest of the people in our culture, it is the intellectual outlook of our whole culture that is here being put to the test. If we should suffer the collapse of some of our cherished beliefs (and the loss of a cherished belief does involve a painful

It is the greatest joy of the man of thought to have explored the explorable and then calmly to revere the inexplorable.

GOETHE

sort of suffering), then it is not only for ourselves that we suffer, but for those many others in our culture who share those beliefs. It is only through such suffering, however, that human thought progresses.

But human thought does progress, and this is what makes the enterprise worthwhile. Many people must have suffered the kind of intellectual agony of which we have been speaking, during the long interval of time that separates us from our primitive ancestors; but there can be little doubt that our way of looking at the world—our world-view—is closer to the truth than the superstitious, animistic, magical views that they are known to have held. If our view is not the whole truth—and it would surely be presumptuous to say that it is—then let us press on toward that elusive goal as best we can. It is the lure of beliefs that are closer to the truth that beckons us on and leaves us dissatisfied with beliefs that are obviously short of that goal.

WILLIAM HALVERSON

> **Authenticity is a kind of honesty or a kind of courage; the authentic individual faces something which the unauthentic individual is afraid to face.**
>
> *JEAN-PAUL SARTRE*

LESSONS:

Charles Beard (1874–1948) was a renowned historian and economist. His colleague, George Counts, tells of a conversation they had in the autumn of 1931.

He and I were motoring over the hills of Connecticut in the vicinity of New Milford. Having been profoundly impressed by the vast range of his knowledge and thought, a range that seemed to embrace the entire human record from ancient times, I asked how long it would take him to tell all he had learned from his lifetime study of history. After contemplating the question a few moments he replied that he "thought" he could do it in "about a week." We drove on a short distance in silence. Whereupon he said he could probably do it in a day. After another brief pause, he reduced the time to half an hour. Finally, bringing his hand down on his knee, he said: "I can tell you all I have learned in a lifetime of study in just three laws of history. And here they are:

"First, whom the gods would destroy they first make mad."

"Second, the mills of the gods grind slowly, yet they grind exceedingly fine."

"Third, the bee fertilizes the flower that it robs."

About ten days later we took a stroll along Riverside Drive in New York City. Evidently he had been giving further thought to my question. At any rate, he said he would like to add a fourth law to his laws of history:

"When it gets dark enough you can see the stars."

GEORGE S. COUNTS
"Charles Beard, The Public Man,"
in Howard K. Beale (ed.),
Charles A. Beard: An Appraisal.

---

11   Just when a humanlike consciousness—in the form of self-awareness—began, we cannot at present tell. Perhaps two million

years ago, perhaps fourteen, perhaps more. But the question is academic. The significant thing is that we are giving birth to, developing, flowering, a seed planted ages ago; and that this is a glorious flowering, whatever the pain we must pay for the seeds of such flowering. After flowering, most flowers die, though most plants do not die but continue to live and grow. This inevitable flowering of man's awareness is totally unavoidable, and like a flower which has gradually, slowly, grown from bud to its moment of opening to the world, there is no turning back; it is flower, or die.

12   Now the cello has stopped. All that can be heard is the ironic funeral march from the first symphony of Mahler. The girl is walking across the desert towards a hill, the only feature in the otherwise gently sloping terrain, apart from a black plume of smoke which is rising distantly in the air. As she gets nearer to this oily cloud of smoke, scurrying human activity can be seen on the ground beneath. Occasionally a gout of bright flame bursts along the ground, and more smoke is added to the cloud rising swiftly in the air. Now the camera, in a tracking shot, reveals a close-up of the girl's face as she walks along. At first lines of concentration furrow her forehead as she tries to make out what is going on, then the concentration is replaced by bewilderment, and then, a little later, by anger. Now the camera is static, and we see the whole scene as the girl walks up.

Men in shirt sleeves are rushing about, their faces grimy and shining with sweat. They look bewildered and panic-stricken, but this is obviously their normal state of mind. On their backs they carry the large chemical tanks of flamethrowers, and the straps have rubbed into their shoulders for so long that they are obviously in great pain. All around the ground is seared and black. It appears that nothing could possibly grow in such a devastated place, but straggly vegetation is visibly thrusting itself up through the soil. Every moment one of the strange plants is beginning to bloom. . . . A bud appears, almost instantaneously, and begins to open. Lush, coloured petals are visible, promising future beauty. But as soon as one of the men sees this he moves up and immerses the plant in a bath of flame from the nozzle of the weapon he is carrying. All that is left when the fire dies away is charred black soil. But after only a few seconds, pushing up through this inhospitable earth, can be seen a new plant.

The girl clearly doesn't like this place, but when one of the men comes close to her, a fevered expression on his face, she lightly touches his arm.

GIRL. What is this? What are you doing?
MAN. Killing them.
GIRL. But—why?
MAN. To stop them from growing. (*The man turns away to spread a carpet of flame, and then turns back to the girl.*) The only way is to kill them. If we weren't doing this good work they'd be spreading all over the desert.
GIRL. But why do you want to stop them?
MAN. We don't want these—these filthy blossoms all over the desert. For one thing they'd encourage laxness—all our men would be too

MAN. And besides which, we're used to the desert. When I see those disgusting petals coming out I feel a strange—tension inside me. What would happen if I gave way to that, and watched them evolving all the way? And anyway, why are you so interested? I don't like the kind of talk you're giving me.

GIRL. It's just that I can't understand you. You're killing something that's beautiful and alive, something that can grow and give you pleasure. . . .

The man looks at the girl with a disgusted expression on his face, and quite deliberately spits at the ground by her feet. Then he turns back to his work. But just before his face goes out of frame his expression can be seen to change from one of disgust to an infinite sadness. The music fades.

LANGDON JONES
"The Eye of the Lens"

The true biologist deals with life, with teaming boisterous life, and learns something from it, learns that the first rule of life is living. The dryballs cannot possibly know a thing every starfish knows in the core of his soul and in the vesicles between his rays.

JOHN STEINBECK

GROWN-UPS ARE VERY STRANGE

When you can measure what you are speaking about, and express it in numbers, you know something about it; but when you cannot measure it, when you cannot express it in numbers, your knowledge is of a meager and unsatisfactory kind: it may be the beginning of knowledge, but you have scarcely, in your thoughts, advanced to the stage of science.

WILLIAM THOMSON, LORD KELVIN
Popular Lectures and Addresses

Grown-ups love figures. When you tell them that you have made a new friend, they never ask you any questions about essential matters. They never say to you, "What does his voice sound like? What games does he love best? Does he collect butterflies?" Instead, they demand: "How old is he? How many brothers has he? How much does he weigh? How much money does his father make?" Only from these figures do they think they have learned anything about him.

ANTOINE DE SAINT-EXUPÉRY
The Little Prince

THE WORLD-RIDDLE

13   Each man tries in his personal, and perhaps desperate, way to make this short life/time meaningful. We identify with the things of

our universe which are comparatively timeless—with the rock-ribbed mountains, the washing oceans, the stars, with evolution, with life itself—in order to appropriate a little part of their time-spans, their seeming immortality. Or we alleviate nonbeing by losing our selves within great causes and great principles and great people; or by becoming a part of the teleocosmic drama of our society or our religion.

Behind all this is the burden of our consciousness of death. We must attempt to be immortal, to be God, and to ease the dread of nonexistence.

But to strive to feel one with the stars—what is this but to die? Stars die. Earth's light will go out; life may dim and vanish, here. No matter: *we are* a part, an ever-so-tiny part, of the infinite program of the universe. I do not deceive myself into thinking I am buying time by longing for the suns or immersing myself in life. *I am* one with the stars. *I am* one with life. I identify, rightly, with all birth and all death of all time. And when I die, I shall not need to feel as though I never was at all; but rather *that* I was, and that is enough. I was a part of it all. I remain a part of all past and all future. I am a moment within the energy-systems of motion and life and purpose.

Does this ease my loneliness? Yes. All this follows naturally from the constantly expanding boundaries of my conscious relatedness: the finite self within the context of the infinite.

14   *What is the meaning of existence?*

For an answer which cannot be expressed the question too cannot be expressed. *The riddle* does not exist. If a question can be put at all, then it *can* also be answered. . . . For doubt can only exist where there is a question; a question only where there is an answer, and this only where something can be *said*. We feel that even if *all possible* scientific questions be answered, the problems of life have still not been touched at all. Of course there is then no question left, and just this is the answer. The solution of the problem of life is seen in the vanishing of this problem. (Is not this the reason why men to whom after long doubting the sense of life became clear, could not then say wherein this sense consisted?)

LUDWIG WITTGENSTEIN

15   The whole world is a circus if you look at it the right way. Every time you watch a rainbow and feel wonder in your heart. Every time you pick up a handful of dust and see not the dust but a mystery, a marvel there in your hand. Every time you stop to think "I'm alive! and being alive is fantastic!" Every time such a thing happens, you're a part of the circus of Dr. Lao.

The 7 Faces of Dr. Lao

REFLECTIONS—

1 Assuming that you have just read through this chapter—text, marginal quotations, boxed vignettes, illustrations, and all—then your responses

---

"What is the Way [Tao]?" Nansen answered, "Your everyday mind is the Way." "How, then, does one get into accord with it?" "If you try to accord, you deviate." Life, he is saying, is not a problem, so why are you asking for a solution?

ALAN WATTS

We shall not cease from
  exploration
And the end of all our exploring
Will be to arrive where we started
And know the place for the first
  time.

T. S. ELIOT
Four Quartets

Omnes Sancti Angeli et Archangeli, intercedite pro nobis.
All ye devoted bodhisattvas, who for us your fellow living beings and for our release have forborne, aeon after aeon, to enter into your rest, tarry with us, we beseech you, yet a little while longer.

ARNOLD TOYNBEE

must be numerous, mixed, and fragmented. Without forcing coherence at this point, what are some of the most luminous meaning-events that linger in your mind? Ask yourself why each item is meaningful.

2 What do you think of Abner Dean's drawing on p. 551: "You missed life"—? Does this drawing apply to anyone you know? *Who* missed *what*?

3 Ponder the quotation from Robert Heinlein (p. 549-QM). How would you answer his question, *"Then why does he look so bored?"*

4 What do you think of the point that Viktor Frankl is making in Sec. 5?

5 Colin Wilson scores a point which, for many of us, is quite meaningful—Sec. 8. What does it say to you?

6 When you compare the statements by Lord Kelvin and Saint-Exupéry (p. 559-Box), what is your first (and most authentic?) response? Can these two points of view be reconciled? Is there room in your life for both?

7 Reflect at length, and with leisure, on the passage from Langdon Jones' "Eye of the Lens" (Sec. 12). Among several possible meanings, what do you think the author is saying?

8 Having arrived at this point—assuming that you have read through the entire textbook—how would you proceed now to answer such a question as "What is the meaning of life?" or "Why are we here?" Are such questions still meaningful questions? If you still feel a bit stymied by such a question, then study carefully, and with a good deal of time and reflection, just the marginal quotations in this final chapter—then return and attempt to answer the question again. Do this several times, if necessary. If no answer emerges, proceed to Postlude.

Furthermore . . .

ANDERSON, MARIANNE S., and LOUIS M. SAVARY, *Passages: A Guide for Pilgrims of the Mind.* Harper, 1973.

DEAN, ABNER, *Abner Dean's Naked People.* Stein & Day, 1963.

FITTS, DUDLEY (trans.), *Poems from the Greek Anthology.* New Directions, 1941.

KAUFMANN, WALTER, *Without Guilt and Justice.* Delta, 1975.

KAZANTZAKIS, NIKOS, *The Saviors of God.* Simon & Schuster, 1960.

KAZANTZAKIS, NIKOS, *The Odyssey: A Modern Sequel.* Simon & Schuster, 1958.

KOPP, SHELDON B., *If You Meet the Buddha on the Road, Kill Him!* Bantam, 1976.

UNGERSMA, A. J., *The Search for Meaning.* Westminster, 1968.

POSTLUDE

The Mahayanas tell the story of a sage
who once stood on a riverbank
looking across at the opposite shore.
Although the far side
was but dimly visible
through the river mists,
he could see that it was
unspeakably beautiful.
The hills were green
and the trees were all in blossom.

So he said to himself,
"I want to go there."
There was a raft tied
at the river's edge.
He untied the raft
and began to paddle
toward the distant shore.

The journey was long and hazardous
for the currents in midstream were swift.
The raging rapids tossed and turned the raft,
and he had to work with all his strength
to maintain his balance.
From the center of the river
both shores were lost from view,
and there were times when he was not sure
which way he was drifting.
But he continued paddling,
and in due time
he reached the far shore.

He got out of the raft and said,
"Ah, at last I am here.
It was a perilous journey,
but now I have reached nirvana."
He looked about him.
The hills were green
and the trees were all in blossom.

Then he turned around and looked back.
He could not see the opposite shore
whence he came.
Nor was there any river to be seen.
And there was no raft.

GLOSSARY

When making use of the following brief definitions of terms, note again what a definition is (see p. 261). Definitions are only *predictions of possible meanings* which words may be given in living contexts. Exact meanings can never be known apart from the concrete situation in which they are used. Therefore, think of the following definitions merely as openers. For further clarification, refer to the Index and note specific contexts in which any particular term is used.

ABSOLUTE A concept of something which is assumed to be free of all qualifications. Whatever is absolute would be underived, complete, perfect, and unconditioned; as such, it could not be modified or changed in any way.

ABSTRACTION A concept, developed in the mind, taking into account only selected characteristics of a set of objects which are thought of as belonging to the same class. Once the mind has created a generalized abstraction (not *this* painting by Gauguin but painting-in-general), the mind is freed from having to deal with particular objects. See pp. 182f.

AGNOSTICISM In epistemology, a term (coined by Thomas Huxley) referring to the deliberate suspension of speculation and judgment about things which cannot be known (e.g., the afterlife or the supernatural). The word can be used to mean "I don't know" or "It cannot be known."

AMBIGUOUS Refers to a word or other symbol which is given different meanings in different contexts. To say that a word is ambiguous often means that one is at a loss to interpret it correctly because he doesn't know the original context in which it was used.

ANALYTIC (1) A twentieth-century philosophic movement whose main concerns are the logical analysis of language and the process of reasoning. (2) In epistemology, a particular kind of statement in which the predicate merely spells out what the subject implies (e.g., "A triangle has three angles"). An analytic statement says nothing about the real world.

ANTHROPOMORPHIC Literally, "in the form of man." The projection of human qualities onto nonhuman objects (e.g., nature, animals, deities). For instance, the Greek gods and goddesses were anthropomorphic, possessing all the physical, mental, and emotional characteristics of mortals.

ANTINOMIAN Literally, "against the law." In the widest sense, refers to those who deliberately choose to exist outside the accepted BTF-patterns of their society. (See pp. 33ff.) In Western religion, the word is often used to refer to religious groups which, considering themselves saved by their faith or special knowledge, hold that they are then above all laws and restrictions.

APOCALYPTIC A specific movement in Western religious thought and literature purporting to reveal the (heretofore hidden) divine plan of history. In the four great Western religions (Zoroastrianism, Judaism, Christianity, and Islam), apocalyptic literature moves within the framework of a cosmic battle taking place between the forces of Good and the forces of Evil, detailing dramatic events in the struggle, and revealing the future progress of the conflict to the eschaton or end-time. See TELEOCOSMOS.

A PRIORI In epistemology, a kind of knowledge not derived from, or dependent upon, experience. Rather, it is a universal and necessary knowledge, such as $7 + 5 = 12$. Kant held that time, too, is a priori; the mind *brings time to* its experience of objects/events and does not derive its notion of time from experience of anything in the real world. Time, that is to say, is *prior to* experience. (Don't confuse a priori knowledge with the notion of "innate ideas" which we are supposedly born with.)

ARGUMENT, PHILOSOPHICAL A sort of dialectical conversation, carried on with others or oneself, by which one attempts to clarify his thinking, especially to clarify the validity of the fact-claims used to support particular ideas or statements. A philosophical argument is not an ego-argument.

ARISTOCENTRIC Refers to an inordinate claim to a position of superiority, for oneself or one's group. From the Greek *aristos* (superlative of *agathos,* "good") meaning "the best of its kind" or "the most to be valued." Aristocentric claims are most often made in behalf of one's ethnic group or "race," one's tribe or nation, or one's religion. See pp. 89–96.

ATHEISM A denial of theism (a-theism); the explicit conclusion that God or gods do not exist. Often a positive statement that the hypothesis of supernatural beings is not required to account for anything observed in human experience.

AUTHORITARIANISM The claim on the part of an individual or institution to be a special source of trustworthy knowledge. In epistemology, the position that our most dependable information derives from, or is validated by, some particular authority. Contrasts with the position that knowledge is best validated by personal experience.

AUTHORITY In epistemology, one of the four basic sources of knowledge. Knowledge which we accept on the authority of others. See pp. 157f.

AUTONOMY The capacity for self-determination; the freedom to operate in terms of one's own volition. Also, functioning harmoniously as an integrated self rather than merely responding inconsistently to disparate environmental stimuli. "Autonomy means the capacity of the individual to make valid choices of his behavior in the light of his needs" (Gail and Snell Putney, *The Adjusted American*).

AXIOLOGY A branch of philosophy concerned with the study of values, their origin and nature.

BELIEF (Unthinking) acceptance of an idea or system of ideas—that is, "blind belief." As in "I *believe* it. Don't confuse me with the facts!" Contrasts with *faith.*

BIOCOSMOS The conception of a universe which would include life as inherent and natural; that is, a cosmos in which life-forms are an integral factor in the overall process of cosmic evolution.

BIOGENESIS The general term for the study of the origin of life. There have been numerous biogenetic theories. ARCHEBIOSIS (chemical evolution) is the theory that life develops from inorganic compounds whenever conditions permit it, both on the earth and (probably) throughout the cosmos.

PANSPERMIA (or transmission) suggests that life drifted to earth from some other world, perhaps in meteorites. SPONTANEOUS GENERATION suggests that fully developed species are produced from nonliving matter. HYLOZOISM is the theory that all matter is alive. CREATIONISM is the theory that life originates only through an act of the supernatural. See pp. 352f.

BRAHMAN A Hindu doctrine of absolute and supreme Reality, as compared with the unreal and illusory nature of this world; Ultimate Reality itself; pure being.

BTF-PATTERNS An abbreviation for Behavior, Thought, and Feeling patterns, the basic elements which together constitute selves and societies.

CAUSALITY An assumption that certain events cause or produce subsequent events. This is an axiomatic assumption of naturalism and a working assumption of science: that nothing happens without prior cause and that the cause-effect principle applies universally.

COHERENCE-TEST A truth-test which states that any fact-claim which coheres with previously accepted facts can be considered to be true.

CONCEPT A mental construct containing all the objects/events which one has classed together according to selected common properties; an abstraction. Contrast with PERCEPT: we have percepts of particular objects/events (*this* seashell, *this* panda, *this* orbit), while a concept is a generalized notion to which the singular object/events belong (seashell, panda, orbit). Most common nouns are concepts.

CONTEXTUALISM In ethics, the school of thought which holds that relevant ethical decisions can be made only within the context of a particular ethical problem where the unique factors of the situation can be taken into account. Contrast with ethical FORMALISM.

CONTINGENT In epistemology, a hypothesis or conclusion which is not *necessarily* true. A conclusion which, being derived from empirical observation, is only probably true. All robins' eggs are *probably* blue, but they are not *necessarily* blue. Contrast with necessary knowledge. See DEDUCTION.

CORRESPONDENCE-TEST A truth-test (developed primarily by Bertrand Russell) which can be used whenever empirical observation is possible. It states that if there is a high degree of correspondence between a (subjective) idea or statement and an (objective) object/event, then the concept can be considered true.

COSMOLOGICAL ARGUMENT An argument for the existence of God, first proposed by Aristotle and further developed by Aquinas. The argument is based on the assumption that causality is absolute and real. Every event must be preceded by another event which is its cause. But it is impossible to think of an infinite regress of causal events. Therefore, there must have been a first cause, an Uncaused Cause which started off this domino-chain of events; this First Cause is defined as God. See p. 517.

COSMOLOGY The study of the nature and structure of the universe. Sometimes used to refer to the study of the origin of the universe, though more correctly this is termed *cosmogony*.

COSMOS From the Greek *kosmos*, "the world" or "the ordered universe." Refers to the entire universe considered as a single, harmonious order; a Gestalt world-system.

CREATIONISM The theory that life originated through an act of the supernatural; carries the implication that life cannot originate through other means. (Theory is not limited to any particular account of life-origins). For various creationist theories see pp. 366ff.

DEDUCTION In logic, the process of drawing out (explicating, making explicit) the implications of one or more premises or statements. Deductive conclusions necessarily follow from the premises. (All bitter fruit is poisonous. Manzanillas are bitter fruit. Therefore, manzanillas are necessarily poisonous.) In deductive logic, the conclusion can be valid (if it has been correctly inferred) and yet be false because the starting premises were false. But if the premises are true and the conclusion is correctly inferred, then the conclusion *must* be both valid and true.

DETERMINISM The assumption or doctrine that every event in the universe has a prior cause and that all effects are at least theoretically predictable if all the causes are known.

DIALECTIC From the Greek *dialektike*, "to converse." The attempt to clarify thought and arrive at facts through a back-and-forth sort of conversation. See ARGUMENT. Also, a thought-process (associated with and propounded by Hegel) wherein ideas attempt to grow and complete themselves through a three-beat rhythm of thesis, antithesis, and synthesis; a back-and-forth progressive movement of thought.

DOUBT, METHODICAL A philosophical method of deliberately disbelieving any idea in order to force it to prove its truth-value with empirical facts and/or rational argument. A way of making fact-claims prove their credentials and of preventing them from being accepted uncritically. Methodical doubt is a helpful corrective to our tendency to take ideas for granted.

DUALISM The view that there exist two related entities, neither of which can be reduced to or identified with the other. In psychology, dualism implies that mind and body are separate entities, different in kind, and that neither can be explained in terms of the other. Metaphysical dualism is the position that there are two orders of reality (usually assumed to be the natural and supernatural), each of which is a distinct and irreducible order.

ECSTASY Greek *ek-stasis*, "standing outside" (of oneself). A mystical mode of consciousness found in almost every religion in which the self is considered to have been displaced by a possessing spirit (usually a good spirit) which brings about a trance or frenzied condition considered to have ultimate religious significance.

EGOCENTRIC ILLUSION An epistemological condition: the fact that each of us perceives himself to be the hub and center of the cosmos, though in reality none of us is such a center. From a perceptual standpoint, the universe would appear to revolve around every perceiving creature, human and nonhuman alike. See pp. 88f.

EGOCENTRIC PREDICAMENT A term coined by the American philosopher Ralph Barton Perry to describe the epistemological fact that each of us is limited to our own perceptual world and cannot move beyond perception to know what the real world is like as it exists apart from perception. Some extreme idealists (e.g., Berkeley) assess this predicament and proceed to the conclusion that the inexperiencible world doesn't exist. Realists usually accept the predicament as a nuisance but proceed to develop a structure of probable facts about the real world which (they assume) lies beyond direct perception.

ÉLAN VITAL Literally, "vital impulse." Term used by Henri Bergson to refer to the impulse-to-life, which, he theorized, directs evolution upward toward the development of higher, more complex forms of life.

EMPATHY The capacity on the part of any creature—man or animal—to assess correctly what another creature is experiencing but without itself sharing the experience. Empathy implies understanding of, but not participation in, another's inner world. See p. 263.

EMPIRICAL In philosophy, the word *empirical* is used in at least two distinct ways. (1) It refers to knowledge acquired by our senses only. Any other knowledge (facts derived by reason, for instance) is not empirical. An "empiricist" would be one who tends to trust the senses (over reason) as our basic source of trustworthy information. In science, there is frequently the added implication that the sense data must be "public facts," that is, subject to repeated experiment and verification. (2) "Empirical" is often used to refer to *any* knowledge gained by *any* human experience (not merely sense experience). This wider definition would include dreams, emotions, religious experiences, and so on; any knowledge derived from these experiences would be called empirical.

EPISTEMIC NAIVETY The condition of one who accepts uncritically his own vast accumulation of data, not yet having come to terms with the contradictions, fictions, and fallacies which are to be found in any large accumulation of disparate fact-claims.

EPISTEMIC Shortened form of epistemological.

EPISTEMOLOGY Branch of philosophy which studies human knowledge. It analyzes the sources of knowledge, processes of thought, truth-tests, fact-claims, value-judgments, etc. A study of what we truly know and don't know.

ESCHATOLOGY Literally, the doctrine of "last things." One's ideas regarding the final events at the "end of time." The Western Zoroastrian-Judaic family of religions holds that history will end through the intervention of supernatural forces. See TELEOCOSMOS and APOCALYPTIC.

ESP Extrasensory perception. See PSI.

ESSENCE The qualities without which any particular object/event would not exist or would be a distinctly different kind of object/event. The qualities necessary for anything to be what it is. (Existentialists are especially concerned to point out that objects may have essences, but that man does not. See pp. 234f.)

ETHNOCENTRISM A sociological term referring to the universal tendency of social groups—tribes, nations, races, cultures, religions—to take their own superiority for granted. See ARISTOCENTRISM.

ETHICS Branch of philosophy which analyzes notions of right and wrong in human relationships. Normative ethics attempts to establish ideals for intent and behavior. The field of ethics is theoretical, in contrast to morality, which refers to one's actual behavior relative to standards by which such behavior is judged to be right and wrong.

EXISTENCE In existentialism, the word *existence* refers to one's experience of vivid, concrete reality in the living present. Often it carries the connotation of being profoundly aware that one is; that to exist is living in, emphasizing, experiencing fully, being intensely involved in the conscious present.

EXISTENTIALISM School of philosophy emerging from the dehumanizing conditions of World War II, but having deep historical roots, especially in the writings of Søren Kierkegaard (1813–1855). Existentialism emphasizes the uniqueness and freedom of the individual person and argues that each person must take full responsibility for his own existence and to "create himself." Most existentialists hold that existence can have meaning only as one participates fully in life. A central motif in existential thought is "the individual versus the crowd."

FACT An idea or statement about which one can feel a high degree of certainty *because,* having been doubted and then subjected to logical and empirical analysis, it still stands. A true idea or statement.

FACT-CLAIM Any idea submitted as a candidate for consideration as an item of human knowledge. In epistemology, a fact-claim becomes a fact only after it has been carefully checked with the truth-tests and logical analysis and has passed muster; only then does it deserve to be called a "fact."

FAITH In philosophical usage, the capacity which enables one to act upon the best facts that he possesses, although they are incomplete and there is no signed guarantee of satisfactory results. In a general sense, faith is the courage to proceed to live—to exist as fully as possible—in terms of possibilities and probabilities rather than absolutes and certainties. Contrast with *belief.*

FALLACY An error in reasoning. In logic, a conclusion arrived at by means of inaccurate reasoning. A logical mistake.

FATALISM The doctrine that every event of our lives is predetermined and that no amount of effort on our part can change anything or make any difference. The source of the predetermination is usually attributed to some vaguely conceived notion of natural causation, though it can be attributed to divine causes. (Originally "fatalism" was inflicted by the three Greek Fates or goddesses of destiny.) Fatalism can be both a mood and a rationalization for submission to conditions over which one feels he has no control.

FINITE Limited. In theology, a limited deity; one that is not omnipotent.

FORMALISM In ethics, the position that there are universal ethical standards that apply to all men; such "laws" are often believed to have been revealed by a deity. Formalistic ethics contrasts with both RELATIVISM and CONTEXTUALISM, which hold that no such universal laws exist.

FREE WILL The theory that man's will is free to make authentic choices that are not predetermined; an affirmation that man's feeling of freedom is accurate and that our choices made between options are genuine decisions. Free will is the doctrine that, somehow, the human consciousness is not subject to the same causal principles which the scientist assumes to operate in the rest of the physical world. Some solution to the controversy over free will versus determinism is a precondition to any discussion of ethics and responsibility. See pp. 239ff.

GOD Roughly synonymous with Ultimate Reality or Ultimate Being. In philosophy the existence of a deity would be a hypothesis developed to account for empirical data or to be supported by rational arguments. It would not be, as in religious systems, the object of uncritical belief.

HEDONISM In ethics, the doctrine that pleasure is the ultimate goal of life which does and should determine our behavior. Philosophical hedonists (e.g., Bentham and Mill) held that man labors under "two sovereign masters": pleasure and pain. Life should be devoted to the avoidance of pain and the augmentation of pleasure, for self and others.

HYLOZOISM Theory held by the earliest Greek philosophers that all matter is alive or in some way possesses life.

IDEALISM Idealism is the theory that reality is primarily mental rather than material; it consists of mind (or Mind), minds, ideas, or selves. There are numerous brands of idealism, no two quite alike. Plato was an idealist since he believed that "ideas" exist in the cosmos quite apart from brains. Christians are similarly idealistic if they believe that "ideas" or "eternal verities" exist in the mind of God. Berkeley was an idealist since he believed that only minds (God's and ours) exist. Hegel was an idealist because he believed the Absolute Mind (a superlogical God of sorts) permeates human activity and that we can "think God's thoughts." Mary Baker Eddy, the founder of Christian Science, was an idealist because she believed that we all exist within the Mind of God, the only Reality. Eastern religions such as Hinduism and Buddhism are idealisms since they hold that life's true purpose (for instance, Zen *satori*, "awareness," or the trance-state of *nirvana*) is achieved only through an odyssey of the mind. Shankara's teaching that this world is maya ("illusion"), "comparable to foam, a mirage, a dream," makes this interpretation of Vedanta the Eastern world's most extreme philosophical idealism.

IMPLY To make statements from which logical inferences can be drawn, but without explicitly stating them. The process of drawing out implications is termed INFERENCE. In everyday usage there is much confusion between *infer* and *imply*. See LOGIC.

INDUCTION In logic, the process of developing generalized explanations, hypotheses, or laws from a collection of facts. Induction is the commonest of our daily procedures for gathering knowledge. It includes the hasty generalizations we are prone to make based upon very limited experience (that is, an inadequate collection of related facts). Inductive conclusions are never necessary (as are deductive conclusions), but only probable. See DEDUCTION, CONTINGENT, and pp. 159f.

INFERENCE An idea which the mind is forced to create after having seen the implications of certain propositions. One infers—draws out, makes explicit—what is implied in a set of premises. The branch of philosophy called logic studies the rules by which we can infer ideas correctly from given premises.

INTUITION (1) A source of knowledge—ideas, remembered facts, hypotheses, solutions to problems—which seem to emerge from the subconscious mind, apparently produced through activity of the subconscious before appearing in the light of consciousness. See pp. 160f. (2) Term used by Bergson to describe the only method he believed could give us an accurate understanding of reality; a process of "intellectual empathy" through which we can understand the duration or unbroken continuum which in fact constitutes physical reality. See p. 421.

INVALID (in·val'id, not in'va·lid) Refers to an idea which has not been inferred correctly; a fallacious conclusion produced by faulty reasoning.

LOGIC Branch of philosophy defined as the study of valid inference; systematic analysis of the correct and incorrect processes of reasoning.

MACROCOSM Refers to man's particular vantage point as he views, and attempts to comprehend, the universe. The macrocosm is man's experiential level of reality as he looks up and down, so to speak: up at cosmic realities (cosmos) and down at microscopic realities (microcosm). Without the aid of instruments man is caught at the macrocosmic level since neither cosmos nor microcosm is directly perceivable.

MATERIALISM The doctrine that everything in the universe is nothing other than various manifestations of matter-in-motion, and, in theory, can be reduced to, and explained by, principles of causality. All the objects/events for which we have such diverse labels—matter, mind, energy, life, and perhaps spirit—are only variant forms of matter-in-motion.

MAYA The Hindu doctrine that this world is unreal; it is mere illusion. All we know are the illusory surface appearances of things. If the material world is unreal, only Brahman or Ultimate Reality is truly real.

METAPHYSICS A branch of philosophy concerned with what actually exists, that is, with what the true nature of things really is. Traditionally, metaphysics has been divided into two subbranches: ONTOLOGY, the study of being, and COSMOLOGY, the study of the cosmos (cosmology is now generally thought of as a branch of astronomy). See ONTOLOGY.

MONISM Any world-view which purports to reduce all existence to a single order of reality; the doctrine that there is but one order of reality, whether it be mind (which would be called "psychical monism") or matter-in-motion ("naturalistic monism"), or some other kind of reality.

MORAL Refers to the way one overtly behaves in his relationships with others. In the most general sense, moral behavior is intended to produce, somewhere, somehow, constructive results; immoral behavior is intended to produce destructive results. Contrast with ETHICS, which is the theoretical study of ideal (normative) relationships.

MYSTIC One who seeks or one who experiences dissolution of ego-self and separateness and feels that his being has merged or become united with Deity, Ultimate Reality, or Nature.

MYSTICISM The school of religion which values the mode of consciousness in which the ego-self is lost and an experience of oneness with Ultimate Reality is attained. Epistemologically, the mystic commonly claims that only through a mystical experience—as opposed to rational or empirical inquiry—can reality be known.

MYTH A story or account, by definition involving some element of the supernatural, which is accepted by a community as a satisfactory answer to, or explanation of, some meaningful question or experience. Historically, myths are held collectively by religious communities, tribes, nations, or the like; but a story can perform the same function for an individual, in which case use of the term *myth* is justifiable. See pp. 497ff.

NAIVE REALISM The uncritical acceptance of one's sense data as representing accurately the nature of the real world; a sort of "blind faith" in what one's senses seem to tell him.

NATURALISM The world-view which holds that there is but a single order of reality, that of matter-in-motion. Naturalism, by definition, excludes the existence of a "supernatural" order of reality.

NIHILISM In epistemology, the doctrine that nothing is knowable, or is worth knowing; the contention that all knowledge is illusory, relative, and meaningless. Similarly, in ethics, nihilism is the doctrine that all moral judgments are irrational, relative, and, finally, meaningless. In a word, nihilism is the belief that there is no knowledge, no value, and no meaning that is of any real worth to man.

NIRVANA A mode of consciousness valued by the Buddhist and Hindu as the supreme goal of human existence. Literally, "extinction of consciousness," but better conceived as a state of consciousness described as an experience of wholeness, peace, and joy. In Hindu and Buddhist doctrine this mode of consciousness will continue after death for one who has reached the point of liberation (*moksha*) from the Wheel of Karma—the "round of rebirths."

OBJECTIVE Refers to whatever exists in the real world apart from our perception of it. Having to do with the perceived object as opposed to the perceiving subject. See SUBJECTIVE.

OCCAM'S RAZOR (Also called the Principle of Parsimony.) One of the fundamental principles of scientific method. It states that, all else being equal, the simplest explanation is the best. That is, in developing inductive hypotheses, the simplest hypothesis which accounts for all relevant data is more likely to be true. Named after the scholastic philosopher William of Occam, who phrased it: "The number of entities should not be needlessly increased."

ONTOLOGICAL ARGUMENT A logical argument for the existence of God developed by St. Anselm of Canterbury (1033–1109). Anselm attempted to prove the existence of God from the nature of thought alone. See pp. 518f.

ONTOLOGY From the Greek *ontos,* "being," and *logos,* "study of." Branch of philosophy which studies the nature of reality or being, especially as applied to living things. The term ontological is commonly used to emphasize the fact that some specific quality is an inescapable aspect of life itself. The fear of death, for instance, is said to be ontological since there is no way—short of the extinction of consciousness—to escape the fear. We could repress it, but the fear would remain a part of our being, buried precariously in the unconscious, where it can become a powerful but unrecognized cause of puzzling behavior.

PANPSYCHISM The doctrine that everything is composed of, or contains, mind or "soul" (*psyche*). Some Western thinkers have speculated that the binding forces within atoms might be, in some way, the operations of mind.

PANSPERMIA The biogenetic theory that life may have developed on earth after having been transferred from other worlds, perhaps by meteorites. See BIOGENESIS, pp. 352f.

PANTHEISM The doctrine that God is All. Pantheists usually hold that God is in all matter or that the totality of all matter is "the body of God."

PARADOX A condition where two mutually exclusive ideas or statements appear to be true; and until the arrival of further data or some sort of resolution, both ideas or statements must be accepted and acted upon.

PARSIMONY, PRINCIPLE OF See OCCAM'S RAZOR.

PERCEPT The first-stage result of the mind's organization of sense data. The mind perceives a concrete object—*this* coin or *this* car—which remains in consciousness as an unnamed, singular object. A percept (or perception) is what is given in consciousness, the object of cognition. Contrast with CONCEPT, in which objects are mentally classed with other objects, and the mind henceforth thinks of the class rather than the object. Contrast also with SENSE DATUM, a raw, unorganized sense-response.

PHILOSOPHY The love of wisdom. From Greek *philein* ("to love") and *sophia* ("wisdom"). Philosophy comprises several distinct disciplines or methods which have in common the goal of improving upon the condition of human knowledge and our knowledge of the human condition.

PLURALISM The world-view holding that there exist more than two orders of reality, each of which is distinct and irreducible. For instance, if one believes that the universe is composed of matter, mind, spirit, and divine-essence, then he would be a pluralist. Compare with MONISM and DUALISM.

PRAGMATIC-TEST The truth-test (developed primarily by William James) which states that if an idea or statement "works"—that is, brings about desirable results—then the idea or statement can be considered true. James held that the truth-value of any idea is to be judged in terms of the results it can produce. See pp. 159ff.

PRAGMATIC PARADOX A human condition in which an idea must be believed to be true in terms of correspondence—that is, one must be convinced that some object/event exists as a real entity—before the idea can be considered to be true on the pragmatic-test. For example, one must believe that immortality exists as a real event (which, one must believe, could be empirically checked, under the right conditions, with the correspondence-test) before the belief in immortality can produce positive results in his life. If he believed it to be true solely on the pragmatic-test, it would in fact *not* be true because it wouldn't "work." See pp. 200ff.

PRAGMATISM An American school of philosophy associated mainly with William James and John Dewey. One of its central themes is that philosophy should be put to work solving the more pressing human problems instead of preoccupying itself in metaphysical speculations. See pp. 42f. According to the pragmatists, truth is tentative and forever changing; truth is the quality of whatever ideas "work" at the present time. See p. 33.

PRECOGNITION Having knowledge of an event supposedly before it happens. See PSI.

PREDESTINATION A theological term referring to divine predeterminism. The doctrine that God has already determined (at least) whether each human soul will be saved or lost, or (at most) that every singular event of existence will occur as planned. A "hard" predestination logically excludes the possibility of free will. See pp. 240ff.

PREDICAMENT A problem condition to which, by definition, there is no solution; a situation which must be accepted. One may be able to deal productively with problems arising from a predicament (e.g., *fear* of nonbeing), but not with the predicament itself (that each of us faces nonbeing).

PREMISE In logic, an idea or statement which, along with other ideas or statements, can lead to a conclusion. In reasoning, a premise is a starting statement, an opener.

PRIMAL FREEDOM Freedom from subjective limitations, thereby enabling one to make authentic choices; freedom from primal limitations. See pp. 242ff.

PRIMARY QUALITIES In epistemology, the qualities, according to John Locke, which inhere in real objects: e.g., weight, motion, shape, extension. Compare with SECONDARY QUALITIES.

PSI Refers to all parapsychological or "paranormal" experiences. Among them: TELEPATHY, the sending of messages (ideas and/or feelings) from one mind to another; CLAIRVOYANCE, the mind's "seeing" an object/event at a distance; PSYCHOKINESIS (PK), "mind over matter," the power of the mind to influence the behavior of objects; PRECOGNITION, knowledge of an event (supposedly) before it takes place. ESP (Extrasensory Perception) is a rough synonym for PSI, though we do not know at present whether such experiences (if they do in fact occur) are truly *extra*sensory

PSYCHE Greek word meaning "soul"; usually thought of as a substantialized, objectified form of the self, though in earlier times and other places the word has been given a bewildering variety of meanings.

PSYCHOKINESIS The power of the mind to influence directly the behavior of objects/events. See PSI.

RATIONAL Roughly synonymous with "reasonable"; the capacity to engage in reasoned inquiry.

RATIONALISM In epistemology, a philosophical tradition that holds that our most dependable information derives from reason rather than from empirical observation. A rationalist is one who trusts reason more than the deceptive "rabble of the senses."

RATIONALIZE The process of developing reasons ("rationales") for holding certain beliefs or performing certain actions—reasons which are not the true reasons but which are more acceptable than the true reasons. One who is subjectively naive will thus delude himself as well as others; one who is subjectively aware may reserve his rationales only for others. By definition, a rationalization is a fallacy engaged in out of need to defend one's thoughts, feelings, or actions. (Don't confuse with RATIONALISM.)

REAL, REALISM Among the most important terms in philosophy. To be real is to exist apart from perception. If I state that the teakwood figurine of the Buddha on my desk is "real," then I am stating the belief that the figurine exists as a "thing-in-itself" quite apart from my perception of it; if I were not perceiving it in any way whatsoever, it would still exist. (This position is *material realism,* and modern use of the term is often restricted to this meaning; *real* therefore refers to material objects or the the physical world in general.) If I should go further and claim that the Cosmic Buddha exists, quite apart from my perception of him (or It), then this is a *theological realism.* If I claim that beauty exists in the orchid or rainbow, apart from my perception (that is, I close my eyes but I am convinced that "beauty" still remains in the rainbow), then I am an *esthetic realist.* Lastly, if I claim that right and wrong (or Good and Evil) actually exist in the real world, then I am a *value realist* or an *ethical realist.*

In common parlance we speak of dreams, headaches, fears, bad vibrations, etc. as "real." "They are *my* realities," we contend. "Don't tell me my head doesn't hurt. My headache is real!" But the headache is not real, as the term is used in philosophy: the headache certainly does not exist apart from your perception of it.

REALITY In epistemology, the totality of all things that exist apart from perception. The real world. See REAL, REALISM. In social science, a fabric of BTF-patterns shared by members of a particular society; all that is *considered* to be real by that social group.

REASON One of many kinds of thinking (others being remembering, day-dreaming, intuiting, dreaming, etc.). The mental process of using known facts to arrive at new facts. In logic, the activity of inferring conclusions from premises.

RELATIVISM In ethics, the belief, based on empirical observation, that what is considered to be right and wrong differs from one society to another and from one person to another. The term usually implies that there are no universal codes of right and wrong. Contrast with FORMALISM. (Don't confuse with Einstein's RELATIVITY.)

RELATIVITY In physics, Einstein's theories of special (1905) and general (1916) relativity. Roughly, a system of mathematics and physics which predicts the behavior of matter-in-motion at high speeds. (Don't confuse with ethical RELATIVISM.)

SAMADHI Literally, "concentration"; a form of meditation. In Hinduism and Buddhism, a trancelike mode of consciousness wherein the mind achieves a blissful, contentless, transpersonal state; the attainment of *atman,* or authentic self-essence.

SATORI In Zen Buddhism, the "moment of awakening" when a mediator realizes the illusory nature of self and separateness; a holistic feeling of mystical oneness. See pp. 217ff.

SCHOLASTICISM A movement in Western ecclesiastical history beginning c. A.D. 1100 and flowering during the thirteenth century, resulting from the recovery of the Greek classics and the revitalized use of rational inquiry following the Dark Ages. A period of renewed intellectual activity within the framework of the accepted truths of medieval Catholic religion. Among the great scholastic philosophers (the "schoolmen") were Anselm of Canterbury, Bernard of Clairvaux, Peter Abelard, Albertus Magnus, and Thomas Aquinas.

SCHOLASTIC METHOD Specifically, the use of reason by the scholastic philosophers, not to discover truth but to explore, explicate, and defend *known* (i.e., revealed) truths. The truths themselves were not subject to doubt or inquiry. See pp. 24ff.

SECONDARY FREEDOM The capacity to make genuine choices without being limited by external restrictions (e.g., economic, social, political). Contrast secondary limitations (which are objective) with primal limitations (which are subjective). See PRIMAL FREEDOM, pp. 242ff.

SECONDARY QUALITIES According to John Locke, qualities which do not inhere in objects/events but are subjective sensations (e.g., color, sound, taste) Compare with PRIMARY QUALITIES.

SELF The conscious subject which experiences, designated by "I" or "ego." The word has frequently been used to refer to some unknown entity which unifies the data of consciousness into a coherent, operational system. Self, however, may be better conceived as the coherent system rather than some hypothetical unifying entity. An ambiguous and problematic concept.

SELF-DETERMINATION In psychology and ethics, the position that one's personal BTF-patterns have antecedent causes, but that such causes may reside within oneself and not in the environment. We can become "self-caused." Self-determination is a middle position between an extreme free will position which denies determinism and a behavioristic position which denies free will.

SEMANTICS Broadly, the study of meaning. A study of the total response of the human organism to symbols of all sorts (words, signs, gestures, etc.). In a narrow sense, the study of words and their meanings.

SENSATION The immediate response of the senses to stimuli. A synonym for SENSE DATUM. (*Sensation* does not refer to emotional responses.)

SENSE DATA Immediate sensory responses as registered in consciousness—patches of color, bits of sound—which are synthesized by the mind into the perception of an object. Sense data (singular, *datum*) are the first raw materials of experience which make their way from our sense receptors to the interpretive areas of the brain, where they are organized into perceptions of particular objects.

SKEPTICISM In epistemology, an attitude of doubt; either a deliberate methodical doubt to force fact-claims to prove themselves or a general doctrine of philosophical agnosticism, a sincere doubt that accurate knowledge is possible.

SOLIPSISM The doctrine that only "I" (the solipsist, of course) exist. A logical (but quite illogical) inference from the conclusion that all we can truly know are our own experiences.

SOUL Roughly, a substantialized, objectified notion of the self. See PSYCHE.

SUBJECTIVE Refers to the subject which experiences, as opposed to the object which is experienced. The term refers to the location of events which constitute the experiencing process (subjective), as opposed to the events which belong to the real world (objective).

SUBSTANCE The ultimate "stuff" (Greek *physis*) of which any object is made; the underlying reality to which primary qualities adhere. The word *substance* is a label applied to the *assumption* that there is a continuing essence in any object which remains immutable through all ephemeral changes in its "perceivable" qualities.

SUMMUM BONUM In ethics, the Ultimate Good of human existence; that is, the final goal toward which all our endeavors should be directed. Various such goals have been proposed: happiness, pleasure, self-actualization, ethical love, soul-salvation, etc.

SUPERNATURAL An order of reality above and outside the natural order. In philosophy, the supernatural is not the object of religious belief; supernaturalists would contend that it is necessary to postulate such an order to account for the complex data of experience. Contrast with NATURALISM; see also MONISM, DUALISM.

SYMPATHY Literally, "to suffer with" another. The capacity not merely to understand what another is experiencing (which is EMPATHY), but the actual duplication, so to speak, in one's own experience of what another is experiencing. See p. 263.

SYNOPTIC From the Greek *sun-optikos,* "seeing the whole together" or "taking a comprehensive view." The attempt to achieve an all-inclusive overview of one's subject matter and to see all its parts in relationship to one another.

TAO In Chinese religion, "The Way"; a sort of cosmic pathway that lies between or within the interactions of the energy-modes Yang and Yin. To discover the Tao is to begin to live in perfect harmony with self and cosmos.

TELEOCOSMOS From the Greek *teleos,* "finished" or "complete" implying purposive design and goal-directed movement; and *kosmos,* "an ordered universe." A world-view with a program which moves with direction and purpose, and in which man plays a major role. The most noteworthy teleocosmic world-views belong to man's religions and resemble cosmic dramas in structure, including a full cast of characters—protagonists and antagonists, gods and demons, supporting roles and bit players—and carefully designed plots leading to a dramatic climax and a dénouement. Man's role is the central element of teleocosmic dramas, though this fact may be obscured by large-scale cosmic events which occur as the drama unfolds. See pp. 500ff.

TELEOLOGICAL ARGUMENT An argument for the existence of God based on the apparent purposive nature of evolutionary movement and/or the design and order of the universe. Order implies an orderer; design implies a designer. The American Personalists considered this to be the strongest empirical argument for the existence of God. See pp. 519f.

TELEOLOGY From the Greek *teleos,* "finished" or "complete." The theory that deliberate purposive activity, rather than mere chance, is involved in some process. The interpretation of any series of events—such as an organism's growth, evolution, or human history—as expressions of purposeful movement; goal-directed, as though planned out and guided toward a present end or ideal. See pp. 359ff.

TELEPATHY Communication of mind with mind via supposedly extrasensory media. See PSI.

THEISM Belief in gods or God. Often used to mean belief in a specific Western doctrine of an omnipotent, omniscient, and personal Deity. Contrast with atheism, the denial that gods or God exist.

THEOLOGY The rational organization of religious beliefs and practices in order to render them logically coherent and meaningful. Theology is an intellectual discipline in contrast to religion which involves one's whole being.

TIME DILATION A phenomenon predicted by Einstein's special theory of relativity: for any object moving at great velocities (relative to the speed of light) time would slow down. See pp. 437ff.

TRUTH "Truth is the approximation of thought to reality" (Brand Blanshard). Truth is a quality possessed by ideas and statements, a quality which is of value to a philosopher only after having been carefully checked with one or more of the truth-tests. The notion of an ethereal, nonspecific (and untestable) truth is meaningless.

VALID In logic, a technical term referring to a conclusion which has been correctly inferred from specific premises.

Validity is the property of an idea or statement which has been correctly derived by logical inference.

VITALISM The doctrine that a "life principle" must suffuse itself (or be injected) into inorganic matter before life-processes can begin. What this "vital" element might be is usually unspecified, but it is often associated with the supernatural.

WORLD-VIEW In a broad sense, one's philosophy of life; an all-inclusive, coherent way of looking at life and the cosmos. From the German *Weltan-schauung,* a sort of unconscious, totalic fabric into which one incorporates all his experiences and through which he sees the world.

CREDITS

I. REFERENCES

Whenever possible, paperback editions have been used since they will usually be more accessible and convenient.

xviii From *A Concise Introduction to Philosophy*, by William Halverson, pp. 18f. Copyright © 1967 by Random House, Inc. Reprinted by permission of the publisher.

1-1

4 Alexei Panshin, *Rite of Passage* (Ace SF, 1968), p. 252.

5 From *The Little Prince* by Antoine de Saint-Exupéry, translated by Katherine Woods, pp. 72f., copyright 1943, 1971, by Harcourt Brace Jovanovich, Inc., and reprinted with their permission.

7 Viktor E. Frankl, *Man's Search for Meaning* (Washington Square, 1963), pp. 167f. Copyright © 1959, 1962 by Viktor E. Frankl. Reprinted by permission of Beacon Press.

From *Out of My Life and Thought* by Albert Schweitzer. Translated by C. T. Campion. Copyright 1933, 1949, © 1961 by Holt, Rinehart and Winston, Inc. Reprinted by permission of Holt, Rinehart, and Winston, Inc.

8 Reprinted from *Psychology Today* Magazine, August 1970, p. 16. Copyright © Ziff-Davis Publishing Company.

9 Gordon Allport. Frankl, *Man's Search for Meaning*, pp. ix–xiii. Reprinted by permission of Beacon Press.

12 Desmond Morris, *The Naked Ape* (McGraw-Hill, 1967), pp. 187, 189, 156, 159.

Konrad Lorenz, *On Aggression* (Bantam, 1967), p. 233. Reprinted by permission of Harcourt Brace Jovanovich, Inc.

15 From "The Undersea World of Jacques Cousteau: The Night of the Squid," ABC-TV, telecast April 12, 1970.

16 René Dubos, *The Torch of Life* (Pocket Books, 1962), p. 15. Reprinted by permission of Trident Press, a division of Simon & Schuster, Inc.

Abraham Maslow, *New Knowledge in Human Values* (Harper, 1959), pp. 123, 126.

17 Program notes by E. C. Stone for the London recording of Richard Strauss' *Also Sprach Zarathustra*, by the Vienna Philharmonic Orchestra, conducted by Herbert von Karajan. (Final italics added.)

From "The Sands of Time," by Robert Wright and George Forrest. Copyright © 1953 Frank Music Corp. 119 West 57th Street, N.Y., N.Y. 10019. International copyright secured. All rights reserved. Used by permission.

1-2

20 Socrates. Plato, *The Apology*, in *The Last Days of Socrates*, trans. Hugh Tredennick (Penguin Classics, 1954), pp. 49–52. Copyright © Hugh Tredennick 1954, 1959, 1969. Reprinted by permission of Penguin Books Ltd. (The opening line of Socrates' defense is from the Jowett translation. See reference for p. 22 below.)

22 Socrates. Plato, *The Apology*, in *The Dialogues of Plato*, trans. Benjamin Jowett (Oxford, 1924).

24 Thomas: John 20:24–29. Paul: 1 Corinthians 1:20; Colossians 2:8; Galatians 3:28.

St. Augustine. Philip Schaff, *History of the Christian Church*, Vol. III, *Nicene and Post-Nicene Christianity* (Eerdmans, 1950 [1910], pp. 998, 1004.

St. Anselm. Schaff, *History*, Vol. V, *The Middle Ages* (1949 [1907]), pp. 600f.

Peter Abelard. Schaff, *History*, Vol. V, pp. 622–624.

25 Arnold J. Toynbee, *A Study of History* (Oxford, 1954), Vol. VII, pp. 729f. Reprinted by permission of Oxford University Press.

28 Socrates. Plato, *The Meno*, in *The Dialogues of Plato*, trans. Benjamin Jowett, Vol. II, p. 47.

28 A. E. Taylor, *Socrates: The Man and His Thought* (Anchor, 1953), p. 81.

Jean Brun, *Socrates* (Walker, 1962), p. 21.

29 Will Durant, *The Story of Civilization* (Simon & Schuster, 1939), Vol. II, p. 366.

30 Bert C. Williams, "On Losing One's Faith," *The Scroll* (Winter 1957), p. 4. Reprinted by permission of the author.

Aristotle. Quotation from B. A. G. Fuller and Sterling McMurrin, *History of Philosophy* (Holt, 1955), p. 172.

32 Erich Fromm, *Marx's Concept of Man* (Frederick Ungar, 1961), p. 3.

Louis Untermeyer, *Makers of the Modern World* (Simon & Schuster, 1955), p. 26.

36 Thomas Merton, *The Way of Chuang Tzu* (New Directions, 1965), p. 10. Copyright © 1965 by the Abbey of Gethsemani. Reprinted by permission of New Directions Publishing Corporation.

Justus Hartnack, *Wittgenstein and Modern Philosophy* (Doubleday Anchor, 1965), p. 8. Translation copyright © by Methuen and Co, Ltd. Reprinted by permission of Doubleday and Co., Inc.

38 Ibid., pp. 4f., 8.

1-3

51 William Harlan Hale, *The Horizon Book of Ancient Greece* (American Heritage, 1965), p. 347.

Félix Martí-Ibáñez, *Tales of Philosophy* (Dell, 1967), p. 33.

Will Durant, *The Story of Civilization* (Simon & Schuster, 1939), Vol. II, p. 523.

1-4

77   Brand Blanshard, "Limited Minds and Unlimited Knowledge." An address to the University Class at Bucknell University. From the *Bucknell University Bulletin.* Used by permission.

78   R. Buckminster Fuller, "Technology and the Human Environment." From Robert Disch (ed.), *The Ecological Conscience: Values for Survival.* Copyright © 1970, pp. 175–176. Reprinted by permission of Prentice-Hall, Inc. Englewood Cliffs, N.J.

80   Isaac Asimov, *View from a Height.* Lancer, 1974, pp. 7–10. Copyright © 1963 by Isaac Asimov. Copyright © 1959, 1960, 1961, 1962 by Mercury Press Inc. Publishers of *The Magazine of Fantasy and Science Fiction,* where these articles originally appeared.

2-1

In Part 2 my indebtedness to others is especially great. The concept of the egocentric illusion is to be found, in various contexts, throughout Toynbee's writings. While the origins of the idea must be credited to him, he is obviously in no way responsible for my elaboration of it.

A substantial amount of material throughout this book, and especially in these chapters, was developed with my wife, Barbara Taylor Christian. I have incorporated many of her observations dealing with personality and growth. Particularly helpful were her concepts on the interaction of intellectual awareness and experience in the making of growth choices and the conditions fostering development of autonomy versus alienation.

88   "The Prayer of the Little Ducks," From *Prayers from the Ark,* by Carmen Bernos de Gasztold, trans. Rumer Godden (Viking, 1962), p. 59. Copyright © 1962 by Rumer Godden. Reprinted by permission of The Viking Press, Inc.

92   Albert Camus, from the preface to *The Myth of Sisyphus* from *The Myth of Sisyphus and Other Essays,* translated by Justin O'Brien. Copyright © 1955 by Alfred A. Knopf, Inc. Reprinted by permission of the publisher.

93   Albert Camus, from the preface to *The Stranger* from *Lyrical and Critical Essays,* edited by Philip Thody, translated by Ellen Conroy Kennedy, Copyright © 1968 by Alfred A. Knopf, Inc. Copyright © 1967 by Hamish Hamilton and Alfred A. Knopf, Inc. Reprinted by permission of the publisher.

93   Paul Horton and Chester Hunt, *Sociology* (McGraw-Hill, 1964), p. 91. Copyright 1964 by McGraw-Hill. Used with permission of McGraw-Hill Book Company.

95   Milton Rokeach, *The Three Christs of Ypsilanti* (Knopf, 1964), pp. 4ff., 315, 313f. Reprinted by permission of Alfred A. Knopf, Inc.

100   Horton and Hunt, *Sociology,* p. 86. Used with permission of McGraw-Hill Book Company.

2-2

105   David Hume, *Treatise of Human Nature,* Book I, Part ii, Sec. 5.

107   Arthur W. Combs (ed.), *Perceiving, Behaving, Becoming: A New Focus for Education,* ASCD 1962 Yearbook, Washington, D.C. (Association for Supervision and Curriculum Development, 1962), p. 84. Copyright © 1962 by the Association for Supervision & Curriculum Development. All rights reserved.

Erich Fromm, *The Art of Loving* (Bantam, 1963), pp. 49ff. Copyright © Harper & Row, Publishers, Inc., and reprinted with their permission.

110   S. I. Hayakawa, "The Fully Functioning Personality," in *Symbol, Status, and Personality* (Harcourt, Brace & World, N.D.), pp. 51ff.

2-3

115   Excerpted from "The Young Monkeys" by Harry and Margaret Harlow in *Psychology Today* Magazine, September 1967. Copyright © 1967 Ziff-Davis Publishing Company.

120   Rollo May, *Love and Will* (Norton, 1969), pp. 165ff.

121   Desmond Morris, *The Naked Ape* (McGraw-Hill, 1967). See Chapter IV, "Exploration."

122   Rogers and Combs. Arthur W. Combs (ed.), *Perceiving, Behaving, Becoming: A New Focus for Education,* ASCD 1962 Yearbook, Washington, D.C. (Association for Supervision and Curriculum Development, 1962), p. 84. © 1962 by the ASCD. All rights reserved.

123   S. I. Hayakawa, "The Fully Functioning Personality," in *Symbol, Status, and Personality* (Harcourt, Brace & World, N.D.), pp. 51ff. (Italics added.)

Combs, *Perceiving, Behaving, Becoming,* pp. 141f. Reprinted by permission of ASCD Publications.

124   Alexei Panshin, *Rite of Passage* (Ace SF, 1968), pp. 241ff. Copyright © 1968 by Alexei Panshin. Used by permission of the author and Henry Morrison Inc., his agents.

126   Gregory Bateson, "Language and Psychotherapy." Quoted from Alan Watts, *Psychotherapy East and West* (Mentor, 1961), p. 105.

127   From *Stop the World—I Want to Get Off.* Words and Music by Leslie Bricusse and Anthony Newley. Copyright © 1961 TRO Essex Music Limited, London, England. Used by permission.

129   From *The Madman,* by Kahlil Gibran. Copyright 1918 by Kahlil Gibran and renewed 1946 by Administrators C.T.A. of Kahlil Gibran Estate and Mary G. Gibran. Reprinted by permission of Alfred A. Knopf, Inc.

2-4

130   William Shakespeare, *As You Like It*, Act II, Sc. 7, ll. 144ff.

134   *Developmental Psychology Today: An Introduction* (CRM Books, 1971), p. 383. From *Psychology Today: An Introduction* (Del Mar, Calif.: CRM Books), © 1970, CRM, Inc.

137   Hudson Hoagland, "Some Biochemical Considerations of Time," and Roland Fischer, "Biological Time," in J. T. Fraser (ed.), *Voices of Time* (George Braziller, 1966), pp. 325 and 360, respectively. Copyright © 1966 by J. T. Fraser. Reprinted by permission of George Braziller, Inc.

142   Sheldon Harnick, *Fiddler on the Roof.* Copyright © 1964 The New York Times Music Corp. (Sunbeam Music Division). All rights administered by the New York Times Music Corp. Used by permission.

147   Erik H. Erikson, "A Healthy Personality for Every Child," in Robert H. Anderson and Harold G. Shane (eds.), *As the Twig is Bent* (Houghton Mifflin, 1971), pp. 136f.

149   Leo Tolstoy, *The Death of Ivan Ilytch*, trans. Aylmer Maude (Oxford). Quoted from Joseph Royce, *The Encapsulated Man* (Van Nostrand, 1964), pp. 108f.

       Newsweek, January 3, 1972, p. 56.

3-1

162   J. Samuel Bois, *The Art of Awareness* (William C. Brown, 1973).

3-2

175   Buckminster Fuller, "This Is the New Invisible World," *TV Guide*, February 6–12, 1970, p. 9.

178   Dr. Willard Geer. From personal conversations. Facts confirmed in a letter dated February 7, 1974: "The loss of the lens did allow UV to get through to the retina and did alter the perception of that eye so much that whenever I enter a room where UV is used I see each UV spotlight and even its beam on its way across the room to the fluorescent paint it is exciting. In the use of the spectroscope I do see spectrum lines in the UV that others cannot see."

3-3

183   S. I. Hayakawa, *Language in Thought and Action* (Harcourt, 1963). Sections 2-9 on abstracting and classifying are heavily indebted to Chapters 10, 11, and 12 of Dr. Hayakawa's book. The story of the animals is a close paraphrase of the account found on pages 214f.

       Lincoln Barnett, *The Universe and Dr. Einstein* (Mentor, 1952), pp. 123f.

184   Hayakawa, *Language in Thought and Action*, p. 216. (Original italics removed.)

       See Ashley Montagu, *Man's Most Dangerous Myth: The Fallacy of Race* (Harper, 1952).

3-4

195   For C. S. Peirce's original article "How to Make Our Ideas Clear," see Walter G. Muelder and Laurence Sears, *The Development of American Philosophy* (Houghton Mifflin, 1940), pp. 341ff.

200   John J. McDermott (ed.), *The Writings of William James* (Modern Library, 1968), p. xxi. The introduction to this anthology contains an excellent brief biography of James.

202   S. I. Hayakawa, *Language in Thought and Action* (Harcourt, 1963), p. 223.

203   William S. and Mabel Lewis Sahakian, *Realms of Philosophy* (Schenkman, 1965), p. 41.

       "My World and Welcome to It," NBC-TV, February 23, 1970.

4-1

208   R. D. Laing, *The Politics of Experience* (Ballantine, 1967), p. 26.

214   Edward B. Fiske, "New Worldview." Reprinted with permission, from the November/December 1971 issue of *The Center Magazine*, a publication of the Center for the Study of Democratic Institutions in Santa Barbara, California, p. 20.

       William James. Quoted from Charles T. Tart (ed.), *Altered States of Consciousness* (John Wiley, 1969), p. 21.

215   Milton H. Erickson, "A Special Inquiry with Aldous Huxley into the Nature and Characteristics of Various States of Consciousness," in Tart, *Altered States of Consciousness*, pp. 45–71.

218   Erich Fromm, D. Suzuki, and di Martino, *Zen Buddhism and Psychoanalysis* (Allen & Unwin, 1960). Quoted from Tart, *Altered States of Consciousness*, p. 490.

219   From a lecture by Terry Allen and used with permission. Requested credit line: "Our Oneness—Mother the Earth . . . Father the Universe."

4-2

223   R. M. MacIver, *The Challenge of the Passing Years: My Encounter with Time* (Simon & Schuster, 1962), p. xxiii. (Italics added.)

224   A. Cornelius Benjamin, "Ideas of Time in the History of Philosophy," in J. T. Fraser (ed.), *Voices of Time* (George Braziller, 1966), p. 4. Copyright © 1966 by

J. T. Fraser. Reprinted by permission of George Braziller, Inc.

Friedrich Waismann, "Analytic-Synthetic," in Richard M. Gale (ed.), *The Philosophy of Time* (Doubleday Anchor, 1967), pp. 55f.

228   St. Augustine, *Confessions*, Book XI. (Any edition.)

229   *Sir Isaac Newton's Mathematical Principles of Natural Philosophy and His System of the World*, trans. Andrew Motte (University of California Press, 1947), p. 6. Quoted from Fraser, *Voices of Time*, p. 18.

Immanuel Kant, *Critique of Pure Reason*, trans. F. Max Müller (Doubleday Anchor, 1966), pp. 29ff.

Benjamin, in Fraser, *Voices of Time*, p. 22. Copyright © 1966 by J. T. Fraser. Reprinted by permission of George Braziller, Inc.

231   Arthur C. Clarke, *Profiles of the Future* (Bantam, 1964), p. 138.

J. B. Priestley, *Man and Time* (Dell, 1968), pp. 205, 288.

232   Louise Robinson Heath, *The Concept of Time* (University of Chicago Press, 1936), p. 199.

233   William James, *Psychology, Briefer Course* (Holt, 1892), p. 280.

Paul Fraisse, *The Psychology of Time*, trans. Jennifer Leith (Harper, 1963), pp. 84f.

236   Carl Rogers, "Toward a Theory of Creativity." From *On Becoming a Person* (Houghton Mifflin), 1961, pp. 353f.

237   Eric Berne, *Games People Play* (Grove, 1964), p. 178.

4-3

239   Carl R. Rogers and Barry Stevens, *Person to Person: The Problem of Being Human* (Real People Press, 1967), p. 47.

240   Paul: see Romans 7:15–24.

244   Bruno Bettelheim, "Joey: A 'Mechanical Boy,'" in *Frontiers of Psychological Research* (Freeman), pp. 223–229. Reprinted from *Scientific American*. Original article dated March 1959.

245   B. F. Skinner, *Beyond Freedom and Dignity* (Knopf, 1971). For similar ideas presented in fiction form, see Skinner's *Walden Two* (Macmillan, 1948).

246   Peter L. Berger, *Invitation to Sociology: A Humanistic Perspective* (Doubleday Anchor, 1963), p. 176

247   Rogers and Stevens, *Person to Person*, p. 50.

249   Robert D. Cumming (ed.), *The Philosophy of Jean-Paul Sartre* (Modern Library, 1966), p. 233.

William Barrett, *Irrational Man* (Doubleday Anchor, 1962), pp. 241f.

4-4

256   *Newsweek*, May 24, 1965. Copyright © Newsweek 1965, and reprinted by permission.

260   Edwin A. Burtt, *Man Seeks the Divine* (Harper, 1957), pp. 137.

261   J. Samuel Bois, *The Art of Awareness* (William C. Brown, 1973).

262   Reuben Abel, *Man Is the Measure* (Macmillan, The Free Press, 1976), p. 84.

263   Leland E. Hinsie and Robert Jean Campbell, *Psychiatric Dictionary* (Oxford, 1960).

J. B. Priestley, *Man and Time* (Dell, 1968), pp. 227f. From the book *Man and Time* by J. B. Priestley © 1964 Aldus Books London. Used by permission.

264   From the book *Psychic Discoveries Behind the Iron Curtain* by Ostrander and Schroeder (Bantam, 1971), pp. 33ff. Copyright © 1970 by Sheila Ostrander and Lynn Schroeder. Published by Prentice-Hall, Inc., Englewood Cliffs, New Jersey. Reprinted by permission of the publisher.

5-1

270   Arnold J. Toynbee, *A Study of History*, 12 vols. (Oxford, 1934–1961).

273   Edward Hallett Carr, "What is History?" (Vintage, 1961).

278ff.   *Time*, November 17, 1952, p. 32.

Arnold J. Toynbee, *An Historian's Approach to Religion* (Oxford, 1957), pp. 243ff., 249.

282   Will Durant, *The Story of Civilization*, Vol. IV, *The Age of Faith* (Simon & Schuster, 1950), pp. 343f.

284   Durant, *The Story of Civilization*, Vol. IV, pp. 343f. The quotations are from Will and Ariel Durant, *The Lessons of History* (Simon & Schuster, 1968), p. 100.

5-2

290   Martin Luther King, Jr. Quoted from Milton Mayer, *On Liberty: Man v. the State* (Center for the Study of Democratic Institutions, 1969), p. 5.

Thoreau. Paul Kurtz (ed.), *American Thought before 1900* (Macmillan, 1966), p. 312.

Martin Luther. Quoted from Joseph Fletcher, *Situation Ethics* (Westminster, 1966), p. 62.

291   Lewis F. Powell, Jr. Quoted from Milton Mayer, *On Liberty*, p. 5.

Immanuel Kant. Ibid., p. 78.

292   Quotation from *The Bold Ones*, NBC-TV.

293   Henry David Thoreau, "On Civil Disobedience," in Paul Kurtz, *American Thought before 1900*, p. 312.

295   *Unam sanctam*, in Henry Bettenson (ed.), *Documents of the Christian Church* (Oxford, 1947), pp. 161ff., 157f.

296   Socrates. Plato, *Crito*, in *The Last Days of Socrates*, trans. Hugh Tredennick (Penguin, 1959), pp. 89ff. Copyright © Hugh Tredennick 1954, 1959, 1969. Reprinted by permission of Penguin Books, Ltd.

298   "Obedience to Authority." By Stanley Milgram, *T. V. Guide*, August 21, 1976, reprinted with permission from *T.V. Guide*® magazine. Copyright © 1976 by Triangle Publications, Inc., Radnor, Pa.

299   Joseph Klausner, *Jesus of Nazareth* (Beacon, 1964), pp. 371, 376, 226, 376.

300   Plato, *The Phaedo*, in *The Great Dialogues of Plato*, trans. W. H. D. Rouse (Mentor, 1956), p. 521.

5-3

303 From *The Madman*, by Kahlil Gibran. Copyright 1918 by Kahlil Gibran and renewed 1946 by Administrators C.T.A. of Kahlil Gibran Estate and Mary G. Gibran. Reprinted by permission of Alfred A. Knopf, Inc.

Ruth Benedict, *Patterns of Culture* (Mentor, 1948), p. 2.

304 Narration from television series, "Primal Man," Part 2 "The Battle for Dominance." David Wolper Productions. Dialogue from filmed experiments at Stanford University by Philip Zimbardo. See also Philip Zimbardo, "The Psychological Power and Pathology of Imprisonment," a statement prepared for the U.S. House of Representatives Committee on the Judiciary: Subcommittee No. 3: Hearings on Prison Reform, San Francisco, October 25, 1971.

307 Carlos Castaneda, *The Teachings of Don Juan: A Yaqui Way of Knowledge* (Ballantine, 1969). Originally published by the University of California Press; reprinted by permission of The Regents of the University of California.

309 Paul Horton and Chester Hunt, *Sociology* (McGraw-Hill, 1964), p. 88.

312 Peter L. Berger and Thomas Luckmann, *The Social Construction of Reality* (Doubleday Anchor, 1967), pp. 175f. (Italics added.)

313 Erich Fromm, *The Revolution of Hope* (Bantam, 1968), pp. 43f. Reprinted by permission of Harper & Row, Publishers, Inc.

314 Norman O. Brown, *Life against Death* (Vintage, 1959), pp. 6–10.

Paul Kurtz (ed.), *American Thought before 1900* (Macmillan, 1966), pp. 15f.

316 Thoreau. Peyton E. Richter (ed.), *Utopias: Social Ideals and Communal Experiments* (Holbrook, 1971), p. 65.

5-4

320 From *The Madman*, by Kahlil Gibran. Copyright 1918 by Kahlil Gibran and renewed 1946 by Administrators C.T.A. of Kahlil Gibran Estate and Mary G. Gibran. Reprinted by permission of Alfred A. Knopf, Inc.

322 From *A Concise Introduction to Philosophy* by William Halverson, pp. 254ff. See xviii above.

323 Kahane. Quoted in *Playboy*, October 1972, p. 69.

324 Bonhoeffer. Quoted from Joseph Fletcher, *Situation Ethics* (Westminster, 1966), p. 33. Also note Bonhoeffer's *Letters and Papers from Prison* (Macmillan, 1953).

This account (§9) is paraphrased from Fletcher, *Situation Ethics*, p. 17.

Ibid., p. 136.

325 *Science News*, April 8, 1972, p. 228. Used by permission of *Science News*.

327f. For a readable account of the "Categorical Imperative," see Lewis White Beck's translation of Kant's *Critique of Practical Reason* (Bobbs-Merrill Library of Liberal Arts, 1956). For a modern formulation of ethical formalism, see Walter G. Muelder, *Moral Law in Christian Social Ethics* (John Knox, 1966).

399ff. For discussions of contextualism, see Joseph Fletcher's books *Situation Ethics* (Westminster, 1966) and *Moral Responsibility* (Westminster, 1967); and for a critical debate of contextualism and formalism, see Harvey Cox (ed.). *The Situation Ethics Debate* (Westminster, 1968).

334 "High Chaparral," NBC-TV. David Dortort, Executive Producer, in association with the National Broadcasting Company, Inc.

337 Albert Schweitzer, *The Teaching of Reverence for Life* (Holt, 1965).

6-1

343 John Keosian, *The Origin of Life* (Reinhold, 1964). p. 47.

347 Irene Kiefer, "Proving we are the stuff of which stars are made." *The Smithsonian* Magazine, May 1972, pp. 50f. Copyright © 1972 The Smithsonian Institution. Reprinted by permission of *The Smithsonian*.

358 Philip Handler (ed.), *Biology and the Future of Man* (Oxford, 1970), p. 504. Reprinted by permission of Oxford University Press, Inc.

359 *Science News*, April 8, 1972, p. 228. Reprinted by permission of *Science News* and the correspondent.

362 Sir Julian Huxley, *Evolution in Action* (Mentor, 1957), p. 13. Reprinted by permission of Harper & Row, Publishers, Inc.

Dubos, *The Torch of Life*, pp. 50f. See 16 above.

363 Handler, *Biology and the Future of Man*, pp. 488f.

Harry Overstreet, *The Enduring Quest* (Norton, 1931), pp. 234f.

6-2

367 Sir James G. Frazer, *Folklore of the Old Testament* (Macmillan, 1923), pp. 3ff. Reprinted by permission of Trinity College, Cambridge.

368 Desmond Morris, *The Naked Ape* (McGraw-Hill, 1967), p. 48.

370 From "Monkeys, Apes and Man," a National Geographic Program, CBS-TV, telecast October 12, 1971. (Italics added.) Printed by permission of The National Geographic Society.

371 Konrad Lorenz, *On Aggression* (Bantam, 1967), pp. 233, 230. Reprinted by permission of Harcourt Brace Jovanovich, Inc.

373 Ashley Montagu, *On Being Human* (Hawthorn, 1966), pp. 101, 97, 96.

375 Philip Handler (ed.), *Biology and the Future of Man* (Oxford, 1970), p. 928.

Sir Julian Huxley, *Evolution in Action* (Mentor, 1953), p. 9. Reprinted by permission of Harper & Row, Publishers, Inc.

377 Handler, *Biology and the Future of Man*, p. 492. Reprinted by permission of Oxford University Press, Inc. (Final italics added.)

6-3

379 From *Out of My Life and Thought* by Albert Schweitzer. Translated by C. T. Campion. Copyright 1933, 1949, © 1961 by Holt, Rinehart and Winston, Inc. Reprinted by permission of Holt, Rinehart and Winston, Inc.

380 *Poems from the Greek Anthology*, translated by Dudley Fitts, p. 114. Copyright 1938, 1941 by New Directions Publishing Corporation. Reprinted by permission of New Directions Publishing Corporation.

382 Dorothy Lee, *Freedom and Culture* (Prentice-Hall, 1959), pp. 163f.

383ff. George S. Sessions, ''Panpsychism versus Modern Materialism.'' Paper delivered at the Conference on ''The Rights of Non-Human Nature'' at Pitzer College, Claremont, California, April 18, 1974. See also George S. Sessions, ''Anthropocentrism and the Environment Crisis'' in the *Humboldt Journal of Social Relations* (Vol. 2, Fall/Winter, 1974). Reprinted by permission of the author.

387 Philip Handler (ed.), *Biology and the Future of Man* (Oxford, 1970), p. 491. Reprinted by permission of Oxford University Press, Inc.

390 Albert Schweitzer, ''The Ethics of Reverence for Life,'' *Christendom*, Vol. 1, No. 2 (Winter 1936). Quoted from Charles R. Joy (ed.), *Albert Schweitzer: An Anthology* (Harper, 1947), p. 270.

Pavel Simonov, ''Dostoevsky as a Social Scientist,'' *Psychology Today*, December 1971, p. 104.

6-4

396 John McHale, *The Future of the Future* (Ballantine, 1971), p. 10. Used by permission.

400 Kahn. *The Futurist*, October, 1975, p. 232. Reprinted from The Futurist. A Journal of Forecasts, Trends and Ideas About The Future, published by the World Future Society.

402 Toffler. *The Futurist*, October 1975, p. 232. Reprinted from The Futurist. A Journal of Forecasts, Trends and Ideas About The Future, published by The World Future Society.

Alvin Toffler, *The Eco-Spasm Report* (Bantam, 1975), p. 101. © 1975 by Alvin Toffler. By permission of Bantam Books Inc.

403 McHale's comment on Clarke: John McHale, *The Future of the Future*, p. 275. Used by permission.

404 Arthur C. Clarke, *Profiles of the Future* (Bantam, 1964), pp. 56, 207. Used by permission.

405 Fred Hoyle, *Encounter with the Future* (Trident, 1965), Chapter II, ''The Anatomy of Doom.'' Copyright © 1965, by Fred Hoyle. Credo Perspectives, planned and edited by Ruth Nanda Anshen. Reprinted by permission of Simon & Schuster, Inc.

407 Ray Bradbury. Quoted from James L. Christian (ed.), *Extraterrestrial Intelligence* (Prometheus, 1976), p. 12.

409 Poem quoted from *Why Man Explores*, a symposium held at California Institute of Technology on July 2, 1976, sponsored by NASA/Langley Research Center. Televised by PBS. Poem reprinted by permission of Ray Bradbury.

410 This selection first appeared in the book: Robert Bundy (ed.), *Images of the Future: The Twenty-first Century and Beyond*. 1976, p. 232, published by Prometheus Books, Buffalo, N.Y. and is reprinted by permission.

411 Robert Bundy (ed.), *Images of the Future*, p. 235. Used by permission.

7-1

417 Account of the baseball game taken from *The Memoirs of Professor R. Kulashto* (Ganymede, 2068), pp. 291ff.

419 Gilbert Newton Lewis, *Valence and the Structure of Atoms and Molecules* (Dover, 1966), p. 18.

Dewey B. Larson, *The Structure of the Physical Universe* (North Pacific Publishers, 1959), p. 1.

421 Sir Arthur Eddington. Quoted from Harry Overstreet, *The Enduring Quest* (Norton, 1931), pp. 27ff.

419 Bertrand Russell, *A History of Western Philosophy* (Allen & Unwin, 1946), p. 48.

422 Ibid., pp. 55ff.

Dialogue between Dr. Dicke and Dr. Ruffini in ''The Princeton Galaxy,'' *Intellectual Digest*, June 1973, p. 27.

424 David S. Saxon and William B. Fretter, *Physics for the Liberal Arts Student* (Holt, 1971), pp. 13–15. Reprinted by permission of the authors.

Walter Scott Houston, *Frontiers of Nuclear Physics* (Wesleyan University Press, 1954), pp. 4f.

426 Werner Heisenberg, ''From Plato to Max Planck,'' *The Atlantic Monthly*, November 1959, p. 113. Copyright © 1959, by The Atlantic Monthly Company, Boston, Mass. Reprinted by permission of the publisher and Dr. Heisenberg.

Norwood Russell Hanson, ''The Dematerialization of Matter.'' Quoted from Paul R. Durbin, O.P., *Philosophy of Science: An Introduction* (McGraw-Hill, 1968), p. 103.

431 Fred Hoyle, *Frontiers of Astronomy* (Mentor, 1957), p. 303.

423 Victor Weisskopf, ''Elementary Particles,'' in Samuel Rapport and Helen Wright (eds.), *Physics* (Washington Square, 1965), p. 215n.

7-2

437 Cornelius Lanczos, ''Einstein and the Role of Theory in Contemporary Physics,'' *American Scientist, 1959*. Quoted from Joseph Royce, *The Encapsulated Man* (Van Nostrand, 1964), p. 64.

439 Martin Gardner, *The Relativity Explosion* (Vintage, 1976), pp. 45 ff. © Martin Gardner and reprinted with his permission.

440 David S. Saxon and William B. Fretter, *Physics for the*

Liberal Arts Student (Holt, 1971). pp. 164f. (See p. 164n.)

443 "The Violent Universe," Public Broadcasting System-TV, April 1969. Produced for British Broadcasting Corporation by Philip Daly and written by Nigel Calder.

444 Gracia Fay Ellwood, *Psychic Visits to the Past* (Signet, 1971). Quotation from back cover.

7-3

457 Fred Hoyle, *Frontiers of Astronomy* (Mentor, 1957). See especially Chapters 19 and 20. On asking how matter might originate, see p. 302. For Hoyle's own counterargument, see *The Nature of the Universe* (Signet, 1955), p. 120.

461 Carl Sagan, *Other Worlds* (Bantam, 1975), p. 153.

465 Martin Gardner, *The Relativity Explosion* (Vintage, 1976), p. 192. © Martin Gardner and reprinted with his permission.

7-4

467 Sir Arthur Eddington, *New Pathways in Science* (University of Michigan Press, 1959), p. 309.

468 Harlow Shapley, *Of Stars and Men* (Washington Square, 1960), pp. 133f., 67. Copyright © 1958 by Harlow Shapley. Reprinted by permission of Beacon Press.
     Ray Bradbury, "The Search for Extraterrestrial Life," *Life* Magazine, October 24, 1960.

475 Isaac Asimov, *Of Matters Great and Small* (ACE, 1976), pp. 19–34.

477 "Six Searches for Extraterrestrial Civilizations," reprinted with permission from *Science News*, the weekly newsmagazine of science, copyright 1976 by Science Service, Inc.

481 Francesco Sizzi is quoted in Oliver Lodge, *Pioneers of Science* (1893), p. 106.

8-1

496 Frederick C. Grant (ed.). *Ancient Roman Religion* (Bobbs-Merrill Library of Liberal Arts, 1957), p. 159.

497 Viktor Frankl, *Man's Search for Meaning* (Washington Square, 1963), pp. 189f. Copyright © 1959, 1962 by Viktor E. Frankl. Reprinted by permission of Beacon Press.

501 Robert W. Smith, *Concepts of Man, Soul, and Immortality in the Gathas of Zarathustra* (1976). Reprinted by permission of the author.

502 Quoted from Bertrand Russell, *Mysticism and Logic* (Doubleday Anchor, 1957), pp. 44f.

503 Sardar Bundahish, 95.5-20.

505 Rudolf Bultmann, "New Testament and Mythology,"
     in Hans Werner Bartsch (ed.), *Kerygma and Myth* (Harper Torchbook, 1961), pp. 1f. Reprinted by permission of Harper & Row, Publishers, Inc.

510 Aldous Huxley, *The Perennial Philosophy* (Harper, 1945).

511 Swami Abhedananda (comp.) *The Sayings of Ramakrishna* (Vedanta Society, 1903), p. 54. Quoted from John B. Noss, *Man's Religions* (Macmillan, 4th ed., 1969), pp. 226f.
     Ibn Arabi. G. F. Moore, *The History of Religions* (Scribner's, 1919), p. 450.

8-2

518 "The Ontological Argument." Reprinted by permission of the author, James L. Catanzaro, Ph.D., California State University, Fullerton.
     This wording of Anselm's "Ontological Argument" follows closely the text of Philip Schaff, *History of the Christian Church*, Vol. V., *The Middle Ages* (Eerdmans, 1949 [1907]).

519 Lecomte du Noüy, *Human Destiny* (Longmans, Green, 1947), p. 87.
     From *The Portable Nietzsche,* translated by Walter Kaufman. Copyright 1954 by The Viking Press, Inc. Reprinted by permission of The Viking Press, Inc.

522 Excerpts from William Hamilton, "The Death of God," *Playboy*, August 1966, pp. 79f. Originally appeared in *Playboy* Magazine; copyright © 1966 by Playboy. Reprinted by permission of *Playboy* and the Reverend William Hamilton.

525 Ernest Hemingway, *For Whom the Bell Tolls* (Scribner's, 1940), p. 41.
     Carl G. Jung, *Psychology and Religion* (Yale University Press, 1938), pp. 113f.

8-3

527f. Ray Bradbury, "The Kilimanjaro Device," from *I Sing the Body Electric!* (Bantam, 1971), pp. 3ff. Reprinted by permission of Harold W. Matson Co., Inc., New York, and the author.

530 James Kidd will. Reproduced courtesy Clerk of the Superior Court, Phoenix.

532 "Miner's Request: Find Proof of Man's Soul," UPI report.

536 Richard W. Doss, "Life and Death in the Biocosmos." From James L. Christian (ed.) *Extraterrestrial Intelligence* (Prometheus, 1976), p. 218. Used by permission.

539 Rikihei Inoguchi and Tadashi Nakajima with Roger Pineau, *The Divine Wind* (Bantam, 1960), pp. 178f. Reprinted by permission of Roger Pineau and the United States Naval Institute.

541 Ray Bradbury in a letter to the author, April 22, 1972.

544 *Poems from the Greek Anthology,* translated by Dudley Fitts, pp. 126, 116, 106, 108, 107
     See Appendix to James L. Christian (ed.), *Extraterrestrial Intelligence*, p. 295. Used by permission.

545 Robert Heinlein, *Time Enough for Love.* Reprinted by

permission of G. P. Putnam's Sons. © 1973 by Robert A. Heinlein, p. 326.

8-4

550 From *The Madman*, by Kahlil Gibran. Copyright 1918 by Kahlil Gibran and renewed 1946 by Administrators C.T.A of Kahlil Gibran Estate and Mary G. Gibran. Reprinted by permission of Alfred A. Knopf, Inc.

Friedrich Nietzsche. Quoted from Erich Heller, "The Modern German Mind: The Legacy of Nietzsche," in Thomas J. J. Altizer (ed.), *Toward a New Christianity: Readings in the Death of God Theology* (Harcourt, 1967), p. 103.

Robert Heinlein, *The Glory Road* (Berkley Medallion, 1970), pp. 34ff. Reprinted by permission of G. P. Putnam's Sons. Copyright © 1963 by Robert Heinlein.

552 Viktor Frankl, *Man's Search for Meaning* (Washington Square, 1963), pp. 122ff.

Jean-Paul Sartre, *La Nausée* (Gallimard, 1938), pp. 162f. The English translation used here is by Kurt F. Reinhardt in his *Existentialist Revolt* (Frederick Ungar, 1952), p. 157.

553 Bertrand Russell, *Mysticism and Logic* (Doubleday Anchor, 1957), pp. 45f.

J. B. Priestley, *Man and Time* (Dell, 1968), p. 323.

555 Nikos Kazantzakis, *The Saviours of God* (Simon & Schuster, 1960), pp. 47f.

Colin Wilson, *Introduction to the New Existentialism* (Houghton Mifflin, 1966), pp. 151, 154.

556 William Halverson, *A Concise Introduction to Philosophy* (Random House, 1967), pp. 215f.

George S. Counts, "Charles Beard, The Public Man," in Howard K. Beale (ed.), *Charles A. Beard: An Appraisal* (Octagon, 1976).

557 Langdon Jones, "The Eye of the Lens," in Michael Moorcock (ed.), *The Best SF Stories from New Worlds, No. 6* (Berkley Medallion, 1971), pp. 69f. Reprinted by permission.

559 These extracts from William Thompson and Saint-Exupéry are quoted from W. Lambert Gardiner, *Psychology: The Story of a Search* (Brooks/Cole, 1970), p. 189, and the flash of genius which juxtaposed these two quotations must be credited to Professor Gardiner.

560 Ludwig Wittgenstein, *Tractatus Logico-Philosophicus* (Routledge & Kegan Paul, 1960), 6.5, 6.51, 6.52, 6.521.

From the motion picture, *The 7 Faces of Dr. Lao* (1964).

II. ILLUSTRATIONS

89   *Saturday Reveiw*, May 27, 1961, p. 17. Reproduced by permission of *Saturday Review*.

98   From *Cave Drawings for the Future*. Copyright © by Abner Dean - 1954. Reproduced by permission of the artist.

99   Bill Mauldin cartoon. Drawing copyrighted 1944, renewed 1972, Bill Mauldin, reproduced by courtesy of Bill Mauldin.

2-2

103   From *What Am I Doing Here?* Copyright © by Abner Dean - 1947. Reproduced by permission of the artist.

104ff   Zen Oxherding Pictures, originally drawn by the Zen Master Kukuan (*c*. A.D. 1100–1200), who also wrote the verse and prose comments for each picture. These modern woodblock prints are by the Zen artist Tomikichiro Tokuriki. From Paul Reps, *Zen Flesh, Zen Bones* (Doubleday Anchor, N.D.), pp. 136–155. Prints and text reprinted by permission of Charles E. Tuttle, Tokyo.

106   *Saturday Review*, January 7, 1961, p. 27. Reproduced by permission of Sidney Harris.

2-3

114   Dr. Harry Harlow and rhesus monkey. Reproduced courtesy of Dr. Harlow and the University of Wisconsin Primate Laboratory.

115   A six-month-old rhesus monkey, raised in isolation from birth—deprived of mother, surrogate mother, and playmates—cowers in fear in the corner of its cage. Photo courtesy the University of Wisconsin Primate Laboratory.

117   *Peanuts* by Charles M. Schulz. Copyright © 1970 The United Feature Syndicate Inc., and used with their permission.

    From *What Am I Doing Here?* Copyright by Abner Dean - 1947. Reproduced by permission of the artist.

119   Paintings by Dick Sargent. Reprinted by permission from *The Saturday Evening Post* © 1954, The Curtis Publishing Company. Photo courtesy Dr. Maurice Riseling, Tustin, California.

120   Pablo Picasso, *Girl before a Mirror* (March 14, 1932). Oil on canvas, 64 × 51¼. Collection, The Museum of Modern Art, New York. Gift of Mrs. Simon Guggenheim. Reproduced by permission.

127   "The Law of Pathei Mathos." Aeschylus, *Agamemnon*, ll. 177–178.

128   *Peanuts* by Charles M. Schulz. Copyright © 1960 The United Feature Syndicate Inc., and used with their permission.

    Edvard Munch, *The Scream* (1893) Nasjonalgalleriet, Oslo. Munch was one of the founders of modern expressionism, and in this painting one can both see and feel the agonized scream. On the margin of a lithograph of *The Scream*, Munch wrote, "I felt a great cry in the whole universe."

129   Chambered Nautilus, courtesy of *The American Museum of Natural History*.

2-4

132   Cover of *Psychology Today*, December 1971. Copyright © 1971 Communications/Research/Machines, Inc. Photography: John Oldenkamp.

138   African boys of Bechuanaland. Photograph by Nat Farbman, *Life* Magazine; copyright © Time Inc. Reproduced by permission.

139   © by Sidney Harris/American Scientist Magazine. Reprinted by permission of the cartoonist, Sidney Harris.

141   From *What Am I Doing Here?* Copyright by Abner Dean - 1947. Reproduced by permission of the artist.

146   *Arizona Highways*, September 1971, p. 15. Reproduced courtesy of the photographer, Joseph Stacey.

152–   Sky maps. From *The Sky Observer's Guide*. Paintings
153   and diagrams by John Polgreen. Copyright © 1965, 1959 by Western Publishing Company, Inc. Used by permission.

3-1

155   Richard Lippold, *Variation Number 7: Full Moon* (1949–50). Brass rods, nickel-chromium, and stainless steel wire, 10 × 6'. Collection, The Museum of Modern Art, New York. Mrs. Simon Guggenheim Fund. Reproduced by permission.

157   Moses with tablets bearing the Commandments. Eighteenth century German wood sculpture. Courtesy of the Photographic Archive of the Jewish Theological Seminary of America, New York.

158   Reproduced by special permission of *Playboy* Magazine. Copyright © 1976 by Playboy. Cartoonist, Boris Drucker.

159   The message sent to the star-cluster in Hercules (M13), 25,000 light-years distance, from the Arecibo Observatory November 16, 1974; devised by Cornell astronomer Frank Drake. At top are the atomic numbers of hydrogen, carbon, nitrogen, oxygen, and phosphorus. Next are the chemical formulas of the DNA molecule, with the double helix winding into the head of a human being. At left is the human's height and, at right, the population of Earth. Below the human figure are the sun and planets of the solar system. At the bottom is depicted the Arecibo radiotelescope that sent the message, and its 1,000-foot diameter.

160   *Peanuts* by Charles M. Schulz. Copyright © 1965 United Feature Syndicate, Inc. and used with their permission.

161   Tarot: "The Ace of Wands" reveals one's future, it is believed; and with the right combination with other cards, it can indicate the beginning of happy new adventures and enterprises. How can such fact-claims be validated?

3-2

165   Bridget Riley, *Current* (1964). Synthetic polymer paint on composition board, 58³/₈ × 58⁷/₈. Collection, The Museum of Modern Art, New York. Philip Johnson Fund. Reproduced by permission.

171   Painting of a sunset on Venus, showing the progressive distortion of the solar image as it would be seen through the dense, lenslike atmosphere of the planet. In what sense is this an example of "sense deception"? Painting reproduced by permission of the artist, Helmut Wimmer.

171ff.   Electromagnetic and sonic spectra. I am grateful to Ronald L. Smith, former director of Tessman Planetarium, Santa Ana College, for assistance in developing this diagram.

176   By Henry Martin, from *Saturday Review*, May 29, 1971. Copyright 1971 by Saturday Review, Inc. Reprinted by permission of the cartoonist.

3-3

183   S. I. Hayakawa. Photo courtesy of Dr. Hayakawa.

184   Village animals redrawn from S. I. Hayakawa, *Language in Thought and Action* (Harcourt, 1963), p. 214. Copyright © Harcourt Brace Jovanovich, Inc., and redrawn with their permission.

186   From *What Am I Doing Here?* Copyright by Abner Dean - 1947. Reproduced by permission of the artist.

187   Cartoon by Dennis Renault. Used by permission.

189   Sky maps. From *The Sky Observer's Guide*. Paintings and diagrams by John Polgreen. Copyright © 1965, 1959 by Western Publishing Company, Inc. Used by permission.

3-4

193   Lord Bertrand Russell (1872–1970). The development of the correspondence-test is credited to Russell. Photo by Lotte Meitner-Graf, London.

206–   Monument Valley. *Arizona Highways*, June 1972, pp.
207   18f. Reproduced courtesy of the photographer, Dick Dietrich.

4-1

214   Gianlorenzo Bernini, *The Ecstasy of St. Theresa* (1645–52). Cornaro Chapel, Church of Sta. Maria della Vittoria.
       Electroencephalograms showing alpha waves. Printouts courtesy Jay W. Klug, Department of Experimental Physiology, Veterans' Administration Hospital, Sepulveda, California.

215   Last letter of the Tibetan alphabet symbolizes the ideal state of a fully awakened consciousness.

218   Statue of Amida Buddha, Kamakura, Japan. This giant bronze, nearly fifty feet high, was cast in A.D. 1252. Photograph by the author.

4-2

226   Salvador Dali, *The Persistence of Memory* (1931). Oil on canvas, 9¹/₂ × 13''. Collection, The Museum of Modern Art, New York. Reproduced by permission.

229   Sir Isaac Newton (1642–1727).

235   Schematic indicating vertical dimensions of the Saturn V moon rocket.

4-3

240   St. Paul: Greek stamp commemorating Paul's visit to Athens *c.* A.D. 50 (Acts 17:16–34).

245   B. F. Skinner. Photo courtesy Dr. Skinner.

247   Carl R. Rogers. Photo courtesy Dr. Rogers.

4-4

254   © Sidney Harris/American Scientist Magazine. Reprinted by permission of the cartoonist, Sidney Harris.

257   *Peanuts* by Charles M. Schulz. Copyright © 1967 by United Feature Syndicate, Inc. and used with their permission.

259   *B.C.* by permission of Johnny Hart and Field Enterprises, Inc.

268–   Photo of Earth, courtesy of NASA.
269

5-1

271   Acropolis in Athens, the Parthenon in the center.

280   Arnold J. Toynbee.

283   Pablo Picasso, *Guernica* (1937, May, early June). Oil on canvas, 11'5¹/₂'' × 25'5³/₄''. Collection, The Museum of Modern Art, New York (on indefinite loan from the estate of the Artist). Reproduced by permission.

5-2

292   Silver denarius of the Roman Emperor Tiberius (A.D. 14–37). This is the type of the tribute coin shown to Jesus.

5-3

305   From *Cave Drawings for the Future.* Copyright © by Abner Dean - 1954. Reproduced by permission of the artist.

308   From *What Am I Doing Here?* Copyright by Abner Dean - 1947. Reproduced by permission of the artist.

312   Four paintings by Louis Wain. © Guttman Maclay Collection, Institute of Psychiatry, London.

315   Paul Klee, *Senecio,* 1922. Kunstmuseum, Basel. © by ADAGP, Paris 1981.

317   Paul Reps, *Zen Telegrams* (Charles E. Tuttle, 1959), p. 38. Reproduced by permission of Charles E. Tuttle, Tokyo.

5-4

336   Photo by Astronaut Thomas K. Mattingly II on April 16, 1972, shortly after *Apollo XVI* headed for the moon. Photo courtesy of NASA.

338   Albert Schweitzer (1875–1965), with Lambaréné Hospital in background.

340–   *Floating City,* reprinted by permission of the artist,
341   Robert McCall.

6-1

344   Dr. Alexander Oparin, pioneer in the field of biochemical evolution. Photo taken by Mrs. Oparin. Reproduced courtesy Dr. Ponnamperuma.

345   Dr. Stanley Miller and the spark-discharge apparatus in which the first amino acids were synthesized in 1953. Photographs courtesy of Dr. Miller.

346   An electron micrograph of a cell-like structure produced from thermal proteinoid in the laboratory of S. W. Fox.

351   Dr. Cyril Ponnamperuma, pioneer in the field of biochemical evolution. Photo taken by Mrs. Oparin. Reproduced courtesy Dr. Ponnamperuma.

352   Trilobites—marine fossil invertebrates—from the Precambrian era, more than 500 million years old. Courtesy of the Smithsonian Institution.

355   Neanderthal skull, named Shanidar I. Excavated by anthropologist Ralph Solecki in a large cave near the village of Shanidar in the high mountains of northern Iraq. This ancestor of modern man, belonging to the species *Homo neanderthalensis,* called "Nandy" by his excavators, was killed some 48,000 years ago by a rock fall. Dr. Solecki's discoveries in this cave have forced a revision of our picture of Neanderthal man. Rather than the dumb brute traditionally pictured, Neanderthals may have been far more sensitive and skilled than previously imagined. One adult man, Shanidar IV, who died about 60,000 years ago, was laid to rest in a tomb in this cave with flowers gathered from the hillsides nearby. Photo courtesy Dr. Solecki.

357   Adaptation and survival: Is this the basic mechanism of evolution? On each tree in these photographs is a peppered moth and a dark moth. On the dark tree trunk, the light-colored moth would be easy prey, but on the lichen-covered trunk, it has become invisible. Photographs from the experiments of Dr. H. B. D. Kettlewell.

360   An Alaskan brown bear with his freshly caught meal, a twenty-eight-inch salmon—"the deadly feast of life." Photography by Leonard Lee Rue III. Reproduced courtesy of the National Audubon Society/ Collection Photo Researchers.

6-2

372   Cover of *The Naked Ape,* by Desmond Morris (Dell, 1969). Illustration by James Bama. Reproduced by permission of Dell Publishing Co., Inc.

374   From *What Am I Doing Here?* Copyright by Abner Dean - 1947. Reproduced by permission of the artist.

376   Paul Reps, *Zen Telegrams* (Charles E. Tuttle, 1959), p. 39. Reproduced by permission of Charles E. Tuttle, Tokyo.

6-3

381   Paul Reps, *Zen Telegrams* (Charles E. Tuttle, 1959), p. 97. Reproduced by permission of Charles E. Tuttle, Tokyo.

390   Drawing by Charles W. Schwartz from *A Sand County Almanac with other essays on conservation from round River,* by Aldo Leopold. Copyright © 1949, 1953, 1966, and renewed in 1977 by Oxford University Press, Inc. Reprinted by permission.

6-4

395   *B.C.* by permission of Johnny Hart and Field Enterprises, Inc.

398   Graph from *Elements of Psychology: A Briefer Course* by Kretch and Crutchfield. Knopf, 1970, p. 319.

401   Life inside a space colony. Painting courtesy NASA/ Ames Research Center.

405   Redrawn from Fred Hoyle, *Encounter with the Future* (Trident, 1965), p. 32. Redrawn by permission of Simon & Schuster, Inc.

410   Redrawn from Philip Handler (ed.), *Biology and the Future of Man,* p. 898. Source: *World Population: A Challenge to the United Nations and Its System of Agencies,* UNA-USA National Policy Panel on World Population, May 1969.

414–   Spiral galaxy NGC 3031 (M 81) in Ursa Major. Photo
415   courtesy Hale Observatories.

7-1

417ff. Snowflakes: a delicate tracery providing spectacular proof that mathematics is indeed "the language of nature." These·are actual photomicrographs taken with the utmost care and in bitter cold, in the latter part of the nineteenth century, by W. A. Bentley, called "the snowflake man." For a fascinating account of how he performed this work of science, see *Audubon* Magazine, January 1971. Photographs reproduced courtesy Mr. John Buechler and the University of Vermont Library, Burlington, Vermont.

420 Cerussite crystals from *Arizona Highways,* February 1975. Photo courtesy Jeff Kurtzeman from the Wayne Darby Collection. Used by permission.

424 Polymethylene crystals, magnified 37,000 times, show that nature grows both "left-handed" and "right-handed" spiral designs. Courtesy of E. I. duPont de Nemours & Co. (Inc.) Wilmington, DE 19898. From Cyril Ponnamperuma, *The Origins of Life* (Dutton, 1972), p. 104.

425 Tortoise (still ahead of Achilles). Drawing by Shannon Christian.

428 Particle streaks. Photo courtesy of NAL.

7-2

438 A galaxy in the constellation Centaurus (NGC 5128), a source of intense radio noise and—perhaps—the actual collision of two galaxies. Reproduced courtesy the Hale Observatories.

441 Quasi-stellar radio source 3C-273; 200-inch photograph. Courtesy Hale Observatories.

442 Light-clocks redrawn from David S. Saxon and William B. Fretter, *Physics for the Liberal Arts Student* (Holt, 1971), p. 165. Redrawn by permission of Holt, Rinehart and Winston, Inc.

443 The original spectrogram referred to in the dialogue from "The Violent Universe" which Maarten Schmidt puzzled over in 1963. "Spectrum of the quasar 3C-273. The lower spectrum consists of hydrogen and helium lines and serves to establish the scale of wavelengths. The upper part is the spectrum of the quasar, a star-like object of magnitude 13. The Balmer lines Hβ, Hγ and Hδ in the quasar spectrum are at longer wavelengths than in the comparison spectrum. The redshift of 16 per cent

corresponds to a distance of two billion light years in the expanding universe." Photo and description courtesy of Dr. Schmidt.

7-3

449 Hebrew cosmos. Redrawn from S. H. Hooke, *In the Beginning,* Vol. VI of *The Clarendon Bible* (Oxford, 1947), p. 20.

450 Egyptian cosmos. From O. Lodge, *Pioneers of Science* (Dover, 1960).

451 Woodcut. From John C. Brandt and Stephen P. Maran, *New Horizons in Astronomy* (Freeman, 1972), p. 82.

452 A medieval diagram of the geocentric (Ptolemaic) universe. Diagram from Peter Appian's *Cosmographia* (1539).

453 The heliocentric (Copernican) cosmos as drawn by Thomas Digges in 1576. In the center of the system is "the sonne," and the other heavenly bodies—though, strangely, not the stars—revolve in circular orbits around the sun. Notice, however, that the moon revolves around the earth. From John C. Brandt and Stephen P. Maran, *New Horizons in Astronomy* (Freeman, 1972), p. 85.

454 Nebula (NGC 6611) in *Scutum Sobieski.* Photo courtesy Mount Wilson and Palomar Observatories.

457 Professor Fred Hoyle. Drawing by Mrs. Juliet Pannett.

458 The Whirlpool galaxy (NGC 5194) in the constellation Canes Venatici, with a smaller satellite galaxy attached to the end of one of the large galaxy's two arms. Photo courtesy the Hale Observatories.

460 A collage of the planet Jupiter and its four moonworlds, photographed by Voyager 1 March, 1979. The four Galilean satellites are (from farthest to nearest) Io, Europa, Ganymede, and Callisto. Photo courtesy NASA.

462 The Lagoon nebula (NGC 6523) in Sagittarius. Photo courtesy of Hale Observatories.

463 A filament of the Veil nebula (NGC 6992) in the constellation Cygnus, the remnant of a supernova explosion. Photo courtesy of Hale Observatories.

464 The impressive Hercules globular cluster (M13) containing some 10,000 stars. Photo courtesy the Hale Observatories.

7-4

470 Artist's concept of ground level view of Cyclops system antennas. Photo courtesy National Aeronautics and Space Administration, Ames Research Center, Moffett Field, California.

476 Ozma radiotelescope from *Extra-Terrestrial Intelligence* edited by James L. Christian (Prometheus Books, 1976).

477 Interstellar dust cloud with stars and planets in process of formation. From *Griffith Observer,* March 1974.

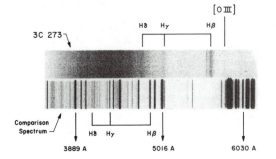

Arecibo. Cornell University photograph by Russ Hamilton.

480   Martian landscape. Photo courtesy NASA.

483   The Voyager record. Photo courtesy NASA.

484   A portion of the Rosette nebula (NGC 2237) in the constellation Monoceros. The small, dark globules in the photograph are dense masses of gas and dust which are contracting into stars; that is, *new stars* are continually being born out of such interstellar and intergalactic matter. Photo courtesy the Hale Observatories.

488–   Eighteenth-century Chinese coin, with the eight tri-
489   grams of the *I Ching* on obverse side. Photo by the author.

8-1

493   Paper currency of the Portuguese colony of Angola (Portuguese West Africa).

495   Note the variety of different, but *associated,* meanings attached to the Greek word *pneuma* and its related forms. From Liddell and Scott's *Greek-English Lexicon* (Oxford, 1889).

498   Cartoon by Clayton D. Powers, *Esquire,* December 1965, p. 213. Copyright © 1965 by Esquire, Inc. Reproduced by permission of *Esquire* Magazine.
       The damaged service module of *Apollo XIII,* April 17, 1970. The explosion in an oxygen tank in Section 4 of the SM forced the crewmen to use the lunar lander as a lifeboat to return home to earth. Photo courtesy of NASA.

503   Detail of painting of Adam and Eve by Lucas Cranach the Elder. Lee Collection, Courtauld Institute Galleries, London. Adam looks rather puzzled by the offer, doesn't he?
       The incredulous horror of a lost soul, having just realized that he has been relegated to hell *for all eternity.* Detail of Michelangelo's Last Judgment in the Sistine Chapel.

8-2

516   IGY postage stamp, detail of hands from Michelangelo's Creation of Adam, from the ceiling of the Sistine Chapel. Solar flares in the background. HANDS: Adam at left, God at right.

519   Cover of *Time,* April 8, 1966. Reprinted by permission from *Time,* The Weekly Newsmagazine; Copyright Time, Inc.

520   Cantonese porcelain factory worker sculpting crucifixes. Photo by the author.

521   Statuette of the Egyptian god Osiris.

523   Cover of *Time,* December 26, 1969. Reprinted by permission from *Time,* The Weekly Newsmagazine; Copyright Time, Inc.

524   Editorial cartoon by Frank Interlandi. Copyright © 1976, Los Angeles Times. Reprinted with permission.

8-3

529   "The Grim Reaper" in Ingmar Bergman's motion picture *The Seventh Seal.* Copyright © 1960 by Ingmar Bergman. From *Four Screenplays by Ingmar Bergman* (Simon & Schuster, 1960). Reprinted by permission of Simon & Schuster, Inc.

530   James Kidd will. Reproduced courtesy Clerk of the Superior Court, Phoenix.

531   King David weeping after having been told of the death of his son (2 Samuel 19:1). In background: Joab, the general of David's army who killed him. Painting by Guy Rowe. From *In Our Image,* by Houston Harte (Oxford, 1949). Reproduced courtesy of Houston Harte.

535   Fresco on wall of the tomb of a nobleman, Menena, at Royal Thebes. The fresco retains its vivid colors after 3,500 years. Note that the faces and parts of the bodies of Menena and his family have been chisled away, thus insuring that the "soul" of each would enter the next life faceless and maimed.

538   "I cannot see what lies ahead. Won't you walk with me." Photo courtesy of John Reseck.

540   Judgment scene before King Osiris. The dog-headed god Anubis is weighing the heart of the deceased—Princess Entiu-ny—against a symbol of Truth; if judged worthy, her spirit can pass on into the western paradise, the Kingdom of Osiris. The goddess Isis, sister of Osiris and compassionate interceder, stands behind the princess.

546   Funeral statuette of the Pharaoh Tutankhamon—exiting into the next life. Photograph, Griffith Institute, Ashmolean Museum, Oxford. Reproduced by permission.

8-4

551   From *What Am I Doing Here?* Copyright by Abner Dean - 1947. Reproduced by permission of the artist.

554   Paul Reps, *Zen Telegrams* (Charles E. Tuttle, 1959), p. 81. Reproduced by permission of Charles E. Tuttle, Tokyo.

557   *Earthrise.* Photo of the blue and white planet, Earth, by the first terran space travelers, December 1968. Taken by crew of *Apollo VIII* when they were 240,000 miles from home. Photo courtesy of NASA.

559   Stonehenge, showing the sunrise trilithon at center left and the moonrise trilithon at center right. Photo by Stephen Perrin.

INDEX TO MARGINAL QUOTATIONS

NAME/SUBJECT INDEX

(Note: Page numbers set in italics refer to illustrations.)